Sustainability Integration for Effective Project Management

Gilbert Silvius
HU University of Applied Sciences Utrecht, The Netherlands & Van Aetsveld, The Netherlands

Jennifer Tharp
Mastodon Consulting, USA

A volume in the Practice, Progress, and Proficiency in Sustainability (PPPS) Book Series

BUSINESS SCIENCE
Reference

Managing Director:	Lindsay Johnston
Editorial Director:	Joel Gamon
Book Production Manager:	Jennifer Yoder
Publishing Systems Analyst:	Adrienne Freeland
Development Editor:	Myla Merkel
Assistant Acquisitions Editor:	Kayla Wolfe
Typesetter:	Christina Henning
Cover Design:	Jason Mull

Published in the United States of America by
   Business Science Reference (an imprint of IGI Global)
   701 E. Chocolate Avenue
   Hershey PA 17033
   Tel: 717-533-8845
   Fax: 717-533-8661
   E-mail: cust@igi-global.com
   Web site: http://www.igi-global.com

Library of Congress Cataloging-in-Publication Data

Sustainability integration for effective project management / Gilbert Silvius and Jennifer Tharp, editor.
   pages cm
 Includes bibliographical references and index.
 Summary: "This book provides a comprehensive understanding of the most important issues, concepts, trends, methodologies, and good practices in sustainability to project management"--Provided by publisher.
  ISBN 978-1-4666-4177-8 (hardcover) -- ISBN 978-1-4666-4178-5 (ebook) -- ISBN 978-1-4666-4179-2 (print & perpetual access) 1. Project management--Environmental aspects. 2. Management--Environmental aspects. I. Silvius, Gilbert. II. Tharp, Jennifer, 1968-

 HD69.P75S873 2013
 658.4'083--dc23

                              2013009514

This book is published in the IGI Global book series Practice, Progress, and Proficiency in Sustainability (PPPS) Book Series (ISSN: Pending; eISSN: Pending)

British Cataloguing in Publication Data
A Cataloguing in Publication record for this book is available from the British Library.

Practice, Progress, and Proficiency in Sustainability (PPPS) Book Series

ISSN: Pending
EISSN: pending

MISSION

In a world where traditional business practices are reconsidered and economic activity is performed in a global context, new areas of economic developments are recognized as the key enablers of wealth and income production. This knowledge of information technologies provides infrastructures, systems, and services towards sustainable development.

The **Practices, Progress, and Proficiency in Sustainability (PPPS) Book Series** focuses on the local and global challenges, business opportunities, and societal needs surrounding international collaboration and sustainable development of technology. This series brings together academics, researchers, entrepreneurs, policy makers and government officers aiming to contribute to the progress and proficiency in sustainability.

COVERAGE

- Eco-Innovation
- Environmental Informatics
- Global Business
- Global Content and Knowledge Repositories
- Green Technology
- ICT and Knowledge for Development
- Knowledge Clusters
- Strategic Management of IT
- Sustainable Development
- Technological Learning

IGI Global is currently accepting manuscripts for publication within this series. To submit a proposal for a volume in this series, please contact our Acquisition Editors at Acquisitions@igi-global.com or visit: http://www.igi-global.com/publish/.

Titles in this Series

For a list of additional titles in this series, please visit: www.igi-global.com

Sustainability Integration for Effective Project Management
Gilbert Silvius (Utrecht University of Applied Sciences, the Netherlands) and Jennifer Tharp (Mastodon Consulting, USA)
Business Science Reference • copyright 2013 • 361pp • H/C (ISBN: 9781466641778) • US $185.00 (our price)

IGI GLOBAL
DISSEMINATOR OF KNOWLEDGE

www.igi-global.com

701 E. Chocolate Ave., Hershey, PA 17033
Order online at www.igi-global.com or call 717-533-8845 x100
To place a standing order for titles released in this series, contact: cust@igi-global.com
Mon-Fri 8:00 am - 5:00 pm (est) or fax 24 hours a day 717-533-8661

Editorial Advisory Board

Table of Contents

Section 1
Considering Project Management through a Sustainability Lens

Section 2
Integrating Sustainability into Project Management

Section 3
Sustainability and the Project Manager

Section 4
Case Studies and Best Practices

Detailed Table of Contents

Section 1
Considering Project Management through a Sustainability Lens

Chapter 1

William T. Craddock, Craddock & Associates, Inc., USA

The purpose of this chapter is to establish the linkages among Business Excellence Models (BEMs), project sustainability, and project success. The particular focus is on how the BEM framework contributes to project sustainability as one element of project success. Although general sustainability definitions vary, most describe a broad perspective that encompasses economic, social, and environmental objectives. This broad perspective fits well with the concepts of both Corporate Social Responsibility (CSR) and Total Quality Management (TQM). Business Excellence Models, with their origins in the TQM movement, provide a framework to address sustainability. Although much of the literature focuses on applying these concepts in a general organizational setting, they also apply to a project organization. Project success criteria can be expanded to include project sustainability, measured both at the time of project closing and later when the overall project benefits are evaluated.

Chapter 2

Lynn A. Keeys, SKEMA Business School, France
Martina Huemann, WU Vienna University of Economics and Business, Austria
Rodney Turner, SKEMA Business School, France

This chapter proposes a conceptual framework for integrating project strategy for Sustainable Development (SD) within the context of corporate sustainability strategy. Project SD strategy is the missing link between SD at the corporate level and project level. The framework draws on a literature review of concepts, definitions, and theories in strategic management, corporate sustainability, and projects. The conceptual framework presented in this book chapter has six key components. These are: (1) corporate sustainability strategy; (2) project understanding of SD and SD business case; (3) strategizing at project initiation stage; (4) project autonomy to negotiate and adapt in the project context; (5) project capability to translate corporate SD strategy to project SD strategy; and (6) project capability in stakeholder management. The premise of the framework is the compatibility of the socially constructed realities of the project and SD, as indicated in SD and project literature. The aim is to help develop new knowledge and insight into how business can integrate SD principles into core business operations such as projects from a process perspective, rather than sustainability content perspective. This chapter is based on doctoral dissertation research by the lead author.

Tom Mochal, TenStep, Inc., USA
Andrea Krasnoff, TenStep, Inc., USA

The world is going green and we are collectively realizing that we do not have an unlimited amount of natural resources to utilize as we have done in the past. Material Handling Industry of America (2007) notes, "Not only do we have climate problems but we are also dealing with a resource depletion issue." However, the project management profession seems to be in its infancy in applying green standards. How can we apply these "green" concepts to our project management discipline? One obvious way is that we can manage green projects more efficiently. For example, if you are the project manager on a project that will result in using less packaging in your products, it would be good if your project completed on time. The sooner that project ends, the sooner the green benefits will be achieved. On the other hand, if you are dealing with projects such as installing a new software package or upgrading network infrastructure, how can these projects become more environmentally friendly? The answer is Green Project Management (GreenPM®). Green project management is a model that allows project managers to think green throughout a project and make decisions that take into account the impact on the environment—if any. It is a way to ingrain "greenthink" (or green thinking) into every project management process. Greenthink connects the environment with the decisions that are made, whether project-related, professional, or in our everyday lives.

Gilbert Silvius, HU University of Applied Sciences Utrecht, The Netherlands & Van Aetsveld, The Netherlands

Sustainability is one of the most important challenges of our time. How can we develop prosperity, without compromising the life of future generations? Companies are integrating sustainability in their marketing, corporate communication, annual reports, and in their actions. The concept of sustainability has more recently also been linked to project management. This chapter explores the concept of sustainability and its application to project management processes. It aims to provide guidance on how the standards of project management should integrate the concepts and principles of sustainability. After a review of the relevant literature on sustainability, its leading principles are identified and applied to the standards for project management processes.

Mohamed Eid, The British University in Egypt, Egypt

The relationship between Project Management (PM) and Sustainable Development (SD) is tested in this chapter through its application on the construction industry. When PM is embedded in construction projects, it has the capacity to be a significant leverage point of great influence, and it becomes one of the cornerstones for rethinking the relationships between PM, SD, and the Construction Industry. The work presented discusses the need for integrating sustainable development into project management processes to ensure a better outcome for the construction industry, which is directly related to the degradation of our quality of life on the economic, social, and environmental levels. The author explores the origins and philosophies behind sustainability, the core of project management processes, the strategic implications of the construction industry practices, and puts forward the "systems thinking and points of leverage" approach to facilitate an efficient environment of integration. Thinking and acting sustainably requires not only incremental change but also a revolution in approach, a shift of perspective; sustainable project management processes are possible to achieve.

Project managers must recognize that socially sustainable development is a key factor in project success and requires far more than public relations or community consultation. Companies are becoming aware of the risk that community dissatisfaction can have on their projects. Communities are becoming increasingly expectant that the management of socially sustainable development, which maximizes the positive outcomes for communities, is incorporated in all types of projects. Planning for social maximization needs to occur at project design phase, and key issues and actions should be placed under the control of the project manager directly. This chapter considers the lessons from managing community impact in the development sector, which can be used to manage social risk for all projects.

There is great concern for social and environmental sustainability. Innovative solutions are needed in addressing the 21st century challenges of globalization, population growth, climate change, and resource scarcity. Corporations become more aware of the importance of sustainable practices by successfully integrating them within non-financial reporting. In the circumstances of the 21st century challenges, corporations start to reconsider both their sustainability and project management approaches. Even though two distinct key-elements of an organization, with importance attributable to the performance of a company, they are interrelated, and sustainability can be integrated within project management. In order to demonstrate this fact, the authors make use of a specific methodology that implies measurement of sustainability integration level, determination of the degree of the project success, and ultimately, computation of Pearson Coefficient for a sample of 35 integrated reports.

Section 2
Integrating Sustainability into Project Management

Project initiation and project management are specific processes of the project-oriented company. In order to improve the performance of these processes in their descriptions as well as in the design of the methods to be applied, the principles of sustainable development can be considered. Templates for some project initiation and project management methods considering SD principles are provided. This chapter is based on the results of the Research Project: SustPM, which was completed in May 2012. The overall research results are published by PMI in the book Project Management & Sustainable Development Principles by Roland Gareis, Martina Huemann, and André Martinuzzi (all WU Vienna).

Chapter 9

Claudia Weninger, WU Vienna, Austria
Martina Huemann, WU Vienna, Austria

The consideration of Sustainable Development (SD) becomes more and more important for investments and the projects which implement those investments. In the project initiation process, the decision regarding the realization of an investment is made. Analyzing the investment is one of the main tasks of the project initiation process. Thus, this process is identified as most important for the integration of SD principles. The authors define SD with the following principles: economic, ecologic, and social-orientation; short, mid, and long term orientation as well as local, regional, and global-orientation. Furthermore, SD is value-based and considers values such as transparency, fairness, trust, etc. In this chapter, the authors describe the concept of responsible and ethical investment, which may also provide the basis for an investment decision within a project's initiation. While global project and program management standards show very limited consideration of comprehensive investment analysis, the authors draw on the Logical Framework Approach used by the World Bank to see how SD principles are considered in investment analysis methods. They then propose the integration of SD principles into the discipline of project initiation. This more holistic approach considers the investment life cycle, the consideration of different stakeholders, and investment method, which explicitly integrates SD principles.

Chapter 10

Alan Brent, Stellenbosch University, South Africa
Carin Tredoux, University of Pretoria, South Africa

Various driving forces originating from society, government, employees, and partners are forcing the enterprise to both incorporate sustainable development in its internal operations and practices, and to align these with the principles thereof. Technology-oriented project management, as a core competency of many enterprises, is not excluded from these requirements. Four cases are explored of how the aspects of sustainability have been addressed by various approaches and tools to enhance the performances of enterprises—in the context of project management in South Africa. The associated challenges are highlighted and the requirement for further work, to address the shortfalls, is outlined. Specifically, by developing methods for understanding the full implications of alternative choices and their relative attractiveness in terms of enhancing the resilience of systems, by extending the field of sustainability science into the field of project management.

Chapter 11

Jennifer Tharp, Mastodon Consulting, USA

As organizations evolve to embrace sustainability objectives, the operations of a company need to evolve to support those new objectives. Since project management is how strategy is executed within an organization, project management's evolution is key to this new reality. In this chapter, the author examine aspects of a sustainability program, common goals between project management and sustainability, and pragmatic implementation guidelines, which help the project manager integrate sustainability into his practices. Special emphasis is placed on each process area of project management, from inception through execution and control. The objectives of this chapter are: (1) translate the fundamental aspects of sustainability to the corporate environment and broader community; (2) understand the risk of ignoring sustainability aspects in projects, as expectations change, both in terms of direct financial loss and longer-term impact; and (3) explore how to integrate sustainability practices into project management knowledge areas.

Chapter 12

Jude Talbot, AMEC, Canada
Ray Venkataraman, Penn State University, USA

The concept of balancing people, planet, and profit to maximize the absolute value of an enterprise is known as sustainability. It is concerned with the economic, social, and environmental effects of an enterprise in the long term. However, in practice, this definition does not provide companies with a meaningful framework to integrate sustainability into their projects, which by definition are one-off endeavors. Given this divide between the long-term nature of sustainability and the temporary nature of projects, companies have found it difficult to incorporate relevant sustainability indicators into project baselines. In this chapter, the authors examine a methodology for integrating sustainability into project baselines for consultants in the industrial and resource extraction fields. The methodology is comprised of an indicator set and a procedure for using the indicator set. This chapter's goal is to help standardize the sustainability process, making it easier to implement and more mainstream. The objectives of this chapter are: (1) identify different sustainability indicator sets and their strengths and weaknesses; (2) explain what a multi-level analytical hierarchy project is and why it is important to integrating sustainability into such projects; and (3) state the steps in a procedure to integrate sustainability into project baselines.

Chapter 13

Gilbert Silvius, HU University of Applied Sciences Utrecht, The Netherlands & Van Aetsveld, The Netherlands
Ron Schipper, Van Aetsveld Project Management and Change, The Netherlands
Snezana Nedeski, Maastricht University, The Netherlands

The relevance of integrating the concepts of sustainability into project management shows from the growing number of studies on this topic. These studies approach the topic mostly from a conceptual, logical, or moral point of view. Given the fact that the relationship between sustainability and project management is still an emerging field of study, these approaches make sense. However, they do not diminish the need for more empirical studies to understand how the concepts of sustainable development are implemented in practice. This chapter reports an analysis of 56 case studies on the integration of the concepts of sustainability in the way organizations initiate, develop, and manage projects. The research question of the study was: To what extent do organizations consider the concepts of sustainability in the initiation, development, and management of projects? The study found an overall average level of sustainability consideration in the actual situation of 25.9%. For the desired situation, this score is almost 10 percent higher, showing an ambition to take sustainability more into consideration. The study also showed that the way sustainability currently is considered in projects should be categorized as the traditional "making things less bad" approach to sustainability integration and not as a more modern "how can we contribute to making things good" approach. However, the scores of the desired situation indicate that the modern approach to corporate responsibility is certainly the ambition of the participating organizations.

Section 3
Sustainability and the Project Manager

Business leaders are embracing sustainability not only as a matter of corporate social responsibility but because it offers opportunities for competitive advantage. As corporate activities are increasingly undertaken in the form of projects, project leaders have the opportunity to assist corporations in achieving their sustainability goals by incorporating sustainable practices in both the products they produce and the practices they use to produce them. Good project management is ultimately concerned with the most effective use of resources, which is a key tenet of sustainability. This chapter provides project leaders with practical guidance for incorporation of sustainable development principles in all aspects of their projects.

In this chapter, the relationship between positive psychology and sustainable project management is discussed. A general description of the field of positive psychology is given. The relationship between positive psychology and the three P's of sustainability (People, Planet, and Profit) is described. Specific attention is paid to hope and optimism as ways to intervene in project teams. Hope and optimism are central concepts in positive psychology. These concepts can help to improve the sustainability of project teams and to stimulate sustainable change.

In this chapter, the authors provide a rationale for asserting a special importance of the project manager with respect to implementing sustainability at their enterprise, due to their being at a key "pivot point." This does not come without challenges, and here the authors convey those specific challenges for project managers. They show that one of these challenges is adopting a sustainability thinking mindset, a mindset that has its roots in the "larger scheme of things, and the long-haul," even though project managers are often (necessarily) focused on their immediate scope, and short-term deliverables for demanding stakeholders. Finally, the authors advise project managers with some specific techniques to overcome the previous challenges.

When the project sponsor is responsible for the definition of the content of the project and the project manager for delivering this content, who then is responsible for incorporating sustainability in the process? Which project governance role has which responsibility to incorporate sustainability aspects in the project management process? This chapter shows how a project manager can influence the way sustainability is implemented in the project and the project management process. This perception is based on the notion that the project manager is intrinsically motivated to work on a sustainable project, and to achieve sustainable results.

Chapter 18

Gilman C. K. Tam, Independent Researcher, Hong Kong

In the two decades since the Earth Summit in 1992, an increasing number of projects have built sustainability considerations into project design and implementation. Project managers without knowledge and guidance on sustainability assessment would find it difficult to drive projects and programs contributing towards a sustainable society. The purpose of this chapter is to devise an assessment tool for project managers incorporating the concept of pillar-based and principles-based sustainability approaches as well as the EIA-driven and objectives-led assessment methodologies. The definitions of sustainability in project management and program management are discussed as basis for the establishment of sustainability evaluation framework. The views of project management community regarding the role of project manager in handling project related sustainability activities are discussed. This chapter contributes to devising a practical assessment tool for project managers in managing project sustainability.

Section 4
Case Studies and Best Practices

Chapter 19

Changes of Projects by Considering the Principles of Sustainable Development Case Study:
Roland Gareis, WU Vienna, Austria & Roland Gareis Consulting, Austria

Permanent organizations, such as companies, divisions, profit, and cost centres, as well as temporary organizations, i.e. projects and programmes, change. Reasons for changes might be new values of organizations such as transparency, empowerment, stakeholder participation, risk-orientation, etc., which are values on which sustainable development is based. Different change types, namely organizational learning, further developing, transforming, and radical re-positioning can be identified and can be described by specific chains of processes. For performing change processes of permanent organizations projects and programmes can be applied. The processes for managing the different changes of projects, in which the principles of SD might be considered, are described. The focus is on the management of transforming a project. The case study: Transforming the Project Hospital North is based on a comprehensive analysis of this project transformation in the book Project Management & Sustainable Development Principles by Roland Gareis, Martina Huemann, and André Martinuzzi (all WU Vienna) published by PMI (Gareis et al. 2013).

Chapter 20

Ramanda Achman, TU Delft, The Netherlands

More projects today are driven by sustainability goals than ever before. The need for sustainability as a critical factor for project success is clear. However, it is interesting to investigate the link between project management and sustainability more comprehensively. Especially by taking into account the importance of stakeholders' involvement in project management activities. Thus, this chapter examines whether stakeholders' perspectives on sustainability can provide a positive contribution to project management practices. Four different projects with goals related to sustainability in the Netherlands are studied and used as case studies to know the differences between the perspectives of stakeholders involved in the projects. One of the findings that was discovered is that the inclusion of "People" and "Planet" performance indicators in the management and delivery of projects is still rarely implemented, although the stakeholders categorize their projects as sustainable projects.

Chapter 21
Ron Schipper, Van Aetsveld Project Management and Change, The Netherlands
Snezana Nedeski, Maastricht University, The Netherlands

Many articles have called attention to the concept of sustainability in project management. However, it still remains a challenge to tie all these very important principles to practice. In this chapter, the main issues with the practical application of sustainability to an actual project are identified, and a method for analysis is presented. Through this method, the authors answer the main question of this chapter: "How can a project and its project management be analyzed for sustainability and how can adequate actions be selected?" The proposed method is then applied to an actual case. In the analysis, an explicit distinction is made between the internal project view of sustainability and external view of sustainability. From the analysis, various conclusions can be drawn.

Chapter 22
Stephanie Steele, USI Group, Australia

This chapter moves outside the traditional methodology of project management, looking more broadly at aspects that influence project sustainability initiatives, including regulation, legislation, brand reputation, government and non-government organisations, and client requirements. Using the example of mercury recycling from fluorescent tubes generated from the Facilities Management (FM) sector in Australia, the relationship between environmental management systems, specifically ISO 14001:2004, and project management aspects are highlighted. The importance of management support, both at a strategic and project level is discussed. The opportunity to create competitive advantage from the sales perspective is demonstrated, through a cost justification and review of client sensitivity to influencing factors, enabling reasoned decision making for a successful, environmentally sustainable initiative.

Chapter 23
Claudia Weninger, WU Vienna, Austria
Martina Huemann, WU Vienna, Austria
Jairo Cardoso de Oliveira, Siemens Ltd, Brazil
Luis Fernando Mendonça Barros Filho, Siemens Ltd, Brazil
Erwin Weitlaner, Siemens AG, Germany

The chapter reports on the case study project of the Engineering, Procurement, and Construction (EPC) of a wind park farm in Brazil from the supplier perspective of Siemens Ltd. In the case study, researchers, together with practitioners, further developed project stakeholder analysis by explicitly integrating Sustainable Development (SD) principles. The chapter offers an operative approach and describes the working form systemic board to better handle the increasing dynamics and complexity in contemporary projects and contexts. For project stakeholder management, the consideration of SD principles means in particular: applying a more comprehensive stakeholder management approach with underpinning values that support sustainable development; integrating economic, ecologic, and social interests of project stakeholders into the project objectives to create shared benefit for the project investor and other project stakeholders; broadening the time perspective to consider not only current stakeholders but also future stakeholders of the investment initialized by the project; broadening the spatial perspective to consider local, regional as well as global impacts of the project for stakeholders; using systemic working forms to allow for making the dynamics and complexities of the project and the project contexts better visible to the project manager, the project team, and the project owner; taking consequences in the project organization which lead to more integrative project organization structures to support cooperation on a project and with its stakeholders.

Chapter 24

Aleksander Janeš, University of Primorska, Slovenia
Armand Faganel, University of Primorska, Slovenia

The purpose of this chapter is to propose a framework that is supporting achievement of the sustainable strategy of the organization. The research frames the methodology that integrates project management and Balanced Scorecard (BSC) in the management system of the organization. In this applicative project research, the authors identified and analyzed the Key Performance Indicators (KPIs) that significantly contribute to the benefits of the business processes exploitation. The involved company executes monitoring of its business performance in the four perspectives of the BSC. With this case study, the authors attempted to get deeper understanding, and to clarify and evaluate the causalities between strategic goals and their respective KPIs. For this purpose, they developed an Error Correction Model with which they performed application on the KPIs and estimated short and long term effects between them. The developed model also supports improvements of the performance management system and monitoring of projects.

Preface

"The most important leadership challenge facing business today is the integration of sustainability into core business functions" (BSR/GlobeScan State of Sustainable Business Poll, 2012). This conclusion, from the 2012 BSR/GlobeScan State of Sustainable Business Poll, outlines the importance of sustainability on global business, and the progress it has made over the past 20 years. Sustainable development emerged from an idealistic concern of pressure groups, and grew into a critical business concern of executives.

An important challenge for these executives is to put sustainability to practice in their core business. Contributing to sustainable development is not the "greenwashing" of current business practices. It is the re-thinking, re-designing, and re-developing of business practices in a more sustainable way. Sustainability therefore means change. Change of business models, products, services, resources, processes, reporting, and behavior. Change that is most often implemented via projects. Relating sustainability to projects and project management therefore makes a lot of sense. It is this relationship that is addressed in this book.

The relationship between sustainability and project management is an emerging field of study that is picking up momentum. Figure 1 provides an overview of publications (books, book chapters, articles in academic journals, and conference papers) on the topic[1]. It shows that the majority of serious publications were published in the last four years, so the insights and knowledge on what the integration of a sustainability orientation on project management are developing.

With insights and knowledge developing, it is useful to create an overview. This book aims to provide this overview. In 24 chapters, the findings and views of over 30 authors are presented. Their contributions cover studies in North America, South America, Australia, West and Central Europe, Asia, and Africa, Some authors have a very practical perspective, whereas others approach the topic more aca-

Figure 1. Overview of publications on the topic of sustainability in projects and project management

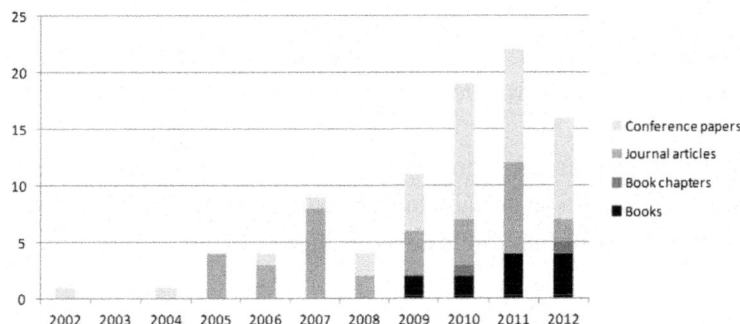

demically. They may have different ideas, consider different aspects, or reach different conclusions. The overview provided in this book is not about providing a single theory, storyline, or "truth." It is about showing relevant insights that provide a foundation for discussion and development. Development of knowledge on the topic of implementing sustainability in, and by, projects and project management. This book is therefore designed to enlighten and inspire project sponsors, project managers, and project teams to understand how sustainability applies to projects and how sustainability practices can be incorporated into project management.

READERSHIP

The first group of professionals that this book addresses is project management professionals. It is this group that will be faced with an increasing demand for demonstrating sustainability in their work.

The responsibility for sustainability in projects, however, also rests with project sponsors, PMO leaders, and other stakeholders in the context of projects. The book therefore also aims to address (senior) management, executives, and sustainability professionals. It is this group that is faced with the implementation of sustainability in the core business practices of their organizations.

The third and final group of professionals this book targets are educators and students in the field of business and project management. They represent the future of their professions and will need to respond with the sustainability challenges that we are faced with. Today and in the future.

ORGANIZATION

This book is structured in four sections, with the following themes:

1. Considering Project Management through a Sustainability Lens
2. Integrating Sustainability into Project Management
3. Sustainability and the Project Manager
4. Case Studies and Best Practices

The next paragraphs provide a short introduction to each chapter.

OVERVIEW

As the book is devoted to a very diverse range of topics contributed by a large number of professionals and academics, it is felt necessary to provide a bird's eye view of the contents of the chapters.

Section 1: "Considering Project Management through a Sustainability Lens." The seven chapters in this section introduce the concepts of sustainability, which have a long-term focus, to project management, with a short-term focus, and finds areas of alignment.

Chapter 1: "How Business Excellence Models Contribute to Project Sustainability and Project Success," establishes links between project sustainability, Business Excellence Models, and project success. The chapter reviews the Baldridge Performance Excellence Program and the European Foundation for Quality Management, for alignment with sustainability considerations. The author finds that establishing the integrative project mindset is critical to ensuring sustainability is a full participant at the table of project success criteria.

Chapter 2: "Integrating Project Strategy for Sustainable Development: A Conceptual Framework," presents a framework for integrating project strategy for sustainable development within the context of corporate sustainability strategy. This framework starts with corporate sustainability strategy and stakeholder relationships, and moves throughout project structures, processes, and activities.

Chapter 3: "GreenPM®: The Basic Principles for Applying an Environmental Dimension to Project Management," describes different concepts for integrating environmental considerations throughout the project lifecycle. Examination is made of the process groups, as well as portfolio management and metrics. Applying principles of environmental sustainability need not be an onerous endeavor, and can ultimately be good for the business as a whole.

Chapter 4: "Sustainability in Project Management Processes," evaluates ways to integrate sustainability principles within project management standards, moving beyond the merely implicit references to sustainability practices within PRINCE2®, the PMBOK® Guide and the ISO 21500 Guidance on project management.

Chapter 5: "How can Sustainable Development Redefine Project Management Processes?" The research described in this chapter proposes a tri-dimensional integration between construction, project management, and sustainable development when approached from a systems thinking point of view.

Chapter 6: "Social Sustainability to Social Benefit: Creating Positive Outcomes through a Social Risk-Based Approach," shows how the incorporation of social risk monitoring can significantly improve the likelihood of a project's success. This chapter argues that sustainability risk should be identified and managed in the same manner as all other project risks.

Chapter 7: "Project Success by Integrating Sustainability in Project Management," concludes the section with a description of the behavioural aspects of integrating sustainability with project management. Published integrated annual reports from 35 organizations are investigated for the level of sustainability disclosure, the degree of success of projects involving sustainability, and the impact of integrating sustainability into project management practices.

Section 2: Titled "Integrating Sustainability into Project Management," consists of six chapters that begin the work of determining how project management processes are changing, and will continue to change, to support sustainability concerns.

Chapter 8: "Re-Thinking Project Initiation and Project Management by Considering Principles of Sustainable Development," it is argued that considering sustainable development principles results in an improved quality of project initiation processes, to determine whether an investment should be made.

Chapter 9: "Project Initiation: Investment Analysis for Sustainable Development," examines responsible and ethical investment, and its possible role in providing the basis for an investment decision within project initiation. The chapter presents holistic approach, which considers the investment life cycle, the interests of different stakeholders and diverse investment methods to integrate sustainability principles in project initiation.

Chapter 10: "Integrating Sustainability into Technology-Oriented Project Management: Cases from South Africa," investigates how sustainability may be addressed in the management of projects, based on the analysis of four cases. The investigation uncovers that sustainability issues cannot be treated as separate from core enterprise activities and practices, as social-ecological systems are the base of all economic activity.

Chapter 11: "Sustainability in Project Management: Practical Applications," describes aspects of sustainability and pragmatically applies them to deliverables and processes throughout the project management lifecycle.

Chapter 12: "Evaluating Sustainability on Projects Using Indicators," examines a proposed methodology for integrating sustainability into project baselines in two industries. Existing indicator sets are analyzed via analytic hierarchy, and a procedure is defined for applying the most appropriate set to a given project.

Chapter 13: "Consideration of Sustainability in Projects and Project Management: An Empirical Study," analyzes 56 case studies, to ask to what extent organizations currently consider the concepts of sustainability in the initiation, development, and management of projects. The study concludes that sustainability is most often considered in terms of business resources, but there are many more opportunities, and desire for realizing them in the future.

Section 3: "Sustainability and the Project Manager," is comprised of five chapters that focus on the project manager as driver for these changes. The drive towards sustainable project management depends on his leadership, attitude, and focus towards integration.

Chapter 14: "Leading Sustainability through Projects," offers practical guidance on what project leaders must do in order to incorporate sustainable development not just in products, but in activities as well. A particular focus is brought to bear on the variance between the temporary nature of projects and the long-term perspective of sustainability.

Chapter 15: "How Positive Psychology can Support Sustainable Project Management," studies project management from a psychological perspective. The chapter posits that positive emotions such as hope and optimism are particularly important for the development of sustainable project management.

Chapter 16: "Project Manager as a Pivot Point for Implementing Sustainability in an Enterprise," focuses on the criticality of the role of the project manager in achieving organizational sustainability, and the importance of developing a new mindset, a new frame of reference, in order to achieve long-term objectives through short-term initiatives. Connections between sustainability thinking and lean methods are used to illustrate this paradigm shift.

Chapter 17: "Sustainability in Project Management: Perceptions of Responsibility," wrestles with the question of who is actually responsible for incorporating sustainability in project management processes, the project manager or the sponsor. Through literature review and case examination, it is determined that intrinsic motivation of the project manager to incorporate sustainability into his work is the decisive factor for effective integration.

Chapter 18: "Sustainability Assessment for Project Managers," a sustainability toolset is revealed, along with guiding principles for assessing sustainability, to encourage positive project impacts. These tools help the project manager better determine how to handle sustainability impacts.

Section 4: "Case Studies and Best Practices," concludes with six chapters that demonstrate work that has already been done on integrating sustainability with project management.

Chapter 19: "Changes of Projects by Considering the Principles of Sustainable Development Case Study: Transforming the Project Hospital North," uses a case to explore how sustainability can be taken into account while managing the transformation of a project. Principles of sustainable development can be considered in changes in projects, and also sustainable development might cause major changes of projects, and may in and of itself be a reason for change.

Chapter 20: "Stakeholders' Perspectives on Sustainability in Project Management," looks at four different projects, with goals related to sustainability, in The Netherlands. The study demonstrates that even projects aligned with sustainability objectives are rarely executed in a socially and environmentally responsible way. Awareness alone is not enough to develop sustainable project management practices, and the stakeholder's own perspective is key.

Chapter 21: "Application of Sustainability Considerations into Practice: The Open Remote Case," examines how a project can be analyzed for sustainability, and how adequate actions can be selected. Conclusions from the case include the fact that applying sustainability in project management gives a broader scope, that lifecycle evaluation is critical, and that sustainability requires leadership and taking action.

Chapter 22: "Drivers for Sustainable Project Management Behaviours in Facilities Management: Fluorescent Tube Business Case Example," moves beyond traditional project management methodology to examine the broader environment around sustainability. What influence do legal and regulatory factors have on sustainability? How about business and governmental factors? This case examines these interdependencies through the initiation and planning phases of a project as it works towards those outcomes.

Chapter 23: "Experimenting with Project Stakeholder Analysis: A Case Study," examines the impacts and complexity of integrating sustainability practices in project stakeholder analysis, using a wind farm project conducted for Siemens.

Chapter 24: "Instruments and Methods for Integrating Sustainability in Project Management: Case Study from Slovenia," the use of a Balanced Score Card (BSC) as an instrument for sustainability integration is examined in a case study. The BSC is a strategic tool for achieving sustainable development and an excellent approach for harmonizing and coordinating projects in order to fulfill the implementation of strategic direction.

CONCLUSION

This book aimed to provide an overview of relevant perspectives, views, and findings on the relationship between sustainability and project management. In that aim, the book succeeds. It brings together the most influential authors on the topic, from different backgrounds and regions, and they provide a variety of approaches and opinions. Therefore, what can we conclude from this overview? Is there a common message? On what do the authors agree? And on what do they disagree?

A first obvious conclusion is that the authors agree it makes sense to connect sustainability to projects and project management. This conclusion may logically be biased, because of the focus of the book, but the fact that so many authors from such different backgrounds share this opinion is meaningful. Also regarding the role of the project manager, the authors seem to agree that this role is pivotal in the consideration of sustainability in projects, despite the fact that the formal responsibility for many aspects of the project may be with the project sponsor.

The authors probably also agree that the widely used standards for project management address the consideration of sustainability aspect only partially and/or implicitly. In fact, one of the critiques on the recently released *Guide to the Project Management Body of Knowledge* (PMBOK®) 5th edition, is that, despite calls and a petition from practitioners and academics, it does not address the relationship between sustainable development and project management properly. One of the logical reasons for this is that the understanding of impact of sustainability on project management principles, concepts, and processes is not developed enough yet. On this aspect, the book makes a good contribution, by providing frameworks, criteria, and consideration, as well as practical instruments, tools, and formats. However, a next step should be to integrate the tools and instruments provided here, in order to provide a foundation for the development of standards.

The tools and instruments provided in, or perhaps derived from, the content of this book will need to be tested and developed further in real life projects. The cases reported in section 4 provide first applications, but it should be concluded that empirical studies on the integration of sustainability in projects and project management is still limited. Studies are mainly interpretive and/or qualitative. In an emerging field of study, this is a logical phase; however, a next step in research on the topic would preferably need to lead to more universal results.

A point of discussion amongst the authors may be the definition of the scope of considering sustainability aspects in projects and project management. Some authors suggest that the concepts of sustainability inevitably imply that the sustainability aspects of the project's deliverables and their effects should be included in the scope of considering sustainability in projects. However, other authors consider the sustainability of the "permanent" organization out-of-scope of the sustainability of the "temporary" organization, the project. Although a point can be made for both views, the editors believe that the two organizations, the permanent one and the project, cannot be isolated from each other. In practice, projects often share resources with the permanent organization, or fall under the same governance regime, making it impossible to have conflicting values. As some authors demonstrate, considering sustainability is most of all a value-based concept.

This observation brings us to our final conclusion: considering sustainability is about values. The question is, what are the values of the project management profession? PMI's Code of Ethics and Professional Conduct paves the way for the further professionalization of project management and formulates clearly and specifically the values that should lead us in our work: responsibility, respect, fairness, and honesty. If we work according to these values, considering sustainability aspects in projects and project management is a logical consequence of our profession. As IPMA Vice-President Mary McKinlay stated at the opening of the 22nd World Congress of the International Project Management Association in 2008: "the further development of the project management profession requires project managers to take responsibility for sustainability". Therefore, it is up to us. All of us!

Gilbert Silvius
HU University of Applied Sciences Utrecht & Van Aetsveld, The Netherlands

Jennifer Tharp
Mastodon Consulting, USA & University of California – Berkeley, USA

REFERENCES

BSR/GlobeScan State of Sustainable Business Poll. (2012). Retrieved from http://www.globescan.com/component/edocman/?task=document.viewdoc&id=43&Itemid=591

McKinlay, M. (2008). *Opening statement.* Paper presented at the 22nd World Congress of the International Project Management Association. Rome, Italy.

ENDNOTES

[1]   The overview of publications is included in the final sections of this book.

Acknowledgment

The editors would like to express their gratitude to all the people who contributed to the book as authors, advisors, reviewers, and developers. It speaks for itself that an overview of relevant views and perspectives can only arise from the willingness of relevant professionals to contribute to the further development of a certain topic. We are happy that so many colleagues, from many different backgrounds and regions, were enthusiastic about the idea to develop this book. Their contributions made the book to what it is: a true overview of the "state of play" of knowledge, perspectives, and insights on the relationship between sustainable development and project management. We are proud of the result and thankful to everyone who made it possible. We would also like to thank the colleagues at IGI Global. Their professionalism, and sometimes patience, was an important condition for the development of this book.

Gilbert Silvius
HU University of Applied Sciences Utrecht and Van Aetsveld, The Netherlands

Jennifer Tharp
Mastodon Consulting, USA & University of California – Berkeley, USA

Section 1
Considering Project Management through a Sustainability Lens

Chapter 1
How Business Excellence Models Contribute to Project Sustainability and Project Success

William T. Craddock
Craddock & Associates, Inc., USA

ABSTRACT

The purpose of this chapter is to establish the linkages among Business Excellence Models (BEMs), project sustainability, and project success. The particular focus is on how the BEM framework contributes to project sustainability as one element of project success. Although general sustainability definitions vary, most describe a broad perspective that encompasses economic, social, and environmental objectives. This broad perspective fits well with the concepts of both Corporate Social Responsibility (CSR) and Total Quality Management (TQM). Business Excellence Models, with their origins in the TQM movement, provide a framework to address sustainability. Although much of the literature focuses on applying these concepts in a general organizational setting, they also apply to a project organization. Project success criteria can be expanded to include project sustainability, measured both at the time of project closing and later when the overall project benefits are evaluated.

INTRODUCTION

The key question this chapter seeks to answer is: How *do* Business Excellence Models (BEMs) contribute to both project sustainability and project success? A secondary question involves the relationship between project sustainability and project success. The path to answer these questions begins with a general discussion of the different views of sustainability and how sustainability is related to the Corporate Social Responsibility (CSR) framework. The connection between the CSR and

DOI: 10.4018/978-1-4666-4177-8.ch001

Total Quality Management (TQM) frameworks is a critical link. Then, the relationship between TQM and BEMs is relatively straight forward. Along the way, these frameworks are extended to a project environment.

The definitions for sustainability vary in their scope. Some have a primarily environmental focus. Examples include Clayton and Radcliffe (1996), Schmitz (2010), and Hopkins (2011). Other definitions highlight three distinct components: economic, social, and environmental. Examples include Elkington (1998), Willard (2002), and Wirtenberg (2011). While there are multiple references that address sustainability in a general sense, there are fewer descriptions of sustainability from a project perspective. One example is the discussion by Silvius, Schipper, and van den Brink (2012) regarding how and why sustainability should be incorporated into project management. They concluded that considering sustainability in project management has implications, including on the level of the organization.

Business Excellence Models provide a framework for performance excellence in any organization. There are many BEMs in use today. Both Grigg and Mann (2008) and Talwar (2011) concluded that the two that are most often cited are the Baldrige Criteria for Performance Excellence (CPE) and the European Foundation for Quality Management (EFQM). Further, these two BEMs both address sustainability, although from different perspectives. Silvius, Schipper, and van den Brink (2012) discussed how the EFQM Model applies to projects. Similar arguments could be made regarding the applicability of the Baldrige CPE Model.

There are over two decades of examples where organizations used BEMs as a framework to achieve organizational excellence. Although there are limited discussions of applying BEMs in a project context, these discussions provide valid arguments to do so. Organizational success

is intuitively linked to organizational excellence. Hendricks and Singhal (2001) examined the impact of Total Quality Management (TQM) programs, as a proxy for BEMs. They found that the winners of TQM Award Programs have better financial performance than firms that had not won the awards. Again, since projects are organizations, BEMs should also facilitate project excellence that increases the likelihood of project success.

Like the definition of sustainability, there are multiple views of what constitutes project success. These multiple views include both a traditional view of project success (based on schedule, cost, and scope performance) as well as metrics that are assessed primarily after the conclusion of the project. Nelson (2005) provided one framework to categorize these two views. Project sustainability can be included in both of these perspectives. Ultimately, the success of the project manager requires managing the expectations of the many project stakeholders. Some stakeholders will likely have expectations for a project's sustainability. A BEM framework will help the project manager address these expectations.

This chapter, then, involves three essential messages. First, Business Excellence Models also apply in a project environment. Second, BEMs provide a framework to address sustainability in organizations, including projects. The final essential message is that BEMs can be utilized to address project sustainability as one contributor to project success.

The organization of this chapter begins with a more detailed discussion of sustainability and its linkages to Corporate Social Responsibility and Total Quality Management. The introduction of Business Excellence Models is a logical extension of the TQM discussion. The two specific BEMs used most frequently are addressed in more detail. Finally, the chapter explores how BEMs address project sustainability and ultimately project success.

SUSTAINABILITY

Barker (1989) defined a paradigm as "a set of rules and regulations that: (1) defines boundaries; and (2) tells you what to do to be successful within those boundaries" (p. 14). From a practical perspective, paradigms are often expressed as definitions, and there are many definitions for sustainability.

Sustainability and Sustainable Development

Indeed, Norton (2005) observed that the multiple definitions are indicative of a larger need for a language to discuss key concepts and priorities for sustainability. More to the point, Bell and Morse (2008) noted "the difficulty that various academic and practitioner communities have had in coming to any agreement about what constitutes sustainability" (p. 181).

Early definitions of sustainability appeared to address environmental or ecological concerns. For example, Hawken (1993) noted: "The word 'sustainability' can be defined in terms of carrying capacity of the ecosystem and described with input-output models of energy and resource consumption" (p. 139). One might argue that this is an outdated definition. However, some more recent definitions have also emphasized an environmental perspective. Schmitz (2010) and Hopkins (2011) are two examples.

The World Commission on Environment and Development (1987) defined sustainable development in *Our Common Future*: "Sustainable development is development that meets the needs of the present without compromising the ability of future generations to meet their own needs" (p. 43). Presley, Meade, and Sarkis (2007) and Deland (2009) noted this is the most accepted definition of sustainability. The World Commission on Environment and Development is frequently referred to as the Brundtland Commission, named after the Chairman of the Commission. Two decades later, the 2005 United Nations World Summit expanded the definition to explicitly include three major components: economic, social, and environmental sustainability. The UN Resolution 60/1 (2005) noted that these three components are "interdependent and mutually reinforcing pillars" (p. 12). As an example of this expanded view, Labuschagne and Brent (2005) rephrased and extended the Brundtland definition as follows: "For the business enterprise, sustainable development means adopting business strategies and activities that meet the needs of the enterprise and its stakeholders today, while protecting, sustaining and enhancing the human and natural resources that will be needed in the future" (p. 160). The "needs" dimension of the Labuschagne and Brent definition encompasses financial resources, human resources, and environmental resources. Similarly, Edwards (2005), who traced the sustainability revolution since the 1800s, observed that it has evolved to a "diverse, worldwide, multicultural and multiperspective revolution built around the Three Es: (1) ecology/environment; (2) economy/employment; and (3) equity/equality" (p. 20).

Elkington (1998) coined the phrase "Triple Bottom Line" to refer to the economic, social, and environmental needs of an organization. Elkington used the terms economic prosperity, environmental quality, and social justice, and then noted that social justice is "the element which business has tended to overlook" (p. 2). Willard (2002) described this triple bottom line as a "three-legged stool" (p. 5). Willard's three legs are economic prosperity, social responsibility, and environmental stewardship.

Wirtenberg (2011) used a Venn diagram to envision the triple bottom line and defined sustainability as the common overlap of the three: "Sustainability thus defined is at the intersection of all three circles, People, Planet, and Profits" (p. 71). Planko and Silvius (2012) also used a Venn diagram with "sustainable" at its center (p. 8). They labeled the intersections between the pairs of variables as "bearable", "equitable", and "viable". All three of these are important, but are not substitutes for sustainable.

Although the Brundtland definition centered on sustainable development, there are differences of opinion regarding whether sustainable development differs from sustainability. Bernhart and Maher (2011) observed that sustainability is an end point and *sustainable development* is the means of getting there" (p. 110). However, other authors used the two terms somewhat interchangeably. Examples include Norton (2005), Deland (2009), and Hitchcock and Willard (2009). This chapter follows the latter practice of using the terms somewhat interchangeably in order to reflect the various treatments in the literature.

Project Sustainability

Pojasek (2007) described business sustainability as follows: "Business sustainability seeks to create long-term shareholder value by embracing the opportunities and managing the risks that result from an organization's economic, environmental, and social responsibilities" (p. 81). Pojasek identified seven attributes of any business activity. These attributes included "performed by people, … influenced by a broad range of stakeholders, … and constrained by limited resources" (p. 82).

Pojasek's attributes also apply to a project context where there is a dependency on people to accomplish work, a wide variety of stakeholders, and resource constraints. In other words, a project can be viewed as a business. With minor changes, the sustainability definition becomes: project sustainability is the process of creating stakeholder value by leveraging the opportunities and risks to balance the project's economic, environmental, and social responsibilities. Projects must address the triple bottom line variables (economics/finances, people, and environment) as do all other organizations. And as with other organizations, the project stakeholders may have differing views of the priorities for these variables.

Badiru (2010) noted that "sustainability is nothing more than prudent resource utilization" (p. 31). This is the central role of a Project Manager – managing resources prudently to accomplish the project objectives within the approved scheduled and budget. More specifically, Badiru placed project sustainability on the same level as project planning, organizing, scheduling, and control. Badiru concluded: "Project sustainability exists in all factors related to the project. Thus, we should always focus on project sustainability." (p. 34). Tharp (2012) used overlapping triangles to visually show the strategic context and relationship of sustainability and project management. The inner triangle represented the traditional project constraints of schedule, cost, and scope. The outer triangle represented the economic, social, and environmental components of sustainability. Tharp also suggested actions a project manager could take to address these three components.

Labuschagne and Brent (2004) addressed project sustainability from a different perspective. Specifically, they evaluated the project evaluation process and determined that the economic component of sustainability is well represented in current project evaluation and approval processes. However, consideration for the social and environmental components is not as evident in project evaluation and approval. They proposed an evaluation framework for these two components to ensure that project evaluations and approvals adequately address all aspects of sustainability. Stated differently, project managers and sponsors address sustainability by ensuring the project approval process rewards projects whose outcome objectives address all three sustainability components.

Finally, Silvius, Schipper, and van den Brink (2012) explored how sustainability can be incorporated into project management using both *PMBOK® Guide* and PRINCE2® terminologies. They also developed a maturity model to assess the extent to which a project addresses sustainability.

Linkage between Sustainability and Corporate Social Responsibility

Corporate Social Responsibility (CSR) also has several definitions. In general, these definitions are similar to the expanded definitions of sustainability. For example, Ghobadian, Gallear, and Hopkins (2007) adopted the definition of CSR that was previously offered by one of the authors:

CSR is concerned with treating the stakeholders of the firm ethically or in a socially responsible manner. Stakeholders exist both within a firm and outside. The aim of social responsibility is to create higher and higher standards of living, while preserving the profitability of the corporation, for its stakeholders both within and outside the corporation (p. 711).

This definition incorporates several key concepts: the roles of stakeholders and their needs/interests, ethical behavior, standards of living, and profitability. The stakeholder needs, including expectations for standards of living and profitability, fit within Elkington's triple bottom line. But the inclusion of ethical behavior in the definition appears to raise the bar on sustainability. For example, McWilliams and Siegel (2001) defined CSR as "actions that appear to further some social good, beyond the interests of the firm and that which is required by law" (p. 117).

Social Responsibility is also addressed in ISO 26000. Bernhart and Maher (2011) noted that "one of the aims of ISO 26000 is to help create uniformity of language" (p. 11). They added: "It may also help to think of *social responsibility* as an organization's responsibility to reach sustainability – an end point, the ultimate destination on the continuum" (p. 11).

Green (2012) offered perhaps the most comprehensive definition of CSR:

The continuing commitment by businesses to behave ethically and contribute to economic development while improving the quality of life of the workplace as well as the local community and society at large; a company's obligation to be accountable to all of its stakeholders in all of its operations and activities (including financial stakeholders as well as suppliers, customers, and employees) with the aim of achieving sustainable development not only in the economic dimension but also in the social and environmental dimensions (p. 34).

The second part of Green's definition incorporated the economic, social, and environmental dimensions, but also went further than the previous definitions of the triple bottom line. Specifically, Green included an organization's obligation to be accountable to all stakeholders for achieving these three dimensions. This obligation was emphasized in the first part of the definition by invoking the ethical commitment to do so. In simple terms, CSR is the self-imposed ethical obligation to balance and meet stakeholder expectations for sustaining economic, social, and environmental resources.

From a project perspective, Green's definition could be slightly rephrased: A Project's Social Responsibility (PSR) is the obligation to achieve the project's objectives and balance the needs of all stakeholders in an ethical manner to ensure financial resources, human resources, and environmental resources are utilized in a way that sustains all three.

Linkage between Corporate Social Responsibility and Total Quality Management

Although the CSR and Total Quality Management (TQM) frameworks are similar, the logic in connecting these two frameworks is not initially obvious. The rationale for connecting them is their similarities. This connection is needed to establish the linkages between sustainability and Business Excellence Models.

Ghobadian, Gallear, and Hopkins (2007) summarized the similarities and differences between the CSR and TQM frameworks. They concluded that CSR and TQM have similar philosophical origins; the two frameworks have significant overlap; and the expected outcomes of each approach are also similar. (p. 704). Based on previous work by two of the authors, they defined TQM (or "business excellence") as follows:

TQM is a structured attempt to re-focus the organisation's behaviour, planning and working practices towards a culture which is employee driven, problem solving, stakeholder oriented, values integrity, and open and fear free. Furthermore, the organisation's business practices are based on seeking continuous improvement, devolution of decision making, removal of functional barriers, eradication of sources of error, team working, honestly, and fact based decision making (p. 706).

Leonard and McAdam (2003) observed that "CSR and quality are strongly linked through such principles as ethics and respect for people" (p. 28). Hazlett, McAdam, and Murray (2007) also identified several similarities between CSR and TQM, including the mutual emphasis on ethics, moral obligations, and a balance of stakeholder voices. They made an argument that moving toward CSR "could be a natural progression for those organisations that have already begun their 'quality journey'" (p. 672).

Finally, Lubin and Esty (2010) declared sustainability as a megatrend, and identified lessons learned from two previous megatrends – the total quality and information technology revolutions. In particular, they listed four stages of value creation as part of the establishing the vision: (1) do old things in new ways; (2) do new things in new ways; (3) transform core business; and (4) create new business models and differentiate (p. 47). Then, Lubin and Esty made the following observation:

Gaining advantage in a megatrend is not just about vision – it's also about execution in five critical areas: leadership, methods, strategy,

management, and reporting. In each area, companies must transition from tactical, ad hoc, and siloed approaches to strategic, systematic, and integrated ones (p. 47).

These five critical areas are an excellent lead-in to the discussion of Business Excellence Models.

BUSINESS EXCELLENCE MODELS

Adebanjo and Mann (2008) described business excellence as "'excellence' in strategies, business practices, and stakeholder-related performance results that have been validated by assessments using proven business excellence models" (p. 16). A Business Excellence Model (BEM), then, is a holistic framework for describing the practices of excellent organizations in a way that allows assessments to determine the strengths and opportunities for improvement in an organization. Some organizations have developed their own BEM. For example, Zhao (2004) described Siemens AG's Top+ Program, their company-wide BEM. Sharma and Talwar (2007) briefly discussed the Xerox Business Excellence Model and the Toyota Production System 4P Model. However, most organizations adopt a BEM that is associated with a National Quality Award.

Grigg and Mann (2008) estimated over 80 nations utilized a BEM as the basis for their National Quality Award (NQA). Grigg and Mann's estimate was further divided into three subsets, with approximately 50 of the 80 nations using the Malcolm Baldrige National Quality Award (MBNQA) model. Another 25 or so nations had adopted the European Foundation for Quality Management (EFQM) model. Stated differently, the MBNQA and the EFQM models were used for approximately 93% of the national BEMs.

In a similar study, Talwar (2011) identified 100 NQAs in 82 different countries. The major BEMs cited are the MBNQA, EFQM, and the Deming Prize. Talwar did not have access to the details of every NQA. However, for the 81 NQAs summarized by Talwar, approximately 80% either fully adopted or used features from the three major BEMs. Talwar noted the structural similarities of the MBNQA and EFQM models, as compared to the Deming Prize. Further, the Deming Prize was cited in less than 10% of these 81 NQAs. Also, Adebanjo and Mann (2008) noted that the Baldrige Criteria for Performance Excellence and the EFQM are the best-known of the BEMs. For these reasons, the MBNQA and EFQM will be the focus of this discussion.

Baldrige Performance Excellence Program

The Malcolm Baldrige National Quality Award was established in 1987, and the Baldrige Criteria for Performance Excellence (CPE) were initially used in 1988 to evaluate applicants for the Malcolm Baldrige Award (Evans & Dean, 2000). The program was recently rebranded as the Baldrige Performance Excellence Program. The program is managed by the U.S. Department of Commerce (via the National Institute of Standards and Technology).

The 2011-2012 version of the Baldrige CPE is described in seven categories. The first six are focused on various processes. The last category addresses results.

1. Leadership
2. Strategic Planning
3. Customer Focus
4. Measurement, Analysis, and Knowledge Management
5. Workforce Focus
6. Operations Focus
7. Results

Both processes and results categories are evaluated. The process evaluations address (1) the overall approach, (2) the deployment of the process, (3) evidence of process learning or improvement, and (4) the integration within the organization. As an organization matures from an overall management perspective, it should begin to incorporate concrete examples across all four of these process attributes.

The results evaluations address (1) the levels of performance, (2) the performance trends, (3) whether comparative data are used for evaluation, and (4) the integration within the organization. Similar to the process evaluations, the results evaluation attributes are a gage of how "mature" an organization is regarding its overall management.

All seven categories are structured from high-level to detailed questions so that an organization can use its responses to determine its level of maturity and key opportunities for improvement. Three versions of the Baldrige CPE are published. The primary version is the *Criteria for Performance Excellence* for use by the business and nonprofit sectors. The other two versions, the *Health Care Criteria for Performance Excellence* and the *Education Criteria for Performance Excellence*, are essentially the same with wording changes to reflect the "customers" and processes for those two sectors.

European Foundation for Quality Management

The European Foundation for Quality Management (EFQM) was established in 1988 (Adebanjo, 2001). The EFQM created the European Quality Award in 1991 in partnership with the European Commission and the European Organization for Quality (Evans & Dean, 2000). Adebanjo noted that the European Quality Award is now known as the EFQM Excellence Award.

The 2010 EFQM Excellence Model is described in nine categories. The first five are focused on various processes. The last four categories address results.

1. Leadership
2. Strategy

3. People
4. Partnerships & Resources
5. Processes, Products and Services
6. Customer Results
7. People Results
8. Society Results
9. Key Results

Similar to the Baldrige CPE, the EFQM assessments are both qualitative and quantitative. The scoring weights are essentially the same. Results represent 45% of the overall Baldrige CPE score, and 50% of the overall EFQM score.

The definitional variations with terms introduced earlier in this chapter also extend to BEMs. For example, some authors viewed BEM and the EFQM as the same, and referred to the EFQM as either the EFQM Business Excellence Model (e.g., Adebanjo, 2001; and Kim, Kumar, & Murphy, 2010) or simply "The Business Excellence Model (e.g., Hughes & Halsall, 2002). This chapter uses BEM to refer to the general framework represented by both the Baldrige CPE and the EFQM Models.

Applying Business Excellence Models to Project Management

Westerveld (2003) examined the EFQM Excellence Model and determined "it becomes clear that because of the unique characteristics of projects the EFQM-model cannot readily be transferred to project situations" (p. 412). The rationale appeared to be two-fold: the difference between the organizational (process) approaches of the EFQM and the *PMBOK® Guide*, and the difference in success criteria (results) between the two. Instead, Westerveld proposed a Project Excellence Model that looked very similar to the EFQM Model.

Similarly, Bryde (2003) proposed a Project Management Performance Assessment (PMPA) Model patterned after the EFQM model. Bryde's rationale was:

There are differences between organisations undertaking projects and those managing operations which suggest that a model more specifically focused on assessing project environments might be more useful and, importantly, perceived as more appropriate by those involved in PM than a general purpose model (pp. 231-232).

Bryde's resulting PMPA model also looked very similar to the EFQM Model. However, Kujala and Artto (2000) offered a different view than both Westerveld and Bryde. Kujala and Artto applied the logic that (1) BEMs apply to enterprises or organizations, and (2) projects are also organizations (albeit temporary ones). Therefore, they concluded that (3) BEMs can also be applied to a project environment. Kujala and Artto then used the Baldrige CPE model (current at that time) to describe in detail how the various processes fit within a project. The EFQM model could also be mapped to a project in a similar manner.

As mentioned in the Introduction, Silvius, Schipper, and van den Brink (2012) discussed how the EFQM Model applies to projects. Specifically, they proposed a four-level Sustainable Project Management Maturity Model along with an assessment instrument. They then combined this Maturity Model with the EFQM excellence maturity levels to "get a sense of the organizational ability to integrate sustainability in projects and project management" (p. 84). A similar analysis could be performed using the Baldrige CPE Model.

Although there are far fewer references that describe the adoption of BEMs for a project context, the logic employed by Kujala and Artto; and Silvius, Schipper, and van den Brink, appears both logical and replicable. The scarcity of the literature in this area should not be interpreted as invalidity of the concept.

The first essential message is that BEMs also apply in a project setting.

How Business Excellence Models Address Sustainability and CSR

Both the Baldrige and EFQM BEMs address sustainability. The Baldrige CPE Model defined sustainability as "your organization's ability to address current business needs and to have the agility and strategic management to prepare successfully for your future business, market, and operating environment" (p 62). The Baldrige CPE further expanded the sustainability considerations to include "workforce capability and capacity, resource availability, technology, knowledge, core competencies, work systems, facilities, and equipment" (p. 62). The environmental and societal responsibilities are included as part of the overall leadership governance and societal responsibilities. In other words, sustainability is infused throughout the criteria. On the other hand, the EFQM Excellence Model addressed sustainability more explicitly. One of the EFQM Model's eight fundamental concepts of excellence is "Taking responsibility for a sustainable future". Specifically, "Excellent organisations embed within their culture an ethical mindset, clear Values and the highest standards for organisational behavior, all of which enable them to strive for economic, social and ecological sustainability" (p 8).

The practices of excellent organizations described in the EFQM criteria include many of the same aspects as the Baldrige CPE. The eight fundamental concepts of excellence in the EFQM Excellence Model are roughly comparable to the Core Values and Concepts that underlie the Baldrige CPE. Both models address aspects of sustainability through these. The Baldrige CPE values include societal responsibility, while the EFQM model concepts include "taking responsibility for a sustainable future", as noted before.

However, Garvare and Isaksson (2001) examined the Baldrige CPE (current at that time) and determined that it was inadequate and needed five additional core values to adequately address a management process for sustainable develop-ment. These additional values are sustainable stakeholder balance, learning excellence, process performance excellence, stakeholdercracy, and transparency. It is true that the Baldrige 2000 CPE did not address sustainability. Sustainability was not in the 2001 glossary, nor was it mentioned as part of the overall leadership category, as it is now addressed in the Baldrige 2011-2012 CPE.

In order to address this shortcoming, Garvare and Isaksson proposed a sustainable development model for organisations that looked very similar to the Baldrige CPE model. The primary difference was that Garvare and Isaksson explicitly created three processes groups: individual excellence, organisational excellence, and societal excellence. Although they did not mention the EFQM Excellence Model, a similar modification could be made for it. However, Pojasek (2007) observed: "The business excellence model is a more suitable springboard for business sustainability than are other commonly used business improvement methods" (p. 84). Pojasek's description of business sustainability and business activities were discussed previously in this chapter. Because these descriptions fit a project organization, as discussed in a previous section, one might conclude that a BEM is also an appropriate vehicle to address project sustainability.

Other authors recognized that current BEMs do address sustainability. For example, Leonard and McAdam (2003) stated that "One of the best examples of quality frameworks that incorporate core elements of CSR is the Malcolm Baldrige *Criteria for Performance Excellence*" (p 31). Similarly, Fibuch and Van Way (2012) observed that the Baldrige *Health Care Criteria for Performance Excellence* "provided a clear model for organizational sustainability" (p. 37). Since all three versions of the Baldrige CPE (Business/Nonprofit, Health Care, and Education) are essentially the same, their observation seems applicable to the overall Baldrige BEM. However, Fibuch and Van Way did suggest further delineation within the model to more explicitly address sustainability. Finally, Castka, Bamber, Bamber, and Sharp (2004) proposed a CSR framework with five elements in a continuously improving system. The five elements were management; strategic planning; measurement and analysis; managing process and systems; and managing change and continuous improvement. The system is connected to stakeholders for both expectations and impacts. If the key stakeholder groups are considered customers and employees, then this model looks very similar to the six process categories of the Baldrige CPE Model.

Collectively, these examples illustrate how BEMs address sustainability. To adopt Lubin and Esty's observation, organizational aspirations are achieved through "execution in five critical areas: leadership, methods, strategy, management, and reporting" (p. 47).

The second essential message of this chapter is that BEMs provide a framework to address sustainability in organizations, including projects. The question now becomes how does this impact project success?

PROJECT SUCCESS

Like sustainability, different paradigms lead to varying and evolving definitions of project success. The traditional view of project success is to achieve all three project constraints represented by the Triple Constraint (sometimes referred to as the Iron Triangle). The third edition of the *Project Management Body of Knowledge (PMBOK® Guide)* (2004) defined the Triple Constraint as "a framework for evaluating competing demands" and noted "The triple constraint is often depicted as a triangle where one of the sides or one of the corners represent one of the parameters being managed by the project team" (p. 378). Ward (2008) went further and defined the triple constraint more specifically: "Term used to identify what generally are regarded as the three most important factors a project manager needs to consider in any project: time, cost, and scope (specifications)" (p. 449).

Jugdev and Müller's (2005) summary of their perspective on the evolution of what constitutes project success could easily apply to other authors writing about project success:

Our views on project success have changed over the years from definitions that were limited to the implementation phase of the project life cycle to definitions that reflect an appreciation of success over the project and product life cycle (p 19).

They noted the traditional triple constraints of time, cost, and scope were all relatively easy to measure at the completion of the project. However, to delay the determination of project success until well past the project completion is difficult under the triple constraint paradigm.

The progression of thought about project success did not evolve quickly or linearly. For example, the third edition of the *PMBOK® Guide* published in 2004 still highlighted the triple constraint. The fourth edition of the *PMBOK® Guide* (2008) noted "Project success is measured by product and project quality, timeliness, budget compliance, and degree of customer satisfaction" (p. 9). Later, the fourth edition described four criteria for a project to be deemed successful, including "balance the competing demands of scope, time, cost, quality, resources, and risk to produce the specified product, service or result" (p. 37). Clearly, the metaphor of the iron triangle to represent the three project constraints may no longer apply.

The evolving view of project success reflects two time components. The first time period ends when the project is completed and closed. The second time period typically begins at project completion, and ends at some point in the future when there is a clearer view of the usefulness of the project results. Cooke-Davies (2002) proposed two definitional distinctions to clarify the two time periods. Project management success can be gauged at the end of the first time component; i.e., when the project ends. Typical metrics include the traditional time, cost, and scope. On the other hand, project success is based on the achievement of the project objectives, some of which cannot be determined until a period of time after the project ends. Nelson (2005) used a similar approach but with different terminology. The traditional time, cost, and product (scope) metrics are considered process criteria, and can be measured at the time of project completion. Outcome criteria are not determined until after the project completion. Nelson's model used three outcome metrics: value, use, and learning. Nelson's study involved the retroactive analyses of Information Technology (IT) projects, so the "use" metric involved whether the intended users were actually using the system. Value involved whether the business case used to justify the project was actually achieved. Learning was a longer-ranged metric: "The project increased stakeholder knowledge and helped prepare the organization for future challenges" (p. 364).

There are other proposed project success frameworks. Bourne (2007), similar to Nelson, retroactively studied project "failures", including the notable Sydney Opera House. As a result, Bourne developed a model that highlighted three pillars of project success. The Delivering Value pillar included the triple constraint plus benefits realization. The Managing Relationships pillar focused on stakeholder expectations. Finally, the Managing Risk pillar addressed corporate governance and procurement. Bourne's primary focus was on managing stakeholder expectations. Siegelaub (2007) also developed a model with six project constraints: the triple constraint (time, cost, and scope) plus quality, benefits, and risk. Baratta (2006) went further and declared: "The Triple Constraint model is both wrong and not useful" (p. 1). Instead, Baratta proposed a new Value Triple Constraint model where value is a function of scope and capability. Capability refers to "the underlying value-added processes used to deliver the project" (p. 5).

Where does project sustainability fall in the palette of project success metrics? The life cycle view of a project typically has a line of demarca-

tion at the project closing. In Nelson's (2005) terminology, the project process metrics can be assessed at that time, but determining the project outcome metrics requires the passage of time. Therefore, project sustainability can be both a process metric and an outcome metric.

Further, BEMs are well-suited to address project success, both process and outcome metrics. The earlier discussion of the Baldrige CPE and EFQM models described how results account for 45 to 50% of the overall BEM assessments. The remainder of the assessments focuses on the processes that lead to these results. To use the Baldrige CPE terminology, these processes are (1) leadership; (2) strategic planning; (3) customer focus; (4) measurement, analysis, and knowledge management; (5) workforce focus; and (6) operations focus. The EFQM processes are similar.

The third essential message of this chapter is that BEMs provide a framework to address project sustainability as one contributor to project success.

Recommendations

Savitz and Weber (2006) defined a sustainable corporation as "one that creates profit for its shareholders while protecting the environment and improving the lives of those with whom it interacts" (p. x). Slightly reworded to reflect a sustainable project organization, this challenges the Project Manager to manage the project to the approved budget while protecting the environment and improving the lives of the project team and all other project stakeholders.

Elkington (2006) used four insects as a metaphor for how organizations approach sustainability: corporate locusts, caterpillars, butterflies, and honeybees. Both the locusts and caterpillars are destructive and degenerative, and decrease returns. Elkington observed: "There are corporate locusts everywhere destroying social and environmental value and undermining the foundations for future economic growth" (pp. 104-105). The destructive impact of caterpillars is more localized and less severe. On the other hand, the butterflies and honeybees are regenerative and increase returns. The primary difference is the reach of their beneficial impact, with honeybees more productive. Elkington's metaphor also seems applicable to project managers, since the leader of an organization generally sets the tone that organization. The major questions, then, are whether the PM is regenerative or destructive, and whether the impacts (favorable or unfavorable) are major or minor. And these questions apply to all three components of sustainability – economic, social, and environmental.

There are simple acts that a project manager can perform to favorably address each of the three components. Economic sustainability is perhaps the easiest to envision (although perhaps more difficult to attain). This is the primary realm of the project manager – actively managing the project expenditures against the approved budget. If this is not done, the project manager and perhaps the project are not sustainable. There are already sufficient tools to help the project manager do this. Social sustainability should also be relatively easy to address, at least from the human resource perspective. Treating project team members "right" is an obvious first step. Approaching all project stakeholders in a respectful manner is another. This does not suggest that the project manager cannot be tough or make tough decisions, when they are needed. The project manager could also engage the team in a community service activity. This does not have to be a lengthy event. Done properly, it can be a beneficial team building exercise as well as an opportunity to benefit others not associated with the project or even the larger organization. Environmental sustainability is also relatively easy, even though some may view it as a waste of effort. Simple acts like reducing the consumption of supplies and recycling wherever possible contribute to this. Team members take their cues from the project manager, and actions speak louder than words. The corollary to this is whenever words and actions disagree, the actions are assumed to be correct.

In short, the project manager can serve as a sustainably conscious leader or as a naysayer who pays lip service to anything not directly related to the project cost, schedule, and scope. One primary influencer is how the project sponsor incents the project manager. Using Elkington's (2006) terminology, the question becomes: What type of insect does the project sponsor want?

The BEM framework can serve as a roadmap for the project manager to achieve excellence across all areas of the project. At a minimum, the criteria can be used as a checklist to consider while preparing the project plan.

FUTURE RESEARCH DIRECTIONS

This chapter has primarily addressed the applicability of BEMs in projects to favorably impact project sustainability and project success. Although some examples are provided from the literature, it would be helpful to have more and more varied applications to validate and illustrate the key points and nuances associated with this.

Other possible next steps include:

- Develop case studies to illustrate how specific projects have addressed this new model.
- Examine organizational examples where the overall performance declined after TQM or CSR was implemented, much like the retrospective analyses of failed projects, and determine if the key learnings can be extrapolated to projects.
- Describe sustainability in the language of a *PMBOK® Guide* process using the inputs, tools & techniques, and outputs terminology.
- Examine both project process and project outcome measures in more detail to see if they can be aggregated to the triple bottom line.

- Incorporate sustainability into a generic balanced scorecard for projects to serve as a template for project planning.

CONCLUSION

The three essential messages of the chapter are:

1. Business Excellence Models (BEMs) also apply in a project environment.
2. BEMs provide a framework to address sustainability in an organization.
3. BEMs can be utilized to address project sustainability as one contributor to project success.

As noted at the beginning of the chapter, Barker's definition of paradigms instructs us how to be successful. As with the general population, project managers and sponsors will have varying opinions (paradigms) regarding the value and importance of sustainability at a project level. Those that are skeptical may concede to include project sustainability in the criteria, but then move to relegate it to a lower priority by orchestrating trade-offs with other project success variables. In particular, there may be a view that economic sustainability is more important than the other two categories of sustainability needs.

Dyllick and Hockerts (2002) warned that short-term tradeoffs among the three dimensions are possible in the near term, but are not sustainable over a longer period: "A single-minded focus on economic sustainability can succeed in the short run; however, in the long run sustainability requires all three dimensions be satisfied simultaneously" (p. 132).

In negotiation, there are generally two possible mindsets. One is a distributive view of the world. In this win-lose paradigm, there is a zero sum relationship between the two negotiating parties. Stated differently, there is an inverse relationship in the value distribution of the deal. For one party to gain, the other party must lose. In a sense, project managers who view the world this way are similar to Elkington's locusts and caterpillars. The other paradigm is an integrative mindset. The value must still be allocated between the parties. The difference is that the total value is first expanded through a collaborative, problem-solving exercise. This is the classical win-win. It is the integrative "both and" view of the world as opposed to the distributive "either-or" mindset. Establishing the integrative project mindset is critical to ensuring sustainability is a full participant at the table of project success criteria. After all, what gets measured gets done. This time, Elkington's butterflies and honeybees come to mind.

Silvius and van den Brink (2011) discussed the integration of sustainability and project management, and made four concluding observations, including "Integrating sustainability stretches the system boundaries of project management" (p. 34). This is certainly true. Adoption curves have pioneers at one end and laggards at the other. When enough evidence regarding the value of project sustainability is incorporated into standards and bodies of knowledge, the bulk of project managers that are between the two ends of the adoption curve will embrace the concept. Business Excellence Models can provide the framework to do so.

REFERENCES

Adebanjo, D. (2001). TQM and business excellence: Is there really a conflict? *Measuring Business Excellence*, *5*(3), 37–40. doi:10.1108/13683040110403961.

Adebanjo, D., & Mann, R. (2008). Business excellence, part 1. *Progressing Business*, *1*(3), 16–20.

Badiru, A. B. (2010). The many languages of sustainability. *Industrial Engineer*, *42*(11), 30–34.

Baldrige Performance Excellence Program. (n.d.b). *2011-2012 criteria for performance excellence*. Gaithersburg, MD: National Institute of Standards and Technology, United States Department of Commerce.

Baldrige Performance Excellence Program. (n.d.a). *2000 criteria for performance excellence*. Gaithersburg, MD: National Institute of Standards and Technology, United States Department of Commerce.

Baratta, A. (2006). *The triple constraint, a triple illusion*. Paper presented at the PMI North America Global Congress. Seattle, WA.

Barker, J. A. (1989). *Discovering the future: The business of paradigms* (3rd ed.). St. Paul, MN: ILI Press.

Bell, J., Masaoka, J., & Zimmerman, S. (2010). *Nonprofit sustainability: Making strategic decisions for financial viability*. San Francisco: Jossey-Bass.

Bell, S., & Morse, S. (2008). *Sustainability indicators: Measuring the immeasurable?* (2nd ed.). London: Earthscan.

Bernhart, M. S., & Maher, F. J. (2011). *ISO 26000 in practice: A user guide*. Milwaukee, WI: ASQ Quality Press.

Bourne, L. (2007). *Avoiding the successful failure*. Paper presented at the PMI Asia-Pacific Global Congress. Hong Kong.

Bryde, D. J. (2003). Modelling project management performance. *International Journal of Quality & Reliability Management, 20*(2), 228–253. doi:10.1108/02656710310456635.

Castka, P., Bamber, C. F., Bamber, D. F., & Sharp, J. M. (2004). Integrating corporate social responsibility (CSR) into ISO management systems – In search of a feasible CSR management system framework. *The TQM Magazine, 16*(3), 216–224. doi:10.1108/09544780410532954.

Clayton, A. M. H., & Radcliffe, N. J. (1996). *Sustainability: A systems approach*. London: Earthscan Publications Limited.

Cooke-Davies, T. (2002). The real success factors in projects. *International Journal of Project Management, 20*(3), 185–190. doi:10.1016/S0263-7863(01)00067-9.

Deland, D. (2009). *Sustainability through project management and net impact*. Paper presented at the PMI 2009 North America Global Congress. Orlando, FL.

Dyllick, T., & Hockerts, K. (2002). Beyond the business case for corporate sustainability. *Business Strategy and the Environment, 11*(2), 130–141. doi:10.1002/bse.323.

Edwards, A. R. (2005). *The sustainability revolution: Portrait of a paradigm shift*. Gabriola Island, Canada: New Society Publishers.

EFQM. (2009). *EFQM excellence model: EFQM model 2010*. Brussels: EFQM.

Elkington, J. (1998). *Cannibals with forks: The triple bottom line of 21st century business*. Gabriola Island, Canada: New Society Publishers.

Elkington, J. (2006). The triple bottom line. In M.J. Epstein & K.O. Hanson (Eds.), The Accountable Organization: Vol. 3: Corporate Social Responsibility (pp. 97-109). Westport, CT: Praeger Publishers.

Epstein, M. J. (2008). *Making sustainability work: Best practices in managing and measuring corporate social, environmental and economic impacts*. San Francisco: Berrett-Koehler Publishers, Inc..

Evans, J. R., & Dean, J. W. Jr. (2000). *Total quality: Management, organization, and strategy* (2nd ed.). Cincinnati, OH: South-Western College Publishing.

Fibuch, E., & Van Way, C. W. III. (2012). Sustainability: A fiduciary responsibility of senior leaders? *Physician Executive, 38*(2), 36–42.

Freeman, R. E., Harrison, J. S., & Wicks, A. C. (2007). *Managing for stakeholders: Survival, reputation, and success*. New Haven, CT: Yale University Press.

Garvare, R., & Isaksson, R. (2001). Sustainable development: Extending the scope of business excellence models. *Measuring Business Excellence*, *5*(3), 11–15. doi:10.1108/13683040110403899.

Ghobadian, A., Gallear, D., & Hopkins, M. (2007). TQM and the CSR nexus. *International Journal of Quality & Reliability Management*, *24*(7), 704–721. doi:10.1108/02656710710774683.

Green, T. (2012). *The dictionary of global sustainability: With case studies on the environmental, economic technological, and social aspects of sustainability*. New York: McGraw-Hill.

Grigg, N., & Mann, R. (2008). Promoting excellence: An international study into creating awareness of business excellence models. *The TQM Journal*, *20*(3), 233–248. doi:10.1108/17542730810867254.

Hawken, P. (1993). *The ecology of commerce: A declaration of sustainability*. New York: HarperBusiness.

Hazlett, S., McAdam, R., & Murray, L. (2007). From quality management to socially responsible organisations: The case for CSR. *International Journal of Quality & Reliability Management*, *24*(7), 669–682. doi:10.1108/02656710710774665.

Hendricks, K. B., & Singhal, V. R. (2001). Firm characteristics, total quality management, and financial performance. *Journal of Operations Management*, *19*(3), 269–285. doi:10.1016/S0272-6963(00)00049-8.

Hitchcock, D., & Willard, M. (2009). *The business guide to sustainability: Practical strategies and tools for organization* (2nd ed.). London: Earthscan.

Hopkins, W. E. (2011). Managing business from a values-based perspective. In S.G. McNall, J.C. Hershauer, & G. Basile (Eds.), The Business of Sustainability, Trends, Policies, Practices, and Stories of Success: Vol. 1: Global Challenges and Opportunities (pp. 143-158). Santa Barbara, CA: Praeger.

Hughes, A., & Halsall, D. N. (2002). Comparison of the 14 deadly diseases and the business excellence model. *Total Quality Management*, *13*(2), 255–263. doi:10.1080/09544120120102487.

Jugdev, K., & Müller, R. (2005). A retrospective look at our evolving understanding of project success. *Project Management Journal*, *36*(4), 19–31.

Juran, J. M., & De Feo, J. A. (2010). *Juran's quality handbook: The complete guide to performance excellence* (6th ed.). New York: McGraw-Hill.

Kim, D. Y., Kumar, V., & Murphy, S. A. (2010). European foundation for quality management business excellence model: An integrative review and research agenda. *International Journal of Quality & Reliability*, *27*(6), 684–701. doi:10.1108/02656711011054551.

Kujala, J., & Artto, K. (2000). *Developing corporate project management practices through quality award framework*. Paper presented at the Project Management Institute Annual Seminars & Symposium. Houston, TX.

Labuschagne, C., & Brett, A. C. (2004). *Sustainable project life cycle management: Aligning project management methodologies with the principles of sustainable development*. Paper presented at the Association for Project Management South Africa Conference. Johannesburg, South Africa.

Labuschagne, C., & Brett, A. C. (2005). Sustainable project life cycle management: The need to integrate life cycles in the manufacturing sector. *International Journal of Project Management*, *23*(2), 159–168. doi:10.1016/j.ijproman.2004.06.003.

Leonard, D., & McAdam, R. (2003). Corporate social responsibility. *Quality Progress*, *36*(10), 27–32.

Lubin, D. A., & Esty, D. C. (2010). Lessons for leaders from previous game-changing megatrends. *Harvard Business Review*, *88*(5), 42–50.

McWilliams, A., & Siegel, D. (2001). Corporate social responsibility: A theory of the firm perspective. *Academy of Management Review*, *26*(1), 117–127.

Nelson, R. R. (2005). Project retrospectives: Evaluating project success, failure, and everything in between. *MIS Quarterly Executive*, *4*(3), 361–372.

Norton, B. G. (2005). *Sustainability: A philosophy of adaptive ecosystem management*. Chicago: The University of Chicago Press. doi:10.7208/chicago/9780226595221.001.0001.

Planko, J., & Silvius, G. (2012). Sustainability in business. In Silvius, G., Schipper, R., Planko, J., van den Brink, J., & Köhler, A. (Eds.), *Sustainability in Project Management* (pp. 7–20). Surrey, UK: Gower Publishing Limited.

Pojasek, R. B. (2007). A framework for business sustainability. *Environmental Quality Management*, *17*(2), 81–88. doi:10.1002/tqem.20168.

Presley, A., Meade, L., & Sarkis, J. (2007). A strategic sustainability methodology for organizational decisions: A reverse logistics illustration. *International Journal of Production Research*, *45*(18-19), 4595–4620. doi:10.1080/00207540701440220.

Project Management Institute. (2004). *A guide to the project management body of knowledge (PMBOK® Guide)* (3rd ed.). Newtown Square, PA: Project Management Institute.

Project Management Institute. (2008). *A guide to the project management body of knowledge (PMBOK® Guide)* (4th ed.). Newtown Square, PA: Project Management Institute.

Prugh, T., Costanza, R., & Daly, H. (2000). *The local politics of global sustainability*. Washington, DC: Island Press.

Savitz, A. W., & Weber, K. (2006). *The triple bottom line: How today's best-run companies are achieving economic, social, and environmental success – And how you can too*. San Francisco: Jossey-Bass.

Schmitz, O. J. (2010). Perspectives on sustainability of ecosystem services and functions. In Graedel, T. E., & van der Voet, E. (Eds.), *Linkages of Sustainability* (pp. 33–46). Cambridge, MA: The MIT Press.

Sharma, A. K., & Talwar, B. (2007). Evolution of universal business excellence model incorporating Vedic philosophy. *Measuring Business Excellence*, *11*(3), 4–20. doi:10.1108/13683040710820719.

Siegelaub, J. M. (2007). *Six (yes six!) constraints: An enhanced model for project control*. Paper presented at the PMI North America Global Congress. Atlanta, GA.

Silvius, A. J. G., & van den Brink, J. (2011). Taking responsibility: The integration of sustainability and project management. In J. Kettunen, U. Hyrkkänen, & A. Lehto (Eds.), *Proceedings from the First CARPE Networking Conference*. Utrecht, The Netherlands: CARPE.

Silvius, G., Schipper, R., & van den Brink, J. (2012). Incorporating sustainability in project management. In Silvius, G., Schipper, R., Planko, J., van den Brink, J., & Köhler, A. (Eds.), *Sustainability in Project Management* (pp. 45–86). Surrey, UK: Gower Publishing Limited.

Talwar, B. (2011). Business excellence models and the path ahead…. *The TQM Journal*, *23*(1), 21–35. doi:10.1108/17542731111097461.

Tharp, J. (2012). *Project management and global sustainability*. Paper presented at the PMI 2012 EMEA Global Congress. Marseille, France.

United Nations. (2005). [World Summit Outcome. New York: UN.]. *Resolution, 60*(1), 2005.

Ward, J. L. (2008). *Dictionary of project management terms* (3rd ed.). Arlington, VA: ESI International.

Westerveld, E. (2003). The project excellence model®: Linking success criteria and critical success factors. *International Journal of Project Management, 21*(6), 411–418. doi:10.1016/S0263-7863(02)00112-6.

Willard, B. (2002). *The sustainability advantage: Seven business case benefits of a triple bottom line*. Gabriola Island, Canada: New Society Publishers.

Wirtenberg, J. (2011). Sustainable enterprise for the 21st century. In S.G. McNall, J.C. Hershauer, & G. Basile (Eds.). The Business of Sustainability, Trends, Policies, Practices, and Stories of Success: Vol. 1: Global Challenges and Opportunities (pp. 67-88). Santa Barbara, CA: Praeger.

World Commission on Environment and Development. (1987). *Our common future*. Oxford, UK: Oxford University Press.

Zhao, F. (2004). Siemens' business excellence model and sustainable development. *Measuring Business Excellence, 8*(2), 55–64. doi:10.1108/13683040410539436.

ADDITIONAL READING

Atkinson, R. (1999). Project management: cost, time and quality, two best guesses and a phenomenon, its [sic] time to accept other success criteria. *International Journal of Project Management, 17*(6), 337–342. doi:10.1016/S0263-7863(98)00069-6.

Bou-Llusar, J. C., Escrig-Tena, A. B., Roca-Puig, V., & Beltrán-Martin, I. (2009). An empirical assessment of the EFQM excellence model: Evaluation as a TQM framework relative to the MBNQA model. *Journal of Operations Management, 27*(1), 1–22. doi:10.1016/j.jom.2008.04.001.

Brown, B. J., Hanson, M. E., Liverman, D. M., & Merideth, R. W. Jr. (1987). Global sustainability: Toward definition. *Environmental Management, 11*(6), 713–719. doi:10.1007/BF01867238.

Constanza, R., & Patten, B. C. (1995). Defining and predicting sustainability. *Ecological Economics, 15*(3), 193–196. doi:10.1016/0921-8009(95)00048-8.

Faber, N., Jorna, R., & Van Engelen, J. (2005). The sustainability of sustainability – A study into the conceptual foundations of the notion of sustainability. *Journal of Environmental Assessment Policy and Management, 7*(1), 1–33. doi:10.1142/S1464333205001955.

Gibson, R. B. (2006). Beyond the pillars: Sustainability assessment as a framework for effective integration of social, economic and ecological considerations in significant decision-making. *Journal of Environmental Assessment Policy and Management, 8*(3), 259–280. doi:10.1142/S1464333206002517.

Jayamaha, N. P., Grigg, N. P., & Mann, R. S. (2008). Empirical validity of Baldrige criteria: New Zealand evidence. *International Journal of Quality & Reliability Management, 25*(5), 477–493. doi:10.1108/02656710810873880.

Joiner, T. A. (2007). Total quality management and performance: The role of organization support and co-worker support. *International Journal of Quality & Reliability Management, 23*(6), 617–207. doi:10.1108/02656710710757808.

Kendra, K., & Taplin, L. J. (2004). Project success: A cultural framework. *Project Management Journal, 35*(1), 30–45.

Kumar, V., Choisne, F., de Grosbois, D., & Kumar, U. (2009). Impact of TQM on company's performance. *International Journal of Quality & Reliability Management, 26*(1), 23–37. doi:10.1108/02656710910924152.

Leonard, D., & McAdam, R. (2002). The role of the business excellence model in operational and strategic decision making. *Management Decision, 40*(1), 17–25. doi:10.1108/00251740210413325.

Linnenluecke, M. K., & Griffiths, A. (2010). Corporate sustainability and organizational culture. *Journal of World Business, 45*(4), 357–366. doi:10.1016/j.jwb.2009.08.006.

Martin, R. L. (2002). The virtue matrix: Calculating the return on corporate responsibility. *Harvard Business Review, 80*(3), 68–75. PMID:11894384.

Munns, A. K., & Bjeirmi, B. F. (1996). The role of project management in achieving project success. *International Journal of Project Management, 14*(2), 81–87. doi:10.1016/0263-7863(95)00057-7.

Oakland, J., Tanner, S., & Gadd, K. (2002). Best practice in business excellence. *Total Quality Management, 13*(8), 1125–1139. doi:10.1080/09544120200000008.

Oakland, J. S. (2003). *Total quality management: Text with cases* (3rd ed.). Boston: Butterworth Heinemann.

Porter, M. E., & Kramer, M. R. (2006). Strategy & society: The link between competitive advantage and corporate social responsibility. *Harvard Business Review, 84*(12), 78–92. PMID:17183795.

Rahschulte, T., & Milhauser, K. (2010). *Beyond the triple constraints: Nine elements defining project success today.* Paper presented at the PMI 2010 North America Global Congress. Washington, DC.

Robson, A., & Mitchell, E. (2007). CSR performance: Driven by TQM implementation, size, sector? *International Journal of Quality & Reliability Management, 24*(7), 722–737. doi:10.1108/02656710710774692.

Savitz, A. W., & Weber, K. (2007). The sustainability sweet spot. *Environmental Quality Management, 17*(2), 17–28. doi:10.1002/tqem.20161.

Seghezzi, H. D. (2001). Business excellence: What is to be done? *Total Quality Management, 12*(7-8), 861–866. doi:10.1080/09544120100000008.

Shenhar, A. J., & Dvir, D. (2007). *Reinventing project management: The diamond approach to successful growth and innovation.* Boston: Harvard Business School Press.

Svensson, G., Wood, G., & Callaghan, M. (2010). A corporate model of sustainable business practices: An ethical perspective. *Journal of World Business, 45*(4), 336–345. doi:10.1016/j.jwb.2009.08.005.

Tharp, J. (2008). *Corporate social responsibility: What it means for the project manager.* Paper presented at the PMI 2008 North America Global Congress. Denver, CO.

Thiry, M. (2012). *How to measure real project success.* Paper presented at the PMI 2012 EMEA Global Congress. Marseille, France.

Weerawardena, J., McDonald, R. E., & Mort, G. S. (2010). Sustainability of nonprofit organizations: An empirical investigation. *Journal of World Business, 45*(4), 346–356. doi:10.1016/j.jwb.2009.08.004.

Wirtenberg, J., Russell, W. G., & Lipsky, D. (Eds.). (2009). *The sustainable enterprise fieldbook: When it all comes together.* New York: AMACOM Books.

KEY TERMS AND DEFINITIONS

Business Excellence Model (BEM): A holistic framework for describing the practices of excellent organizations in a way that allows assessments to determine the strengths and opportunities for improvement in an organization.

Corporate Social Responsibility (CSR): The self-imposed ethical obligation to balance and meet stakeholder expectations for sustaining economic, social, and environmental resources.

Project Social Responsibility (PSR): The process to achieve the project's objectives and balance the needs of all stakeholders in an ethical manner to ensure financial resources, human resources, and environmental resources are utilized in a way that sustains all three.

Project Success: The determination that the project met the criteria established at the beginning of the project by the primary stakeholders.

Project Sustainability: The process of creating stakeholder value by leveraging the opportunities and risks to balance the project's economic, environmental, and social responsibilities.

Sustainability: A balanced approach to ensure an organization's financial, social (human), and environmental resources are sustained for both the present and future times.

Total Quality Management (TQM): A framework to ensure all aspects of total quality are addressed within an organization.

Triple Bottom Line: The three primary components of sustainability: financial, social (human), and environmental resources.

Chapter 2
Integrating Project Strategy for Sustainable Development:
A Conceptual Framework

Lynn A. Keeys
SKEMA Business School, France

Martina Huemann
WU Vienna University of Economics and Business, Austria

Rodney Turner
SKEMA Business School, France

ABSTRACT

This chapter proposes a conceptual framework for integrating project strategy for Sustainable Development (SD) within the context of corporate sustainability strategy. Project SD strategy is the missing link between SD at the corporate level and project level. The framework draws on a literature review of concepts, definitions, and theories in strategic management, corporate sustainability, and projects. The conceptual framework presented in this book chapter has six key components. These are: (1) corporate sustainability strategy; (2) project understanding of SD and SD business case; (3) strategizing at project initiation stage; (4) project autonomy to negotiate and adapt in the project context; (5) project capability to translate corporate SD strategy to project SD strategy; and (6) project capability in stakeholder management. The premise of the framework is the compatibility of the socially constructed realities of the project and SD, as indicated in SD and project literature. The aim is to help develop new knowledge and insight into how business can integrate SD principles into core business operations such as projects from a process perspective, rather than sustainability content perspective. This chapter is based on doctoral dissertation research by the lead author.

DOI: 10.4018/978-1-4666-4177-8.ch002

INTRODUCTION

Projects, as important business operations, have not escaped the 21ˢᵗ century challenge of ensuring sustainable development. Interest and efforts in integrating sustainable development (SD) in projects is growing yet still scant. SD, the process of balancing financial profitability interests of organizations with larger societal concerns for economic development, environmental safeguards and satisfaction of societal needs in the short, medium and long-term, is yet to be the standard practice in projects (Gareis, Huemann & Weninger, 2010; Silvius, Schipper, Planko, van den Brink, & Kohler, 2012). We distinguish SD (the process) from sustainability (the outcome) which is "an ideal of development efforts" which is constantly changing based on the ethics and values of stakeholders (Bagheri & Hjorth, 2007, p. 84). Therefore, SD is a stakeholder-focused process that projects must enter.

Addressing SD in projects is not only a concern and challenge at the project level. "A project is not an island (Engwall, 2002)." Society requires that the project's parent or investor organization move towards sustainable business operations and mainstream SD in core operations and activities. This is the 21ˢᵗ century business challenge. Organizations initiate investments with projects to produce products, services or change. Projects operate within the corporate or organizational context. SD is a systems issue and as such understanding of the SD problem flows from larger systems to smaller systems (Bagheri & Hjorth, 2007). Projects are smaller systems within the organizational or corporate structure. Thus, projects as core business operations are contributors to as well as the subject of corporate SD. Projects are able to engage stakeholders in the project context and identify more closely stakeholder SD concerns. As such, projects are able to inform and form corporate SD strategic aims. We believe that this suggests the integration of SD principles in projects is associated with a symbi-

otic, interdependent relationship with corporate SD (usually called corporate sustainability). Thus, SD in projects needs a strategic focus for success (Englund & Graham, 1999). Most businesses to date have not been successful in achieving this focus, integration (Ebner & Baumgartner, 2010) and interdependency. Project SD strategy is the missing link or strategic nexus that integrates corporate and project SD (See Figure 1).

Why does this lack of strategic SD integration and interdependence exist in projects? Two thirds of chief executive officers in a major survey on corporate SD reported they need assistance in the execution of SD strategy, i.e., integrating or embedding SD in its core operations (UN Global Compact-Accenture, 2010). Researchers have concluded that organizations generally do not only know how to integrate into core business operations; they also lack clear SD strategies to address the issues (Ebner & Baumgartner, 2010). Corporations often manage SD as a "side-lined" activity, outside of the rigor of core strategic and business processes (Epstein, 2008). The lack of clear strategy uncovers as well notions of norms, ethics, risk, costs and commitment related to SD. This influences how an organization plans, integrates and implements SD in projects.

Thus, we propose a conceptual framework for integrating project strategy for sustainable development, arising from SD strategy at the corporate level. The objective is to create SD strategy that arises from a cyclical, iterative process, linking project SD with corporate SD. We believe this process approach will aid the mainstreaming of SD principles in projects in a way that contributes to and refines corporate sustainability aims. A cyclical process of strategic alignment, emergence and realignment characterizes this relationship at the organizational and project levels. The framework, for purposes of this chapter, assumes the development of project SD strategy within one sponsor/investor organization that has an articulated commitment to SD through a corporate sustainability strategy. We use the term sponsor/investor to

Figure 1. Strategic link between corporate and project SD (Adapted from Ebner & Baumgartner, 2010) (Keeys, forthcoming 2014)

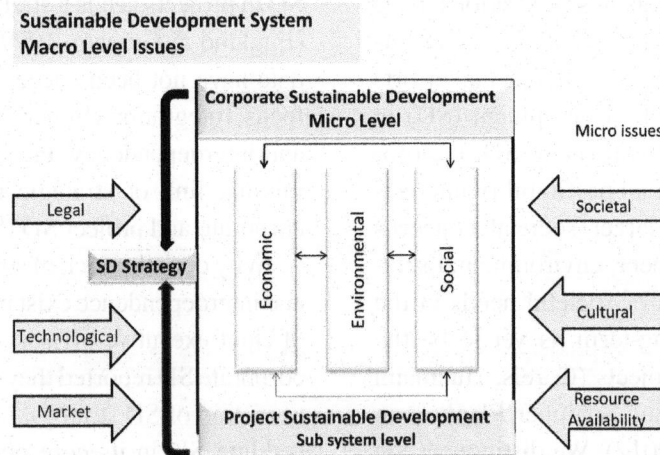

enable the identification of an often-key project role within the investor organization—the leading force behind the project embodied in a senior executive or a department. The presentation of the framework concludes with a discussion of the implications for application in different settings and for project and project management processes and areas for further development.

THE PROJECT SD INTEGRATION CHALLENGE

Project management and corporate sustainability research acknowledges that corporate support for SD influences how SD principles are addressed within projects and in core business operations in general (Gareis, Huemann, & Martinuzzi, 2011). Here we define a project as a temporary organization, involved in value creation and social processes, to which a parent or investor organization provides resources for bringing about a strategically important benefit (Turner, 2009; Gareis et al. 2010). Projects are linked with strategy through their value creation processes. However, the relationship between the integration of SD principles in projects and SD strategy at the

corporate level appears unaddressed in research and practice (See Figure 2). Sustainable development in projects is not addressed usually within the context of corporate sustainability strategy. This is an important oversight.

Researchers and practitioners have tended to address project SD outside of corporate SD strategy and the challenge of holistic SD mainstreaming. Project research largely focuses on specific sustainability aspect or pillars, i.e., environmental or social, on selected industries--manufacturing

Figure 2. Project and corporate SD strategy practice and research gap (Keeys, forthcoming 2014)

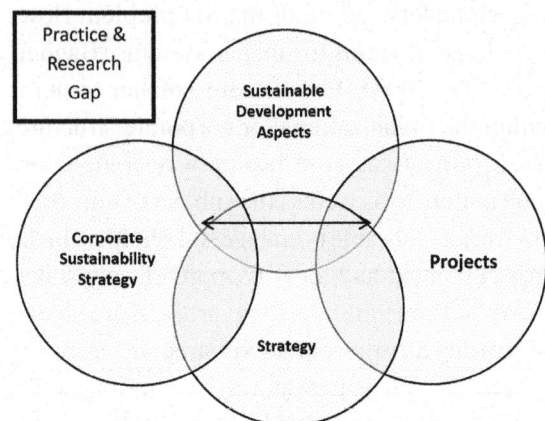

(Labuschagne, Brent & Claasen, 2005) and construction (Edum-Fotwoe & Price, 2008) or on techniques, i.e., project life cycle management (Labuschagne & Brent, 2004) and value engineering (Al-Saleh & Taleb, 2010). Presley, Meade, and Sarkis (2007) propose an "activity-based" decision-making framework as a strategic tool for evaluating a project's contribution to corporate SD, without reference to project SD strategy. Research on integrating SD principles in project management standards, reported by Gareis et al. (2010) begins to touch on the strategic issue of project SD by proposing to integrate SD at the project assignment stage of the project management process. This is where the investment idea is assessed, decisions made and project initiated. However, the project assignment process might inadvertently overlook corporate sustainability strategy because it is often not part of the business case for the project or core strategic processes of the organization. Without explicitly developing project SD approaches within the integrated context of SD strategy at the corporate and project level, SD integration in projects will not be robust and enduring to move projects as a value creation process and organizations to improved sustainability.

The following summary of literature on corporate sustainability, strategy and projects will help to illuminate some of the issues surrounding the development of project SD strategy and its integration at the corporate level.

COMPLEXITY OF CORPORATE SUSTAINABILITY

Content and Process

Corporate sustainability is SD at the micro level (Ebner & Baumgartner, 2010). As such, it inherits the rich complexity, multidisciplinary content, value basis, large spatial and temporal orientation, and ambiguity of the SD concept. Brundtland (World Commission on Environment and Development, 1987) defined SD as "the process of development that meets the needs of the present without compromising the ability of future generations to meet their own needs" (p. 1). Economic development, environmental safeguards, and satisfaction of social needs are the three SD pillars.

As a societal concept, SD requires identification and specification of issues and needs for whom over an indefinite timespan (present to future) and space (micro and macro; local, national, regional, and global). Macro level issues comprise global concerns such as climate change, pollution control, corporate conduct, human rights and poverty reduction. Corporations, operating at the micro level of SD must refer to macro level issues while addressing micro or local, national and regional issues. Local issues are influenced by policy and legal frameworks, market participants (such as customers, supply chain, competitors), shareholders, employees, government, special interest organizations and local communities. These in turn influence macro SD concerns. Micro issues are steeped in the local culture (within and outside the corporation) and political and natural environmental context (Ebner & Baumgartner, 2010). The concept sustainability (in contrast to SD) is the state of actually addressing these issues and meeting needs in a way that enables life to flourish within the short, medium and long term, grounded in ideals of intra- and inter- generational justice (Clifton & Amran, 2011). This state of sustainability (content) is in continual flux and stakeholder participation (needs for whom) is at the centre of the SD process. Corporations have found it difficult to translate the SD content definition to the corporate setting and to make the holistic SD concept operational and mainstreamed in core business.

In research on integrating SD principles in project management standards, Gareis, Huemann and Martinuzzi (forthcoming in 2013) address this definitional complexity by distilling process-related guiding principles of SD. These are: (1) holistic approach of balancing economic, social and ecologic orientation, (2) short-, mid- and long-term orientation, (3) local, regional, and global orientation, (4) risk reducing, (5) values and ethics based, and (6) participation and capacity building. This process definition, viewed alongside the SD content definition, appears useful for considering the management process for integrating SD principles in projects and other core business operations.

Variations in Definition, Knowledge, and Practice

Although corporate sustainability is called SD at the micro level, researchers have offered a variety of definitions, revealing the varied nature of corporate sustainability. Dyllick and Hockerts (2002) use the Brundtland definition: "meeting the needs of a firm's direct and indirect stakeholders (such as shareholders, employees, clients, pressure groups, communities) without compromising its ability to meet the needs of future stakeholders as well" (p. 131). Dunphy, Griffiths, and Benn (2007) define corporate sustainability in phases, distinguishing corporate sustainability—a corporation that survives through "excellent return to investors" and the sustaining corporation—concerned with sustainable world goals and how it contributes to them (p. 16). Dunphy, Griffiths and Benn link these two concepts, as a business will cease to exist unless it is moving towards the sustaining corporation state. In this context, corporate sustainability can be seen as "responsible business behavior," anchored in a stakeholder-oriented approach and ethics (Avram & Kuhne, 2008).

Not all organizations understand or practice corporate SD in the same manner. In fact, Linnenluecke, Russell, and Griffiths (2009) found that understanding of SD and SD practices at top levels of an organization can differ from the lower levels

where different employee subcultures operate and SD initiatives occur. They noted that employee understanding of corporate sustainability strategy is the best indicator of whether there is an holistic understanding of SD in a organization.

Understanding the nature of corporate SD terminology and intent is necessary for determining the starting point for SD at the project level. In practice, corporate sustainability struggles for a commonly understood term. Ebner and Baumgartner (2006) found multiple usages related to corporate sustainability, corporate social responsibility and SD. These usages relate to SD as the Brundtland definition and triple bottom line; SD as societal concern with Corporate Social Responsibility (CSR) as firm-level concern; CSR as SD at the firm level; and CSR as the social dimension of SD. Added to this is SD as addressing environmental concerns, or as in "corporate greening." These definitional terms reveal whether organizations and the public see SD as something that must be addressed in core business or as sidelined as part of the philanthropic division of the business or the responsibility of government.

Businesses have identified this variation in terms and practice as an important barrier to the integration of SD principles in core business activities (UN Global Compact-Accenture, 2010). This definitional barrier applies to projects as well. Some researchers suggest corporate SD needs standard terms (Ebner & Baumgartner). Others maintain that standard definitions are not appropriate and that social context, culture, values and the development state of the organization will influence the organization's definition and view of SD (Van Marrewijk, 2003). Project sponsors/investors and managers need to be aware of and understand these differing terms, as they influence how SD issues are identified by business, understood by stakeholders, whether they are structured within strategy and mainstreamed in projects and core business activities.

Corporate Sustainability Strategy: Organizational SD Compass

Corporate sustainability or SD strategy acts as a compass, indicating an organization's direction in integrating or mainstreaming SD principles. Corporate SD strategy is a relatively recent concept, having roots in the important paradigm shift in strategic management literature in the 90s, embodied in Hart's "natural resource-based view" of the firm (Hart, 1995). Hart viewed sustainable competitive advantage as rooted in three interconnected internal capabilities linked to managing "environmentally-oriented resources"—pollution prevention, product stewardship (incorporation of stakeholder perspective into the design and development of products), and sustainable development (p. 991). Hart proposed that pollution prevention and product stewardship are embedded in SD that indicates a higher level of organization SD commitment.

Since Hart, certain values and principles are associated with good practice in corporate sustainability strategy. Transparency, stakeholder dialogue and sustainability reporting are considered key aspects of SD strategy (Robert et al., 2002). Many consider the following four core principles as essential for guiding SD strategy at the corporate level. These are: (1) backcasting: an approach to strategy formulation based on planning backwards from the vision of the desirable future SD outcome (not prediction-based); (2) flexible platforms: creating investments that add value in the same direction in the future; (3) good return on investment; and (4) precautionary principle: using caution when unsure of the environmental impact (p. 202). These principles, when part of SD strategy, influence how projects identify objectives, determine value and benefits, and manage risks when identifying SD concerns with stakeholders.

Corporate SD strategy progresses along phases or levels towards sustainability. At the earliest phase or level, firms focus on compliance with minimum SD standards that society sets in order to avoid sanctions and reduce risk. Firms transition to legitimization or "license to operate" strategies that additionally emphasize good stakeholder reporting and voluntary compliance. Dunphy, Griffiths and Benn view this as a transition stage towards improving efficiency through improved SD processes. In the later phases, firms make SD an integral part of business strategy. However, firms distinguish themselves by motivation: SD as a source of self-interest, competitive advantage and SD as the ideology of the "sustaining" firm. Ebner and Baumgartner (2010) refer to the later phases as visionary strategy where firms demonstrate a high commitment to SD in two types of strategy. Conventional visionary strategy is externally motivated by market opportunities while systemic visionary strategy is inwardly motivated, augmenting the market view with organizational values that lead to holistic SD becoming part of the resource base of the firm. It is only in these last phases that organizations direct SD strategy towards full mainstreaming of holistic SD principles.

Stakeholder Management: Composition, Competition, and Cooperation

Stakeholder managerment is a core feature of strategic management and operates prominantly in the concept of SD and corporate SD.. Freeman developed this concept to help managers to develop new strategic directions and to identify opportunities within an unstable setting (Freeman & McVea, 2001). Freeman defined stakeholders broadly as "any group or individual who is affected by or can affect the achievement of an organization's objective (p. 4)." Since Freeman's broad definition, corporations have tended to narrowly view stakeholders as organization shareholders and direct beneficiaries (Clifton & Amran, 2011). Stakeholder relations have been rooted in reducing complexity and risk and not focused on identifying opportunities created from stakeholder relationships. When corporations do broadly view stakeholders, they separate "business stakeholders" from "SD stakeholders" which means that a broad stakeholder approach is not considered in corporate business strategy (Freeman & McVea).

Corporate SD strategy calls for organizational adaptive capability to broadly identify, work with, manage and integrate the diverse groups and networks of stakeholders for the long-term success of the firm and society (Lorbach, van Bakel, Whiteman & Rotmans, 2010). This adaptive capability is important for translating macro SD issues into micro ones, of concern to stakeholders at the local level where corporations operate (Bagheri & Hjorth, 2007). The stakeholder approach requires that managers actively handle relationships in a way that integrates individual stakeholder concerns, promotes "shared interest" and, as a strategic management process, does not rely on prediction of outcome (Freeman & McVea). The quality of stakeholder participation and sustainability progress depend on stakeholder knowledge (Birkin, Polesie & Lewis, 2009). The lack of stakeholder knowledge should not deter an organization's stakeholder management efforts. SD principles of transparency and participation mean that organizations have the responsibility to inform and contribute to joint learning with stakeholders. This implies cooperation, collaboration, adaptation and emergence in defining SD issues and strategic directions with stakeholders. However, according to Audebrand (2010), current metaphors that permeate strategic management education still rest in warfare terminology. This conceptualization of stakeholder relations in the market does not facilitate the development of the aforementioned adaptive capability.

PROJECTS AND SD: STRUGGLE FOR COMPATIBILITY

Projects are becoming appreciated as temporary organizations steeped in social and value creation processes, with a long-term perspective (Winter, Smith, Morris & Cicmil, 2006). These are important characteristics potentially compatible with the stakeholder approach, long-term view, and shared value characteristics of SD. As temporary organizations, projects are social systems and have organizational characteristics as "open systems." Projects have distinct boundaries and operate in dynamic internal and external contexts characterized by complex stakeholder networks (Artto, Kujala, Dietrich & Martinsuo, 2008). These stakeholder networks have varying perceptions of what constitutes value and benefit. As SD involves creating a sense of "shared value" with stakeholders, a project can interact, learn, broker, and adapt with these groups as integral to its social and value creation processes. As a smaller system within its parent organization, in direct contact with stakeholder concerns, a project has the capability to do this with much more flexibility and clarity than the larger parent organization, when it has the autonomy to do so (Artto et al., 2008).

However, this potential compatibility between projects and SD is constrained by the more traditional view, innate nature of projects as organizational instruments with short-term perspective, and project perception of risk as only negative abbreviation of project objectives. Project management approaches, such as SCRUM and Agile, epitomizes this short-term perspective where the maximum time horizon can be 90 days (Morris, 2008). This perspective is rooted in the actual temporary nature of projects and the definition of projects that emphasize the creation of a specific product or service within schedule and budget (iron triangle) as its primary if not sole function. The view of the project life cycle as static rather than evolving and iterative also helps to engrain this short-term perspective. Experts generally agree on five phases: (1) concept/project definition (initiation or front end), (2) feasibility, (3) design and appraisal, (4) execution and control, and (5) close out (Turner, 2009). The project lifecycle is connected with the life cycle of the product, service or process it creates. This should give a project a medium-to-long-term perspective. Ironically, this is often not the case.

The longer-term perspective of SD and the need to broaden stakeholder inclusion in the definition of value and benefit present a heightened sense of uncertainy and risk for projects. Nevertheless, projects may be especially capable of navigating this terrain due to project management processes that emphasize control through the various project phases. However, social construction of sustainable products and services, implied by broad stakeholder involvement, would call for projects to relinquish "prediction" of the outcome for "co-creation" based on the concept of social learning and finding shared value (Wiltbank, Dew, Read & Sarasvathy, 2007). This means that projects would need to be more open and "entrepreneurial" with stakeholders in identifying and finding solutions in response to opportunities presented by stakeholders SD concerns. This will require combining soft system processes for interacting with stakeholders (Checkland & Winter, 2005) with hard system processes for choosing technology for specific products or services for project SD content.

This struggle for compatibility between SD and projects manifests itself in the sphere of project SD strategy, where the parent or investor organization's perspective on projects and strategy unfold.

Projects and Strategy: Alignment and Emergence

Two main perspectives concerning projects and strategy impact on SD strategy at the project level—projects as implementors of organizational strategy and projects as shapers of strategy. Many have questioned the strategic nature of individual projects, suggesting that a project can only contribute to strategy through programs or portfolio of projects (Archer & Ghasemzadeh, 2004). However, there is growing recognition of the strategic nature of individual projects and the contribution to organizational strategy (Morris, 2008). Mintzberg and Waters (1985) defined strategy as "a pattern in a stream of decisions" and "actions (p. 257)." Importantly, strategy can be deliberate, as in planning, or emergent as in learning and adapting in a dynamic context (Mintzberg, Ahstrand & Lampel, 1998). Williams and Samset (2010) suggest that projects struggle to maintain strategic alignment with the planned organizational (and project strategy) when turbulence exists in the project context. In the SD context, this turbulence is created by the fluctuating nature of SD, the tension between multiple networks of project stakeholders, diversity of value and benefit concepts and aims of the parent or investor organization concerning SD objectives. Shenhar et al. (2007) suggest that corporate and project strategy should be mutually supporting. Therefore, we propose that alignment and emergence are both applicable to the relationship between SD strategy at the corporate and project level.

Projects as Implementors of Planned Strategy: Alignment

Based on strategic alignment theory and project management standards, project SD strategy should flow from the corporate level. Projects are key instruments for improving business performance and for obtaining competitive advantage. Sustainable projects (integrating holistic SD principles) contribute to competitive advantage (Gareis et al., 2010). Projects are linked to strategy through a traditional process of strategic alignment—moving from organizational strategy to business strategy from which comprehensive project strategy is developed at the early project stage, i.e., project initiation which is often called the project front end (Morris & Jamieson, 2005). From an alignment perspective, project strategy is "the definition of position, means, and guidelines of what to do and how to do it, to achieve the highest competitive advantage and the best value from the project (Shenhar et al., 2007, p.65)." The business case provides the justification for the project and provides direction for the project strategy. Thus, project strategy that is aligned with corporate and business strategy is viewed as having the greatest chance of creating benefits for the organization.

Projects as Shapers of Strategy through Emergence

Projects can emerge strategy through a process of negotiating, learning and adapting in its project context. This can entail joint action and co-creation with customers and other stakeholders (Wiltbank et al., 2006). Going beyond the strategic alignment concept, projects can create "holistic project strategy" where the project has the possibility to "operate as an autonomous organization, to seek survival and success in an uncertain and complex environment, and to consider strategic options possibly with multiple strong stakeholders" (Artto et al., p. 8). When it has a high level of autonomy in its parent organization, a project establishes its own culture, objectives, and goals within the complex stakeholder network. In this context, projects can "...emerge and shape their strategy through the co-evolution of different stakeholders' interests and shape-- rather than being shaped by – their context (p.54)." In achieving this, a project would make its context endogenous rather than exogenous to the project in order to co-create with stakeholders (Wiltbank et al., 2006). The project would be able to exploit unexpected occurrences or problems as opportunities (Porter & Kramer, 2006).

The ability of a project to establish its own strategy makes projects "strategic" and not tactical (Artto et al., p. 7). From this angle, project strategy is "a direction in a project that contributes to success of the project in its environment" (p. 8). Mintzberg and Walters (1985) support this perspective of emergent strategy-- strategy cannot be "centrally controlled" or "pre-planned" in contexts characterized by diverse organizational actors, complexity, and unpredictability.

When projects shape strategy, they introduce particular project and organizational challenges. Engwall (2003) observes that "... radically new projects might challenge the existing capabilities, knowledge bases, and institutional structures of an organization" (p. 802). This suggests that projects will need to develop adaptive capabilities (including knowledge, skills, and tools) appropriate for emerging strategy. Projects will need to look beyond short-term outputs to understanding the concerns of the end user. The SD strategy approaches of backcasting and flexible investment also help projects to take this longer-term view required for SD. Both approaches require new ways of coordination, control and communication with stakeholders that reflect SD values.

Project Initiation Stage: Strategy Alignment and Emergence

The project initiation is a pivotal stage in establishing project strategy, and thus project SD strategy within the context of organization investment.

The project initiation begins "... when the initial idea is conceived, and proceeds to generate information, consolidate stakeholders' views and positions and arrive at the final decision as to whether or not to finance the project" (Williams & Samset, 2010, p.44). At the initiation stage, the project is conceptual and unplanned. The decisions regarding project initiation are usually taken at the project portfolio level, where organizations manage multiple projects to achieve organization strategic investment goals. At the portfolio level, organizations would consider if a project is related to multiple projects that support a single investment or is a single investment instrument.

The project initiation stage links the lifecycles of the project and investment. Project management standards and researchers often do not make a distinction between projects and investments. Here, we distinguish the project from its investment lifecycle context, so that it can be explicitly rooted within the context of the longer-term investment business case (For purposes of simplicity, we are assuming that one project initiates one investment). We acknowledge the fusing of phases—project initiation (definition and feasibility) and investment initiation. Placed within this context, this fusing enables a project to consider the long-term investment perspective so necessary in strategizing to contribute to corporate SD and to meet societal SD demands (See Figure 3).

The lack of adequate attention at the project initiation stage often accounts for project failure and the inability to create value for the organization (Morris, 2008). It is at this point in the project that strategy begins to unfold, traditionally based on the business case (for sponsor/investor organization) which articulates corporate strategic aims, including SD—alignment and begins to shape strategy based on its stakeholder context— emergence. At this stage, the project is linked to the business objectives of the sponsor/investor by way of the project purpose, scope, and output (Turner 2009). The sponsor/investor organization makes the final choice of project, guided by the anticipated effect of the project that includes its SD effect (Williams & Samset, 2010). The project strategy—"what to do and how to do it"—is formed to ensure best value and competitive advantage for the organization and to determine success or failure criteria (Shenhar et al., 2007). SD objectives and measures of success are pertinent at this stage, as the initial point for establishing project SD strategy.

Project Strategizing

The process that an organization chooses to formulate SD strategy at the project initiation stage is equally important to the content of project SD strategy. Here we can consider some approaches from the "strategy as practice" (see Whittington, 2003) or "strategizing" camp of strategic management regarding formulating strategy in pluralistic contexts where multiple objectives, values, and diffused power operate.

Figure 3. Project long-term investment perspective for developing project strategy at initiation (Keeys, forthcoming 2014)

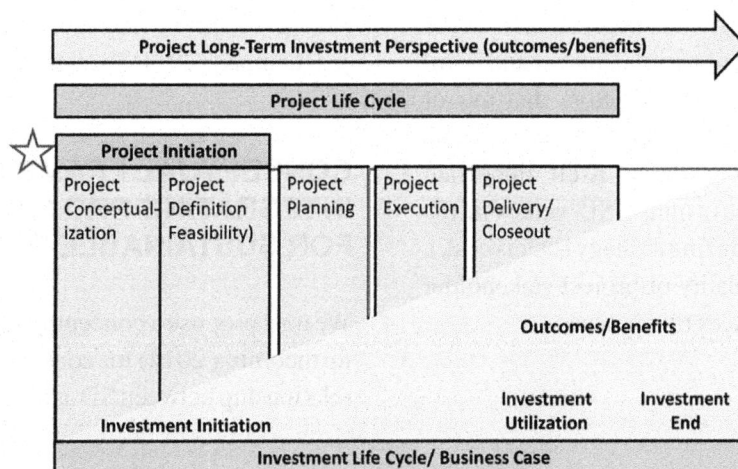

The diversity of SD stakeholders creates a pluralistic context for projects as temporary organizations. As an open system, a project has links to internal parent organization stakeholders and external stakeholder networks. This would include multiple investors and supply chains as well. The multi-disciplinary content of SD means that stakeholders may have independent ideas and possibly better information as to what constitutes "correct" SD approaches and priorities in their subject domain. Although it is evident that the organizational stakeholder (sponsor/investor organization) has power, power is also diffused among the players in SD context for the project, including the project team itself.

In the pluralistic context, strategizing researchers propose that organizations create value-based networks that incorporate multiple (divergent and dissenting) stakeholder points of view. Strategizing in this pluralistic context calls for accommodation of values brought about through routines and conversations (Denis, Langley & Rouleau, 2007). This accommodation would entail bridging the market value system with the SD value system (Denis et al.). Developing project SD strategy could mean that the project: first, identify and internalize stakeholders; second, construct its stakeholder network based on the attributes of the project; and third, tailor project routines, methodologies and activities so to help forge value accommodation with its stakeholders. These project routines and activities could include project processes, plans, meetings, focus groups, workshops, reports shaped by approaches to coordination, control and communication with stakeholder actors that mirror SD principles (Spee & Jarzabkowski, 2006). The strategizing process becomes itself important for "affirming or reaffirming" SD values in the project and for legitimizing strategy (Denis et al.). The approach and quality of project stakeholder management influences this process.

Project Stakeholder Management

Agreement with stakeholders on what constitutes project success has become a key condition of project success (Jugdev & Muller, 2005), and as such is important for SD success. However, the nature of SD calls for changing traditional project stakeholder approaches. In project management, the approach to stakeholder management has primarily been to use stakeholders as resources for projects or to subject stakeholders to project needs (management of stakeholder approach). Eskerod and Huemann's (2010) analysis of stakeholder practices promoted by project management standards reveals primarily a risk management perspective rather than one premised on the opportunities presented by stakeholder concerns. This approach is evident in a case study done by Banerjee and Bonnefous (2011) of the French nuclear industry where a corporation employed stakeholder strategies that would enhance its position, mitigate obstructive stakeholders, and maintain passivity of non-interested stakeholders. From the narrow point of view of the project sponsor/investor organization, this is important for ensuring achievement of project value against goals. However, this stakeholder approach had no effect on how the organization handled SD issues. SD requires a broader perspective—shared value within the longer-term view of SD and organization success. Consequently, a management for stakeholder approach which views stakeholders as having legitimate interests of their own (Eskerod & Huemann, 2011) is equally required.

CONCEPTUAL FRAMEWORK FOR INTEGRATING PROJECT STRATEGY FOR SUSTAINABLE DEVELOPMENT

We now propose a conceptual framework (Keeys, forthcoming 2014) for considering the symbiotic relationship between SD at the corporate and project levels and for integrating project SD strategy. The key components of the framework are:

1. Corporate sustainability strategy.
2. Project understanding of SD and SD business case.
3. Strategizing at project initiation stage.
4. Project autonomy to negotiate and adapt in the project context.
5. Project capability to translate corporate SD strategy to project SD strategy.
6. Project capability in stakeholder management.

The conceptual framework links SD corporate and project SD strategy and thus presents an approach to closing the practice and research gap identified in Figure 2. Figure 4 shows the framework components contributing to the formulation of project SD strategy, which enters into a cyclical and iterative process with corporate SD strategy. This process starts with the alignment of the corporate SD strategy. Through the project's beneficial interaction with stakeholders, the project is able to refine or adapt and emerge

SD strategy as appropriate for its context and go through a process of realignment with corporate SD strategy to improve corporate strategy processes. The degree of autonomy of the project within its parent organization and the knowledge and understanding of key project personnel, such as the project sponsor/investor and project manager, are important elements for the success of this process. We view the adaptive capabilities of the project, primarily embodied in the project manager and project sponsor/investor as pivotal to the efficacy of this framework. Sustainability is a moving target and requires organizational adaptive capabilities to adjust to the evolving circumstances (Bagheri & Hjorth, 2007). According to Hollings (Bagheri & Hjorth, 2007):

Sustainability is the capacity to create, test and maintain adaptive capability. Development is the process of creating, testing, and maintaining opportunity. The phrase that combines the two, SD, therefore refers to the goal of fostering adaptive capabilities while simultaneously creating opportunities (p.84).

Figure 4. Conceptual framework: a cyclical-iterative approach project SD strategy (Keeys, forthcoming 2014)

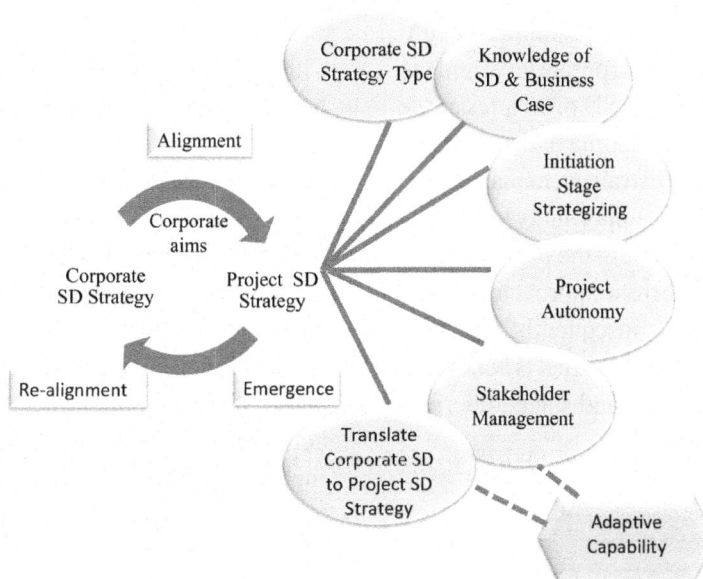

This appears pertinent to the work of the project manager and project sponsor/investor to respond to the evolving challenges of integrating SD principles in projects.

Corporate Sustainability Strategy: Setting Initial SD Aims

We have shown that the type of corporate SD strategy determines whether and how organizations will integrate SD principles in projects. The project sponsor/investor, project manager, as well as overall team, will understand the mission, values, objectives and overall aim of the direct project stakeholders, and this will establish a foundation from which to initiate discussions on possible SD issues, objectives, and criteria for overall success of the project. However, the corporate strategy might not prioritize mainstreaming SD principles in core business operations such as projects. The consideration of corporate sustainability at this stage marks only the initial yet insufficient conditions for formulating appropriate project SD strategy.

Project Knowledge of SD and Business Case

In order to formulate project SD strategy, the project manager and sponsor/investor need to understand SD strategy at the corporate level and the business case for integrating SD principles at the project level. With understanding and sensitivity to SD issues and corporate strategy, managers and sponsors/investors have the opportunity to become "critical thinkers," questioning the normative assumptions behind the current approaches in the project when warrented. Consequently, they help to foster SD change (Denis et al.) that is beneficial for the project, organization and stakeholders.

Strategizing at Project Initiation Stage

Project SD strategy is best defined at the initiation stage. It is important that the process for strategizing (formulating strategy) itself reflect SD principles as a means to reflect and confirm project commitment to SD. However, because of the wider network of stakeholders beyond the project team, and sponsor/investor, the strategy is only beginning to emerge. This pluralistic context requires project autonomy for appropriate strategizing for project success throughout project.

Project Autonomy to Negotiate and Adapt in the Project Context

The degree of project autonomy will determine to what extent the project will identify and respond to SD concerns through appropriate project SD strategy to achieve success for the project in its context. Autonomy enables the project to take advantage of rich information that manifests in project planning and implementation as the project evolves and interacts with stakeholders.

Project Capability to Translate Corporate SD Objectives to Project SD Strategy

This means that the project manager will need to be capable of defining strategy at the project level, often considered contrary to the traditional role of the project manager. Project managers do not always participate in project initiation decisions and thus may not contribute to project SD strategy at that stage. The project manager oversees daily routines and activities to take SD objectives at the corporate and business strategic levels and makes sense of them in the project. These routines and activities will contribute to corporate strategizing through dialogue, reports and other project comunication methods. This capability to translate corporate SD strategy to project strategy is closely related to stakeholder management capability.

Project Capability in Stakeholder Management

The choice of "management of stakeholders" or "management for stakeholders" approach influences the project SD strategy. Organizations will not be able to meet all stakeholder expectations. The capability to make acceptable trade-offs, recognizing the legitimate interest of stakeholders, in a transparent way as part of stakeholder management is vital.

FUTURE DIRECTIONS

Based on a review of literature in strategy, projects and SD, we have proposed a conceptual framework for understanding how organizations can integrate project strategy for SD, starting with corporate sustainability strategy and then through beneficial interaction with stakeholders. This conceptual framework identifies the process nature and the project capabilities for linking SD at the corporate and project level. Our perspective is that projects can achieve compatibility with integrating SD principles in a robust way and contribute to ongoing corporate mainstreaming of SD.

This conceptual framework can be discussed from different perspectives.

Multiple Organization Settings

We have presented the framework as applied to one sponsor/investor organization but have alluded to its application with multiple investor organizations and their supply chains. In a multiple organization setting, it will be important for the sponsor/investor organization to apply this framework not only to its own organization but also to use it to guide the creation of project structures, processes and activities for the entire project or-

ganization. This is not unlike its application for a single sponsor/investor organization. Moreover, the sponsor/investor will need to do this during the project initiation phase, as well as planning and implementation phases. Further, the sponsor/investor will need to identify and accommodate the project stakeholder views, such as investors, their supply chains and sub-contractors. Communication approaches, including workshops, project start-up and other meetings and project documentation, such as project plans and project contracts, become important instruments for building in SD principles. These approaches will support the autonomy of the project organization to guide the emergence of appropriate SD strategy with stakeholders.

Different Industry Settings

The framework is intended to be generic and adaptable within different organizational and industry settings. The framework does not consider the specific SD content of projects. The intent of the framework is to help organizations to take a process approach to ensuring that SD principles are considered holistically in projects. This process approach coupled with SD content and project technical processes will enable organizations to identify SD issues with stakeholders to improve value of their products and services and meet societal concerns.

Organizations without Corporate SD Strategies

Because we believe that projects provide a strategic nexus for corporate SD and stakeholder concerns, projects can actually help organizations to identify important SD issues related to core business and contribute to the development of appropriate SD strategy at the corporate level. Thus, organizations without SD strategies can adapt this framework, so that the starting place is the project level rather than the corporate level. Once the iterative process in developing project SD strategy is in play, information arising from the project level can feed corporate strategic processes.

SD Knowledge of Project Manager

The level of SD knowledge we propose is commensurate with what a project manager would normally require to understand the project business case to be an effective manager. However, SD is a new, multidisciplinary subject area. We would propose that organizations consider a sustainability expert embedded in the project team. This sustainability expert would advise the project manager, as well as sponsor/investor, on more specific aspects of SD principles and issues and the associated ways of working with stakeholders that project processes and activities should reflect. This does not alleviate the need for the project manager to develop knowledge and understanding of corporate strategy in the SD context. It enriches project knowledge.

CONCLUSION

Corporate SD represents a new management paradigm for innovation. This innovation occurs by viewing the concerns of stakeholders as opportunities to create shared value and developing approaches that enable firms to interact with SD stakeholders in ways that give emergence to these opportunities. This can only happen by mainstreaming SD principles in core business operations, such as projects. Society is demanding this, and this paradigm shift is an enduring one. Projects are at the forefront of making this happen. Closing the practice and research gap between SD strategy at the corporate level and SD strategy at the project level, to paraphrase Hollings (Bagheri & Hjorth, 2007), helps to foster the capabilities in formulating SD strategy at the project and corporate level that simultaneously

create opportunities for the corporation to move successfully along the SD path.

This leading role for projects means a different lens for viewing projects, project strategy and project managers within this important SD management paradigm. Projects are important sources of management and strategic innovation for organizations. Researchers are already looking at projects in this manner (Winter et al., 2006). While strategic alignment between projects and parent organizations is still good business practice, projects need flexibility to respond in a competitive manner in dynamic and uncertain situations, such as presented by SD, where interests go beyond internal project and organizational issues. Strategy formulation will require strategic ambidexterity—alignment and emergence. This is already happening implicitly in projects as few strategies are implemented exactly as planned. Project change control processes enable changes and refinements that can make projects more competitive yet projects and parent organizations have yet to view this as formulating strategy in the context and process of work and beneficial interaction with stakeholders. SD demands require projects to think of strategy and scope in the longer-term interrelationship between SD and business aims. Thus, sponsors/investors and project managers will become more sensitive to the longer-term impact of project decisions and the opportunities potentially presented by broader stakeholder interactions for charting new strategic directions.

As SD strategy formulation moves from the corporate level to the project level, corporate management will need to acknowledge and prepare the middle management project manager for the role as strategist within the project context. The project manager will have to balance carefully this strategist role with the priorities of achieving the project outputs. However, this balancing must be with the longer-term view of sustainable outcomes. Thus, project managers will need to be prepared to understand implications of project decisions, activities and routines for SD strategy formulation. In fact, it is through project decisions, actions, routines, tools and techniques that strategy emerges as a pattern in projects and strategizing occurs. This contributes not only to strategy praxis (how strategy is done) at the project level, but to praxis at the corporate level of the parent organization as well. Researchers can fruitfully pursue the area of strategy sensemaking at the project level to help project managers to most effectively carry out this new role in the SD management paradigm. Additionally, change management would be an important area of research underlying the move to this new paradigm. Ultimately, SD as the new management paradigm clearly points to the important and pivotal role for projects to contribute to the short, medium and long-term sustainability of the corporation.

REFERENCES

Archer, N., & Ghasemzadeh, E. (2004). Project portfolio selection and management. In Morris, P., & Pinto, J. (Eds.), *The Wiley guide to managing projects*. New York, NY: John Wiley & Sons, Inc..

Artto, K., Kujala, J., Dietrich, P., & Martinsuo, M. (2008). What is project strategy? *International Journal of Project Management*, *26*, 4–12. doi:10.1016/j.ijproman.2007.07.006.

Avram, D., & Kuhne, S. (2008). Implementing responsible business behaviour from a strategic management perspective: developing a framework for Austrian SMEs. *Journal of Business Ethics*, *82*, 463–475. doi:10.1007/s10551-008-9897-7.

Bagheri, A., & Hjorth, P. (2007). Planning for sustainable development: a paradigm shift towards a process-based approach. *Sustainable Development*, *15*, 83–96. doi:10.1002/sd.310.

Banerjee, S. B., & Bonnefous, A.-M. (2011). Stakeholder management and sustainability strategies in the French nuclear industry. *Business Strategy and the Environment*, *2*, 124–140. doi:10.1002/bse.681.

Birkin, F., Polesi, T., & Lewis, L. (2009). A new business model for sustainable development: an exploratory study using the theory of constraints in Nordic organizations. *Business Strategy and the Environment*, *18*, 277–290. doi:10.1002/bse.581.

Checkland, P., & Winter, M. (2005). Process and content: Two ways of using SSM. *The Journal of the Operational Research Society*, 1–7.

Clifton, D., & Amran, A. (2011). The stakeholder approach: a sustainability perspective. *Journal of Business Ethics*, *98*, 121–136. doi:10.1007/s10551-010-0538-6.

Denis, J.-L., Langley, A., & Rouleau, L. (2007). Strategizing in pluralistic contexts: Rethinking theoretical frames. *Human Relations*, *60*(1), 179–215. doi:10.1177/0018726707075288.

Dunphy, D., Griffiths, A., & Benn, S. (2007). *Organizational change for corporate sustainability*. Abingdon, UK: Routledge.

Dyllick, T., & Hockerts, K. (2002). Beyond the business case for corporate sustainability. *Business Strategy and the Environment*, *11*, 130–141. doi:10.1002/bse.323.

Ebner, D., & Baumgartner, R. (2010). Corporate sustainability strategies: Sustainability profiles and maturity levels. *Sustainable Development*, *18*, 76–89. doi:10.1002/sd.447.

Ebner, D., & Baumgartner, R. J. (2006). *The relationship between sustainable development and corporate social responsibility*. Paper presented at the Corporate Responsibility Research Conference 2006. Dublin, Ireland. Retrieved from http://www.crrconference.org.

Edum-Fotwoe, E., & Price, A. (2008). A social ontology for appraising sustainability of construction projects and developments. *International Journal of Project Management, 27*(4), 313–322. doi:10.1016/j.ijproman.2008.04.003.

Englund, R., & Graham, R. (1999). From experience: Linking projects to strategy. *Journal of Product Innovation Management, 16*, 52–64. doi:10.1016/S0737-6782(98)00046-0.

Engwall, M. (2003). No project is an island. *Research Policy, 32*, 789–808. doi:10.1016/S0048-7333(02)00088-4.

Epstein, M. J. (2008). *Making sustainability work: Best practices in managing and measuring corporate social, environmental, and economic impacts.* Sheffield, UK: Greenleaf Publishing Limited.

Eskerod, P., & Huemann, M. (2011). *Project management stakeholder practices—In the light of modern stakeholder theory and sustainability principles.* Paper presented at Nordic Academy of Management Meeting. Stockholm, Sweden.

Freeman, R. E., & McVea, J. (2001). *A stakeholder approach to strategic management.* Retrieved May 25, 2012, from http://papers.ssrn.com/paper.taf?abstract_id=263511

Gareis, R. (2005). *Happy projects!* Vienna: Manz Velog.

Gareis, R., Huemann, M., & Martinuzzi, A. (2011). What can project management learn from considering sustainability principles? *Project Perspectives.* ISSN 1445-4178

Gareis, R., Huemann, M., Martinuzzi, A., Weninger, C., & Sedlacko, M. (2013). *Rethinking project management.* Newtown Square, PA: Project Management Institute.

Gareis, R., Huemann, M., & Weninger, C. (2010). The consideration of sustainability principles in the project assignment process: An analysis of project management approaches. Paper presented at IPMA World Congress. Istanbul, Turkey.

Hart, S. L. (1995). A natural-resource-based view of the firm. *Academy of Management Review, 20*(4), 986–1014.

Jugdev, K., & Muller, R. (2005). A retrospective look at our evolving understanding of project success. *Project Management Journal, 36*, 4–19.

Keeys, L. (in progress; forthcoming 2014). *Considering corporate sustainability strategy in projects.* Unpublished doctoral dissertation, SKEMA Business School. Lille, France.

Labuschagne, C., & Brent, A. (2004). *Sustainable project life cycle management: Aligning project management methodologies with the principles of sustainable development.* Paper presented at PMSA International Conference. Johannesburg, South Africa.

Labuschagne, C., Brent, A., & Claasen, S. J. (2005). Environmental and social impact considerations for sustainable project life cycle management in the process industry. *Corporate Social Responsibility and Environmental Management, 12*, 38–54. doi:10.1002/csr.76.

Linneluecke, M., Russell, S., & Griffiths, A. (2009). Subcultures and sustainability practices: The impact on understanding corporate sustainability. *Business Strategy and the Environment, 18*, 432–452. doi:10.1002/bse.609.

Lorbach, D., van Bakel, J., Whiteman, G., & Rotmans, J. (2010). Business strategies for transitions towards sustainable systems. *Business Strategy and the Environment, 133*, 133–146.

Mintzberg, H., Ahstrand, B., & Lampel, J. (1998). *Strategy safari.* Edinburgh, UK: Pearson Education Limited.

Mintzberg, H., & Walters, J. (1985). Of strategies, deliberate and emergent. *Strategic Management Journal, 6*, 257–272. doi:10.1002/smj.4250060306.

Morris, P. (2008). *Implementing strategy through project management: Managing the front-end.* Unpublished manuscript.

Morris, P., & Jamieson, A. (2005). Moving from corporate strategy to project strategy. *Project Management Journal, 36*(4), 5–18.

Porter, M. E., & Kramer, M. R. (2006). Strategy and society: The link between competitive advantage and corporate social responsibility. *Harvard Business Review*, 78–92. PMID:17183795.

Presley, A., Meade, L., & Sarkis, J. (2007). A strategic sustainability justification methodology for organizational decisions: A reverse logistics illustration. *International Journal of Production Research, 4*(18-19), 4595–4620. doi:10.1080/00207540701440220.

Robert, K.-H., Schmidt-Bleek, B., de Larderel, A., Basile, G., Jansen, J. L., & Kuehr, R. et al. (2002). Strategic sustainable development—Selection, design and synergies of applied tools. *Journal of Cleaner Production, 10*, 197–214. doi:10.1016/S0959-6526(01)00061-0.

Shenhar, A., Dvir, D., Guth, W., Lechler, T., Milosevic, D., & Patanakul, P. Stefanovic, J. (2007). Project strategy: The missing link. In A. J. Shenhar, D. Milosev, D. Dvir, & H. Thamhain (Eds.), Linking Project Management to Business Strategy. Newtown Square, PA: Project Management Institute.

Silvius, G., Schipper, R., Planko, J., van den Brink, J., & Kohler, A. (2012). *Sustainability in project management.* Surrey, UK: Gower Publishing Limited.

Spee, A. P., & Jarzabkowski, P. (2009). Using strategy tools as boundary objects. *Strategic Organization, 7*(2), 223–232. doi:10.1177/1476127009102674.

Turner, R. (2009). *Handbook of project management* (3rd ed.). New York, NY: McGraw-Hill.

U.N. Global Compact-Accenture. (2010). *A new era of sustainability: UN global compact-accenture CEO Study.* New York: Accenture and UN Global Compact.

Van Marrewijk, M. (2003). Concepts and definitions of CSR and corporate sustainability: Between agency and communion. *Journal of Business Ethics, 44*(2), 95–105. doi:10.1023/A:1023331212247.

Whittington, R. (2003). The work of strategizing and organizing: For a practice perspective. *Strategic Organization, 1*(1), 117–125.

Williams, T., & Samset, K. (2010). Issues in front-end decision-making on projects. *Project Management Journal, 41*(2), 38–49. doi:10.1002/pmj.20160.

Wiltbank, R., Dew, N., Read, S., & Sarasvathy, S. (2006). What to do next? The case for non-prescriptive strategy. *Strategic Management Journal, 27*, 981–998. doi:10.1002/smj.555.

Winter, M., Smith, C., Morris, P., & Cicmil, S. (2006). Directions for future research in project management: The main findings of a UK government-funded research network. *International Journal of Project Management, 24*, 638–649. doi:10.1016/j.ijproman.2006.08.009.

KEY TERMS AND DEFINITIONS

Corporate Sustainable Development: Process of balancing financial profitability interests of an organization with larger societal concerns for economic development, environmental safeguards and satisfaction of societal needs in the short, medium and long-term. The focus is on both internal stakeholders (shareholders and employees) and external stakeholders who are impacted by the organization's activities.

Corporate Sustainable Development Strategy (Corporate Sustainability Strategy): Expressed intentions and actions, usually communicated in the form of a plan that lay out the organization's vision, objectives, and approach for integrating sustainable development principles in core business activities and for meeting the economic, environmental and social needs of internal and external stakeholders in the short, medium and long term (corporate sustainability).

Emergent Strategy: Strategy formulated through learning and adaption (as opposed to planning) as the organization interacts with its stakeholders to make sense of and take decisions on a competitive way forward, often in dynamic, complex, uncertain contexts, where prediction is weak and stakeholders diverse and many.

Project Autonomy: Degree to which a project can discern and choose approaches that may be distinct from the parent organization strategic plan, which will enable it to respond to challenges in such a way as to forge a competitive path to success in its stakeholder context.

Project Stakeholder Management: Manner used by the project to identify, interact with and address internal and external stakeholder concerns, either from the perspective of positive or negative influence on the project or opportunity to create new strategic direction and shared valued from legitimate stakeholder interests.

Project Strategy: Expressed intentions and actions, usually communicated in the form of a plan that lay out the project's vision, objectives, and approach for achieving success for the project in its operating context. This strategy is usually aligned with planned parent organizational strategy but also can emerge from project actions in its context.

Project Sustainable Development Strategy: Expressed intentions and actions, usually communicated in the form of a plan that lay out the project's vision, objectives, and approach for integrating sustainable development principles in project activities and for obtaining competitive and sustainable project outcomes.

Strategizing: Routines, approaches, techniques, tools, and activities used by an organization as a whole or individual staff to make strategy for the organization—in other words, what people do to create strategy.

Chapter 3

GreenPM®:
The Basic Principles for Applying an Environmental Dimension to Project Management

Tom Mochal
TenStep, Inc., USA

Andrea Krasnoff
TenStep, Inc., USA

ABSTRACT

The world is going green and we are collectively realizing that we do not have an unlimited amount of natural resources to utilize as we have done in the past. Material Handling Industry of America (2007) notes, "Not only do we have climate problems but we are also dealing with a resource depletion issue." However, the project management profession seems to be in its infancy in applying green standards. How can we apply these "green" concepts to our project management discipline? One obvious way is that we can manage green projects more efficiently. For example, if you are the project manager on a project that will result in using less packaging in your products, it would be good if your project completed on time. The sooner that project ends, the sooner the green benefits will be achieved. On the other hand, if you are dealing with projects such as installing a new software package or upgrading network infrastructure, how can these projects become more environmentally friendly? The answer is Green Project Management (GreenPM®). Green project management is a model that allows project managers to think green throughout a project and make decisions that take into account the impact on the environment—if any. It is a way to ingrain "greenthink" (or green thinking) into every project management process. Greenthink connects the environment with the decisions that are made, whether project-related, professional, or in our everyday lives.

DOI: 10.4018/978-1-4666-4177-8.ch003

INTRODUCTION

Green, environment, sustainability – these are words that continue to become more and more common in everyday vocabulary. Esty and Winston (2006) state they were told by a McDonald's Executive, "In a prosperous society, you really have only two assets: people…and the ecosystem around them. Both need to be carefully tended."(p.32). Natural resources are limited and there are steps to preserve these resources. In private life, some of the most common environment-related discussions include neighborhood and school recycling programs, environmentally friendly vehicles, carpooling, and water usage. Businesses primarily focused in sustainable industries have also been adopters of green standards, whether in new product development, collaborating throughout their supply chains, or working with environmental groups. Material Handling Industry of America (2007) states "There are many facets of the supply chain that could be improved by looking at it from a sustainability standpoint. The first issue that sustainable companies are focusing on is the design and production of the product.", and Velis and Linich (2012) state "Leading companies create value by modifying their supply chains to manage five key inputs and outputs: energy, carbon, water, materials, and waste."

Increasingly, organizations think green and strive for sustainable results. Interbrand produces a report, *Best Global Green Brands 2012*, noting the top globally green brands and in describing its methodology states that "Sustainability has proven to be a strategic and profitable aspect of business and a brand-strengthening asset, as long as organizations take measurable steps to reduce their social and environmental impact and credibly convey benefits that are relevant to consumers." Additionally, there are many organizations who have adopted the International Organization for Standardization (ISO) for environmental management systems, ISO 14001:2004. The International Organization for Standardization (2010) noted in *ISO 9001 certifications top one million mark, food safety and information security continue meteoric increase,* "Up to the end of December 2009, at least 223 149 ISO 14001:2004 certificates had been issued in 159 countries and economies. Annual growth is stabilized at almost the same level as in 2008 – 34 334 in 2009, compared to 34 242 in 2008, when the total was 188 815 in 155 countries and economies."

With this focus on creating sustainable products, the question that arises is how this focus on green can be extended to all projects. Is thinking green in project management as common and apparent if the result is not an obvious environmentally friendly product? With people and organizations more environmentally conscious, there is an opportunity to continue the practice of thinking about and applying environmental decisions to each specific project conducted within an organization.

This chapter proposes a model/concept that adopts or promotes green thinking in project management. It shares ideas for placing the environment into the project management profession and how organizations' existing processes may be extended to incorporate GreenPM:

- Supporting ISO 14000 Standards Through Project Management Processes
- A Closer Look: Applying Greenthink to Project Management Processes
- Taking Green Projects to the Next Level in Your Organization: PMOs and Portfolio Management

BACKGROUND

Companies incorporate sustainability ideas into business strategies. As noted in Environmental Leader (2010) "Large U.S. companies continue to be involved in sustainability, and most companies see an alignment between sustainability and their overall business strategy, according to a new report and related podcast from Deloitte." Companies undertake projects, and therefore use project management practices, to help move toward their business strategies. Therefore, it seems that there is a natural fit to extend the environmental dimension into project management. Ideas and research for thinking green in project management continue to surface although the widespread practical application of diligently considering an environmental dimension in structured project management processes, to our knowledge, remains a future hope.

GreenPM (green project management), a model introduced and defined by TenStep, Inc., is a concept in its infancy with a goal of incorporating an organization's environmental policies into project management processes. The point about GreenPM is not that every decision is made in favor of the one that is most environmentally friendly. The point is that the environment is factored in and evaluated, rather than being ignored. Decisions might be made the same as today. But there might be some decisions that are made differently. If more organizations use GreenPM, this new way of thinking and assessing projects implications could be propagated to all projects, not just the more obvious projects that are undertaken to create sustainable products.

The challenge with green thinking in project management, and therefore with GreenPM, is educating the project management profession that there is a place for environmental considerations to be factored into project discussions and decisions. The profession includes a large number of individuals. As noted in *PMI Today*, The Project Management Institute (2012) documents there are "482,015" project managers worldwide holding the Project Management Professional (PMP) credential (p.4). There are others practicing project management who do not hold the credential. And, project stakeholders include many individuals in addition to the project managers. Therefore green thinking in project management needs to reach a wide, global audience. It also requires ongoing education, communication and awareness, and governance, to ensure the practices are adopted and applied. GreenPM is a culture change to the profession, and any culture change can be challenging to an organization. It takes sponsorship and staying power.

By adopting these environment-related considerations into project management processes and their supporting templates, decisions can incorporate a thought for the environment. Whether or not the resulting project decisions change from what may have been decided prior to incorporating greenthink, it enables everyone to be more cognizant and better stewards of potential environmental impacts in their decision making processes. For example, often when discussing project decisions and impacts, schedule and budget come to mind. These are evaluated before proceeding with project decisions. The environment should become another routine area discussed and evaluated.

SUPPORTING ISO 14000 STANDARDS THROUGH PROJECT MANAGEMENT PROCESSES

Since the 1990s there is an increasing focus on sustaining the environment. The International Organization for Standardization (ISO) established ISO 14000 standards for the environmental field in 1996. Most recently revised in 2004, these standards are voluntary and global. As noted before by ISO (2010) in the 2008 and 2009 results, companies are earning the ISO 14001 certification. It is also common for these companies to request an environmental focus from their supply chain partners. According to Material Handling Industry of America (2007) "One of the bigger issues facing companies these days is the actions of suppliers. Companies today are being held accountable for environmental problems created by suppliers… Many companies are performing environmental audits or implementing "rules of conduct" to check the actions of their suppliers."

Like the more mature ISO 9000 standards for quality management, the environmental model follows a continuous improvement process. As noted by ISO in the *Management Systems Standards*, "All ISO's management system standards are based on the principle of continual improvement." As opposed to a defined environmental performance level, the ISO 14001:2004 environmental standard provides a framework for organizations to act in a manner that enables each to comply with its own environmentally defined standards. ISO14001:2004 defines a set of elements for defining and deploying an Environmental Management System (EMS), to help an organization improve its overall environmental performance. The Standard enables each organization to establish its target levels of performance and performance measurements, assisting in the creation of an organizational EMS. The EMS describes an approach for how a company will conduct itself in a sustainable manner.

Employees in the project management profession can learn from their company's approach to environmental awareness. If a company has an EMS or defined environmental processes, extending this to project management may not be a huge leap. Some of the culture change to think green and consider the environment is already established. The next step is to consider how environmental management applies to project management. It is possible that new questions could be asked or new decisions could be made if everyone involved in a project (project manager, sponsor, team members, key stakeholders, etc.) participated in greenthink. Environmentally friendly and sustainable thinking such as GreenPM can be applied to all projects, although all projects' outcomes cannot be expected to have the same level of environmental performance or gain.

A CLOSER LOOK: APPLYING GREENTHINK TO PROJECT MANAGEMENT PROCESSES

In its, *A Guide to the Project Management Body of Knowledge (PMBOK® Guide) Fourth Edition*, The Project Management Institute, Inc. (2008) identifies nine knowledge areas of project management which are comprised of project management processes and are commonly covered in a project management methodology. These knowledge areas are:

- **Project Integration Management:** Focuses on the integrated and coordinated nature of the project management processes. It is the area that assesses the implication of a decision on the other project areas. For example, when adding scope to a project, the result could introduce new risk, require additional resources, add time and/or cost to the project, define new quality requirements for the added scope, or introduce the need to procure resources with a specific skill.
- **Project Scope Management:** Focuses the project on the agreed upon work required to complete the project, and adhering to this defined scope of work.
- **Project Time Management:** Defines the project schedule and manages the project completion to this schedule.
- **Project Cost Management:** Defines the project budget requirements and manages the project to this budget.
- **Project Quality Management:** Defines how to meet the customer's expectations for quality and manages the project to meet these quality expectations.
- **Project Human Resource Management:** Focuses on the people aspect of the project, including identifying, obtaining, and managing the project human resources.

- **Project Communications Management:** Defines and implements the communications required to meet all stakeholder needs of being informed about the project.
- **Project Risk Management:** Defines the uncertainties that may occur during the project and how to minimize these if they will impede the project or maximize these if they are project opportunities.
- **Project Procurement Management:** Includes identifying, purchasing, acquiring, and managing products and/or services that are needed from outside the project team.

The following sections are aligned to the knowledge areas within the PMBOK® Guide. The examples show how environmental thinking could be applied to each of these knowledge areas. These examples are not comprehensive, but they provide concrete ways to extend the project management processes to include an environmental dimension.

Project Integration Management

The most likely part of Integration Management that can incorporate greenthink is Integrated Change Control. This is the process where all changes are evaluated and their affects on other project management processes are considered. The environment should be an aspect that is evaluated with each change and factored into each decision making process.

Project Charters, one of the main deliverables in this area, infrequently (or never) contain a section on environmental concerns. Therefore, most project managers never give it a thought as they are defining the project. It is likely that few project sponsors give it a thought either. But perhaps there are ways that your project can be greener. For instance, if you are upgrading your network infrastructure, it is likely that some of your equipment will be obsolete. Ten years ago,

you might take the old equipment and bury it in the middle of a big dumpster. However, maybe the better choice is to seek out a recycling company. It might even increase project costs, however; if you identify the recycling need up-front you can build the cost into your estimate. The business strategy and objective for the project may have considered this and determined that the brand reputation may improve or the bottom line may increase due to the focus on the environment. Dell is a perfect example. As a user of their printers, when purchasing cartridges they always provide self-addressed, postage paid recyclable envelopes to ship back used cartridges. Whatever their underlying reason, this is a demonstration of their environmental consideration.

Have you considered environmental performance goals in your Project Charter? Any project should be able to state whether it is related to some aspect of the environment and if so, how the project aligns with the company's EMS. Your project may or may not be related to the environment, but the consideration here is metrics management. Determine what project scorecard metrics are applicable to your project and whether to include any related to the environment. Plan the activities into your project to capture, measure, report, and improve on your findings. You could then summarize how all projects' deliverables align to the environmental targets. Would the consolidation of these findings provide another level of environmental awareness that does not exist today?

A second key deliverable, the Project Management Plan, should include environmental. The Project Management Plan is the "how" – how the project will be executed, monitored, controlled, and closed. Taking the time during planning to include how environmental aspects will be incorporated and supported throughout the project management processes may help to align a company's projects to its EMS standards through its understanding of the EMS and its planning of how environment-related decisions will be addressed.

Successful projects begin with defining the work and gaining Stakeholder agreement on the project and how it will be conducted. Greenthink starts at the beginning of the project so it will be planned in and managed throughout the project lifecycle.

Project Scope Management

One thing is inevitable – you will experience change on your projects. Scope changes if not properly managed, are a common cause of project challenges or failures. For this reason they receive a significant amount of project attention. Most scope change processes currently take into account the business value of the change and the impact to the project. Let's now add a third factor – the impact on the environment. With the added dimension of environmental impact to value and project impact, there are a couple of possible outcomes.

- There are no real environmental impacts. In this case, the process is the same as today. This may be the outcome of the vast majority of instances.
- There is an impact on the environment, but the scope change is approved as is because of the business value. Again same process as today, but the environment was considered.
- There is an impact on the environment, and the sponsor makes a different decision because of it. Perhaps the scope change request is modified to lessen the environmental impact. Perhaps the scope change request is not approved.

You see that in some percentage of cases, the sponsor might make different decisions on scope change requests if he only knew the impact of the change on the environment. Therefore, let's bring this information to the people who need to make project decisions, so they can at least consider environmental impact when they are making decisions.

The beginning of this Chapter discusses the example of installing a software package upgrade and how the environment may not be an obvious factor in such a project. However, consider that the project is now in the testing phase, and that the infrastructure and application design were architected to package specification. Testing identifies an issue that requires a package change which cannot be completed in the timetable for your company's go-live date. Your Sponsor decides to invest in additional hardware to alleviate the application issue. Will you determine whether to proceed based on the hardware's cost and schedule to implement within the project schedule? Or, will you also assess whether the type of hardware needed aligns to your company's environmental standards, and consider this dimension in your decision making?

When defining the project scope, all of the work is defined into the resulting Work Breakdown Structure (WBS). You may also add new work packages to your WBS for demonstrating performance-related gains that align with your company's environmental policy. For example, if you are manufacturing a new widget, you may want to demonstrate that you are decreasing the amount of scrap that has been historically measured in the manufacturing plant.

With rollout of the PMBOK® Guide Fourth Edition is the introduction of Collecting Requirements. If you are gathering green requirements, you consider environmental requirements and an understanding of the importance or priority of these requirements. Not every project or deliverable will have environmental requirements, but you may find some instances where this is applicable. Here is an example of how this may work.

- **Elicitation:** When preparing to gather requirements, you identify the stakeholders who will provide you with requirements. Does your organization have an environmental management group? Does your organization have an environmental policy? If the answer is yes, you may want to spend some time understanding how your deliverable aligns to the organization's environmental approach.

- For example, if you are working on a marketing project to create branded give-aways at trade shows, are the give-aways aligned with the organization's environmental policy? If you were not practicing GreenPM, you may previously have provided brochures and CDs (an example) to anyone who came by your booth at the trade show. Did anyone consider whether the brochures were on recycled paper and how they may be disposed? Did anyone investigate what is used in manufacturing the CDs and cases? Are the cases manufactured with recycled plastic?

- If you are practicing GreenPM, in preparation for eliciting requirements you would understand your organization's environmental policy and environmental stakeholders. You may include questions that help you collect information in consideration of the environment. You could ask the stakeholders what the environment requirements are for the trade show give-aways and understand the priorities of these requirements. Perhaps your organization has defined recycling and the use of recyclable materials as an environmental priority. If we consider the brochure and CD as an example, perhaps they are valid give-aways as long as the brochure is on recyclable paper and the CD is packaged in recyclable plastic.

- **Validation:** With GreenPM, as you review and consolidate requirements, you may determine inconsistencies in information. For example, what if a key stakeholder wanted to continue with CD distribution at trade shows but the environment stakeholder disagreed due to the non-recyclable materials currently used? You may determine that you now have a requirement to distribute CDs but find a new manufacturer who uses recyclable plastic covers. GreenPM could validate that the requirements align with any organizational environmental policy that has been established.

- **Specification:** When prioritizing requirements, GreenPM practitioners include the organization's environmental policy in weighting and ranking requirements. If a CD manufacturer could not be found to manufacture the CD covers within the defined project budget, and if this environmental requirement was a top priority, it is possible that an alternative give-away would be identified and the CD will no longer be created. If GreenPM is not practiced or the environment requirement for the CD case is not a high priority, then the CD may still be used.

- **Verification:** With GreenPM, you may educate your Sponsor on the environmental considerations that were taken into account in defining the requirements. Perhaps you even have a section of a Business Requirements Report template that highlights these.

GreenPM is not suggesting that you create a new way to gather requirements. You may incorporate environmental considerations into your existing process. If there is no environmental impact on your project deliverables, then you continue gathering requirements similar to what you are doing today. If there is an environmental consideration in your project deliverable, then you can consider which environment-related stakeholders can provide information for your project to consider, the weight and ranking of the environment factors on your deliverables, and whether you need to adjust any requirements or your deliverables due to the environmental factors.

Projects cannot be delivered successfully without proper scope definition and management throughout the project. GreenPM prompts the environmental thinking early on in the project, so no green-related work required on the project is overlooked. It also enables you to be mindful of the environment in your decisions of what you are delivering.

Project Time Management and Project Cost Management

The most common areas assessed for project impact are time and cost. The PMBOK® Guide knowledge area of project time management describes the processes related to the project schedule, from definition to creation to change control. Adopting a green project management methodology may now include activities in support of your company's environmental policy or EMS. Plan the time for these activities into your project schedule. If your WBS identified measuring performance-related gains for your deliverables, add the associated activities to your project schedule to measure, capture, and report on your findings.

When considering the knowledge area for project cost management, your projects can include costs for environment-related processes or activities on the project. A recycling program investment for product lifecycle and disposal, such as network cables or printer cartridges, may be costs included when planning the project budget.

With so much attention to achieving project schedules and budgets, taking the time to plan the environment factors into your project and determine the activities, schedule, and associated costs, can result in achieving both you environmental project goals along with the desired schedule and costs.

Project Quality Management

There are two levels of quality management programs – each of which can accommodate GreenPM concepts. One is focused at an organization level and one is focused on a project level. As stated in the PMBOK® Guide, quality initiatives at an organizational level include Six Sigma or the Capability Maturity Model Integrated (CMMI). Individual project teams don't implement large scale quality programs such as Six Sigma on their own. This is normally completed at an organization level.

It makes sense that if you have a Six Sigma initiative in your organization; you are going to need to adopt Six Sigma principles on your project. Similarly, if you are practicing GreenPM you should first look to see if your organization has an Environmental Management Policy (or something similar). If so, then you should make sure that your project aligns to these environmental policies and standards as well.

The second aspect of quality is the specific quality criteria that make sense for your specific project. The project Quality Management Plan focuses on the stakeholders' expectations (requirements) of quality and the resulting activities needed to meet these expectations. If you are practicing GreenPM, you should seek to expand this discussion of quality to discuss the environmental considerations of the project. This does not mean that every project will have environmental considerations. However, if you start to ask the questions and start to raise awareness, you might be surprised to learn that there may be green areas of interest to your stakeholders.

When you understand the environmental expectations of your customer, you can take these into account as project quality requirements. These can be addressed through your project as you address all other requirements that you have gathered.

Project quality assurance and project quality control may also include activities in support of the environment. For example, a project quality audit may confirm that the processes performed are in support of the company's environmental policy. You may incorporate a quality control checklist to validate deliverable quality. Perhaps it makes sense for your checklist to include questions that tie in environmental aspects to the deliverable you are building. One idea could be to ensure that you use recycled paper to create your project paper-based deliverables. This is a small thing but could have a large impact when multiplied over hundreds or thousands of projects.

Let's further explore a Green Project Audit. An organization that follows GreenPM may look to enhance its project auditing process. If there is a predefined quality assurance checklist used to conduct project audits on all projects, the checklist can be updated to include questions that verify that projects are complying with the defined green processes. Examples of some questions include:

- Do the project management processes or project management deliverable templates include environment considerations, (i.e., environmental implications resulting from specific project situations)?
- Can the project demonstrate its alignment to the organization's environmental policy or environmental management system, if any?
- Are environment stakeholders identified and participating in project communications?
- Are environment stakeholders involved in defining business requirements?
- Are environment stakeholders involved in deliverable review and acceptance?
- Are any project environmental factors a consideration for determining whether to continue to proceed in each phase gate review?

It is likely that environment goals and metrics will not exactly follow the best practices of current quality management processes. However, there are areas of similarity and concepts that can be adapted. As green becomes more routine within the world of project management, there will be further understanding for how to best apply and adapt current project management processes into a structured, proactive approach for managing environment-related aspects to our projects, and contribute to our organization's environment policies and goals.

Project Human Resource Management

Esty and Winston (2006) state that "By examining their businesses through an environmental "lens," managers can avoid expensive problems and create substantial value" (p.3). This environmental lens should be extended to all stakeholders, project managers, and project teams so that environmental awareness becomes a part of doing project business.

If practicing GreenPM, educate project team members on the project management processes that consider the environment. It is also an opportunity to educate them on your company's EMS. Since project team members are often involved in analyzing situations and alternatives and providing recommendations, their introduction to greenthink could help them recognize environmental impacts in their work.

The "people" aspect of a project can often be the most difficult to manage. Informing, educating, and including your team in your company's environmental culture can help you account for all environmental considerations throughout your project.

Project Communications Management

Project communications focus on how to create, share, and retain project information. The most common aspects for communications include knowing your stakeholders, determining your communications throughout your project, and providing project status.

When planning project communications, you look at the stakeholders involved in your project and determine the type and frequency of communications needed for the various stakeholder groups. The additional question asked in thinking green in project management is whether there are any "green" stakeholders that are relevant to the project. In most cases the answer may be "no". That is, most projects may not have any obvious connections with the environment or green concepts. However on some projects you might realize that there are some additional stakeholders that are interested in your project from a green perspective. Some examples of green stakeholders:

- **Your Internal Environmental Management Group:** Check the mandate for this group to see the types of areas they are interested in. You might be surprised that they could have an interest in many projects if the project manager and sponsor asked the question.
- **Facilities Organization:** If your project touches on the Facilities organization, you may well have some green implications. The Facilities group is interested in recycling, waste handling, trash removal, office moves, cleaning, and much more. Of course, most projects don't have a need to engage the facilities group. But if you do, they may very well have green policies that you will want to take into account on your project.
- **Procurement:** If your project will work with vendors, make sure that the vendors meet any green requirements that have been established by the Procurement Organization.

- **The Public or Public Agencies:** If your project impacts the public, or a public agency, you may well fall under some environmental scrutiny. For instance, let's assume your project requires a survey to gather stakeholder feedback. If the survey is only internal to your company then only your company would be interested in the format of the survey. However, if the survey goes to the public, you may get held to a higher environmental standard.

The prior stakeholders are examples of how to determine if you may have some stakeholders that are interested in the environmental aspects of your project. Some of them may be stakeholders anyway and you will just need to be aware of their green interests as well. However, in some cases, thinking green about project management will allow you to include some stakeholders that you may not have identified before.

If you are thinking green, you simply ask if there is any environmental impact for each communication option. Generally speaking you will probably find that most of your communications plan does not have any impact on the environment. However, sometimes you will find some impact. This also does not mean that you automatically change your mind. However, after evaluating any environmental impact, you might find other options that are as equally effective and do not have the same environmental impact. Here are a few examples of how this might play out.

- You decide that you will hold a quarterly status meeting of all management stakeholders. Normally this is in your office conference room. However, on your project you decide to have the meeting offsite. There are advantages to being able to get people away from their offices so they can concentrate on your project for a couple hours. After asking the simple GreenPM question, you realize that holding the meeting offsite will result in 12 people having to drive 10 miles each way to the offsite facility. This has some impact on gasoline supplies and air pollution. After identifying this environmental impact, you might decide to leave the meeting in the off-site facility. However, now that you are more aware of the environmental impact, perhaps you will decide to have the meeting in the office conference room instead.

- You decide to hand out sample CDs to all of the employees attending a training class. The CDs are cheap – less than $.25 each. After doing a quick environmental impact check, you see that there is a small impact to the environment from the CDs that will generally be thrown in the trash within 30 days. Faced with this reality you no longer just consider costs. This leads you to think a little more and realize that it is just as effective to send people an email with a link so that the material can be downloaded – eliminating the CD altogether.

- You want to create a project dashboard for your sponsor and other senior executives. The initial requirements state that this will be available online. After looking quickly from an environmental impact you do not see any implications. So you quickly move on.

GreenPM does not require you to change how you create a Communications Plan. You simply ask a quick question on whether there is any environmental impact associated with each communication option.

Green communication is much broader than trying to reduce paper on your project. Greenthink means considering green concepts in all aspects of communication, including status reporting and status meetings. Your status report should include a new section describing anything that your project encounters that is related to the environment. For example, describe any issues or risks that have an environmental impact. You could also report on how your project is aligning to your company's Environmental Management System (EMS). This status report section is also the place to brag about things you are doing that result in positive impact to the environment.

Providing status also includes status meetings. Incorporating greenthink would mean that each status meeting should have an agenda topic to discuss recent or upcoming items that have environmental implications. Being aware of these items might allow you to make environmentally friendlier decisions.

Communication accounts for the majority of our time on a project. Green communications help maintain the environmental considerations throughout the project.

Project Risk Management

Risk management is the process of evaluating each risk for probability and impact, and then responding to the risks that are most important to the project. Green risk management fits into this model very cleanly, by extending the "impact" side of the equation and look for any project risks that have an impact on the environment. It is likely that there will be no environmental risks on most projects. However, if you ask the right questions perhaps some risks are identified that you had not thought of before. You may identify some risks that are defined with a different impact level and therefore a different risk rating and risk response strategy that may not have been considered previously.

You might see things like the following:

- Prototyping a new technology. If the new technology does not prove to be a solution, you may then resort to an existing technology. Prior to GreenPM, you may have considered the risk to be associated with a schedule and/or budget impact. By considering the environment, you may recognize that additional resources (electrical power) used for you prototype that otherwise would have been avoided. If your company's environmental policy is looking to reduce its use of such a resource, then the prototype results may now include an environmental impact in addition to a schedule and/or budget impact.

- Considering a schedule risk if you cannot rely on overtime as an alternative for getting a project back on schedule. While this has never been a recommended best practice in project management, overtime is often a reality based on project constraints (e.g., schedule, scope, and budget). If your company's environmental policy includes an objective to maintain or reduce its use of natural resources, then overtime could impact this electrical power and water usage. Now, your Sponsor may determine that the project team should not work overtime.

- Replacing desktop computers could result in dumping of toxic chemicals into landfills. Perhaps you can make sure that the company you use to dispose of the old computers has a policy to extract the toxic components, recycle as much as possible and dispose of the remainder in an environmentally friendly manner.

- A manufacturing process might have a risk of releasing pollution to a local stream. Understanding the nature of this risk might result in more safeguards.

- A construction project may currently be most interested in the cost of materials. Using greenthink you might start to think more about the waste generated on the job, the disposal of excess materials, the runoff of paint and a host of other environmental concerns.

It is important to state again that the purpose of GreenPM is not that all of these decisions are made in a way that is environmentally friendly. The point is that the environmental impacts are recognized and any questions about these impacts are explored. The sponsor and senior stakeholders will still make the best decisions as they do today. But maybe, just maybe, they will make different decisions in some cases based on the environmental impact.

Project Procurement Management

Procurement refers to the aspects of project management related to obtaining goods and services from outside companies. This specifically refers to vendors and suppliers. Procurement is an area that project managers definitely need to understand at some level, and it is an area into which the project manager will give input. However, in many, and perhaps most companies and organizations, procurement is an area that the project manager does not own. The project manager normally does not have the authority to enter into contracts on behalf of the company, and he normally is not asked to administer the contracts once they are in place.

If you are purchasing goods or services on your project, you should determine your project procurement strategy and plans. In some cases, you will simply follow the procurement contracts and plans that are already established by your company or your organization. For instance, you may purchase hardware from companies using a standard company contract. You may acquire contactors using your company's preferred vendor list under prior master contractor agreements. In some cases, you will need to work with your Procurement Department to establish your own project-level vendor management plans.

If the organization is adopting a green procurement approach to all of its purchases, green procurement may be owned, defined, and deployed through its Procurement department. When practicing GreenPM on specific projects first determine whether your organization has an Environmental Management Policy (or something similar) and green procurement processes aligned to your environmental standards. If so, then you should make sure that your project aligns to these environmental policies and green procurement processes as well.

Green procurement also relates to the specific purchases that are needed for our project. Beginning with the Procurement Management Plan, it is important to understand and note any organizational policies and standards you are adopting on your project. The Procurement Management Plan describes how items will be procured on your project and the approach you will use to managing vendors. If a project manager is practicing GreenPM, he should describe the aspects of the project's procurement management process that will consider the environment. For example, you may identify how you expect vendors to adhere to your environment processes (such as GreenPM) or meet your environment requirements. There are a number of areas within procurement that can be enhanced to consider the environment and help you establish a green procurement approach. Following are some ideas:

- As you gather and rank the needs against which you will evaluate vendors, you can now include environment criteria that the vendors need to meet. You can also establish the weighting factors for these needs and ultimately rate the vendors on their ability to meet your environmental requirements.
- In Requests For Proposals (RFPs), you may include information on your organization's environmental focus (such as describing your GreenPM processes) and have the vendor comment on how they will align to these, or make a general inquiry regarding the vendor's use of green in its project management processes. Each vendor should be able to explain and demonstrate how they can accomplish your environmental goals.
- Map the vendor capabilities against your requirements and weighting factors, including the environment requirements that you have established. Using GreenPM, it is possible that your vendor selection may result in a different vendor. For example, if your environment requirements are weighted high, it is possible that there is a vendor with a significant focus in this area who perhaps would not have been your top ranked vendor without environment requirements. Therefore, if you did not consider environmental factors in your evaluation, you may not be determining the vendors who can meet your top needs. Then again, it is possible that the environment requirements and weighting factors may not have any impact on the vendor results and your vendor selection.
- Throughout the life of the project, validate that the vendor is proceeding as planned and agreed. This includes confirming that the vendor is following green project management processes (GreenPM) and meeting any defined environment criteria for deliverable completion. Procurement audits can be used to validate the compliance to your expected standards and processes.

Procurement is not simple and organizations seek to continually streamline and improve their procurement approaches. It is possible that green procurement is in its infancy and may add another dimension or complexity to improving procurement processes. However, if the results have a positive effect on the environment and possibly achieving your organization's environmental policy, isn't it worth the effort?

Recap: Greenthink and Project Management Processes

GreenPM® is the marriage of project management processes with greenthink. Since GreenPM can be embedded into the PMBOK® Guide nine knowledge areas, it appears a natural next step to incorporate the environment into project management processes. It is a reasonable extension of existing project management methodologies and processes, rather than a completely new concept.

As green becomes more routine within the world of project management, the profession will further understand how to best apply and adapt current project management processes into a structured, proactive approach for managing environment-related aspects to projects, and contribute to an organization's environment policies and goals.

TAKING GREENPM TO THE NEXT LEVEL: PROJECT MANAGEMENT OFFICES AND PORTFOLIO MANAGEMENT

The basis of GreenPM is incorporating green thinking into project management methodology. However, it should also be factored into Project Management Offices (PMOs) and Portfolio Management processes. As a "homeroom" for projects, PMOs often attempt to deploy common processes. One of the future roles of a PMO may be to help a company implement environmentally friendly practices. A portfolio management process provides a way to select, prioritize, authorize and manage the totality of work in the organization, including project work. Organizations with environmental strategies can evaluate and align their work with this criterion in mind.

How Can Your PMO Apply Greenthink?

Project management is an enabler to help you implement projects more successfully. You will need the project management resources in your organization to help you achieve successful project implementation. This is a long-term effort and often includes standard processes, training, and coaching, as a few common items for sustaining project management. A PMO is often established to serve as a base for all project management needs.

As the advocate for project management in organizations, PMOs already have a natural role as supporters and promoters of various standards and processes within their organizations. It seems that there is a logical next step for PMOs to advocate and align environment-related items into its project management initiatives. Companies that already incorporate environmental processes such as an Environmental Management System (EMS) and have established PMOs may be better positioned to incorporate the environmental discipline into their project management methodology. They already operate within established processes in both of these areas. The next step could be to determine how best to incorporate environmental aspects into the PMO.

- **Processes and Methodology:** A PMO usually owns the project management methodology, but can also have responsibility for portfolio management, business planning, development lifecycle and other organizational methodologies. These processes can be modified to determine when green thinking may be applicable. The PMO should not write processes that mandate environmental costs at the expense of providing business value. Instead, the emphasis should be placed on understanding when environmental factors should be considered.

- **Training:** Many PMOs are responsible for training the staff to build competencies and ensure good processes and techniques are understood and practiced. This training can be reviewed two ways. First, environmental awareness should be encouraged and taught to the staff. Second, the staff should be trained in how the new green practices have been integrated into existing processes.

- **Project and Organizational Assessments:** Many PMOs currently are responsible for assessing projects and organizations to determine how well they are adhering to standards and policies. These project audits could be expanded to also validate how well each project team is following the company's environmental standards and policies.

- **Metrics and Best Practices:** The PMO would be the logical place to coordinate the collection and consolidation of metrics (measures) related to green processes. The PMO can also collect green key learnings from projects to help formulate a set of green best practices that will be applicable to all projects.

- **Environmental Management System (EMS) Representative:** Organizations that are serious about incorporating green practices usually have created an EMS. The EMS provides guidance for all of the departmental initiatives related to environmental policies. The EMS usually requires broad participation and buy-in across the company. A representative from the PMO would be a logical candidate for the EMS Steering Committee.

In our everyday lives, we all recognize that the environment is a shared, global responsibility. Organizations can also continue to extend their environmental responsibilities throughout their departments. PMOs can be one of these additional avenues for organizations to champion their environmental focus. All projects cannot achieve the same level of environmental gain but it seems that all projects can consider an environmental component.

Making Portfolio Management Green

No organization or department has the resources to meet all of its business needs. This is true in the best of times. It certainly is even truer when times are tough. The typical response to managing scarce resources against an unlimited demand is to come up with some type of prioritization process to ensure that you approve and fund the work that will provide the most value. "Portfolio management" differs from traditional approaches in that it borrows ideas and approaches from the allocation and management of our financial portfolio and applies these to the allocation and management of our work.

There are a number of ways that greenthink can be deployed in the portfolio management process. Let's first look at the processes associated with business planning – that is the process to determine what work is authorized and funded for the upcoming year.

- **Green Customers and Stakeholders:** You need to identify your customers and stakeholders when you are creating your portfolio management processes. Depending on your organization, it is possible that you may have a direct green customer. For instance, your environmental organization may be a direct customer of your organization. However, it is more likely that if you have such a focused group, they would be identified as a stakeholder. Of course, if you do not plan to apply any green concepts to your portfolio management process, then there would be no reason to identify a green stakeholder. However, if you are going to apply some green concepts, then there may be a green stakeholder.

- **Green Categories:** Categories are ways that work is balanced. For example, you may create project categories of high, medium and low risk so that you can determine the mix of high, medium and low risk projects. Likewise you might want to balance the money that you are spending on corporate projects with the money you are spending on projects that primarily benefit your field organization. You can now add a category for whether the project had green benefits. Perhaps you could have a company policy that 50% of your projects will have some (maybe not entirely) environmental benefit. Categories allow you to allocate funding based on a strategic mix.

- **Alignment:** All of the work for the coming year should be aligned to your organizational goals and strategies. Therefore if you really want to make sure that projects have a positive environmental impact, you should describe at least one goal or strategy that has an environmental component. It is not possible to achieve a goal or strategy without projects aligned to do the work. So, by making sure that the environment is a part of the organization goals and strategies, you are also making sure that at least some green projects are authorized and executed in the future.

Green portfolio management still involves understanding the work and the resources, but with environmental input. The work of the portfolio at any given time has already gone through a green filter. This includes not just project work, but all of the work of the portfolio – including operational, support, management, etc. This baseline of work is prioritized during the business planning process and new work is handled through similar processes throughout the year. Greenthink can be applied to this work by including environmental cost/benefit (if any) in the Business Case. The company goals and strategies can also include environmental statements, which will influence how work is aligned.

The other side of the equation involves the management of the portfolio - the resources that are applied to the work. Here there is an opportunity to apply traditional green thinking, including understanding the environmental impact of the resources in use.

- **Employees:** People may not be considered green or non-green, but the way you utilize them can be. For instance if you are flying an employee into your headquarters on as weekly basis, you would have to say that this is not very environmentally friendly. On the other hand if your company has a policy of allowing all staff to work from home one or more days per week, this might be considered environmentally friendly.

- **Contractors:** Similarly, there may be ways to utilize contractors that are more environmentally friendly that other ways. In addition, your company can influence the environmental policies of the contracting companies. For example, you could require that each of your contract vendors develop an environmental policy.

- **Equipment/Hardware:** The purchase of equipment or hardware could be greener by including environmental impact and sustainability into the purchasing process. This could include a percentage of the equipment being made from recycled material, or that the vendor has a program for recycling the equipment when it is no longer needed. Of course, the equipment must meet the business needs and be cost effective.

- **Supplies:** Supplies are usually seen as commodities. This includes paper, pens, ink, toner, etc. These supplied can also be very hard on the environment since they tend to be discarded to landfills. The good news is that with a little foresight and green thinking, most all supplies can be recycled and utilized in a very environmentally friendly manner.

It is important to remember the basic point about green portfolio management. All decisions are still based on business value and business needs. The green aspects of the decision are just one more element of the decision making process.

GreenPM is focused on the right way to manage projects. Green portfolio management will ensure that the right projects are authorized and executed. Together they can provide a powerful set of guiding forces to help a company become greener in the future.

CONCLUSION

The implementation of GreenPM is not a major disruptive event. It is designed to be non-threatening and easy to implement. After all, more information is included and evaluated into the decision making process, but ultimately the same people are making decisions that appear to be best for the business.

On the other hand, the hope is that there will be a culture shift as greenthink becomes more embedded. More and more people will be making more and more decisions taking into account any environmental inputs. It only stands to reason that there will be some decisions that will be made differently. But these will be natural given the situation. So what does it take to successfully implement GreenPM?

- **Strong Sponsorship:** This is not just a feature of GreenPM. This is actually a requirement for all culture change initiatives. Let's face it. People don't like to change. It takes a strong sponsor with the leadership, vision and staying power to give the initiative a chance.
- **A Commitment to Try:** You need to be open to a slightly new way of thinking and some slightly new aspects to your current processes. If you are not willing to try, you will never be successful.
- **Training:** It's true – thinking green about project management is a little esoteric. Most people are not going to get the main focus right away. You will need to have some training available. The training does not need to be extensive. You are not training people in fundamental project management. You do need to make sure people understand what they are doing and how the process works.
- **Process Updates:** To really be successful an organization should do a minimum amount of work embedding the green approach into the appropriate templates and processes. This will help reinforce and standardize what needs to be done. Of course, as you extend GreenPM further into the organization, you will need to be more sophisticated in your implementation. You can provide different levels of training, collect metrics showing the results, respond to resistance, and launch a multi-faceted Communications Plan. Again, this is common with any organizational change initiative – not specific with GreenPM.

The bottom line is that an organization can get on board with GreenPM and implement it with very little investment of money. In fact, it can also be implemented with very little commitment of time as well. When it is all said and done it is just not that hard. The key is to find a sponsor with the vision and drive to get the process started.

GreenPM techniques and processes are in its early stages. The point is not to invent (many) new project management processes. The point is to adopt GreenPM into existing project management methodologies. Green thinking is part of the ISO 14000 standard. Since companies are now applying this thinking through their environmental policies and Environmental Management Systems, the question is how best to apply it on your projects in support of your company's environmental direction.

Applying GreenPM enables everyone to be more cognizant and better stewards of potential environmental impacts in their decision making processes. It does not mean that all resulting project decisions will change from what may have been prior to incorporating greenthink. Ultimately it is up to the sponsor and client organization to make the final decisions. Over time, the project management profession may begin to understand how many decisions might be made differently if the environmental impact (if any) is taken into account. These different decisions, multiplied by tens of thousands each day across the world, can make a difference.

FUTURE RESEARCH DIRECTIONS

Since the concept of GreenPM is in the early stages, the current challenge is adopting it and demonstrating the value of it. As organizations use green processes on projects and communicate results, both within their companies as well as to their industries and supply chains, there may be more understanding of what can result from its application.

Whether it is piloting projects within a company, industry, or supply chain, applying GreenPM and implementing a continuous improvement process may begin to quantify its value. The concepts appear to have validity, what will the results be when they become more of a common practice?

As with any culture change initiative, the success of GreenPM lies in the Sponsorship and deployment model. A multi-faceted deployment with periodic assessment and continuous improvement practices may help sustain the use of GreenPM. Ultimately the results may help expand this into other companies, industries and public sector areas.

REFERENCES

Environmental Leader. (2010). *Executives link sustainability with business strategy*. Retrieved from http://www.environmentalleader.com/2010/07/30/executives-link-sustainability-with-business-strategy/

Esty, D. C., & Winston, A. S. (2006). *Green to gold*. New Haven, CT: Yale University Press.

Interbrand. (2012). *Methodology*. Retrieved from http://www.interbrand.com/en/best-global-brands/Best-Global-Green-Brands/2012-Report/bggb-2012-methodology.aspx

International Organization for Standardization. (2010). *ISO 9001 certifications top one million mark, food safety and information security continue meteoric increase*. Retrieved from http://www.iso.org/iso/news.htm?refid=Ref1363

International Organization for Standardization. (2012a). *ISO 14001:2004*. Retrieved from http://www.iso.org/iso/iso_catalogue/catalogue_ics/catalogue_detail_ics.htm?csnumber=31807

International Organization for Standardization. (2012b). *Management systems standards.* Retrieved from http://www.iso.org/iso/home/standards/management-standards.htm

Material Handling Industry of America. (2007). *The green supply chain.* Retrieved from http://mhia.org/news/industry/7056/the-green-supply-chain

Project Management Institute, Inc. (2008). *A guide to the project management body of knowledge (PMBOK® guide)* (4th ed.). Newtown Square, PA: Project Management Institute, Inc..

Project Management Institute, Inc. (2012). *PMI today.* Newtown Square, PA: Project Management Institute, Inc..

Velis, E., & Linich, D. (2012). *The evolving supply chain: Lean and green.* Retrieved from http://www.interbrand.com/en/best-global-brands/Best-Global-Green-Brands/2012-Report/the-evolving-supply-chain.aspx

ADDITIONAL READING

Esty, D. C., & Winston, A. S. (2006). *Green to gold.* New Haven, CT: Yale University Press.

Green PM®. (n.d.). *TenStep, Inc.* Retrieved from www.green-pm.com

Interbrand. (n.d.). Retrieved from http://www.interbrand.com/en/best-global-brands/Best-Global-Green-Brands/2012-Report.aspx

International Organization for Standardization (ISO). (n.d.). Retrieved from www.iso.org

TenStep PMO Implementation. (n.d.). Retrieved from http://www.pmostep.com/0.0.0PMOStepHomepage.htm

TenStep Portfolio Management Framework. (n.d.). Retrieved from http://www.portfoliostep.com/0.0.0PortfolioStepHomepage.htm

TenStep® Project Management Process. (n.d.). Retrieved from http://www.tenstep.com/open/0.0.0TenStepHomepage.html

KEY TERMS AND DEFINITIONS

GreenPM®: A model that allows project managers to think green throughout a project and make decisions that take into account the impact on the environment – if any.

Greenthink: Thinking about the environment and sustainability in decisions we make in projects, in our organization and in general in our lives.

Chapter 4
Sustainability in Project Management Processes

Gilbert Silvius
HU University of Applied Sciences Utrecht, The Netherlands & Van Aetsveld, The Netherlands

ABSTRACT

Sustainability is one of the most important challenges of our time. How can we develop prosperity, without compromising the life of future generations? Companies are integrating sustainability in their marketing, corporate communication, annual reports, and in their actions. The concept of sustainability has more recently also been linked to project management. This chapter explores the concept of sustainability and its application to project management processes. It aims to provide guidance on how the standards of project management should integrate the concepts and principles of sustainability. After a review of the relevant literature on sustainability, its leading principles are identified and applied to the standards for project management processes.

INTRODUCTION

Sustainability is recognized by the United Nations as one of the most important challenges of our time (Glenn and Gordon, 1998). The pressure on companies to broaden reporting and accountability from economic performance for shareholders, to sustainability performance for all stakeholders has increased substantially (Visser, 2002). Some authors even imply that a strategy focused solely on shareholder value is not longer viable (Kennedy, 2000). Following the success of Al Gore's 'An Inconvenient Truth', awareness seems to be growing that a change of mindset is needed, both in consumer behavior as in corporate policies. How can we develop prosperity without compromising

DOI: 10.4018/978-1-4666-4177-8.ch004

the life of future generations? Proactively or reactively, companies are looking for ways to integrate ideas of sustainability in their marketing, corporate communications, annual reports and in their actions (Hedstrom et al., 1998; Holliday, 2001).

Sustainability, in this organizational context, can be defined as "Adopting business strategies and activities that meet the needs of the enterprise and its stake-holders today while protecting, sustaining and enhancing the human and natural resources that will be needed in the future" (International Institute for Sustainable Development and Deloitte & Touche 1992). The concerns about sustainability indicate that the current way of producing, organizing, consuming, living, etc. may have negative effects on the future. In short, the cur-rent business processes of organizations are not sustainable. Therefore, these processes need to change. And they need to change in a sustainable way.

A frequently used practice of realizing change in organizations is by creating temporary, task oriented organizations called projects (Lundin and Söderholm, 1995; Turner and Muller, 2003). Therefore it makes sense to link the concept of sustainability to project management (Association for Project Management, 2006; Maltzman and Shirley, 2010; Gareis et al., 2011; Silvius et al., 2012). In one of the first publications that discusses the relationship of sustainability and project management, the British Association for Project Management recognizes that "the planet earth is in a perilous position with a range of fundamental sustainability threats" and "Project and Programme Managers are significantly placed to make contributions to Sustainable Management practices" (Association for Project Management, 2006). However, Eid concludes in his study on sustainable development and project management that the standards for project management "fail to seriously address the sustainability agenda" (Eid, 2009).

This chapter explores the integration of the concepts of sustainability in project management processes as identified by the most-prominent standards for project management. It aims to identify the relationship between sustainability and project management and to provide guidance on how the processes and standards of project management should integrate the concepts and principles of sustainability.

THE CONCEPTS OF SUSTAINABILITY

The balance between economic growth and social wellbeing has been around as a political and managerial challenge for over 150 years (Dyllick and Hockerts, 2002). Also the concern for the wise use of natural resources and our planet emerged already many decades ago, with Carson's book "Silent Spring" (Carson, 1962) as a launching hallmark. In 1972, the 'Club of Rome', an independent think tank, published its book "The Limits to Growth" (Meadows et al., 1972). In the book, the authors concluded that if the world's population and economy would continue to grow at their current speeds, our planet's natural resources would approach depletion. The Limits to Growth fuelled a public debate, leading to installation of the UN 'World Commission on Development and Environment', named the Brundtland Commission after its chair. In their report, the Brundtland commission defines sustainable development as "development that meets the needs of the present without compromising the ability of future generations to meet their own needs" (World Commission on Environment and Development, 1987). By stating that "In its broadest sense, sustainable development strategy aims at promoting harmony among human beings and between humanity and nature", the report implies that sustainability requires also a social and an environmental perspective, next to the economical perspective, on development and performance.

The visions that none of the development goals of economic growth, social wellbeing and a wise use of natural resources, can be reached without considering and effecting the other two, got widely accepted (Keating, 1993). In his book "Cannibals with Forks: the Triple Bottom Line of 21st Century Business", identifies John Elkington, this as the 'triple bottom line' or 'Triple-P (People, Planet, Profit)' concept: Sustainability is about the balance or harmony between economic sustainability, social sustainability and environmental sustainability (Elkington, 1997).

This triple bottom line has grown to be one of the key elements, or principles, of sustainability. But from the definitions described prior, more principles can be derived. For example Dyllick and Hockerts (2002) identify three "key elements of corporate sustainability": Integrating the economic, ecological and social aspects into the firm's strategy, Integrating short-term and long-term aspects and Consuming the income and not the capital. Gareis et al. (2011) define sustainability with the following principles: economic, social and ecologic orientation; short-, mid- and long-term orientation; local, regional and global orientation; value orientation. The recently launched ISO26000 guideline on social responsibility mentions accountability, transparency, ethical behavior, respect for stakeholders' interests, respect for rule of law, respect for international norms of behavior and respect for human rights as 'principles' of sustainability.

After considering these sets of elements or principles, Silvius et al. (2012) conclude six principles of sustainability. These six principles are:

- *Sustainability is about balancing or harmonizing social, environmental and economical interests.* In order to contribute to sustainable development, a company should satisfy all 'three pillars' of sustainability: social, environment and economic. The dimensions are interrelated, that is, they influence each other in various ways. Based on the thinking in Willard's model of stages of sustainability, organizations, organizations can have a reactive approach to this principle and try to 'balance' so-

cial, economic and environmental aspects by trading off the negative effects of doing business for a somewhat lower profit. For example, compensating CO2 emissions by planting new trees or compensating unhealthy work pressure with higher salaries. A more proactive approach to sustainability looks at how organizations create a 'harmony' of social, environmental and economic aspects in their activities. This approach is not about compensating bad effects, but about creating good effects.

- *Sustainability is about both short-term and long-term orientation.* A sustainable company should consider both short-term and long-term consequences of their actions, and not only focus on short-term gains. Firms listed on the stock market may especially be tempted to focus on short-term gains, trying to increase performance from quarterly report to quarterly report, and thereby loosing long-term vision. This principle focuses the attention to the full lifespan of the matter at hand.

An important notion with regards to this principle is that the economical perspective, because of discounting of future cash flows, values short-term effects more than long-term effects. In economic theory, an immediate cash flow holds more value than a future cash flow, thereby emphasizing the value of short-term benefits. However, social impacts or environmental degradation because of business decisions, may not occur before the long-term.

- *Sustainability is about local and global orientation.* The increasing globalization of economies effects the geographical area that organizations influence. Intentionally or not, many organizations are influenced by international stakeholders whether these are competitors, suppliers or (potential) customers. The behavior and actions of organizations therefore have an effect on economical, social and environmental aspects, both locally and globally. 'In order to efficiently address these nested and interlinked processes sustainable development has to be a coordinated effort playing out across several levels, ranging from the global to the regional and the local' (Gareis et al., 2011).

- *Sustainability is about consuming income, not capital.* Sustainability implies that nature's ability to produce or generate resources or energy remains intact. The 'source and sink' functions of the environment should not be degraded. Meaning that the extraction of renewable resources should not exceed the rate at which they are renewed, and the absorptive capacity of the environment to assimilate waste should not be exceeded (Gilbert et al., 1996). The economic equivalent of this principle is common knowledge in finance and business. Financial managers know that a company which does not use its income to pay for its costs, but instead uses its capital, will soon be insolvent. The principle may also be applied to the social perspectives. Organizations should also not 'deplete' people's ability to produce or generate labour or knowledge by physical or mental exhaustion. In order to be sustainable, companies have to manage not only their economic capital, but also their social and environmental capital.
- *Sustainability is about transparency and accountability.* The principle of transparency implies that an organization is open about its policies, decisions and actions, including the environmental and social effects of those actions and policies. This implies that organizations provide timely, clear and relevant information to their stakeholders so that the stakeholders can evaluate the organization's actions and can

address potential issues with these actions. The principle of accountability is logically connected to this proactive stakeholder engagement. This principle implies that an organization is responsible for its policies, decisions and actions and the effect of them on environment and society. The principle also implies that an organization accepts this responsibility and is willing to be held accountable for these policies, decisions and actions.

- *Sustainability is about personal values and ethics.* As discussed earlier, a key element of sustainability is change: change towards more sustainable (business) practices. As argued by Robinson (2004) and Martens (2006), sustainable development is inevitably a normative concept, reflecting values and ethical considerations of society. Part of change needed for more a sustainable development, will therefore also be the implicit or explicit set of values that we as professionals, business leaders or consumers have and that influence or lead our behavior. Nelmara Arbex, Deputy Director of the Global Reporting Initiative, puts it simple and clear: 'In order to change the way we DO things, we need to change the way we VIEW things' (Silvius et al., 2012).

These sustainability principles provide guidance for the analysis of the impact of the concepts of sustainability in project management process standards in the following paragraphs.

PROJECT MANAGEMENT PROCESSES AND STANDARDS

Project Management Standards

Standards form an important building block of any profession (Crawford, 2007). They capture the body of knowledge that provide guidance for individuals and organizations practicing the profession and for the development of professionals. For projects and project management, several standards can be identified. Some relate to the process of performing or managing projects, some to the competences or qualifications of the project manager and some to the organization that commissions projects.

For the purpose of this chapter, we selected two broadly used standards of project management processes, and one developing standard, as our object of analysis. The two broadly used standards are the Project Management Institute's project management body of knowledge (PMBOK® Guide) and the Office of Government Commerce's PRojects In Controlled Environments (PRINCE2®). These two standards were selected on the criteria:

1. **Usage:** Commonly and internationally used.
2. **Endorsement:** By an international organization.
3. **Recognition:** As a project management standard.

In Europe, PRINCE2® is the leading standard for management of projects (Zoete, 2009), whereas the PMBOK® Guide may be the globally the most recognized standard for project management.

The PMBOK® Guide (Project Management Institute, 2008) is often considered as the most influential standard on project management, because of the distribution of the Guide and the popularity of the related Project Management Professional (PMP®) certification process. The PMBOK® Guide defines project management 'best practices' in terms of processes, inputs, outputs and formats.

PRINCE2® (Office of the Government Commerce, 2009) is a structured approach to project management, originally developed in 1989 for the government of the United Kingdom. It was released in 1996 as a generic project management methodology. PRINCE2® combined the original PROMPT methodology, which evolved into the PRINCE methodology, with IBM's MITP (managing the implementation of the total project) methodology. PRINCE2® provides a methodology for managing projects within a clearly defined framework. It describes project management principles, themes and processes (Office of the Government Commerce (2009).

The third standard we include in this chapter is the recently released ISO 21500:2012 Guidance on project management (International Organization for Standardization, 2012). We selected this standard because of its potential as an overarching standard on project management.

Project Management Processes

The PMBOK® Guide recognizes five project management process groups or clusters:

- Initiating Processes
- Planning Processes
- Executing Processes
- Closing Processes
- Monitoring & Controlling Processes.

And although these process groups suggest a project life cycle, they do not necessarily represent the phasing of the project. Projects appear in many variations and "there is no single way to define the ideal structure for a project" (Project Management Institute, 2009). The project management process groups may therefore depict a full project life cycle or the nature of the project management processes in a certain stage or phase of the project.

PRINCE2® bases its identification of project management processes on the project life cycle. The processes describe a step by step progression throughout the project lifecycle, from getting started till project closure. Each process provides checklists and formats of recommended activities, products and related responsibilities. The eight project management process groups that PRINCE2® recognizes are:

- Starting Up a Project
- Initiating a Project
- Planning
- Managing Project Delivery
- Controlling a Stage
- Managing Stage Boundaries
- Directing a Project
- Closing a Project

These eight process groups are detailed in 45 (sub) processes.

ISO 21500 also selected a life cycle approach to identifying project management processes. The process groups identified in the ISO 21500 resemble those of the PMBOK® Guide: Initiating; Planning; Implementing; Controlling and Closing. The term 'Implementing' was preferred above 'Executing', as the corresponding PM-BOK® Guide process group is labeled, because 'executing' translates quite harsh in various other languages. Within the five process groups, a total of 39 project management processes are identified.

When comparing these standards, the process groups show great similarity. Table 1 presents an overview of the process groups. Especially in

Table 1. Comparison of project management process groups as identified by the standards for project management processes considered in this chapter

PMBOK® Guide	PRINCE 2®	ISO 21500
Initiating Processes	Starting up a Project	Initiating
	Initiating a Project	
Planning Processes	Planning	Planning
Executing Processes	Managing Project Delivery	Implementing
	Managing Stage Boundaries	
	Directing a Project	
Monitoring & Controlling Processes	Controlling a Stage	Controlling
Closing Processes	Closing a Project	Closing

the process groups 'Initiating', 'Controlling' and 'Closing', the three standards are almost identical. For the 'Planning' and 'Executing/Managing/Implementing' process groups, the differences between the standards appear to be more notable, but the nature of these processes, a iterative cycle of planning, managing and executing, is shared by all three standards.

Given the similarities of the three standards, we will use a generic project life cycle based identification of process groups (initiating, planning, executing, controlling, closing) as our baseline for analyzing the impact of sustainability on project management processes.

INTEGRATING SUSTAINABILITY IN PROJECT MANAGEMENT PROCESSES

The principles of sustainability identified earlier can be expected to have an impact on the way projects are performed and managed. For example in the identification of relevant stakeholders, in the recognition of benefits in the business case, or in the assessment of risks. In the study by Eid (2009), a forum of project management practitioners was asked about their assessment of the impact of sustainable development on project management processes. More specifically, for each project management process group (initiating, planning, executing, controlling, closing) the study asked their views on the area of integration of sustainability aspects. The questions asked were:

- To which account do the scope and objectives of the project (more or less the project content) provide opportunities for integrating sustainability?
- To which account do the actual processes of delivering and managing the project (the project process) provide opportunities for integrating sustainability?

Figure 1 shows the result of Eid's study.

From this study it can be concluded that the respondents see opportunities for the integration of sustainability in all process groups of project management. The area of integration of sustainability aspects, however, differs:

- The initiating and planning stages of the project provide opportunities for integrating the concepts of sustainability into the *content* of the project.
- The executing and controlling stages of the project provide opportunity for integrating the concepts of sustainability in the *process* of the project.

This outcome is not unexpected, since the aspects of sustainability are best integrated from the origins of the process, system or asset that is defined as the intended project result.

A more specific assessment of the impact of sustainability aspects and principles on the project management processes is presented in the following section (Silvius et al., 2012). This section analyses confronts the project management processes of a generic project life cycle, on their inclusion of the six principles of sustainability. The terminology is based on the PMBOK® Guide.

- *Sustainability is about balancing or harmonizing social, environmental and economical interests.* This principle provides additional perspectives on the content and process of the project. It logically influences both the content and the process of the project. Hence, it may be expected that this principle has a high impact on almost all project management processes. For example, balancing social, environmental and economical interests will influence the project initiating processes in terms of the intended project result and the identification of stakeholders. Also in the project planning stage, providing additional perspectives will logically affect processes like defining the requirements, scope, activities, quality and risks of the project. Taking into account social and environmental criteria will logically also affect the organization of the project and the criteria for materials and supplier selection.

All considerations that apply to the project planning stage of the project will also affect the project execution phase. For example, additional perspectives on quality, will logically also influence the quality assurance process. And applying

Figure 1. The best areas to integrate sustainable development into project management (based on Eid, 2009)

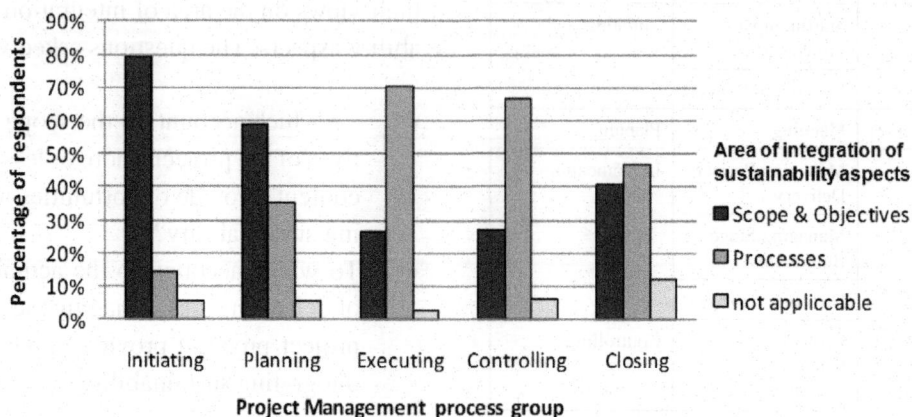

social criteria like equal opportunity, also apply in the project execution stage, when organizing and managing the project team.

The project monitoring and control processes may be less strongly affected by the inclusion of social and environmental aspects. Of course the project content that is being monitored is influenced by the principal, but the monitoring and controlling processes itself not that much. One exception to this is the reporting process. The project's progress reports will definitely be influenced by the principle, for example by including reporting items that refer to the social and environmental aspects. Inclusion of these aspects will also influence the process of data gathering and preparing the report.

Taking into account social and environmental criteria is not expected to influence the project closing processes.

- *Sustainability is about both short-term and long-term orientation.* Also this principle provides an additional perspective on the content and the process of the project. For example including the long term future as a consideration may influence the selection of materials used in the project, favoring more eco-friendly materials. In this regard, the principle seemingly overlaps with the balancing social, environmental and economical interests principle, but it adds a time scale to these interests. Adding this time scale logically impacts almost all project management processes in the project initiating and project planning stages, like defining intended result, requirements, scope, stakeholders, activities, quality and risks of the project.

In the project execution stage, adding a long term perspective could include developing team members beyond the needs of the project, but thereby building the organization's strength to perform projects. This would influence the pro-

cesses of managing and developing the project team. Another consideration that is emphasized by the short term and long term process is the acceptance of the change in products, services, systems, processes, resources or procedures that the project includes. It is impossible to narrow this down to one process in the project. The acceptance of the project result is influenced by the way all project management processes are executed.

Following the reasoning stated earlier, the project monitoring and control processes may be less strongly affected by the inclusion of the short term and long term perspective. In the project closing stage, the short term and long term principle may be expected to emphasize the hand-over of the project result to the permanent organization and the acceptance of the organizational change that the project created.

- *Sustainability is about local and global orientation.* In a similar way as the first two principles, also this principle provides a specific perspective on the content and the process of the project. For example the global aspects of a project may include the labor conditions of organizations in the supply chain that may reside in low-cost countries like India, China or Africa. Local aspects may include engaging with stakeholders in the local community about the effect of the project (for example noise or traffic related to the project) on their living environment. Since considering the local and global perspective can impact again both the content and the process of the project, almost all project management processes in the project initiating, planning and execution stages may be affected by this.

The project monitoring and control processes may be less strongly affected by the inclusion of this perspective. As may the closing stage of the project.

- *Sustainability is about consuming income, not capital. This principle of sustainability provides guidance for the* materials and resources in the project. For example by selecting eco-friendly materials to be used in the project. The impact of this principle therefore concerns the content of the project, thereby logically impacting the processes of the project planning stage.

But the principle also applies to the processes of the project execution stage. For example by caring for the well-being of the project team members or other stakeholders of the project. The result-oriented nature of projects, combined with often limited resources, may create high work pressure for the team members or suppliers involved. If this pressure leads to fall-out of team members, this should also be considered as 'consuming capital', since it affects a person's future ability to perform. The impact of this principle therefore also concern the processes of the project execution stage. The impact of this principle on the project initiating, monitoring and controlling and the project closing phase may be less obvious.

- *Sustainability is about transparency and accountability. The principle of transparency and accountability does not* provide a new or different perspective on the project's content or process, but concerns the openness and pro-activeness in information and communication towards stakeholders and the general public. This principle therefore logically applies to all project management processes. It concerns 'how' processes are done, but also 'what' is done in terms of communicating en engaging with stakeholders.
- *Sustainability is about personal values and ethics. Following a similar reasoning as the last principle* prior, also the principle of values and ethics logically applies to all project management processes and stages. It is not that much about 'what' is done, but most of all about 'how' this is done.

Table 2 summarizes the impact of the sustainability principles analyzed before. The expected impact is indicated as 'High', 'Moderate' and 'Low'.

Based on this analysis, the following 'areas of impact' can be concluded.

Table 2. Expected effect of sustainability principles on project management processes (Silvius et al., 2012)

	Sustainability Principles					
	Harmonizing Social, Environmental and Economical Interests	Both Short Term and Long Term	Local and Global	Consuming Income, Not Capital	Transparency and Accountability	Personal Values and Ethics
Project Initiating	High Impact	High Impact	High Impact	Low Impact	High Impact	High Impact
Project Planning	High Impact	High Impact	High Impact	High Impact	High Impact	High Impact
Project Executing	High Impact	High Impact	High Impact	High Impact	High Impact	High Impact
Project Monitoring and Controlling	Moderate Impact	Low Impact	Low Impact	Low Impact	High Impact	High Impact
Project Closing	Low Impact	High Impact	Low Impact	Low Impact	High Impact	High Impact

Project Context

Project management processes should address questions like How do the principles and aspects of sustainability influence the societal and organizational context of the project? And How is this influence relevant or translated to the project?

The PMBOK® Guide mentions in paragraph 1.8, Enterprise Environmental Factors, the organization's human resources and marketplace conditions as "internal or external environmental factors that surround or influence a project's success". But the paragraph fails to more explicitly identify potential social or environmental interest resulting from sustainability policies as factors of influence.

PRINCE2® addresses the project context in several processes during the start-up and initiation stages of the project. The business case and intended project result may logically be linked to organizational goals and strategy. No mentioning is made of a larger societal context of the project.

Also in ISO 21500, the context and concepts of projects are described mainly from an organizational strategy realization perspective.

Stakeholders

The principles of sustainability, more specific the principles 'balancing or harmonizing social, environmental and economical interests', 'both short term and long term' and 'both local and global', will likely increase the number of stakeholders of the project. Typical 'sustainability stakeholders' may be environmental protection pressure groups, human rights groups, nongovernmental organizations, etc.

The PMBOK® Guide lacks in paragraph 2.3, Stakeholders, or in the definition of stakeholders in the Glossary, any reference to typical sustainability stakeholders as environmental protection pressure groups, human rights groups or nongovernmental organizations. Also chapter 10, Project Communications Management, fails to recognize

these potential stakeholders when it discusses stakeholder communication.

In PRINCE2®, the identification of stakeholders is mentioned in different processes of the initial stages of the project. Also the communication to stakeholders is addressed explicitly. There is no explicit recognition of potential stakeholders representing the environmental and/or social aspects of the project.

ISO 21500 uses a broad definition of potential stakeholders, a "person, group or organization that has interests in or can affect, be affected by, or perceive themselves to be affected by any aspect of the project" and makes an explicit reference to "Special Interest Groups" as potential stakeholders.

Project Content

Integrating the principles of sustainability will influence the definition of the result, objective, conditions and success factors of the project. For example the inclusion of environmental or social aspects in the project's objective and intended result.

In the introduction of chapter 3 Project Management Processes, the PMBOK® Guide mentions a few criteria for a successful project. Here it is mentioned that the project manager should be able to "balance the competing demands of scope, time, cost, quality, resources and risk". In this section the PMBOK® Guide fails to recognize the social and environmental aspects as relevant factors in project success.

PRINCE2® mentions six project performance variables. These variables do not mention sustainability aspects explicitly, but they may be included in performance variables 'quality' and 'benefits'.

ISO 21500 positions the content, goal and outcome of the project in the context of the organizational strategy. No reference is made to the content of this strategy or the project.

Business Case

The influence of the principles of sustainability on the project content, will need to be reflected also in the project justification. The business case of the project may need to be expanded to include also non financial factors that refer to for example social or environmental aspects.

Paragraph 4.1.1. of the PMBOK® Guide, Develop Project Charter, mentions "Ecological impacts" and "Social needs" as potential benefits of a project when it discussed the business case.

In PRINCE2®, the business case has a central role. In all stages of the project, specific processes are identified to define or update the business case. In the business case, benefits are addressed in general, without specifically addressing potential social or environmental benefits.

ISO 21500 mentions the business case as the justification for the investment in the project. Reference to a holistic view on justification is made by stating that the evaluation "may include multiple criteria including financial investment appraisal techniques and qualitative criteria such as strategic alignment, social impact, and environmental impact."

Project Success

In the introduction of chapter 3 Project Management Processes, the PMBOK® Guide mentions a few criteria for a successful project. Here it is mentioned that the project manager should be able to "balance the competing demands of scope, time, cost, quality, resources and risk". In this section the PMBOK® Guide fails to recognize the social and environmental aspects as relevant factors in project success.

PRINCE2® mentions six project performance variables. These variables do not mention sustainability aspects explicitly, but they may be included in performance variables 'quality' and 'benefits'.

ISO 21500 mentions "comply with requirements to satisfy the project sponsor, customers and other stakeholders" as an important criterion for project success. Following the 'broad' definition of stakeholders mentioned earlier, this statement may support a holistic view on project success.

Project Reporting

Since the project progress reports logically follow the definition of scope, objective, critical success factors, business case, etc. from the project initiating and planning processes, also the project reporting processes will be influenced by the inclusion of sustainability aspects.

Project reporting processes can be found in the PMBOK® Guide in paragraph 3.6.8. Report Performance and paragraph 10.5 Report Performance. In these sections, project reporting focuses on progress and changes in the areas scope, schedule, cost and quality of the project. Reporting on sustainability aspects is not explicitly addressed, nor is the principle of transparency.

The 'Report highlights' process as part of 'Controlling a stage' of PRINCE2®, reports the progress of the project in terms of the work packages, issues and changes. Reporting on sustainability aspects is not addressed, nor is the principle of sustainability.

In ISO 21500, progress reports and inspection reports are frequently mentioned as inputs or outputs of processes without being detailed. Reporting on sustainability aspects is not addressed, nor is the principle of transparency.

Materials and Procurement

Also the processes concerned with materials and procurement provide a logical opportunity to integrate aspects of sustainability, for example non-bribery and ethical behavior in the selection of suppliers.

Processes related to the selection of materials and procurement can be found in different sections of the PMBOK® Guide. For example paragraph 3.4.20 Plan procurements, paragraph 3.5.8. Conduct procurements, chapter 12 Project Procurement Management. None of these sections include any references to sustainability aspects in for example the selection of suppliers or the selection of materials.

In PRINCE2®, materials and procurement are implicitly included in work-packages. No reference is made to the selection of materials and suppliers, based on sustainability criteria.

In ISO 21500, references to materials, procurement and suppliers are all related to a controlled execution of the project. In process 4.3.36 Select Suppliers, no reference is made to social or environmental criteria that may be considered in supplier selection.

Risk Management

With the inclusion of environmental and social aspects in the project's objective, scope and or conditions, logically also the assessment of potential risks will need to evolve.

Chapter 11 of the PMBOK® Guide, Project Risk Management, mentions a process and several techniques to identify risks. However, these techniques do not mention the possibility of environmental and/or social risks.

In PRINCE2®, risk, as one of the central themes, is addressed in many processes throughout the project life cycle. However, no explicit reference is made to environmental and/or social risks.

Also ISO 21500 makes no explicit reference to environmental and/or social risks.

Project Team

Another area of impact of sustainability is the project organization and management of the project team. Especially the social aspects of sustainability, such as equal opportunity and personal development, can be put to practice in the management of the project team.

Chapter 9 of the PMBOK® Guide, Project Human Resource Management, shows little consideration of social sustainability aspects such as life-work balance, equal opportunity, part time job opportunities, etc. Paragraph 9.2.2., however, pays attention to 'virtual teams' and links this to team members working from home offices, potentially with mobility limitations or disabilities. Also the personal development of team members is addressed. The objective for this development, however, is the performance of the project team, without considering the effectiveness of team members in their professional life after the project.

PRINCE2® pays ample attention to the management and development of the project team. It does mention 'Design and appoint the project management team', but in later stages no reference is made.

ISO 21500 mentions that "the project manager, when possible, should take into consideration factors such as skills and expertise, different personalities, and group dynamics when establishing the project team". No reference is made social sustainability aspects such as life-work balance, equal opportunity, part time job opportunities, etc. Process 4.3.18 does mention the development of the project team.

Organizational Learning

A final area of impact of sustainability is the degree to which the organization learns from the project. Sustainability also suggests minimizing waste. Organizations should therefore learn from their projects in order to not 'waste' energy, resources and materials on their mistakes in projects.

Paragraph 2.4.3 of the PMBOK® Guide mentions 'Historical information and lessons learned' as part of the 'Corporate Knowledge Base' of the organization. However, this section lacks a more explicit reference to organizational learning or knowledge management in order to improve an organization's competence in doing projects.

In PRINCE2®, the 'Lessons log' and the 'Lessons report' explicitly capture the lessons learned in a project. These lessons are explicitly addressed in the starting up stage of a project in the process 'Capture previous lessons'.

ISO 21500 also includes a 'Collect lessons learned' process, covering the capturing, compiling, formalising, storing and dissemination of experiences to benefit current and future projects. The planning processes mention lessons learned as an input.

INTEGRATING SUSTAINABILITY IN PROJECT MANAGEMENT PROCESS STANDARDS

Now that we have assessed the potential project management processes and related areas on which the aspects of sustainability may have a logical impact, a next step is to understand how this impact is covered in the current project management standards. Table 3 shows an overview of the areas of impact, how these are included in PMBOK® Guide, PRINCE2® and ISO 21500, how these impacts should be addressed in 'true' sustainable project management.

Reflecting on the previous analysis, we can conclude that on the logical areas of impact, the standards of project management processes (*PMBOK® Guide*, PRINCE2® and ISO 21500) refer mostly implicit to sustainability considerations. More explicit identification of especially environmental and social aspects is lacking. Furthermore, the standards of project management place emphasis on the processes of project management and consider the content of the project (objective, intended result, deliverable) as given. Integrating the concepts of sustainability, however, suggests

that not just the process of delivering the project is considered, but also the content of the project itself. The integration of sustainability in projects and project management therefore requires an elaborated view of the profession.

CONCLUSION

Projects can make a contribution to the sustainable development of organizations. It should therefore be expected that the concepts and principles of sustainability are reflected in projects and project management and their standards. Reflecting on our analysis, we can conclude that on the logical areas of impact, the standards of project management processes (PMBOK® Guide, PRINCE2®, and ISO 21500) refer mostly implicit to sustainability considerations. More explicit identification of especially environmental and social aspects is lacking. And since, the standards of project management place emphasis on the processes of project management, the content of the project (objective, intended result, deliverable) is mostly considered as given. Integrating the concepts of sustainability, however, suggests that not just the process of delivering the project is considered, but also the content of the project itself.

It is clear that still a lot of work has to be done on the implications of Sustainable Project Management and that there is a growing need of expertise, criteria and concepts to practically implement the concept in the management of projects.

FUTURE RESEARCH DIRECTIONS

Future research may elaborate on the impact of sustainability on the project management processes by providing process descriptions, formats, and enhanced standards. However, as with many standards, it should be taken into account that

Table 3. Overview of the impact of sustainability on the project management processes

Area of impact	PMBOK® Guide	PRINCE2®	ISO 21500	Sustainable Project Management
Project context	Section 1.8, Enterprise Environmental Factors, mentions the organization's human resources and marketplace conditions as "internal or external environmental factors that surround or influence a project's success". But the section fails to more explicitly identify potential social or environmental interest resulting from sustainability policies as factors of influence.	PRINCE2® addresses the project context in several processes during the start-up and initiation stages of the project. The business case and intended project result may logically be linked to organizational goals and strategy. No mentioning is made of a larger societal context of the project.	Clause 3 describes the context and concepts of projects mainly from an organizational strategy realization perspective. However, section 3.5 mentions the 'Project Environment', including "factors outside the organiza-tional boundary such as socio-economic, geographical, political, regulatory, technolo-gical and ecological". It is stated that the project team should consider these factors.	The context of the project is addressed in relationship to the organization's strategy, but also in relationship to society as a whole.
Stake-holders	In Section 2.3, Stakeholders, or the definition of stakeholders in the Glossary, any reference to typical sustainability stakeholders as environmental pressure groups, human rights groups or nongovern-mental organizations are lacking. Chapter 10, Project Communications Management, also fails to recognize these potential stakeholders when it discusses stakeholder communication.	The identification of stakeholders is mentioned in different processes of the initial stages of the project. Also the communication to stakeholders is addressed explicitly. There is no explicit recognition of potential stakeholders representing the environmental and/or social aspects of the project.	Stakeholder is defined as a "person, group or organization that has interests in or can affect, be affected by, or perceive themselves to be affected by any aspect of the project'. In the Figure showing potential stakeholders reference is made to "Special Interest Groups", without elaborating on this in the text of the guideline.	In the identification of potential stakeholders, explicit notion is made of potential stakeholders representing the environmental and/ or social aspects of the project. Communication with stakeholders includes proactive engagement with potential stakeholders.
Project content	The *PMBOK® Guide* covers the project management processes and therefore does not refer to the content of the project, other that when mentioning the goal, objective, deliverable, business case and success criteria of projects, as mentioned in other parts of this table.	Also PRINCE2® does not refer to the content of the project specifically.	ISO 21500 positions the content, goal and outcome of the project in the context of the organizational strategy. No reference is made to the content of this strategy or the project.	The content, intended result and success criteria are based on a holistic view of the project, including sustainability perspectives as 'economical, environmental and social', 'short term and long term' and 'local and global'.
Business case	Section 4.1.1., Develop Project Charter, mentions "Ecological impacts" and "Social needs" as potential benefits of a project when it discussed the business case.	The business case has a central role in PRINCE2®. In all stages of the project, specific processes are identified to define or update the business case. In the business case, benefits are addressed in general, without specifically addressing potential social or environmental benefits.	Section 3.4.2 mentions the business case as the justification for the investment in the project. Reference to a holistic view on justification is made by stating that the evaluation "may include multiple criteria including financial investment appraisal techniques and qualitative	The business case addresses the 'triple bottom line' of economic, social and environmental benefits. Investment evaluation is done based on a multi-criteria approach of both quantitative and qualitative criteria.

continued on following page

Table 3. Continued

Area of impact	PMBOK® Guide	PRINCE2®	ISO 21500	Sustainable Project Management
Business case			criteria such as strategic alignment, social impact, and environmental impact."	
Project success	In the introduction of chapter 3 Project Management Processes, the *PMBOK® Guide* mentions a few criteria for a successful project. Here it is mentioned that the project manager should be able to "balance the competing demands of scope, time, cost, quality, resources and risk". In this section the *PMBOK® Guide* fails to recognize the social and environmental aspects as relevant factors in project success.	PRINCE2® mentions six project performance variables. These variables do not mention sustainability aspects explicitly, but they may be included in performance variables 'quality' and 'benefits'.	As an important criterion for project success is mentioned: "comply with requirements to satisfy the project sponsor, customers and other stakeholders". Following the 'broad' definition of stakeholders mentioned above, this statement provides an holistic view on project success.	The definition and perception of project success take into account the 'triple bottom line' of economic, social and environmental benefits as laid out in the business case, both in the short term as in the long term. This implies that the success of the project is assessed based on the life cycle of the project and its result.
Project reporting	Project reporting processes can be found in the *PMBOK® Guide* in section 3.6.8. Report Performance and section 10.5 Report Performance. In these sections, project reporting focuses on progress and changes in the areas scope, schedule, cost and quality of the project. Reporting on sustainability aspects is not explicitly addressed, nor is the principle of transparency.	The 'Report highlights' process as part of 'Controlling a stage' reports the progress of the project in terms of the work packages, issues and changes. Reporting on sustainability aspects is not addressed, nor is the principle of transparency.	Progress reports and inspection reports are frequently mentioned as inputs or outputs of processes without being detailed. Reporting on sustainability aspects is not addressed, nor is the principle of transparency.	Project reporting is pro-active and transparent. Project progress is reported on different aspects of the project, including environmental and social aspects.
Materials and procure-ment	Processes related to the selection of materials and procurement can be found in different sections of the *PMBOK® Guide*. For example section 3.4.20 Plan procurements, section 3.5.8. Conduct procurements, chapter 12 Project Procurement Management. None of these sections include any references to sustainability aspects in for example the selection of suppliers or the selection of materials.	Materials and procurement are implicitly included in work-packages. No reference is made to the selection of materials and suppliers, based on sustainability criteria.	References to materials, procurement and suppliers are all related to a controlled execution of the project. In process 4.3.36 Select Suppliers, no reference is made to social or environmental criteria that may be considered in supplier selection.	In the selection of materials and suppliers for the project, these decisions are also based on environmental and social considerations.
Risk manage-ment	Chapter 11, Project Risk Management, of the *PMBOK® Guide*, does mention a process and several techniques to iden tify risks. However, these techniques do not mention the possibility of environmental and/or social risks.	Also Risk, as one of the central themes in PRINCE2®, is addressed in many processes throughout the project life cycle. However, no explicit reference is made to environmental and/or social risks.	Section 3.5 Project Environment mentions risks imposed by factors outside the organizational boundary. And section 3.11 Project Constraints mentions that consensus on the "level of acceptable risk exposure " should be reached among	The risk identification and risk management processes include the identification and man agement of environmental and/or social risks. These processes consider risks in relation to the

continued on following page

Table 3. Continued

Area of impact	PMBOK® Guide	PRINCE2®	ISO 21500	Sustainable Project Management
Risk management			key project stakeholders. However, no explicit reference is made to environmental and/or social risks.	objectives and goals of the project, but also in relation to the interests of stakeholders.
Project team	Chapter 9 of the *PMBOK® Guide*, Project Human Resource Management, shows little consideration of social sustainability aspects such as life-work balance, equal opportunity, part time job opportunities, etc. Section 9.2.2., however, pays attention to 'virtual teams' and links this to team members working from home offices, potentially with mobility limitations or disabilities. Also the personal development of team members is addressed. The objective for this development, however, is the performance of the project team, without considering the effectiveness of team members in their professional life after the project.	PRINCE2® pays ample attention to the management and development of the project team. It does mention 'Design and appoint the project management team', but in later stages no reference is made.	Process 4.3.15 Establish Project Team, mentions that "the project manager, when possible, should take into consideration factors such as skills and expertise, different personalities, and group dynamics when establishing the project team". No reference is made social sustainability aspects such as life-work balance, equal opportunity, part time job opportunities, etc. Process 4.3.18 does mention the development of the project team.	The management and development of project team members is aimed at preparing them for their role in the project and keeping them fit for this role. But also considers the effectiveness of team members in their personal and professional life after the project.
Organisational learning	Section 2.4.3 mentions 'Historical information and lessons learned' as part of the 'Corporate Knowledge Base' of the organization. However, this section lacks a more explicit reference to organizational learning or knowledge management in order to improve an organization's competence in doing projects.	The 'Lessons log' and the 'Lessons report' explicitly capture the lessons learned in a project. These lessons are explicitly addressed in the starting up stage of a project in the process 'Capture previous lessons'.	Process 4.3.8 Collect lessons learned, covers the capturing, compiling, formalising, storing and dissemination of experiences to benefit current and future projects. The planning processes mention lessons learned as an input.	Lessons learned and previous experiences are explicitly captured during project execution and closing and are made to use in the initiation and start-up of new projects. This is done to improve an organization's competence in doing projects.

the integration of sustainability concepts may be specific to the context of the project. The fact that most standards for sustainability indicators developed context specific or industry specific sets of indicators, supports this view. It is for that reason that there is a demand for in depth case studies to understand what the implications of integrating sustainability into project management processes really entails.

REFERENCES

Association for Project Management. (2006). *APM supports sustainability outlooks*.

Carson, R. (1962). *Silent spring*. Boston: Houghton Mifflin.

Crawford, L. (2007). Global body of project management knowledge and standards. In Morris & Pinto (Eds.), The Wiley Guide to Managing Projects. New York: Wiley.

de Zoete, L. (2010, April). PMBOK of prince 2. *Automatisering Gids*.

Dyllick, T., & Hockerts, K. (2002). Beyond the business case for corporate sustainability. *Business Strategy and the Environment, 11*, 130–141. doi:10.1002/bse.323.

Eid, M. (2009). *Sustainable development & project management*. Cologne, Germany: Lambert Academic Publishing.

Elkington, J. (1997). *Cannibals with forks: The triple bottom line of 21st century business*. Oxford: Capstone Publishing Ltc.

Gareis, R. (2010). Changes of organizations by projects. *International Journal of Project Management, 28*, 314–327. doi:10.1016/j.ijproman.2010.01.002.

Gareis, R., Heumann, M., & Martinuzzi, A. (2009). *Relating sustainable development and project management*. Berlin: IRNOP IX.

Gareis, R., Huemann, M., & Martinuzzi, A. (2011). What can project management learn from considering sustainability principles? *Project Perspectives, 33*, 60–65.

Gilbert, R., Stevenson, D., Girardet, H., & Stern, R. (Eds.). (1996). *Making cities work: The role of local authorities in the urban environment*. Earthscan Publications Ltd..

Glenn, J. C., & Gordon, T. J. (1998). *State of the future: Issues and opportunities*. Washington, DC: American Council for the United Nations University.

Holliday, C. (2001, September). Sustainable growth, the DuPont way. *Harvard Business Review*, 129–134. PMID:11550629.

International Institute for Sustainable Development & Deloitte and Touche. (1992). *Business strategy for sustainable development: Leadership and accountability for the 90s*. Winnipeg, Canada: International Institute for Sustainable Development.

International Organization for Standardization. (2012). [Geneva: ISO.]. *ISO, 21500*, 2012.

Keating, M. (1993). *The earth summit's agenda for change*. Geneva: Centre for our Common Future.

Kennedy, A. (2000). *The end of shareholder value: Corporations at the crossroads*. New York: Basic Books.

Knoepfel, H. (Ed.). (2010). Survival and sustainability as challenges for projects. Zurich: International Project Management Association (IPMA).

Lundin, R. A., & Söderholm, A. (1995). A theory of the temporary organization. *Scandinavian Journal of Management, 11*, 437–455. doi:10.1016/0956-5221(95)00036-U.

Maltzman, R., & Shirley, D. (2010). *Green project management*. Boca Raton, FL: CRC Press. doi:10.1201/EBK1439830017.

Martens, P. (2006). Sustainability: Science or fiction? *Sustainability: Science, Practice, &. Policy, 2*(1), 1–5.

Meadows, D. H., Meadows, D. L., Randers, J., & Behrens, W. W. (1972). *The limits to growth*. Universe Books.

Office of the Government Commerce. (2009). *Managing successful projects with PRINCE2*. Norwich: Author.

Project Management Institute. (2008). *A guide to project management body of knowledge' (PMBOK guide)* (4th ed.). Newtown Square, PA: Project Management Institute.

Robinson, J. (2004). Squaring the circle: On the very idea of sustainable development. *Ecological Economics, 48*(4), 369–384. doi:10.1016/j.ecolecon.2003.10.017.

Russell, J. (2008). Corporate social responsibility: What it means for the project manager. In *Proceedings of PMI Europe Congress*. Malta: Project Management Institute.

Silvius, A. J. G., Schipper, R., Planko, J., van der Brink, J., & Köhler, A. (2012). *Sustainability in project management*. Farnham, UK: Gower Publishing.

Silvius, A. J. G., van der Brink, J., & Köhler, A. (2009). Views on sustainable project management. In Kähköhnen, K., Kazi, A. S., & Rekola, M. (Eds.), *Human Side of Projects in Modern Business*. Helsinki, Finland: IPMA Scientific Research Paper Series.

Turner, J. R., & Müller, R. (2003). On the nature of the project as a temporary organization. *International Journal of Project Management, 21*(3), 1–8. doi:10.1016/S0263-7863(02)00020-0.

Visser, W. T. (2002). Sustainability reporting in South Africa. *Corporate Environmental Strategy, 9*(1), 79–85. doi:10.1016/S1066-7938(01)00157-9.

White, D., & Fortune, J. (2002). Current practice in project management: An empirical study. *International Journal of Project Management, 20*(1), 1–11. doi:10.1016/S0263-7863(00)00029-6.

World Commission on Environment and Development. (1987). *Our common future*. Oxford, UK: Oxford University Press.

Chapter 5
How Can Sustainable Development Redefine Project Management Processes?

Mohamed Eid
The British University in Egypt, Egypt

ABSTRACT

The relationship between Project Management (PM) and Sustainable Development (SD) is tested in this chapter through its application on the construction industry. When PM is embedded in construction projects, it has the capacity to be a significant leverage point of great influence, and it becomes one of the cornerstones for rethinking the relationships between PM, SD, and the Construction Industry. The work presented discusses the need for integrating sustainable development into project management processes to ensure a better outcome for the construction industry, which is directly related to the degradation of our quality of life on the economic, social, and environmental levels. The author explores the origins and philosophies behind sustainability, the core of project management processes, the strategic implications of the construction industry practices, and puts forward the "systems thinking and points of leverage" approach to facilitate an efficient environment of integration. Thinking and acting sustainably requires not only incremental change but also a revolution in approach, a shift of perspective; sustainable project management processes are possible to achieve.

INTRODUCTION

The major issues facing the world are mostly from the effect of human development activities. Economic instability, widespread social exclusion and inequalities and global environmental degradation mean the world is fighting for a better quality of life for all present and future generations. In order to start facing up to these challenges, the global community has to realize that these problems are no longer specific to certain countries at a national level, but in fact, they

DOI: 10.4018/978-1-4666-4177-8.ch005

have now risen to a global scale. When tackling such huge issues, everyone has a significant role to play. Enhancing our quality of life will not be achieved unless the world's communities rise to the challenge and contribute individually as well as collectively to a better quality of life, each within their field of expertise. Acknowledging that there are always better ways of practice, and that the wheel of development never stops, this thesis embarks on researching and studying the construction industry's practices and indeed challenging the impacts of global development on our quality of life. The research tackles the need for changing the strategies, policies, and standards which normally control the practices and guide the projects from inception to completion (Eid, 2009, pp.1-2).

Sustainable development is emerging as an important agenda for better practice in the construction industry; an industry that in conjuction with the built environment—which constitutes more than one half of the real capital—they are the main consumers of resources in energy and materials (CIB, 1999). The relationship between construction and sustainability has created new performance agendas driven by sustainable construction guidelines.

With projects increasing in complexity, needs and standards to be fulfilled, project management has grown to be an essential and vital tool for managing and delivering those projects, meeting if not exceeding expectations. This underpins the major contributions of project management to our quality of life which justifies its increasing recognition as a profession and practice. The work presented herein describes a suggested relationship between sustainability, project management, and construction. The author puts forward a rich environment encircling this relationship based on fundamental criteria that embrace the opportunities for introducing "change"; this milieu is the systems thinking approach. This is implemented by identifying the places within this system (leverage points) where the earlier the change is

introduced to its early fundamental stages, the better and more efficient is the impact expected to derive in terms of the overall performance of the system (Eid, 2009)[1].

The research reported in this chapter examines the potential of a tri-dimensional integration to explore the way forward for construction, project management, and sustainable development to contribute effectively to a better quality of life. This is investigated to unveil whether or not it would have fundamental impact on the three professions in general and in turn, enhance their contributions to people's quality of life.

BACKGROUND: DEFINING THE THREE DIMENSIONS OF THE RELATIONSHIP AND THE ENCIRCLING MILIEU

Figure 1 represents the first part of the methodology, the research uses a Venn diagram on three-sets to exhibit the existing and proposed relationships between the three dimensions of the relationship in question; the construction industry, sustainable

Figure 1. Establishing the relationships between the four pillars of the research

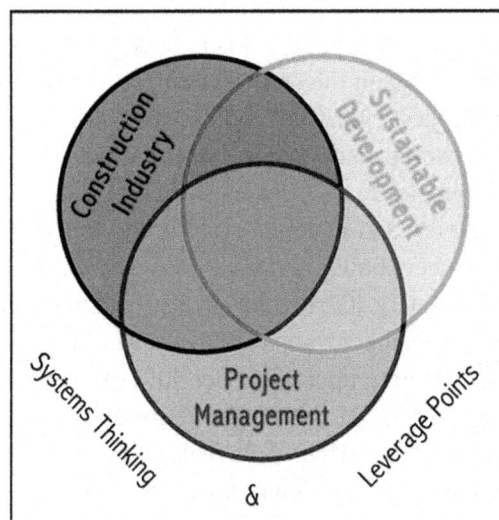

development and project management, while the encircling milieu is the systems thinking theories and leverage points.

THE CONSTRUCTION INDUSTRY

The construction industry is a major constituent of the European Union's economy (The Commission of the European Parliament, 2002). The construction sector is an active and dynamic industry throughout Europe, but one that contains a large number of hazards and risks. It plays a very important role in the economic well-being of the European Union, representing approximately 11% of Community GDP (Gross Domestic Product) in 1996 (The European Union Online; Europa). In spite of a slow-down in the rate of increase of productivity, the construction industry remains the largest industrial sector in the community, ahead of the foodstuffs and chemicals industries and it is crucial in producing investment goods. It accounted for 10% of GDP and 48.5% of Gross Fixed Capital Formation in 2000 (European Construction Industry Federation (FIEC). It is also the largest sector in terms of employment, providing jobs for 8.8 million people (7% of the working population), and gives rise to 2.5 million construction related jobs, and 14.3 million other service jobs, acquiring 28.5% of industrial employment. In the EU, 26 million workers depend, directly or indirectly, on the construction sector making it the biggest industrial employer in Europe. It is a fact that the construction industry and the built environment are the main consumers of resources (i.e. energy and materials) within the European Union where buildings are estimated to consume approximately 40% of total energy. Buildings are also responsible for some 30% of CO_2 emissions – and generate approximately 40% of all man-made waste (CIB, 1999). The destruction of the resource base and the whole scale pollution of the life support systems upon which continued human development depends are among the consequences of operating economic limits beyond ecological limits (Royal Commission on Environmental Pollution (RCEP), 2000).

As addressed in the Egan Report, leading companies in other sectors (and a very small number of leading UK construction companies) are already measuring, and taking systematic steps to manage, their sustainability impacts. These companies recognize that a reorientation towards sustainable development is essential for ensuring their long-term viability. However, most companies within the UK construction industry appear to be missing opportunities for taking a more pro-active role, within their broader sphere of influence, in helping to provide a sustainable built environment (The Construction Task Force, 1998).

An urgent need—and a considerable opportunity—exists to include sustainable development as an explicit objective into existing and new initiatives. This could be facilitated by including indicators of sustainability (such as those being developed by CIRIA, BSRIA and others) into the Key Performance Indicators (KPIs) framework put forward in "Rethinking Construction".

The construction industry has successfully passed the milestone of recognizing the importance of integrating sustainable development into the core of the industry's practices. Creating sustainable agendas for the industry is a vital step forward towards the implementation of change in the culture of the industry and attitudes towards a sustainable future. The scale of the UK construction industry, its immediate environmental and resource use impacts, coupled with the influence of its products on the nation's quality of life, make it a key player in delivering sustainable development (Eid, 2000).

The implementation of sustainable development agendas and the business case behind the integration demonstrate that the business case for sustainable construction has many opportunities to create environmental and social improvements whilst increasing profits and market shares which can create new sources of employment and ensure better business benefits and sustainable economic base and beneficial impacts. The industry is facing up to its weaknesses and building upon its strengths, and, it has not yet used its full potential for change and doing things differently. The construction industry was part of the problem of delivering a better quality of life for people and there was a persisting need to make the industry part of the solution. Integrating sustainable development into the construction industry practices and indeed into the culture of the industry was, and still is, the biggest challenge facing the industry (Eid, 2009).

SUSTAINABLE DEVELOPMENT

Sustainable development goes beyond environmental awareness; it tackles social and economic aspects as well as the environment, hence, this section discusses the ways in which sustainable development touches upon our daily activities. Sustainable development represents a vital element of the integration proposed in order to attain sustainable construction practice and more specifically in the management of projects. European and British policies for sustainable development are quite similar in their commitment to the implications which sustainable development might introduce within social, environmental and economic trends, but whatever the policies are, sustainable development faces significant challenges in defining its "Business Case".

In order to achieve an effective implementation of sustainable development and face up to the challenge, putting these strategies into action demands the response of different sectors in society. More sector-specific initiatives are needed to allow the sustainable development framework to touch on the everyday aspects of life. They must provide environments in which people live and work enjoyably and efficiently and which encourage working and social communities to flourish.

The construction industry stands a great potential for change because "Sustainable Construction" is about much more than the fabric of the built environment. Housing and the social, commercial and transport infrastructures around them must all be built in ways that are sustainable in environmental and economic as well as in social terms. They must add value to the quality of life for the individual and the community (Eid, 2009).

The "Business Case" for sustainable development stands as a major challenge for businesses to accept and embrace sustainability into their financial planning and economic development (WBCSD, 2002). In general, sustainable development calls for more efficiency, higher standards of quality in delivering social progress, protecting the environment and ensuring economic growth. The new paradigm of sustainable progress and acceptance of businesses to the concept of more involvement of sustainable development into their financial planning and core commitment has provided a significant opportunity for government sectors to follow suit. But this has proven yet as challenging as it was for general businesses to concur. For the construction industry, the challenge for construction businesses to embrace sustainable practices is still in its early phase and more needs to be done. From the previous analysis of the interconnections between business and sustainability, it emerges that the concept of sustainable development is closely linked to efficiency and competitiveness (The UK Government, 2003).

Sustainable development is not incompatible – and can be mutually supportive- with competitiveness. Business has many "win-win" opportunities to create and/or social improvement whilst increasing profits and market share(James, 2000).

Sustainable business practice is the way forward and this will reflect on the different business sectors including the construction industry and its sustainable approach. Sustainable Development has established itself as the road to a better future and a better quality of life. With all the contributing factors to its current popularity, it highlights for governments, businesses, and society the importance of not only future development on the economic level but also on the social and environmental levels. The reasons behind the emergence of sustainable development, its importance to and its impact on our lives, demonstrate that although future and continuous development is the aim of all nations, it cannot follow the same strategies of the past with no regard for the environmental, and social impacts. It has to be generated by the need for a change of attitude. National economies can no longer envisage development without considering the social and environmental aspects. Businesses have to integrate the sustainable development triple bottom line into the core of their financial plans.

The construction industry plays a major role in any nation's development and therefore, the potential it holds for sustainable approaches to a better performance is immense. Achieving more sustainability into the construction processes is possible by breaking down the existing system without losing perspective of the holistic nature of the construction processes. By breaking down the system, it is possible to identify where the sustainability gaps exist and work on better implementation for these gaps. Within the construction industry, project management stands as a significant stage of all projects and it is the role of the following chapter to introduce the functions of project management in general and more specifically within construction practices (Eid, 2009).

PROJECT MANAGEMENT

In the construction industry as well as in all other industries, project management applications have proved indispensable for the continuous progress of better performance along with the undeniable need for its existence among the early phases of projects. The effective involvement of project management processes in projects is shown as an essential factor of success in delivering/exceeding stakeholders'/clients' expectations and needs. The Project Management Institute (PMI) created a project management reference that is undeniably one of the most comprehensive bodies of knowledge for PM; the Guide to the Project Management Body of Knowledge (PMBOK).

The purpose of project management described for the construction industry is to add significant and specific value to the process of delivering construction projects. PM adds significant opportunities for better and more efficient completion. Whether on small or large scale projects, they both share the same properties of "projects" described earlier, but the contribution of PM to the successful completion does not vary relatively to their sizes. For construction and all other fields, projects are not only confined to major undertakings or large scale projects but they come in all sizes, varying in time plans, resources, goals and areas of applications.

While it is true that major projects have provided the impetus for identifying and studying the principles of effective project management, these principles are nevertheless just as applicable to small projects as to larger projects (Wideman, 1995, p.72).

The importance of the project management's contribution remains the same whatever the scale or area of application. This contribution is underpinned by a core of knowledge and guidelines which generally remain the same but only vary in their applications according to the field of incorporation.

Due to the increasing demand on PM and since the skills required to manage projects successfully have multiple dimensions, models of the project management body of knowledge needed to be identified. Models which guide practitioners or academics working or researching on PM to identify the core basics of PM processes, stages and enable them to apply its basics to all fields and areas of application given that the management team is always responsible for determining what is appropriate for any specific project.

During the late 1980s and early 1990s, a significant increase of interest in knowledge management originated from a convergence of at least four interrelated trends: the first as described by Argyris and Schön (1978) is the development of organizational learning, the second is an emphasis on re-engineering and re-invention of business processes as expressed by Davenport (1993) and Hammer and Champy (1993). The third trend is the total amount of advances in information technology such as computational speed and Web applications as explained by Snider and Nissen (2003) and the fourth trend being the associated development of information systems management theory and practice. These four trends have resulted, together, in an awareness of and attention to knowledge, particularly in the private sector, as an organizational asset or resource that may be leveraged for competitive advantage as illustrated in the work of Grant (1996) and Spender (1996).

The bodies of knowledge, in the case of project management, represent generally accepted sets of skills and tools that all certified professionals should possess (Sneider & Nissen, 2003). However, the studies mentioned before, deal with knowledge as something that is capable of being transferred, shared, or transformed in the context of any specific business sector (Berger & Luckman, 1967).

This fluid view of knowledge is at odds with the more static view implied by the bodies of knowledge of professional fields. This is tempered by recognition that none of the several project management bodies of knowledge describe themselves as complete and exhaustive repositories of all project management knowledge (Wirth & Tryloff, 1995).

The main reasons behind choosing The Project Management Institute PMBOK for this research study are (Eid, 2009):

- In comparison to the previously mentioned BOKs of project management, the PMBOK® guide excels in its breakdown of application areas of project management and processes. The level of details provided in the PMBOK is not matched by any other BOK, specifically in the illustration of interactions between processes through the corresponding lists of inputs, tools & techniques and outputs.

- PMBOK allows a simple application to the circumstances of the construction industry and therefore an easy path to the successful completion of construction projects following the core knowledge of project management described in PMBOK.

- The new Construction Extension to PMBOK, is another demonstration of the important partnership between PM and construction practices, hence the new document details the additional knowledge areas which are more specific to construction.

- The practices and the project management of construction projects were one of the resources on which the original PMBOK was based. The involvement of construction from the early beginnings of PMBOK as an important body of PM knowledge makes the final document even more relevant to this research and touches on many sides of the industry.

- Unlike any of the international PM bodies of knowledge, no other PM initiatives had ventured in creating a PM document specific to construction as PMI pioneered in creating the Construction Extension to PMBOK.

- Due to the international exposure of PMBOK, it covers the practices of project management in many countries over the world including the UK, which makes its body of knowledge more applicable to more countries and industries than any other PM body of knowledge.

The essence of project management has been identified by PMBOK; the project management knowledge areas, their component processes along with their inputs, tools and techniques and outputs. These component processes and lists represent the initial information which project management processes deal with, to incorporate them into the PM life cycle. The construction industry holds within its practices significant opportunities that allow project management processes to contribute more sustainably into its framework. But after displaying all the knowledge areas from the PMBOK and adding the new areas from the Construction Extension, the combined knowledge areas from both publications do not portray any serious commitment to sustainable construction.

Integrating sustainability strategies into the PM life cycle has to start from within the core of project management processes, following the theory of systems thinking. The sooner sustainability changes are integrated into project management, the more significant and stronger the impact we can expect. The following chapter examines "Systems Thinking" as the tool which will facilitate the integration as the vehicle to assist the integration of sustainable development into the project management processes for construction projects (Eid, 2009).

SYSTEMS THINKING AND LEVERAGE POINTS

General systems theory was introduced in the 1940s by Ludwig Von Berttalanffy, but has been vastly expanded since its inception (Cummings, 1980). It developed as a response to rapid technological complexities that confronted engineering and science. It was a radical departure from traditional science which dealt with cause and effect explanations (Gardner & Demello, 1993).

Systems thinking viewed an organization and its respective environment, as a complex whole of interrelating, interdependent parts. It stressed the relationships and the processes that make up the organizational contact, rather than the separate entities or the sum of the parts (Cummings, 1980).

Leverage points allow individuals to identify the opportunities in existing systems/organizations where "change" could be implemented to lead the system to the long planned goals and objectives. Senge describes them as places to pursue the goals in a way that takes advantage of, instead of working against, the systemic structures around them (Senge, 1999).

Leverage points are seen as opportunities in existing systems where embedded actions and changes can lead to significant, enduring improvements. Donella Meadows describes Leverage points as:

Places within a complex system where a small shift in one thing can produce big changes in everything (Meadows, 1999).

The reason behind the identification of leverage points and places to intervene in a system, is mostly because individuals and participants in systems need to study where changes can be implemented and the manner in which these changes should be introduced as well as the nature of these changes. Senge and Meadows, both argue that small changes and well-focused actions can produce significant, enduring improvements if they are introduced to the system in the right place, with the right value needed and at the right time (Senge, 1999).

The lead taken in sustainable development has changed the global reality and commitment to a better future, and has also affected the commitment of private and public sectors in pushing forward the application of a smooth transition from environmental management systems to sustainable management systems. The initiation of development of such management systems highlights the potential role and contribution of conventional business and public sector organizations in corporate and public environmental, social and economic management for all practices. The conversion of environmental management systems to sustainable management systems, represent a smooth transition to face the new global challenge, embracing sustainable business thinking, tools and techniques to identify, evaluate and improve social, economic and environmental organizational commitment.

It is not only about environmental concerns, but it is about a better future on the three parallel strands of economic, social and environmental concerns. Sustainable approach to management systems is proven to be a valid contribution to sustainable performance which aligns with the arguments for implementing sustainability into the project management process, from the early phases of any project, as advised by Meadows. Achieving a more effective impact is possible when the change is implemented from the early stages using the right leverage points. The next stage of this thesis illustrates the interaction between the three pillars of this research (i.e. Project Management, Sustainable Development and Construction Industry's Practices) within a tri-dimensional framework to achieve a more sustainable project management process for construction practices

starting from the earliest phases of projects. Systems thinking and its theory's basics and the identification of leverage points will act as the "milieu" which will allow the tri-dimensional integration to take place and will fortify their existing relationships (Eid, 2009).

RETHINKING THE RELATIONSHIPS: THE TRI-DIMENSIONAL INTEGRATION

Figure 2 represents a mirrored image of the same Venn diagram; the image on the left entails the intersections between the three dimensions of the relationship while the image on the right explains how these intersections are manifested by the enclosed case studies or initiatives.

The body of the chapter relies on three distinctive case studies as a fundamental part of the methodology of the research. The first practical application portrays the Egan Agenda's Drivers from a systems thinking point of view; when integrating SD into construction practices, it generates a sustainable construction agenda.

Figure 2. The tri-dimensional integration

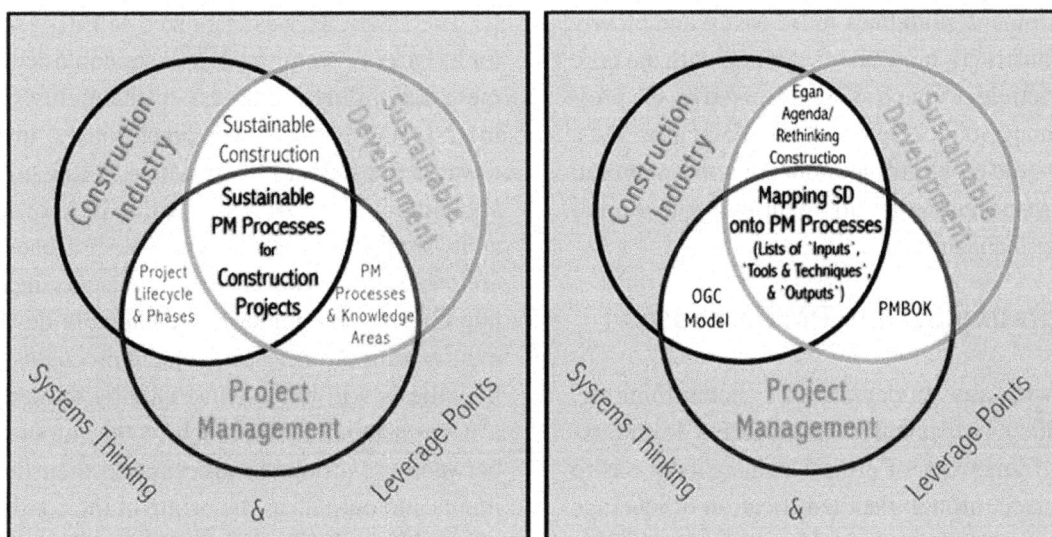

The second case study is the identification of leverage points within one of the most important phases of all construction projects; the procurement stage. This is demonstrated as an example to the integration between PM and construction practices. Project lifecycles and phases are demonstrated through the procurement stage to attain a more sustainable application to the project phase in question (i.e. procurement) through the identification of sustainability gaps within an existing Government model which should have been following Government's sustainable initiatives (OGC Model).

The final case study application withdraws the research into its fundamental conclusion; integrating SD into PM processes for construction projects. The case study examines the notions of a sustainable development approach to the PMBOK processes and knowledge areas and describes the way forward to implement the desired change into the core knowledge of PM to envisage an efficient implementation of SD guidelines into the PM standards of the PMBOK. The integration explores the potential of a holistic approach to strategic project management and show how a systems thinking approach to PM processes would enhance PM's contribution to construction projects.

As a governing milieu, systems thinking theories would allow the Integration of sustainable development guidelines more easily and clearly into construction processes starting with the core of its activities which are represented by the project management knowledge areas and processes. This would highlight the connections between and among sustainable development, construction and project management.

Integrating SD into PM Processes

Following the guidelines of systems thinking, introducing sustainable development to the existing framework of project management has to take place through the identification of leverage points within the system. This takes the analysis back to the components of project management as a functioning system, to the fundamental parts out of which it is formed; the processes and their interactions which rely on their inputs and outputs. Implementing a significant change such as "sustainable development" into project management has to take place from within its core of knowledge or paradigm out of which the project management process arises.

This research relies on changing the interactions between the lists of inputs and the lists of outputs through embedding sustainable development guidelines, indicators and measuring tools into the list of tools and techniques of all the PM processes and their knowledge areas listed in the PMBOK. Leverage point 2 (the mindset or paradigm out of which the system arises) is a very high point on Meadows list in terms of the effectiveness of the implementation of the desired change. This point of leverage allows the change to take place from within the sources of the system. However small this change could be, its effectiveness is expected to be of very high significance because the change is introduced to the core of the system. This will mean therefore that all subsequent activities, knowledge areas, process groups, project processes, project management practices and ultimately, the construction projects would be affected by the impact of this change.

The PMBOK was criticized in this research for its lack of commitment to sustainable development and failure to address sustainability issues more seriously and direct practitioners' interest towards the global pressure for a better sustainable future. PMBOK holds, within its knowledge areas, significant opportunities to embrace sustainability; the following analysis represents the main hypothesis for integrating sustainable development within project management processes. The hypothesis will be demonstrated by introducing a new sustainable approach to the interactions between the groups of process and their lists of inputs and outputs as the origin of the continuity of the whole PM functioning system.

As shown in Figure 3, when analyzing each process, the PMBOK displays the interactions between the list of inputs and outputs by listing the suggested tools & techniques which facilitate the transformation of inputs to outputs. For all combined fifty two processes, PMBOK uses the format shown in Figure 3 to display the linear interconnections among the lists of inputs, tools and techniques and outputs for each process. The example shown in the figure is for the first process of "Initiation" which is part of the knowledge area of "Project Scope Management" and the Process Group of "Initiation".

The argument is based on adding sustainable development guidelines, indicators and measuring tools to the original list of tools and techniques for each corresponding process. Clearly, it is not an attempt to substitute the existing list but to add sustainability drivers to its content to enhance and direct all of the interactions towards sustainable development.

Figure 3 displays the transformation from the PMBOK format at the top, to an illustration of the proposed sustainable approach to the PM process at the middle and then finally at the bottom of the figure an illustration of the new sustainable

Figure 3. The proposed phases of integrating SD into PM processes

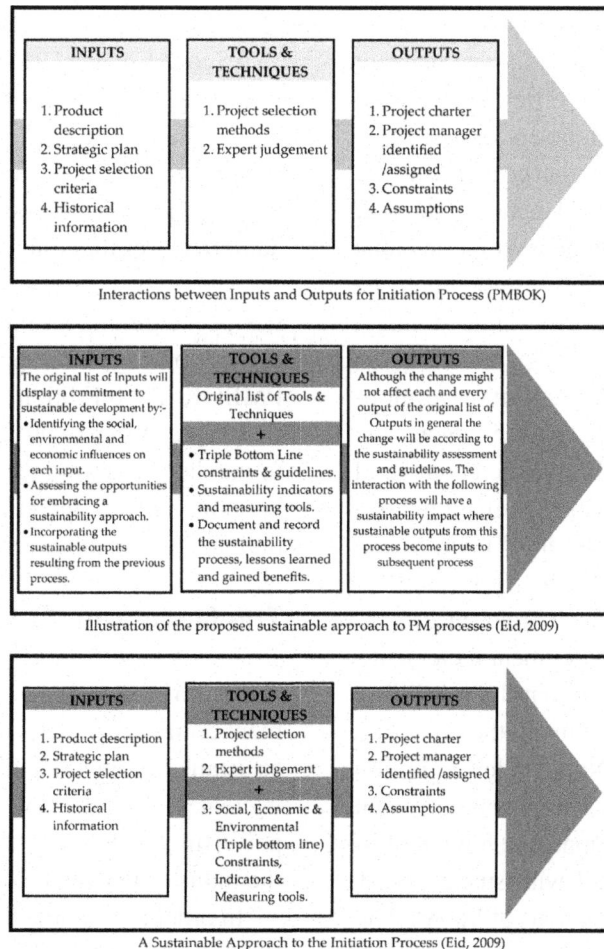

Interactions between Inputs and Outputs for Initiation Process (PMBOK)

Illustration of the proposed sustainable approach to PM processes (Eid, 2009)

A Sustainable Approach to the Initiation Process (Eid, 2009)

approach to the Initiation PM process. From the figure, it is now obvious that the approach is applicable to the processes and relies on adding sustainable development guidelines, indicators and tools to the lists of tools and techniques and also assesses the opportunities for change starting from the inputs.

In order to move forward, it is vital at this stage to map the opportunities for integrating sustainable development to the general as well as the specific elementary origin of construction PM processes; the knowledge areas.

Mapping the Opportunities for SD to PM Processes and Knowledge Areas

The knowledge areas, as the origin of PM processes, hold within them the core catalyst for change in performance. This also represents a very efficient leverage point on Meadows' efficiency scale to introduce sustainable development to the whole process and guarantee significant positive impact.

The matrix shown in Table 1 demonstrates that the relevance of each knowledge area to sustainable development is not necessarily the same among its own processes (e.g. for 6- Project Time Management; "6.1 Activity Definition", "6.4 Schedule Development" and "6.8 Progress Curve Development") nor is the relevance constant among the three elements of sustainability when compared for one process (e.g. "7.2 Cost Estimating": relevance of "* *" "medium relevance" to the Social element, relevance of "* * *" "high relevance" to the Economic element and finally, relevance of "*" "low relevance" to the Environmental element). This, of course, does not rule out the possibility of similarities in relevance among the processes nor does it rule out the "None" relevant option (e.g. Claim Identification). The table is not meant to be exclusive, but to demonstrate how the PM processes can be integrated with sustainability and to identify the potential areas of knowledge, which lead to a more sustainable approach.

The matrix lays out the knowledge areas and their processes in terms of any project's main five process groups (Initiating to Closing).

In line with the theories of systems thinking and leverage points, it is apparent that the highest relevance and potential for integrating sustainable development exists within the Initiating and Planning Process Groups. This is the most efficient leverage point where the project is still in its early phases of creating the scope, generating the project's plans, identifying the risks and producing the rules. As explained earlier, these process groups keep repeating the cycle from Initiating processes to Closing processes for every stage of the project, hence the appearance of high relevance and potential points during the Executing and the Controlling Processes (e.g. "14.2 Environmental Assurance" for the Environmental bottom line, "5.5 Scope Change Control" for the three bottom lines and "7.4 Cost Control" for the Economic bottom line). The high potential for integration at this stage is underpinned by the significance of the process itself and its contribution to and authority over the following process.

Although the matrix presents the possibilities of integrating sustainable development into project management process provided in the PMBOK (2000 Edition), a chance was provided for PM practitioners, professionals, academics and researchers to introduce their own professional opinions on this integration's hypothesis in an online questionnaire.

The Questionnaire

There is a persisting need for the project management community to act upon the conviction that a sustainable approach is possible and as shown, it creates a whole new and significantly more powerful role for project management; to guide the industry to even better performance.

In order to examine further these possibilities and opportunities for sustainable project manage-

Table 1. Matrix of mapping sustainability opportunities to PM processes and knowledge areas

	SOCIAL		ECONOMIC		ENVIRONMENTAL	
	PM Processes	**Relevance**	**PM Processes**	**Relevance**	**PM Processes**	**Relevance**
1. INITIATING	5.1 Initiation	* * *	5.1 Initiation	* * *	5.1 Initiation	* * *
2. PLANNING	4.1 Project Plan Development	* * *	4.1 Project Plan Development	* * *	4.1 Project Plan Development	* * *
	5.2 Scope Planning	* * *	5.2 Scope Planning	* * *	5.2 Scope Planning	* * *
	5.3 Scope Definition	* * *	5.3 Scope Definition	* * *	5.3 Scope Definition	* * *
	6.1 Activity Definition	* * *	6.1 Activity Definition	* * *	6.1 Activity Definition	* * *
	6.2 Activity Sequencing	* *	6.2 Activity Sequencing	* * *	6.2 Activity Sequencing	* *
	6.3 Activity Duration Estimating	* *	6.3 Activity Duration Estimating	* *	6.3 Activity Duration Estimating	* *
	6.4 Schedule Development	* *	6.4 Schedule Development	* *	6.4 Schedule Development	* *
	7.1 Resource Planning	* * *	7.1 Resource Planning	* * *	7.1 Resource Planning	* * *
	7.2 Cost Estimating	* *	7.2 Cost Estimating	* * *	7.2 Cost Estimating	*
	7.3 Cost Budgeting	None	7.3 Cost Budgeting	* * *	7.3 Cost Budgeting	None
	8.1 Quality Planning	* *	8.1 Quality Planning	* *	8.1 Quality Planning	* *
	9.1 Organisational Planning	* * *	9.1 Organisational Planning	* *	9.1 Organisational Planning	*
	9.2 Staff Acquisition	* * *	9.2 Staff Acquisition	* *	9.2 Staff Acquisition	*
	10.1 Communication Planning	* *	10.1 Communication Planning	*	10.1 Communication Planning	*
	11.1 Risk Management Planning	* * *	11.1 Risk Management Planning	* * *	11.1 Risk Management Planning	* * *
	11.2 Risk Identification	* * *	11.2 Risk Identification	* * *	11.2 Risk Identification	* * *
	11.3 Qualitative Risk Analysis	* *	11.3 Qualitative Risk Analysis	* * *	11.3 Qualitative Risk Analysis	* *
	11.4 Quantitative Risk Analysis	* *	11.4 Quantitative Risk Analysis	* * *	11.4 Quantitative Risk Analysis	* *
	11.5 Risk Response Planning	* *	11.5 Risk Response Planning	* * *	11.5 Risk Response Planning	* *
	12.1 Procurement Planning	* *	12.1 Procurement Planning	* * *	12.1 Procurement Planning	* *
	13.1 Safety Plan Development	* * *	13.1 Safety Plan Development	* *	13.1 Safety Plan Development	* * *
	14.1 Environmental Planning	* *	14.1 Environmental Planning	* *	14.1 Environmental Planning	* * *
	15.1 Financial Planning	*	15.1 Financial Planning	* * *	15.1 Financial Planning	*
	16.1 Claim Identification	None	16.1 Claim Identification	* *	16.1 Claim Identification	None
	16.2 Claim Quantification	None	16.2 Claim Quantification	* *	16.2 Claim Quantification	None
3. EXECUTING	4.2 Project Plan Execution	* * *	4.2 Project Plan Execution	* * *	4.2 Project Plan Execution	* * *
	6.6 Activity Weights Definition	* *	6.6 Activity Weights Definition	* *	6.6 Activity Weights Definition	* *
	8.2 Quality Assurance	* *	8.2 Quality Assurance	* *	8.2 Quality Assurance	* *
	9.3 Team Development	* * *	9.3 Team Development	None	9.3 Team Development	* *

continued on following page

Table 1. Continued

	SOCIAL		ECONOMIC		ENVIRONMENTAL	
	PM Processes	**Relevance**	**PM Processes**	**Relevance**	**PM Processes**	**Relevance**
3. EXECUTING	10.2 Information Distribution	*	10.2 Information Distribution	* *	10.2 Information Distribution	*
	12.4 Source Selection	* *	12.4 Source Selection	* * *	12.4 Source Selection	* *
	13.2 Safety Plan Execution	* * *	13.2 Safety Plan Execution	* *	13.2 Safety Plan Execution	* *
	14.2 Environmental Assurance	*	14.2 Environmental Assurance	*	14.2 Environmental Assurance	* * *
4. CONTROLLING	4.3 Integrated Change Control	*	4.3 Integrated Change Control	*	4.3 Integrated Change Control	*
	5.4 Scope Verification	* * *	5.4 Scope Verification	* * *	5.4 Scope Verification	* * *
	5.5 Scope Change Control	* * *	5.5 Scope Change Control	* * *	5.5 Scope Change Control	* * *
	6.5 Schedule Control	* *	6.5 Schedule Control	* *	6.5 Schedule Control	* *
	6.7 Progress Curve Development	None	6.7 Progress Curve Development	None	6.7 Progress Curve Development	None
	6.8 Progress Monitoring	None	6.8 Progress Monitoring	None	6.8 Progress Monitoring	None
	7.4 Cost Control	*	7.4 Cost Control	* * *	7.4 Cost Control	*
	8.3 Quality Control	* *	8.3 Quality Control	* *	8.3 Quality Control	* *
	10.3 Performance Reporting	*	10.3 Performance Reporting	* *	10.3 Performance Reporting	*
	11.6 Risk Monitoring & Control	* *	11.6 Risk Monitoring & Control	* *	11.6 Risk Monitoring & Control	* *
	14.3 Environmental Control	*	14.3 Environmental Control	*	14.3 Environmental Control	* * *
	15.2 Financial Control	*	15.2 Financial Control	* * *	15.2 Financial Control	*
	16.3 Claim Prevention	*	16.3 Claim Prevention	*	16.3 Claim Prevention	*
5. CLOSING	Relevance of Sustainability Approach to this Process Group is significantly minor not only because this stage consists mainly of the legal aspects of the project but also because it is too late to incorporate sustainability at this phase of administrative closure and contract closeout (ineffective leverage points). The only relevance for future projects is to document and record all lessons learned including gained sustainability benefits.					

ment processes, the research now moves forward to examine the results of an online survey made accessible to PM practitioners, professionals and academics which attempts to discover the potential and identification of a sustainable approach. An online questionnaire was created discussing the proposed set of arguments as an invitation for all project management users to agree and/or disagree with the hypothesis. The questionnaire is also an opportunity to share the views of the international audience on the sustainable approach to an international PM document publication such as the PMI's PMBOK.

The overall objective of the questionnaire was to investigate the views of the respondents on the possibilities and the opportunities for integrating sustainable development into project management processes listed in the PMBOK (2000 Edition). The broad as well sophisticated nature of the area covered by the questionnaire meant that the targeted audience should represent a specific class of respondents; PM practitioners, professionals, academics and/or researchers. The questionnaire examines specific aspects of project management with specific interest in the PMBOK processes; this implied that the respondents should be familiar of the contents of the PMBOK and preferably well into practicing its guidelines.

There were two versions of the questionnaire, a detailed version entailing all fifty two numerous processes from the PMBOK which demanded the inputs and full dedication of certain type of respondents to complete it. The second version was a much less detailed document which took about 20 minutes to complete (this version can be found in the only annex to this chapter). Both versions followed the same design, methodology, format and answering techniques. The primary difference is that the final version does not contain the detailed illustration of the interactions of each process from "Inputs" to "Outputs" through the involvement of the lists of "Tools and Techniques" but rather a general outlook on the process without its lists of interactions.

Questionnaire Findings

Table 2 summarizes the answers retrieved from the first part of section 5 of the questionnaire. To illustrate all the answers, the same matrix used before in Table 1 has been re-introduced to map the opportunities and the relevancy of sustainable development to each of the PM processes. In this section, but with minor changes although following the same framework, the responses were compiled to calculate the percentage of respondents who chose any of the possible selections (A, B, C).

The outcome of the compilation demonstrates that "B" is the most popular choice. Hence, for 79.5% of the listed processes, the respondents thought that when sustainable development guidelines would be added to the list of "tools and techniques" of these processes, there will be considerable changes to their lists of outputs and therefore guide the overall performance towards sustainability. This significant majority supports the argument that endorses the integration of SD into PM processes. The analysis of the responses clearly shows that the respondents agree that the

Table 2. Matrix of the respondents' selections concerning mapping the opportunities and the impact of integrating SD into PM processes

	Selection A		Selection B		Selection C	
	PM Processes	**%**	**PM Processes**	**%**	**PM Processes**	**%**
1- INITIATING	5.1 Initiation	**82.4**	5.1 Initiation	**11.8**	5.1 Initiation	**5.9**
2- PLANNING	4.1 Project Plan Development	**76.5**	4.1 Project Plan Development	**20.6**	4.1 Project Plan Development	**2.9**
	5.2 Scope Planning	**82.4**	5.2 Scope Planning	**17.6**	5.2 Scope Planning	**0**
	5.3 Scope Definition	**67.6**	5.3 Scope Definition	**32.4**	5.3 Scope Definition	**0**
	6.1 Activity Definition	**41.2**	6.1 Activity Definition	**41.2**	6.1 Activity Definition	**17.6**
	6.2 Activity Sequencing	**20.6**	6.2 Activity Sequencing	**52.9**	6.2 Activity Sequencing	**26.5**
	6.3 Activity Duration Estimating	**11.8**	6.3 Activity Duration Estimating	**44.1**	6.3 Activity Duration Estimating	**44.1**
	6.4 Schedule Development	**20.6**	6.4 Schedule Development	**50**	6.4 Schedule Development	**29.4**
	7.1 Resource Planning	**55.9**	7.1 Resource Planning	**32.4**	7.1 Resource Planning	**11.7**
	7.2 Cost Estimating	**44.1**	7.2 Cost Estimating	**44.1**	7.2 Cost Estimating	**11.8**

continued on following page

Table 2. Continued

	Selection A		Selection B		Selection C	
	PM Processes	%	PM Processes	%	PM Processes	%
2- PLANNING	7.3 Cost Budgeting	17.7	7.3 Cost Budgeting	64.7	7.3 Cost Budgeting	17.7
	8.1 Quality Planning	59.4	8.1 Quality Planning	37.5	8.1 Quality Planning	3.1
	9.1 Organisational Planning	23.5	9.1 Organisational Planning	47.1	9.1 Organisational Planning	29.4
	9.2 Staff Acquisition	20.6	9.2 Staff Acquisition	52.9	9.2 Staff Acquisition	26.5
	10.1 Communication Planning	35.3	10.1 Communication Planning	50	10.1 Communication Planning	14.7
	11.1 Risk Management Planning	61.8	11.1 Risk Management Planning	38.2	11.1 Risk Management Planning	0
	11.2 Risk Identification	67.6	11.2 Risk Identification	29.4	11.2 Risk Identification	3
	11.3 Qualitative Risk Analysis	26.5	11.3 Qualitative Risk Analysis	64.7	11.3 Qualitative Risk Analysis	8.8
	11.4 Quantitative Risk Analysis	20.6	11.4 Quantitative Risk Analysis	61.8	11.4 Quantitative Risk Analysis	17.6
	11.5 Risk Response Planning	35.3	11.5 Risk Response Planning	55.9	11.5 Risk Response Planning	8.8
	12.1 Procurement Planning	48.5	12.1 Procurement Planning	48.5	12.1 Procurement Planning	3
	12.2 Solicitation Planning	33.3	12.2 Solicitation Planning	60.6	12.2 Solicitation Planning	6.1
3- EXECUTING	4.2 Project Plan Execution	26.5	4.2 Project Plan Execution	67.6	4.2 Project Plan Execution	5.9
	8.2 Quality Assurance	30.3	8.2 Quality Assurance	63.6	8.2 Quality Assurance	6.1
	9.3 Team Development	20.6	9.3 Team Development	52.9	9.3 Team Development	26.5
	10.2 Information Distribution	32.6	10.2 Information Distribution	50	10.2 Information Distribution	17.6
	12.3 Solicitation	15.2	12.3 Solicitation	57.6	12.3 Solicitation	27.2
	12.4 Source Selection	33.3	12.4 Source Selection	51.5	12.4 Source Selection	15.2
	12.5 Contract Administration	21.2	12.5 Contract Administration	57.6	12.5 Contract Administration	21.2
4- CONTROLLING	4.3 Integrated Change Control	23.5	4.3 Integrated Change Control	70.6	4.3 Integrated Change Control	5.9
	5.4 Scope Verification	35.3	5.4 Scope Verification	55.9	5.4 Scope Verification	8.8
	5.5 Scope Change Control	29.4	5.5 Scope Change Control	70.6	5.5 Scope Change Control	0
	6.5 Schedule Control	11.8	6.5 Schedule Control	44.1	6.5 Schedule Control	44.1
	7.4 Cost Control	23.5	7.4 Cost Control	50	7.4 Cost Control	26.5
	8.3 Quality Control	30.3	8.3 Quality Control	45.5	8.3 Quality Control	24.2
	10.3 Performance Reporting	11.7	10.3 Performance Reporting	55.9	10.3 Performance Reporting	32.4
	11.6 Risk Monitoring & Control	15.2	11.6 Risk Monitoring & Control	66.7	11.6 Risk Monitoring & Control	18.1
5- CLOSING	10.4 Administrative Closure	5.8	10.4 Administrative Closure	47.1	10.4 Administrative Closure	47.1
	12.6 Contract Closeout	3	12.6 Contract Closeout	60.6	12.6 Contract Closeout	36.4

Table 3. Summarizes the results taken from the respondents' answered questionnaires with a rating scale based on: A= significant sustainable outputs which enhance sustainable performance; B = considerable changes to outputs and guiding performance towards sustainability; C = resulting outputs have no modification or enhancement of sustainability

PM Knowledge Areas	PM Component Processes	Majority of Respondents chose: -	%
Project Integration Management	Project Plan Development	A	76.5
	Project Plan Execution	B	67.6
	Integrated Change Control	B	70.6
Project Scope Management	Initiation	A	82.4
	Scope Planning	A	82.4
	Scope Definition	A	67.6
	Scope Verification	B	55.9
	Scope Change Control	B	70.6
Project Time Management	Activity Definition	A/B	41.2
	Activity Sequencing	B	52.9
	Activity Duration Estimating	B/C	44.1
	Schedule Development	B	50
	Schedule Control	B/C	44.1
Project Cost Management	Resource Planning	A	55.9
	Cost Estimating	A/B	44.1
	Cost Budgeting	B	64.7
	Cost Control	B	50
Project Quality Management	Quality Planning	A	59.4
	Quality Assurance	B	63.6
	Quality Control	B	45.5
Project Human Resource Management	Organisational Planning	B	47.1
	Staff Acquisition	B	52.9
	Team Development	B	52.9

continued in following column

Table 3. Continued

PM Knowledge Areas	PM Component Processes	Majority of Respondents chose: -	%
Project Communications Management	Communications Planning	B	50
	Information Distribution	B	50
	Performance Reporting	B	55.9
	Administrative Closure	B/C	47.1
Project Risk Management	Risk Management Planning	A	61.8
	Risk Identification	A	67.6
	Qualitative Risk Analysis	B	64.7
	Quantitative Risk Analysis	B	61.8
	Risk Response Planning	B	55.9
	Risk Monitoring & Control	B	66.7
Project Procurement Management	Procurement Planning	A/B	48.5
	Solicitation Planning	B	60.6
	Solicitation	B	57.6
	Source Selection	B	51.5
	Contract Administration	B	57.6
	Contract Closeout	B	60.6

processes hold within them efficient leverage points for introducing SD to PM practices.

From Table 3, another conclusion is apparent; among the other two selections (A, C); the respondents seem more leaning towards choosing (A) rather than (C). In fact, only two processes out of the thirty nine had a majority choice of (C) denying them the opportunity for SD enhancement (i.e. Activity Duration Estimating and Schedule Control). In this case, the majority of choice was equally divided between (B) and (C) and never for (C) alone. This analysis underpins the research's findings of the great potential that exists within the processes to embrace sustainable development guidelines and therefore, enhance the overall performance of project management.

The respondents' feedback on each section of the questionnaire was very informative in many ways. This enhanced the outcome of the analysis of the responses. The responses were analyzed with a clear approach in mind which allowed the statistical analysis to represent, in an honest and fair way, the participants' point of views and professional feedback.

From the statistical analysis of the responses, it is evident that the respondents acknowledge the possibilities for integrating sustainable development into project management processes and support the positive impact this integration would have on the overall performance of PM within construction in specific and in all fields in general.

Significant majority of the participants identified several valid opportunities within PM processes listed in the PMBOK which have been identified earlier within the approach of this research. The outcome of the questionnaire's analysis has strengthened this research's hypothesis and identified the ways in which project management, as significant profession in the current modern age, should contribute to the global commitment for sustainable development within all fields. Therefore, since the PMBOK is considered as an international source of project management standards, a way forward for enhancing the PM pledge to embrace a sustainable approach to its practices, is to have sustainable criteria implications on the contents of the PMBOK. These implications have to be transferred and applied to the lists of PM processes and knowledge area. This would serve the whole PM profession with a document of standards that embraces sustainable development. In this case, changing PM practices to sustainable PM practices would have originated from the source out of which PM practices arise; the sustainable approach to PM standards.

FUTURE RESEARCH DIRECTIONS

The built environment could benefit from the involvement of several disciplines in its creation. The construction industry is the main executer of the elements which define the built environment, but the involvement of sustainable development guidelines should not be limited to construction practices or the contribution of project management processes into construction projects, but future work should tackle the other elements which contribute to the built environment such as architecture, commerce, and manufacturing. Further research should look into the progress of these disciplines along the years to reveal different ways of improving their performances. This would ultimately result in a better quality of life which does not only rely on the impact of construction but an overall response from the built environment.

In the practice of construction projects, new case studies should be identified to demonstrate the potential benefits which exist in the implementation of sustainable PM guidelines. This research introduced and tested the desired change of SD guidelines into the standards of PM. This change was intended to be introduced to the policies and strategies of practice before heading to the real life projects. The research makes the initial step towards the implementation phase but it is no longer about enforcing new initiatives on the construction sector, and expecting stakeholders to justify their business cases within these regulations. Further research should be done to examine the practical implementation of this research's recommendation on real life case studies. Future work should concentrate on the identification of stakeholders/ clients who would be interested in implementation such recommendations on different scales of projects (i.e. large, medium or small scale projects). This would add an additional dimension to the findings to reveal whether or not the scale of the impact of such change in policies would differ in the case of large scale projects from its impact in the case of small scale projects.

For developing countries, in the preliminary implementation of sustainable regulatory frameworks, there is a greater opportunity and a more efficient leverage point than in the case of developed economies. For the latter, it is a chance to reshape existing frameworks and disseminating such knowledge to the developing countries. The developing world, paradoxically, has greater prospects for effective change in the application of existing expertise through new frameworks, conceived with sustainability as a key integral component. This contrasts with the difficulties the western hemisphere has in grafting sustainable policy to entrenched methodologies.

CONCLUSION

This chapter has discussed the decision making level of current construction projects including project management practice. The involvement of project management in construction projects is fundamental, although not exclusive, to the successful completion of projects. When embraced from the initial phases of a project, project management standards ensure a systematic breakdown of all activities to fit into a comprehensive, detailed plan for the project as a whole, from initiation to completion and closure.

This research has demonstrated that project management, when embedded in construction projects, has the capacity to be a significant leverage point of such great influence that it is the cornerstone for rethinking the relationships between the three main elements of the integration.

The study has defined and examined the proposal of a tri-dimensional integration between construction, project management and sustainable development when approached from a systems thinking point of view. The main focus of the research is not only to explain the potential and the benefits of such integration. It also tested the criteria on which the integration is based and offers guidance concerning the practical aspects of

construction, and project management practices, in the form of illustrative examples taken from current initiatives and practice standards.

REFERENCES

Argyris, C., & Schon, D. (1978). *Organizational learning: A theory of action perspective.* Reading, MA: Addison-Wesley Publication.

Berger, P., & Luckman, T. (1967). *The social construction of reality.* Hoboken, NJ: Anchor Publications.

CIB. (1999). *Agenda 21 on sustainable construction.* CIB Report Publication 237.

Cummings, T. (1980). *Systems theory of organizational development.* New York: Wiley Publications Ltd..

Davenport, T. (1993). *Process innovation: Reengineering work through information technology.* Boston, MA: Harvard Publications.

Eid, M. (2000). A review of project management & sustainable development for construction projects. *EAR Journal, 27.*

Eid, M. (2009). *Sustainable development & project management: Rethinking relationships in the construction industry, integrating sustainable development into project management processes.* Koln, Germany: Lambert Academic Publishing.

European Construction Industry Federation (FIEC). (n.d.). Retrieved June 2002, from http://www.fiec.org/main.html

Gardner, B., & Demello, S. (1993). Systems thinking in action. *The Healthcare Forum Journal, 36*(4). PMID:10127050.

Grant, R. (1996). Toward a knowledge based theory of the firm. *Strategic Management Journal, 17.*

Hammer, M., & Champy, J. (1993). *Reengineering the corporation: A manifesto for business revolution*. New York: Harper Business School Press. doi:10.1016/S0007-6813(05)80064-3.

James, P. (2000). *Business, eco-efficiency and sustainable development*. Lisbon: The European Commission.

Meadows, D. (1999). *Leverage points, places to intervene in a system*. New York: The Sustainability Institute.

Royal Commission on Environmental Pollution (RCEP). (2000). *Energy - The changing climate*. London: RCEP.

Senge, P. (1999). *The fifth discipline field book, strategies and tools for building a learning organization*. London: Nicholas Braeley Publishing Limited.

Senge, P. (1999). *The fifth discipline, the art & practice of the learning organization*. London: Randome House Business Books.

Sneider, K. F., & Nissen, M. E. (2003). Beyond the body of knowledge: Knowledge-flow approach to project management theory and practice. *Project Management Journal, 34*(2).

Spender, J. (1996). Making knowledge the basis of a dynamic theory of the firm. *Strategic Management Journal*, 17.

The, U. K. Government. (2003). Sustainable development fact sheets: The UK government's policy for SD for UK businesses. London: Her Majesty's Stationery Office (DETR).

The Commission of the European Parliament. (2002). *The competitiveness of the construction industry*. Brussels: European Union.

The Construction Task Force. (1998). *Rethinking construction*. London: DETR.

The European Union Online. Europa. (n.d.). *The European commission*. Retrieved June 2002, from http://europa.eu.int/comm/enterprise/construction/it/connet/connet.htm

Wideman, R. M. (1995). Criteria for a project management body of knowledge. *International Journal of Project Management, 13*(2), 72. doi:10.1016/0263-7863(94)00020-D.

Wirth, I., & Tryloff, D. (1995). Preliminary comparison of six efforts to document the project management body of knowledge. *International Journal of Project Management, 13*, 109–118. doi:10.1016/0263-7863(95)00003-9.

World Business Council for Sustainable Development. (2002). *The business case for sustainable development, making a difference toward the Johannesburg summit 2002 and beyond*. Switzerland: WBCSD.

World Business Council for Sustainable Development (WBCSD). (2002). *The business case for sustainable development, making a difference toward the Johannesburg summit 2002 and beyond*. Switzerland: WBCSD.

ENDNOTES

[1] This chapter is based on an existing published PhD Thesis by the same author; the Thesis was concluded in 2004 at the University of Edinburgh, Scotland, UK. The book was published in 2009 by Lambert Academic Publishing AG & Co. KG and licensors. ISBN: 978-3-8383-1578-2.

Chapter 6
Social Sustainability to Social Benefit:
Creating Positive Outcomes through a Social Risk–Based Approach

Jessica-Louise Winnall
Winnall Consulting, Australia

ABSTRACT

Project managers must recognize that socially sustainable development is a key factor in project success and requires far more than public relations or community consultation. Companies are becoming aware of the risk that community dissatisfaction can have on their projects. Communities are becoming increasingly expectant that the management of socially sustainable development, which maximizes the positive outcomes for communities, is incorporated in all types of projects. Planning for social maximization needs to occur at project design phase, and key issues and actions should be placed under the control of the project manager directly. This chapter considers the lessons from managing community impact in the development sector, which can be used to manage social risk for all projects.

INTRODUCTION

When examining risk in a project management context, our common considerations are financial (Smithson, 1998), logistical (Caron et al., 1998) and occasionally reputational (Fombrun et al., 2000), yet the most significant risks for many projects increasingly fit into the reputational category (Raftery, 2003). Social impacts however demonstrate are a whole range of factors which can result in the failure of an otherwise successful project.

Social impact is often given a perfunctory assessment with only legislated and regulatory risks addressed. Technical staff also often naively assume themselves capable of anticipating a project's social impact, placing the project itself at risk (Clark et al., 2004). By considering the potential risks that social impacts pose upon projects, organisations have an opportunity to move beyond those projects which merely sustain and create to those which truly benefit communities (Clark et al., 2004). This approach is not just for large government projects or for projects in the

DOI: 10.4018/978-1-4666-4177-8.ch006

development sector; it can be applied to projects of all sizes and disciplines. Risks and their impacts, when handled correctly, can become project opportunities, where the potential impact becomes a measurably improved chance of a positive outcome (Vancaly, 2004).

This chapter will explore the ways in which the incorporation of social risk monitoring can significantly improve the likelihood of a project's success. In relation to the concept of socially sustainable development, projects are now considered to have a moral responsibility to create a net positive impact on the communities in which they operate. Resource extraction companies, for example, are moving away from the application of traditional risk mitigation approaches towards the maximization of positive outcomes for communities.

Social monitoring indicators such as those of human rights, gender and social and economic impact should be incorporated in overall project management. Projects in the development sector (whose primary aim is social change) have incorporated social risks and impacts in order to maximize socially sustainable development and, as the World Bank states, many lessons exist for all major projects in this regard. Communities now expect that the management of socially sustainable development, which maximize the positive outcomes for communities, is incorporated in all types of projects (Heltberg et al., 2012).

Increasingly, companies and governments are becoming aware of their impact on the communities in which they work. Moreover, communities have become aware of their ability to halt projects which they perceive as not meeting their social and economic needs. Companies realise that in order to develop a 'social licence to operate' they must develop positive long term relationships with their most vociferous critics (Wheeler et al., 2000) but what this term means is as ambiguous as the dress code 'business casual. Developing a social licence to operate is not just necessary to demonstrate good

corporate social responsibility but is a sensible approach for the risk adverse project manager. Too often social risks are ignored or understated by project management, though even rudimentary definitions of risk in the project context imply that they are as important as financial or logistical challenges. The US Department of Defence defines a risk as 'an uncertain event or condition that, if it occurs, has a positive or negative effect on a project's objectives' ("Risk management guide," 2006) and what is less certain than public opinion?

It is important to highlight the need to assess and measure potential social impact and to incorporate a monitoring system within existing project management frameworks. In recent times, projects have had a social and economic impact assessment which may then be incorporated into a risk management plan that remains the responsibility of the community relations manager. It is the design and application of effective monitoring, however, that is the required next step in creating positive outcomes for communities involved in and around projects.

This chapter will give an outline of the context of risk management and sustainable development in the context of social sustainability, including a brief discussion on the corporate social responsibility and the 'social licence to operate'. The following section will provide a summary of the changing context of development theory, and the move towards incorporating all projects in the context of traditional development. It will also briefly consider the challenges associated with the identification of social risk. From this background, the chapter will examine some case studies of failure to recognise social risk and one project which has turned its challenges into social benefit, focussing on project accountability, and establishing a 'social licence to operate'. Though the lessons of these projects, the chapter will then set out a method to monitor and to manage social risks in project management.

DEFINITIONS AND CONTEXT

Definitions of 'sustainable development' are becoming more complex and specific to particular circumstances as theorists and practitioners grapple with the challenges that arise from the concept. Definitions no longer rest upon the United Nations' 1983 exhortation that we 'not compromise the future'. The responsibility remains with all project managers to ensure that their projects do not have a negative effect on their stakeholders (both those who are directly and those indirectly affected). Further, in relation to the concept of socially sustainable development, projects are now considered to have a moral responsibility to create a net positive impact on the communities in which they operate. Resource extraction companies, for example, are moving away from the application of traditional risk mitigation approaches towards the maximization of positive outcomes for communities.

Risk management is not a new concept in project management, yet project managers rarely incorporate social risks into their risk management plans. A robust risk assessment should not be limited to social risks. Nonetheless, it is important to recognise this category of risks. All risks including social risks need to be assessed for probability and impact, and risk management can be seen as a significant driver in social sustainability (Reinhardt, 1999).

The monitoring of project impact in the development sector can provide practical tools for the management of social risk in a range of project contexts. It is pertinent then, to understand the formulation of monitoring in the development sector.

Understanding the "Development" Context

The dominant theory of development for many years—modernization theory—equated development with modernization. Both dependency theorists, and the New Right, whose neoliberalism eclipsed modernization theory as the dominant development discourse, felt this definition was too limited. Dependency theorists believed that development included social, not just economic aspects and the New Right felt that development should promote individual liberty. Each school believed that their definition could be universally applied to the developing world. As Simon says:

Definitions are contextual, and contingent upon the ideological, epistemological or methodological orientation of their purveyors (Simon, 1997).

Modernization (Rostow, 1964; Leys, 1996), assumes that development is 'an automatic slide' (Rostow, 1971) and essentially asserts that development occurs within a capitalist context. According to the modernization school development is the process of industrial-driven modernization from a static, traditional society, to a high consumption welfare state (Rostow, 1964). Although countries could industrialize under a capitalist or communist model, the final stage of modernity—a high-consumer society—could only flourish under capitalism (Rostow, 1964). In his companion work *Politics and the Stages of Economic Growth*, Rostow (1971) labels democracy as 'the touchstone of dignity and modernity'.

Conversely, dependency theory assumes that development will pass through capitalism and result in socialism, and that *independence* is the greatest wish of development. Afro-Caribbean theorists Frantz Fanon and Walter Rodney (Fanon, 1963, 1971; Rodney, 1972) particularly shared the view that development was an historic process, although one which would pass through capitalism and result in socialism. A further element central to Rodney's definition of development was that it had to be *independent,* otherwise the third world would continue in a state of underdevelopment, stymied by neo-colonial capitalism. Without genuine independence, the resources central to development, industry and natural resources, would be controlled by former colonials and their puppets; the local bourgeoisie (Rodney, 1972; Fanon, 1963). We see here the beginnings of the need for a 'social licence to operate' albeit in a very specific circumstance.

Finally, the new right presents individual liberty as the wish of Development, and consequently supports the development of minimalist governments. The New Right then, with its absence of economic construct, is the most appropriate to transfer to other contexts. Rodney defines development as:

An overall social process which is dependent upon the outcome of man's efforts to deal with his natural environment (Rodney, 1972).

The New Right argues that although industrialization facilitates development, it does not constitute development. Development, according to philosopher Robert Nozick and author Ayn Rand, is the promotion of individual liberty (Rand, 1964; Nozick, 1974). Coupled with the economics of Milton Friedman which trumpeted a free market void of government interference (Perira, 1995), this resulted in a 'hollowed out' or minimalist state(Molyneux, 2008). Nozick (1974) argues that a state should be organized so an individual's dignity and rights are not violated by any other member of that society, including the state itself. Hence, a government should provide only security, as any other tax-funded service for the social good coerces individuals to act in ways they may not wish to. As Rand (1964) argues:

Only individual men have the right to decide when or whether they wish to help others; society—as an organised political system—has no rights in that matter at all.

The welfare state which Rosotow (1971) felt was central to a developed society, is labelled by Rand 'dictatorial presumptiveness.'

Sustainable Development

Academic understanding of 'sustainable development' is evolving and becoming more specific to particular circumstances and more complex as theorists and practitioners grapple with the challenges that arise from the concept. Definitions no longer simply rely on the 1983 UN assumption that we 'not compromise[e] the future'. In the 1980s, the World Bank adopted the neoliberal based structural adjustment, it 'bent its own operations to the logic of the American state.' Thus, we see the risk of failing to understand the social construct in which a project operates, beginning to (Harrison, 2001) affect this industry. The neoliberal definition of development is not only a political ideology presented as an universal theory of development, its assumptions reflect its geographical context. A minimal government is only possible if there is a strong private sector to act as a substitute. As many countries who adopted structural adjustment programs in the 1980s did not have an alternative private sector, the gaps created by the programs entrenched inequality and poverty (Harrison, 2001; Malhorta, 2000). This often presented as civil tension and conflict later on, impacting the ability of the private sector to operate.

The 'lost decade' in Latin America saw mass inequality and poverty. Coming from a decade of oil shocks, recessions and debt crises, structural adjustment 'erode[d] the social sector at precisely the moment when its expansion was most needed' (Molyneux, 2008). Hence, exporting political ideology as a definition of development can be incredibly detrimental. The link between the development theory and the impact of resource wealth then, has long been recognised by students of development studies, and is increasingly being recognised by the resource industry, in terms of social licence to operate, and also in terms of social risk.

CHALLENGES WITH SOCIAL RISK IDENTIFICATION

The global minerals and extraction industry continues to become increasingly aware of the risks that community challenges can present to a project, and these are becoming increasingly enunciated in the academic arena (Evans et al., 2007). Once the risks are identified, the project manager must establish how to determine if they are materializing (before they do).

Risk cues are used by project managers across the board but they can be harder to identify for social risks where the link between community opinion and project output is not always clear (Clark et al., 2004). This is where it is necessary to have a strong understanding and relationship with the community the project is located within. Then, as a project progresses, managers will be able to determine if a risk element has become an issue. If they don't know these cues, however, it is very possible a risk could fester, silently materialize and affect the project, even if there are good contingencies in place.

In the development sector in the 1990s, government bureaucracies had swollen, decreasing efficiency and Keynesian economics was losing popularity (Perira, 1995). This goes some way to explaining the disenchantment with government and faith in markets but does not explain the movement towards the need for a social licence to operate, or to encourage community ownership of projects.

A famous noteworthy failure to identify social risk in a project context is the Rio Tinto Panguna mine in Bougainville. The social impact assessment conducted was minimal at best and the company (as was common at the time) made a series of assumptions about land ownership based on the PNG norm. Through these assumptions they failed to realise that in Bougainville, land secession is matrilineal and made a compensation agreement with the male leaders. Civil war ensued over the compensation offered by the project, and 20,000 people died.

As Rio Tinto raises the possibility of re-entering Bougainville these risks remain significant. The government of Papua New Guinea are supportive of reopening the mine which will maximise the commercial income of the State, whereas the landowners are still withholding customary law approval. A robust social risk assessment undertaken in conjunction with a detailed anthropological study may have alleviated some of this risk.

It is far too easy to assume that in a developed country context, community consultation alone is sufficient to reduce this risk. While community consultation can assist in many cases, risks remain. Often community consultation is undertaken by those without skills sufficient in identifying risks, or community consultation runs parallel to project management and the information is not fed back to project management sufficiently or expediently.

Another noteworthy failure to address social impact occurred in Kingaroy, Australia ("Kingaroy groundwater test," 2010). The Kingaroy Cougar Energy Underground Coal Gasification plant came under significant public scrutiny when high benzene and toluene levels arose in soil as an apparent result of the plant. This significantly affected not only the social impact of the Cougar Energy Project, but of all resources projects in Queensland and nationally. This project also demonstrates the need to consider social risks in a project-wide manner. The supposedly dangerously high levels of heavy metals found in the groundwater and soil surrounding the plant resulted in substantial flow-on effects to cattle and other industries. Yet high levels of these metals already existed in the soil and groundwater around Kingaroy. Without oversimplifying matters, greater communication between community and groundwater groups could have reduced the potential impact to a social one rather than just a chemical issue. This is not to say that the impact could have been avoided, but the far reaching consequences may have been reduced.

This month, tests around the plant demonstrated acceptable levels of heavy metals, but the negative social perceptions have already occurred, creating future challenges for the project.

Accountability and a "Social License to Operate"

It is easy to highlight all the times a project hasn't had an effective social risk analysis, but that is not the whole picture. As mentioned earlier, the increased recognition of social risk is improving, but as yet is still largely ineffective. Simply gaining a 'social licence to operate' is not sufficient to avoid the risks associated with program and project development. We need to anticipate and monitor these risks along with other project risks.

Robert Chambers (1997) argues that projects owe their primary accountability to the people at whom the interventions are aimed- the users. This is not to say that there is consensus on the application of monitoring social impact—the *counter bureaucracy* argument suggests that the increased compliance requirements that this monitoring would need comes at a necessary cost to delivering technical results (Natsios, 2010). Financial monitoring systems have been identified as effectively reducing the risk of fraud and related damage to image (Hoefer, 2000). Not all companies recognize the damage to image that can come from ineffective social risk management.

Gormley (1996) refers to this increased desire for reporting the 'counter bureaucracy' as 'a relatively durable government agency whose principal mission is to monitor, criticize, and improve the performance of other government agencies.' Gormley attributes the rise of these counter bureaucracies to the growing unhappiness with the effectiveness, efficiency and transparency of traditional bureaucracies, at least in the public

perception. He also observes the rise of counter bureaucracies as an US based phenomenon. Whilst he sees wide spread unease with bureaucracies, other nations have found different ways to deal with them.

Monitoring and Evaluation of Social Risk

Monitoring and evaluation and risk management usually remain in the control of the engineering group, and there remains no question as to whether this is necessary. They test the tensile strength of the end product, the load bearing and other factors. Project Managers monitor financial spending in order to ensure cost-effectiveness, and we monitor our timeframes in search of the elusive 'on time on budget' project. These are certainly necessary in project development, but they miss significant social challenges.

Increasingly, companies and governments are becoming aware of their impact on the communities in which they work. Moreover communities are becoming aware of their ability to halt projects which do not meet their social and economic needs. In recent times, projects have had a social and economic impact assessment, which may then be incorporated into a risk management plan which remains the responsibility of the community relations manager. However, it is the design and application of effective monitoring that is the required next step to creating positive outcomes for communities in and around project areas. It is important to monitor changing social patterns in order to ensure early warning for changes in a projects social risk profile.

Benefits of Collaboration

Boutilier and Svendsen (2000)developed a case study of a Forestry Project in Clayquote Sound, Canada, which analysed the seven year development of the relationship between a forestry company and a coalition of environmental stakeholder groups (who opposed the clear cutting of old growth forests in British Columbia). An evaluation of the project found that the move from interorganizational conflict to collaboration required an intervening interpersonal stage in which individuals from each side were given an opportunity to develop mutual trust.

Events suggest third parties can catalyze the transitions into, and out of, the interpersonal trust stage.

One of Canada's largest forestry companies, MacMillan Bloedel, formed a relationship with an informal coalition of environmental non-governmental organizations. The relationship was only formed, however after the environmental non-governmental organizations executed a successful international campaign which prevented MacMillan Bloedel from clear cutting old growth forests in Clayoquot Sound on Vancouver Island in British Columbia, Canada. The conflict climaxed in 1993, with the largest act of civil disobedience in Canadian history, when logging roads were blockaded and more than 800 people were arrested.

By 1999, MacMillan Bloedel ended clear cutting in Clayoquot and instead was operating an eco-friendly logging company, Iisaak Forest Resources, which was jointly owned with the local First Nations (i.e. North American Indian) bands. Greenpeace and other ENGO signed a Memorandum of Understanding (MOU) that committed them to helping Iisaak develop a market for forest products and services from Clayoquot. In examining this case, the Boutilier and Svendsen article determines that stakeholders should focus, first, on structural factors to end the conflict, second interpersonal trust to understand stakeholders' views, and third, on shared values and cognitive frameworks to spark collaboration (Boutilier and Svendsen, 2000). This does not go far enough, however, and does not meet the crux of the problem: That the company should have anticipated the widespread objection to clear cutting in Clayoquot and instigated appropriate reduction and mitiga-

tion strategies. We can certainly assume that they would have had a risk management strategy in place for financing or approvals, so why ignore such a significant risk?

It might be argued that the profitability of the Iisaak model is lower than that of clear cutting. While this may be the case initially, the long term profitability would be better under the Iisaak model (without considering the six year period in which the project was blocked.

As the *Clayoquot* experience demonstrates, working with stakeholders can result in significant benefits for the community through cooperation. In this case the project has gone ahead, and the environmental non-governmental organizations are supporting the project through assisting them increasing their market share. Significant and sustainable employment opportunities have also been provided to the First Nations people. So how do we ensure that more projects have these types of social benefits?

It is the responsibility of the project manager to gather, quantify and monitor all risks that could affect the project, including monitoring social change (under the guidance of a qualified individual). In developing states this could include factors measured by Transparency International (corruption) or various UN agencies (child mortality, access to clean drinking water, education levels). In developed states these can be collected through the national bureaux of statistics, other government departments, or focus groups.

A SOCIAL RISK MANAGEMENT PLAN

Social risk identification should be established within the project's overall management plan. Project managers should start with their robust risk management framework, and ensure that social risks are adequately identified and managed within their broader risk management plan. This section will consider the adaptation of a traditional risk management plan for social risks. Georgia State University PMO (2005) has identified several strategy options that the project team can take to neutralize negative risks and maximize opportunities identified through risk management (Elkington and Fennell, 1998).

This model provides an example of the importance of socializing risks with project stakeholders (including communities). In the following summaries, these strategies for overall risk management have been adapted in order to manage social risk.

- **Acceptance:** In cases where the project team has either decided not to alter the project to avoid the risk, or there are no alternatives to dealing with the risks. In a social context this may be unavoidable relocation (although some groups maintain that no compulsory relocation is acceptable).

- **Avoid:** Put simply, don't take on a project where the damage to social communities or the company is too high. This strategy would be used with detailed and informed participation of the community. In terms of collaboration, some companies have begun to build bridges to environmental advocacy groups in order to acquire new information and ideas, forestall negative media coverage, and win credibility with the public, stake holders and pressure groups.

- **Mitigate:** Mitigation refers to those additional actions which lessen the impact that a risk may have on a project. Technically, this might include another round of quality testing. When measuring social risk this might mean early involvement with stakeholders and communities to develop a win-win outcome, a 'plan B' that is acceptable to the project outcomes and the community. This strategy would be used with detailed informed participation by the community. The most proactive companies have embraced environmental principles

as a stimulus for innovation in efficient resource allocation and in product and service development (Lovins et al., 1999).

- **Transfer:** In order to transfer the social risk, a project manager would move the risk to a third party. Transfer is interesting in the context of risks, and positive risks 'opportunities'. Transferring benefits to the community (e.g. a road to and from a mine may allow additional commerce or benefits to the local community, and could be transferred at the start and finish of a project).

- **Exploit:** Taking full advantage of a possible opportunity for a project, educating stakeholders to the potential of the possible impacts of the project could be a way of exploiting the risk, as the acceptance of the known is greater than the potential worry of the unknown.

- **Share:** Similar to a transference strategy in which the positive opportunities of a project can be shared with a third party. One example of a share strategy would be to form a joint venture that includes all stakeholders so that the full potential of the opportunity is developed. Countless mining companies demonstrate a 'share' approach when they develop project infrastructure integral to their project's success but which they open to government and community users, allowing a net benefit. The identification and sharing of opportunities for local entrepreneurs to act outside or parallel to the project would have a positive social impact ("Enduring Value", 2004; Peck and Sinding, 2003).

- **Enhance:** A strategy that increases the impact of an opportunity as well as the likelihood that the opportunity will happen. This will require the project team to alter the project plan to make sure that the opportunity discussed is a reality and increases the benefits of the full project.

CONCLUSION

It is not simply through ensuring ethical project management that a project manager can manage their social risk profile, nor is good corporate responsibility sufficient justification for monitoring social indicators. In fact, it is far simpler than that. It is a matter of pragmatic risk management and monitoring. What makes it even simpler is that the model already exists.

Project managers must recognize that socially sustainable development is a key factor in project success, and requires far more than public relations or community consultation. Planning for social maximization needs to occur at project design and planning phases, and key issues and actions should be placed under the control of the project manager directly.

Projects in a developing country context (or any fragile community) have been aware of this for some time and there is a raft of documentation of 'monitoring results', 'measuring change' and 'evaluating effectiveness of development results'. These same indicators which are used in a development context to measure the effectiveness of official development assistance can be used as indicators of social risk (and often are in the resources sector).

In this way—through identifying social risks early and recognizing the needs of various stakeholders project managers can ensure that what started out as social risks to their project can both ensure project success and result in social benefits.

Project managers who are accredited (for example through the PMP or PRINCE2 systems) must agree to ensure ethical behaviour of themselves and others through project management. This alone is not enough to ensure that a project is successful, but is congruent with the requirement to include social risks into the project management process.

By considering potential project impacts as presenting risks to the project, organisations have an opportunity to move beyond social sustainability to social acceptance and the support of stakeholders, and so create projects which truly social benefits communities. This approach is not just for large government projects or for projects in the development sector, but can be applied to all projects in all disciplines.

REFERENCES

Boutilier, R. G., & Svendsen, A. C. (2000). *From conflict to collaboration: Stakeholder bridging and bonding in clayoquot sound*. Burnaby, Canada: Simon Fraser University at Harbour Centre.

Caron, F., Marchet, G., & Perego, A. (1998). Project logistics: Integrating the procurement and construction processes. *International Journal of Project Management, 16*(5), 311–319. doi:10.1016/S0263-7863(97)00029-X.

Chambers, R. (1997). *Who's reality counts?* London: Intermediate Technology Publications.

Clark, C., Rosenzweig, W., Long, D., & Olsen, S. (2004). *Double bottom line project report: Addressing social impact in double bottom line methods*. New York: Rockerfeller Foundation.

Elkington, J., & Fennell, S. (1998). Partners for sustainability. *Greener Management International, (24),* 48-60.

Evans, R., Brereton, D., & Joy, J. (2007). Risk assessment as a tool to explore sustainable development issues: Lessons from the Australian coal industry. *International Journal of Risk Assessment and Management, 7*(5), 607–619. doi:10.1504/IJRAM.2007.014089.

Fanon, F. (1963). *The wretched of the earth*. Middlesex, UK: Penguin.

Fanon, F. (1970). *Toward the African revolution*. London: Penguin Books.

Fombrun, C. J., Gardberg, N. A., & Barnett, M. L. (2000). Opportunity platforms and safety nets: Corporate citizenship and reputational risk. *Business and Society Review*, *105*(1), 85–106. doi:10.1111/0045-3609.00066.

Georgia State University. (2005). *Risk management*. Retrieved from http://www2.gsu.edu/~wwwpmo/risk_management.html

Gormley, W. T. (1996, November). Counter-bureaucracies in theory and practice. *Administration & Society*, 275–298. doi:10.1177/009539979602800301.

Harrison, G. (2001). Administering market friendly growth? Liberal populism and the world bank's involvement in administrative reform in sub-Saharan Africa. *Review of International Political Economy*, *8*(3), 528–547. doi:10.1080/09692290110055867.

Heltberg, R., Hossain, N., Reva, A., & Turk, C. (2012). *Anatomy of coping: Evidence from people living through the crises of 2008-11*. Washington, DC: World Bank.

Hoefer, R. (2000). Accountability in action? Program evaluation in nonprofit human service agencies. *Nonprofit Management & Leadership*, *11*(2). doi:10.1002/nml.11203.

Leys, C. (1996). *The rise and fall of development theory*. Bloomington, IN: Indiana University Press.

Lovins, Lovins, & Hawken. (1999). *Natural capitalism: Creating the next industrial revolution*. New York: Little Brown and Company, UK.

Malhotra, K. (2000). NGOs without aid: Beyond the global soup kitchen. *Third World Quarterly*, *21*(4), 665–668. doi:10.1080/713701062.

Minerals Council of Australia (MCA). (2004). *Enduring value: Guidance for implementation*. Canberra, Australia: MCA.

Molyneux, M. (2008). The 'neoliberal turn' and the new social policy in Latin America: How neoliberal, now new? *Development and Change*, *39*(5), 775–797. doi:10.1111/j.1467-7660.2008.00505.x.

Natsios, A. (2010). The clash of the counter-bureaucracy and development. *Center for Global Development*. Retrieved from www.cgdev.org/content/publications/detail/1424271

Nozick, R. (1974). *Anarchy, state and utopia*. Oxford, UK: Basil Blackwell.

Peck, P., & Sinding, K. (2003). Environmental and social disclosure and data richness in the mining industry. *Business Strategy and the Environment*, *12*, 131–146. doi:10.1002/bse.358.

Perira, L. C. B. (1995). Development economics and the world banks' identity crisis. *Review of International Political Economy*, *2*(2), 218–219.

Queensland Government. (2010). *Kingaroy groundwater test results remain at safe low levels*. Retrieved from http://www.derm.qld.gov.au/media-room/2010/08/kingaroy-testing-02-08.html

Raftery, J. (2003). *Risk analysis in project management*. London: Chapman and Hall.

Rand, A. (1964). *The virtue of selfishness: A new concept of egoism*. New York: New American Library.

Reinhardt, F. (1999). Market failure and the environmental policies of firms: Economic rationales for 'beyond compliance' behaviour. *Journal of Industrial Ecology*, *3*, 9–21. doi:10.1162/108819899569368.

Rodney, W. (1972). How Europe underdeveloped Africa. Dar es Salaam, Tanzalia: Tanzania Publishing House.

Rostow, W. (1964). *The stages of economic growth: A noncommunist manifesto*. Cambridge, UK: Cambridge University Press.

Rostow, W. (1971). *Politics and the Stages of growth*. Cambridge, UK: Cambridge University Press. doi:10.1017/CBO9780511562778.

Simon, D. (1997). Reconsidered: New directions in development thinking. *Geografiska Annaler. Series B, Human Geography, 79*(4), 183–201. doi:10.1111/j.0435-3684.1997.00018.x.

Smithson, C. W. (1998). *Managing financial risk: A guide to derivative products, financial engineering and value maximisation* (3rd ed.). New York: McGraw Hill Professional.

United States of America Defense Acquisition. (2006). *Risk management guide for department of defense acquisition* (6th ed.). Washington, DC: United States of America Defense Acquisition University.

Vancaly, F. (2004). International principles for social impact assessment. *Impact Assessment and Project Appraisal, 21*(1), 5–12. doi:10.3152/147154603781766491.

Wheeler, R., Fabig, H., & Boele, R. (2000). Shell, Nigeria and the Ogoni: A study in unsustainable development: In analysis and implications of Royal Dutch/Shell group strategy. *Sustainable Development, 9*(4), 177–196. doi:10.1002/sd.172.

Chapter 7
Project Success by Integrating Sustainability in Project Management

Tiron-Tudor Adriana
Babes-Bolyai University, Romania

Dragu Ioana-Maria
Babes-Bolyai University, Romania

ABSTRACT

There is great concern for social and environmental sustainability. Innovative solutions are needed in addressing the 21st century challenges of globalization, population growth, climate change, and resource scarcity. Corporations become more aware of the importance of sustainable practices by successfully integrating them within non-financial reporting. In the circumstances of the 21st century challenges, corporations start to reconsider both their sustainability and project management approaches. Even though two distinct key-elements of an organization, with importance attributable to the performance of a company, they are interrelated, and sustainability can be integrated within project management. In order to demonstrate this fact, the authors make use of a specific methodology that implies measurement of sustainability integration level, determination of the degree of the project success, and ultimately, computation of Pearson Coefficient for a sample of 35 integrated reports.

INTRODUCTION

This chapter focuses on sustainability impact on the success of the projects developed by companies. We aim to demonstrate that by integrating sustainability practice within project management, objectives and targets will be successfully attained and the achievements are in line with the expectations.

Our topic has been subject to a review of scientific literature. After an extensive documentation process, we have selected the most relevant views on integrating sustainability within project management and how this resulted in successful projects. The section of literature review provides a background on sustainability theory and practice, integrated reporting, corporate disclosure and modalities to measure the degree of success in

DOI: 10.4018/978-1-4666-4177-8.ch007

terms of sustainability determinants. It provides the reader with definitions, classifications and discussion upon opinions and arguments issued by scholars or scientists. Finally, it comprises some personal views on the matter and makes reference to the case study presented forward.

The disclosure of integrated reports brings many controversies in terms of sustainability and project management. Problems arise when information is not presented properly, or is confusing. We believe that improvements can still be made with respect to disclosure on sustainability aspects. The case study explains the development of the hypothesis and the methodology used in testing the initial assumption. We also provide a detailed presentation of the sample companies and we mention the arguments for selecting those specific corporations.

The results are quite controversial, as the success of projects is not always connected to sustainability inclusion. However, in the majority of cases, we obtained a direct impact from sustainability. Therefore, there is evidence that sustainability may induce the success in project management, even though there could be other factors of influence. We estimate that corporations applying sustainability practice contribute, in a high or low degree, to successful outcomes and achievements.

The detailed analysis on the results of our study represents the basis for solutions and recommendations. We believe that sustainability is a solution for incorporating future benefits, and therefore we highly recommend companies to adopt sustainability in their project management in order to become successful. Disclosure improvements are also necessary, as users of reports and stakeholders can provide constructive feedback upon the efforts made by corporations publishing integrated reports to integrate sustainability information/sustainability reports within their integrated reports.

This chapter presents all the mentioned aspects, centered on its main objectives: determining the level of sustainability disclosure, establishing the degree of success for projects involving sustainability, and estimating the impact of integrating sustainability practice into project management on successful outcomes.

BACKGROUND

Defining Sustainability

In an attempt to define *sustainability*, most scholars emerge towards environmental and social concerns (Sijtsma, 2006; D'Amato et. al, 2009; Gary et al., 2011). However, the notion means more than "how green and socially responsible a company has been" (Gary et al., 2011, p.99), being integrated within the organization structures (D'Amato et. al, 2009; Gary et al., 2011) and even managed as a risk related issue (Gary et al., 2011). Sustainability is closely related to sustainable development of the society that according to Kuhlman & Farrington (2010) can be presented as a centre of three dimensions: economic, social and environmental, harmonizing welfare with resource scarcity and environmental damage, on one hand and fulfilling civilization needs without compromising the future (Hansmann, 2010). We agree on the second, broader definition on sustainability that connects this notion to sustainable development and incorporates people, planet and profit.

As Hasmann (2010) argues, sustainable developed has evolved from the eternal conflict between individual interests and public interests. Therefore, the main challenge has been to relate sustainability- in terms of progress, technology and improved standards of living, with sustainability- that means acting responsibly and maintaining this relationship for long term (Kuhlman & Farrington, 2010). This leads to the necessity for the reconciliation of social, economic and climate aspects (Tovey, 2009). In our view, corporations face similar challenges when developing projects and they have to consider all the three pillars of sustainable development if they want to achieve success.

The study developed by Nidumolu et al (2009) signals the advantages of sustainability practices, as companies reduce costs and increase revenues. They consider that organizations gain competitive advantage, being able to "rethink business models, products, technologies, processes" (p.1). We argue that their results represent evidence for the fact that successful projects with both economic and social-environmental benefits can be determined by sustainability behaviour.

Han et al. (2012) argues that sustainability brings innovation and original solutions. Focusing on the vision of a sustainable future in the circumstances of large industrialized cities, their main purpose is to outline the importance of innovation for sustainability. In our opinion, sustainability and innovation are highly correlated and are both essential for project management. Similar studies that discuss sustainable development and urban social sustainability present two distinct perspectives, of social equity and community sustainability (Dempsey et. al, 2011) and describe the progress of cities, organizations and products, underlining the concepts of social sustainability in terms of urban development (Weingaertner, 2011).

In View of Integrated Reporting

The idea of integrated reporting originated from the Accounting for Sustainability Project and has been supported by the International Integrated Reporting Committee. Further on, integration is considered to be a process of sustainability enhancement or environmental and social inclusiveness (Gary et al., 2011). In our view, this statement explains the true meaning of an integrated report and discusses the connection between sustainability and integrating reporting. If sustainability is composed, by definition, from

two main coordinates- the economic and social aspects1, and the notion of *integrated* is determined by the same elements, as mentioned previously, the facts lead us to the conclusion that integrated reports include sustainability information.

It is expected that more companies will enroll for integrated reporting. In this concern Brown Gooding (2012) makes some remarks on the basis of the integrated annual report issued by Altron Company, mentioning the competitive advantage of such a report along with other benefits, of incorporating responsibility, ethics and corporate citizenship. We agree on the fact that integrated reporting contributes to an organization's fulfillment in achieving its objectives and even developing successful projects.

Integrated reports are meant to establish a dialogue between the company and its stakeholders (Oberholzer, 2012) and one of its most important functions is communication. From the perspective of the current research, the information from the integrated annual reports regarding projects development and implementation is essential in order for the organizations to communicate effectively not only the resources and the manner in which they are used, but most important the outcomes or results and its effects on long-term.

Evidence from literature (Azcárate et al., 2011) reveals the existence of integrated indicators that measure the extent in which the organizations conduct of operations affect the process of sustainable development. We consider that corporations are directly accountable for their actions and their impact on sustainable development should be indicated as reference for the sustainability practice level.

Similarities between integrated reporting and sustainability are highlighted by Katelijne Van Wensen et. al. (2011) who defines integrated reports as being those sustainability reports that address all the needs and expectations of the stakeholders. Thereof, sustainability information is integrated within the annual report of the company—that becomes an integrated report, consistent of both financial and non-financial information. Although GRI has issued a set of guidelines for sustainability reporting, new reporting trends demand for integration (Benoit & Niederman, 2010), and therefore inclusiveness of relevant non-financial information so that the convergence between the financial and non-financial elements is made in a concise, clear and proper way.

The study developed by Harvard Business School upon companies that published the first annual integrated reports reveals that problems may arise from stakeholders' perspective, as the attitude towards them should be re-considered. The same study discusses the GRI achievement in harmonizing sustainability with integrated reporting. Adams and Simnett (2011) considers that integrated reporting is to be enhanced by most of the Australian non-for profit organizations.

Remarks on Corporate Disclosure

In recent times, academics become interested in connecting sustainability and financial performance (Uwuigbe et al., 2011), either by stating the expectations from reporting on sustainability (Godschalk, 2011) or by identifying positive correlations between disclosure on environmental issues and performance (Hossain et al., 2006).

If financial performance is influence by sustainability disclosure, when we turn to stakeholder engagement results are contradictory. Research has revealed that reputation or stakeholder perspective does not have a relevant impact on sustainability reporting (Michelon, 2007).

Evidence for improvements made in sustainability reporting practices are outlined by Michael (2009) who performs an analysis on eight Australian companies, considering certain criteria, namely: organizational profile, environmental social and governance performance metrics, governance and economic strategy, report parameters, headquarter location. The scholar found that sustainability reporting has encountered a

remarkable evolution in time, although mentioning subjectivity and possible misinterpretation as research limitations.

The academics Marks and Dyk (2011) examined sustainability reporting in South Africa. Their research sample assumed firms qualified as members of the Johannesburg Securities Exchange Socially Responsible Investment Index for the year 2009. A deep documentation throw international literature demonstrated that few corporations provided assurance for sustainability reporting.

Fonseca et al. (2011) outlines sustainability reporting trends in Canada, and determines GRI indicators for a sample of reports published by universities. According to the academic, only seven out of 25 analysed universities publish sustainability reports.

Sustainability reporting has registered a remarkable evolution (Kolk, 2003) and more companies are willing to adopt this practice. Htaybat (2010) developed a study on corporate online reporting by testing 272 corporations on disclosure upon financial and non-financial elements. Performing computations of an unweighted disclosure index, the scholar found that only 70% from the sample presented corporate online reports.

Academics have implemented econometric models for correlating environmental disclosure with performance. Positive connection resulted from the values registered by the environmental performance indicators from the perspective of IFRS mandatory disclosure (Clarkson et al., 2007; Tsalavoutas, 2009; Michelon, 2007).

Project Management and Sustainability

Project management can be defined as the set of functions—planning, organizing, and administrating inputs—in an attempt to pursue given objectives. Successful projects can be achieved by the proper implementation of project management. Management of activities, resources, time and effort, as well as intermediate products is essential for developing projects. Furthermore, communication represents the determinant for the resulted output, by deciding upon success or failure. Analysis on project management tools—Microsoft Project, Architecture of Integrated Information Systems, Microsoft Power Point, Microsoft Outlook—shows that an integrated variant of these systems is needed. Examination upon such a combined variant presents the outputs resulted from MidManager, an information system technology used in project management, from the perspectives of project managers, team projects, participants, communication. The investigation implied a series of benefits for adopting this system, and the value added to the initiated and developed projects has been considerable (Van Der Merwe & Bussin, 2006).

Awareness is brought on the importance of integrating sustainability aspects into project management by implementing community development and social projects or by focusing on innovation and commitment for sustainability (D'Amato et. al, 2009). From planning, and continuing with execution and evaluation, projects should involve not only the social element, but they also have to be environmental consistent (Godschalk, 2011) and provide "sound environmental management practices" (Dam, 2008, p. 37).

Sijtsma (2006) provides insights on project evaluation from sustainability point of view. The academician performs both cost-benefit and multi criteria analysis for establishing the sustainability degree of projects, also noting the trade-off between alternatives when promoting sustainability. Another interesting perspective of sustainability is conferred by Hossain et al. (2006) and regards mainly projects in development stage or future outcomes and their commitment to sustainability.

According to Riemer and Meyer (2009: 4), the process of project management involves five main criteria, namely:

- Initiation
- Planning
- Implementation
- Monitoring and Controlling
- Closing

Discussion on Success Measurement in terms of Sustainability Determinants

There have been many attempts to quantify the impact or benefits of projects from a sustainability perspective. Michael (2009) provides discussions on the implementation of social and community indicators, while Benoît and Niederman (2010) states the need for projects' impact assessment in the circumstances of environmental damage and believes that a framework for sustainability reporting should incorporate indicators that can be used for measuring sustainability levels for extensive projects.

In order to integrate sustainability practice into project management, corporations have to apply certain stages, namely (Riemer & Meyer, 2009):

1. Setting the sustainability expectations.
2. Opportunities of reducing costs.
3. Sustainability risks management.
4. Value maximization.
5. Sustainability requirements that are to be to accomplished.
6. Engagement to suppliers and sub-contractors.
7. Motivate the project team.

The measuring scale for project success involves two perspectives and can be presented as follows (DeLone & McLean, 2003):

1. Project Management Success
   a. Targeting time and cost- fulfilment with initial objectives.
   b. Setting quality standards for the processes involved in project management.

c.   Engagement to stakeholders.
2. Project/Product Success
    a.   Establishing strategic organizational objectives and their compliance.
    b.   Understanding the needs of users.
    c.   Stakeholder engagement from product perspective.

MAIN FOCUS OF THE CHAPTER: ISSUES, CONTROVERSIES, PROBLEMS

Preliminary Aspects

It is argued that projects add to the sustainability of organisations because they realise innovations, but there is more to it. Not all organisational changes can be considered sustainable and not all products or services produced with the results of projects add to sustainability. Therefore we need to create a common understanding of the complex concept of Sustainable Project Management. (Gilbert Silvius).

We initiate the problem statement of this chapter by presenting the approach of Professor Gilbert Sivius who argues that sustainability does not result from change or innovation, but from a mixture of sustainable products, services and actions. Therefore, the main issues of the current work involve investigation upon sustainability levels of projects developed by corporations and the correlation to the achievements of established objectives-project success. The research is meant to contribute to the progress of sustainable project management.

Controversies can appear from eventual non-correlations or high project management sustainability and low success rates. We intend to test the mentioned issues on a sample of integrated reports. We agree that annual integrated reports represent a reliable source for information disclosure examination from the perspective of sustain-

ability integration within project management. The integrated reports contain relevant information regarding future projects or in development ones. In addition, we mention that by projects we understand any action undertaken by the corporation that upholds certain objectives and targets as well as the directions for fulfilling these goals.

Nowadays, corporations feel the need to reconsider their policies on integrating sustainable development within project management. Labuschagne and Brent (2006) concentrate on assessing life cycle impact and present their Social Impact Indicator (SII) which is tested on South Africa. The findings suggest low levels of information regarding social impact concluding that further research is still necessary to provide the right indicator for measuring project life cycle management. From a practical perspective, an interesting controversy is introduced by Riemer and Meier (2009) who aim to integrate sustainability within project management, from environmental, social and economic point of view. The scholars argue that sustainable projects become one of the main objectives for large corporations and successful projects are determined by enhancement of sustainability. Sustainability integration into project management is best presented in Figure 1.

The first stage in project management integration assumes a complete *understanding of sustainability expectations*, by including corporate social responsibility, environmental, health and safety issues, product quality and a code of conduct. The mentioned elements have to be included within planning and execution of the projects. Thereof, *scope* and *time* are two joined parameters that measure the understanding of sustainability expectations, as a purpose of sustainability integration into project management, and assume a time scale planning and execution schedule. A secondary item is represented by opportunities of *reducing costs* in terms of materials, energy, water, waste, penalties or injuries, reputation, biodiversity, etc. Another important element consists of *sustainability risk management and value maxi-*

Figure 1. Integrating sustainability within project management (Source: adapted from Riemer and Meier (2009, p. 6))

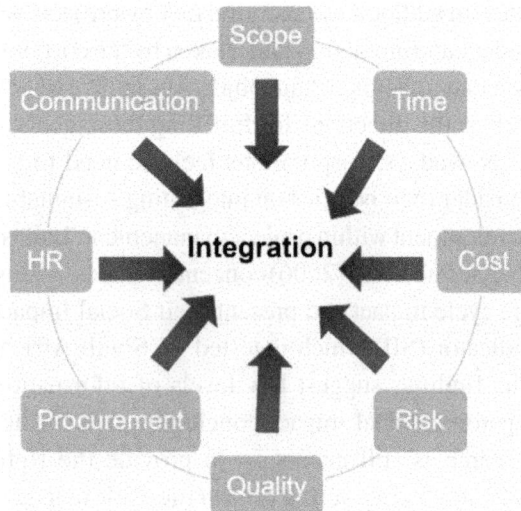

mization. Sustainability risk comprises environmental, social and economic as well as health and safety risks. Value maximization can be achieved when these risks become opportunities. *Sustainability requirements* have to be complied and applied in the proper manner. *Procurement guidelines and supply chain influence* should also be on the list of project management enhancement of sustainability. Motivation of the project team is essential and can be attained only through inclusion, involvement, communication, training, and incentives. Finally, *communication* with stakeholders is the most critical point as corporations should start from their needs and expectations and also ask for feedback in order to maintain a transparent line in reporting. Thereof, integration of sustainability asks for additions in a basic project management model (e.g. expectations, requirements, and motivations).

DeLone and McLean (2003) define project management success from three perspectives: time, budget and specifications (illustrated in Figure 2).

Figure 2 describes project management success by extending the three dimensions of time, budget and specification to stakeholder engagement and quality. However, this approach fails in explaining the relation between inputs and outputs of project management, between resources and processing, and final benefits or impacts, connecting project management quality with user satisfaction and impact.

Figure 2 represents a replication of the seven criteria for defining project management success and project/product success:

- Project Management Success
  - **Targeting Time and Cost-Fulfilment with Initial Objectives:** Means system created versus experienced.
  - **Setting Quality Standards for the Processes Involved in Project Management:** Relates to information quality and system quality.
  - **Engagement to Stakeholders**: Refers to user satisfaction.
- Project/Product Success
  - **Establishing Strategic Organizational Objectives and Their Compliance:** Is in fact the system created.
  - **Understanding the Needs of Users:** Shows user satisfaction.
  - **Stakeholder Engagement from Product Perspective:** Represents the organizational impact.

The connection between Figure 2 and the seven criteria for sustainability integration in project management can be explained as follows:

1. **Setting the Sustainability Expectations:** This is related to stakeholders and user satisfaction.
2. **Opportunities of Reducing Costs:** Will impact the internal environment of the organization and the organization is to benefit from this initiative.
3. **Sustainability Risks Management:** Concerns organizational impact.

Figure 2. Success for project management (Source: DeLone and McLean (2003, p. 12))

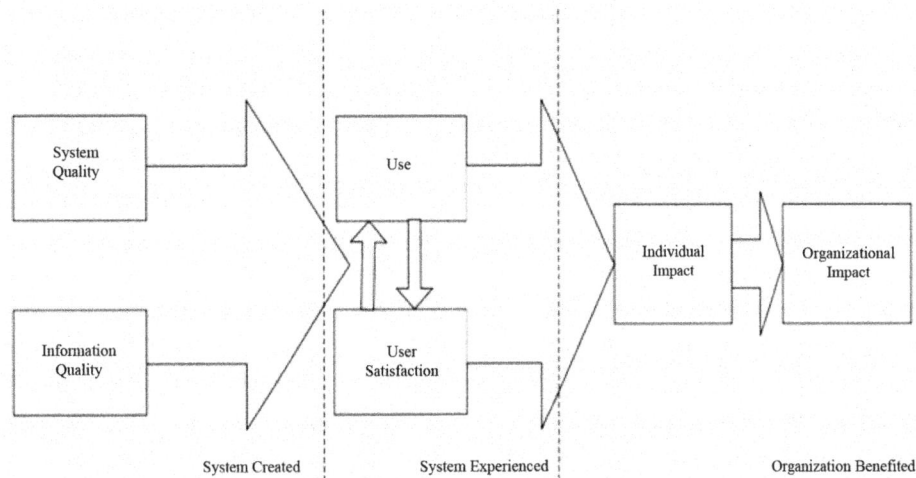

4. **Value Maximization:** Relates to stakeholders and organizational impact and organization benefits.
5. **Sustainability Requirements that are to be to Accomplished:** Refers to created versus experienced system.
6. **Engagement to Suppliers and Sub-Contractors:** Enhances organizational impact.
7. **Motivate the Project Team:** Contributes to organizational benefits.

In view of the previously presented items, our case study presents the long-time impact of the short-time project cycle and benefit of integrating the sustainability criteria in project management.

METHODOLOGY

This research starts from the hypothesis that *the success of a project depends on integrating sustainability within project management*. Therefore, we suppose that those companies whose project management involves highly integrated sustainability practices obtain high quality projects.

We aim to test the elements of project sustainability integration- *setting the sustainability*

expectations; opportunities of reducing costs; sustainability risks management; value maximization; sustainability requirements that are to be to accomplished; engagement to suppliers and sub-contractors; motivate the project team and success level- *targeting time and cost-fulfillment with initial objectives; setting quality standards for the processes involved in project management; engagement to stakeholders; establishing strategic organizational objectives and their compliance; understanding the needs of users; stakeholder engagement from product perspective* on our sample of companies, as to investigate whether or not they qualify for developing sustainability projects. Furthermore, we consider each element as equal in importance, thus representing 1/7 or 14.29%. We denote with one the cases when a certain condition is accomplished, and 0, when it is not. Finally, we obtain a score representing the level of sustainability integration within project management. The maximum value that can be obtained is 100% or 100 points, and the minimum 14.29% or 14.29 points (or 0%, in case none of the elements is present, which most probably will not be the case as we discuss integrated reports).

The second part of the research involves determining the degree of the project success, based on the measuring scale. In this case, we intend to allocate 50% to each of the two components of the project success- project management success and project/product success-. Moving to the three sub-categories of the main elements, their weight will be equally distributed, as 1/3 or 33.5%. Therefore, the highest possible amount represents 100% (100 points) and the minimum is 33.5% (33.5 points).

Finally, we try to establish if there can be sign of correlation between the level of sustainability integration within project management and the success of these projects. The research method implies the determination of the Pearson Correlation Coefficient, as a fraction of covariance for our variables- sustainability integration and success level- and the product of their standard deviation, as follows:

$$\rho_{X,Y} = \text{cov}(X,Y) / \sigma_X\sigma_Y (1)$$

X represents the level of sustainability integration within project management, while Y defines the project success.

The main argument for choosing this particular coefficient relies in the fact that it has been previously used in similar papers that discuss project management and sustainability issues (Kranjac, et al., 2011).

Sample Selection

The corporations included in the current study have been selected based on the criteria that they publish integrated annual reports. We discussed previously that according to our sources from literature, integrated reporting upholds sustainability information, even that referring to project management. Therefore, we tested the elements mentioned in the hypothesis section, by analysing the information disclosed in the integrated reports. In addition, we applied the methodology presented earlier.

We discuss a number of 35 annual integrated reports for years 2009 and 2010 published by corporations from various industries: informa-

tion technology, chemicals, mining, banking and assurance, electricity, communication, medicine, aerospace, agriculture, retail, construction, electronics, real estate and cosmetics.

Table 1 presents our sample of companies.

All the previously listed companies have initiated and implemented projects that uphold sustainability elements during the period 2009-2010. This section comprises a trespassing on the main projects and their implications. In year 2010, Philips developed the EcoVision 5, and found a series of solutions for cost reduction or increase in economic value, focusing on environmental quality, programmes and targets for sustainability and providing support for green products. The same year, Potash Group was initiating projects on water quality, while RB Platinum was concentrating on energy-consumption targets establishing DSM programmes. Standard Bank was fighting for business sustainability on long term, by showing environmental concern. UTC has implemented a set of programmes such as PurePower PW1000G for energy reduction or ACE with the goals of lowering costs, increase customer satisfaction and efficiency. Vodacom initiated programmes for product innovation and access to research, Wolesely created projects for energy reductions and Xstrata meant to support the community. Eskom was mainly concerned by economic development projects, Altron believed in continuous sustainability, and Anglo Platinum had the Modikwa project on initiating value. BASF developed the safety Quality Assessment System, Logica involved in community programmes, Capita concentrated on energy cost reductions and Gold Field provided programmes for the purpose of health, education and community support. Great Portland managed projects for environment and community, while Novo Nordisk became part of AA1000 framework for accountability. AEP contributed to the Carbon Disclosure Project and Amlin was initiating community programmes. Implats concentrated on performance assessment, and Massmart believed in sustainability perfor-

Table 1. Sample description

Crt. No.	Year	Country	Industry	Company	Document title	Website
1	2010	USA	Electricity	AEP	2010 Annul Report	www.aep.com
2	2009	South Africa	Electronics	Altron	Integrated Report 2010	www.altron.com
3	2010	South Africa	Electronics	Altron	Integrated Report 2011	www.altron.com
4	2009	UK	Banking and assurance	Amlin plc	Amlin plc AnnualReport 2009	www.amlin.com
5	2010	UK	Banking and insurance	Amlin plc	Annual Report 2010	www.amlin.com
6	2009	South Africa	Mining	Anglo Platinum	Annual Report 2009	www.angloplatinum.com
7	2010	South Africa	Mining	Anglo Platinum	Integrated Annual Report 2009	www.angloplatinum.com
8	2009	Germany	Chemicals	BASF	Annual Report 2010	www.basf.com
9	2010	Germany	Chemicals	BASF	Integrated Report	www.basf.com
10	2009	UK	Banking and insurance	Capita Group	Annual Report and Accounts 2009	www.capita.co.uk
11	2010	UK	Banking and insurance	Capita Group	Annual Report 2010	www.capita.co.uk
12	2009	South Africa	Electricity	Eskom	Annual Report 2009	www.eskom.co.za
13	2010	South Africa	Electricity	Eskom	Integrated Report 2010	www.eskom.co.za
14	2009	South Africa	Mining	Gold Fields	Integrated Annual Report 2009	www.goldfields.com
15	2010	South Africa	Mining	Gold Fields	Integrated Annual Report 2010	www.goldfields.com
16	2009	UK	Real Estate	Great Portland Estate	Annaul Report 2009	www.greatportlandestate.com
17	2010	UK	Real Estate	Great Portland Estate	Annual Report 2010	www.greatportlandestate.com
18	2010	South Africa	Mining	Implats	Integrated Annual Report 2010	www.implats.co.za
19	2009	UK	Information Technology	Logica plc	Annual Report and Accounts 2009	www.logica.com
20	2010	UK	Information Technology	Logica plc	Annual Report and Accounts 2010	www.logica.com
21	2010	South Africa	Retail	Massmart	2010 Annual Report	www.massmart.com
22	2009	Finland	Mining	Metso Corporation	Annual Report 2009	www.metsocorporation.com
23	2009	UK	Electricity	National Grid	Annual Report and Accounts 2009	www.nationalgrid.com
24	2010	UK	Electricity	National Grid	Annual Report and Accounts 2010	www.nationalgrid.com
25	2010	Brazil	Cosmetics	Natura	Natura Report 2010	www.natura.com
26	2009	Denmark	Medicine	Novo Nordisk	Annual Report 2009	www.novonordisk.com
27	2010	Denmark	Medicine	Novo Nordisk	Annual Report 2010	www.novonordisk.com
28	2010	Netherlands	Electronics	Philips	Annual Report 2010	www.philips.com
29	2009	Canada	Agriculture	Potash Group	Fiancial Review 2009	www.potashgroup.com
30	2010	South Africa	Mining	RB Platinum	Integrated Annual Report 2011	www.bafikenglatinum.co.za

continued on following page

Table 1. Continued

Crt. No.	Year	Country	Industry	Company	Document title	Website
31	2010	South Africa	Banking and insurance	Standard Bank	Integrated Report	www.standardbank.com
32	2010	USA	Aerospace and industrial	UTC	Annual Report 2010- Financial and Corporate Resonsibility Performance	www.utc.com
33	2010	South Africa	Communication	Vodacom	Integrated Report	www.vodacom.com
34	2010	UK	Construction	Wolesely	Annual Report and Accounts 2010	www.wolesely.com
35	2010	Switzerland	Mining	Xstrata plc	Annual Report 2010	www.xstrata.com

Source: authors' own projections

mance and commitment, while Natura was more attached to environmental causes.

Solutions and Recommendation

This section is meant to present our solutions and recommendations for the problem statement of sustainable project management. We investigate the findings upon the current research implementation by aiming to demonstrate the connection between integrating sustainability within project management and enhancing benefits from successful projects. Our results represent the basis for providing the proper solutions and recommendations.

We add that all the stages of the current research- data gathering, analysis of integrated reports and data processing, external computations and correlation checking, have been separately performed by two different persons, both authors of the current chapter and in the end, we discussed and agreed upon the right variant. Therefore, this study has been reviewed and peer-review by its authors- two distinct persons, so that subjectivity could be eliminated from the list of limitations.

The fundamentals of this study represent corporate disclosure within integrated annual reports regarding project management sustainability and achievements of successful projects. The main challenge of the research is to provide incentives for adoption and improvement of sustainable

project management by organizations. However, research limitations still exist, in the form of considering disclosure aspects instead of real actions performed by corporations (for instance, it is possible that they comply with a certain element from our scale, but do not mention this information within the integrated report because it represents an internal and confidential type of information). This limitation can provide partial explanations for the final results of the study that is to be detailed further in the corresponding section. We continue with the presentation of our findings regarding project management sustainability integration and its correlation to successful projects and enhanced benefits.

First of all, we discuss the level of project management sustainability integration, by analysing the seven elements that contribute to the determination of projects sustainability: setting the sustainability expectations, opportunities of reducing costs, sustainability risk management, value maximization, sustainability requirements to be accomplished, suppliers and sub-contractors engagement and motivation of project team. Thereof, Table 2 contains the determination sustainability integration in project management. The last column has been completed with the percentage that ascertains the level for integrating sustainability within projects initiation and development. We searched through the whole content of the integrated reports for the seven elements that contribute to sustainability of project management. For each one of the seven items, we nominated a score of 1 in case the information has been disclosed, and 0, where no evidence was found. Same importance has been attributed to all of the items, so that sustainable project management level was established by adding all the elements and dividing the result by seven. Fluctuating between 40% and 100%, the degree of sustainability integration within project management does seem to change, although with some exemptions (Altron, Amlin, National Grid), from a year to another for the same company. This could result in a controversy, as generally those corporations that apply for a sustainable project management are believed to be constant in their policies for sustainability, and it would have unusual to find a change in this perspective. However, this is not the case for Anglo Platinum, BASF, Capita Group, Eskom, Gold Fields, Great Portland Estate, Logica, Novo Nordisk. If some of them register declines in the level for sustainable project management (Anglo Platinum, BASF, Gold Fields, Logica, Novo Nordisk), the others have witnessed improvements in this respect (Capita Group, Eskom, Great Portland).

Complete sustainability integration within projects initiatives and developments (100% degree) is registered by five corporations from our entire sample, namely: BASF (2009), Eskom (2010), Gold Fields (2009), Logica (2009) and Novo Nordisk (2009). High levels for sustainable project management (86%) are achieved by Altron, Anglo Platinum (2009), Capita Group, Gold Fields (2010), Implats, Logica (2010), National Grid, Philips, RB Platinum and Vodacom. Strong evidence for sustainability of projects is also found in the 10 companies with 71% sustainability integration within project managemement: Amlin, BAFS, Capita Group, Great Portland Estate (2010), Massmart, Metso Corporation, Natura, Standard Bank, Wolesely, Xstrata. Smaller percentages, around half level-integration register Anglo Platinum (2010), Eskom (2009), Great Portland Estate (2009), Novo Nordisk (2010),

Potash Group (2009), UTC. The only case under 50% (43%) is represented by AEP, the electricity company from USA.

All of the 35 annual reports disclose information upon *setting the sustainability expectation regarding* project management, while 27 present the *opportunities of cost reduction* generated by sustainable projects. Also, out of our sample of 35 reports, only 23 mention *sustainability risk management*, the concept of *value maximization* being detailed in 30 cases and *sustainability requirements* in 24. *Suppliers and sub-contractors engagement* has been underlined by 22 of integrated reports, and in 28 cases *project teams are motivated*.

The next stage to sustainability integration into project management involves measurement for projects success (See Table 3). The six components of success scale are targeting time and cost fulfilment, quality standards, engagement to stakeholders, strategic organizational objectives and compliance, need of users, product perspective stakeholder engagement. If Altron and National Grid companies maintain their 100% success rate, Amlin, Anglo Platinum and National Grid register a decrease in success levels from 2009 to 2010, while BASF, Capita Group, Eskom, Gold Fields, Great Portland Estate and Logica increase the degree of project success for the same period. Out of 35 integrated reports, 16 disclose information that results in a scale of 100% projects success (Altron, Anglo Platinum 2009, BASF 2010, Capita Group 2010, Eskom 2010, Gold Fields 2010, Great Portland Estate 2010, Implats, Metso Corporation, National Grid, Natura 2010, Novo Nordisk, Philips and Standard Bank. High success levels of 83% are met for Amlin 2009, BASF 2009, Capita Group 2009, Eskom 2009, Gold Fields 2009, Great Portland Estate 2009, Logica 2010, Massmart, National Grid, RB Platinum, Vodacom, Wolesely. AEP, Amplin 2010, Logica 2009, Potash Group, UTC and Xstrata register 67% success of project management implementation, while Anglo Platinum 2010 performed only

Table 2. Projects and sustainability

Crt. No.	Year	Company	Ettting the sustainability expectations	Opportunities of reducing costs	Sustainability risks management	Value maximization	Sustainability requirements that are to be to accomplished	Engagement to suppliers and sub-contractors	Motivate the project team	Sustainability Integration
1	2010	AEP	1	1	1	0	0	0	0	43%
2	2009	Altron	1	1	1	1	1	1	0	86%
3	2010	Altron	1	1	1	1	0	1	1	86%
4	2009	Amlin plc	1	0	1	1	1	0	1	71%
5	2010	Amlin plc	1	0	1	1	1	0	1	71%
6	2009	Anglo Platinum	1	1	1	1	1	0	1	86%
7	2010	Anglo Platinum	1	1	1	0	0	1	0	57%
8	2009	BASF	1	1	1	1	1	1	1	100%
9	2010	BASF	1	1	1	1	1	0	0	71%
10	2009	Capita Group	1	0	1	1	0	1	1	71%
11	2010	Capita Group	1	1	1	1	0	1	1	86%
12	2009	Eskom	1	1	1	1	0	0	0	57%
13	2010	Eskom	1	1	1	1	1	1	1	100%
14	2009	Gold Fields	1	1	1	1	1	1	1	100%
15	2010	Gold Fields	1	1	1	1	1	0	1	86%
16	2009	Great Portland Estate	1	0	0	0	1	1	1	57%
17	2010	Great Portland Estate	1	0	1	1	1	0	1	71%
18	2010	Implats	1	0	1	1	1	1	1	86%
19	2009	Logica plc	1	1	1	1	1	1	1	100%
20	2010	Logica plc	1	1	1	1	1	0	1	86%
21	2010	Massmart	1	1	0	1	0	1	1	71%
22	2009	Metso Corporation	1	1	1	1	0	0	1	71%
23	2009	National Grid	1	1	1	1	0	1	1	86%
24	2010	National Grid	1	1	0	1	1	1	1	86%
25	2010	Natura	1	0	0	1	1	1	1	71%
26	2009	Novo Nordisk	1	1	1	1	1	1	1	100%
27	2010	Novo Nordisk	1	1	0	0	1	0	1	57%
28	2010	Philips	1	1	0	1	1	1	1	86%
29	2009	Potash Group	1	0	0	1	1	0	1	57%
30	2010	RB Platinum	1	1	1	1	1	1	0	86%
31	2010	Standard Bank	1	1	0	1	0	1	1	71%
32	2010	UTC	1	1	0	0	1	1	0	57%
33	2010	Vodacom	1	1	0	1	1	1	1	86%
34	2010	Wolesely	1	1	0	1	0	1	1	71%
35	2010	Xstrata plc	1	1	0	1	1	0	1	71%
			35	27	23	30	24	22	28	

Source: authors' own projection

Table 3. Measuring projects success

Crt. No.	Year	Company	targeting time and cost- fulfilment with initial objectives	setting quality standards for the processes involved in project management	Engagement to stakeholders	establishing strategic organizational objectives and their compliance	understanding the needs of users	Stakeholder engagement from product perspective	Projects Success (%)
1	2010	AEP	1	1	0	1	0	1	67%
2	2009	Altron	1	1	1	1	1	1	100%
3	2010	Altron	1	1	1	1	1	1	100%
4	2009	Amlin plc	1	1	1	1	0	1	83%
5	2010	Amlin plc	0	0	1	1	1	1	67%
6	2009	Anglo Platinum	1	1	1	1	1	1	100%
7	2010	Anglo Platinum	1	1	1	0	0	0	50%
8	2009	BASF	1	1	1	0	1	1	83%
9	2010	BASF	1	1	1	1	1	1	100%
10	2009	Capita Group	1	1	1	1	1	0	83%
11	2010	Capita Group	1	1	1	1	1	1	100%
12	2009	Eskom	1	1	1	1	1	0	83%
13	2010	Eskom	1	1	1	1	1	1	100%
14	2009	Gold Fields	1	1	1	1	0	1	83%
15	2010	Gold Fields	1	1	1	1	1	1	100%
16	2009	Great Portland Estate	1	1	1	1	1	0	83%
17	2010	Great Portland Estate	1	1	1	1	1	1	100%
18	2010	Implats	1	1	1	1	1	1	100%
19	2009	Logica plc	1	0	1	1	1	0	67%
20	2010	Logica plc	1	1	1	1	1	0	83%
21	2010	Massmart	1	1	1	1	0	1	83%
22	2009	Metso Corporation	1	1	1	1	1	1	100%
23	2009	National Grid	1	1	1	1	1	1	100%
24	2010	National Grid	1	1	1	1	1	0	83%
25	2010	Natura	1	1	1	1	1	1	100%
26	2009	Novo Nordisk	1	1	1	1	1	1	100%
27	2010	Novo Nordisk	1	1	1	1	1	1	100%
28	2010	Philips	1	1	1	1	1	1	100%
29	2009	Potash Corp	1	1	1	1	0	0	67%
30	2010	RB Platinum	1	1	1	1	0	1	83%
31	2010	Standard Bank	1	1	1	1	1	1	100%
32	2010	UTC	1	0	1	0	1	1	67%
33	2010	Vodacom	1	0	1	1	1	1	83%
34	2010	Wolesely	1	0	1	1	1	1	83%
35	2010	Xstrata plc	1	0	1	1	0	1	67%
			34	29	34	32	27	27	

Source: authors' own projection

50%. Information concerning *targeting time and cost fulfilment with the initial objectives* as well as *stakeholder engagement* has been disclosed within 34 integrated reports, while in 29 of the cases companies claim to set *quality standards* for their projects. *Strategic organizational objectives* are mentioned in 32 reports. *The needs of reports and product sustainability* are outlined in 27 cases, out of 35.

Correlation is established after determination of sustainable project management and measurement of projects success (See Table 4). At first sight, sustainability integration within project management is not always correlated to successful projects. It seems that sometimes 100% sustainability integration generates only 67% or 83%

successful outcome. Similarly, 86%, 71%, and even 57% sustainability levels lead to 100% success. In the other cases, values fluctuate approximately in a constant trend. However, the controversial findings suggest that there are situations when projects success can be determined by other external or internal factors, besides sustainability. In this respect, further research is needed to reveal the key drivers of projects success. Although not perfectly correlated, we can state that sustainable project management participates directly, indeed, at obtaining successful outcomes, maintaining a high influence on the projects results and benefits. Similar, if high sustainability integration degree did not always result in high success levels this does not mean

Table 4. Correlation

Country	Industry	Company	Sustainability Integration	Projects Success	Sustainability Integration (%)	Projects Success (%)
UK	Information Technology	Logica plc	1.00	0.67	100%	67%
Germany	Chemicals	BASF	1.00	0.83	100%	83%
South Africa	Mining	Gold Fields	1.00	0.83	100%	83%
South Africa	Mining	Anglo Platinum	0.57	0.50	57%	50%
Switzerland	Mining	Xstrata plc	0.71	0.67	71%	67%
UK	Banking and insurance	Amlin plc	0.71	0.67	71%	67%
UK	Information Technology	Logica plc	0.86	0.83	86%	83%
UK	Electricity	National Grid	0.86	0.83	86%	83%
South Africa	Mining	RB Platinum	0.86	0.83	86%	83%
South Africa	Communication	Vodacom	0.86	0.83	86%	83%
South Africa	Electricity	Eskom	1.00	1.00	100%	100%
Denmark	Medicine	Novo Nordisk	1.00	1.00	100%	100%
USA	Aerospace and industrial	UTC	0.57	0.67	57%	67%
Canada	Agriculture	Potash Group	0.57	0.67	57%	67%
UK	Banking and assurance	Amlin plc	0.71	0.83	71%	83%
UK	Banking and insurance	Capita Group	0.71	0.83	71%	83%
South Africa	Retail	Massmart	0.71	0.83	71%	83%

continued on following page

Table 4. Continued

Country	Industry	Company	Sustainability Integration	Projects Success	Sustainability Integration (%)	Projects Success (%)
UK	Construction	Wolesely	0.71	0.83	71%	83%
South Africa	Electronics	Altron	0.86	1.00	86%	100%
South Africa	Electronics	Altron	0.86	1.00	86%	100%
South Africa	Mining	Anglo Platinum	0.86	1.00	86%	100%
UK	Banking and insurance	Capita Group	0.86	1.00	86%	100%
South Africa	Mining	Gold Fields	0.86	1.00	86%	100%
South Africa	Mining	Implats	0.86	1.00	86%	100%
UK	Electricity	National Grid	0.86	1.00	86%	100%
Netherlands	Electronics	Philips	0.86	1.00	86%	100%
USA	Electricity	AEP	0.43	0.67	43%	67%
South Africa	Electricity	Eskom	0.57	0.83	57%	83%
UK	Real Estate	Great Portland Estate	0.57	0.83	57%	83%
Germany	Chemicals	BASF	0.71	1.00	71%	100%
UK	Real Estate	Great Portland Estate	0.71	1.00	71%	100%
Finland	Mining	Metso Corporation	0.71	1.00	71%	100%
Brazil	Cosmetics	Natura	0.71	1.00	71%	100%
South Africa	Banking and insurance	Standard Bank	0.71	1.00	71%	100%
Denmark	Medicine	Novo Nordisk	0.57	1.00	57%	100%

(Source: authors' own calculations)

that sustainable project management is not essential for projects success. A possible explanation is that the successful scales were lowered by external circumstances or exceptional situations. Finally, we underline again that our dataset information has been gathered based on disclosure in integrated reports, which means that we fundament our findings on what it has been mentioned within the report, and not what the corporation did in reality. In addition, it is possible that they have adjusted certain information, or omitted some elements. We admit that if interviews were applied to these organizations results may have been different. Thereof, possibilities for future research related to this theme can be easily expanded.

On the whole, the two compared variables—sustainability integration within project management and projects success—seem to fluctuate in the same trend and there are no significant discrepancies between them (See Figure 3).

However, when performing the computation for Pearson Correlation Coefficient, we obtained a value of 0.38. As this result approaches 0, it can represent evidence for non-correlation. In addition, we explain this outcome from the perspective of imperfect disclosure, as corporations may offset certain elements by omission.

Table 5 presets our results from the state perspective. The figures provide evidence for the correlation between the analysed variables. Figure 4 best illustrates this correlation for the 10 countries implied in our study: United Kingdom, Germany, South Africa, Switzerland, Denmark, USA, Canada, Netherlands, Finland, and Brazil.

Table 6 shows the correlation by sectors of activity: information technology, chemicals, mining, banking and assurance, electricity, commu-

Figure 3. Correlation between sustainability integration within project management and projects success (Source: developed by the authors)

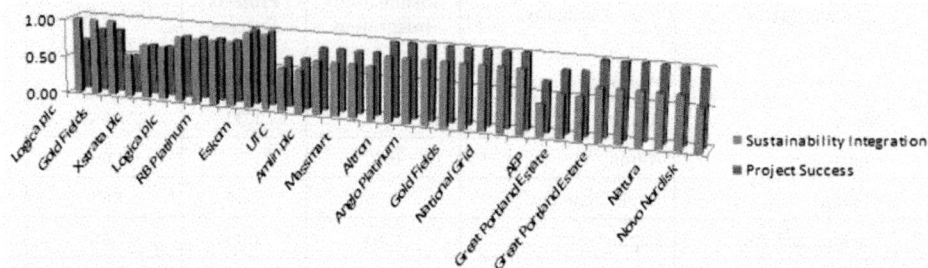

Table 5. Correlation by country

Country	Sustainability Integration	Projects Success
UK	8.57	9.33
Germany	1.71	1.83
South Africa	10.57	11.67
Switzerland	0.71	0.67
Denmark	1.57	2.00
USA	1.00	1.33
Canada	0.57	0.67
Netherlands	0.86	1.00
Finland	0.71	1.00
Brazil	0.71	1.00

Source: authors' own calculations

Figure 4. Sustainability integration and projects success at state level (Source: developed by the authors)

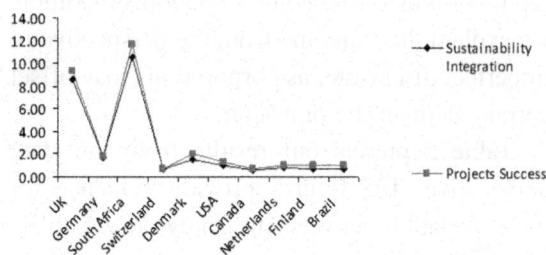

nication, medicine, aerospace, agriculture, retail, construction, electronics, real estate and cosmet-

ics. High correlation is indeed registered from an industry perspective, as it results from Figure 5.

The current research findings illustrate that the best solution for successful projects is represented by sustainability. Therefore, we highly recommend corporations to adopt and improve sustainability policies and integrate them within project management. Our results demonstrate that sustainable project management leads to success. A secondary recommendation or advice would

Table 6. Correlation by industry (Source: author's own calculations)

Industry	Sustainability Integration	Projects Success
Information Technology	1.86	1.50
Chemicals	1.71	1.83
Mining	6.43	6.83
Banking and insurance	3.71	4.33
Electricity	3.71	4.33
Communication	0.86	0.83
Medicine	1.57	2.00
Aerospace	0.57	0.67
Agriculture	0.57	0.67
Retail	0.71	0.83
Construction	0.71	0.83
Electronics	2.57	3.00
Real Estate	1.29	1.83
Cosmetics	0.71	1.00

Figure 5. Correlation from industry perspective (Source: developed by the authors)

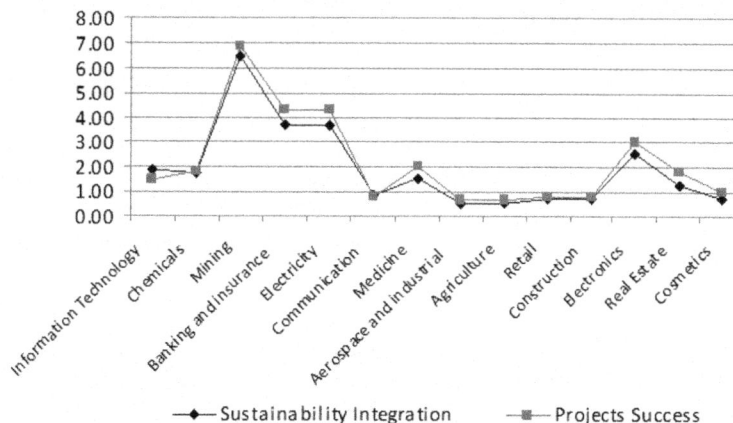

be made in terms of disclosure items. In our view, organizations should focus more on the elements they disclose and the modality in which information is presented or mentioned. This has to be made in a clear, concise and precise way, and main outlines should not be, by any means, omitted, especially when project management involved. In this respect, we consider that even for integrated reports, there is place for improvements to be made and progress still can be done from corporate disclosure perspectives.

FUTURE RESEARCH DIRECTIONS

The main purpose of this Chapter was to present the influence of sustainability integration in project management on the degree of project success. The results showed a direct link between sustainability and the success in project management. Therefore, sustainability practice contributes to successful outcomes and achievements. We consider that the corporate behaviour of integrating sustainability within project management is meant to emerge in future successful projects. Given the demonstrated benefits provided by sustainability integration, we can assume that companies will reclassify their policies regarding sustainability. Thereof, it is

likely for us to witness a change in perspective, and a revolution in the near future as globalization will contribute to the new tendencies of sustainable project management to expand worldwide.

We discussed sustainability as a solution for successful project management. Improvements in sustainability information could be measured further in future studies on the background of the information published in annual reports. Research should be expanded in the direction of feedback received from users of reports and stakeholders, so disclosure quality and reporting transparency is critical for any case study. Thereof, we highly encourage future research in the field of sustainability and project management that should contribute to the development of attitudes, behaviour, and finally accountability regarding sustainable development. Studies on sustainability reporting practice and disclosure as well as project management interference ought to be considered a valuable contribution to both international literatures in the sphere of sustainable project management and on a practical scale, influencing organizations in acting in a responsible way towards people, planet and profit.

In order to be validated, our model of correlating sustainability integration into project management with measurement of project success has to be continuously tested on enlarged samples and populations. By underlining the benefits of sustainable project management, corporations will become aware of the importance of sustainability and will be more motivated to implement or improve sustainable practice.

RESEARCH LIMITATIONS

This research is not meant to observe the physical behaviour of corporations in terms of adopting sustainability for project management purposes, but to concentrate only on the disclosure aspects. This means that we cannot be sure that a certain company complies with the information presented in the integrated report, and is possible that they do not include all the mentioned elements regarding sustainability. However, we can only rely on those facts published in annual reports, as evidence for our case study. Therefore, we investigate the information presented in 35 integrated reports in search for elements that prove the integration of sustainability practice into project management and show measurements of projects success.

Our sample is subject to geographical bias, as 75% of the companies are headquartered in South Africa and United Kingdom. This homogenous distribution is explained by the limited access to reports in English, state implication or pressure regarding sustainability information and its integration within the annual report, the industry factor (e.g. oil and gas companies are more willing to demonstrate their sustainability with respect to environment), and ultimately corporations' attitude towards stakeholders and the importance and relevance attributed to non-financial information in connection with the financial aspects.

CONCLUSION

The main purpose of this chapter has been to discuss the integration of sustainability within project management as a determinant of project success. We assumed that there is a correlation between sustainable project management and successful projects. The methodology for testing our hypothesis involved determination of the level for sustainability integration within project management as well as measurement of success scales for a sample of 35 integrated annual reports. We provided a background of studies and books as well as other sources from literature that represented the starting point for our research. Scholars and academics worldwide presented the concept of sustainability, integrated reporting, disclosure and project management by emphasis on case studies that illustrate their purpose and importance. We also noted the issues, controversies, and items that interrelate with our main objective, mentioning research limitation in terms of analysis upon corporate disclosure; thereof we investigated only what corporations have communicated through their annual reports and it is possible for omissions or misinterpretations to have occurred.

Our findings suggest strong correlations for the criteria of country and industry, while the general study on corporations has issued certain controversies. We identified cases when successful projects were not necessarily induced by sustainability, and the other way around, sustainable practice did not lead to success. We concluded that there should be other factors influencing projects outcomes, either by contributing to a higher success level, or by contracting it and thus reducing the scale of successful projects.

Finally, we argue that further research development is needed and the current study could represent an initial step in finding the road to sustainable project management, by harmonizing profit—in terms of corporate interests, with people and planet- environmental and social aspects of sustainability.

REFERENCES

Adams, S., & Simnett, R. (2011). Integrated reporting: An opportunity for Australia's not-for-profit sector. *Australian Accounting Review, 21*(3), 292–301. doi:10.1111/j.1835-2561.2011.00143.x.

Azcárate, F., Carrasco, F., & Fernández, M. (2011). The role of integrated indicators in exhibiting business contribution to sustainable development: A survey of sustainability reporting initiatives. *Spanish Accounting Review, 14*, 213–240.

Benoît, C., & Niederman, G. V. (2010). *Social sustainability assessment literature review*. Measurement Science.

Brent, A., & Labuschagne, C. (2006). Social indicators for sustainable project and technology life cycle management in the process industry. *The International Journal of Life Cycle Assessment, 11*(1), 3–15. doi:10.1065/lca2006.01.233.

Brown Gooding, S. (n.d.). One company's shift to integrated reporting. *Communication World*. Retrieved from www.iabc.com/cw

D'Amato, A., Henderson, S., & Florence, S. (2009). *Corporate social responsibility and sustainable business- A guide to leadership tasks and functions*. Greensboro, NC: CCL Press.

Dam, L. (2008). *Corporate social responsibility and financial markets*. (Unpublished doctoral dissertation). University of Rijks. Groningen, The Netherlands.

Deloitte. (2011). *Integrated reporting: A better view?*. Deloitte.

Delone, W. H., & McLean, E. R. (2003). Model of information systems success: A ten-year update. *Journal of Management Information Systems, 19*(4), 9–30.

Dempsey, N., Bramley, G., Powe, S., & Brown, C. (2011). The social dimension of sustainable development: Defining urban social sustainability. *Sustainable Development, 19*(5), 289–300. doi:10.1002/sd.417.

Eccles, R.G., Krzus, M.P., & Tapscott, D. (2010). *One report: Integrated reporting for sustainable strategy.*

Fonseca, A., Macdonald, A., Dandy, E., & Valenti, P. (2011). The state of sustainability reporting at Canadian universities. *International Journal of Sustainability in Higher Education, 12*(1). doi:10.1108/14676371111098285.

Gary, C.M., Fagerström, A., & Hassel, L.G. (n.d.). Accounting for sustainability: What's next? A research agenda. *The Annals of the University of Oradea: Economic Sciences, 1*, 97-111.

Godschalk, S. K. B. (2011). *An assessment of the relationship between environmental and financial reporting by South African listed companies in the mining sector*. (Unpublished doctoral dissertation). University of Pretoria. Pretoria, South Africa.

Hansmann, R. (2010). Sustainability learning: An introduction to the concept and its motivational aspects. *Sustainability, 2*(9), 2873–2897. doi:10.3390/su2092873.

Harvard Business School. (2010, October). *A workshop on integrated reporting- Framework and action plan*. Boston: Harvard.

Hossain, M., Islam, K., & Andrew, J. (2006). Corporate social and environmental disclosure in developing countries: Evidence from Bangladesh. In *Proceedings of the Asian Pacific Conference on International Accounting Issues*. Hawaii, HI: IEEE.

Htaybat, K. (2011). Corporate online reporting in 2010: A case study in Jordan. *Journal of Financial Reporting and Accounting, 9*(1).

Kolk, A. (2003). Trends in sustainability reporting by the fortune global 250. *Business Strategy and the Environment, 12*(5), 279–291. doi:10.1002/bse.370.

Kranjac, M., Henny, C., & Sikimić, U. (2011). European funds as fact of sustainable development in central eastern European countries. *Economics and Organization, 8*(3), 301–312.

Kuhlman, T., & Farrington, J. (2010). What is sustainability? *Sustainability, 2*(11), 3436–3448. doi:10.3390/su2113436.

Loo, R. (2003). A multi-level casual model for best practices in project management. *Benchmarking: An International Journal, 10*, 29–36. doi:10.1108/14635770310457520.

Marx, B., & Dyk, V. (2011). Sustainability reporting and assurance: An analysis of assurance practices in South Africa. *Meditari Accountancy Research, 19*(1).

Michael, J. (2009). *Best practice CR&S reporting in the real estate industry.* (Unpublished master's thesis). Ryeron University, Toronto, Canada.

Michelon, G. (2007). *Sustainability disclosure and reputation: A comparative study.* Paper presented at the IV Workshop on Disclosure to Financial Markets. Padova, Italy.

Nidumolu, R., Prahalad, C. K., & Rangaswami, M. R. (2009). Why sustainability is now the key driver of innovation. *Harvard Business Review.*

Oberholzer, A. (n.d.). Integrated reporting: Why should you care? *Communication World.* Retrieved from www.iabc.com/cw

Riemer, S., & Meyer, S. (2009, October 15). Integrating sustainability in project management- A practical approach. *Strategies to Sustainability.*

Sijtsma, F. (2006). *Project evaluation, sustainability and accountability.* REG- publication 27.

Sustainability SA. (n.d.). Retrieved from http://www.sustainabilitysa.org/IntegratedReporting/ReferenceSourcesonIntegratedReporting.aspx

Tovey, H. (2009). Sustainability: A platform for debate. *Sustainability, 1*(1), 14–18. doi:10.3390/su1010014.

Uwuigbe, U., Uwuigbe, O., & Aiayi, A. O. (2011). Corporate social responsibility disclosures by environmentally visible corporations: A study of selected firms in Nigeria. *European Journal of Business and Management, 3*(9), 9–17.

Van Der Merwe, S., & Bussin, M. (2006). An evaluation of a communication, facilitation and project management tool to enhance the effectiveness of project execution. *Journal of Human Resource Management, 4*(3), 48–54.

Weingaertner, C., & Moberg, A. (2011). Exploring social sustainability: Learning from perspectives on urban development and companies and products. *Sustainable Development, 10.*

ADDITIONAL READING

Bellringer, A., Ball, A., & Craig, R. (2011). Reasons for sustainability reporting by New Zealand local governments. *Sustainability Accounting, Management and Policy Journal, 2*(1).

Clarkson, P. M., Li, Y., Richardson, G. D., & Vasvari, V. P. (2007). Revisiting the relation between environmental performance and environmental disclosure: An empirical analysis. *Accounting, Organizations and Society*.

Eccles, R. G., Cheng, B., & Saltzman, D. (2010). *The landscape of integrated reporting: Reflections and next steps*. Boston: Harvard Business School.

Eccles, R. G., Krzus, M. P., & Tapscott, D. (2010). One report: Integrated reporting for sustainable strategy. ISBN: 978-0-470-58751-5

Fahmi, F. M., & Omar, N. (2005). Corporate reporting on minority shareholders information and its implication on shareholders activism in Malaysia. *Journal of Financial Reporting and Accounting*, *3*(1). doi:10.1108/19852510580000335.

Freedman, M., & Stagliano, A. J. (2004). Environmental reporting and the resurrection of social accounting. *Advances in Public Interest Accounting, 10*.

Gray, R. (2006). Social, environmental and sustainability reporting and organisational value creation? Whose value? Whose creation? *Accounting, Auditing & Accountability Journal*, *19*(6), 793–819. doi:10.1108/09513570610709872.

Jara, E. G., Ebrero, A. C., & Zapata, R. E. (2011). Effect of international financial reporting standards on financial information quality. *Journal of Financial Reporting and Accounting*, *9*(2). doi:10.1108/19852511111173121.

Jones, K. L. (2010). The game of fraudulent financial reporting: Accounting for ethics. *Advances in Public Interest Accounting, 15*.

Lamoreaux, M. G. (2010, August). Accounting groups back integrating sustainability, financial reports. *Journal of Accountancy*.

Selvi, Y., Wagner, E., & Türel, A. (2010). Corporate social responsibility in the time of financial crisis: Evidence from Turkey. *Annales Universitatis Apulensis Series Oeconomica*, *12*(1), 281–290.

Tsalavoutas, I. (2009). *The adoption of IFRS by Greek listed companies: Financial statements effects, level of compliance and value relevance*. Edinburgh, UK: The University of Edinburgh.

KEY TERMS AND DEFINITIONS

Corporate Disclosure: Consists of the main tool of communication between companies and users or stakeholders, by publishing or presenting information within available sources, such as annual reports, sustainability reports, CSR reports, Websites, press, etc.

Integrated Reporting: Can be defined as the new attitude towards reporting in which financial information is synchronised with the non-financial one in a concise, clear and precise way, eliminating ambiguities from classical reports.

Project Management: Represents the process of planning, implementing, monitoring and controlling of activities and resources with the purpose of fulfilling targets and objectives.

Project Success: Represents the full achievement of all targets and objectives established in the initial stage of a project.

Sustainability: Refers to the state of harmonizing people, planet and profit by integrating economic, social and environmental interests as a result of organizations' accountability and corporate responsibility.

Sustainability Integration: Means the process of integrating sustainability elements within an established framework.

Sustainable Project Management: Can be outlined as the procedure of integrating sustainability and sustainable development into project management and enhancing long-term benefits.

ENDNOTES

[1] Nevertheless, the environmental aspect is regarded as part of the social pillar.

Section 2
Integrating Sustainability into Project Management

Chapter 8
Re–Thinking Project Initiation and Project Management by Considering Principles of Sustainable Development

Roland Gareis
WU Vienna, Austria & Roland Gareis Consulting, Austria

ABSTRACT

Project initiation and project management are specific processes of the project-oriented company. In order to improve the performance of these processes in their descriptions as well as in the design of the methods to be applied, the principles of sustainable development can be considered. Templates for some project initiation and project management methods considering SD principles are provided. This chapter is based on the results of the Research Project: SustPM, which was completed in May 2012. The overall research results are published by PMI in the book Project Management & Sustainable Development Principles by Roland Gareis, Martina Huemann, and André Martinuzzi (all WU Vienna)[1].

INTRODUCTION

In this chapter the objectives, tasks, and the responsibilities for the project initiation process[2] and the project management process are described. Sustainable development as a societal concept is introduced and its transfer to companies is reflected. The demand to operationalize SD for companies by applying its principles in processes and projects is defined. Basic SD principles, namely values-based, economic, ecologic, and social oriented, short-term, mid-term, and long-term oriented as well as local, regional, and global oriented, are described and considered in the project initiation process as well as in the project management process. It is argued, that considering SD principles results in an improved quality of these processes. For the application of some methods considering SD principles templates are provided.

SD is perceived as a new management paradigm to cope with the complexity and dynamics of organizations. It is of relevance for permanent but also for temporary organizations, i.e. for projects and programs.

DOI: 10.4018/978-1-4666-4177-8.ch008

PROJECT INITIATION PROCESS AND PROJECT MANAGEMENT PROCESS

Project initiation and project management are specific processes of the project-oriented company. A diferentiation between the project initiation process and the project management process is necessary, as these processes have different objectives, different tasks, and require different organizations for their performances.

Project Initiation Process

The project initiation process is a process belonging to the group of project portfolio management processes. The initiation of a new project adds to an existing project portfolio of a company and therefore has to be analyzed within this context.

The objectives of the project initiation process are to decide if an investment is to be made or not, and to decide about the appropriate organization for initiating the investment. This can be the base organization of a company, a project, a chain of projects, a network of projects or a program (of projects). The tasks of the project initiation process are to analyze an investment, to make a decision regarding the realization of an investment, to define the organization, which shall initiate the investment, to make a decision regarding the appropriate organization, to initiate the investment with, and to assign a manager and a team with a project or a program (Gareis 2005: 447).

The project initiation process starts with the formulation of a need or an opportunity for an investment, and ends with the assignment of a project to a project manager or a project team (Gido/Clements 2008; Samset 2008; Wijnen/Kor 2000: 89). Problem formulation, investment analysis, understanding stakeholders´ views, investment decisions, and project definition are mentioned as tasks to be accomplished in the project initiation phase (Samset 2008). Figure 1

shows the tasks of the project initiation process. The project initiation process is performed by a project initiation team, which is assigned by an investment promoter (See Figure 2).

Outputs of the project initiation process are the investment analysis, the investment decision, the organization decision, the rough project management plan, and the project charter.

The project initiation process is performed by a project initiation team, which is assigned by an investment promoter (Figure 2). The investment promoter, who is interested in the investment, assigns a project initiation team. In the design of the project initiation process, the members of the project initiation team, the communication structures, and the methods to be applied in the process have to be defined. It also has to be assured that the values of the organizations and the individuals involved in the project initiation process fit.

Project Management Process

Project management is a management process to be differentiated from the content-related processes of a project. The project management process includes the sub-processes project planning, project executing, project monitoring and controlling, and project closing, and possibly resolving a project discontinuity.

The objectives of the project management process are to perform the project according to the project objectives, contribute to the optimization of the results of the investment initiated by the project, and manage the project complexity as well as the project dynamics by adjusting the project boundaries, and managing the project-context relationships (Andersen 2008; Gareis 2005; Sahlin-Andersson/Söderholm 2002). The project management process starts when the project has been assigned by the project sponsor to the project manager or the project team, and ends after the closing sub-process with the project approval by the project sponsor (See Figure 3). The

Figure 1. Project initiation process (Gareis, et al., 2013)

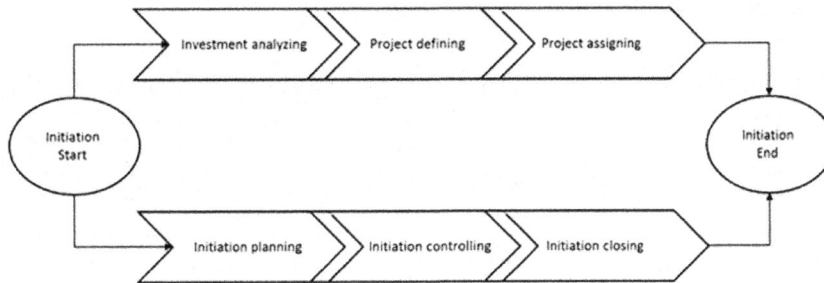

Figure 2. Responsibility matrix of the project initiation process (Gareis, et al., 2013)

Responsibility / Tasks	Investment Promoter	Initiation Team	PM Office	Investment Decision Committee	Project portfolio Group	Expert Pool Managers	Project / Program Sponsor	Project / Program Manager	Representatives important stakeholder
Investment analysis									
Gathering information about investment and alternatives	C	P							C
Development business case, cost benefit analysis etc.		P							
Analysing relationships to other investments		P							
Developing the investment proposal		P	C						
Performing investment decision meeting		C		P					C
Communicating investment decision	I	I		P	I				I
Project defining									
Development PM plan draft including e.g. project objectives, project start and end, project budget, project roles, WBS, bar chart, stakeholder analysis and project contexts		P			C	C			
Development project proposal		P	C		C				
Decision about appropriate project organisation		P	C						
Project assigning									
Assignment project sponsor		P	C		C				
Assignment of project	I						P	C	I

Figure 3. Project management process (Gareis, 2005, p. 58)

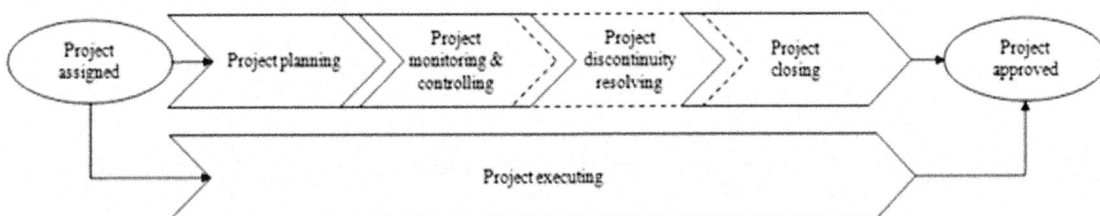

responsibilities for performing the project management process have to be differentiated by the sub-processes. As an example the responsibilities for performing the project planning sub-process are shown in Figure 4.

Traditional project management focuses on the management of the project schedule, costs, and scope (Turner, et al., 2010). The understanding of a project as a social system and temporary organization promotes a more holistic project definition. Not only the project scope, the schedule, and the project costs, but also the project organization and culture, the project personnel and infrastructure, project contexts, such as stakeholders, relationships to the company strategies and to other projects, as well as the design of the project management process are considered in project management.

SUSTAINABLE DEVELOPMENT

Sustainable Development (SD) is a normative concept, which was originally developed for the society overall. The application of the concept for companies is called corporate sustainability or corporate social responsibility. Based on the definition of some general principles of SD the concept cannot only be applied for permanent organizations, but also for temporary organizations, i.e. projects and programs.

Sustainable Development: A Societal Concept

The concept of SD has acquired wide attention following the publication of the so-called Brundtland Report by the World Commission

Figure 4. Responsibility matrix of the project planning process (Gareis, 2005)(P: Performing. I: Being Informed. C: Contributing.)

Tasks	Project sponsor	Project manager	Project team	Project team members	Expert pool manager	Representatives of stakeholders
Preparing the project planning communication						
Checking project assignment and results of the pre-project phase		P				
Selecting project planning communication form		P				
Selecting project team members		P			C	
Selecting PM methods and templates to be used		P				
Agreeing with the project sponsor on start process	C	P				
Preparing project team workshop and project sponsor meeting		P		C		
Inviting project team workshop participants		P		I	C	
Documenting the results of the pre-project phase		P		C		C
Developing drafts of project management documents		P		C		C
Developing information for project team workshop		P		C		
Performing the project planning communication						
Distributing information to project team workshop participants		P		I		I
Performing project team workshop	C		P			C
Further developing the project management documents		P				
Performing project sponsor meeting	C	P		C		C
Follow-up to the project planning communication						
Finalizing the project management documents (PM plan)		P		P		
Agreeing with project sponsor on PM plan	C	P				
Initial project marketing	C	P		C		C
Distributing the PM plan	I	P		I	I	I
Performing first work packages (in parallel)				P		C

for Environment and Development in 1987. The report defines SD as "development that meets the needs of the present without compromising the ability of future generations to meet their own needs" (WCED, 1987, p. 41).

SD is a normative concept (see e.g. Adams 2006; Davidson 2000; Martens 2006; Meadowcroft 2007; Robinson 2004) and thus is representing values and ethical considerations. The basic values of sustainable development are inter and intra-generational equity, transparency, fairness, trust, and innovation (Global Reporting Initiative 2011). These values are defined at a societal level. They cannot be transferred to companies directly, interpretation is required. "Sustainable development when incorporated by the organization is called corporate sustainability and it contains, like sustainable development, all three pillars: economic, ecological and social" (Baumgartner/ Ebner 2010: 77).

During the last years, businesses committed themselves to implement the concept of sustainable development as an active corporate engagement that goes beyond legal compliance. Critiques, such as Porter and Kramer (2011) argue that corporate sustainability initiatives performed by many organizations can be understood as paying a lip service only. Often philanthropic activities are provided in order to do "good" for the society. Serious SD means to integrate SD principles into services, products, and processes of a company, means to "re-think the business".

Principles of Sustainable Development

Although many different definitions of SD can be found in the literature, some basic guiding principles can be identified. Content related definitions and process related definitions of sustainability are differentiated. Content related definitions refer to climate change, clean energy, public health, social inclusion (e.g. EU SDS, 2006). A more generic, process related definition of SD considers the

following SD principles: economic, ecologic, and social oriented, short-term, mid-term, and long-term oriented, local, regional, and global oriented as well as values-based (Gareis et al. 2013).

The attempt to equally consider the three dimensions economic, ecologic, and social is called the 'triple bottom line', which was well established in *Agenda 21*. A holistic understanding of corporate sustainability requires an integration of economic, social, and environmental perspectives (Elkington 1997; Linnenluecke et al. 2009).

The SD of social systems over time and the consideration of the needs of future generations are in direct contradiction with the today's ever shortening time horizon of decision-makers. Sustainability requires the company to be profitable in the long-term (Linnenluecke et al. 2009). For a company to develop sustainably, it becomes necessary to balance its operations across geographic and institutional scales (ranging from the local through national and regional to global) as well as through its entire value chain (see e.g. Hartman 1998; Wolters 2003).

Sustainable Development and Projects

SD is of relevance for different social systems such as societies, regions, and companies, but also for temporary organizations, i.e. for projects and programs. While there has been consideration of SD for companies, projects and programs did not get too much attention.

Some research contributes to the understanding of SD in projects, where the focus lays on the content and the project results. Impact assessments to measure project results have been developed, and the relevance of project management for managing SD projects receives increasing attention in practice and research (Martinuzzi/Krumay 2012). Little attention is paid to the consideration of SD in the project initiation and in the project management process (see also Silvius et al. 2012).

In the *Research Project 'SustPM'* it was argued, that the SD principles, namely economic, ecologic, and social-oriented, short term, mid-term, and long term-oriented, local, regional, and global-oriented, as well as values-based, can be considered in the project initiation process and in the project management process in order to improve the quality of these processes, and by this indirectly improve the quality of the project results (Gareis et al. 2013).

PROJECT INITIATION CONSIDERING SUSTAINABLE DEVELOPMENT PRINCIPLES

In this paragraph concepts and models regarding the consideration of SD principles in the project initiation process are described. Objectives for the design of the project initiation process and for the application of investment analysis and project management methods are defined. A template for the application of the investment analysis considering SD principles is shown.

Design of the Project Initiation Process Considering SD Principles

In the design of the project initiation process, the tasks to be performed, the responsibilities for these tasks, the communication structures, and the methods to be applied in the process are defined. The design of the project initiation process influences its quality and its results. The consideration of SD principles in the project initiation process implies stakeholder participation, the application of a cost-benefit analysis, the analysis of the investment context, a holistic definition of the project boundaries, and the analysis of the different project contexts.

Participation of stakeholders in the project initiation process can ensure good process results and the acceptance of these results by the stakeholders.

Therefore, in the design of the project initiation process, appropriate stakeholder participation has to be organized. Possible forms of stakeholder participation are:

- Periodic stakeholder information about results of the initiation process.
- Invitations of stakeholders to participate in analysis and planning meetings and workshops.
- Invitations of representatives of stakeholders to become members of the initiation team.

In meetings and workshops, representatives of stakeholders can contribute e.g. by providing information, by sharing expectations, by giving feedback to results. A participatory management approach can contribute to the quality of the relationships with the stakeholders, can assure commitment and a better quality of the results, and can reduce risks. In order to assure a transparent decision-making, the decision criteria and the decision-makers shall be defined.

A holistic and consistent application of investment analysis methods and of project management methods is the basis for a good investment decision and a good organization decision. Therefore, in the design of the project initiation process, an appropriate application of investment analysis methods and project management methods is assured.

The basis for considering SD principles in the project initiation process are fitting values of the organizations and of the individuals involved. SD is a values-based concept. The SD principles, namely economic, ecologic, and social-oriented, short term, mid-term, and long term-oriented, local, regional, and global-oriented, as well as additional values such as transparent, empowered, faire, etc. represent a new management paradigm. Therefore, it is challenging to assure fitting values of the organizations and of the individuals involved in the project initiation process. But sharing this set of values is the basis for the consideration of the SD principles in the project initiation process by the project initiation team. The values need to be clarified, interpreted, and communicated to the team members.

In addition to the flow chart and the responsibility matrix shown in Figures 1 and 2, the boundaries and the contexts as well as the consequences of the project initiation process can be described in a process facts sheet (See Figure 5).

Investment Analysis Considering SD Principles

There are investments in new services and products, but also investments in further developments of markets, infrastructures, the organization, personnel, and stakeholder relations. An investment decision is the start event and the completed de-investment can be defined as end event of the investment life cycle.

An investment analysis is the basis for a decision regarding the realization of an investment. The consequences considered, which are caused by

Figure 5. Facts of the project initiation process

Process:	Project Initiation Process		
Process boundaries			
Process start event	Decision to analyze an investment by project initiator	**Process end event**	Project assigned to project manager and to project team by the project sponsor
Economic objectives	• Decision to invest considering investment alternatives and relationships to other investments. • Decision about the appropriate organization (line organization, working group, project, network of projects, program) to implement the investment considering the existing project portfolio. • Assignment of a project sponsor. • Assignment of the project to a project manager and a project team by the project sponsor.		
Ecologic objectives	• Consideration of the local, regional and global ecologic impacts of the investment. • Consideration of the local, regional and global ecologic impacts of the project initiating the investment.		
Social objectives	• Consideration of the local, regional and global social impacts of the investment. • Consideration of the local, regional and global social impacts of the project initiating the investment. • Assuring stakeholder participation in the initiation process		
Non-objectives	• Developing a detailed project management plan for the project to be initiated.		
Process duration	2 weeks to 4 months		
Process costs	20 to 400 person days plus € x.- for other expenses		
Relationship to other processes	Strategic planning, creating an investment idea; project management; investment controlling; project portfolio coordination		

Impact	X short-term	mid-term	long-term	**Interpretation**	
	X local	Regional	global		

Stakeholder		Stakeholder risks
Investment initiator	+	Realization of investment
	-	Not involved in investment decision process
User	+	If involved: support own investment interests
	-	Not involved in decision process
Members of the future project organization	+	Interesting work
	-	Wrong decision about organization form (project / program)
Competitor	+	...
	-	...
Supplier	+	...
	-	...

an investment, influence the investment decision. While traditional investment methods, such as the business case analysis, focus on economic criteria such as costs, cash flows, or amortization rates (Geyer et al. 2003; Hirth 2008), the cost benefit analysis (Drews/Hillebrand 2007; Gareis 2005) and the social cost benefit analysis (Brent 2006) take a more holistic approach and include social aspects. Methods like the environmental impact analysis (Barthwal 2002; Morris/Therivel 1995) focus on ecologic aspects.

If only short to mid-term cash flows of the investor are considered, a different investment decision might result than if long-term costs and benefits of different stakeholders are taken into account. Considering SD principles in the investment analysis means:

- To analyze economic, ecologic, and social costs and benefits of the investment for the investor but also for selected stakeholders.
- To consider short, mid, and long-term consequences of an investment.
- To consider local, regional, as well as global consequences of an investment.
- To use a social discount factor for discounting future costs and benefits in order to consider the interests of future generations.

A template for a holistic investment analysis considering SD principles is shown in Figure 6. The represented holistic approach is based

- On the consideration of the investor's perspective as well as the perspectives of stakeholders.
- On the consideration of costs and benefits relating to the different dimensions of an investor's organization, such as its services and products, technologies, organization, personnel, infrastructure, financing and budget, and its relations with stakeholders.

- On the identification of the consequences of the investment differentiated in economic, ecologic, and social as well as in local, regional, and global.

The identification of these consequences of an investment assures, that these different dimensions are transparent and are considered in the analysis as well as in decision making.

If reasonable the costs and benefits of an investment are to be evaluated monetarily. If this is not possible indicators, to assure quantitative evaluations, but also qualitative descriptions of costs and benefits are to be applied. Monetary and non-monetary decision criteria can be considered in a multi-criteria decision analysis in order to calculate an overall utility ratio of an investment.

An investment should not be analyzed independently from other investments. It can be related to other investments in the investment portfolio of the investor, but also to investments from other organizations. The consideration of relationships of an investment to other investments is important as the costs and the benefits of the considered investment may be influenced by the other investments.

A more detailed description of the features of an investment analysis which considers SD principles can be found in the chapter: *Project initiation – Investment analysis for sustainable development* in this book.

Project Definition Considering SD Principles

The project definition is to be understood as a rough planning of the structures and the contexts of a project to be performed in order to initiate an investment. The project definition determines what a project includes and provides clarity regarding the project boundaries, which arises upon explicit exclusion of those issues that do not belong to the project (Engwall 2003; Sahlin-Andersson/

Figure 6. Investment analysis considering SD principles

Investment Analysis									
Investor's Perspective									
Cost/Benefit Type	Cost Description	Benefit Description	Consequence						Monetary Evaluation
			Economic	Ecologic	Social	Local	Regional	Global	
Services, products									
Technologies									
Organization									
Personnel									
Infrastructure									
Financing, Budget									
Relations to Stakeholders									
Stakeholders' Perspectives									
Stakeholder	Cost Description	Benefit Description	Consequence						Monetary Evaluation
			Economic	Ecologic	Social	Local	Regional	Global	
Stakeholder 1									
Stakeholder 2									
Stakeholder n									
Investment ratios									
Monetary cost-benefit ratio from the investor's perspective:									
Utility ratio from the investor's perspective:									
Monetary cost-benefit ratio including the stakeholders' perspectives:									
Utility ratio including the stakeholders' perspectives:									

Söderholm 2002). In the project initiation process the project management plan for the project to be performed is developed in a rough form. Once the project is assigned, the project management documents are further detailed and possibly additional documents are developed in the starting process.

Project boundaries and project contexts can be defined according to a content, a time, and a social dimension. The content-related project boundary is defined by the project objectives, the objects of consideration and the work breakdown structure. The time-related boundary is defined by the project start and the project end event, and the social-related boundary is defined by the membership in the project organization and by the project culture.

By developing a new product or implementing a new IT application a project delivers a change for the investor. Therefore, all of the dimensions of the identity of an investor organization, which are affected, are to be considered when defining the project scope. Identity dimensions of a company are its services, products and technolo-

gies, its organization, culture and personnel, its infrastructure, budget and financing, as well as the relations to its contexts. All or some of these dimensions might be affected by an investment and therefore have to be considered in the project that is initiating this investment. If measures for dealing with consequences of an investment for stakeholders are considered in the project scope, investor external concerns are internalized.

The project boundaries become clear by differentiating the project from its contexts. The content-related project context is defined by the investment, the strategies of the investor and the relations to other projects. The time-related context is defined by the decisions made in the pre-project phase and the expectations about the post-project phase as well as possibly by chains of projects. The social-related context is defined by the project stakeholders.

The long-term orientation of SD contradicts the short and mid-term orientation of projects and programs. This contradiction can be resolved by understanding that a project contributes to realize long-term investment objectives. A project is supposed to provide results that lead to a positive benefit-cost ratio of the investment. An investment may be initiated by a single project or by a chain of projects. An example for a chain of projects initiating an investment is a conception project followed by an implementation project.

PROJECT MANAGEMENT CONSIDERING SD PRINCIPLES

Relevant dimensions of the project management process for considering SD principles are the process design, the project contexts, and the project structures. Concepts for the design of the project management process and for managing the project contexts and structures are described. Templates for the application of some project management methods considering SD principles are provided.

Design of the Project Management Process Considering SD Principles

In the design of the project management process, the tasks to be performed, the responsibilities for these tasks and the methods to be applied in the process are defined. Outputs of the project management process are the project management documents resulting from the project planning, the project executing, the project monitoring & controlling, and the closing process, the communications of the project organization, and the relationships with project stakeholders.

The consideration of SD principles in the project management process implies stakeholder participation, a holistic and consistent application of project management methods, and the assurance of fitting SD-related values of the involved organizations and individuals. The consideration of SD principles in designing the project management process improves the quality of the process, and by this indirectly improves the quality of the project results.

In the design of the project management process, a consistent application of project management methods is assured. The holistic and consistent application of project management methods ensures the quality of the project management results by traceability and transparency. It allows for structural clearness and thus provides orientation to the members of the project organization.

Projects are complex and dynamic. The selection of adequate working forms to cope with the project complexity is a task in the design of the project management process. Analog working forms, such as systemic constellations, role plays, drawing pictures, etc., can be applied in addition to traditional digital working forms, such as assignments, plans, reports, mails, etc.

In addition to the flow chart and the responsibility matrix shown in Figures 3 and 4, the boundaries and the contexts as well as the consequences of the project management process can be described in a process facts sheet (See Figure 7).

The consideration of SD principles is of relevance for all project management sub-processes, i.e. for project planning, executing, monitoring & controlling, and project closing. Based on the rough project management plan developed in the project initiation process, these project management documents are further detailed and actualized in the project planning. The consideration of SD principles is especially important in project planning. Decisions made in project planning are of relevance for all other project management sub-processes.

Managing Relationships to Project Contexts Considering SD Principles

Project contexts to be considered in project management are the investment, which is initiated by the project, other projects, with which the project has relationships, and project stakeholders.

The success of a project is depending to a high degree on the management of the project stakeholder relations. A project stakeholder analysis considering SD principles includes directly and

Figure 7. Facts of the project management process

Process: Process boundaries	Project Management Process			
Process start event	Project assigned by the project sponsor to the project manager and the project team	**Process end event**	Project approved by the project sponsor	
Economic objectives	• Professional management of the project; efficient performance of the sub-processes project planning, project monitoring & controlling, project executing, and project closing; possibly resolution of a project discontinuity • Management of the project complexity, the project dynamics, and the relationships to project contexts • Optimizing the economic consequences of the investment initiated by the project			
Ecologic objectives	• Considering the (local, regional and global) ecologic consequences of the project • Optimizing the ecologic consequences of the investment initiated by the project			
Social objectives	• Considering the (local, regional and global) social consequences of the project • Assuring stakeholder participation in the project management process • Optimizing the social consequences of the investment initiated by the project			
Non-objectives	• Performing content-related processes (e.g. procurement, engineering)			
Process duration	According to the project duration			
Process costs	• x person days • € y.- for other expenses			
Relationship to other processes	Project initiation, content-related project processes, investment controlling, project portfolio coordination, strategic planning			
Impact	short-term	X mid-term	long-term	**Interpretation**
	X local	Regional	global	

Stakeholder		Stakeholder risks	
Members of the project organization		+	Gaining experience, Take over responsibility
		-	Wrong design of project organization for dealing w/ complexity / dynamic
User		+	Direct influence on project result(s) possible
		-	Participation of project stakeholders not appropriate
Supplier		+	Transparent structures for the cooperation throughout the process
		-	Lack of commitment to the developed project management methods
Competitor		+	...
		-	...
Authorities		+	...
		-	...

indirectly affected stakeholders, considers relationships between stakeholders, and analyzes the impacts of a project for stakeholders. Freeman et al. (2010) differentiate a traditional management of stakeholders approach with a more participatory management for stakeholders approach. The management of stakeholders approach means to consider stakeholders because of their harm potential to the project. The management for stakeholders approach promotes stakeholder engagement and represents a participative understanding.

A project stakeholder analysis explicitly considering economic, ecologic, and social as well as local, regional, and global expectations is introduced in the chapter "Experimenting with project stakeholder analysis: A case study" in this book.

Managing Project Structures Considering SD Principles

Project structures are understood as the project objectives, project strategies, project scope, project schedule, project resources, project budget, project risks, project organization, project culture, project personnel, and project infrastructure (Gareis 2005).

The scope of a project is defined by the objects of consideration, the work breakdown structure, and by work package definitions. A holistic definition of the project scope is based on those identity dimensions of an investor organization, which are affected by an investment, such as services and products, technologies, the organization, personnel, infrastructure, or budgeting and financing. All closely coupled dimensions are to be considered. Figure 8 shows a template of objects of consideration plan, which differentiates relevant objects by the prior identity dimensions and by economic and ecologic consequences.

To ensure a holistic understanding of the content-related project objectives, these are based on the objects of consideration of a project. That means, that the project objectives can be differentiated into services and products-related objectives, technology-related objectives, organization-related objectives, personnel- related objectives, etc.

A differentiation into economic, ecologic, and social-related project objectives further assures the consideration of SD principles. The members of the project organization are not only responsible to achieve the economic objectives, but also the ecologic and social project objectives. Figure 9 shows a template of a project objectives plan considering SD principles.

Realistic and complete project management plans (work breakdown structure, schedule, cost plan, risk plan, etc.) provide a model of the reality to which the members of the project organization shall work. Realistic assumptions and honest reporting meet the values of transparency and fairness in the communication with members of

the project organization and with representatives of projects stakeholders. These project management documents provide orientation to the members of the project organization.

In identifying project risks, a differentiation in economic, ecologic, and social risks as well as in local, regional, and global risks allows for differentiated risk response measures. Not only the risks for a project from the project stakeholders, but also the risks for the project stakeholders are analyzed and managed.

Elements for the organizational design of projects, such as empowerment, integration, and partnering, consider SD principles. Project team members, the project team, and the project overall can be empowered, i.e. to be given decision authorities. An empowered project has a certain autonomy, which also results in a higher responsibility of the members of the project organization. A project organization that integrates representatives of stakeholders allows for coping with the complexity and the dynamics of the project. Common project objectives, common project documents, and common communication structures promote the quality of the cooperation in the project.

The project sponsor, the project manager, and the project team members have responsibilities for considering SD principles in projects. An

Figure 8. Objects of consideration plan considering SD principle (Gareis, et al., 2013)

Objects of Consideration				
Object type	Object		Con-sequence	
			Economic	*Ecologic*
Services and products	• ...		...	...
Technologies	• ...		...	...
Organization	• ...		...	...
Personnel	• ...		...	...
Infrastructure (buildings, rooms, ICT)	• ...		...	...
Budgeting and financing	• ...		...	...

Figure 9. Project objectives plan considering SD principles (Gareis, et al., 2013)

Project Objectives Plan		
Objective	**Con-sequence**	
	Economic	*Ecologic*
Services and products-related project objectives		
• …		
Technology –related project objectives		
• …		
Organization-related objectives		
•		
Personnel-related objectives		
•		
Infrastructure (buildings, rooms, ICT) –related project objectives		
• …		
Budgeting and financing-related objectives		
Stakeholder-related project objectives (**social**)		
…		

integration of these responsibilities in the project role descriptions provides orientation to the role players and contributes to the operationalization of SD principles.

CONCLUSION

SD can be perceived as a new management paradigm that is not only of relevance for permanent organizations, such as companies or divisions of companies, but also for temporary organizations contributing to the survival of companies, i.e. projects and programs. Principles of SD, namely values-based, economic, ecologic, and social oriented, short-term, mid-term, and long-term oriented as well as local, regional, and global oriented, can be considered in the project initiation process and in the project management process in order to improve the quality of these processes.

The differentiation between the project initiation process and the project management process is necessary, as these processes have different objectives, different tasks, and different organizations for their performance. The objectives of the project initiation process are to decide if an investment is to be made or not, and to make a decision about the appropriate organization for initiating the investment. The objectives of the project management process are to successfully perform a project according to the project objectives, contribute to the optimization of the results of the investment initiated by the project, and manage the project complexity as well as the project dynamics. From the point of view of SD the project initiation process is more important than the project management process, given that the strategic investment and organization decisions are made in this process.

REFERENCES

Adams, W. M. (2006). *The future of sustainability: Re-thinking environment and development in the twenty-first century. The World Conservation Union*. IUCN.

Andersen, E. (2008). *Rethinking project management–An organisational perspective*. FT Press.

Barthwal, R. R. (2002). *Environmental impact assessment*. New Delhi: New Age International.

Baumgartner, R. J., & Ebner, D. (2010). Corporate sustainability strategies: Sustainability profiles and maturity levels. *Sustainable Development, 18*(2), 76–89. doi:10.1002/sd.447.

Brent, R. (2006). *Applied cost-benefit analysis.* Cheltenham, UK: Edward Elgar Publishing Limited.

Davidson, J. (2000). Sustainable development: Business as usual or a new way of living? *Environmental Ethics, 22*(1), 45–71.

Drews, G., & Hillebrand, N. (2007). *Lexikon der projektmanagement-methoden.* Haufe Verlag.

Elkington, J. (1997). *Cannibals with forks: The triple bottom line of 21st century business.* Oxford, UK: Capstone Publishing Limited.

Engwall, M. (2003). No project is an island: linking projects to history and context. *Research Policy, 32*(5), 789–808. doi:10.1016/S0048-7333(02)00088-4.

European Council. (2006). *Review of the EU sustainable development strategy (EU SDS – renewed strategy).* European Council.

Freeman, R. E., Harrison, J. S., Wicks, A. C., Parmar, B. L., & De Colle, S. (2010). *Stakeholder theory: The state of the art.* Cambridge, UK: Cambridge University Press. doi:10.1017/CBO9780511815768.

Gareis, R. (2005). *Happy projects!* Vienna: Manz.

Gareis, R., Huemann, M., Martinuzzi, A., Weninger, C., & Sedlacko, M. (2013). *Project management & sustainable development principles.* Newtown Square, PA: Project Management Institute.

Geyer, A., Hanke, M., Littich, E., & Nettekoven, M. (2003). *Grundlagen der finanzierung.* Linde.

Gido, J., & Clements, J. P. (2008). *Successful project management.* South-Western Pub..

Global Reporting Initiative. G. (2011). Sustainability reporting guidelines version 3.1. Amsterdam, The Netherlands: Global Reporting Initiative.

Hartman, F. (1998). *The nature and role of projects in the next 20 years: Research issues and problems.* Calgary, Canada: Project Management Specialization, University of Calgary.

Hirth, H. (2008). *Grundzüge der finanzierung und investition.* München, Germany: Oldenbourg Wissenschaftsverlag GmbH..

Linnenluecke, M. K., Russell, S. V., & Griffiths, A. (2009). Subcultures and sustainability practices: The impact on understanding corporate sustainability. *Business Strategy and the Environment, 18*(7), 432–452. doi:10.1002/bse.609.

Martens, P. (2006). Sustainability: Science or fiction? *Sustainability: Science Practice and Policy, 2*(1), 36–41.

Martinuzzi, A., & Krumay, B. (2012). The good, the bad and the successful - How CSR leads to competitive advantage and organizational transformation. *Journal of Organizational Change Management.*

Meadowcroft, J. (2007). Who is in charge here? Governance for sustainable development in a complex world. *Journal of Environmental Policy and Planning, 9*(3), 299–314. doi:10.1080/15239080701631544.

Morris, P., & Therivel, R. (1995). *Methods of environmental impact assessment.* Vancouver, Canada: University of British Columbia Press.

Porter, M. E., & Kramer, M. R. (2011). The big idea: Creating shared value. *Harvard Business Review, 89*(1-2).

Robinson, J. (2004). Squaring the circle? Some thoughts on the idea of sustainable development. *Ecological Economics*, *48*(4), 369–384. doi:10.1016/j.ecolecon.2003.10.017.

Sahlin-Andersson, K., & Söderholm, A. (2002). *Beyond project management: New perspectives on the temporary-permanent dilemma.* Malmö: Liber.

Samset, K. (2008). How to overcome major weaknesses in mega-projects: The Norwegian approach. In Decision-making on mega-projects: Cost-benefit analysis, planning and innovation, (pp. 173-188).

Silvius, G., Van den Brink, J., Schipper, R., Köhler, A., & Planko, J. (2012). *Sustainability in project management*. Gower.

Turner, R. J., Huemann, M., Anbari, F. T., & Bredillet, C. N. (2010). *Perspectives on projects*. New York: Routledge.

Wijnen, G., & Kor, R. (2000). *Managing unique assignments: A team approach to projects and programmes*. Aldershot, UK: Gower.

Wolters, T. (2003). Transforming international product chains into channels of sustainable production: The imperative of sustainable chain management. *Greener Management International*, *43*, 6–13.

World Commission on Environment and Development. (1987). *Our common future*. Oxford, UK: World Commission on Environment and Development.

ENDNOTES

[1] The concepts introduced in this chapter are based on the results of the Research Project: SustPM. This project was performed between January 2010 and May 2012 in cooperation between the PROJEKTMANAGEMENT GROUP, WU Vienna and the Research Institute for Managing Sustainability, WU Vienna. The objectives of this research project were to analyze the consideration of Sustainable Development (SD) principles in international project management standards, to develop hypotheses and models regarding the consideration of SD principles in the project initiation process and in the project management process, and to interpret quality improvements achieved by considering SD principles in the project initiation process and in the project management process. The results of the research project are published by PMI in the book *Project Management & Sustainable Development Principles* by Roland Gareis, Martina Huemann, and Andrè Martinuzzi with the assistance of Claudia Weninger and Michal Sedlacko.

[2] The consideration of SD principles applies to projects but also to programs. To make the reading of this text easier only projects are addressed. Therefore, the process "project initiation" is not called "project or program initiation".

Chapter 9
Project Initiation:
Investment Analysis for Sustainable Development

Claudia Weninger
WU Vienna, Austria

Martina Huemann
WU Vienna, Austria

ABSTRACT

The consideration of Sustainable Development (SD) becomes more and more important for investments and the projects which implement those investments. In the project initiation process, the decision regarding the realization of an investment is made. Analyzing the investment is one of the main tasks of the project initiation process. Thus, this process is identified as most important for the integration of SD principles. The authors define SD with the following principles: economic, ecologic, and social-orientation; short, mid, and long term orientation as well as local, regional, and global-orientation. Furthermore, SD is value-based and considers values such as transparency, fairness, trust, etc. In this chapter, the authors describe the concept of responsible and ethical investment, which may also provide the basis for an investment decision within a project's initiation. While global project and program management standards show very limited consideration of comprehensive investment analysis, the authors draw on the Logical Framework Approach used by the World Bank to see how SD principles are considered in investment analysis methods. They then propose the integration of SD principles into the discipline of project initiation. This more holistic approach considers the investment life cycle, the consideration of different stakeholders, and investment method, which explicitly integrates SD principles.

DOI: 10.4018/978-1-4666-4177-8.ch009

INTRODUCTION

The Brundtland Report defines Sustainable Development (SD) as "development that meets the needs of the present without compromising the ability of future generations to meet their own needs" (World Commission on Environment and Development 1987: 41). The challenge lays in operationalizing the meaning of SD for projects which are per definition temporary and only of short to mid-term duration, while SD is long term oriented.

The long term perspective can be brought into projects, when considering the investment initiated by the project. Gareis et al. (2013) propose that the highest potential of influence to consider SD in a project is taken in the project initiation process, when the investment decision is taken. Thus it is essential that SD principles are considered in the investment analysis to take an adequate decision and to contribute to the SD of the investor´s organization and other relevant stakeholders.

In the context of project management, process related rather than content related definitions of SD are of relevance, therefore we consider the SD principles (Gareis et al. 2013) economic, ecologic and social-orientation; short, mid and long term-orientation; local, regional and global-orientation as well as values-based as those principles relevant for SD in the initiation of a project.[1]

We analyzed project and program management standards such as PMBOK® Guide, the Standard for Program Management (both Project Management Institute 2008a), PRINCE 2, Managing Successful Programmes (both Office of Government Commerce 2009) as well as ICB (International Project Management Association 2006) for their explicit and implicit consideration of SD principles in the investment analysis. We found little evidence of considering SD principles, therefore we turned to the Logical Framework Approach (*LFA*) (Norad 1999; The World Bank 1997), used by the World Bank, to see what we can learn from the initiation of development projects regarding investment analysis.

Typical investment analysis methods only focus on economic aspects, and are therefore rather limited. We discuss different investment analysis methods such as business case analysis, cost benefit analysis, social cost benefit analysis as well as the environmental impact analysis and see how SD principles are considered.

Based on the concept of responsible investment and what we could learn from the initiation of development projects, we propose a more holistic project investment analysis which considers SD principles. We argue that it is not enough to consider SD principles only in the investment analysis itself, but also the consideration of different stakeholder perspectives in the investment decision is essential.

This chapter is structured as following. First, we clarify the term investment as well as responsible and ethical investment. Then we discuss the difference between project and investment and introduce the project initiation process and important investment analysis methods. After briefly presenting our analyses results of project and program management standards, we more describe the *LFA* and analyze how SD principles are considered in the initiation of development projects. Then we indicate potentials to implement SD principles in the investment life cycle and propose a more holistic approach of project initiation, which considers the investment method as well as the design of the initiation process of a project.

INVESTMENT AND PROJECT

Investment

Different definitions of the term *investment* exist. Traditionally, the finance sectors defines investments very narrowly as "the purchase of a financial product or other item of value with an expectation of favorable future returns. In general terms, investment means the use of money in the hope of making more money (Webfinance 2010).

The business sector describes it as the purchase or development of a product or service with the hope of improving future business (Investorwords 2011). Investments are characterized by a number of payments and can be perceived as long-term investigation in real assets e.g. investments in buildings, machines and also in customer relationships or products (Gareis 2005). Organizations invest in objects because they expect the financial returns from the investment to be greater than the money they invested initially (Mills/Turner 1995: 3).

Responsible and Ethical INVESTMENT

In the 1970s the concept of responsible investments was developed by societal and environmental activists in the United States. Responsible investments are defined as *"[…] the integration of Environmental, Societal, and Governance (ESG) issues into investment decision-making"* (Louche/Lydenberg 2011: 2). This approach is mostly used by the finance sector for monetary investments. The key characteristics of responsible investments can be defined as following (Louche/Lydenberg 2011: 17)

- *Responsible investment encourages a long-term perspective […]*
- *RI adopts a stakeholder perspective […]*
- *Responsible investment encourages interaction between society and corporation […]*

Furthermore Louche and Lydenberg (2011) defined four different motivations for using the concept of responsible investments. The first motivation is avoiding profiting from unethical behavior, the second is to encourage corporations to enter positive business lines or to develop strong stakeholder relations. Furthermore responsible investments avoid underperforming stocks and seek to change the corporate behavior.

In 2005 UN General Secretary Kofi Annan invited representatives of the biggest global investors to develop responsible investment principles (PRI). The principles were developed between 2005 and 2006 in workshops and individual works. The result of this development process was a list of principles that are used as guiding principles for responsible investments. These are (UN Global Compact/UNEP Finance Initiative 2006: 6):

- *We will incorporate ESG[2] issues into investment analysis and decision-making processes.*
- *We will be active owners and incorporate ESG issues into our ownership policies and practices.*
- *We will seek appropriate disclosure on ESG issues by the entities in which we invest.*
- *We will promote acceptance and implementation of the Principles within the investment industry.*
- *We will work together to enhance our effectiveness in implementing the Principles.*
- *We will each report on our activities and progress towards implementing the Principles.*

For all principles different actions and measures were defined. The use of these guiding principles is optional for companies but increased attention is observable in the business sector.

In addition to the concept of responsible investments the concept of ethical investments was developed. Ethical investment combines the model of sustainability, environment, responsibility and ethics in its overall process and in the investment methods (O'rourke 2003). These investments are defined as "[…] the integration of personal values, social considerations and economic factors into the investment decision" (Michelson et al. 2004: 1).

The concepts of responsible investment as well as ethical investment focuses both on the integration of SD in the investment analysis method as well as in its overall processes. The concept of responsible investment is more holistic and should be integrated in all organizational units of a company. While responsible investments focus on environmental, social and governance issues the concept of ethical investment focuses also on the integration of personal values such as fairness in the investment decision. Furthermore ethical investments have a big focus on responsibility (regarding stakeholder, the environment, etc.) and ethics. One big difference is that UN Global Compact developed responsible investment principles and therefore made them more visible for the business sector. Companies can use the principles as guiding principles for the integration of responsible investments in the company. Furthermore they can use these guiding principles for the realization of more sustainable investments initiated by projects.

Both concepts can be used as basis for the integration of SD principles into the project initiation.

Differentiating Investment and Project

In literature different understandings of projects exist. We use the definition provided by Gareis (2005: 41) who defines a project is a temporary organization for the performance of a relatively unique, short to medium term strategic business process of medium or large scope. It is perceived as a social system and social construct.

In project management literature the project and the investment is often not differentiated. This differentiation is important because the management of the investment and the management of a project require different processes, roles and methods. Furthermore this differentiation allows to clearly differentiating between the project initiation process, the project management process and the investment life cycle. In general the project initiation process includes two main decisions. First, a decision regarding the realization of an investment and second the decision regarding

the organization form in which the investment is to be initiated (Gareis 2005). Both processes (project initiation and project management) are business processes. These processes fulfill different objectives, require different tasks for their performance, and different organizations are responsible for their performance. Furthermore different stakeholders are important for the investment and the project. The long term orientation of investments contradicts with the short term orientation of projects. Further it is important to clearly differentiate investment and project costs and benefits. Investment costs include in addition to the costs for investment initiation also costs for operating and maintain the investment.

Figure 1 shows how project and investment can be differentiated and related to each other.

Investments can be initiated by a single project, a chain of projects or by programs (Gareis 2005).

INITIATING A PROJECT

Initiation Process for a Project[3]

The initiation process of a project starts with the investment analysis and ends with the development of the project charter. The main objectives of the initiation process are to make a decision regarding the realization of an investment, to generate information about the investment and to define the project. Figure 2 shows the initiation process for a project after Gareis et al. (2013).

The description of the investment idea or the problem formulation lays the basis for the investment analysis. For the investment analysis, different methods exist, such as the business case analysis, cost benefit analysis, social cost benefit analysis, and environmental impact analysis. These methods are briefly described later.

The results of the investment analysis and the definition of the investment idea are the basis for the development of an investment proposal. The investment proposal is an important communica-

Figure 1. Investment and project (Gareis, 2005, p. 456)

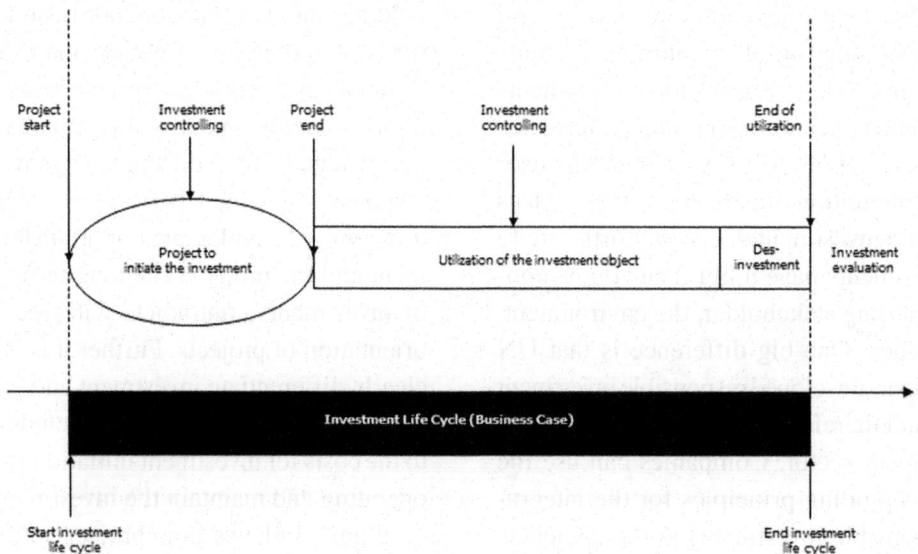

Figure 2. Initiation process for a project (Gareis, et al., 2013)

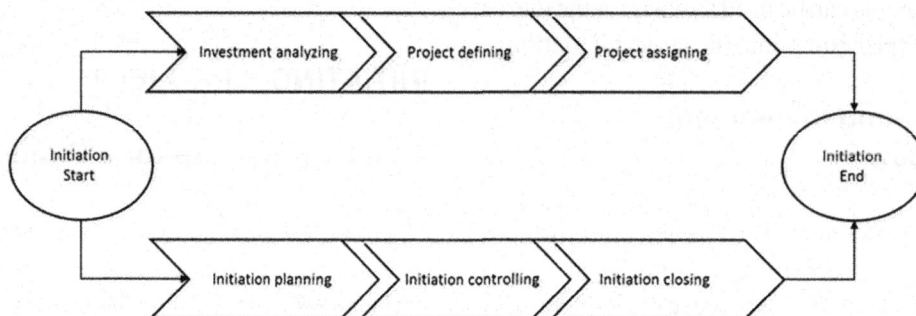

tion document. The customer, the company board, and other important stakeholders achieve central information from this document (Robb 2007). This document set the ground for the investment decision.

A positive investment decision represents the start point for the development of the project proposal. One important step in the development of the project proposal is the project definition. A project must be differentiated from its context (Gareis 2005). The project definition determines what a project includes and is very important for a successful performance of a project (Cano/Lidon 2011; Kähkönen 1999). This method provides a common understanding of the project boundaries (Wijnen/Kor 2000). In the project proposal, general structures of the project become clear and are the basis for the initiation of a project (Steyn 2003). Furthermore the project proposal lays the basis for the project decision.

If the project decision is yes, the project charter is developed. This document is a further development of the project proposal and is a formal summary of important project information between the project manager and the project owner. Signing the project assignment is the start event for the project that initializes the investment (Gido/Clements 2008).

Investment Analysis as Central Method of Project Initiation

As described previous the investment analysis lays the basis for the decision regarding the realization of an investment. Different investment methods exist such as:

Business Case Analysis

A business case analysis is a very traditional and only economic based analysis method. It considers the cash in-flows and out-flows and possible an investment calculation or a simulation. Only cash-effective consequences of the investment are considered and typically analyzed as well as rated with static or dynamic investment calculations such as net present value, internal rate of return or the annuity method. In contrast to static investments methods dynamic investment methods are payment flow oriented and consider a wider investment period (Hirth 2008).

Cost Benefit Analysis

The main objective of the cost benefit analysis is to find the investment with the best costs and benefits relation (Drews/Hillebrand 2007). It is important to analyze at least one alternative to each investment. In this analysis method different types of costs and benefits are analyzed. These are direct costs and benefits; indirect costs and benefits; tangible costs and benefits; intangible costs and benefits.

Social Cost Benefit Analysis

The social cost benefit analysis is a further development of the original cost benefit analysis. Brent (2006) describes the social cost benefit analysis as more holistic in comparison to a traditional cost benefit analysis as it is more long-term oriented and prefers future generations in the social discount factor.

Environmental Impact Analysis

Ecologic aspects are not considered in the previously described analysis methods. It is the main focus of the environmental impact analysis to consider the environmental impact which is caused by the investment. To cover environmental impacts of the investment in the planning phase and minimize their negative impact is the main objective of this analysis (Morris/Therivel 1995).

Consideration of SD Principles in Investment Analysis Methods

The investment analysis methods described prior consider SD principles in different degrees. Table 1 gives a short summary about the relation of SD principles to different investment analysis methods. Traditional methods, such as the business case analysis or the cost benefit analysis, focus only on economic principles and are short to mid-term oriented. The social cost benefit analysis is a more holistic further development of the classic cost benefit analysis and considers also social principles. Furthermore, a wider investment period and a social discount factor are considered. Ecologic principles are not considered in the social cost benefit analysis. The environmental impact analysis considers ecologic as well as social factors and is mid to long term oriented.

Companies often use traditional investment analysis methods. Therefore, most investment decisions are based on economic and short-term aspects.

PM STANDARDS AND INVESTMENT ANALYSIS

Global recognized project management standards offered by international project management associations have a big influence on the practices of the project management community (Hodgson/Muzio 2011). Most of the standards are developed

Table 1. The consideration of sustainability principles in investment methods

SD Principle Investment analysis method	Economic, ecologic and social orientation	Short, mid, and long term orientation	Local, regional, and global orientation
Business Case Analysis	Consideration of economic principles	Short term orientation	-
Cost Benefit Analysis	Consideration of economic principles	Short to mid term orientation	-
Social Cost Benefit Analysis	Consideration of economic and social principles	Mid term orientation	-
Environmental Impact Analysis	Consideration of ecologic as well as social principles	Mid to long term orientation	Local, regional as well as global orientation

by practitioners and aim to represent best or common practices across organizations and industries within the field (Garcia 2005).

Standards are the basis for the certification of project and program manager and thus these standards reflect a common understanding of project initiation and project management. Furthermore these standards offer a generic project management approach.

We analyzed globally recognized project and program management standards if and how they consider SD principles in the investment analysis. Furthermore, we analyzed documents that influence the investment analysis of a project. Table 2 provides an overview over the analyzed documents:

We structure the analysis as following. First, we analyzed which investment analysis methods are considered in the standards. Then we analyzed how stakeholders are considered in the performance of the investment analysis as well as in the decision process. Furthermore, we analyzed which values are the basis for using the analysis method. Table 3 provides a summary about the analysis results. The results are discussed briefly.

Investment Analysis Method: All standards consider a business case as central method for analysis of the investment, while the focus mainly lays on economic aspects. The *PMBOK® Guide* as well as *the Standard for Programme*

Table 2. Overview analyzed documents

Organization	Documents	Initiation Process
Project Management Institute (PMI)	A Guide to the Project Management Body of Knowledge (PMBOK® Guide) (Project Management Institute 2008a)	Initiating Process Group
	The Standard for Program Management (Project Management Institute 2008b)	Initiating Process Group
	Code of Ethics and Professional Conduct (Project Management Institute 2006)	
International Project Management Association (IPMA)	International Competency Baseline 3.0 (ICB) (International Project Management Association 2006)	Project development phase
Office of Government Commerce (OGC)	Managing Successful Projects with PRINCE2 (PRINCE2) (Office of Government Commerce 2009)	Starting Up A Project process
	Managing Successful Programmes (MSP) (Office of Government Commerce 2007)	Identifying a Programme
	Management of Value (MoV) (Office of Government Commerce 2010)	

Table 3. Summary analysis results

Organization	Document	Investment Analysis Method	Additional methods/ documents	Consideration of SD principles	Consideration of values	Stakeholder involvement
Project Management Institute (PMI)	PMBOK® Guide (PMI 2008a)	Business case; cost benefit analysis		Traditional cost benefit analysis – focus on economic principles; business case document considers customer requests, technological advances, legal requirements, environmental impacts and social needs.	Consideration of Code of Ethics in all decisions.	Involvement in project charter development. No involvement in investment decision process.
	The Standard for Programme Management (PMI 2008b)	Business case; cost benefit analysis; feasibility study	Feasibility study; comparative advantage analysis	Cost benefit analysis includes in addition to traditional financial costs and benefits also the description of non-financial benefits.	Consideration of Code of Ethics in all decisions.	No involvement in investment decision process.
International Project Management Association (IPMA)	ICB (IPMA 2006)	Business case	Environmental impact plan;	Traditional business case –focus on economic principles. Ecologic principles are considered in the environmental impact plan.	Behavioral competence part in ICB – values like ethics, values appreciation and reliability are listed and need to be considered in all decisions.	Involvement in development of business case. No involvement in investment decision process.
Office of Government Commerce (OGC)	PRINCE2 (OGC 2009)	Business case; cost benefit analysis	Investment appraisal	Benefit of an investment can be described with non-monetary facts – social and ecologic description of benefit possible. Consideration of long-term costs in investment appraisal.	Management of Value as guiding framework for all decisions. Stakeholder participation is mentioned as relevant but not integrated in standards.	Involvement of stakeholder in development of business case. No involvement in investment decision process.
	MSP(OGC 2007)	Business case; cost benefit analysis		Benefit of an investment can be described with non-monetary facts – social and ecologic description of benefit possible.	Management of Value as guiding framework for all decisions. Stakeholder participation is mentioned as relevant but not integrated in standards.	Involvement of stakeholder in development of business case. No involvement in investment decision process.

Management describes in addition to the monetary and economical results of the cost benefit analysis, other principles like customer requests, technological advances, legal requirements, as well as environmental impacts and social needs.

In addition to the business case the *PMBOK® Guide, the Standard for Programme Management, PRINCE 2* as well as *MSP* describes a cost benefit analysis. In the *PMBOK® Guide* the cost benefit analysis is not described in detail, the assumption taken is that a traditional cost benefit analysis taken. In contrast to that *the Standard for Program Management* the described cost benefit analysis includes, in addition to the traditional financial cost and benefits, also the description of non-financial benefits such as increased market share. Thus a qualitative benefit description is possible.

PRINCE2 as well as *MSP* provide no detailed description of the cost and benefit analysis but indicate that the benefit of an investment can also be described in non-monetary facts. Thus the benefits of an investment are described in a qualitative way and the consideration of intangible costs and benefits is possible. This is allows better to consider social and ecologic issues, as these are often not easy express monetary and therefore are not considered in traditional cost benefit analysis.

In addition to the business case the *ICB* describes an environmental impact plan. In the environmental impact plan ecologic principles are analyzed and considered.

Involvement of Stakeholder: All standards recommend an involvement of stakeholders during the development of the business case. Stakeholder interests are not considered in the investment analysis and therefore are not considered in the investment decision. Furthermore, stakeholders are not involved in the investment decision process. Stakeholder participation is mentioned as relevant in the MoV but not integrated in *PRINCE2* or *MSP*.

Consideration of Values: Behavior and decisions are driven by values. Thus the investment decision is driven by values of organizations or communities as well as personal values of individuals taking the investment decision. Values are often only implicitly traceable in standards. Nevertheless, some values are explicitly defined in standards e.g. ethics in the *ICB*. Other values are not integrated in the standards itself but explicitly mentioned in additional documents, e.g. the code of ethics of PMI. These additional documents are guiding documents for the standards and need to be considered in every decision. One limitation of these documents is the focus on the project

manager as the investment decision is made e.g. by the project portfolio group and not by the project manager itself. Thus these documents are very limited considered when analyzing the investment. OGC developed the MoV as a guiding framework for benefit management in project and programs. It focuses on values like stakeholder participation and mentions that the economic, ecologic as well as social orientation is relevant. This document should be used as guiding framework for all decision and lays the basis for *PRINCE2* and *MSP*.

Summarizing our findings, all standards describe a business case to evaluate an investment. In some standards further investment analysis methods are recommended e.g. the environmental impact plan. Further developments of traditional investment analysis methods such as the social cost benefits analysis are not recommended. SD principles are implicitly considered but there is no explicit consideration in the investment decision.

LOOKING OUTSIDE THE PM STANDARDS WORLD: THE LOGICAL FRAMEWORK APPROACH

The previously discussed standards offer a generic project management approach (i.e., applicable for all project types) and do not consider different contexts (e.g., industries or project types) (Garcia 2005). Furthermore because they didn't provide much evidence for the consideration of SD principles in the project initiation, we were looking for recognized project management approach, which would per nature of the project consider SD principles. SD is an important issue in regional development projects (Stockmann 1997). A well known approach for these projects is the Logical Framework Approach (*LFA*) (Norad 1999) which is applied by the World Bank (The World Bank 1997).

The participative process design of the *LFA* is based on a participatory analysis (stakeholder analysis) as first step of the initiation process. All important stakeholders are invited to participate in the process and contribute actively to the decision regarding the realization of an investment. The LFA defines important stakeholders as all organizations and individuals that are necessary to fully understand the investment and/or that have an interest regarding the investment. Each stakeholder has the possibility to define investment ideas and to share his/her opinion.

In the *LFA* a more holistic cost benefit analysis considering economic, social as well as ecologic principles described. The cost benefit analysis described in the *LFA* defines the following criteria: total costs, benefits to main stakeholder, probability of achieving objectives, and social risks (Norad 1999; The World Bank 1997). Furthermore, the *LFA* defines following possible additional criteria (See Table 4).

A central value of the *LFA* is transparency. Problems, causes and effects are analyzed and communicated to the stakeholders. This open and transparent communication form leads to a more holistic investment decision because the identified problem, cause and effects can be considered in the decision.

Values like participation, transparency and acceptance are very important in the *LFA*. No decision is done without the confirmation of the stakeholders. A high social responsibility about countries but also about the stakeholders itself is observable.

The described cost benefit analysis in the *LFA* is a potential to further develop investment analysis methods for other project types. Nevertheless, one limitation of the *LFA* is its focus only on the project initiation and not the consideration of managing the whole investment life cycle.

PROPOSING A COMPREHENSIVE INVESTMENT ANALYSIS METHOD

The traditional cost benefit analysis and its further developments can be used as basis for the integration of SD principles into the investment analysis of a project. The use of a comprehensive investment analysis method considering SD principles lays the basis for a holistic and sustainable investment.

The selection of an adequate investment analysis method that fits to the organizational need and ensures a high flexibility to include SD aspects is the basis for a holistic investment decision. Traditional investment analysis methods consider only economic aspects and some methods are not flexible in integrating SD principles. Further developments such as the social cost benefit analysis are more holistic and focus also on social cost and benefits but don't allow the description of ecologic aspects. Environmental Impact Assessments focus on social and ecologic aspects but exclude economic aspects. Approaches from multilateral development agencies focus on the consideration of SD principles in the project initiation, especially when analyzing the investment. The social cost benefit analysis methods from UNIDO or the World Bank (Bruce et al. 1976; Dasgupta et al. 1972; Little/Mirrlees 1974; Squire/Van Der Tak 1975), the concept of responsible investments (Louche/Lydenberg 2011), ethical investments (Michelson et al. 2004; O'rourke 2003), or the *LFA* (Norad 1999) are good examples of how SD principles can be integrated into investment analysis methods.

Table 4. Criteria according to the investment analysis of LFA (Norad, 1999, p. 44)

Criteria type	Criteria
Technical	Appropriateness, use of local resources, market suitability, etc.
Financial	Costs, financial sustainability, foreign exchange needs, etc.
Economic	Economic return, cost effectiveness, etc.
Institutional	Capacity, capability, technical assistance, etc.
Social/ distributional	Distribution of costs and benefits, gender issues, socio-cultural constraints, local involvement, and motivation, etc.
Environmental	Environmental effects, environmental costs vs. benefits

Based on our analysis of standards and the literature, we summarize the following topics as important for a comprehensive investment analysis method:

- The consideration of a stakeholder perspective.
- A qualitative and non-monetary cost benefit description.
- The consideration of economic, ecologic, social as well as local, regional and global consequences when analyzing the investment.
- Costs and benefits for the investment but also for the project initiating the investment.

The Consideration of a Stakeholder Perspective: It is one guiding principles of responsible investment to adopt a stakeholder perspective in the investment analysis. This means that e.g. the costs and benefits of the stakeholders are considered. Knowing costs and benefits of important stakeholder allows one the one hand to consider these aspects when making the investment decision and on the other hand allows to plan actions and measures to minimize the costs of the stakeholders. Stakeholder costs are often non-monetary e.g. noise disturbance during construction and therefore not considered in traditional investment analysis methods. Gareis et al (2013) mentioned the importance to analyze the stakeholder perspective when analyzing the investment.

A Qualitative and Non-Monetary Cost Benefit Description: To allow a qualitative and non-monetary description of costs and benefits is one further step to reach a more holistic investment analysis method. In *PRINCE2* and *MSP* a non-monetary description of benefits is possible. Therefore the consideration of ecologic and especially social factors is possible. Another result of a qualitative description is a better description of costs and benefits of different stakeholder. This is important because stakeholder often have non-monetary costs such as noise disturbance during construction.

The Consideration of Economic, Ecologic, Social as well as Local, Regional and Global Orientation: Traditionally costs and benefits are only economic based. The qualitative and non-monetary cost and benefit description allow the consideration of ecologic as well as social costs and benefits. This is important as investments, which have a focus on social or ecologic aspects, becomes more important. The analysis is more balanced and other facts get a higher visibility. Furthermore it is possible to classify costs and benefits in the spacial scale and differentiate them into local, regional and global. This is also important as social or especially ecologic costs sometime have little influence on the local level but a high influence on the regional or global level. It is also possible to have a combination of two or more aspects e.g. local and regional. E.g. a new factory may have influence on local but also on regional level. Gareis et al (2013) defined the consideration of economic, ecologic and social as well as local, regional and global consequences as basis for a comprehensive investment analysis. Furthermore they defined the short, mid and long term orientation as essential.

Costs and Benefits for the Investment but also for the Project Initiating the Investment: Investments in contrast to project or programs are long term oriented. Thus it is not possible to differentiate the costs and benefits of an investment into short, mid and long term. But different costs and benefits during investment initiation and after investment initiation exits. Different costs and benefits during investment initiation and utilization exist such as noise disturbance of neighbors during construction of a hospital. This differentiation is more important for the stakeholder perspective than the investor perspective. The costs during investment initiation represent the costs of the project and are mostly very economic driven. But for stakeholder different costs and benefits during investment initiation and after initiation exists. Knowing the stakeholder costs during investment imitation increase potentials to define measures and actions to minimize these costs. Furthermore potentials for optimizing stakeholder benefits during and after investment initiation can be identified. Costs during investment initiation are linked to risks for stakeholder during project performance. Risks can have a positive or a negative meaning. The awareness of these risks gives the possibility to plan measures and actions to minimize the risks and therefore the costs.

Table 5 shows one possible way to explicitly consider SD principles when analyzing an investment. As basis for the development of the investment analysis a stakeholder analysis needs to be done. The investor perspective can be done as a draft in internal workshops and meetings. It is suggested to do the final analysis together with important stakeholder in workshops and actively involve them in the investment decision process. This integration lays the basis for an open and transparent decision process. Based on the identity model of organizations (Gareis/Stummer 2008) the costs and benefits of the investment are analyzed. This first step represents the investor perspective and focus on costs and benefits for the investor itself when realizing the investment. It is possible to describe the costs and benefits in a monetary or non-monetary way. Thus tangible as well as intangible costs and benefits can be considered. In a next step the cost and benefit type is selected. It is possible that one cost or benefit is a combination between different types e.g. that one benefit is social as well as economic. The evaluation of the described costs and benefits can also be done in a monetary or non-monetary way. As described before, a differentiation between costs and benefits during and after investment initiation is made.

In a next step the stakeholder perspective is analyzed. Thus the costs and benefits of important stakeholder are analyzed and evaluated. The costs and benefits can be described in a qualitative and non-monetary way and can relate to more than one type e.g. to social and economic. This section can be perceived as most important part for stakeholder because in this part it is possible

to explicitly consider the costs and benefits of stakeholder. The active involvement of important stakeholder in this section is absolutely necessary to achieve meaningful and authentic information. A good balance between costs and benefits of stakeholders is the basis for a high acceptance regarding the investment. This information is also important for the future project manager as it give information how stakeholder may react during project performance. Furthermore this information can be used as basis for different actions and measures. It may also be considered when developing a communication plan. An important differentiation between costs and benefits is the previously described differentiation between costs and benefits during and after investment initiation. One advantage of this differentiation is the possibility to define specific measures and actions to minimize stakeholder costs and maximize stakeholder benefits. The definition of optimal measures requires this differentiation.

CONSEQUENCES FOR THE DESIGN OF THE INITIATION PROCESS

The application of a comprehensive investment analysis method has considerable effects on designing the initiation process of a project, which includes a clear differentiation between project and investment and stakeholder participation and engagement.

Clear Differentiation between Project and Investment: A clear differentiation between project and investment is the basis for the development of an adequate organizational design to ensure a holistic understanding of the investment. In point 3.3. the differentiation between investment and project was explained. As described before, these processes fulfill different objectives, require different tasks for their performance, and different organizations are responsible for their performance.

Table 5. Further developed cost benefit analysis

INVESTMENT ANALYSIS

INVESTOR PERSPECTIVE

| Cost/Benefit type | Cost/Benefit during investment initiation | | | | | | | | | Cost/Benefit of investment | | | | | | | | | |
| | Cost description | Benefit description | Type | | | | | | Evaluation | Cost description | Benefit description | Type | | | | | | Evaluation |
			Economic	Ecologic	Social	Local	Regional	Global				Economic	Ecologic	Social	Local	Regional	Global	
Services																		
Technologies																		
Organization																		
Personnel																		
Infrastructure																		
Finance																		
Relations to Stakeholders																		

STAKEHOLDER PERSPECTIVE

| Stakeholder | Cost description | Benefit description | Type | | | | | | Evaluation | Cost description | Benefit description | Type | | | | | | Evaluation |
			Economic	Ecologic	Social	Local	Regional	Global				Economic	Ecologic	Social	Local	Regional	Global	

Investment ratios

Cost-benefit ratio for the investor:

Amortization period for the investor:

Overall cost-benefit ratio:

Overall amortization period:

Furthermore the clear differentiation of project and investment allows the management of the whole investment life cycle. The management of the whole investment is done by a business analyst. The business analyst supports the investment from the idea until the deinvestment. Furthermore the business analyst consults the performance of the investment analysis. During project performance it is necessary that the project manager communicates with the business analyst.

Stakeholder participation and engagement in the project initiation process especially in the investment analysis process leads to a better acceptance regarding the investment and regarding the project that initiates the investment.

The consideration of stakeholder in the analysis process of the investment is the first step to achieve a more holistic and sustainable investment. The development of strong stakeholder relations is a main driver of responsible investments. A participative process design allows a more holistic and transparent decision process (Gareis et al 2013). The analysis of important stakeholders is the basis for such an involvement. The *LFA* shows that the involvement of stakeholders in the process allows them to define criteria for the analysis that are important for them. Stakeholders are involved in the whole initiation and decision process. Via workshops, a strong participatory process design is realized. All decisions are made along with the workshop participants. A transparent investment decision leads to a higher acceptance of stakeholders regarding the investment. The outcome of a higher acceptance is to minimize risks.

Stakeholder participation and a comprehensive stakeholder management represent one of the biggest potentials to integrate SD principles into the project initiation process as well as into the project management process. In this field increasing research interest is observable (e.g. Eskerod/ Huemann 2012; Gareis et al. 2013; Huemann et al. 2014). Huemann and Eskerod (2012) discuss the importance of a comprehensive project stakeholder management and the integration of stakeholder in decision processes.

CONCLUSION

The project initiation process starts with the investment analysis and ends with the assignment of the project. Analyzing the investment is one main key task of this process. For this analysis different methods exists. Traditional methods such as the business case analysis or the cost benefit analysis consider only economic aspects and are short to mid-term oriented. Further developments such as the social cost benefit analysis consider also social costs and benefits are have a wider investment period. The environmental impact analysis considers social as well as ecologic aspects and is long-term oriented.

The concept of responsible investments is mostly used for financial investments. The concept tries to integrate economic, social as well as ecologic aspects in the investment analysis. Furthermore it encourages a long-term perspective and adopts a stakeholder perspective when analyzing the investment. The concept of ethical investments considers personal values and social considerations in addition to economic aspects.

Globally recognized project and program management standards represent a common understanding and knowledge in the project management community. All analyzed standards describe the business case analysis as basis for the investment decision. Some standards recommend further investment analysis methods but do not describe them in detail. All standards do not explicitly consider SD principles when analyzing the investment.

The Logical Framework Approach (*LFA*) (Norad 1999; The World Bank 1997) is used by the World Bank mostly for initiating regional development projects. The *LFA* uses a participative process design to perform the investment analysis.

Important stakeholders are actively involved in the investment decision process and the project definition. The described cost benefit analysis considers economic, social as well as ecologic aspects. The chapter proposes a more comprehensive investment analysis method based on the explicit consideration of SD principles, which includes

- The consideration of a stakeholder perspective.
- A qualitative and non-monetary cost benefit description.
- The consideration of economic, ecologic, social as well as local, regional and global consequences.
- Costs and benefits for the investment but also for the project initiating the investment.

The application of a comprehensive investment analysis method has considerable effects on designing the initiation process of a project, which includes a clear differentiation between project and investment and stakeholder participation and engagement.

REFERENCES

Brent, R. (2006). *Applied cost-benefit analysis*. Cheltenham, UK: Edward Elgar Publishing Limited.

Cano, J. L., & Lidon, I. (2011). Guided reflection on project definition. *International Journal of Project Management*, *29*(5), 525–536. doi:10.1016/j.ijproman.2010.04.008.

Drews, G., & Hillebrand, N. (2007). *Lexikon der projektmanagement-methoden*. Haufe Verlag.

Eskerod, P., & Huemann, M. (2012). Sustainable development and project stakeholder management: What standards say. *International Journal of Managing Projects in Business*.

Garcia, S. (2005). How standards enable adoption of project management practice. *IEEE Software*, *22*(5), 22–29. doi:10.1109/MS.2005.122.

Gareis, R. (2005). *Happy projects!* Vienna: Manz.

Gareis, R., Huemann, M., Martinuzzi, A., Weninger, C., & Sedlacko, M. (2013). *Project management & sustainable development principles*. Newtown Square, PA: Project Management Institute.

Gareis, R., & Stummer, M. (2008). *Processes & projects*. Wien: Manz.

Gido, J., & Clements, J. P. (2008). *Successful project management*. South-Western Pub..

Global Compact, U. N. UNEP Finance Initiative. (2006). *Principles for Responsible investment*. Paris: UNEP.

Hirth, H. (2008). *Grundzüge der finanzierung und investition*. München, Germany: Oldenbourg Wissenschaftsverlag GmbH..

Hodgson, D., & Muzio, D. (2011). Prospects for professionalism in project management. In Morris, Pinto, & Söderlund (Eds.), The Oxford Handbook of Project Management. New York: Oxford University Press.

Huemann, M., Eskerod, P., Weninger, C., & Aagaard, A. (2014). *Rethinking project stakeholder management*. Newtown Square, PA: Project Management Institute.

International Project Management Association. (2006). *International Competency Baseline ver. 3.0*. Zürich: IPMA.

InvestorWords. (2011). *Definition investment*. Retrieved from http://www.investorwords.com/2599/investment.html

Kähkönen, K. (1999). Multi-character model of the construction project definition process. *Automation in Construction*, *8*(6), 625–632. doi:10.1016/S0926-5805(98)00111-3.

Louche, C., & Lydenberg, S. D. (2011). *Dilemmas in responsible investment*. Greenleaf Publishing Limited.

Michelson, G., Wailes, N., Van Der Laan, S., & Frost, G. (2004). Ethical investment processes and outcomes. *Journal of Business Ethics, 52*(1), 1–10. doi:10.1023/B:BUSI.0000033103.12560.be.

Mills, R., & Turner, R. (1995). Projects for shareholder value. In Turner (Ed.), The commercial project manager. London: McGraw-Hill Book Company.

Morris, P., & Therivel, R. (1995). *Methods of environmental impact assessment*. Vancouver: University of British Columbia Press.

NORAD. N. A. f. D. C. (1999). The logical framework approach: Handbook for objectives-oriented planning (4th ed.). Oslo, Norway: Tykk and Kopisenteret AS.

O'Rourke, A. (2003). The message and methods of ethical investment. *Journal of Cleaner Production, 11*(6), 683–693. doi:10.1016/S0959-6526(02)00105-1.

Office of Government Commerce. (2007). *Managing successful programmes*. London: The Stationery Office.

Office of Government Commerce. (2009). *Managing successful projects with PRINCE2*. London: Stationery Office.

Office of Government Commerce. (2010). *Management of value*. London: The Stationery Office.

Project Management Institute. (2006). *Code of ethics and professional conduct*. Newtown Square, PA: Project Management Institute.

Project Management Institute. (2008a). *A guide to the project management body of knowledge*. Newtown Square, PA: Project Management Institute.

Project Management Institute. (2008b). *The standard for program management*. Newton Square, PA: Project Management Institute.

Robb, L. (2007). Project proposal and initiation. In Turner (Ed.), Gower Handbook of Project Management. Aderlshot, UK: Gower.

Steyn, H. (2003). *Project management: A multi-disciplinary approach*. Pretoria, South Africa: FPM Publisher.

Stockmann, R. (1997). The sustainability of development projects: An impact assessment of German vocational-training projects in Latin America. *World Development, 25*(11), 1767–1784. doi:10.1016/S0305-750X(97)00067-3.

The World Bank. (1997). *The logframe handbook: A logical framework approach to project cycle management*. Washington, DC: OECD.

WebFinance. I. (2010). *InvestorWords - Investment*. Retrieved from http://www.investorwords.com/2599/investment.html

Wijnen, G., & Kor, R. (2000). *Managing unique assignments: A team approach to projects and programmes*. Aldershot, UK: Gower.

World Commission on Environment and Development. (1987). *Our common future*. Oxford, UK: World Commission on Environment and Development.

ENDNOTES

[1] A detailed description about the SD principles defined by Gareis et al. (2013) can be found in chapter 8 – "Re-thinking Project Initiation and Project Management by Considering Principles of Sustainable Development" written by Roland Gareis.

[2] ESG: Environmental Social and Governance

[3] A detailed description of the project initiation process can be found in chapter 8 – "Re-thinking Project Initiation and Project Management by Considering Principles of Sustainable Development" written by Roland Gareis.

Chapter 10
Integrating Sustainability into Technology–Oriented Project Management:
Cases from South Africa

Alan Brent
Stellenbosch University, South Africa

Carin Tredoux
University of Pretoria, South Africa

ABSTRACT

Various driving forces originating from society, government, employees, and partners are forcing the enterprise to both incorporate sustainable development in its internal operations and practices, and to align these with the principles thereof. Technology-oriented project management, as a core competency of many enterprises, is not excluded from these requirements. Four cases are explored of how the aspects of sustainability have been addressed by various approaches and tools to enhance the performances of enterprises—in the context of project management in South Africa. The associated challenges are highlighted and the requirement for further work, to address the shortfalls, is outlined. Specifically, by developing methods for understanding the full implications of alternative choices and their relative attractiveness in terms of enhancing the resilience of systems, by extending the field of sustainability science into the field of project management.

INTRODUCTION

Over the past decade, sustainability has moved from the domain of the few, to the domain of the many. Sustainability now features in the discussions of top enterprise leaders, and is amongst the most thoroughly researched topics and has been a powerful undercurrent running through the pages of the enterprise media (KPMG, 2011). Indeed, a recent survey indicates that many enterprises now report profits that are derived from sustainability activities (Haanaes et al., 2012). Despite this, there remains no widespread agreement on the precise meaning of sustainability for enterprises, or how

DOI: 10.4018/978-1-4666-4177-8.ch010

exactly to achieve it (Aras and Crowther, 2009). Similarly, there is widespread disagreement in the literature on the contribution of enhanced environmental and social performance on the financial performance of individual entities. Nevertheless, there has been increasing recognition of, and response to, the pressures of adding social and environmental bottom lines to the conventional financial focus; primarily to address the demands of increasing global competition (Eweje, 2011). The objective of this chapter is thus to investigate how sustainability issues may be addressed in the management of projects, based on the experiences of some cases in the South African context.

BACKGROUND

The World Business Council for Sustainable Development, in its outlook to 2050 (WBCSD, 2010), provides a sobering insight into the many environmental and social changes that will bring about both risks and opportunities for enterprises in the search for global sustainable growth. Climate Change, specifically, is highlighted as the major challenge that directly impacts, and interacts with, all other challenges, such as (affordable) energy and fuel, material resource scarcity, water scarcity, population growth, urbanisation, wealth, food security, ecosystem decline, and deforestation. The principles of sustainable development are subsequently proposed that offer enterprises the notion of being able to reconcile environmental protection and socio-economic development with improved enterprise performance. The enterprise community has responded in various strategic ways to this call, eliciting a wide range of sustainability action types, or categories, alternatively termed: Corporate Responsibility, Corporate Social Responsibility (CSR), Corporate Citizenship, Business Ethics, Stakeholder Relations Management, Corporate Environmental Management, Business and Society, and Corporate Sustainability (Berns et al., 2009), to name but a few.

Current enterprise-operational approaches and practices in this domain vary and range from attempts to adapt production processes to minimize resource use and environmental pollution, and/ or to improve relations with the community and other stakeholder groups (Gonzales-Benito & Gonzales-Benito, 2008). Initially sustainability practices began as a means of organisations responding to compliance requirements to the fact that organizations now want to deploy sustainability programmes to reap greater shareholder value (Haanaes et al., 2012). Rather than treating sustainability efforts exclusively as a response to legal and regulatory requirements, more organizations are now integrating sustainability activities into how they manage reputation risk, generate cost savings and ensure long-term profitability and competitive advantage. Corporate sustainability programmes are also expanding in numbers across the spectrum of company size and industry sectors. No longer solely the domain of the large-scale industry or large multinational conglomerates, enterprises of all types and size are increasingly implementing sustainability programmes and practices (Berns et al., 2009). For example, manufacturing companies may emphasize reducing emissions, decreasing water consumption, and recycling by-products, while service firms may focus on customer relationships, employee development, and community service (Reilly & Weirup, 2010). As corporations comply with stringent regulations, they must protect or enhance their ethical image, avoid serious liabilities, satisfy the safety concerns of employees, respond to government regulators and shareholders, and develop new enterprise opportunities in order to remain competitive (Eweje, 2011).

Technology-Oriented Project Management, Conceptually and in Practice

Technology-oriented project management addresses the effective identification, selection, acquisition, development, exploitation and protection of technologies in the form of product, process, and infrastructure, which are needed to sustain the competitive advantage of regional sectors in accordance with sector, regional, national, and international sustainable development objectives. The management process is conceptualized in Figure 1, the details of which are provided elsewhere (Brent & Pretorius, 2008). It commences with idea generations, whereby ideas enter the wide end of a funnel and are then screened along the funnel through scientific and engineering performance criteria with the objective of identifying, selecting and economically exploiting innovations (Wheelwright & Clark, 1992). The first screening phase of the funnel, namely pre-feasibility and feasibility, occurs through a formal research and development (R&D) life cycle with idea, assessment, research and scale-up phases and associated decision gates, which are typical of R&D institutions (Swasdio et al., 2004). The final R&D decision is to commence – or not – with the Development, Implementation, and Exploitation (DIE) of the R&D output (Roelofse & Pretorius, 2003). Many tools and methods are applied in the DIE phases to support business-orientated decision gates (in a project life cycle) to optimize and maximize the return on innovations (Roelofse & Pretorius, 2003). Through the market-uptake cycle (Nieto et al., 1998), many different technology life cycles are associated with the innovation – and project (Labuschagne & Brent, 2005), that is the life cycles of process and physical assets that manufacture or produce products and/or services and the life cycles of the products and/or services themselves.

Approaches to Address the Risks and Opportunities

A holistic understanding of the sustainable development implications during the market-uptake cycle of innovations (See Figure 1) is required during the pre-feasibility and feasibility phases of the technology life cycle; bringing practical solutions to sustainable development problems requires a trans-disciplinary knowledge base and a holistic management approach (Klein, 2004). Therefore, during these phases, conventional tools and approaches have been adapted that can assist with the identification of risks and opportunities for planning and strategising purposes within a project (and an enterprise). For example, Table 1 summarises some of the tools and approaches used by enterprises to assess and improve performances.

Aim of the Chapter

The chapter describes how some of the approaches and tools pertaining to sustainability (as underlined in Table 1), have been used in technology-oriented project management practices in the South African context. The aim is to draw on these cases to: (1) identify the major challenges with the approaches and tools; and (2) to conceptualise an improved framework of how sustainability issues may be addressed in the management of projects.

Technology-Oriented project management cases in South Africa

Case 1: Sustainable Agriculture Project Selection

The degradation of natural resources has a direct and significant impact on those living in rural areas. The resultant increasing pressure that is placed on the livelihoods of rural people leads to desperate and poor agricultural practices, which in turn cause further degradation of natural resources. The LandCare programme of the South African national government aims to address these problems by facilitating rural agricultural projects that are sustainable in the long-term. However, the previous project success rate was testimony to poorly planned projects, with few projects completed on time, within the budget and of acceptable quality. Only a small number of projects were taken further after project closure, placing a large question mark on the sustainability

Figure 1. Technology life-cycle interventions and associated evaluated systems (Source: Brent and Pretorius (2008))

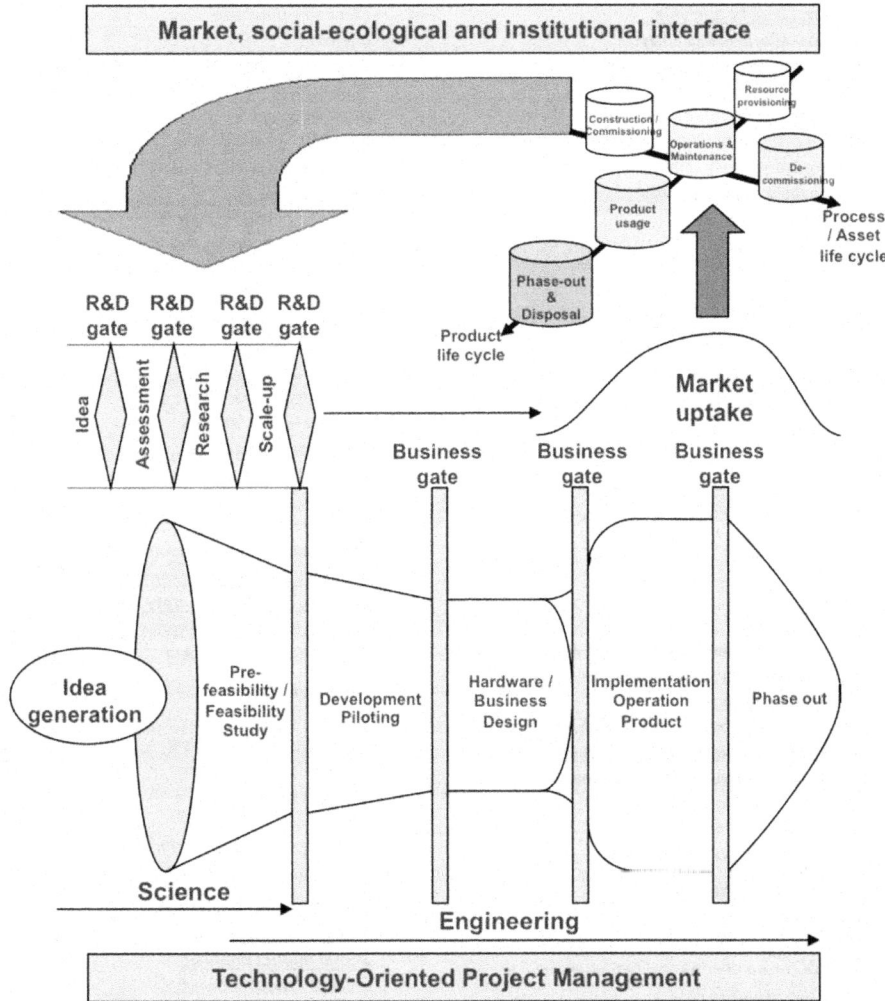

of the LandCare programme in general. Mulder and Brent (2006) subsequently reported on the development of new selection criteria, as well as an appropriate evaluation procedure, in order to filter project proposals effectively and ensure sustainable project performances, and to compile the best possible LandCare programme portfolio.

The use of appropriate project selection criteria aims to identify proper projects that will be funded and implemented. These criteria also guide project planners as to what is required in a project plan. Although this is by no means a guarantee that projects will be successfully implemented, good project plans significantly improve the chances of project success.

The new project selection criteria (See Table 2) were developed through a review of literature, (then) existing criteria applied in previously selected projects, and interviews with key stakeholders during project site visits. These site visits were also used to determine criterion weights, which were calculated using the Analytical Hierarchy Process (AHP), a known Multi-Criteria Decision Analysis (MCDA) technique. The established set of criteria

Table 1. Typical approaches and tools used by the enterprise to improve performances

Economic Analysis	Information Monitoring
Cost benefit analysis	*Electronic database*
Cost effectiveness analysis	*Internet*
Lifecycle cost assessment	**_Technical/ scientific literature reviews_**
Return on investments	*Patent searches*
Net present value	*IP asset valuation*
Internal rate of return	
Breakeven point analysis	**Technical performance assessment**
Payback period analysis	*Statistical analysis*
Residual income	*Bayesian confidence profile analysis*
Total savings	**_Surveys/questionnaires_**
Increasing returns analysis	*Trial use periods*
Technology value pyramid	*Beta testing*
Real options	*Technology decomposition theory*
Technology balance sheet	*S-curve analysis*
	Human factors analysis
Decision analysis	*Ergonomics studies*
Multi-criteria decision analysis (MCDA)	*Ease-of-use studies*
Multi-attribute utility theory	*Outcomes research*
Scoring	*Technometrics*
Group decision support systems	
Delphi/group Delphi	**Risk assessment**
Analytic hierarchy process	*Simulation modelling and analysis*
Q-sort	**_Probabilistic risk assessment_**
Decision trees	**_Environ, health and safety studies_**
Fuzzy logic	*Risk-based decision trees*
	Litigation risk assessment
Systems engineering/ systems analysis	
Technology system studies	**Market analysis**
System dynamics	*Fusion method*
Simulation modelling and analysis	*Market push/pull analysis*
Project management techniques	*Surveys/questionnaires*
Systems optimization techniques	*S-curves analysis*
Linear, integer and	*Scenario analysis*
non-linear programming	*Multigenerational tech diffusion*
Technology portfolio analysis	
	Externalities/impact analysis
Technology forecasting	**_Externalities analysis_**
S-curve analysis	**_Social impact analysis_**
Delphi/ **_Analytic hierarchy process_**/*Q-sort*	*Political impact analysis*
R&D researcher hazard rate analysis	**_Environmental impact analysis_**
Trend extrapolation	**_Cultural impact analysis_**
Correlation and causal methods	**_Integrated impact assessment_**
Probabilistic methods	**_Life cycle analysis_**
Monte Carlo simulation	
Roadmapping	

Sources: de Piante Henriksen (1997) and Tran (2007)

was applied to three project developments in South Africa, through which an evaluation procedure is further demonstrated (Mulder & Brent, 2006). Thereby a successful project portfolio can be ensured that is dedicated to all three components of sustainable development in rural areas.

A scaling factor (-1 to +1) is assigned to each criterion (of Table 2), based on an introduced 'class' change in a community after project imple-

mentation (see Appendix A in Mulder, 2003). Community members and the Provincial Department of Agriculture jointly determine the current baseline class, regarding the state of the criterion in the community. The community's needs regarding the criterion class are then identified through a process of participation. Thereafter, the project's impact on the criterion is determined, namely how the project would affect the class of the criterion.

Table 2. Developed selection criteria for development, agriculture-oriented projects in rural areas of South Africa

Social sustainability	Economic sustainability	Environmental sustainability	Technical feasibility
Representation **Community participation** **Leadership** **Household food security** **Employment opportunities** **Skills development** **LandCare awareness and education**	**Return on investment** **Return on environment** **Community contribution** **Management level** **Profitability**	**Air resources** • Air quality • Noise **Water resources** • Quantity • Quality **Soil resources** • Soil loss • Soil condition **Plant resources** • Biodiversity of plant species • Plant production • Plant management **Animal resources** • Biodiversity of animal species • Animal production • Animal management **Waste management** • Waste generation • Waste disposal	**Project plan** • Work breakdown structure • Schedule • Budget layout • Quality management • Risk management • Plans and specifications **Appropriateness of technology** **Address prime causes**

Source: Mulder and Brent (2006)

A single class difference indicates a moderate change, while a class difference of two or more indicates a significant change. The conformance of the class change to the community needs is assessed on a similar scale.

By following this process both the project performance and conformity to community needs are evaluated. Some of these indicators require a subjective evaluation by project management expertise, specifically for determining effects and comparing these to a baseline. Other criteria such as representation, community participation, leadership, and community contribution do not require baseline information as performances are directly measured.

Technical sustainability indicators are either a go or a no-go decision for the entire project with respect to its projected sustainability. This component is subsequently not included in the sustainability evaluation procedure.

These indicators are subjective, but the evaluation and project selection process is consistent as only one committee evaluates all the project proposals. The evaluation committee may choose not to fund a project if the overall project performance and conformance to community needs are not deemed adequate. For such an overall evaluation weighting values for the different social, economic and environmental criteria and indicators are required.

For each of the social, environmental and economic sustainability groups, the AHP model is based on a pair wise weighting approach (Kamal, 2001), whereby the selection criteria of a group are compared to each other to establish the criterion contribution (priority vector) to the objectives, namely to maximise the sustainability performance of the LandCare programme.

The application of the selection criteria and evaluation procedure to the development projects showed that the developed selection criteria could be used to evaluate project proposals effectively (Mulder & Brent, 2006). The incorporation of both overall project impact, as well as conformity to community needs, in the procedure facilitates more informed decisions. It was also showed that the required investment for a project is, to a large extent, directly proportionate to the specific impact desired. It is therefore often the case that a larger investment in a project brings about a more significant or positive change. In this regard, the following recommendations can be made:

- When the evaluation of selection criteria for a specific project indicates that the outcome of project implementation is expected to exceed the community needs on one of the components, the initial funding allocated to that component will be excessive. The excess funding can then be applied to other project components, which, according to the project evaluation, will not achieve the community needs. In this regard, it may prove valuable to consider alternative technologies or practices to determine if community needs cannot be addressed more effectively.

- The project selection criteria could also be applied in the monitoring and evaluation of LandCare projects. As the system has been tested and data already gathered, the impact of agricultural practices and other technologies or projects on natural resources can be more accurately determined.

Case 1 emphasises the general challenge of conducting a subjective, trade-off analysis, without understanding, necessarily, the interactions of different criteria associated with a project.

Case 2: Appraising Social Aspects of Projects in the Process Industry

The inclusion of social aspects in both the sustainability debate and practice has received less attention compared to the focus on the other two dimensions of sustainable development, namely economic and environmental performances, especially from a business perspective. In the process industry sector the tools that have focused on

social justice and related sustainability aspects have mainly addressed business sustainable development reporting, operational conditions, and product social life cycle assessments. Brent and Labuschagne (2007) subsequently introduce methods that have been developed to consider social sustainability aspects in the initial phases of projects in the process industry, namely in the design stage of technological systems, whereby a proactive approach in industry can be ensured.

First, a framework of appropriate criteria was developed to assess the sustainability performances of projects, as shown in Figure 2 (Labuschagne et al., 2005). The framework is divided into different levels to address the separate aspects of corporate responsibility strategy in terms of sustainability. The rationale of these levels is described in detail elsewhere (Labuschagne et al., 2005). The framework has been validated and verified by means of project managers in the process industry (Labuschagne and Brent, 2008).

The projects that were used to validate and verify the framework also confirmed that information availability and the standardisation of categories remain problematic (Brent & Labuschagne, 2007). Thus, it is proposed that social sustainability should be incorporated into project management methodologies in phases, commencing with questionnaires and checklists following more traditional risk approaches. An indicator method can be implemented at a later stage when information is more readily available.

An example of a questionnaire is shown in Figure 3 and a checklist in Table 3; the other questionnaires and checklists can be found elsewhere (Labuschagne, 2005: 431). A summary of the main activities and deliverables prompted by the checklists and questionnaires are shown in Figures 4 and 5. Questionnaires and checklists promoting social impact and risk identification should thus be incorporated in project management methodologies as the first step towards addressing the social sustainability of projects. The second step would encompass the implementation of the evaluation

Figure 2. Levels 1 to 4 of the developed sustainability assessment framework (Source: Labuschagne et al. (2005))

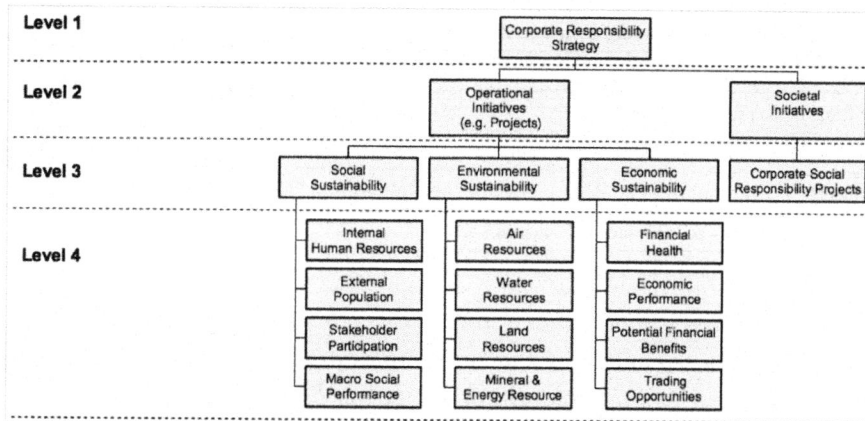

Figure 3. Example of a social questionnaire (pre-feasibility project life cycle phase) (Source: Brent and Labuschagne (2007))

Questionnaire					
		Yes	No	Uncertain	Deliverable
	Activities				
1	Has the company strategy/approach with regards to technology intensive vs employee intensive been communicated to the design team?				
2	Has the company strategy/approach with regards to Health & Safety Practices been communicated to the Design Team?				
3	Does the project require Research & Development support?				
3.1	If yes, interact with R&D department to clarify project roles.				Clear project roles
3.2	If yes, will the R&D be funded by the project or by the mother company?				
4	Is the project an opportunity for current employees to develop their expertise?				
4.1	If yes, decide on how to choose the most suitable project team members				Project Team defined
5	Has all stakeholders (internally and externally) been identified?				List of Stakeholders
5.1	Has internal stakeholders been informed of the Project Kick-off?				
	Possible Impacts or Sources thereof				
6	Can the project result in possible inflow of people to the region?				
7	What is the regulatory set-up in the proposed country?				
8	Are there any known cultural properties that might be affected by the project?				
8.1	If yes, is this a critical concern based on risk evaluation? (Use the Social Risk Assessment Grid as developed by the World Bank)				

Likelihood of Occurrence				
High	R	R	MP	K
Substantial	R	R	MP	MP
Moderate	I	R	T	T
Low	I	R	T	T
	Low	Moderate	Substantial	High

Importance of Risk

K – Killer Concern Assumption
R – Review and Reconsider
MP – Modify Plan – Take action by mitigating
I – Ignore
T=Triggers (Establish indicator, if reached address impact by measures of compensation, etc.)

Table 3. Example of a social checklist (pre-feasibility project life cycle phase)

Checklist			
Has the following been done?	*Yes*	*No*	*Uncertain*
Communicate all relevant strategies to design team			
Clarify the role of R&D in the project			
Identify individuals for project team in accordance with competencies and career paths			
Identify all stakeholders			
Complete questionnaire and identify possible areas of concern			

Source: Brent and Labuschagne (2007)

Figure 4. Summary of proposed activities and deliverables prompted by questionnaires and checklists for project life cycle phases 1 to 3 (Source: Brent and Labuschagne (2007))

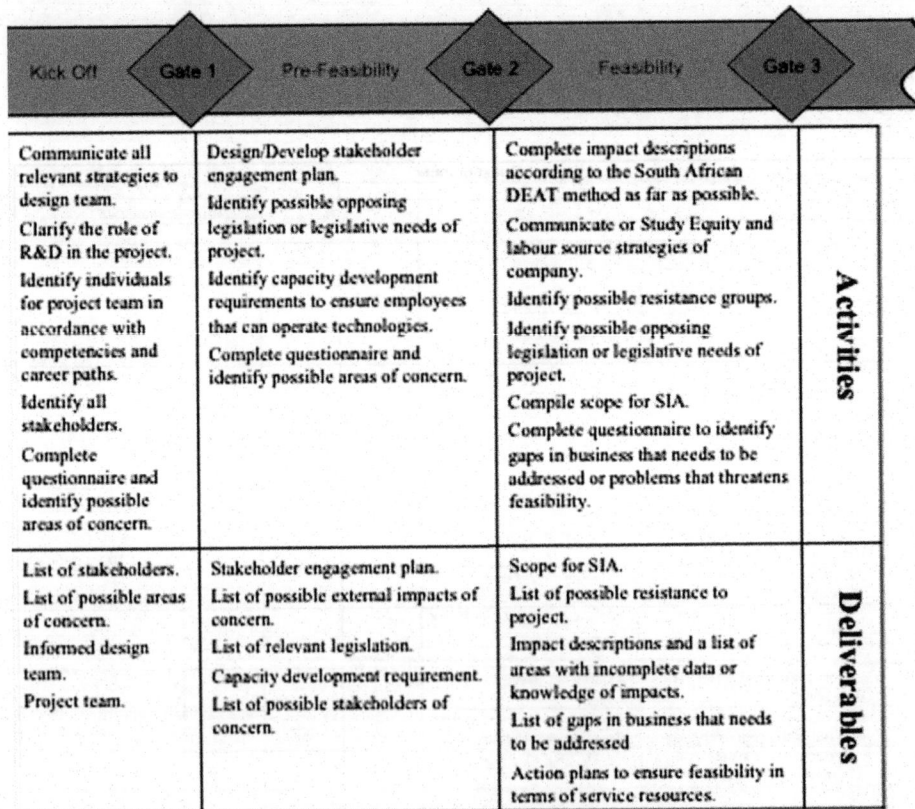

method or indicator approach in project management methodologies. However, this can only occur once the paradigm shift of internalising external social impacts has taken place and the database of social information has been broadened, which would solve most problems associated with the indicator method (See Case 3). Figure 6 shows at which stages in the life cycle the various proposed tools could be used.

The implications on project management, and specifically project evaluation methods, have been described (Labuschagne, 2005: 173). Specifi-

Figure 5. Summary of proposed activities and deliverables prompted by questionnaires and checklists for project life cycle phase 4 to 6 (Source: Brent and Labushagne (2007))

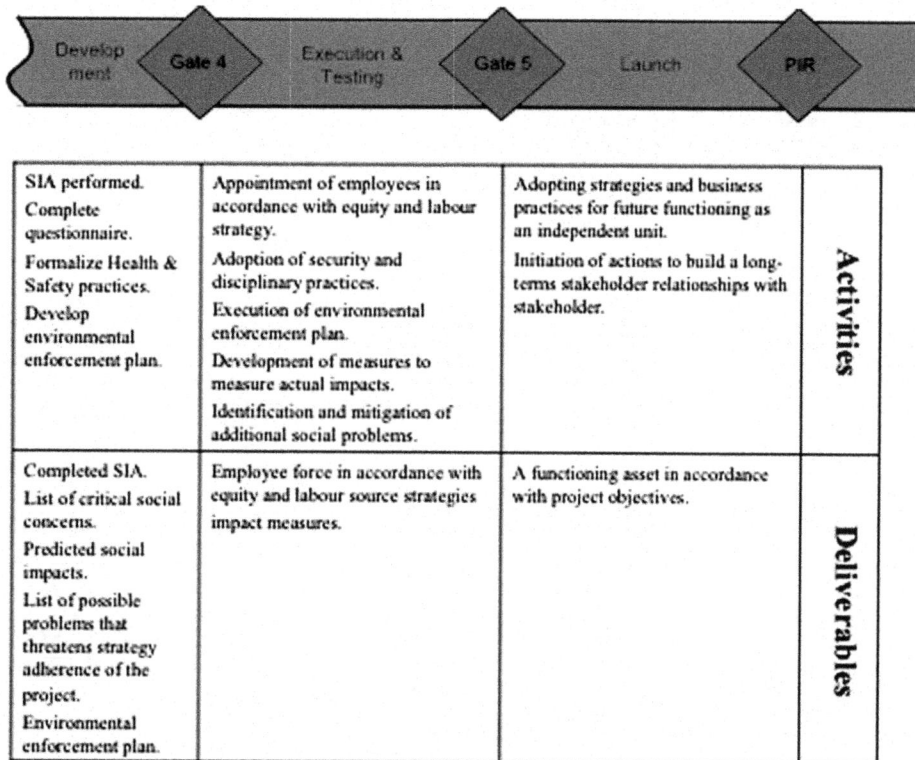

			Activities
SIA performed. Complete questionnaire. Formalize Health & Safety practices. Develop environmental enforcement plan.	Appointment of employees in accordance with equity and labour strategy. Adoption of security and disciplinary practices. Execution of environmental enforcement plan. Development of measures to measure actual impacts. Identification and mitigation of additional social problems.	Adopting strategies and business practices for future functioning as an independent unit. Initiation of actions to build a long-terms stakeholder relationships with stakeholder.	
Completed SIA. List of critical social concerns. Predicted social impacts. List of possible problems that threatens strategy adherence of the project. Environmental enforcement plan.	Employee force in accordance with equity and labour source strategies impact measures.	A functioning asset in accordance with project objectives.	**Deliverables**

Figure 6. The use of the proposed tools over the project life cycle (Source: Brent and Labuschagne (2007))

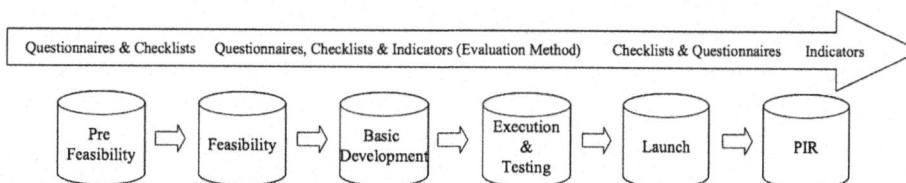

cally, gate review questions have been introduced to determine whether a business should proceed with a project, or not (See Figure 7). A number of decision-making techniques can then be used during the project gate review; similar to what has been described in Case 1.

Case 2 emphasises the need to maintain a systems perspective, and make decisions in a project life cycle, without being able to (necessarily) quantify all sustainability aspects of a project.

Case 3: Evaluating Project Externality Costs in the Metallurgical Sector

It has been suggested that if a proposed project may cause environmental harm, the total cost of damages need to be included in the economic appraisal of the project (Silva & Pagiola, 2003). Therefore, in principle, economic analyses carried out to ascertain the viability of projects should also take into account all the costs and benefits generated by the projects, including environmental

Figure 7. Proposed gate questions in the project life cycle to address social sustainability (Source: Labushagne (2005, p. 175))

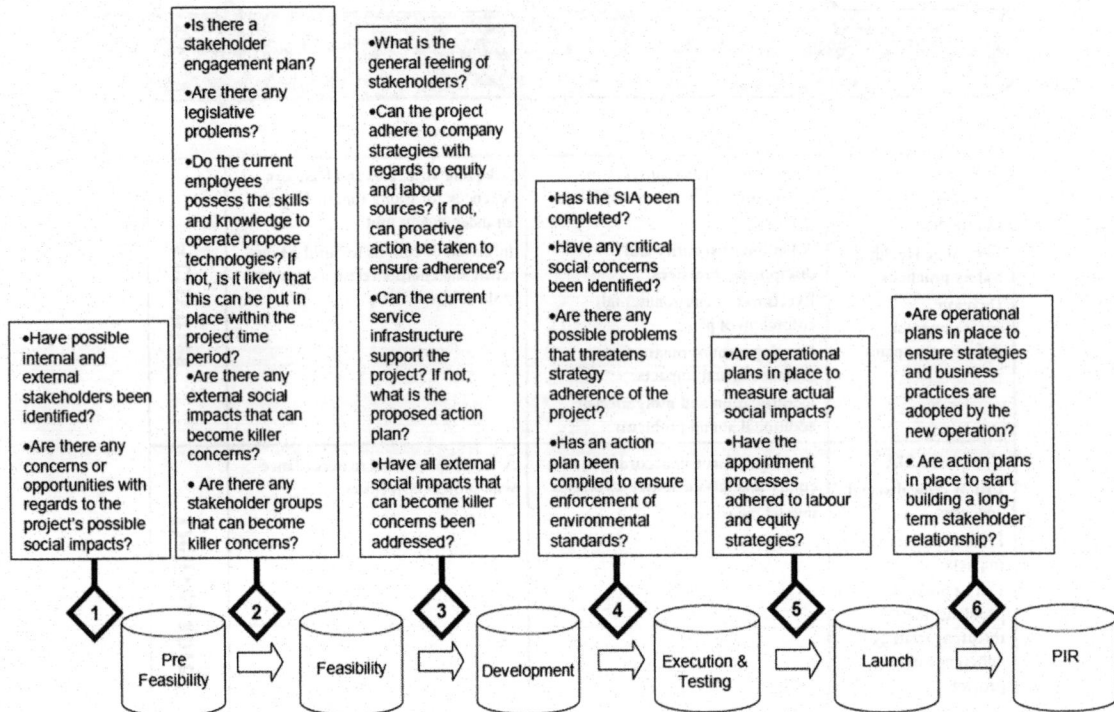

positive or negative impacts from cradle-to-grave. Literature argues that in the past environmental impacts of projects were not considered as part of economic assessment practices, making projects appear artificially more attractive than they were. Some of the reasons for not incorporating externality costs in the economic assessments of projects included a lack of appropriate methodologies to value the impacts (Van Erck, 2003) and environmental issues being viewed as a constraint to business (Wingard, 2001). Nevertheless, Nyoka & Brent (2007) set out to ascertain whether an appropriate method could be established, and specifically for project evaluation in the metallurgical sector of South Africa.

The integrated frameworks and proposed criteria to assess the sustainability of a deployed technology (from Case 2) was utilised (Labuschagne et al., 2005). The environmental impacts associated with a technology life cycle system were grouped into the four main criteria of air, water, land, and mined abiotic resources as summarised in Table 4 (Brent et al., 2006, 2007).

A monetary valuation method for the four criteria (See Table 5), based on the economic Cost Benefit Analysis (CBA) procedure (Blignaut, 1995; van Pelt, 1993), which was developed for the manufacturing sector and specifically for technology-oriented project management purposes (Brent et al., 2006; 2007), was then used (Nyoka & Brent, 2007).

A cash flow analysis and Net Present Values (NPV) were calculated for an expected project life of twenty years. The total potential external costs were then deducted from the projected cash flows of the project. Figure 8 illustrates how damage costs are integrated in the economic evaluation, which has been described in detail elsewhere (Brent et al., 2006, 2007).

Table 4. Environmental criteria definitions

Criteria	Definition
Environmental Sustainability	**The environmental dimension concerns an organization's impacts on the environment due to an introduced technology. It has an external focus and addresses impacts on air, water, land and mined abiotic resources.**
Air Resources	Air Resources assess a technology's contribution to regional air quality effects (e.g. visibility, smell, noise levels, etc.) as well as to global effects such as global warming and stratospheric ozone depletion.
Water Resources	Water Resources assess the availability of clean and safe water by focusing on a technology's impacts on the quantity and quality of water.
Land Resources	Land Resources assess a technology's impacts on the quantity and quality of land resources, including aspects such as biodiversity, erosion, transformation and rehabilitation ability, etc.
Mined Abiotic Resources	Mined Abiotic Resources assess a technology's contribution to the depletion of non-renewable mineral and energy resources.

Source: Nyoka and Brent (2007)

Table 5. Economic CBA procedure

Step	Description
Step 1 Inventory	Costs and benefits that are imposed by a company (as a by-product of its economic activity) on third parties are identified.
Step 2 Monetary Valuation	*Cost approaches:* Cost approaches assess actual costs or hypothetical expenditures aimed at reducing or eliminating impacts. *Benefit approaches:* "Benefit approaches", analyse how changes in environmental and social quality affect income or wealth generation in society; one technique that is used is to calculate opportunity costs to preserve an asset, e.g. relocating an industrial plant to secure an ecological sensitive area.
Step 3 Discounting	Environmental damages of present actions will occur many years from now. The higher the discount rate, the lower the value that will be attached to these damages. The discount rate for externalities is highly debated, and is addressed in the case study of this paper.
Step 4 Risk/Uncertainty	Case probabilities can be assigned to the likelihood that an event (industrial accident) will occur, or little is known about future impacts.

Source: Nyoka and Brent (2007)

Figure 8. Schematic model for incorporating externalities into project economic analysis (Source: Nyoka and Brent (2007))

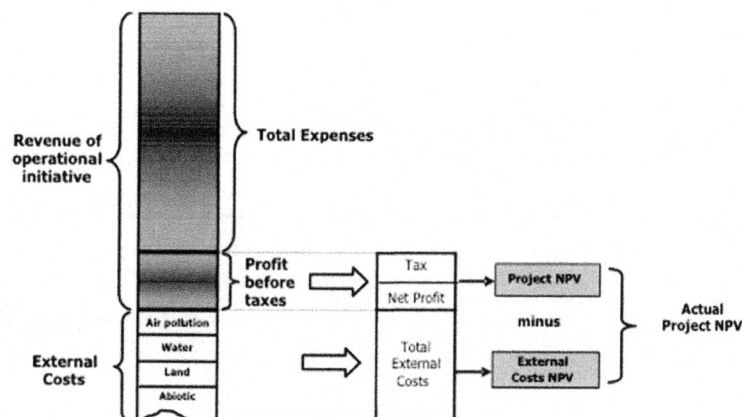

The application of the approach for incorporating externalities into project financial analyses was demonstrated for a steel production project, the details of which was available (Nyoka, 2005).

The monetary evaluation approach highlighted atmospheric pollution as the largest environmental impact associated with the specific project. The site rehabilitation costs that have to be incurred, as it is a regulatory requirement of the national government, and, together with land use during the operational lifecycle phase, are the second largest externalities. Additionally, water is a scarce resource in South Africa; hence the externality cost of water is also of significance. In general, it was found that the negative impacts on the environmental dimension, if accounted for in monetary terms, have a considerable influence on the economic viability of the project.

Due to the long time perspective, estimates of externality costs are very sensitive to the discount rate used for estimating the present value of future damage costs. Figure 9 shows the influence of the discount rate on the economic viability of a project. Though low discount rates theoretically

appear more robust in promoting project sustainability, the chosen discount rate may considerably influence the long-term economic viability of a deployed technology. This underlines the importance of the choice of the discount rate for discounting externality costs, which is much debated in literature. The implication of lower discount rates is that higher net present damage costs are obtained, due to elevated weighting of the present values of future losses and vice versa.

The monetary valuation procedure shows certain limitations. Firstly, it is not possible to express the concept of environmental sustainability in monetary terms in a comprehensive manner. Thereby, not all of the aspects that are considered relevant to assess environmental performances can be measured. Secondly, the values used by the different indicators have to be evaluated on a case-by-case basis and reported in a transparent manner. Also, the uncertainty of the data that is obtained, and on which the procedure is based, may strongly influence the usability of an environmental performance assessment's results; for example, future damage costs will change

Figure 9. Effect of discount rate on the net present value of damages associated with the case study (Source: Nyoka and Brent (2007))

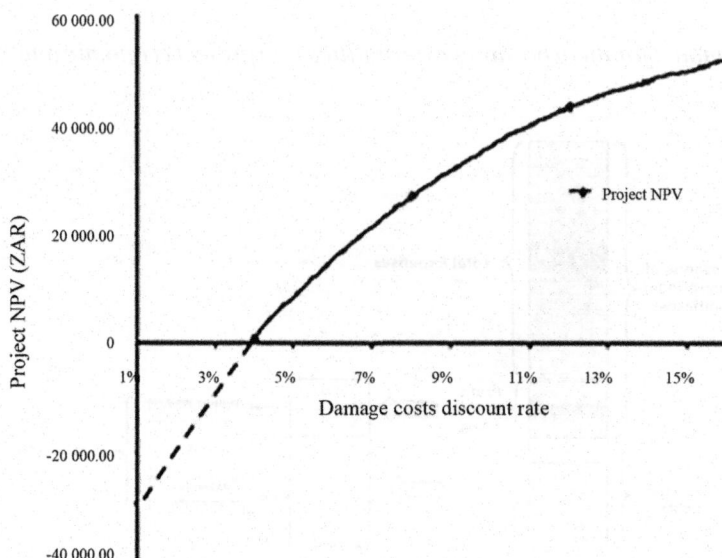

with the fluctuations of the markets. However, this does not mean that the procedure is incapable of improving the understanding of a technology's environmental performance.

Case 3 emphasises the risk of reducing all sustainability aspects of a project to one common denominator, such as a monetary value, that may be more understandable to decision-makers.

Case 4: A System Dynamics Approach to the Sustainability Assessment of Renewable Energy Project Developments

Several renewable energy technologies have reached, or are approaching, maturity that can be utilised for small- and large-scale applications. Biodiesel, a cleaner burning replacement fuel, is argued to potentially contribute to sustainable development in many countries and regions of the world. Biodiesel development projects, however, entail complex interactions of actors such as the technology developers, government at different levels, communities, as well as the natural environment; different actions or responses in the greater system might hinder or undermine the positive effects of such a development. Given such complexity, an integrated and holistic technology assessment approach is indispensible to determine the potential effects of biodiesel development on sustainability in general, which can then inform and enhance proper project planning and management.

Musango and Brent (2011) argue that there is no such formal and coherent approach from a sustainability perspective. Tools such as life cycle assessment and the ecological footprint assessment attempt to jointly analyse industrial and environmental systems; however, most of these techniques focus on the impact of emissions, measured in terms of resource consumption and waste emissions, while ignoring the consequence and contribution to the ecosystem (Bakshi & Fiksel, 2003). Likewise, environmental management systems and environmental due diligence tools are often not fully attuned to the risks and opportunities arising from the degradation of ecosystems and the services they provide (WBCSD, 2008).

System dynamics, however, is an interdisciplinary and transdisciplinary approach that is based on the theory of system structures (Sterman, 2000). System dynamics represents complex systems and analyses their dynamic behaviour over time. The approach has gained popularity due to its focus on the structure and its flexibility, and its potential as an intermediate level tool in technology assessment is recognized (Wolstenholme, 2003).

Recently, several studies have used system dynamics to analyse renewable and alternative energy related issues. Similarly, Musango et al. (2011) utilised a Bioenergy Technology Sustainability Assessment (BIOTSA) model, which is the first system dynamics approach in South Africa for this sector, but focussing on biodiesel development projects. The major interactions considered between society, economy and environmental systems of a biodiesel production development are presented in Figure 10: (1) the society component that includes population, community acceptance and employment, which are relevant for the specific social system; (2) the economic component, which invests capital and labour for biodiesel production in the specific economy; and (3) the environmental components, which determine the key resources that are used, such as land, water, energy and biodiesel related wastes. Musango et al. (2011) gathered the required information and data on the economic, environmental and social conditions for the specific context from various sources. A number of sub-models were developed to simulate the overall system; for example, Figure 11 illustrates the sub-model of community perception – and acceptance.

Qualitative validation using expert opinion was used to assess the model usefulness, importance and quality. The BIOTSA model baseline results and scenarios were subsequently presented at a number of forums. During these dis-

Figure 10. Society-economy-environment interactions in biodiesel production development (Source: Musango et al. (2011))

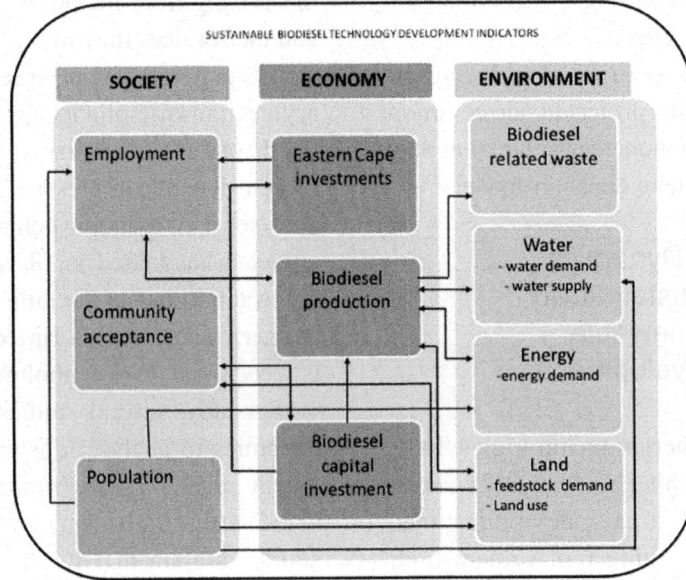

Figure 11. The stock and flow diagram of the community perception sub-model (Source: Musango et al. (2011))

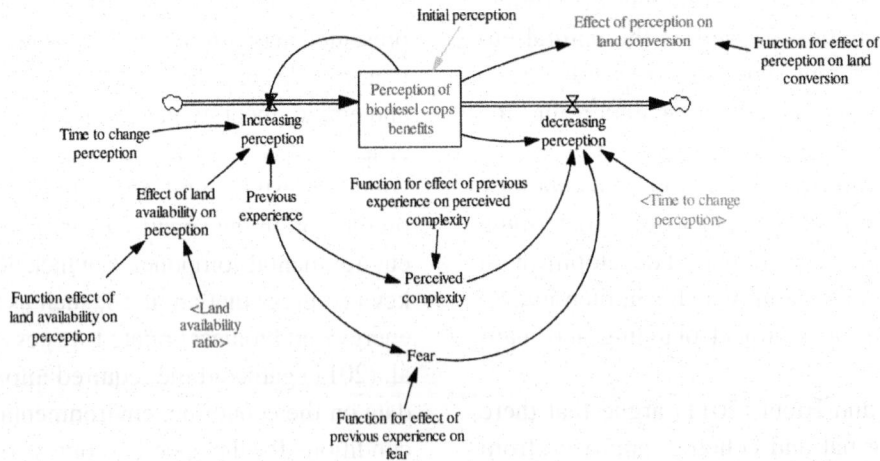

cussions, suggestions were highlighted for improving the model from both technical and practical points of view.

Overall it was highlighted that computer simulations only provide a simple representation of the reality that is being investigated. Thus, they do not capture all the inherent aspects of the reality; hence resulting in some limitations. Some of the specific limitations of the BIOTSA model, for example, are:

Biodiesel Market: The biodiesel production chain consists of crop production, biodiesel production and biodiesel market as illustrated in Figure 12. The biodiesel market can either be

Figure 12. Illustration of the biodiesel production chain (Source: Musango et al. (2011))

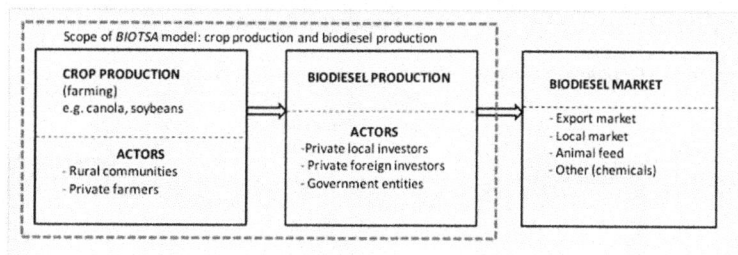

export-oriented or for local consumption. By-products from biodiesel production can be used as animal feed and in the chemical industry. While the BIOTSA model considers a project aimed for the export market, the boundary is limited to the crop production and biodiesel production chain (See Figure 12).

The dynamics of the export market was not taken into account although it could influence the selected sustainability indicators. However, the biodiesel production is not mainly dependent on the outside (export) market but on local conditions such as land availability, community perception and local incentives for investments.

- **Implicit Farming Activities:** The BIOTSA model assumes that the community can easily alter the fallow land to biofuel crop land as long as they have the acceptance to convert this land. The whole social process such as training of the community on the new farming activity was not considered.
- **Feedstock Logistics:** There are a number of feedstock logistics that are involved in the biodiesel production such as biomass collection, pre-processing, storage, and transportation. This was not included in the BIOTSA model due to the lack of such information in the South African situation.
- **Employment:** Biodiesel production development is also claimed to create employment in the farming communities. The BIOTSA model does not consider this type

of employment and only employment in the biodiesel production processes is considered. This was because the level of information on employment in the whole supply chain is unavailable. In addition, given the land that is planned for biodiesel crop production is in the rural areas, it would be difficult to determine the extent to which this employment would be created and thus this was excluded from the model. However, it is possible and important to include when assessing a medium-scale and small-scale biodiesel production development.

Regardless of the limitations and the challenges discussed, the BIOTSA model does provide insights for assessing the impact of biodiesel development on the sustainability indicators and opportunities to improve the value chain.

Case 4 emphasise that techniques that do attemt to undestand the related systems of projects inherently fall short in terms of them being cumbersome and complicated to engage with.

FUTURE RESEARCH DIRECTIONS

To analyse and determine risks and opportunities associated with sustainability aspects requires new approaches to understand interconnectedness in a global world, most notably the systems and nexus approaches to sustainability (See Figure 13) that comprises of the (KPMG, 2012):

Figure 13. The systems and nexus approach (Source: KPMG (2012))

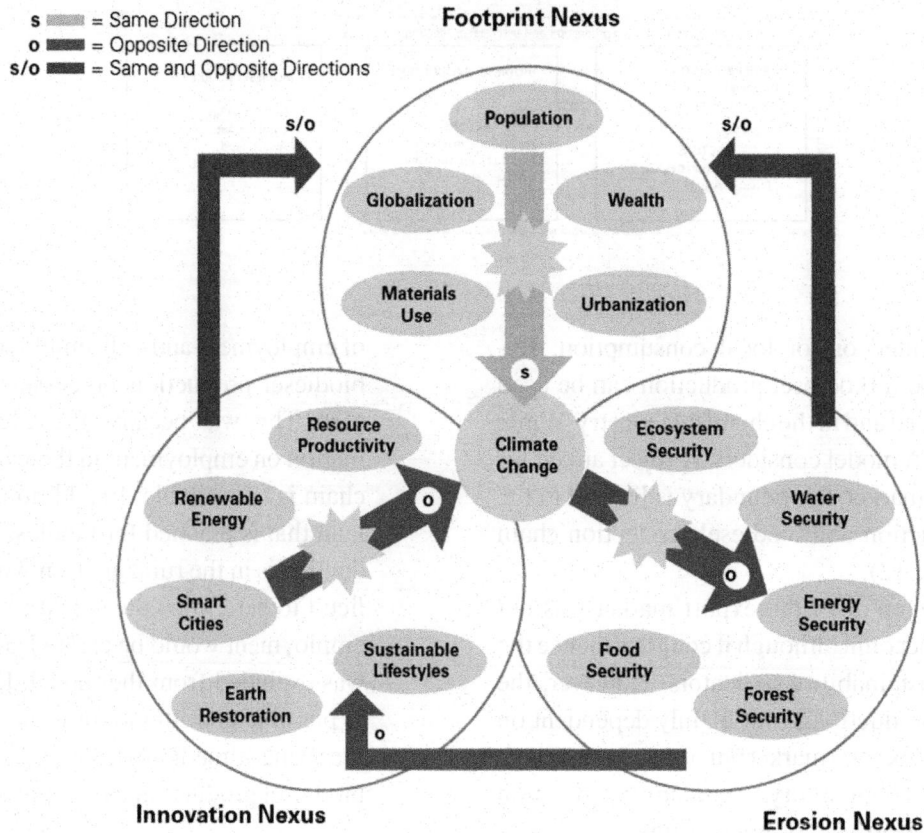

- **Footprint Nexus:** The forces driving the escalating "footprint of mankind on the planet";
- **Erosion Nexus:** The resulting changes in the natural systems on which we (as business) depend; and
- **Innovation Nexus:** The opportunity to address sustainability challenges through business innovation.

Thereby the notion of moving the paradigm of 'business as usual' into the social-ecological context, so as to better understand and address risk and uncertainty to promote resilience of the system, and thereby the sustainability of the enterprise, may be achieved. Despite the clear link between ecological health, social well-being and enterprise resilience, corporate sustainability practices have, for the most part, remained fragmented, non-strategic, and insular. Unfortunately, this mindset will do little to reduce the real risks that the enterprise faces today due to global changes and the nexus. An important research priority, from a project management perspective, is therefore the development of appropriate modelling and decision-making approaches and tools that support dynamic, adaptive management, rather than static optimisation. These approaches and tools need to determine the points of intervention of a project in the larger social-ecological system whereby the resilience of the enterprise can be increased through desired configurations to meet future changes. This requires methods for understanding the full implications of alternative choices and their relative attractiveness in terms of enhancing the resilience of systems, by extending the field of sustainability science into the field of project management (See Figure 14).

CONCLUSION

Society needs the public and private sectors to engage in the sustainability arena. This will, however, not happen because of an optional executive commitment to an abstract concept. The sectors will engage in the notion of sustainability only if it is a good strategy (Gilding, 2005). However, in many ways it may be argued that sustainability is the only strategy left to pursue (KPMG, 2012). Sustainability issues cannot be treated as separate from core enterprise activities and practices, as social-ecological systems are the base of all economic activity. Without communities there will be no enterprises. If environmental resources are not managed according to a sustainable strategy, primary industry activities will not take place, thereby breaking the whole chain of industrial

(and other entrepreneurial) activities. Enterprises should thus think further than pure profit – society needs capitalism with a soul. The focus should be on free enterprise in partnership with other stakeholders. Sustainable development is about balance, namely balancing the economic needs within the natural environment's limits without negatively impacting on intergenerational equity. It is thus concluded that all enterprises should address sustainability aspects, but not at the expense of losing perspective of the their reason for existence – their economic licence to operate.

If it (the enterprise) does not make profits, it will not survive; equally if it thinks only about profits, it will not survive either, since it has to think about the long-term, its goods and services, and the people who touch it. -Lorde Browne as cited by Macalister (2005).

This chapter investigated the approaches and tools that have been used to address sustainability aspects in project management practices (in the South African context). A number of challenges

Figure 14. The extension of the sustainability science field to project management

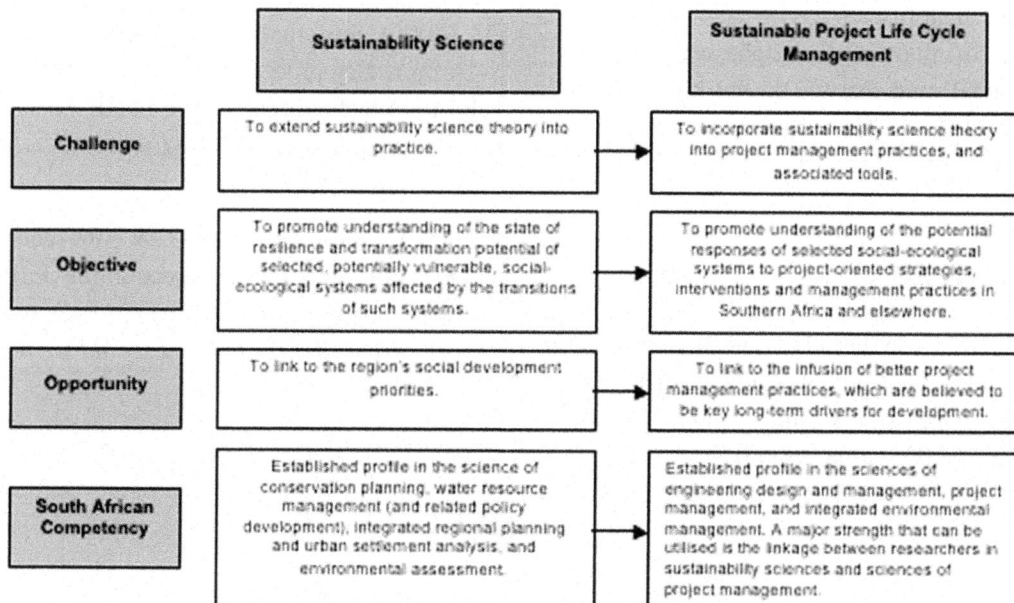

are highlighted to utilise such approaches and tools. It is concluded that, conceptually, the critical principles upon which to base these new approaches to dealing with the fundamental uncertainty, from a sustainability perspective, within project management practices include:

- Acknowledging and adopting a systems approach to the management of a project by recognising the relationships and interactions between the social and ecological systems relevant to the project.
- Diversifying project management practices and processes to expose and enable the enterprise to exploit positive outcomes associated with uncertainty and to minimise the exposure of the impacts of negative consequences of uncertainty, whilst maximising positive impacts.
- Educating and convincing shareholders of these aspects so as to get support for these initiatives.

The latter is important because it is likely that the implementation of new approaches and procedures that fulfill the previous requirements will incur upfront net economic costs and longer-term future benefits.

It is also important to emphasise that these are the 'ideal' and that we do not know all the answers, and thus requires an openness to principle of adaptive learning.

REFERENCES

Aras, G., & Crowther, D. (2009). Corporate sustainability reporting: A study in disingenuity? *Journal of Business Ethics*, *84*(1), 279–288. doi:10.1007/s10551-008-9806-0.

Bakshi, B. R., & Fiksel, J. (2003). The quest for sustainability: Challenges for process systems engineering. *AIChE Journal. American Institute of Chemical Engineers*, *49*(6), 1350–1358. doi:10.1002/aic.690490602.

Berns, M., Townend, A., Khayat, Z., Balagopal, B., Reeves, M, Hopkins, M.S., & Kruschwitz, N. (2009, Fall). The business of sustainability: What it means to managers now. *MIT Sloan Management Review*.

Blignaut, J. N. (1995). *Environmental accounting in South Africa*. (Doctoral thesis) University of Pretoria, Pretoria, South Africa.

Brent, A. C., & Labuschagne, C. (2007). An appraisal of social aspects in project and technology life cycle management in the process industry. *Management of Environmental Quality: An International Journal*, *18*(4), 413–426. doi:10.1108/14777830710753811.

Brent, A. C., & Pretorius, M. W. (2008). Sustainable development and technology management. In M.H. Sherif, & Khalil (Eds.), Management of technology innovation and value creation, (vol. 2, pp. 185-204). Hoboken, NJ: World Scientific.

Brent, A. C., van Erck, R. P. G., & Labuschagne, C. (2006). Sustainability cost accounting: Part 1 – A monetary procedure to evaluate the sustainability of technologies in the South African process industry. *South African Journal of Industrial Engineering*, *17*(2), 35–51.

Brent, A. C., van Erck, R. P. G., & Labuschagne, C. (2007). Sustainability cost accounting: Part 2 – A case study in the South African process industry. *South African Journal of Industrial Engineering*, *18*(1), 1–17.

De Piante Henriksen, A. (1997). A technology assessment primer for management of technology. *International Journal of Technology Management*, *13*, 615–638. doi:10.1504/IJTM.1997.001681.

Eweje, G. (2011). A shift in corporate practice? Facilitating sustainability strategy in companies. *Corporate Social Responsibility and Environmental Management*, *18*, 125–136. doi:10.1002/csr.268.

Gilding, P. (2005). The profit motive is pure enough. *The Australian*. Retrieved June 6, 2012, from http://www.onlineopinion.com.au/author.asp?id=3806

Gonzales-Benito, J., & Gonzales-Benito, O. (2008). Operation management practices linked to the adoption of ISO 14001: An empirical analysis of Spanish manufacturers. *International Journal of Production Economics*, *113*, 60–73. doi:10.1016/j.ijpe.2007.02.051.

Haanaes, K., Reeves, M., von Strengvelken, I., Audretsch, M., Kiron, D., & Kruschwitz, N. (2012, Winter). Sustainability nears a tipping point. *MIT Sloan Management Review*.

Kamal, M. A.-S. A.-H. (2001). Application of the AHP in project management. *International Journal of Project Management*, *19*, 19–27. doi:10.1016/S0263-7863(99)00038-1.

Klein, J. T. (2004). Prospects for transdisciplinarity. *Futures*, *36*, 515–526. doi:10.1016/j.futures.2003.10.007.

KPMG. (2011). *Corporate sustainability: A progress report*. Retrieved May 20, 2012, from http://www.kpmg.com/sustainability

KPMG. (2012). *Expect the unexpected: Building business value in a changing world*. Retrieved May 20, 2012, from http://www.kpmg.com/sustainability

Labuschagne, C. (2005). *Sustainable project life cycle management: Incorporating social criteria in decision making*. (PhD Thesis). University of Pretoria, Pretoria, South Africa. Retrieved June 2, 2012, from http://upetd.up.ac.za/thesis/available/etd-10112005-083255

Labuschagne, C., & Brent, A. C. (2005). Sustainable project life cycle management: The need to integrate life cycles in the manufacturing sector. *International Journal of Project Management*, *23*, 159–168. doi:10.1016/j.ijproman.2004.06.003.

Labuschagne, C., & Brent, A. C. (2008). An industry perspective of the completeness and relevance of a social assessment framework for project and technology management in the manufacturing sector. *Journal of Cleaner Production*, *16*, 253–262. doi:10.1016/j.jclepro.2006.07.028.

Labuschagne, C., Brent, A. C., & van Erck, R. P. G. (2005). Assessing the sustainability performance of industries. *Journal of Cleaner Production*, *13*(4), 373–385. doi:10.1016/j.jclepro.2003.10.007.

Macalister, T. (2005). Browne lauds the noble purpose of making money. *The Guardian*. Retrieved June 6, 2012, from http://www.guardian.co.uk/business/2005/feb/oilandpetrol.news

Mulder, J. (2003). *Project selection criteria for LandCare projects*. (Masters dissertation). University of Pretoria, Pretoria, South Africa.

Mulder, J., & Brent, A. C. (2006). Selection of sustainable agriculture projects in South Africa: Case studies in the LandCare programme. *Journal of Sustainable Agriculture*, *28*(2), 55–84. doi:10.1300/J064v28n02_06.

Musango, J. K., & Brent, A. C. (2011). Assessing the sustainability of energy technological systems in Southern Africa: A review and way forward. *Technology in Society*, *33*, 145–155. doi:10.1016/j.techsoc.2011.03.011.

Musango, J. K., Brent, A. C., Amigun, B., Pretorius, L., & Müller, H. (2011). Technology sustainability assessment of biodiesel development in South Africa: A system dynamics approach. *Energy*, *36*, 6922–6940. doi:10.1016/j.energy.2011.09.028.

Nieto, M., Lopez, F., & Cruz, F. (1998). Performance analysis of technology using the S curve model: The case of digital signal processing (DSP) technologies. *Technovation*, *18*, 439–457. doi:10.1016/S0166-4972(98)00021-2.

Nyoka, M. (2005). *Internalising environmental costs: A case study of the minerals extraction industry in South Africa*. (Masters thesis). University of Pretoria, Pretoria, South Africa.

Nyoka, M., & Brent, A. C. (2007). Application of an environmental valuation approach to incorporate externality costs in decision making of the metallurgical sector. *Journal of the South African Institute of Mining and Metallurgy*, *107*(10), 663–669.

Reilly, A., & Weirup, A. (2010). Sustainability initiatives, social media activity, and organizational culture: An exploratory study. *Journal of Sustainability and Green Business*. Retrieved May 29, 2012, from http://ww.w.aabri.com/manuscripts/10621.pdf

Roelofse, A. J., & Pretorius, M. W. (2003). A generalised innovation model for large organizations. In *Proceedings of PICMET*. Portland, OR: PICMET.

Silva, P., & Pagiola, S. (2003). A review of the valuation of environmental costs and benefits in World Bank projects. *Environmental Economic Series*, *94*. Retrieved June 2, 2012, from http://econwpa.wustl.edu:80/eps/othr/papers/0502/0502007.pdf

Sterman, J. D. (2000). *Business dynamics: Systems thinking and modelling for a complex world*. New York: McGraw-Hill/Irwin.

Swasdio, U., Islam, N., & Krairit, D. (2004). Commercialization of technologies developed in public research and development institutes: The case of Thailand. *IEEE Engineering Management Conference Proceedings*, *2*, 617-621.

Tran, T. A. (2007). Review of methods and tools applied in technology assessment literature. In *Proceedings of PICMET*. Portland, OR: PICMET.

Van Erck, R. P. G. (2003). *Monetary evaluation of business sustainability, case study: GTL fuel production in South Africa*. (Masters thesis). Technical University of Eindhoven, Eindhoven, The Netherlands.

Van Pelt, M. J. F. (1993). Ecologically sustainable development and project appraisal in developing countries. *Ecological Economics*, *7*, 19–42. doi:10.1016/0921-8009(93)90018-2.

Wheelwright, S. C., & Clark, K. B. (1992). *Revolutionizing product development*. New York: The Free Press.

Wingard, C. H. (2001). *Financial performance of environmentally responsible South African listed companies*. (Doctoral thesis). University of Pretoria, Pretoria, South Africa.

Wolstenholme, E. F. (2003). The use of system dynamics as a tool for intermediate level technology evaluation: Three case studies. *Journal of Engineering and Technology Management*, *20*, 193–204. doi:10.1016/S0923-4748(03)00018-3.

World Business Council for Sustainable Development (WBCSD). (2008). *Guidelines for identifying business risks and opportunities arising from ecosystem change*. Conches-Geneva: WBCSD.

World Business Council for Sustainable Development (WBCSD). (2010). *Vision 2050: The new agenda for business.* Retrieved May 20, 2012, from http://www.wbcsd.org/vision2050.aspx

KEY TERMS AND DEFINITIONS

Adaptive Capacity: Is determined by the ability of institutions and networks to learn, and store knowledge and experience; creative flexibility in decision-making and problem solving; and the existence of power structures that are responsive and consider the needs of all stakeholders.

Adaptive Management: Is an iterative process of optimal decision-making in the face of uncertainty, with the aim to reduce that uncertainty over time via system monitoring.

Complexity: Deals with the study of complex systems, which are composed of many elements that interact in complex ways, and the ability to model complex interaction structures with few parameters.

Externality: Is a consequence of an economic activity that is experienced by unrelated third parties. An externality can be either positive or negative.

Resilience: Is the resistance and robustness of an integrated system against surprises, which includes risk-based measures and precautionary regulations and the capacity to buffer change, learn and develop.

Sustainable Development: Is about balancing the economic needs within the natural environment's limits without negatively impacting on intergenerational equity.

Sustainability Science: Recognizes the negative and positive feedback loops associated with socio-ecological systems and technology and the role of technological life cycles to enhance the sustainability of complex socio-ecological systems.

Technology: Is a way or ways of carrying through any economic purpose and may exist as pure method or pure information or it may be embodied in physical products or processes.

Technology Management: Addresses the effective identification, selection, acquisition, development, exploitation, and protection of technologies in the form of product, process and infrastructure, which are needed to sustain the competitive advantage of regional sectors in accordance with sector, regional, national and international sustainable development objectives.

Chapter 11
Sustainability in Project Management:
Practical Applications

Jennifer Tharp
Mastodon Consulting, USA

ABSTRACT

As organizations evolve to embrace sustainability objectives, the operations of a company need to evolve to support those new objectives. Since project management is how strategy is executed within an organization, project management's evolution is key to this new reality. In this chapter, the author examines aspects of a sustainability program, common goals between project management and sustainability, and pragmatic implementation guidelines, which help the project manager integrate sustainability into his practices. Special emphasis is placed on each process area of project management, from inception through execution and control. The objectives of this chapter are: (1) translate the fundamental aspects of sustainability to the corporate environment and broader community; (2) understand the risk of ignoring sustainability aspects in projects, as expectations change, both in terms of direct financial loss and longer-term impact; and (3) explore how to integrate sustainability practices into project management knowledge areas.

INTRODUCTION

To do their jobs well, project managers must be fiscally sustainable – managing time and budget – as well as socially and environmentally sustainable – managing resources. But project managers usually only look at these impacts within their own projects – as if they were islands, unrelated to the rest of the company and the broader community. Placing project management in the correct strategic context helps project managers and teams see the big picture, to make the right decisions for their projects for their organization and for the broader community.

DOI: 10.4018/978-1-4666-4177-8.ch011

Project managers are experts at execution, but sustainability is a pretty new idea for many of us, and we're not sure how to integrate it into our day-to-day lives as project managers. This chapter will focus on the tactical elements – how we as project managers can modify the project management practices we already use to work in a more sustainable manner.

This chapter will examine the business need for sustainability, and how a project manager can be a critical factor in its execution. How does the work of the project manager change to embrace this new reality?

THE BUSINESS MANDATE FOR SUSTAINABILITY

It is tempting to think that what your company does has nothing to do with the broader community, but in reality, corporations and society depend on each other. Communities need corporations to give their people employment and infrastructure, and corporations need healthy societies to provide a capable workforce. This mutual dependence is the reason why business decisions must follow the principle of shared value – the activities a company does must benefit the society it operates in, and vice versa (Porter, 2006, p. 5). Stakeholders of the broader corporation – shareholders, suppliers, customers, partners, regulators, activists, labor unions, employees, community members, and government – expect companies to be accountable for their own operations, but also for the performance of their entire supply chain.

A sustainable focus helps a company achieve basic fundamentals of good business practice. This helps an organization be able to assess risks more effectively, and to become more proactive in dealing with these risks. As a result, sustainability not only becomes a necessary value of organizations, but it is quickly becoming integrated into the business goals and objectives of organizations. In order for businesses to be successful in the future, then they must consider social, environmental,

and supply issues wherever they operate, and wherever their suppliers and customers operate (Porter & Kramer, 2006).

There are further advantages to the business that operates sustainably. Many companies wait until a law is passed which prohibits something, before they change their behavior. But a company that acts in advance of legislation, instead of merely reacting to laws that have already been passed, avoids risks to its reputation, and can gain strategic competitive advantage over their rivals (Barton, 2011). Also, working on societal problems related to the business can help spark innovative thinking by exposing employees to new ideas and perspectives (Kanter, 2010). An organization's focus on sustainability can result in improved corporate reputation, higher brand equity, better risk management and increased access to capital, and is vital to attracting and retaining top talent.

THE TIE WITH PROJECT MANAGEMENT

When we think about introducing sustainability into an organization, we tend to think of purely operational concerns – the amount of paper used by the copier, turning the lights off at night. But projects are how the company evolves, changes, and reaches strategic objectives. It's these actions that are most critical to the company's work, and where sustainability needs to get a toehold.

Projects are temporary in nature, so it's not intuitive that there would be a connection with the long-term orientation of sustainability. However, all projects take place within a strategic context, and there are both internal and external environmental factors that surround or influence a project's success. Understanding the framework in which the project takes place helps ensure that work is carried out in alignment with the goals of the enterprise and managed in accordance with the established practice methodologies of the organization. (PMI, 2008, p 45)

These factors may enhance or constrain project management options and may have a positive or negative influence on the outcome (Figure 1). In much the same way that a project manager must balance cost, schedule and scope, there are trade-offs that must be made between the economic, social and environmental factors surrounding a project.

Being responsible for economic sustainability means moving beyond the simple ROI for the project, and ensuring that it fits in the overall strategy for the firm. What are the key economic drivers for the organization? How does this project contribute to those drivers? How will this initiative, once deployed, contribute to the long-term fiscal viability of the organization? These factors need to be part of any project business case, as metrics are the driver for strategic outcomes.

Just as the project manager must understand the business benefits the project yields, he is also accountable for any long-term impacts of his projects. Project managers have traditionally focused on the process of getting from an idea to an implemented project. We haven't scrutinized longer-term issues, such as what happens to the product as it's manufactured, used and disposed of. This implies taking responsibility for the results of the project, including the sustainability aspects of that result. The developed product or service

Figure 1. Sustainability: strategic context for project management

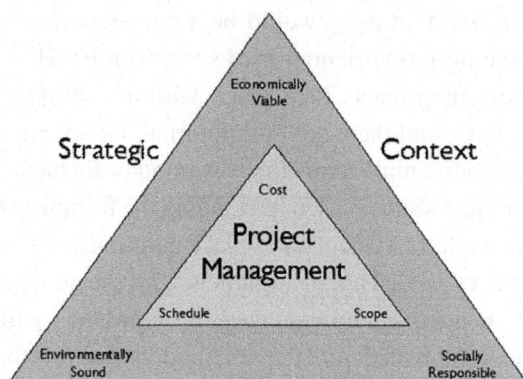

does not go away once we hand it over. It has an impact on the world, a useful period of operation and ultimate disposal.

Ensuring a project is socially sustainable involves reflecting on organizational culture, structure, and processes, existing human resource skills and personnel practices, both inside the firm and throughout the value chain (Porter and Kramer, 2006). In this way, the PM can play a pivotal role in sustainability. Being familiar with the details of day-to-day operations and execution, the project manager is in a position to perceive and analyze socially relevant issues and situations that may not be obvious to senior management. For example, the project manager knows from firsthand experience that norms and laws, culture and traditions may render a project very different in execution and outcome from what it is in other countries, including his company's home country (Tharp Russell, 2008).

Incorporating sustainability into project management helps us cope with the complexity of projects, reduces project crisis situations, project cancellations and interruptions, and the fluctuation of project personnel, creates a competitive advantage and economic benefits and promotes sustainable project results (Gareis et al., 2010).

Former PMI President Greg Balestrero noted, "Social responsibility is no longer the whim of an environmentally sensitive CEO. It has become a mandate for all organizations in every operation. Project managers must recognize and address this mandate now and into the future." (Hunsberger, 2008)

Responsibilities of a Project Manager

The experienced project manager takes a systems view of his project, looking at all factors, inside and outside, over the entire lifecycle of the project. Project managers are the ones who direct the consumption of resources in a project, and the ones who can instill a life cycle mentality into the project from its inception to its ultimate disposal.

PMI's Code of Ethics and Professional Conduct states: "We make decisions and take actions based on the best interest of society, public safety, and the environment." This aspirational statement demonstrates the importance of balancing sustainability with other project management priorities (PMI, undated).

PMI, as an organization, also follows the strategic principle: PMI shall take actions and make decisions in a socially and environmentally responsible way (PMI, 2009, p 9).

ASPECTS OF SUSTAINABILITY

When it embraces sustainability, a company takes responsibility for the impact of its activities on customers, employees, shareholders, communities and the environment through all aspects of its operations.

A sustainable focus recognizes the interdependence between companies and the broader society, and encompasses the following aspects:

- **Human Rights:** Human rights are inalienable fundamental rights to which a person is entitled, just by the nature of being human. As project managers, we must consider:
  - Does our project protect stakeholders from discrimination of vulnerable groups and other civil rights violations?
  - Are there effective policies to prevent harassment?
  - Human rights include freedom of speech, including right to assembly. Do your company, and all vendors and suppliers on the project, allow workers to speak out for better pay or better working conditions?
  - What about freedom from slavery? Many organizations have had issues with indentured servants, often for-

eigners, not being paid fair wages. How can you be sure this issue doesn't affect your company, and companies in your value chain?

- **Labor Practices:** Conditions of work, health and safety, and development and training.
  - Where Human Rights (previously) encompasses the freedom of speech to speak out against poor conditions – what about protecting them from poor conditions to begin with?
  - Do your project teams and subcontractors have fair pay, living wages, and job opportunities?
  - Do project members inside and outside your firm have freedom of association and the right to collective bargaining for employees?

- **The Environment:** Sustainable resource use, pollution prevention and climate change mitigation.
  - Are life cycle value assessments done for assets and product development?
  - Are you using sustainable practices, cradle to cradle, to develop new products and sell to new markets?

- **Fair Operating Practices:** Anti-corruption, fair competition, and respect for property rights.
  - Most countries have anti-bribery laws on the books, but they might not be enforced. Does your project have strict, enforced rules against corruption?
  - Is your project transparent with partners and prospective partners? Are partners selected in a fair and transparent manner? Does your project respect intellectual and other property of others?
  - What is your project's relationship with government agencies and other external organizations?

- **Consumer Issues:** Fair contractual practices, dispute resolution and fair marketing.
  - Does your project represent itself honestly to the rest of the organization?
  - If the project is to develop a product or service, is it represented honestly to customers? Do you offer a way for unhappy consumers to seek redress?
  - Does your project team negotiate contracts with others in your value chain fairly?
- **Community Involvement and Engagement:** Employee training and skills development, wealth and income creation and community involvement.
  - Does your project actively manage stakeholders, inside and outside the firm?
  - Do you ensure that your project team members get the training they need to advance in their own professional development, outside of immediate project goals (ISO, 2010)?

Over the remainder of this chapter, we will discuss how and when to evaluate some of these core issues as part of sustainable project management.

INCORPORATING SUSTAINABILITY INTO PROJECT MANAGEMENT PRACTICES

Project managers are instrumental in achieving strategic goals, as they hold the path to execution. For an organization to realize sustainability goals, sustainability principles must be integrated in every step of the project management framework, from project selection through risk and communication management.

Portfolio Management and Project Selection

Projects, within programs or portfolios, are a means of achieving organizational goals and objectives, often in the context of a strategic plan. One goal of portfolio management is to maximize the value of the portfolio by the careful examination of its components—the constituent programs, projects, and other related work. In this way, an organization's strategic plan becomes the primary factor guiding investments in projects (PMI, 2008, p 40-41).

Project Portfolio Management is the bridge between project management and organizational imperatives such as sustainability. When managers use sustainability objectives as a basis for determining which projects are selected and given priority, the end result is that only those projects that move towards those long-term goals will be undertaken.

Inclusion of Sustainability Objectives Within the Project Charter

The Project Charter formally authorizes a project, and documents initial high-level requirements that satisfy the stakeholders' needs and expectations. The charter determines what success looks like, as it includes the objectives that must be met for the project to be considered successful.

Integrating the principles of sustainability in the project charter will help define the result, objective, conditions and success factors of the project. The content, intended result and success criteria are based on a holistic view of the project, including sustainability perspectives as 'economical, environmental and social', 'short term and long term' and 'local and global' (Silvius, G, Schipper, R, Planko, J, van den Brink, J & Köhler, A, p 49-51). Within the charter, the project manager translates the goals of the organization into a project outcome that effectively and efficiently meets the goals of the organization and the broad set of project stakeholders (Mochal, 2010).

Guiding principles for the project, and team values may be enshrined within the project, as the firm's organizational strategy and core values are translated to project outcomes. These outcomes are extended beyond the usual charter elements of cost, schedule and resource declarations, to include sustainability objectives of the project, which keep the other objectives in balance.

By balancing sustainability constraints with other project goals in the charter – for example, we will get this effort done in this time frame without forcing employees to work weekends – the project is set up for success at the outset.

Stakeholder Identification and Management

Stakeholders are persons or organizations (e.g., customers, sponsors, the performing organization, or the public), who are actively involved in the project or whose interests may be positively or negatively affected by the performance or completion of the project. (PMI, 2008, p 53)

Project managers have traditionally had a narrow view of stakeholders, looking primarily at those within the organization who are most directly impacted by the activities of a project, such as team members, customers and the sponsor.

However, a holistic view defines a stakeholder as anyone with power, legitimacy, and urgency over a project, and/or its longer-term impacts (Mitchell, 1997, p 873). Stakeholders bear power and influence over the project, how it is formed, how problems are solved, and the end result of the project. Stakeholders who are located outside of the company, who represent community, social or environmental interests, have very little direct power, so it is incumbent on the project manager to carefully identify the salient interests who should be incorporated into project stakeholders. It's critical to include these stakeholders, as "in

the long run, those who do not use power in a manner which society considers responsible will tend to lose it" (Davis, 1973, p 314).

Supporting the principles of sustainability – balancing social, environmental and economical interests, both short term and long term and both local and global – will increase the number of stakeholders of the project. Typical "sustainability stakeholders" may be environmental protection pressure groups, human rights groups, nongovernmental organizations, etc. In order to perform the project successfully, the project manager needs to acquire the buy-in of the stakeholders. This means the project manager must have conceptual and operational knowledge about the knowledge domains of the now extended stakeholders group (Silvius, 2012). The project manager also benefits from this direct engagement, as he gains powerful expertise outside his traditional domain, which strengthens not just the project, but also his firm as a whole.

In including external stakeholders, project managers need to evaluate:

- Are all groups or individuals affected by the project been identified, and have the impacts on them been assessed?
- Are stakeholder meetings organized?
- Are there community forums, information brochures and/or information Websites?
- Do stakeholders have an effect during the project, or during the lifecycle of the eventual product or service? (Oehlmann, 2010)

Truly active stakeholder management isn't limited to what the stakeholders expect from the project, but also includes what the project expects from the stakeholder.

An illustration of the principle of extended stakeholder engagement in a sustainable environment follows:

In this past year, in the wake of the Gulf accident, what has surprised you?

Well, timelines have gotten longer. When I was an engineer back in the '80s working for this company, when you moved into a new project you focused on the technical aspects — getting the permits involved, figuring out if you could actually drill in water this deep, could you produce in this type of environment. Those are all still big parts of the equation, but they're maybe half of the equation. The other half is about communities and stakeholders. What are the needs of communities where you want to work? What do they think and how involved are they? This is a shift from being a company where you basically looked at the world and said, 'Trust me. I'm going to do it the right way.' Now we have stakeholders whose point of view is, 'Show me and involve me. Make me part of this. I'm going to be part of these decisions going forward.' It changes everything. It changes the way we think as a company. It raises our performance. And it changes the timeline of these projects.

…We deal quite a bit with native groups, with indigenous people, first nations and others. We've learned a lot in this process about not only how we should approach those areas, but what the values are in those kinds of communities.

When I look at an investment proposal now, it still covers the technical issues, of course. It certainly covers the financial issues. But fully half of that proposal deals with what I would call the nontechnical risk. The social performance, the sustainability issues — how have those been taken into account? What are the headline issues? How are we dealing with them? How will we mitigate the risk associated with those? What's the cost of that, and how long does that take? - Marvin Odum, President of Shell Oil (Hopkins, 2011).

Careful identification and management of stakeholders is critical to developing a sustainable project structure and culture, as all decisions flow from there. For example, the project manager de-velops requirements by defining and documenting stakeholders' needs to meet the project objectives. The project's success is directly influenced by the care taken in capturing and managing project and product requirements. (PMI, 2008, p 135).

Human Resources Management

As project managers improve the competencies, team interaction, and the overall team environment to enhance project performance, they also need to look at the broader picture – to look beyond the artificial barriers of the project itself and evaluate human resource implications in the larger community, and over the lifecycle of the product that the project is creating.

Human resource elements already tend to get short attention from project managers, partially because most project teams are in a matrix environment, where team members do not report directly to the project manager. So the project manager primarily addresses human resource management via team building, recognition and rewards, and occasionally professional development of team members.

However, a longer-term, sustainable focus requires the project manager address these elements for project team members:

- Work-life balance, training, personnel administration policies, meetings and travel.
- Equity, quality and enhancement of the work environment, education, ethics, skill development and social inclusion.
- Sufficient income for team members to economically support themselves and their families, family services, health and safety, worker rights, respect, transparency and honesty (Morgese, no date).

Sustainability principles should be built into the roles and responsibilities of the project manager and team members.

That is a lot to put on one project manager, and much of it outside the PM's direct control, but not outside of his influence. By being aware of these issues, he can raise them directly to line management, or address them, as he is able to, within the confines of the project.

However, his responsibility does not stop there. There are also human resource management issues for the broader stakeholder community. The organization cannot claim to have a sustainability focus if vendors and suppliers do not uphold the same principles in raw material development that the purchasing organization follows.

Procurement Management

Project Procurement Management includes the contract management and change control processes required to develop and administer contracts or purchase orders issued by authorized project team members (PMI, 2008, p 343)

Project managers are encouraged to evaluate the following when planning procurement activities:

- Marketplace conditions.
- Products, services, and results that are available in the marketplace.
- Suppliers, including past performance or reputation.
- Typical terms and conditions for products, services, and results or for the specific industry.
- Unique local requirements (PMI, 2008, p 350).

Project managers are advised that the complexity and level of detail of the procurement documents should be consistent with the value of, and risks associated with, the planned procurement (PMI, 2008, p 357). Project managers are accustomed to factoring risk into procurement documents,

and using those documents to transfer risk to the seller, or otherwise manage risk. However, those risks have traditionally been limited to risks to the project itself, and its constraints of schedule, cost, and scope. If an organization is moving towards a sustainable, long-term view of its business, it makes sense that those values be reflected in procurement contracts as well, in areas such as bribery, child labor, and similar factors that could pose risk to the firm as a whole.

Operationally, organizations tend to look at waste reduction as a solitary activity. However, it's only when it's integrated into the organization, and throughout project management, that the organization begins to look at the entire supply and value chain – to reduce the amount purchased in order to reduce the amount wasted.

- Do supplier evaluations include sustainability criteria?
- Are obligations and appointments regarding sustainability encoded in contracts?
- How transparent is the entire supply chain, in terms of sustainability priorities?

Risk Management

As traditionally defined, risk is an uncertain event or condition that, if it occurs, has an effect on at least one project objective: scope, schedule, cost, or quality (PMI, 2008, p 305). However, if we are to look at not just the project implementation, but also its effect over its entire lifecycle on the community and the organization at large, it is clear that we must examine risk more broadly.

A risk orientation serves as an excellent basis for sustainable thinking. Risks arising from environmental problems or social discontent surrounding a project can be extremely costly in terms of delays and stoppages, negative publicity, threats to operating license, and significant unforeseen expenditures. At the same time, reputational damage to a company can far exceed the immediate cost impacts of a single project.

In much the same way that different companies and industries face different kinds of project risks, sustainability risks can vary significantly. For example, extractive industries may have more environmental risks, while textile firms have more risks in terms of social sustainability. To evaluate what is at stake, companies must scan the whole value chain, looking, for example, at the way they source raw materials and make and sell their products.

To determine sustainability risks, think about the full range of activities that happen under your project.

1. Identify the activities of your company, itself, and the activities of vendors, suppliers and contractors.
2. Examine the range of ways in which the project's decisions and activities can cause impacts on sustainability.
3. Identify the societal expectations of responsible behavior concerning these impacts.
4. Be sure to include issues that relate to day-to-day activities as well as those that might arise only occasionally under very specific circumstances.

The challenge is to find a way for project managers to incorporate an awareness of sustainability risks more systematically into their core decision-making processes. In this way, the risk management process informs portfolio and project management.

Communication Management

Project Communications Management includes the processes required to ensure timely and appropriate generation, collection, distribution, storage, retrieval, and ultimate disposition of project information. Project managers spend the majority of their time communicating with team members and other project stakeholders. Effective communication creates a bridge between diverse stakeholders involved in a project, connecting various cultural and organizational backgrounds, different levels of expertise, and various perspectives and interests in the project execution or outcome (PMI, 2008, p 273).

Communications, encompassing project reporting, presentation, records and lessons learned, will ensure that the project stakeholders are informed about the sustainability aspects of the project.

Communication management includes:

*   Actively managing the expectations of stakeholders to increase the likelihood of project acceptance by negotiating and influencing their desires to achieve and maintain the project goals.
*   Addressing concerns that have not become issues yet, usually related to the anticipation of future problems. These concerns need to be uncovered and discussed, and the risks need to be assessed.
*   Clarifying and resolving issues that have been identified. The resolution may result in a change request or may be addressed outside of the project, for example, postponed for another project or phase or deferred to another organizational entity (PMI, 2008, p 291).

Project managers must consider:

*   How should the project communicate with the extended stakeholders – activist groups, NGO's, governmental agencies or community members who will want to know about the project and its impacts?
*   How will information be received and processed from those extended stakeholders?
*   How can we ensure engagement at the appropriate level?

CONCLUSION: CHALLENGES AND OPPORTUNITIES

Business leaders have become involved in sustainability not only because their companies have so much to add, but also because they have a strategic interest in doing so. Social and political forces, after all, can alter an industry's strategic landscape fundamentally; they can torpedo the reputations of businesses that have been caught unawares and are seen as being culpable; and they can create valuable market opportunities by highlighting unmet social needs and new consumer preferences (Bonini, 2006).

For too long, project management has operated independently of its broader business context. Only focused on tactical execution, project managers evaluated their initiatives as if they had no life outside their defined beginning and end. This has limited the career development of project managers, as well as job satisfaction.

Similarly, companies also operated like islands. Ignoring negative externalities (costs borne by society at large for its actions), organizations relentlessly pursued shareholder value, at the expense of stakeholder interests.

Those days are over.

Project managers must align their projects with organizational strategy, and organizational strategy has changed to encompass the interests of the broader stakeholder community, encompassing sustainability concerns.

If you don't do this work the right way on the front end, you actually never get a good project. It never works out in the long run. So you have to do this work up front. What I have to do as a company leader is push the education and the thinking of our project managers, our project developers, in that direction. If we can get our people thinking sufficiently from that point of view, not just working

with stakeholders and listening to what they say but actually anticipating their needs, anticipating these "nontechnical" risks and opportunities — and if we can get more people skilled in that way — then the more successful we'll be, the shorter these project timelines will be, the more trust in Shell there will be. And all of that will continue to improve over time. This change will be catalytic. - Marvin Odum, President of Shell Oil (Hopkins, 2011).

REFERENCES

Balestrero, G., & Gedansky, L. (2008). *Contributing to a sustainable world: White Paper for setting PMI strategy on global sustainability and determining organizational social responsibility.* Draft document, unpublished.

Barton, D. (2011). Capitalism for the long term. *Harvard Business Review.* Retrieved on July 4, 2011 from http://hbr.org/2011/03/capitalism-for-the-long-term/ar/1

Berns, M., Bussey, K., Murray, S., & Vismans, D. (2011, Winter). Sustainability: The 'embracers' seize advantage. *MIT Sloan Management Review.*

Bonini, S., Mendonca, L., & Oppenheim, J. (2006). When social issues become strategic. *McKinsey Quarterly.* Retrieved on July 4, 2011 from https://www.mckinseyquarterly.com/When_social_issues_become_strategic_1763

Davis, K. (1973). The case for and against business assumption of social responsibility. *Academy of Management Journal, 16,* 312–322. doi:10.2307/255331.

Epstein, M. (2008). *Making sustainability work.* Sheffield, UK: Greenleaf Publishing.

Gareis, R., Heumann, & Martinuzzi, A. (2010). *Relating sustainable development and project management: A conceptual model.*

Goleman, D. (2009). Why investors should consider sustainability risk management. *Harvard Business Review*. Retrieved on July 4, 2011 from http://blogs.hbr.org/cs/2009/10/investors_consider_sustainabil.html

Hedberg, C., & von Malmborg. (2003). The global reporting initiative and corporate sustainability reporting in Swedish companies. *Corporate Social Responsibility and Environmental Management, 10*(3), 153–164. doi:10.1002/csr.38.

Hopkins, M. (2011). From trust me to show me: Moving sustainability at shell oil from priority to core value. *MIT Sloan Management Review*. Retrieved on July 4, 2011 from http://sloanreview.mit.edu/the-magazine/2011-spring/52317/moving-sustainability-at-shell-oil-from-priority-to-core-value/?utm_source=Publicaster&utm_medium=email&utm_campaign=Sust%20Enews%20March%2017%202011&utm_term=Read+more+

Hunsberger, K. (2008). The sustainability mandate. *PMI Voices on Project Management*. Retrieved on July 4, 2011 from http://blogs.pmi.org/blog/voices_on_project_management/2008/10/the-sustainability-mandate.html

ISO 26000. (2010). *Guidance on social responsibility*. Geneva: International Organization for Standardization.

Kanter, R. M. (2010). How to do well and do good. *MIT Sloan Management Review*. Retrieved on July 4, 2011 from http://sloanreview.mit.edu/the-magazine/2010-fall/52118/how-to-do-well-and-do-good/

Lacy, P., Cooper, T., Hayward, R., & Neuberger, L. (2010). A new era of sustainability: CEO reflections on progress to date, challenges ahead and the impact of the journey toward a sustainable economy. In UN Global Compact-Accenture CEO Study. New York: UN.

Maltzman, R., & Shirley, D. (2011). *Green project management*. Boca Raton, FL: CRC Press.

Mitchell, R., Agle, B., & Wood, D. (1997). Toward a theory of stakeholder identification and salience: Defining the principle of who and what really counts. *Academy of Management Review, 22*(4).

Mochal, T., Krasnoff, A., Maltzman, R., & Shirley, D. (2010). Open letter to authors of PMI PMBOK guide V5 regarding green PM. *ICPM Blogs*. Retrieved July 11, 2011 from http://www.theicpm.com/component/content/article/152-blogs/3600-open-letter-to-authors-of-pmi-pmbok-guide-v5-regarding-green-pm

Morgese, P. (n.d.). Integrating global sustainability into project management: The human resource knowledge area. *PMI Global Sustainability Community of Practice*. Retrieved July 11, 2011 from http://sustainability.vc.pmi.org/Community/Blogs/tabid/376/entryid/648/Integrating-global-sustainability-into-project-management-the-human-resource-knowledge-area.aspx

NetImpact. (2009). Making your impact at work: A practical guide to changing the world from inside any company. *NetImpact*. Retrieved July 11, 2011 from http://netimpact.org/associations/4342/files/MakingYourImpactatWork.pdf

NetImpact. (2011). Corporate careers that make a difference. *NetImpact*. Retrieved July 11, 2011 from http://netimpact.org/associations/4342/files/CorporateCareersThatMakeaDifference_v2.pdf

Norman, W., & MacDonald, C. (2003). Getting to the bottom of triple bottom line. *Business Ethics Quarterly*. Retrieved July 10 from www.business-ethics.ca/3bl/triple-bottom-line.pdf

Oehlmann, I. (2010). *The sustainable footprint methodology: Including sustainability in the project management of the bergermeer gas storage project*. Delft, The Netherlands: Delft University of Technology Faculty of Technology, Policy and Management.

Organisation for Economic Co-Operation and Development. (2001). Corporate social responsibility: Partners for progress. *OECD Publishing*. Retrieved on July 6, 2011 from http://www.oecd.org/document/37/0,3746, en_2649_34417_2429925_1_1_1_1_,00.html

Porter, M. E., & Kramer. (2006, December). Strategy and society – The link between competitive advantage and corporate social responsibility. *Harvard Business Review*, 1–14. PMID:17183795.

Project Management Institute. (2008). *A guide to the project management body of knowledge (PMBOK Guide)* (4th ed.). Newtown Square, PA: PMI.

Project Management Institute. (2009). *Strategic plan*. Newtown Square, PA: PMI.

Project Management Institute. (n.d.). *PMI code of ethics and professional conduct*. Newtown Square, PA: PMI. Retrieved from http://www.pmi.org/About-Us/Ethics/~/media/PDF/Ethics/ap_pmicodeofethics.ashx

Silvius, G., Schipper, R., Planko, J., van den Brink, J., & Köhler, A. (2012). *Sustainability in projects and project management*. Surrey, UK: Gower.

Silvius, G., van den Brink, J., & Köhler, A. (2009). Views on sustainable project management. *Human Side of Projects in Modern Business*. IPMA Scientific Research Paper Series.

Tharp, J. (2007). *Align project management with organizational strategy*. Hong Kong: PMI Global Congress.

Tharp, R. J. (2008). *Corporate social responsibility: What it means for the project manager*. Denver, CO: PMI Global Congress.

WBCSD. (2000). Corporate social responsibility: Making good business sense. *World Business Council for Sustainable Development*. Retrieved on June 30, 2011 from http://www.wbcsd.org/templates/TemplateWBCSD5/layout.asp?type=p&MenuId=MTE0OQ

Werbach, A. (2009). *Strategy for sustainability*. Boston: Harvard Business Press.

Chapter 12
Evaluating Sustainability on Projects Using Indicators

Jude Talbot
AMEC, Canada

Ray Venkataraman
Penn State University, USA

ABSTRACT

The concept of balancing people, planet, and profit to maximize the absolute value of an enterprise is known as sustainability. It is concerned with the economic, social, and environmental effects of an enterprise in the long term. However, in practice, this definition does not provide companies with a meaningful framework to integrate sustainability into their projects, which by definition are one-off endeavors. Given this divide between the long-term nature of sustainability and the temporary nature of projects, companies have found it difficult to incorporate relevant sustainability indicators into project baselines. In this chapter, the authors examine a methodology for integrating sustainability into project baselines for consultants in the industrial and resource extraction fields. The methodology is comprised of an indicator set and a procedure for using the indicator set. This chapter's goal is to help standardize the sustainability process, making it easier to implement and more mainstream.

The objectives of this chapter are: (1) identify different sustainability indicator sets and their strengths and weaknesses; (2) explain what a multi-level analytical hierarchy project is and why it is important to integrating sustainability into such projects; and (3) state the steps in a procedure to integrate sustainability into project baselines.

INTRODUCTION

The 1987 World Commission on Economic Development, the Brundtland Commission (Brundtland, 1987), provided the most common working definition of sustainability as the balancing of people, planet, and profit to maximize the absolute value of an undertaking. This definition forms the foundation of sustainability programs at the executive level in many corporations. A majority of major corporations now provide a public sustainability report, or a sustainability section in their annual

DOI: 10.4018/978-1-4666-4177-8.ch012

report, that is organized around the Bruntland definition and outlines how the company incorporates sustainability in their operations.

One problem with the Bruntland definition is that it does not provide good day to day guidance for attempting to integrate sustainability into a company's operations and/or projects. One definition of a project is a temporary undertaking that has a specific objective and a definite beginning and end, with the key focus often being the creation of a unique product or service (Labuschagne & Brent, 2005). Sustainability, however, has a long term orientation and this direct contrast with the short term nature of projects creates an imbalance that makes it challenging to incorporate sustainability into projects in a meaningful and measureable way.

It is becoming more common for project organizations to drive sustainability deep into their organizations by conducting projects such as building new facilities or designing new production methods to achieve internal sustainability objectives or targets. These projects are usually very company-specific and are not applicable outside the organization, except in a general sense. There are few, if any, large consulting companies in the resource extraction or industrial sphere that have driven sustainability deeply into their processes and, therefore, can offer their clients a range of sustainability services within their project execution philosophies. It is also very rare to find a large engineering company with sustainability offerings that contain documented processes, procedures, indicators, and methodologies.

This chapter examines sustainability indicators through the lens of one global engineering, consulting, and project management services organization. This organization is one of the leaders in its peer group in regards to sustainability and for a number of years has been the world sector leader on the Dow Jones Sustainability World Index. This organization works on world scale projects for many global resource companies, which are very advanced organizations when it comes to corporate sustainability and therefore demand high sustainability acumen from their consultants. In addition to these highly advanced sustainability clients, this consulting organization also has clients that are not yet mature in the sustainability field. These clients are looking to their consultants to guide them in improving their sustainability practices.

Given the global landscape, there is an opportunity for this consulting firm to be a leader in driving sustainability deeper, and perhaps fully, into its processes and project execution. Doing this would differentiate this firm from its competitors when pursuing new projects, both from a reputational standpoint and, for some clients, from a material standpoint.

The goal of this chapter is to assist in standardizing the sustainability process, making it easier to implement and more mainstream. Along with an examination of a number of current indicator sets in use, this chapter will show a proposed indicator set for use by consulting engineers and their resource extraction and industrial clients on projects in industries such as oil and gas, mining, manufacturing, and pulp and paper. The indicator sets examined will include those used by the International Federation of Consulting Engineers (PSM), the Global Reporting Initiative (G3), the US Green Building Council (LEED), the International Finance Corporation (IFC), the Ceres and Tellus Institute (FRP), and the Mining Association of Canada (TSM). The proposed indicator set is a sub-set of indicators that are used by existing sustainability indicator sets and is tailored to be applicable to industrial or resource extraction projects.

The chapter will conclude by evaluating the implementation of the indicator set and implementation process against a current design build project in the transportation industry.

Because each project is, by definition, unique, the proposed indicator has been developed to be broader in scope than the majority of projects would require. Project dimensions such as industry type, stakeholder requirements, location, and the owner's sustainability culture will determine the exact indicator set for each project. One of the first steps in using such an indicator set is for the engineering consultant to work with the client to determine which indicators are applicable to the project in question and whether new indicators will be needed. For a project to be successful, this step must be done up front at the beginning of a project.

SUSTAINABILITY IN PROJECTS

The traditional top-down and bottom-up approaches to incorporate sustainability within the organization, to a large extent, have not been effective. In order to integrate sustainability into the evaluation process, practical tools are needed to align business methodologies with the principles of sustainable development (Gladwin, Kennelly, & Krause 1995). Project management methodologies, which are core business methodologies for most companies are not excluded from this requirement (Labuschagne & Brent, 2005). In addition, there is a definite need to develop indicators that can be used in decision-making processes to ensure that projects are managed according to practices that will contribute to sustainable development (Warhurst, 2003).

There is a growing body of research literature that examines the interface between project management and sustainability. However, this body of work is still small and there has not been a lot of research done into integrating sustainability into project management processes and specifically into a framework that is useful for consultants involved in resource extraction or industrial projects. According to the United Nations Environment Programme 2002 report, industry needs to develop a set of sustainability indices, against which it can benchmark performance towards increased sustainability. An indicator is defined

as an operational representation of an attribute (quality, characteristic, property) of a system (Moldan & Billharz, 1997). An index of sustainability indicators is defined as an amalgam of more than one indicator (Liverman, Hanson, Brown, & Meredith, 1988).

Existing Sustainability Indicator Frameworks

One of the more useful starting points for building a framework that can be used for selecting sustainability indicators on projects was produced by Koo and Ariaratnam. Their example was specific to a water main replacement project but their concepts are generally applicable. There are four steps in the process.

1. Define the project details.
2. Determine the spatial and temporal project boundaries.
3. Identify the indicators (using existing indicator lists as a basis).
4. Analyze the indicator attributes for assessment.

Using the analytical hierarchy process, originally developed by Saaty (1980), on the indicator set we get the matrix represented in Figure 1.

When there are options that are well defined, like in some municipal construction projects, the analytical hierarchy process can work very well. However, in most natural resource extraction and industrial consulting projects, the options are not known with any degree of certainty during the initial definition or feasibility study phases because the variables are not defined in enough detail. In other words, it is difficult to use the analytical hierarchy process in most resource extraction and industrial projects because it is during the feasibility study phase, or perhaps even in earlier phases, that many of the significant decisions regarding project sustainability indicators are made.

Figure 1. Project sustainability requirements matrix for qualitative indicator analysis

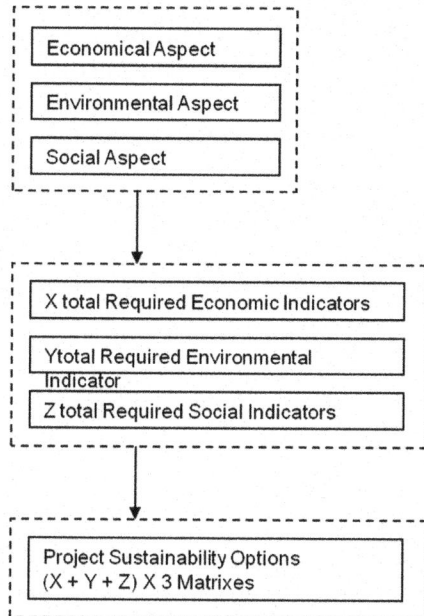

1. Categorizing the indicators into economic, environmental, and social categories.
2. Creating sub categories for direct and indirect accounts within each of the categories in step one. Direct accounts show benefits/expenditures that are internal to the organization undertaking the project. Indirect accounts show externalities or benefits/expenditures that are external to the organization undertaking the project.
3. Determine what information is already collected via the firm's existing project accounting methods and can be restated in a project sustainability report and determine what additional information requires collection.

Sustainability in Project Management in the Resource Sector

Labuschagne, Brent, and van Erck (2007) have developed a framework that can be used to organize indicators into categories. This methodology gives us a very good starting point for developing a framework for evaluating sustainability for consultants in natural resource extraction and industrial projects at the project level. The key to this methodology is to break the three pillars of sustainability: economic, environmental, and social, into sub categories containing groups of indicators. For example, social sustainability indicators could be broken up into the sub-categories of:

- Internal Human Resources
- External Populations
- Land Resources
- Macro Social Performance

Most indicator sets that have been published use this multi-level grouping approach. One key point that is often overlooked when setting up an indicator set however, is that the level at which indicators are tracked cannot contain too many indicators or the indicator set will be too difficult to track in a project setting. This point is made implicitly in

Accounting of Sustainability Indicators on Projects

While the Global Reporting Initiative (GRI) is the accepted global standard for corporate sustainability reporting, there is currently no such standard for project sustainability reporting or management. In most organizations, a bespoke process is built from the ground up to handle each project's sustainability aspirations, with little learning and/or data used from past projects. Sustainability data collection is difficult, which leads to wasted resources throughout the project lifecycle.

Casella Stanger, Forum for the Future, and Carillion plc (Stranger, Forum for the Future, & Carillion plc, 2002) provide a framework for the final step of the process outlined in the previous section, which they have called sustainability accounting. The framework was developed for construction projects but is generally applicable. There are three steps in this framework.

Figure 1. None of the indicator sets discussed next contain a manageable number of indicators on the tracking level, and hence are very difficult to track at the project level. An unmanageable number of indicators to track is seen as a leading cause of poor uptake of the indicator sets on projects by consulting organizations. Labuschagne, Brent, and van Erck (2007) help solve this problem by identifying related groups of indicators at the lowest level, resulting in a small enough data set for accurate and transparent decision making process on whether sustainability has been achieved for the project. The sustainability indicators section of this chapter shows a framework that can be used by consultants on natural resource extraction and industrial projects.

SUSTAINABILITY INDICATOR SETS

The Global Reporting Initiative (GRI) is considered the global standard for corporate sustainability reports (APEG BC, 2005; Labuschagne, Brent, & van Erck, 2007). However, at the beginning of 2012 there were over 100 recognized indicator sets for measuring sustainability. Some of these indicator sets cut across industry boundaries, while others are specific to a single industry/geography. This multitude of indicator sets shows that there is currently no standardization of sustainability indicators, accounting practices, and measurement tools for consultant companies to use on resource extraction and manufacturing projects.

Representative indicator sets that have some applicability to natural resource extraction or industrial industries are reviewed in this section to give an overview of the tools that are currently available for consultants and their clients to work with. Each indicator set is introduced and a table describes the strengths and weaknesses for each.

- **Global Reporting Initiative (GRI):** G3 Reporting Guidelines

In 1997, the United Nations Environment Programme, along with the United States non-governmental organization, created the GRI as a Coalition for Environmentally responsible Economics. The mission of the GRI is to make economic, environmental, and social impacts transparent and a fundamental component in effective stakeholder relations by providing a trusted and credible framework for sustainability reporting that can be used by organizations of any size, sector, or location (Global Reporting Initiative, 2002).

- **Ceres and the Tellus Institute:** Facilities Reporting Project

In order to develop consistent, comparable, and credible economic, environmental and social reporting guidance for individual facilities in the United States the Facility Reporting Project (FRP) was launched as a multi-stakeholder effort by Ceres and the Tellus Institute in 2003. (Facilities Reporting Project, 2004). The structure, indicators, and guidance contained in the FRP have been designed to match up with the GRI sustainability reporting indicators and guidance so that facilities in an organization can report against the FRP and roll up to a corporate GRI report.

- **International Finance Corporation:** Performance Standards for Social and Environmental Sustainability

The International Finance Corporation (IFC) is an organization that is part of the World Bank. The IFC's vision and purpose are that people should have the opportunity to escape poverty and improve their lives. The IFC performance standards apply to all the projects it finances. There are eight performance standards.

1. Social and Environmental Assessment and Management System
2. Labour and Working Conditions

3. Pollution Prevention and Abatement
4. Community Health, Safety and Security
5. Land Acquisition and Involuntary Resettlement
6. Biodiversity Conservation and Sustainable Natural Resource Management
7. Indigenous Peoples
8. Cultural Heritage (International Finance Corporation, 2006)

- **International Federation of Consulting Engineers:** Project Sustainability Management Guidelines

The International Federation of Consulting Engineers (FIDIC) has published a Project Sustainability Management (PSM) process, indicator set, and guidance as the basis for the development of a system to integrate sustainability into projects. In the PSM process, the project owner and engineer balance the owner's project vision against cost and available alternatives, by working together to select appropriate project goals and indicators for sustainable development which are linked back to higher level goals. Objectives for sustainable development are therefore addressed in much the same way as other project objectives are addressed in the project's quality plan.

PSM also provides a methodology for benchmarking sustainable development project performance, and for ensuring that advances in one dimension of sustainable development are not accomplished at the expense of another (International Federation of Consulting Engineers, 2004).

- **Towards Sustainable Mining:** Performance Indicators

Towards sustainable mining (TSM) is an initiative of the Mining Association of Canada. It has come up with a set of indicators that is geared towards the issues that its members, the mining industry within Canada, face on their projects and operations. The focus areas for these indicators are:

1. Tailings Management
2. Energy use and Greenhouse Gas Emissions Management
3. Aboriginal and Community Outreach
4. Crisis Management Planning
5. Biodiversity Conservation Management
6. Safety and Health

- **Green Building Council:** Leadership in Energy and Environmental Design Indicators

The Leadership in Energy and Environmental Design (LEED) indicator set is a green building rating system that encourages and accelerates global adoption of sustainable green building and development practices through the creation and implementation of universally understood and accepted tools and performance criteria in occupied buildings (Canadian Green Building Council – LEED, 2009). This indicator set is not designed to be applicable to natural resource extraction and industrial projects, however, LEED is a very well-known indicator set in North America and it is often one of the first things that clients reference for integrating sustainability on a project.

- Envision Rating System for Sustainable Infrastructure

Envision provides a holistic framework for evaluating and rating the community, environmental, and economic benefits of all types and sizes of infrastructure projects. The Envision rating system evaluates, grades, and gives recognition to infrastructure projects that use transformational, collaborative approaches to assess the sustainability indicators over the course of the project's life cycle (Sustainable Infrastructure, 2012).

The Envision system is very similar to the LEED in that it is a voluntary program containing a prescriptive set of indicators, and projects are given a rating based on how many indicators they are able to achieve on the project. Therefore, from the perspective of this chapter, it has the same strengths and weaknesses as the LEED rating system.

INDICATOR SET'S STRENGTHS AND WEAKNESSES

Each of these indicator sets has advantages that can be used when managing natural resources extraction and industrial projects and each set also has weaknesses that reduce the effectiveness of these indicator sets when managing sustainability on these projects. Table 1 outlines these strengths and weaknesses.

SUSTAINABILITY INDICATOR SET SELECTION

There are three main criteria for choosing which indicators from the indicator sets discussed in the previous section to include in the indicator set in this chapter. These criteria are as follows.

- The indicators can be measured in a project setting.
- The indicators are relevant to natural resources extraction and industrial projects.
- The indicators have applicability to a wide range of natural resources extraction and industrial settings.

In many cases indicators were duplicated between the different indicators sets. When this occurred, the indicator that was most clearly written and simplest to track on a consulting project was chosen. To make this indicator set applicable to as wide a range of projects as possible, the indicators are not filtered with a view for what type of project a consultant may encounter. They can be customized for each project depending on the project location, the client, and other factors.

Economic Indicators

This set includes only economic indicators that focus on the project's economic impact outside of the project, e.g. items that have an economic

Table 1. Indicator set strengths and weaknesses

Indicator Set	Strengths	Weaknesses
GRI/FRP	• role as the global standard for corporate sustainability reports • reporting project sustainability against the GRI may lead to alignment between corporate and project sustainability outcomes.	• some indicators are difficult to report against, especially in a project setting and • the guidance provided by the GRI tends to be too general.
IFC Performance Standards	• the standards are complete and there is a framework presented that can be used to track achievement • they are specifically designed for World Bank Projects, and often apply to industrial and resource extraction projects.	• the guidance does not contain suggestions for tracking measures to implement on projects • the guidelines are written in a way that makes it difficult to track achievement using simple data sets.
FIDIC PSM Guidelines	• conceptually, the guidelines were designed to cover effects of the project from a whole society perspective, which could help prevent a project from focussing on one area such as water pollution while neglecting other areas of sustainability • FIDIC's analysis starts from envisioning integrating sustainability into the project management processes and ensures that as many of the indicators as possible is associated with measurable success criteria.	• many of the measurable success criteria are too broad and/or difficult to measure at the project level. • while the whole society perspective of the guidelines and the focus on project management processes is an excellent way to approach the problem of integrating sustainability into projects, the end result is that the tracking indicators set is not conducive to efficient project management.
TSM	• excellent baseline for mining projects • indicators mostly well written for project use.	• much of the indicator set is very specific to the mining industry.
LEED/ Envision	• success criteria are easily measureable • success criteria are generally applicable.	• much of the indicator set specific to occupied buildings and infrastructure.

impact on external stakeholders. Economic indicators that are part of the project normally have well defined processes that do not need duplication. In addition, the evaluation of performance in the area of community capital is of utmost importance in evaluating the social sustainability of a project as it has been implied that the core of sustainability is how people feel about their surroundings and their way of life. These perceptions can directly influence stakeholder participation initiatives (Labuschagne, Brent, & van Erck, 2007).

Environmental Indicators

Environmental sustainability is not a new concept to most resource extraction and industrial organizations. Therefore, this is the most developed dimension of sustainability in the indicator sets studied. In fact, indicator sets such as LEED have been designed to be almost exclusively environmentally focused. The number and breadth of environmental indicators made it necessary to only focus on those indicators that were applicable to resource extraction or industrial projects.

Social Indicators

Compared to environmental sustainability, less work has been done on social sustainability as it applies to business (Edum-Fotwe & Price, 2008), which means that there is little or no consensus on what social sustainability means and how to best apply it in a project setting. A consequence of this is a multitude of social sustainability indicators that have a different focus for different indicator sets. One benefit of this excess of indicators and focuses is that it is unlikely that any one project will address all the indicators and the list created for this chapter can be customized and shortened for most projects.

Another consequence of the lack of consensus around social sustainability is that there are usually few, if any, well-defined processes to apply social sustainability in a project setting. Therefore, unlike the economic dimension indicators, we look at

social business sustainability from both an internal and external perspectives. The internal focus concerns the health and well being of employees, disciplinary practices, and equity and human rights aspects in employee sourcing. Training and development opportunities for employees are also included. The external focus concerns the impact of the project on three different levels of society: local, regional, and national communities, as applicable (Labuschange, Brent, & van Erck, 2007).

Indicator Organization

The total set of indicators for tracking sustainability in natural resource extraction and industrial projects consists of approximately 300 unique indicators. No project could effectively manage this task without an inordinate amount of resources. Simply sorting through this number of indicators and selecting the appropriate ones provides project management a challenge that hinders sustainability implementation and measurement on projects. To make this process feasible, another higher level, called high level sustainability themes, on the indicator hierarchy is required. Sustainability themes are groups of indicators that cover a portion of the project, such as minimizing or eliminating air emissions. When a theme is to be addressed in a project, the indicators within this theme are reviewed to determine which ones apply on the project.

The list of sustainability themes in each dimension is given in Appendix 1. Due to space considerations, an example of one sustainability indicator that applies to each indicator is presented in Appendix 2. In total, there are approximately 300 indicators in the indicator set, which is considerably more comprehensive than the 26 given in Appendix 2. The indicators presented were included because they apply to a wide range of resource extraction and manufacturing projects; however each indicator within the theme is unique and covers a different item that could be part of the project. For example there are fourteen indicators within the Minimize or Eliminate Air emissions including indicators on counting, auditing, and minimizing greenhouse gases and on other gasses such as ozone depleting substances.

HOW TO USE THE INDICATOR SET

Procedure for Using the Indicator Set

Natural resources and industrial projects can implement this indicator set by following a simple procedure.

1. Determine the project's stakeholders and their requirements.
2. Sort these requirements into the indicator set's high level sustainability themes, creating new themes if necessary.
3. For each theme that is applicable to the project, determine which of the theme's indicators are best suited for tracking the project's sustainability achievement. Create new indicators if necessary.
4. Assign ownership for each indicator and define when in the project the indicator will be completed.
5. Create success criteria for each selected indicator and determine the information required to measure achievement.
6. Collect project information and track the project's progress in completing the indicators.
7. Report on the indicator set at regular intervals, preferably as part of the regular project report.

Key aspects of this procedure are explained next.

Determining Stakeholders

As a general rule, engineering consultants do not own the assets that they design in their projects. They also don't often operate these facilities without a separate business group taking part under different arrangements. It is even rarer that they are associated with the marketing, handling, and development of the products that are developed as a result of their projects. However, it is….the asset life cycle resulting from the project, and the subsequent product life cycle resulting from the asset that have economic, social, and environmental consequences, which are in turn associated with an implemented project (Labuschagne & Brent, 2005). Therefore, in all dimensions of sustainability on a project, it is important for a project to define [the project's] stakeholders. Treating stakeholders in an ethically and socially responsible manner has been seen as the core of CSR (corporate sustainability) (Hopkins 2002). Additionally, stakeholder management has been regarded as the tool to connect strategy to social and ethical issues (Wartick, 1998). Because of this, a complete indicator set for sustainability cannot be achieved when the project stakeholders, along with their needs and desires, are not all identified. Stakeholders are people or groups that have, or believe they have, legitimate claims against substantive aspects of the project. A stake is an interest or share or claim in a project; it can range from informal interest in the undertaking at one extreme, to a legal claim of ownership at the other extreme (Cleland 1998).

The methodology for selecting project stakeholders is covered elsewhere including in Winch 2004 (Winch, 2004) and is not the focus of this chapter. However it is imperative that only after the project stakeholders have been determined that indicator selection for the project can proceed.

Assigning Indicator Responsibility

From the perspective of the consultant's role on an industrial or natural resources extraction project, all indicators in a project need to contain project information such as how to measure the indicator, when in the project to address the indicator, and where the responsibility is for the indicator's achievement. Two examples of indicators with responsibilities assigned and with project lifecycle stages for measurement identified are presented in Figure 2.

A natural resources extraction or industrial project is often broken down into the following project phases.

- **Idea Generation:** Generate the idea for a new project and prepare the initial proposal that describes the business need. This phase does not require a formal project plan.
- **Pre-Feasibility:** Evaluate the existing proposal in terms of financial, operational, and technical viability as well as against the company's strategy. Overlap or synergy with other projects should also be checked out.

- **Feasibility:** Identify and define the optimum solution to address the business need. All areas of the solution must be analyzed and assessed to determine killer concerns and risks.
- **Development and Execution or Engineering and Construction:** Design, develop, create, and build the chosen solution. Also develop the supporting system manuals, business processes, and training for the solution during this phase.
- **Commissioning:** Test the solution in an operational environment to validate the acceptance and capabilities of the solution.
- **Launch or Start-Up:** Hand over to the customer (internal or external) and thus release to the operational environment. This phase also marks the beginning of operational support.

Figure 2. Examples of sustainability indicators organization

	Example 1	Example 2
Dimension	Environmental	Social
High Level Theme	Comply with all applicable environmental regulations	Maintain a crisis communication plan
Indicator	List categories of environmental permits in effect at the project and their issuing authorities. Describe the scope of these permits and how stakeholders can access them.	Establish a local crisis management team, with defined roles and responsibilities.
Owner	Consultant or project owner	Project owner, with consultant involvement.
Project Lifecycle Phase for Measurement	Pre-Feasability with a review at every stage until commissioning.	Every stage where there is a site presence. Review plan at every stage.

- **Post Implementation Review or Project Follow-Up Review:** Assess the project after sufficient time (9-15 months), to determine if the benefits were delivered and what the impact of the project was on the business. Capture lessons learned for future reference.

Two examples of sustainability indicators organization in a project setting with responsibility assigned and lifecycle stage for measurement identified are shown in Figure 2.

PRACTICAL SIGNIFICANCE OF SUSTAINABILITY INDICATORS

An example of the robustness and usefulness of the indicator set can be seen when checking the use of the set and high-level themes by a design build project in the transportation sector. This project includes the design, procurement, and construction, by a consortium of engineering and construction companies, of a road through a medium sized Canadian city. Its purpose is to strengthen transportation and trade links, reduce road congestion, and foster economic growth. The road's strategic importance for economic growth, urban location, and unique ecological context necessitate strong design and planning principles to guide infrastructure development. It is to be a state-of-the-art facility within a contextually sensitive landscape setting that has ecological integrity, builds physical and cultural connections, and establishes a sustainable network of amenities that can be enjoyed by present and future generations. The legacy of the project will not only be its significant contribution as a trade and transportation route, but also include the establishment of a contiguous and sustainable green space system that contributes to the quality of life in the community and supports the re-establishment of an ecologically rich landscape.

High Level Themes and Specific Indicators

Table 2 shows that many of the high level themes applied to the project.

For each of the applicable themes, the specific objective that is applicable to the project has been recorded. In addition a SMART (Specific, Measurable, Achievable, Relevant, and Time-bound) indicator with a specific target, who in the project is responsible for the indicator, and the frequency of measurement are included. For example:

- **Sustainability Aspect:** Environmental
- **High Level Theme:** Minimize or eliminate energy use and procure energy from renewable sources
- **Specific Indicator:** Reduce overall energy use of the road and associated green space
- **SMART Indicator:** Electrical use in KWhr/year
- **Target:** 35,533,480 KWhr/year
- **Owner:** OM&R Manager
- **Frequency:** Annual

Review of the Project Indicators

Using the methodology and indicator set described in this chapter, and incorporating the Green Roads indicator set as well as the indicator set in this chapter, the project determined that there were a total of 33 indicators for the 14 applicable high level themes. Most of the specific indicators used on the project, such as the previous example maps directly to economic indicator 4.17, are taken straight from the indicator set in the appendix. In other cases new indicators have been written within a theme to meet the specific requirements of the project. This is to be expected in any large scale project as when this indicator set and implementation procedure are used as the indicator set will normally have applicable themes and indicators for most, but normally not all of the project stakeholder needs.

Table 2. High level themes applicability to the project

Number	Social	Environmental	Economic
1	**Applicable**: Maintain community health, safety, and security	**Applicable**: Manage natural resources in a sustainable manner to promote conservation and maintain biodiversity	Not Applicable: Provide economic opportunities for the local community - employment
2	**Applicable**: Maintain a crisis communication plan	**Applicable**: Comply with all applicable environmental regulations	**Applicable**: Provide economic opportunities for the local community - supply chain
3	**Applicable**: Preserve cultural heritage	**Applicable**: Minimize or eliminate air emissions	Not Applicable: Determine the local taxation and infrastructure benefits and impacts of the project
4	**Applicable**: Create a social and environmental management system to IFC standards	**Applicable**: Minimize or eliminate energy use and procure energy from renewable sources	**Applicable**: Design the project to maximize its lifespan with a minimum level of care and maintenance
5	**Applicable**: Maintain effective communication with local stakeholders	**Applicable**: Water pollution: discharges, effluents, and spills	Not Applicable: General economic considerations
6	**Implicitly Applicable**: Maintain human rights standards	Not Applicable: Fresh water withdrawal and recycling	
7	Not Applicable: Enable positive outcomes for indigenous peoples	**Applicable**: Waste and hazardous waste control, minimization, or elimination	
8	**Implicitly Applicable**: Ensure decent work and labour practices are adhered to	Not Applicable: Transportation to and from site	
9	Not Applicable: Eliminate, minimize, or fairly compensate for land acquisition and involuntary settlement	Not Applicable: Indoor environmental quality - occupied buildings only	
10	**Applicable**: Take responsibility for impacts of the projects outputs (products and services)		
11	Not Applicable: Contribute to local/national housing and educational system		

Note that two social themes, maintaining human right standards and ensure decent work and labour practices are adhered to were implicitly applicable because this project is being conducted in Canada where there are already strong baseline laws, standards, and culture that ensure that virtually all projects meet the requirements for these themes. Additionally, two of the not applicable economic indicators, provide economic opportunities for the local community – employment and determine the local taxation and infrastructure benefits and impacts of the project were both applicable to the project but did not have specific indicators written for them. For the first of these indicators, there was a target for youth employment, but no specification that it needed to be local. For the second indicator, it was inherent in the project's purpose and baseline assumptions so it is not being specifically tracked as part of the project.

FUTURE DIRECTIONS

One possible area for future study can be found in the procedure presented in the last section, namely creating a list of sustainability indicator success criteria that can be used on projects. The unique nature of each project means that this list cannot be all-inclusive, but building the list will highlight what information is needed for tracking and achieving sustainability, and will give projects a common starting point. Efforts could then be directed towards investigating integration of sustainability reporting into project reports to streamline information collection in projects and ease project management.

Another possible area of further study is determining the utility of this sustainability indicator set and methodology both in more resource extraction and industrial projects and in other industries. There may be common sustainability indicators shared by most industries and discovering these similarities and leveraging the material presented in this chapter will assist in making project sustainability management a defined and accepted aspect of project management.

CHAPTER SUMMARY

There is an imbalance between the long term nature of sustainability and the unique, finite nature of projects, which makes it difficult to incorporate meaningful sustainability indicators into project execution plans. Specifically there is not yet a standardized method of measuring sustainability on consulting projects in resource extraction and industrial industries.

This chapter has examined such a method centered on an indicator set based on existing sustainability indicators sets. The indicator set used set contains approximately 300 indicators, too many to manage in a project setting, so the indicators are grouped as high level themes organized around the three aspects of sustainability, social,

environmental, and economic. Projects can use a sub-set of these indicators to measure and report the attainment of sustainability on the project.

This chapter also outlines, with examples, a process to use the indicator set to create project specific SMART objectives that have specific owners and are addressed at specific points in the project lifecycle.

After reading this chapter you should be able to:

- Identify different sustainability indicator sets and their strengths and weaknesses.
- Explain what a multi-level analytical hierarchy project is and why it is important to integrating sustainability into such projects.
- Develop a procedure to integrate the sustainability into project baselines.

REFERENCES

Association of Professional Engineering and Geoscience. B.C. (2004). Part 3e: Practice specific module - Consulting engineering and geosciences. In Sustainability in Professional Engineering and Geoscience: A Primer. Academic Press.

Brundtland, G. E. (1987). *Our common future: The world commission on environment and development*. Oxford, UK: Oxford University Press.

Canadian Green Building Council - LEED. (2009). Retrieved from http://www.cagbc.org/AM/Template.cfm?Section=LEED

Cleland, D. I. (1998). Stakeholder management. In *Project Management Handbook*. San Francisco, CA: Jossey Bass.

Facilities Reporting Project. (2004). Retrieved from https://www.ceres.org/resources/reports/facility-reporting-project-sustainability-reporting-guidance/view

Gladwin, T. N., Kennelly, J. J., & Krause, T.-S. (1995). Shifting paradigms for sustainable development: Implications for management theory and research. *Academy of Management Review*, *20*(4), 874–907.

Global Reporting Initiative. (2002). *GRI sustainability reporting guidelines*. Boston: GRI.

Hopkins, M. J. D. (2002). Sustainability in the internal operations of companies. *Corporate Environmental Strategy*, *9*(4), 398–408. doi:10.1016/S1066-7938(02)00121-5.

International Federation of Consulting Engineers. (2004). Retrieved from http://www1.fidic.org/bookshop/account/reading_pdf.asp?sesskey=0&productcode=FI-EN-T-AA-10&range=0&f=IENTAA&p=2&n=Project+Sustainability+Management+Guidelines%2C+2004

International Finance Corporation. (2006). Retrieved from http://www1.ifc.org/wps/wcm/connect/5159190048855a4f85b4d76a6515bb18/SustainabilityPolicy.pdf?MOD=AJPERES&CACHEID=5159190048855a4f85b4d76a6515bb18

Labuschagne, C., & Brent, A. C. (2005). Sustainable project life cycle management: The need to integrate life cycles in the manufacturing sector. *International Journal of Project Management*, *23*(2), 159–168. doi:10.1016/j.ijproman.2004.06.003.

Labuschagne, C., Brent, A.C., & van Erck Ron, P.G. (2007). *Assessing performance of industries*. Pretoria, South Africa: University of Petroria openUP.

Liverman, D. M., Hanson, M. E., Brown, B. J., & Meredith, R. W. Jr. (1988). Global sustainability: Toward measurement. *Environmental Management*, *20*(2), 133–143. doi:10.1007/BF01873382.

Moldan, & Billharz, S. (Eds.). (1997). Indicators and their use: Information for decision making sustainability indicators: Report on the project on indicators for sustainable development. Chichester, UK: Academic Press.

Saaty, T. T. (1990). *The analytic hierarchy process*. New York: McGraw-Hill.

Stranger, C. (2002). *Sustainability accounting in the construction industry*. London: Ciria Publishing Services.

Sunter, W. V. A. C. (2002). *Beyond reasonable greed: Why sustainable business is a much better idea*. Cape Town, South Africa: Human & Rousseau Tafelberg.

Sustainable Infrastructure. (2012). Retrieved from http://www.sustainableinfrastructure.org/rating/index.cfm

Warhurst, A. (2003). *Sustainability indicators and sustainability performance management*. Mining, Minerals and Sustainable Development.

Wartick, S. L. W. D. J. (Ed.). (1998). International business and society. Malden, MA: Blackwell.

Winch, G. M. (2004). *Managing project stakeholders*. Hoboken, NJ: John Wiley & Sons.

ADDITIONAL READING

Abood, K. A. (2007, March). *Sustainable and green ports: Application of sustainability principles to port development and operation*. Paper presented at Ports 2007 30 Years of Sharing Ideas. New York, NY.

Ashley, R., Blackwood, D., Butler, D., Jowitt, P., Davies, J., & Smith, H. et al. (2008). Making asset investment decisions for wastewater systems that include sustainability. *Journal of Environmental Engineering*, *134*(3). doi:10.1061/(ASCE)0733-9372(2008)134:3(200).

Beheiry, S. M. A., Chong, W. K., & Haas, C. T. (2006). Examining the business impact of owner commitment to sustainability. *Journal of Construction Engineering and Management*, *132*(4). doi:10.1061/(ASCE)0733-9364(2006)132:4(384).

Brundtland, G. E. (1987). *Our common future: The world commission on environment and development.* Oxford, UK: Oxford University Press.

Cleland, D. I. (1998). Stakeholder management. In *Project Management Handbook.* San Francisco, CA: Jossey Bass.

Dandy, G., Roberts, A., Hewiston, C., & Chrystie, P. (2006). *Sustainability objectives for the optimization of water distribution networks.* Paper presented at 8th Annual Water Distribution Systems Analysis Symposium. Cincinnati, OH.

Gladwin, T. N., Kennelly, J. J., & Krause, T.-S. (1995). Shifting paradigms for sustainable development: Implications for management theory and research. *Academy of Management Review*, *20*(4), 874–907.

Hopkins, M. J. D. (2002). Sustainability in the internal operations of companies. *Corporate Environmental Strategy*, *9*(4), 398–408. doi:10.1016/S1066-7938(02)00121-5.

Koo, D. H., & Ariaratnam, S. T. (2008). Application of a sustainability model for assessing water main replacement options. *Journal of Construction Engineering and Management*, *134*(8). doi:10.1061/(ASCE)0733-9364(2008)134:8(563).

Labuschagne, C., & Brent, A. C. (2005). Sustainable project life cycle management: The need to integrate life cycles in the manufacturing sector. *International Journal of Project Management*, *23*(2), 159–168. doi:10.1016/j.ijproman.2004.06.003.

Labuschagne, C., Brent, A.C., & van Erck Ron, P.G. (2007). *Assessing performance of industries.* Pretoria, South Africa: University of Petroria openUP.

Saaty, T. T. (1990). *The analytic hierarchy process.* New York: McGraw-Hill.

Sunter, W. V. C. (2002). *Beyond reasonable greed: Why sustainable business is a much better idea.* Cape Town, South Africa: Human & Rousseau Tafelberg.

Talbot, J., & Venkataraman, R. R. (2011). Integration of sustainability principles into project baselines using a comprehensive indicator set. *International Business & Economics Research Journal*, *10*(9), 29–40.

KEY TERMS AND DEFINITIONS

Global Reporting Initiative (GRI): A nonprofit organization that promotes economic, environmental, and social sustainability. GRI provides all companies and organizations with a comprehensive sustainability reporting framework that is widely used around the world.

Indicator: An operational representation of an attribute (quality, characteristic, property) of a system.

Indicator Set: An amalgam of more than one indicator.

SMART Objective: An objective that is Specific, Measurable, Achievable, Relevant, and Time-bound.

Stakeholder: People or groups that have, or believe they have, legitimate claims against substantive aspects of the project. A stake is an interest or share or claim in a project; it can range from informal interest in the undertaking at one extreme, to a legal claim of ownership at the other extreme.

Success Criteria: A method of measuring achievement of an indicator on a project. To be most effective, a success criterion should contain a SMART objective.

Sustainability: The concept of balancing people, planet, and profit to maximize the absolute value of an enterprise.

Sustainability Dimension: An aspect of sustainability. Traditionally sustainability is separated into three dimensions, social, environmental, and economic. However, alternate schemes exist with the most common including an operational dimension in addition to the usual three.

APPENDIX 1

Table 3. High level sustainability themes

Social	Environmental	Economic
Maintain community health, safety, and security	Manage natural resources in a sustainable manner to promote conservation and maintain biodiversity	Provide economic opportunities for the local community - employment
Maintain a crisis communication plan	Comply with all applicable environmental regulations	Provide economic opportunities for the local community - supply chain
Preserve cultural heritage	Minimize or eliminate air emissions	Determine the local taxation and infrastructure benefits and impacts of the project
Create a social and environmental management system to IFC standards	Minimize or eliminate energy use and procure energy from renewable sources	Design the project to maximize its lifespan with a minimum level of care and maintenance
Maintain effective communication with local stakeholders	Water pollution: discharges, effluents, and spills	General economic considerations
Maintain human rights standards	Fresh water withdrawal and recycling	
Enable positive outcomes for indigenous peoples	Waste and hazardous waste control, minimization, or elimination	
Ensure decent work and labour practices are adhered to	Transportation to and from site	
Eliminate, minimize, or fairly compensate for land acquisition and involuntary settlement	Indoor Environmental Quality - occupied buildings only	
Take responsibility for impacts of the projects outputs (products and services)		
Contribute to local/national housing and educational system		

APPENDIX 2

Table 4. Sustainability indicator list

Dimension	Theme	Possible Project Indicators	Source
Social	Maintain community health, safety, and security	The client will prevent or minimize the potential for community exposure to water-borne, water based, water-related, vector-borne disease, and other diseases that could result from project activities.	IFC
Social	Maintain a crisis communication plan	The President and CEO has endorsed and demonstrated support for crisis management planning.	TSM
Social	Preserve cultural heritage	The client is responsible for siting and designing a project to avoid significant damage to cultural heritage. The client will not disturb any chance finds further until an assessment by a competent specialist is made and actions are identified.	IFC
Social	Create a social and environmental management system to IFC standards	The management program will be accompanied by an action plan where specific mitigation measures and actions necessary to comply with applicable laws and regulations.	IFC
Social	Maintain effective communication with local stakeholders	The communication and engagement process includes formal agreements with stakeholders respecting the process for dialogue.	TSM
Social	Maintain human rights standards	Operations identified as having significant risk for incidents of child labour, and measures taken to contribute to the elimination of child labour.	GRI
Social	Enable positive outcomes for indigenous peoples	The client will identify all communities of Indigenous Peoples who may be affected by the project within the project's area of influence, as well as the nature and degree of the expected social, cultural, and environmental impacts on them, and avoid adverse impacts whenever feasible.	IFC
Social	Ensure decent work and labour practices are adhered to	Ratio of basic salary of men to women by employee category.	GRI
Social	Eliminate, minimize, or fairly compensate for land acquisition and involuntary settlement	When displacement cannot be avoided, the client will offer displaced persons and communities compensation for loss of assets at full replacement cost and other assistance to help them improve or restore their standards of living or livelihoods.	IFC
Social	Take responsibility for impacts of the projects outputs (products and services)	Monetary value of significant fines and total number of non-monetary with laws and regulations concerning the provision and use of products and product services.	GRI
Social	Contribute to local/national housing and educational system	Contribution to K-12 education by building facilities and incorporating auxiliary programmes in the project.	FIDIC
Environmental	Manage natural resources in a sustainable manner to promote conservation and maintain biodiversity	Effect of the project on arable and permanent crop land area.	FIDIC
Environmental	Comply with all applicable environmental regulations	List categories of environmental permits in effect at the project and their issuing authorities. Describe the scope of these permits and how stakeholders can access them.	FRP
Environmental	Minimize or eliminate air emissions	The organizational level of accountability for GHG emissions management.	TSM

continued on following page

Table 4. Continued

Dimension	Theme	Possible Project Indicators	Source
Environmental	Minimize or eliminate energy use and procure energy from renewable sources	In addition to fundamental building systems commissioning, hire an independent agent for the commissioning, conduct reviews of the contract documents prior to issuing and the contractor submittals, provide the owner with a single manual for recommissioning the building, and have a system in place for dealing with follow up commissioning items and indoor air quality issues.	LEED
Environmental	Water pollution: discharges, effluents, and spills	Total number and volume of significant spills.	GRI
Environmental	Fresh water withdrawal and recycling	Concentration of faecal coliform in freshwater.	FIDIC
Environmental	Waste and hazardous waste control, minimization, or elimination	Weight of transported, imported, exported, or treated waste deemed hazardous under the terms of the Basel Convention Annex I, II, II, and VIII, and percentage of transported waste shipped internationally.	GRI
Environmental	Transportation to and from site	Provide showers for 5% and secure bicycle storage for 15% of building occupants.	LEED
Environmental	Indoor Environmental Quality - occupied buildings only	Install a permanent carbon dioxide monitoring system that provides feedback on space ventilation performance in a format that affords operational adjustments. Follow CO_2 differential guidelines in ASHRAE 62-2001, Appendix C.	LEED
Environmental	General environmental considerations	Initiatives to mitigate environmental impacts of products and services, and extent of impact mitigation.	GRI
Economic	Provide economic opportunities for the local community - employment	Effect of project on GDP per capita.	FIDIC
Economics	Provide economic opportunities for the local community - supply chain	Cost and percentage of all goods, materials, and services purchased locally.	FRP
Economics	Determine the local taxation and infrastructure benefits and impacts of the project	Development and impact of infrastructure investments and services provided primarily for public benefit through commercial, in-kind, or pro bono engagement.	GRI
Economic	Design the project to maximize its lifespan with a minimum level of care and maintenance	Durability of the constructed works.	FIDIC
Economic	General economic considerations	Financial implications and other risks and opportunities for the organization's activities due to climate change.	GRI

Chapter 13
Consideration of Sustainability in Projects and Project Management:
An Empirical Study

Gilbert Silvius
HU University of Applied Sciences Utrecht, The Netherlands & Van Aetsveld, The Netherlands

Ron Schipper
Van Aetsveld Project Management and Change, The Netherlands

Snezana Nedeski
Maastricht University, The Netherlands

ABSTRACT

The relevance of integrating the concepts of sustainability into project management shows from the growing number of studies on this topic. These studies approach the topic mostly from a conceptual, logical, or moral point of view. Given the fact that the relationship between sustainability and project management is still an emerging field of study, these approaches make sense. However, they do not diminish the need for more empirical studies to understand how the concepts of sustainable development are implemented in practice. This chapter reports an analysis of 56 case studies on the integration of the concepts of sustainability in the way organizations initiate, develop, and manage projects. The research question of the study was: To what extent do organizations consider the concepts of sustainability in the initiation, development, and management of projects? The study found an overall average level of sustainability consideration in the actual situation of 25.9%. For the desired situation, this score is almost 10 percent higher, showing an ambition to take sustainability more into consideration. The study also showed that the way sustainability currently is considered in projects should be categorized as the traditional "making things less bad" approach to sustainability integration and not as a more modern "how can we contribute to making things good" approach. However, the scores of the desired situation indicate that the modern approach to corporate responsibility is certainly the ambition of the participating organizations.

DOI: 10.4018/978-1-4666-4177-8.ch013

INTRODUCTION

Sustainability is recognized as one of the most important challenges of our time. Awareness seems to be growing that a change of mindset is needed, both in behavior and in policies. How can we develop prosperity without compromising the future? This growing awareness may, or should, influence projects and project management (Labuschagne and Brent, 2006; Gareis et al. 2009, 2011; Silvius et al. 2009, 2012). Association for Project Management (past-) Chairman Tom Taylor recognizes that "The planet earth is in a perilous position with a range of fundamental sustainability threats," and "Project and Programme Managers are significantly placed to make contributions to Sustainable Management practices" (Association for Project Management 2006). And at the 22nd World Congress of the International Project Management Association (IPMA) in 2008, IPMA Vice-President Mary McKinlay stated in the opening keynote speech, "The further development of the project management profession requires project managers to take responsibility for sustainability" (McKinlay 2008). It is for that reason inevitable that 'sustainability' will find its way to project management methodologies and practices in the very near future. *But how is this responsibility put to practice?*

Studies on the integration of the concepts of sustainability are mostly interpretive, giving meaning to how the concepts of sustainability *could* be interpreted in the context of projects (for example Barnard et al, 2011; Maltzman and Shirley, 2010; Gareis et al., 2011, Oehlmann, 2011), or normative, prescribing how sustainability *should* be integrated into projects (for example, Silvius et al., 2012; Labuschagne and Brent, 2006). These studies approach the integration of the concepts of sustainability into project management from a conceptual, logical or moral point of view. Given the fact that the relationship between sustainability and project management is still an emerging field of study (Gareis et al. 2009), these approaches

make sense. However, they do not diminish the need for more empirical studies to understand how the concepts of sustainable development are implemented in practice.

The study reported in this chapter aims to do just that. It reports an empirical analysis of 56 case studies on how organizations consider sustainability in their projects and project management. The cases were assessed, using the maturity model for sustainability integration in projects and project management of Silvius and Schipper (2010). Based on the concepts of sustainability, this maturity model assesses the level of consideration of sustainability in projects and project management, in terms of resources, business processes, business model and products/services. It thereby answers the research question: *To what extent, do organizations consider the concepts of sustainability in the initiation, development and management of projects?*

The remainder of this chapter is organized as follows. First the reader will be introduced to the maturity model that was used in the study. In the following section, the design of the study will be revealed and an overview of the participating organizations will be provided. The section Findings presents the results of the study and the section Analysis analyzes these findings. The chapter is concluded with a reflection on what the results tell us about the consideration of sustainability in projects and project management.

THE SUSTAINABILITY IN PROJECT MANAGEMENT MATURITY MODEL

Maturity models are a practical way to 'translate' complex concepts into organizational capabilities and to raise awareness for potential development. They provide guidance for action plans and allow organizations to monitor their progress (Dinsmore, 1998). Most maturity models are derived from the Software Engineering Institute's Capability Maturity Model (Carnegie Mellon Software

Engineering Institute, 2002) and thereby based on the maturity of processes. For example, project management maturity is, in this context, a measure for the organization's ability to perform project management and related processes in a controlled and optimized way. For the goals our sustainability maturity model, however, Silvius and Schipper (2010) developed a maturity model that addresses the consideration of sustainability aspects more specifically.

The model is based on two dimensions. The first dimension is that of the aspects, or criteria, of sustainability, the second that of the level or depth of considering sustainability.

Dimension 1: Criteria of Sustainability

Sustainability in the context of sustainable development is defined by the World Commission on Environment and Development (1987) as "forms of progress that meet the needs of the present without compromising the ability of future generations to meet their needs". This broad definition emphasizes the aspect of future orientation as a basic element of sustainability. This care for the future implies a wise use of natural resources and other aspects regarding the environmental footprint. However, sustainability requires not just an environmental "green" perspective, but also a social one. Elkington (1997), recognizes this in his 'triple bottom line' or 'Triple-P (People, Planet, Profit)' concept (Figure 1): Sustainability is about the balance or harmony between economic sustainability, social sustainability and environmental sustainability (Elkington, 1997).

Elaborating on the three perspectives of the Triple-P concept, several organizations developed frameworks of indicators that would allow organizations to evaluate the sustainability aspects of different policies and projects, as well as to monitor progress. In fact, the literature on these models is a veritable jungle of different approaches and numerous case studies (Olsson et

Figure 1. The triple-P concept of sustainability

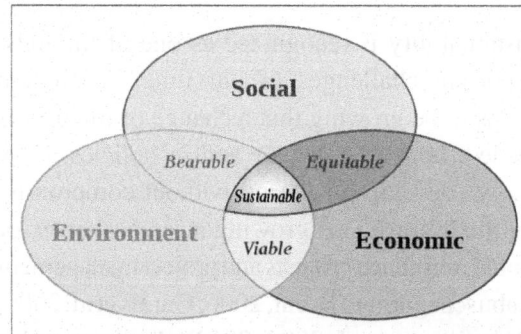

al, 2004). A widely used framework in (external) sustainability reporting is the Sustainability Reporting Guidelines by the Global Reporting Initiative (GRI). The GRI is a non-profit organization that pioneered the Sustainability Reporting Guidelines (SRG). Companies can use the SRG to indicate to shareholders and consumers their economic, social, and environmental performance. GRI's objective is to facilitate sustainability reporting for companies and thereby stimulate them to operate more sustainably. The SRG framework consists of an extensive set of indicators, from which companies can select a set that is relevant to their operations or industry.

At the 2010 IPMA Expert Seminar 'Survival and Sustainability as Challenges for Project" (Knoepfel, 2010), one of the goals was to 'translate' the concepts of sustainability to practically applicable tools for project management professionals. Based on the SRG, the participants of the seminar developed a 'Sustainability Checklist' for projects and project managers. Table 1 provides this Sustainability Checklist. The maturity model by Silvius and Schipper adopted this checklist as operationalization of the criteria of sustainability.

Dimension 2: Level of Consideration

The second dimension of the maturity model is that of level, or depth, of consideration of sustainability. This dimension is based on the observation

Table 1. A checklist for integrating sustainability in projects and project management (Knoepfel, 2010)

Economic Sustainability	Return on Investment	- Direct financial benefits/Net Present Value - Strategic value
	Business Agility	- Flexibility/Optionality in the project - Increased business flexibility
Environmental Sustainability	Transport	- Local procurement/supplier selection - Digital communication - Travelling - Transport
	Energy	- Energy used - Emission/CO2 from energy used
	Water	- Water usage - Recycling
	Waste	- Recycling - Disposal
	Materials and resources	- Reusability - Incorporated energy - Supplier selection
Social Sustainability	Labour Practices and Decent Work	- Employment - Labour/Management relations - Health and Safety - Training and Education - Organizational learning
	Human Rights	- Non-discrimination - Diversity and Equal opportunity - Freedom of association - Child labour - Forced and compulsory labour
	Society and Customers	- Community support - Public policy/Compliance - Customer health and safety - Products and services labelling - Market communication and Advertising - Customer privacy
	Ethical behaviour	- Investment and Procurement practices - Bribery and corruption - Anti-competition behaviour

that sustainability can be considered on different levels. A first logical level is the level of resources. For example using resources that provide the same functionality, but are less harmful for the environment, like using hybrid cars instead of normal fueled cars. These actions can reduce the less sustainable effects of operating the organization, but do not take away the cause of non-sustainability. A second level of consideration is therefore the business process in which the resources are used. A more sustainable business process takes away

the cause of non-sustainable effects instead of just limiting or compensating them. For example optimizing a service management process in such a way that less travel is required.

A third level of consideration is looking at the way the products or services are delivered: the business model. For example changing from a strictly off-line business model to a combined on-line and off-line business model, may have favorable effects on sustainability because of the fact that on-line shoppers travel less than off-line shoppers. A fourth and final level of consideration takes into account not only the business process or model to deliver products and services, but also the products and services themselves. How can products and services be innovated to contribute to a more sustainable society. For example a product that learns children to respect nature.

Figure 2 illustrates the four levels of consideration of the maturity model.

The different levels of consideration reflect the more modern views on sustainability in which the challenge is not to make 'bad' products, services and processes 'less bad', but to make them good.

Assessing Maturity

The maturity assessment uses a questionnaire consisting of 31 questions in four sections. The first three sections cover descriptive questions regarding the respondent, the project that is assessed and the organizational context of the project. The fourth section consists of the actual assessment questions. The model assesses the level (business resources, business process, business model, products/services) on which the different

Figure 2. The levels of consideration

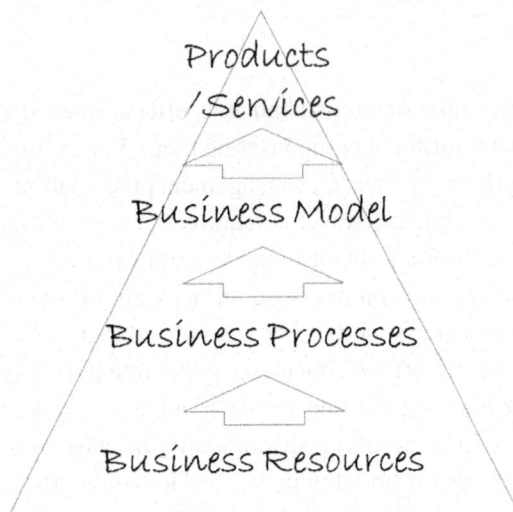

aspects of sustainability are considered in the project. The sustainability aspects are derived from the sustainability checklist and are grouped in economical aspects, environmental aspects and social aspects. Presenting the project's maturity separately on these three pillars of sustainability is a deliberate choice in order to address the regional differences mentioned earlier and the ambitions or values an organization may have. Figure 3 shows the conceptual model of the assessment.

For each sustainability aspect an assessment of the current situation and the desired situation is asked. This provides guidance for improvement. Some example questions from the assessment are in Box 1 (The full questionnaire is added to the Appendix of this chapter).

In the questionnaire, answers B to E correspond to the earlier mentioned levels of consideration (B: business resources, C: business process, D: business model, E: products/services). Answers A correspond to 'non existing', meaning that this aspects of sustainability is not specifically taken into account. Answers B to E were formulated to be non-cumulative, meaning that the respondents could 'tick' multiple answers. Answer A, the 'non-existing' answer, logically does not combine with any of the answers B to E.

The assessment is reported in a graphical way, showing both the actual levels and the desired levels of integration of the sustainability aspects. Based on the report, organizations can discuss their ambition levels (the desired situation) on the different perspectives, develop an action plan to bridge the gap between actual levels of maturity and desired levels and to monitor their progress.

RESEARCH DESIGN

Given the interpretive and normative nature of the available insights on the topic, we selected an exploratory approach to the empirical study, based on a quantitative analysis of the maturity assessments.

Figure 3. Conceptual model of the assessment (Silvius and Schipper, 2010)

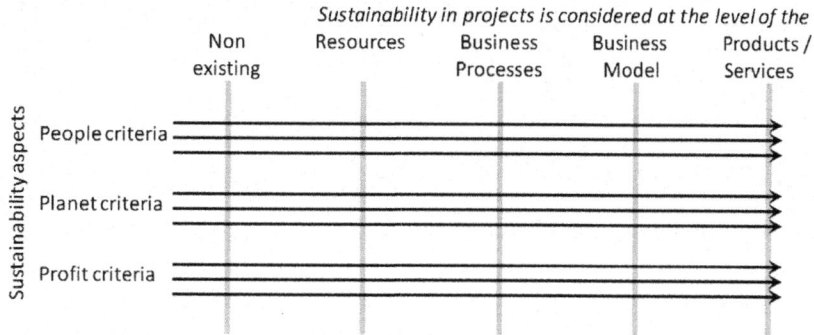

Box 1. Sample questionnaire

In which way does the project try to minimize its waste?

	Actual situation	Desired situation	
A.	[ ]	[ ]	No specific policies on this point.
B.	[ ]	[ ]	Waste in the project is separated in recyclable and non-recyclable and collected by the local waste handling companies.
C.	[ ]	[ ]	The project has policies (e.g. double sided printing) to minimize waste and waste in the project is separated.
D.	[ ]	[ ]	The project is designed to minimize waste and necessary waste is as much as possible recycled in the project itself.
E.	[ ]	[ ]	The project and the result it delivers are designed to minimize waste and necessary waste is as much as possible recycled in the project or result itself.

To what extent does the project apply policies or standards for diversity and equal opportunity that reflects the society it operates in?

	Actual situation	Desired situation	
A.	[ ]	[ ]	The project does not have any specific policies on diversity and equal opportunity, but complies with the standards and regulations of the organization it operates in.
B.	[ ]	[ ]	The project explicitly seeks diversity and complies with applicable standards and regulations on equal opportunity in terms of gender, race, religion, etc.
C.	[ ]	[ ]	The project actively (re) designs its work processes in a way (e.g. by designing part-time jobs) that diversity and equal opportunity are promoted and stimulated.
D.	[ ]	[ ]	The project actively (re) designs its work processes in a way (e.g. by designing part-time jobs) that diversity and equal opportunity are promoted and stimulated, and requires its suppliers to practice diversity practices and provide equal opportunity in terms of gender, race, religion, etc.
E.	[ ]	[ ]	The project's result is designed to improve diversity and equal opportunity in the society it operates in and this reflects in the way the project is executed and in its suppliers and users.

Data Collection

The maturity assessments were performed over the period October 2010 to December 2011 and followed the process suggested by Silvius and Schipper (2010). Data was collected using structured interviews based on the questionnaire of the maturity model (enclosed as Appendix). Respondents were typically project managers, project sponsors and other key stakeholders. An important condition was that the respondent was in a position to give an informed answer to the questions of the assessment.

Sample

The study included maturity assessments of 56 projects in 46 organizations. Table 2 presents the details of the participating organizations in the study, showing that the study covered a broad range of industries and company sizes.

The majority of the participating organizations was located in Europe (40). The non-European organizations were located in Asia (5) and the United States (1). 59% of the organizations operated internationally.

Descriptives

The maturity assessments assessed the consideration of sustainability aspects in actual projects in the before-mentioned organizations.

Type of the Projects

78% of the projects were characterized as building and/or construction projects, and 22% of the projects as organizational change and/or information technology (IT) projects. Approximately 73% of the projects were international, or multinational, projects.

Size of the Projects

Figure 4 provides an overview of the (financial) size of the projects in terms of project budget. This Figure shows that the majority of the projects in the sample had a budget of either < 1 Million € or between 10 and 100 Million €. Given this distribution, we consider the results of the study representative for both large and smaller projects.

FINDINGS

People Perspective

Figure 5 provides the findings of the study summarized for the People perspective. In the graph, a 100% score on a certain level of consideration indicates that all organizations in the study scored this level of consideration on all eight questions

Table 2. Overview of organizations participating in the study

Industry/sector	Number of employees						Total
	<51	51-200	201-500	501-1000	1001-5000	>5000	
Agriculture				1			1
Building & Construction	3			1		1	5
Education		1		1	2		4
Energy					1		1
Engineering & Installation				1			1
Financial services						1	1
Health Care					2	1	3
ICT Services	2	2					4
Manufacturing					2	1	3
Professional services	5	1			2		8
Public		1			1		2
Real Estate	2	1	2		3		8
Retail	1					1	2
Tourism & Hospitality			1				1
Transport & Logistics						2	2
Total	13	6	3	4	13	7	46

Figure 4. Overview of the financial budgets of the assessed projects

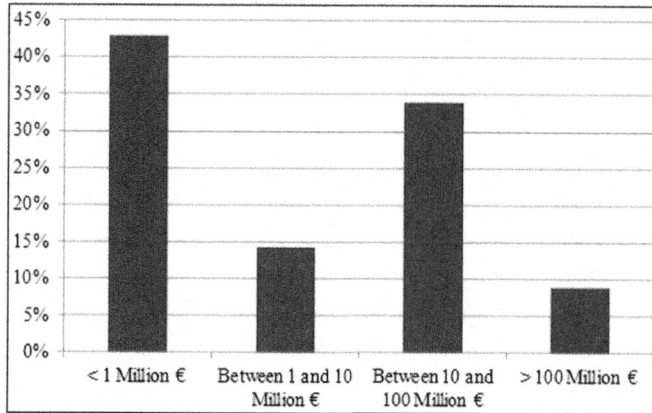

Figure 5. The results of the study for the people perspective

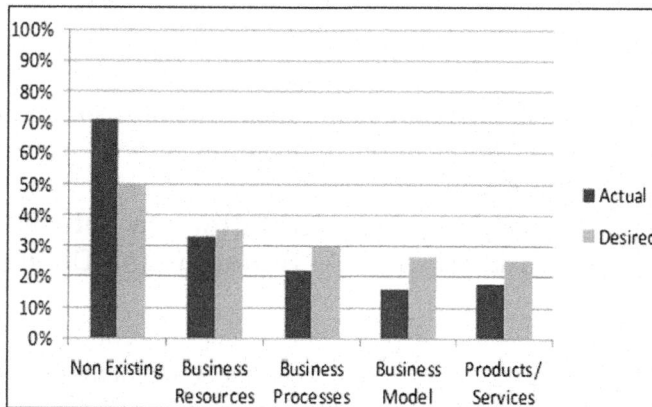

of the people perspective. A 100% score therefore suggests that the people perspective is fully considered on this level of consideration, by all participating organizations. A 50% score indicates that the people perspectives is only half taken into account on this level of consideration. The graph shows both the actual as the desired situation.

Figure 5 shows that the Desired scores are for all levels of consideration higher than the Actual scores, except for the 'non existing' category, indicating that there is clearly an ambition in the participating organizations to consider sustainability more substantially in their projects. Both Desired and Actual scores are strongest on the Business Resources level

Planet Perspective

Figure 6 shows the results for the Planet perspective.

Also the results on the Planet perspectives show higher scores for the Desired situation than for the Actual situation, indicating an ambition to consider sustainability more than today. The pattern of the Actual scores over the four levels of consideration shows resemblance with the scores on the People profile. The Desired scores, however, shows highest scores on the business process and business model level.

Figure 6. The results of the study for the planet perspective

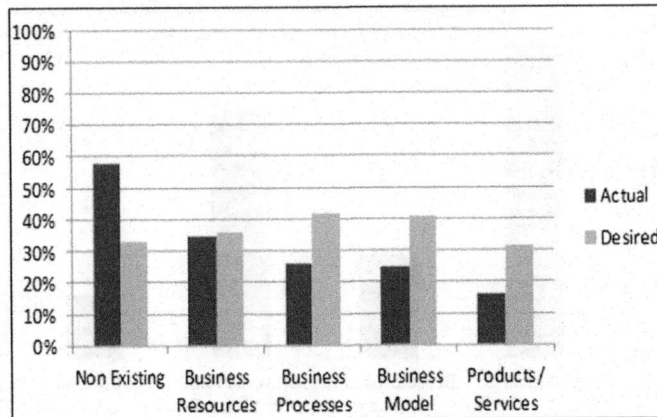

Profit Perspective

And finally, Figure 7 shows the results for the Profit perspective.

Not surprisingly, the Profit perspective shows the relatively highest scores on the consideration levels. Also on this perspective, the desired scores are higher than the Actual scores, with exception of the business resources level, and of course the non existing level.

ANALYSIS

Based on the findings on the three perspectives, this section discusses a few observations that can be made.

Overall Level of Consideration

A first observation should be that the highest scores recorded in the study are for the 'non existing' category, indicating that sustainability is not completely considered in the projects in the sample. On average, non existing scored 57% for the actual situation and 36% for the desired situation.

When considering the different levels of consideration, the B to E answer categories, an overall average level of sustainability consideration,

regardless of what consideration level or perspective, in the actual situation of 25.9% was found. For the desired situation, this score is almost 10 percent higher: 34.9%. These scores do not seem to be quite high and are in line with the scores found for the non existing option.

Differences between Actual Situation and Desired Situation

A visual inspection of Figures 5, 6 and 7 shows that the scores of the Desired situation are consistently higher than the Actual situation, on the four levels of consideration for all three perspectives, with the exception of the business resources level of the Profit perspective. Overall, the Desired situation scores 9 percent points higher than the Actual situation (35% versus 26%). This indicates a clear ambition of the participating organizations to consider sustainability more in their projects. Table 3 illustrates this ambition, by presenting the Actual and Desired levels of sustainability consideration by perspective.

From this table it shows that the largest 'gap' between Desired and Actual situation is for the planet perspective (13%). This result may indicate that in the Western world, sustainability, is very much associated with the environmental 'green' concerns.

Figure 7. The results of the study for the profit perspective

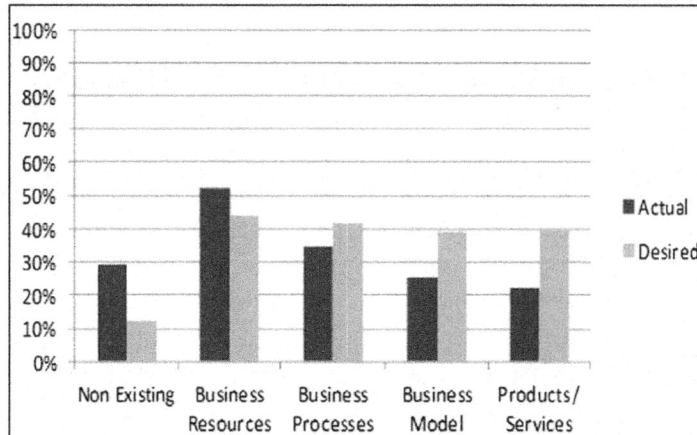

Differences between the Levels of Consideration

The results shown in Figures 5, 6, and 7 more or less all show the same pattern over the different levels of consideration, in the sense that the consideration of sustainability aspects appears to be highest on the resources level and lowest on the products/services level. This pattern corresponds with the traditional 'less bad' view of considering sustainability. However, from the scores of the desired level of consideration, the ambition to consider sustainability on a more proactive level shows.

When comparing actual and desired levels of consideration in Table 3, the gaps on the business processes, business model and products/services levels, are substantial (respectively 11%, 12%, and 13%), whereas the gap on the business resources level is negligible. This outcome indicates that the participating organizations understood that the current 'resources' orientation in considering sustainability should be complemented by a more modern 'corporate responsibility' orientation, in which organizations ask themselves how their business model, products and services can contribute to sustainable development.

Table 3. Actual and desired levels of sustainability consideration

		Level of consideration					
		Non Existing	*Business Resources*	*Business Processes*	*Business Model*	*Products / Services*	*Total*
People perspective	Actual	71%	33%	22%	16%	18%	**22%**
	Desired	*49%*	*35%*	*30%*	*27%*	*25%*	***29%***
Planet perspective	Actual	58%	35%	26%	25%	16%	**25%**
	Desired	*33%*	*36%*	*42%*	*41%*	*31%*	***38%***
Profit perspective	Actual	29%	52%	35%	25%	22%	**34%**
	Desired	*12%*	*44%*	*42%*	*39%*	*40%*	***41%***
Overall	Actual	57%	38%	26%	21%	18%	**26%**
	Desired	*36%*	*37%*	*37%*	*35%*	*31%*	***35%***

Differences between the Three Perspectives

Visually it appears from Figures 5, 6, and 7 that the profit perspective, scores the highest level of consideration, followed by the planet perspective and the people perspective. This dominant position of the profit perspective is not unexpected. Also the lowest scores for the people perspective is not entirely unexpected, given the fact the majority of the firms in the sample were European. In Europe, the labor conditions and social aspects are relatively well taken care of, and 'sustainability' is often identified with 'green'. In other regions and cultures, the people perspective may score higher.

Contextual Factors

Organizational Strategy

The influence of the strategy of the organization with regards to sustainability had a noticeable effect on the level of sustainability consideration. The organizations that do not mention the consideration of sustainability in their strategy scored an overall level of sustainability consideration (actual situation) that is considerably (more than 10%) lower than the organizations that include some mention of sustainability consideration in their strategy. However, for the Desired situation, both groups score approximately equal scores (32.2% and 31.6%), indicating that the ambition of the organizations on the consideration of sustainability in projects seems to be independent of the mentioning of sustainability in the strategy.

Type of Project

Regarding the type of the project, a distinction was made in building and/or construction projects, and organizational change and/or IT projects. Tables 4 and 5 show the levels of consideration for these two types of projects.

Tables 4 and 5 show that the level of consideration of sustainability is higher in building and/or construction projects than in organizational change and/or IT projects. From the three perspectives, the planet perspective scores highest and the people perspective lowest. Again, this corresponds with the traditional 'less bad' view of sustainability, in which sustainability is mainly seen as 'green' or 'eco-friendly', providing criteria for the materials used in a project and the characteristics of the project deliverable (for example energy efficiency).

CONCLUSION

This chapter reported an analysis of 56 case studies on the integration of the concepts of sustainability in the way organizations initiate, develop and manage projects. The research question of the study was: To what extent, do organizations consider the concepts of sustainability in the initiation, development and management of projects? The study uses the maturity model for sustainability integration that was presented at the 2010 IPMA World Congress for the assessment of the level of sustainability consideration.

The study found an overall average level of sustainability consideration in the Actual situation of 25.9%. For the Desired situation, this score is almost 10 percent higher, showing an ambition to take sustainability more into consideration. Given this ambition, it should be expected that the consideration of sustainability in projects will develop further in the future. The study also found that the mentioning of sustainability in the organization's strategy is related to a higher actual level of sustainability consideration in projects, but is not related to the desired level of consideration.

The results of the study indicated that sustainability is most of all considered on the level of the business resources, corresponding with a traditional 'less bad' approach to sustainability,

Table 4. Actual and desired levels of sustainability consideration of building and/or construction projects

		Level of consideration					
		Non Existing	*Business Resources*	*Business Processes*	*Business Model*	*Products / Services*	*Total*
People perspective	Actual	59%	30%	20%	14%	15%	**20%**
	Desired	*45%*	*33%*	*26%*	*23%*	*23%*	*26%*
Planet perspective	Actual	59%	51%	34%	32%	19%	**34%**
	Desired	*38%*	*53%*	*60%*	*52%*	*36%*	*50%*
Profit perspective	Actual	24%	52%	33%	21%	23%	**32%**
	Desired	*16%*	*44%*	*40%*	*36%*	*39%*	*40%*
Overall	Actual	52%	42%	28%	22%	18%	**28%**
	Desired	*37%*	*42%*	*41%*	*36%*	*31%*	*38%*

Table 5. Actual and desired levels of sustainability consideration of organizational change and/or IT projects

		Level of consideration					
		Non Existing	*Business Resources*	*Business Processes*	*Business Model*	*Products / Services*	*Total*
People perspective	Actual	73%	11%	18%	10%	11%	**13%**
	Desired	*55%*	*28%*	*21%*	*20%*	*25%*	*23%*
Planet perspective	Actual	103%	16%	17%	14%	10%	**14%**
	Desired	*56%*	*29%*	*31%*	*37%*	*30%*	*32%*
Profit perspective	Actual	53%	50%	40%	33%	18%	**35%**
	Desired	*8%*	*60%*	*60%*	*58%*	*38%*	*54%*
Overall	Actual	79%	21%	22%	16%	12%	**18%**
	Desired	*45%*	*35%*	*33%*	*34%*	*29%*	*33%*

and not on the level of the product or service, that would correspond with a more modern social responsibility approach. The results also indicate that the people perspective is least considered. Given the fact that the majority of firms in the sample was European, this is not entirely unexpected. In other regions and cultures, the people perspective may score higher.

From the previous conclusion we can also conclude that in the near future the attention for sustainability in projects will grow. Sustainability is an emerging trend, now moving from reputational strategy towards business orientation. The personal values of individual project managers and sponsor and the formal attention from company strategy will drive this ambition.

FUTURE RESEARCH DIRECTIONS

In the study of the impact of sustainability on projects and project management there is a clear need for more empirical work to understand how organizations consider the concepts of sustainability impact projects and project management. The study reported in this chapter found that organizations demonstrate quite a conservative view on sustainability. Further research is needed to:

1. Test whether this is confirmed in a larger sample.
2. Test whether this finding is consistent over different industries.
3. Monitor how this view develops in time.

REFERENCES

Association for Project Management. (2006). *APM supports sustainability outlooks*. Retrieved from http://www.apm.org.uk/page.asp?categoryID=4

Barnard, L. T., Ackles, B., & Haner, J. L. (2011). *Making sense of sustainability project management*. Explorus Group Inc..

Carnegie Mellon Software Engineering Institute. (2002). *Capability maturity models*. Retrieved from http://www.sei.cmu.edu/cmmi/

Dinsmore, P. C. (1998). How grown-up is your organization? *PM Network, 12*(6), 24–26.

Elkington, J. (1997). *Cannibals with forks: The triple bottom line of 21st century business*. Oxford, UK: Capstone Publishing.

Gareis, R., Huemann, M., & Martinuzzi, R.-A. (2009). *Relating sustainable development and project management*. Berlin: IRNOP IX.

Gareis, R., Huemann, M., Martinuzzi, R.-A., Sedlacko, M., & Weninger, C. (2011). *The SustPM matrix: Relating sustainability principles to project assignment and project management*. Paper presented at EURAM11. Talinn.

Knoepfel, H. (Ed.). (2010). *Survival and sustainability as challenges for projects*. Zurich, Switzerland: International Project Management Association.

Labuschagne, C., & Brent, A. C. (2006). Social indicators for sustainable project and technology life cycle management in the process industry. *International Journal of Life Cycle Assessment, 11*(1), 3–15. doi:10.1065/lca2006.01.233.

Maltzman, R., & Shirley, D. (2010). *Green project management*. Boca Raton, FL: CRC Press. doi:10.1201/EBK1439830017.

McKinlay, M. (2008). *Where is project management running to...?* Paper presented at the 22nd World Congress of the International Project Management Association. Rome, Italy.

Oehlmann, I. (2011). *The sustainable footprint methodology*. Cologne, Germany: Lambert Academic Publishing.

Olsson, J. A., Hilding-Rydevik, T., Aalbu, H., & Bradley, K. (2004). *Indicators for sustainable development. Discussion paper*. European Regional Network on Sustainable Development.

Silvius, A. J. G. (2012). *Update May 2012 overview of literature on sustainability in projects and project management*. Retrieved from http://www.slideshare.net/GilbertSilvius/update-may-2012-overview-of-literature-on-sustainability-in-projects-and-project-management

Silvius, A. J. G., Brink, J., & Köhler, A. (2009). Views on sustainable project management. In Kähköhnen, Kazi, & Rekola (Eds.), Human Side of Projects in Modern Business. Helsinki, Finland: IPMA Scientific Research Paper Series.

Silvius, A. J. G., & Schipper, R. (2010). *A maturity model for integrating sustainability in projects and project management*. Paper presented at the 24th IPMA World Congress. Istanbul, Turkey.

Silvius, A. J. G., Schipper, R., Planko, J., van den Brink, J., & Köhler, A. (2012). *Sustainability in project management*. Gower Publishing.

World Commission on Environment and Development. (1987). *Our common future*. Oxford, UK: Oxford University Press.

APPENDIX

QUESTIONNAIRE OF THE SUSTAINABLE PROJECT MANAGEMENT MATURITY MODEL

The questionnaire in Table 6 consists of four sections and in total 31 questions. The first three sections cover descriptive questions regarding the respondent, the project that is assessed and the organizational context of the project. The fourth section consists of the actual assessment questions.

Table 6. Sustainable project management questionnaire

Section I. Questions regarding the respondent (4 questions)		
1.	*What is your gender?* Select only one answer	
	A.	Male
	B.	Female
2.	*What is your age?* Select only one answer	
	A.	< 25 years
	B.	25-34 years
	C.	35-44 years
	D.	45-54 years
	E.	55-64 years
	F.	65 years or over
3.	*In which domain is your position?* Select only one answer	
	A.	General Management
	B.	Commercial Management
	C.	Financial Management
	D.	IT Management
	E.	Project, Program or Portfolio Management
	F.	Business Development
	G.	Consulting
	H.	Training or Education
	I.	Other
4.	*What level would you say your position is?* Select only one answer	
	A.	Strategic Management
	B.	Tactical Management
	C.	Operational Management
	D.	Non-Management
	E.	Other

continued on following page

Table 6. Continued

			Section II. Questions regarding the project (6 questions)
5.			*What type of project is assessed?* Select only one answer
	A.		Building & Construction Public Infrastructure
	B.		Building & Construction Real Estate
	C.		Building & Construction Development
	D.		Organizational Change
	E.		Information Technology
	F.		Research and Development
	G.		Other
6.			*In what industry sector does the project take place?* Select only one answer
	A.		Agriculture
	B.		Industry
	C.		Energy
	D.		Building & Construction
	E.		Healthcare
	F.		Wholesale & Retail
	G.		Logistic Services
	H.		Financial Services
	I.		Facility & Real Estate Services
	J.		Legal Services
	K.		HR Services
	L.		ICT & Communication Services
	M.		Consulting
	N.		Public Administration
	O.		Education & Training
	P.		Other
7.			*Is the project international?* Select only one answer
	A.		No
	B.		Yes, th esult of the project has international aspects
	C.		Yes, the resources working on the project are international
	D.		Yes, the suppliers in the project are international
8.			*In which geographical regions will the project have an impact?* Multiple answers allowed
	A.		Europe
	B.		North America
	C.		Central and/or South America
	D.		Asia
	E.		Africa
	F.		Australia
9.			*What is the approximate size of the project budget?* Select only one answer

continued on following page

Table 6. Continued

	A.			< 1 Million €
	B.			Between 1 and 10 Million €
	C.			Between 10 and 100 Million €
	D.			> 100 Million €
10.	*How many business partners (suppliers, subcontractors, etc.) will participate in the project?* Select only one answer			
	A.			0
	B.			1-5
	C.			6-15
	D.			16-50
	E.			>50
Section III. Questions regarding the organizational context of the project (2 questions)				
11.	*What is the position of sustainability in the strategy of the organization that commissions the project?* Multiple answers allowed. Please tick all answers that are applicable.			
	A.			The strategy of the organization does not include any statements or ambitions regarding sustainability.
	B.			The strategy of the organization mentions a wise use of natural resources and/or social responsibility as one of the guiding principles
	C.			The strategy of the organization mentions a wise use of natural resources and/or social responsibility as one of the guiding principles for *the (design of the) business processes* of the organization.
	D.			The strategy of the organization mentions a wise use of natural resources and/or social responsibility as one of the guiding principles for *the (design of the) business model* of the organization.
	E.			The strategy of the organization mentions a wise use of natural resources and/or social responsibility as one of the guiding principles for *the (development of) products and services* of the organization.
12.	*Does the organization that commissions the project have any form of sustainability reporting?* Multiple answers allowed. Please tick all answers that are applicable.			
	A.			No, the organization does not have any specific form of sustainability reporting.
	B.			Yes, the organization reports on their contribution *as a part or section of the regular company reports* (e.g. the Annual Report).
	C.			Yes, the organization reports on their contribution *as a separate periodic sustainability report in a self-developed format.*
	D.			Yes, the organization reports on their contribution as a separate periodic sustainability report in a format that is *based on the sustainability reporting guidelines of the GRI.*
Section IV. Questions regarding the assessment of sustainability aspects in the project				
In all questions, multiple answers are allowed. Please tick all answers that are applicable for the project. *Please answer all questions two times. The first time for the actual situation. The second time for the 'desired' situation as you would prefer it.*				
Profit perspective (4 questions)				
13.	**Direct (financial) benefits** *Which types of benefits are recognized in the business case of the project?* Multiple answers allowed. Please tick all answers that are applicable.			
		Actual Situation	Desired Situation	
	A.			Benefits are not explicitly recognized or no business cases are made for the project.

continued on following page

Table 6. Continued

		Actual Situation	Desired Situation	
	B.			Benefits are recognized in terms of *cost savings or reduced use of resources*.
	C.			Benefits are recognized in terms of *improved business processes*.
	D.			Benefits are recognized in terms of *extra revenues from new business models for existing products and services*.
	E.			Benefits are recognized in terms of *extra revenues from innovated products or services*.
14.	**Managerial flexibility and optionality** *To what extent does the project allow for future decision making and real options?* Multiple answers allowed. Please tick all answers that are applicable.			
		Actual Situation	Desired Situation	
	A.			Projects are designed as optimal as possible, given our current knowledge. Future decisions may or may not be included in this design, but are not a design criterion as such.
	B.			Projects are designed as optimal as possible, and decisions regarding *materials, resources and suppliers* are made as late as possible to allow for flexibility in the execution of the project.
	C.			Projects are designed as optimal as possible, and decisions regarding *project (production) processes and outsourcing partners* are made as late as possible to allow for flexibility in the execution of the project.
	D.			Projects are designed as optimal as possible, and the *exact requirements of the project deliverables* are made as late as possible to allow for flexibility in the execution of the project.
	E.			Projects are designed as optimal as possible, and the *exact requirements of the project goal, result and deliverables* are made as late as possible to allow for flexibility in the execution of the project.
15.	**Project reporting** *Which items are reflected in the project's (progress) reports?* Multiple answers allowed. Please tick all answers that are applicable.			
		Actual Situation	Desired Situation	
	A.			The project does not formally report progress.
	B.			The project (progress) reports show items such as *activities commenced, activities completed, budget spent, budget still required, total budget, issues and risks*, all in terms of 'plan' and 'actual'.
	C.			The project (progress) reports show also *lessons learned and improvements to the project*.
	D.			The project (progress) reports show also *suggestions to (radically) change the way the project is being designed an delivered*.
	E.			The project (progress) reports show also *changes (e.g. market conditions) that may have an effect on the value and business case of the project's result*.
16.	**Investment evaluation** *Which evaluation methods are used in the selection of projects?* Multiple answers allowed. Please tick all answers that are applicable.			
		Actual Situation	Desired Situation	
	A.			No formal selection methods are used, projects are selected based on the availability of funds to invest.
	B.			Projects are evaluated and selected predominantly based on the *pay-back period* of the investment.

continued on following page

Table 6. Continued

		Actual Situation	Desired Situation	
	C.			Projects are evaluated and selected predominantly based on the *return on investment or net present value* of the investment.
	D.			Projects are evaluated and selected predominantly based o their *long term strategic value, in combination with their short/medium term returns.*
	E.			Projects are evaluated and selected predominantly based on a balanced set of quantitative and qualitative criteria that reflect both long term and short term perspectives and also *economical, social and environmental aspects.*
	**Planet perspective (7 questions)**			
17.	**Procurement** ***Based on which criteria are suppliers for the project selected?*** Multiple answers allowed. Please tick all answers that are applicable.			
		Actual Situation	Desired Situation	
	A.			Suppliers for the project are selected based on *price.*
	B.			Suppliers for the project are selected based on *location for minimizing transport.*
	C.			Suppliers for the project are selected based on *their own use of natural resources and policies to enhance environmental sustainability.*
	D.			Suppliers for the project are selected based on how *their know -how and partnership helps our project to be delivered in a more sustainable way.*
	E.			Suppliers for the project are selected based on how *their know -how and partnership helps our product and services to aid sustainability.*
18.	**Materials** ***Based on which criteria are materials for the project selected?*** Multiple answers allowed. Please tick all answers that are applicable.			
		Actual Situation	Desired Situation	
	A.			Materials for the project are selected based on *technical and functional requirements and their costs.*
	B.			Materials for the project are also selected based on the *waste* they cause in and for the project.
	C.			Materials for the project are also selected based on the *energy consumption and/or pollution incorporated in the materials because of their production process.*
	D.			Materials for the project are also selected based on the *energy consumption and/ or pollution incorporated in the materials because of their production and logistics processes.*
	E.			Materials for the project are also selected based on their *reuse capabilities and value.*
19.	**Energy** ***Does the project have any specific policies regarding its energy consumption?*** Multiple answers allowed. Please tick all answers that are applicable.			
		Actual Situation	Desired Situation	
	A.			Next to general policies on energy consumption within the organization, the project does not have specific policies and the energy consumption.
	B.			There are policies in the project to promote the *smart use of energy* and where possible, *energy saving equipment* is used.
	C.			Where possible, energy consumption is *actively kept to a minimum* and the necessary energy used is acquired as *'green' energy.*

continued on following page

Table 6. Continued

		Actual Situation	Desired Situation	
	D.			Minimizing energy consumption is *one of the parameters in the design of the project delivery processes.*
	E.			Minimizing energy consumption is one of the parameters in the design of the *project deliverable and result.*
20.	**Water** **Does the project have any specific policies regarding its water consumption and pollution?** Multiple answers allowed. Please tick all answers that are applicable.			
		Actual Situation	Desired Situation	
	A.			Next to general policies on water consumption and pollution within the organization, the project does not have specific policies.
	B.			There are policies in the project to promote the *smart use* of water and where possible, *water saving equipment* is used.
	C.			Water consumption is *actively kept to a minimum* and where possible, the project recycles its water and/or purifies it.
	D.			Minimizing water consumption and pollution is one of the parameters in the *design of the project delivery processes.* The necessary water used is recycled and/or purified before disposal.
	E.			Minimizing water consumption and pollution is one of the parameters in the *design of the project deliverable and result.* The project result actively minimizes water consumption and pollution and the necessary water used is recycled and/or purified before disposal.
21.	**Waste** **In which way does the project try to minimize its waste?** Multiple answers allowed. Please tick all answers that are applicable.			
		Actual Situation	Desired Situation	
	A.			No specific policies on this point.
	B.			*Waste in the project is separated* in recyclable and non-recyclable and collected by the local waste handling companies.
	C.			The project has *policies (e.g. double sided printing) to minimize waste.*
	D.			The *project delivery processes are designed to minimize waste* and necessary waste is as much as possible recycled in the project itself.
	E.			The *project deliverable and result are designed to minimize waste* and necessary waste is as much as possible recycled in the deliverable itself.
22.	**Travel** **To what extent does the project apply travel policies that consider environmental aspects?** Multiple answers allowed. Please tick all answers that are applicable.			
		Actual Situation	Desired Situation	
	A.			Travelling in the project is based on necessity for the project's activities and deliverables. Means of travel are selected on costs and time.
	B.			Travelling in the project is based on necessity for the project's activities and deliverables, *but means of travel are selected considering environmental aspects.*
	C.			Travelling in the project is based on necessity and minimized by *actively promoting and facilitating the use of alternatives* for travelling (e.g. video conferencing).
	D.			The *project delivery processes* are designed to minimize travelling in the project.
	E.			The *project deliverable and result* are designed to minimize travelling.

continued on following page

Table 6. Continued

		Actual Situation	Desired Situation	
23.	**Project reporting** *Does the project's (progress) reports reflect indicators of environmental sustainability?* Multiple answers allowed. Please tick all answers that are applicable.			
	A.			The project does not formally report progress.
	B.			The project (progress) reports reflect indicators of environmental sustainability with respect to *used (physical) resources*.
	C.			The project (progress) reports reflect indicators of environmental sustainability with respect to *the project delivery process*.
	D.			The project (progress) reports reflect indicators of environmental sustainability with respect to *the project deliverable or result*.
	E.			The project (progress) reports reflect indicators of environmental sustainability with respect to the *use and disposal of the project deliverable or result*.
People perspective (8 questions)				
24.	**Labor practices and decent work** *To what extent does the project apply policies or standards for labour practices and decent work?* Multiple answers allowed. Please tick all answers that are applicable.			
	A.			The project complies with applicable standards and regulations on labour practices or decent work.
	B.			The project also requires *its suppliers and partners* to practice good labour practices and decent work.
	C.			The project actively *(re) designs its project delivery processes* in a way that labour practices are improved and/or on a high level.
	D.			The *project's deliverable and result* is designed to improve labour practices and decent work in the organization that commissioned the project.
	E.			The *project's deliverable and result* is designed to improve labour practices and decent work in the community in which the result is used or aimed at.
25.	**Health and safety** *To what extent does the project apply policies or standards for health and safety?* Multiple answers allowed. Please tick all answers that are applicable.			
	A.			The project complies with applicable standards and regulations on health and safety.
	B.			The project also requires *its suppliers and partners* to practice good health and safety practices.
	C.			The project actively *(re) designs its project delivery processes* in a way that health and safety risks are minimized.
	D.			The *project's deliverable and result* is designed to improve health and safety conditions in the organization that commissioned the project.
	E.			The *project's deliverable and result* is designed to improve health and safety conditions in the community in which the result is used or aimed at.

continued on following page

Table 6. Continued

		Actual Situation	Desired Situation	
26.	**Training, education and organizational learning** *To what extent does the project includes training, education and development of stakeholders?* Multiple answers allowed. Please tick all answers that are applicable.			
	A.			The project includes activities for training and education of *end users* as part of the project's deliverables (if applicable).
	B.			The project includes activities for training and education of *team members for improved individual and team performance in the project.*
	C.			The project includes activities for training and education of team members and partners for improved individual and team performance *after the project has finished.*
	D.			The project includes activities for *developing the (project) competences of all stakeholders* involved.
	E.			The project's result involves or includes activities for the *development of the community* that is effected by the project or the project result.
27.	**Diversity and equal opportunity** *To what extent does the project apply policies or standards for diversity and equal opportunity that reflects the society it operates in?* Multiple answers allowed. Please tick all answers that are applicable.			
		Actual Situation	Desired Situation	
	A.			The project complies with applicable standards and regulations on equal opportunity in terms of gender, race, religion, etc.
	B.			The project also requires *its suppliers and partners* to practice diversity practices and provide equal opportunity in terms of gender, race, religion, etc.
	C.			The project actively (re) designs *its project delivery processes* in a way (e.g. by designing part-time jobs) that diversity and equal opportunity are promoted and stimulated.
	D.			The *project's deliverable and result are designed to improve* diversity and equal opportunity in the organization that commissioned the project.
	E.			The *project's deliverable and result are designed to improve* diversity and equal opportunity in the community in which the result is used or aimed at.
28.	**Human rights** *To what extent does the project apply policies or standards for respecting and improving human rights like non-discrimination, freedom of association and no child labor?* Multiple answers allowed. Please tick all answers that are applicable.			
		Actual Situation	Desired Situation	
	A.			The project complies with applicable standards and regulations on human rights and stimulates improvement of these rights where applicable.
	B.			The project also requires *its suppliers and partners* to respect and improve human rights where possible.
	C.			The project actively (re) designs *its project delivery processes* in a way that human rights are improved and/or on a high level.
	D.			The *project's deliverable and result are designed* to respect and improve human rights in the organization that commissioned the project.

continued on following page

Table 6. Continued

		Actual Situation	Desired Situation	
	E.			The *project's deliverable and result are designed* to respect and improve human rights in the community in which the result is used or aimed at.
29.	**Society and customers** *To what extent does the project take a social responsibility towards the society it operates in?* Multiple answers allowed. Please tick all answers that are applicable.			
		Actual Situation	Desired Situation	
	A.			For the *general acceptance* of the project and its results, the project recognizes a social responsibility towards the external stakeholders in the society it operates in.
	B.			The project also requires *its suppliers and partners* to take on social responsibility towards the external stakeholders in the society they operates in.
	C.			The project actively (re) designs *its project delivery processes* in a way that translates its social responsibility towards the external stakeholders in the society it operates in.
	D.			The *project's deliverable and result are designed* in a way that translates its social responsibility towards the external stakeholders in the society it operates in.
	E.			The *project's deliverable and result are designed* in a way that translates its social responsibility towards the total society.
30.	**Bribery and anti-competitive behaviour** *To what extent does the project reject bribery and anti-competitive behaviour?* Multiple answers allowed. Please tick all answers that are applicable.			
		Actual Situation	Desired Situation	
	A.			The project rejects bribery and anti-competitive behaviour and holds responsible team members accountable.
	B.			The project also requires *its suppliers and partners* to reject bribery and anti-competitive behaviour.
	C.			The project actively *(re) designs its project delivery processes and trains its project* members to prevent bribery and anti-competitive behaviour.
	D.			The project actively *(re) designs its project deliverable and results* in a way that bribery and anti-competitive behaviour is prevented in the organization that commissioned the project.
	E.			The project actively *(re) designs its project deliverable and results* in a way that bribery and anti-competitive behaviour is prevented in the community in which the result is used or aimed at.
31.	**Project reporting** *Does the project's (progress) reports reflect indicators of social sustainability?* Multiple answers allowed. Please tick all answers that are applicable.			
		Actual Situation	Desired Situation	
	A.			The project does not formally report progress.
	B.			The project (progress) reports reflect indicators of social sustainability with respect to *used (physical) resources.*
	C.			The project (progress) reports reflect indicators of social sustainability with respect to *the project delivery process.*
	D.			The project (progress) reports reflect indicators of social sustainability with respect to *the project deliverable or result.*
	E.			The project (progress) reports reflect indicators of social sustainability with respect to the *use and disposal of the project deliverable or result.*

Section 3
Sustainability and the Project Manager

Chapter 14
Leading Sustainability through Projects

Lynn Crawford
Bond University, Australia & Australia and Human Systems International Limited, Australia

ABSTRACT

Business leaders are embracing sustainability not only as a matter of corporate social responsibility but because it offers opportunities for competitive advantage. As corporate activities are increasingly undertaken in the form of projects, project leaders have the opportunity to assist corporations in achieving their sustainability goals by incorporating sustainable practices in both the products they produce and the practices they use to produce them. Good project management is ultimately concerned with the most effective use of resources, which is a key tenet of sustainability. This chapter provides project leaders with practical guidance for incorporation of sustainable development principles in all aspects of their projects.

INTRODUCTION

Sustainability is gaining ground as a key concern of corporations. It is being embraced by business leaders not only as a matter of corporate social responsibility but because it offers opportunities for competitive advantage. As an increasing number of organizations are project based and even those entities that retain more functional structures are implementing strategies, organizational changes, sustainability initiatives and other corporate activities in the form of projects, there is significant potential for leadership in sustainability to be taken by the project management community.

DOI: 10.4018/978-1-4666-4177-8.ch014

In addition to the significant amount of corporate activity being undertaken through projects, there are aspects of project management that inherently support sustainability initiatives. One such aspect is that good project management is ultimately concerned with the most effective use of resources which is a key tenet of sustainability. Another is that transparency and disclosure are central requirements of sustainability reporting and good project management processes and practices provide transparency and an excellent audit trail for bringing sustainability achievements to account.

Unless specifically stated as a project requirement, project managers may feel they are limited by the objectives of their projects from incorporating sustainability principles. The aim of this chapter is to highlight the increasing importance of corporate social responsibility and sustainability to organizations in terms of competitive advantage, good governance and survival, and the many practical ways in which project managers can take a leadership role in sustainability through all of their projects.

BACKGROUND

In offering the most widely accepted and used definition of sustainability, the Brundtland Report (The World Commission on Environment and Development, 1987) specifically states that consideration should not be limited to physical sustainability but should include every aspect of social, political and economic activity, positioning sustainability as a key aspect of corporate social responsibility (CSR). Corporate concern about social responsibility tends to be seen as a relatively recent phenomenon, but a belief that businesses have obligations to the society in which they operate can be traced back to the early twentieth century. There is a link here with project management because the earliest management scholar to address this issue was Henry Gantt, best known to project managers for creation of the Gantt or bar chart. As early as 1919 Henry Gantt advocated that companies should serve society (Whetten et al. 2007).

Business was slow to respond to such ideas. It was not until the second half of the twentieth century, following publication of a Harvard Business Review article on the subject (David, 1949), that there was any interest shown in incorporating ideas of social responsibility into management education. Growing popularity of the concept of corporate social responsibility during the 1950s and 60s was vigorously criticized by economist Milton Friedman who articulated the widely held view that "the proper social responsibility of business is to focus on wealth creation, and to leave other social institutions to solve social problems" (Whetten et al., 2007, p. 380).

Serious concern for the effects of global population explosion, pollution and poverty emerged in the early 1970s and the first United Nations major conference on environmental issues was held in 1972. In the early 1990s, corporate social and environmental responsibilities were recognized in the concept of the Triple Bottom Line, which expands traditional financial corporate reporting to include environmental and social performance (Elkington, 1994; Garnaut, 2008). The World Business Council for Sustainable Development, a global association of around 200 international companies, was created in 1995.

In the 21st century, the strength of public support for social responsibility and sustainability, amplified by social media, was such that being seen to be doing the right thing became a motivator of corporate sustainability initiatives. A variety of factors are forcing companies to translate good intentions into positive action. Investors are recognizing links between social responsibility and economic viability of companies (Prairie, 2011), and shareholder demands for corporate accountability are emerging as key drivers of sustainability initiatives (Ernst & Young, 2011; Mell & Mathiasen, 2011).

Various forms of regulation such as carbon tax and emissions trading schemes are being introduced in a number of countries as a contribution to reducing "the risks of dangerous climate change" (Mills, 2008). Regardless of how conservative such schemes may be, they will need to be addressed by organizations in order to minimize the economic impact on business. Even where there are no formal regulations, initiatives such as the Carbon Disclosure Project (CDP) are using the measurement and sharing of environmental information to influence market forces towards a more sustainable economy. The CDP is an independent not-for-profit organization that works with a growing number of institutional investors (655 investors in 2012 accounting for US$78 trillion in assets) and claims to have the largest collection globally of self reported climate change data. Companies voluntarily participating in the CDP Carbon Performance Leadership Index in 2012 included BMW, Nestlé, Lockheed Martin, Unilever and France Telecom (Carbon Disclosure Project (CDP), 2013).

Employers face a prolonged skilled labor shortage and the challenge of attracting and retaining talent in an extremely competitive market (Salt, 2007). Prospective employees, and especially those of Generation Y, are increasingly concerned about their employer's attitude to the environment. In a survey of 2,774 college students and recent graduates in the United States, 81% said it was important to work for a green company by which they mean companies that are either green-friendly, green-conscious or green-certified, and 79% reported that they would be more likely to accept a job offer at a green company over another company, when evaluating two similar job offers (Business Wire, 2008). Consumers are also increasingly looking for "green" services, products and investments.

It is no longer possible for business to ignore the impact of social and environmental responsibility, as regulations increasingly enforce it; strengthening focus on corporate governance in many cases requires it; shareholders are expecting it; competitive forces are driving it and employees, consumers and investors are beginning to demand it;

In summary, sustainable development is now recognized as vital to our future and business leaders have increasingly embraced corporate social responsibility (CSR) and sustainability not only because they are increasingly required to do so by regulation and market forces, but because it offers opportunities for competitive advantage (Prairie, 2011).

Projects are central to social responsibility and sustainability endeavors of corporations. One aspect of this is that many corporate strategies, including CSR and sustainability initiatives, are implemented through projects or programs (Morris & Jamieson, 2005; Dietrich & Lehtonen, 2005). Another significant aspect is that projects have 'become a common form of work organization in all sectors of the economy'(Lindgren & Packendorff, 2006), not just for project based organizations for which projects are core business but for those organizations that remain largely structured along traditional functional lines but increasingly rely on projects to carry out a range of activities (Bredin, 2008). Cumulatively, this positions the management of projects as a key business process.

One of the challenges of sustainability is that it requires a change in perspective from the short to the long term when making decisions and taking action at all levels of endeavor. The thinking of many project managers is limited by the objectives and time frame of their project and they have difficulty seeing what role they might have in terms of sustainability except where their project specifically requires it, as for a building that clients say must be designed to achieve a particular sustainability or "green" rating or certification (U.S. Green Building Council, 2013; BRE Global Limited, 2012; Green Building Council of Australia (GBCA), 2013). But the relevance of sustainability is not restricted to environmental concerns and projects with physical end products.

As much corporate activity is undertaken in the form of projects, and projects are the means of delivering corporate strategy, sustainability principles need to be embedded in the products and processes of projects if corporations are to achieve their sustainability goals. Further, the term project management is increasingly interpreted as encompassing management of the corporate project portfolio, which is central to decision making about the use of corporate and other resources. If corporations are to achieve their sustainability goals, project leaders must contribute by looking beyond the short term and incorporating sustainable practices not only in the products they produce but in the processes and practices they use to produce them.

Instead of passively accepting that sustainability initiatives are out of scope unless specifically included in project objectives, project managers should provide leadership by actively considering sustainability principles in all project decisions. The following sections of this chapter address the need for project managers to take personal responsibility and proactively incorporate sustainability into their projects. Specific actions that are within the control of the project manager and can contribute to corporate sustainability goals are identified.

TAKING PERSONAL RESPONSIBILITY FOR SUSTAINABILITY

A key tenet of sustainability is that everyone must take individual responsibility for the future by including the long term view in day to day decisions and action. The Chairman of the Business Council for Sustainable Development said, well over a decade ago that "sustainability requires that we pay attention to the entire life cycles of our products and to the specific and changing needs of our customers" (Schmidheiny and Business Council for Sustainable Development, 1992 in Elkington, 1994, p. 91). This document also points out that for sustainability to be achieved, business must play a central role. While business is either volunteering or being forced by shareholders, by the market and by regulation to demonstrate their commitment to CSR and sustainability, and adjust their strategies and reporting arrangements accordingly in order to effectively execute their strategies, the devil is in the details. They need every individual within their organization to play their part. For this to happen there is a need for people, including people in projects, to "accept that the responsibility for tackling these problems is theirs" (Elkington, 1994, p.90).

Reaching this level of acceptance and associated action is not always easy. We will all have experienced or observed the following stages in this journey: ignorance, awakening, denial, guilt reduction or displacement behavior/tokenism, conversion and finally, integration (Elkington, 1994). All of these stages can be seen in the project management community. Anyone reading this will respond according to their own position in this continuum. There will be relatively few who are totally ignorant of the issues, but many projects managers will consider that action on sustainability is out of their control, that it is not in the budget and not part of their remit. Unless theirs is a sustainable development or social welfare project, issues of CSR and sustainability will not be on their agenda and they will be unwilling to potentially alienate clients and senior managers by even talking about such issues. Project managers have been known to actively deny that sustainability has any relevance in the assessment of the performance and success of their projects. There will be those at the tokenism stage who are prepared to pay lip service, to include environmental awareness statements in the signature on their emails and to provide data to clients and sponsors, when required, to satisfy triple bottom line reporting. And finally there are those who have reached the conversion stage and recognize that they can make contributions to sustainability in almost every aspect of the process and product of their projects. Some will be at the integration stage, taking a leadership role, and considering sustainability in every decision and action on their projects.

TAKING ACTION FOR THE FUTURE

For individual project managers, getting to the conversion stage may never happen, it may be very slow, or it could have been reached just by reading this chapter and acknowledging the very practical role that those involved in projects can play in contributing to sustainability and the achievement of personal, corporate and legislated goals in terms of their responsibility to society and a sustainable future. The next challenge is how to put this into action in the project context.

Scope

If we accept that the management of projects is a responsibility that is shared by general and project management and that it operates at the level of the organization's portfolio(s) of projects and programs, at the program level and at the level of the individual project, then we can consider what specific contributions might be made at each level. We also need to think about issues of sustainability not just in terms of the product of the project but in terms of the process by which the product is achieved. And when making project related decisions and actions we need to take a long term view, thinking beyond the handover of the product of a project to consider its full life cycle.

Portfolio View and Strategic Alignment

Following the principle that implementation of sustainability requires everyone to take personal responsibility, although the frame of reference extends well beyond the scope of an individual project manager's role, let's look at what the project manager can do. First they can look at their organization's annual report and see how the organization is reporting against the triple bottom line of finance, society and the environment. What does the organization say its goals and actions are in terms of CSR and sustainability? What is the organization's strategy and in what way, if any, are they claiming a commitment to economic, social and environmental sustainability? If the business has no apparent commitment to sustainability then this is an opportunity to point out, in a polite, helpful and politically sensitive way, the potential threats of increased costs if they have no strategy to deal with their carbon footprint – particularly in the face of current or potential legislation to reduce emissions; of damage to their reputation and their ability to sell their products and employ staff if they have no policies addressing social and environmental sustainability. If, as is most likely, the organization has a stated policy on CSR and sustainability then this becomes a starting point for securing corporate support, when required, for decisions and recommendations that are sustainability sensitive and responsible.

Project management is essentially about the most effective use of resources, which is fundamental to sustainability, so the conversion to a proactive role in sustainability is in many ways a natural progression for the project manager. At the portfolio level, economic, social and environmental sustainability considerations should be factored into all decisions concerning project selection, prioritization, and resourcing. Such considerations should form part of the business case for each proposed initiative. If the organization doesn't ask for this to form part of the business case, then the project or program manager, in preparing a business case, can take the initiative by including it and perhaps suggesting that such considerations become part of the corporate business case template. If your role is in a portfolio, program or project office then you have many opportunities to provide leadership in sustainability by ensuring that it is considered, where sensible, in templates, processes, procedures and in measures for performance reporting. This will be particularly useful in organizations that are reporting, at corporate level, against a triple bottom line.

Performance Measurement and Reporting

Performance measurement and reporting is a very useful place to start getting traction for sustainability in organizations as it rolls up to the public face of the business, its interaction with shareholders and ability to provide evidence that it is doing what it says it will do. Although corporate sustainability policies are reportedly rare and most companies don't report on sustainability (AICPA/ UNC Kenan-Flagler, 2008) the pressure to do so is mounting. The accounting profession is taking a serious interest in sustainability reporting and providing advice to its members (American Institute of Certified Public Accountants (AICPA), 2007; CPA Australia, 2005). For those companies that report on sustainability, the primary frame

of reference is the Global Reporting Initiative which registered an increase of 22 percent in the number of GRI Reports on their list during 2010 (Global Reporting Initiative (GRI), 2012). Other voluntary sustainability reports include the Carbon Disclosure Project (CDP) (Carbon Disclosure Project, 2013) mentioned earlier in this chapter.

GRI is a worldwide, multi-stakeholder network that is collaborating to create and continuously improve a sustainability reporting framework as a basis for facilitating transparency and accountability by organizations – companies, public agencies, non-profits - of all sizes and sectors, across the world. This reporting framework provides a useful guide to the definition of sustainability and where to look to take action and measure performance. Definitions and indicators are summarized in Table 1 which is provided in the form of a checklist for focus on sustainability in projects. Knowing that your organization is either currently reporting or will in the not too distant future, be reporting against this framework provides you with an opportunity to get started and be ready to provide the relevant information. This framework can also

Table 1. Checklist for focus on sustainability in projects (adapted from Global Reporting Initiative, 2011)

	Economic	Environmental	Labour Practices & Decent Work	Human Rights	Society	Product Responsibility
Definition	Impacts on the economic conditions of its stakeholders and on economic systems at local, national, and global levels	Impacts on living and non-living natural systems, including ecosystems, land, air, and water.	Impacts an organization has on the social systems within which it operates	Extent to which human rights are considered in investment and supplier/contractor selection practices	Impacts organizations have on the communities in which they operate, and disclosing how the risks that may arise from interactions with other social institutions are managed and mediated	Aspects of a reporting organization's products and services that directly affect customers, namely, health and safety, information and labeling, marketing, and privacy
Indicators	• Flow of capital among different stakeholders; • Main economic impacts of the organization throughout society.	• Materials; • Energy; • Water; • Biodiversity; • Emissions, Effluents, and Waste; • Products and Services; • Compliance; • Transport; • Overall	• Employment; • Labor/Management Relations; • Occupational Health and Safety; • Training and Education; • Diversity and Equal Opportunity.	• Investment and Procurement Practices; • Non-discrimination; • Freedom of Association and Collective Bargaining; • Abolition of Child Labor; • Prevention of Forced and Compulsory Labor; • Complaints and Grievance Practices; • Security Practices; • Indigenous Rights.	• Community; • Corruption; • Public Policy; • Anti-Competitive Behavior; • Compliance.	• Customer Health and Safety; • Product and Service Labeling; • Marketing Communications; • Customer Privacy; • Compliance.

act as a guide to decision making in every aspect of your project management role. Some ideas for doing this are provided in the next section of the paper.

Practical Application to Projects

Using Table 1 as a checklist, project managers can think through the various aspects of their role to see how consideration of these issues can influence the incorporation of concepts of sustainability in their projects. Some ideas are provided next and further guidance, specifically for the project context can be found in papers by Tom Taylor (2008) and Jennifer Tharp (2008) and on the Website of the Association for Project Management (2012)

Risk and Stakeholder Management

Program and project managers are familiar with techniques for risk and stakeholder management. Risk identification can be extended to include the relevant issues and considerations shown in Table 1. Proposals for mitigation should be developed in a similar vein. From the sustainability perspective, the identification of relevant stakeholders may need to be broadened and identification and evaluation of their interests may require a difference in treatment. In any case, the attention to both risk and stakeholder management that are part of standard project management practices can be brought to account as evidence of a corporate commitment to sustainability.

Project Brief and Requirements

As mentioned previously, many project managers believe that they have little control over the time, cost and quality objectives for their projects. But often the project manager has to develop the brief for their project, identify or clarify requirements and write, amend or re-confirm the objectives. There is an opportunity here to engage the client and other stakeholders in a shared commitment to address sustainability in all its aspects.

Planning

Planning is home ground for the project manager and involves a multitude of decisions each of which may involve a number of options that can be evaluated from a sustainability perspective. The challenge to take action in the present with the welfare of the future in mind may encourage creativity and lead to better solutions. The long term view may also encourage involvement of end users and other stakeholders in the planning process to ensure that their interests are addressed and that the product of the project, when handed over, will be accepted, used and where relevant, disposed of in as resource sensitive a manner as possible. Planning should encompass the entire life cycle of the product of the project where this is a physical end product, a service, a system or a change.

Resourcing and Procurement

Resourcing and procurement are areas rich with possibility for consideration of sustainability. Initial resourcing decisions may well have been made at the portfolio level and are often not fully within the control of either the program or project manager but there will still be opportunities for sensitive decision making. Resources such as materials, space, power and the like clearly have implications for the project and therefore the corporate carbon footprint. Environmentally friendly recommendations and choices can be made and careful creative planning with this in mind can have surprisingly good results. The improvements in carbon footprint may not be large but every little bit counts. Resources and services should where possible be procured from sources that espouse and demonstrate a commitment to CSR and sustainability. This not only improves the carbon footprint of your project but it sends a message to suppliers that encourages them to take these issues seriously. It sends a strong and important message about your company's commitment to CSR, enhancing their reputation.

Human Resources

Human resources on projects are often overlooked when it comes to thinking about sustainability yet this is an area where most project managers will be able to have an impact. Apart from the issues listed under Social in Table 1, the project manager can actively consider the workload and work life balance of the project team. Is the pace of work sustainable? Can virtual teamwork be used more effectively to minimize travel, improving the carbon footprint and potentially improving work/life balance? Are team members developing their knowledge and skills for work on future projects? Capturing and sharing of lessons learned and continuous improvement can be seen as contributions to sustainability as they involve taking action in the present for the benefit of future projects.

Transparency

Good governance as well as sustainability initiatives such as the Global Reporting Initiative and Carbon Disclosure Project focus on the need for disclosure and transparency. One of the challenges that project management practices face in organizations is that they inherently provide transparency and an audit trail of decision making, action and performance. This has not always been attractive to senior management who, for a variety of reasons, often prefer "black boxes" to transparency of process. But tightening of corporate governance requirements (OECD, 2004) has made this position untenable and highlighted the value of project management in terms of governance (Crawford & Helm, 2009) as well as supporting the disclosure requirements of sustainability reporting.

These are only a few ideas for sustainability action that are within the control of most project managers in most projects. By using Table 1 as a checklist, project managers will be able to find many more practical opportunities for leading sustainability through projects.

CONCLUSION

Project leadership for sustainability starts with each individual taking personal responsibility and thinking about the consequences of decisions and actions in terms of sustainability (refer Table 1). From here it can be embedded in processes and practices but the most important thing will always be people thinking through their actions and understanding that everything we do is part of a system and the interconnectedness of all things (Adams, 2005). To lead the process and to ensure that every decision, however small, is guided by sustainability thinking and principles, we need to ensure that everyone involved in our projects is taking sustainability into account in everything they do. One way of doing this is to treat sustainability as we have been treating occupational health and safety for some time. Give a sustainability briefing at the start of your project; ensure every member of the team has sustainability training; that sustainability is acknowledged in meetings; that sustainability is acknowledged in project governance and is a consistent theme in decision making. It is important however to ensure that this is not tokenism but is fully integrated. The best way of doing this, as a leader, is to be a good role model.

The aim of this chapter has been to start project managers thinking seriously about incorporation of sustainability principles in their projects, to give them some ideas about action they can take for immediate impact, and where to go for further information. Concern for sustainability is not about to go away. It is a rising tide. Organizations are becoming increasingly aware of their need to provide evidence of commitment to sustainability and project managers are well placed to play a leadership role in the process.

REFERENCES

Adams, D. (2005). *The hitchhiker's guide to the galaxy*. Toronto: Ballantine Books.

AICPA/UNC Kenan-Flagler. (2008). *AICPA business and industry economic outlook survey 3Q 2008*. Retrieved from http://fmcenter.aicpa. org/NR/rdonlyres/2CAEEC67-79F4-4472-93B4-5AEB0502A1E1/0/3QEconomicOutlookSurveyChartsFinal.pdf

American Institute of Certified Public Accountants. (AICPA). (2007). *FAQs on sustainability reporting*. Retrieved from http://www.aicpa.org/innovation/baas/environ/faq.htm

Association for Project Management. (2012). *Sustainability in project management*. Association for Project Management.

Australia, C. P. A. (2005). *Sustainability reporting: Practices, performance and potential*. Melbourne, Australia: CPA Australia.

BRE Global Limited. (2012). *The world's leading design and assessment method for sustainable buildings*. Building Research Establishment Ltd (trading as BRE).

Bredin, K. (2008). People capability of project-based organisations: A conceptual framework. *International Journal of Project Management, 26*(5), 566–576. doi:10.1016/j.ijproman.2008.05.002.

Business Wire. (2008). *Four out of five college students and recent grads prefer jobs at green companies*. Retrieved from http://findarticles.com/p/articles/mi_m0EIN/is_2008_August_4/ai_n27968336

Carbon Disclosure Project (CDP). (2013). *CDP 2012 performance scores*. Retrieved from https://www.cdproject.net/en-US/Results/Pages/CDP-2012-performance-scores.aspx

Crawford, L. H., & Helm, J. (2009). Government and governance: The value of project management in the public sector. *Project Management Journal, 40*(1), 73–87. doi:10.1002/pmj.20107.

David, D. K. (1949). Business responsibilities in an uncertain world. *Harvard Business Review, 27*(1), 1–8.

Dietrich, P., & Lehtonen, P. (2005). Successful management of strategic intentions through multiple projects - Reflections from empirical study. *International Journal of Project Management, 23*(5), 386–391. doi:10.1016/j.ijproman.2005.03.002.

Elkington, J. (1994). Towards the sustainable corporation: Win-win-win business strategies for sustainable development. *California Management Review, 36*(2), 90–100. Retrieved from http://search.ebscohost.com/login.aspx?direct=true&db=buh&AN=9410213932&site=ehost-live doi:10.2307/41165746.

Ernst & Young. (2011). *Climate change and sustainability: Shareholders press boards on social and environmental risks: Is your company prepared?* Ernst & Young LLP.

Garnaut, R. (2008). *Garnaut climate change review update: Bulletin 3*. Retrieved from http://www.garnautreview.org.au/CA25734E0016A131/WebObj/FINALAuguste-bulletin_29Aug08/$File/FINAL%20August%20e-bulletin_29%20Aug%2008.pdf

Global Reporting Initiative (GRI). (2011). *Sustainability reporting guidelines*. Global Reporting Initiative.

Global Reporting Initiative (GRI). (2012). *A new phase: The growth of sustainability reporting: GRI's year in review 2010/11*. Global Reporting Initiative.

Green Building Council of Australia (GBCA). (2013). *Green star overview.* Green Building Council of Australia.

Lindgren, M., & Packendorff, J. (2006). What's new in new forms of organizing? On the construction of gender in project-based work. *Journal of Management Studies, 43*(4), 841–866. doi:10.1111/j.1467-6486.2006.00613.x.

Mell, E., & Mathiasen, C. (2011). *U.S. proxy season review 2011: Environmental & social issues.* Retrieved from http://www.issgovernance.com/files/private/2011ProxySeasonReviewES.pdf

Mills, K. (2008). *Demographic change has led to a shortage of skills and given employees the upper hand.* Retrieved from http://cio.co.nz/cio.nsf/focus/59F02885E3360D57CC25737E0082526F

Morris, P. W. G., & Jamieson, A. (2005). Moving from corporate strategy to project strategy. *Project Management Journal, 36*(4), 5-18. Retrieved from http://search.ebscohost.com/login.aspx?direct=true&db=buh&AN=19561978&site=ehost-live

OECD. (2004). *OECD principles of corporate governance* (Revised ed.). Paris, France: OECD.

Prairie, P. (2011, December 28). Top corporate sustainability trends to watch in 2012. *Fast Company.*

Salt, B. (2007). *Beyond the baby boomers: The rise of generation Y - Opportunities and challenges for the funds management industry.* Melbourne, Australia: KPMG International. Retrieved from http://www.bernardsalt.com.au/pdf/Beyond_the_Baby_Boomers.pdf

Taylor, T. (2008). *A sustainability checklist for managers of projects.* Retrieved from http://www.pmforum.org/library/papers/2008/PDFs/Taylor-1-08.pdf

Tharp, J. (2008). Corporate social responsibility: What it means for the project manager. In *Proceedings of PMI Europe Congress.* Philadelphia, PA: Project Management Insitute.

U.S. Green Building Council. (2013). *LEED rating systems. U.S.* Green Building Council.

Chapter 15
How Positive Psychology can Support Sustainable Project Management

Jasper C. van den Brink
HU University of Applied Sciences Utrecht, The Netherlands

ABSTRACT

In this chapter, the relationship between positive psychology and sustainable project management is discussed. A general description of the field of positive psychology is given. The relationship between positive psychology and the three P's of sustainability (People, Planet, and Profit) is described. Specific attention is paid to hope and optimism as ways to intervene in project teams. Hope and optimism are central concepts in positive psychology. These concepts can help to improve the sustainability of project teams and to stimulate sustainable change.

INTRODUCTION AND BACKGROUND

In this chapter, sustainable project management is studied from a psychological perspective. The field of project management evolved from the use of mathematical calculation models to a field concerned with change management and the roll of behavior involved in these change processes (Silvius & Schipper 2012). We can see an increasing awareness that human behavior is crucial for project success (Kahkonen et al., 2009), therefore human behavior is the central perspective for this chapter.

The knowledge from the new scientific field of positive psychology will be used to study sustainable project management. More specifically, attention will be paid to the role of positive emotions, optimism and hope. This knowledge will provide us with insights in the way positive psychological approaches to project management will increase the sustainability of projects.

This perspective is taken because a large number of studies both on sustainability and project management are 'problem focused'. They are concentrating on ways to prevent problems, like risk management (Raz & Michael, 2001), stress

DOI: 10.4018/978-1-4666-4177-8.ch015

in projects (Aitken & Crawford, 2007) or the difficulties faced when sustainable behavior is being promoted (Dovers, 1995).

In this chapter, it will be argued that this problem focus, with its perspective on problems and negative emotions, is not fruitful. To deal with the challenges of sustainable project management, a positive approach is needed. Grounded in the science of positive psychology and using the concepts of positive emotions, optimism, and hope. The chapter will answer the question: *How can positive psychology support positive project management?*

In the following section attention will be paid to the relationship between positive psychology, projects and positive emotions, one of the central concepts of positive psychology. The next section will describe the link between positive emotions and sustainability, using the division between people, planet and profit. In the third section the focus will be on ways to influence sustainable behavior by influencing positive emotions, special attention will be paid to the powerful concepts of optimism and hope. This chapter ends with concluding remarks and suggestions for further research.

PROJECTS, POSITIVE PSYCHOLOGY AND POSITIVE EMOTIONS

Projects

In the organizational theory many different definitions of projects are being used. In this chapter we use the widely used definition by Turner (1993): 'Projects are an endeavor in which human, material and financial resources are organized in a novel way, to undertake a unique scope of work, of given specification, within constraints of cost and time, so as to achieve beneficial change defined by quantitative and qualitative objectives'.

Two things are important in this definition when it comes to the topic of this paper: first of all projects are endeavors in which human resources are being organized. And secondly, the purpose of projects is to achieve change. These are two components that will be addressed in this chapter.

Projects are endeavors in which human resources are being organized, this means that human behavior is an important component of projects. Paying attention to this part of project management is crucial for successful projects (El Saaba, 2001; Pant & Baroudi, 2008; Pasian, 2011; Suhonen & Paasivaara, 2011).

Realizing that projects are change instruments is important when it comes to sustainable organizations. At this moment sustainable organizations are not mainstream. Implementing sustainability into organizations urges for an explicit change perspective. Projects seem to be the perfect vehicle to drive this change, due to the explicit change perspective of project management.

Positive Psychology

Positive psychology is a movement in the field of psychology that was coined by Martin Seligman, the former chairman of the American Psychological Association (APA) who is widely seen as one of the founding fathers of this movement. Positive psychology was a reaction to the dominant orientation of psychology on problems, sickness, and negative deviant behavior.

The movement of positive psychology is focusing on 'positive' research questions like 'why do people get into a flow while working' (Csikszentmihaiyi, 1990), 'why are people happy' (Lyubomirsky, 2001, 2007) or 'what are the roots of positive deviant behavior in organizations' (Cameron 2008). The reason to study this positive behavior is not to disqualify the 'negative' research in traditional psychology but to complement the traditional research with a different perspective (Seligman 1998).

Even though many authors state that this movement was started with the speech of Seligman (1998) for the APA, the movements has got roots that are found much earlier in the history of psychology. The humanistic psychology with leading figures like Abraham Maslow and Carl Rogers was a good example of such earlier research. Positive emotions have been researched way before the speech of Seligman in 1998 (e.g. Isen & Daubman, 1984). But the study of these positive topics has increased enormously since the beginning of this century.

A special branch of positive psychology is the positive study of organizations. This special branch is applying the traditional more individual perspective of positive psychology on organizations and organizational change (Cameron, Dutton & Quin, 2003; Cameron & Spreitzer, 2012; Linley, Harrington & Garcea, 2010; Nelson & Cooper, 2007). It pays attention to various subject like positive cooperation (Losada & Heapy, 2004), positive deviance (Wooten & Cameron, 2010), thriving (Spreitzer & Sutcliffe, 207), and work engagement (Rothbard & Patil, 2012).

Positive Emotions

One important finding of both the individual and the organizational positive psychology is the importance of positive emotions on the behavior of people. Positive emotions lead to a wide variety of positive effects that are beneficial for project teams (Lyubomirsky, King, & Diener, 2005).

The concept of positive emotions is closely related to the broader concept of happiness. Happiness is one of the most widely researched concepts in positive psychology. The Oxford English dictionary defines happiness as as 'The state of pleasurable content or mind, which results from success or the attainment of what is considered good'. This definition is immediately showing the close link between sustainability and happiness. For many people sustainability is considered 'good' and is therefore stimulating the happiness

of the people pursuing it. In this chapter we will mainly focus on positive emotions, or as they are described in the psychological discourse 'positive affect'. In this chapter we will use the definition of Luyubomirski, King, and Diener (2005) of positive emotion 'a state of positive mood or emotion'. In many cases happiness and positive affect are considered to be interchangeable concepts (see Lyubomirski et al., 2005).

POSITIVE EMOTIONS AND SUSTAINABLE PROJECT MANAGEMENT

In this chapter sustainability will be defined using the PPP concept (Elkington, 1997) A concept widely used in the business world. The three P's are the three dimensions of People, Planet, and Profit. People refers to social equity, Plant to environmental protection and Profit to economic prosperity. The PPP concept implies that all three of these factors should be in balance when making business and project decisions.

The benefits of positive emotions cover wide area of topics like assertiveness (Schimmack et al., 2004), martial state (Harker and Keltner, 2001), life expectancy (Danner, Snowdon, and Friesen, 2001), openness (Dovido et al., 1995; Johnson and Frederickson, 2005; Stroessner et al., 2005) and teamwork (Rhee & Yoon, 2012). These benefits are related to all three areas of sustainability as being described by the three P's, People, Planet, and Profit. In the next part of this chapter the relationship between these three areas and positive emotions will be explored.

People

The people side of sustainable project management is often described as (among other subjects) taking care of the people in third world countries and applying to the labor laws in your own country (Planko & Silvius, 2012). For many project teams these conditions are not that relevant because the project team cannot easily influence them. Many projects in the western world have little impact on people in third world countries and many project teams have no influence on the general labor conditions in the organization they belong to. But all project teams and project managers do have influence on the happiness and the amount of positive emotions being experienced by their own project members. The way the work is organized, the way communication and relations are being managed, the way the goals of the project are being developed and formulated are all of influence on the happiness of the project members involved.

This happiness has value on its own as is increasingly being acknowledged by governments and organizations. There is a growing debate about the use of Gross national happiness as an indicator for government policy next to the economical indicators like Gross national income or the employment level (Bates, 2009). With Bhutan as the first example of a state that takes this indicator seriously. Stimulating positive emotions and happiness among the project members is a very effective way of promoting the well being of the project members (the people side of project management).

But happiness and positive emotions leads to a number of very desirable secondary effects as well as described earlier. Overall we can see that happy project members benefit from their happiness in a great number of ways. This means that stimulating positive emotions among project members is an effective way to influence a number of other factor that are being associated with the well being of personnel.

The effect of happiness in the project team is not being limited to the direct project team. Research has shown that emotions of people are contagious (Ashkanasy & Ashton-James, 2007 ;Bono & Ilies, 2006; Johnson 2009; Loyd-Walker & Walker, 2011). When a project member shows positive emotions this will influence the emotions of the people around him, both inside the project team as well as outside of the project. This means that stimulating positive emotions among project members is not only beneficial for the project members themselves but for the community around them as well (Fowler & Christakis, 2008).

Planet

A second effect of positive emotions and happiness is the increase of pro social behavior (Aknin, Dunn & Norton, 2011). Pro social behavior is often associated with environmental behavior (Corral-Verdugo, Mireles-Acosta, Tapia-Fonllem, Fraijo-Sing, 2011). By stimulating positive emotions the chances of pro social and environmental behavior in projects are being increased.

Various authors have studied the direct link between environmental behavior and happiness. They show that environmental behavior is positively related to happiness (Brown, Kasser, 2005; Corral-Verdugo et al., 2011). It is though unclear whether environmental behavior leads to positive emotions and happiness as is suggested by various authors or vice versa. See for example the studies by the Prat and Ashford (2003) and Wrizesniewski (2003) that both show the importance of meaningful activities for happiness. There is a fair change that relationships in both directions exist. This would mean that positive emotions lead to environmental behavior which leads again to positive emotions.

Profit

The good news from a traditional business perspective is the fact that positive emotions lead to more productive workers (Zelenmski, Murphy and Jenkins, 2008), they spent less time on sick leave, work more hours and are less likely to leave to another job (Price-Jones, 2010). Staw and Barsade (1993) showed in an experiment that managers who have a positive disposition are better both in decision making and in interpersonal tasks. Van den Brink (2013) studied the relationship between behavioral competences of project managers and positive emotions. IPMA ICB3 (2006) identifies 19 behavioral competences, some of which are categories under technical competences[1]. These competences are seen as the core competences that project managers need in order to be successful. From the 19 behavioral competences van den Brink found that 16 had a proven positive relationship with positive emotions. Which means that those competences were positively influenced by positive emotions. These competences cover topic like leadership, negotiation, relaxation and openness.

A study by Losada and Heaphy (2004) showed that there is a direct link between the use of positive language and the effectiveness of management teams. Losada studied the communication of management teams. He divided the teams in three groups, based on profitability, 360 feedback for the managers and customer satisfaction. Teams that had the highest scores in all three categories were seen as top teams. Teams with low scores on all three categories were labeled as low performing teams. The other teams were in the middle category. Losada and his team studied the positive/negative communication ratio. Examples of positive communications were compliments and supportive comments. Examples of negative communication were sarcasm, criticism etc.. Losada and his team found that het top performing teams had a minimum ratio of 3:1 positive: negative language. The other teams had ratios much lower with the lowest performing teams having ratios that could drop below the 1:1 ratio. This observation research showed the importance of positive communication for the effectiveness of management teams. It is very likely that the same mechanism will apply to project teams.

The overall conclusion is that positive emotions lead to more effective behavior on the work floor in general and as a sustainable project manager in particular. This leads to the question how to influence these positive emotions?

INFLUENCING POSITIVE EMOTIONS TO SUPPORT SUSTAINABLE PROJECT MANAGEMENT

This section will focus on one specific type of intervention that can be particularly useful for sustainable project management: the fostering of hope and optimism. Hope and optimism are two concepts that are in the core of the positive psychology debate (Peterson & Seligman, 2004). One of the first and most influential books in this movement was actually about optimism (Seligman 1991).

Hope and optimism are specifically important for the development of sustainable project management. This is due to two reasons: One: sustainable change can't rely solely on traditional change approaches. Two: sustainable project management benefits from positive emotions. One effective way to stimulate positive emotions is by fostering hope and optimism.

In project management change management is an important topic, since project management's aim is to implement change. We know that change can lead to feelings of confusion, insecurity and fear (Piderit, 2000). Dominant perspectives on change (e.g. Kotter, 1996) argue that a sense of urgency should be created in order to 'get things moving'. People need a feeling of crisis in order to be willing to change.

The problem with sustainable change is that by most people no acute sense of urgency is felt because they don't see the everyday effects of unsustainable behavior. Global warming is a problem but for most people on the planet (or at least in the western world) it doesn't effect their day to day live. Child labor is a problem but very few people see the effects of child labor on a regular basis. Since most sustainability problems are abstract, big and far away most people don't feel they have the influence to effectively chance them. This means that the traditional approaches to change do not work when it comes to sustainability. Sustainability is to abstract and far away to create a sense of urgency with most people.

We need a different approach: people have to choose to be sustainable. The have to believe it is useful and effective to work in a sustainable way. This means that we should not create a sense of urgency but a sense of hope and optimism that we can have influence. Without the hope for change sustainable project management will not succeed. In this chapter we will explore how optimism and hope can be used to facilitate organization development. What are the chances and limitations of using optimism during organizational development? And how can we stimulate optimism in organizations?

What are Hope and Optimism?

Dr. Martin Luther King is probably one of the best examples of the force of hope and optimism when it comes to change. With his famous speech at Lincoln Memorial in Washington DC he showed the power of spreading hope and optimism to fuel change. And he was successful, since a year later the Civil Right Act was passed by the Congress.

In recent years hope and optimism are a theme with an increased attention from researchers (Snyder 2000). Optimism is no longer an approach that is disrupting a realistic view on reality (Snyder 2000). It is increasingly seen as a way to improve and facilitate change both on the individual and on the organizational level (Lopez, Ciarlelli, Cofman, Stone & Wyatt, 2000). Especially the recent growth of the field of positive psychology is stimulating research on this topics.

Optimism and hope are intuitively clear concepts for many people, but when studied in detail turn out to be more complex constructs. Various authors have defined these concepts. The research on optimism is dominated by three researchers: Seligman, Scheier and Carver. The discussion on hope is heavily influenced by the research of Snyder.

Seligman (1991) is describing the difference between pessimists and optimists as a difference in the explanatory style. The main question is how people explain what is happening around them. How do the interpret the events happening to them? This means that optimism concerned to Seligman is actually an activity of looking back and interpreting the history instead of directly predicting the future. But the way you perceive the events that happen to you will influence the optimistic or pessimistic approach of the future. They define how much control you feel on future events.

According to Seligman optimists and pessimists differ in their explanatory style on three aspects: permanence, pervasiveness and personalization (See Table 1). Explanatory style is the habitual way that an individual explains setbacks and failures (Schulman, 1999). Optimists and pessimists tend to explain events in opposite ways. Where optimists explain events in favor of their own position pessimists do the opposite.

Permanence

Is an event permanent or temporary? Pessimists believe bad events are permanent and good events are temporary. Optimists believe good events are permanent and bad events are temporary.

Pervasiveness

Is an event isolated or generalized to other events/other areas of live? Pessimists will generalize bad events to other areas of live and will isolate good events. Optimists will generalize good events and isolate negative events.

Personalization

Is an event internalized (the cause is sought inside of the person) or externalized (the cause is sought outside the person)? Pessimists internalize negative events and externalize positive events. Optimists internalize good events and externalize negative events.

Table 1. Optimistic and pessimistic explanation style

		Optimistic explanation	Pessimistic explanation
Permanence	Good event	Permanent	Temporary
	Bad event	Temporary	Permanent
Pervasiveness	Good event	Generalizing	Isolating
	Bad event	Isolating	Generalizing
Personalization	Good event	Internalized	Externalized
	Bad event	Externalized	Internalized

For example: optimists will explain signals of obstruction of their plans to implement sustainable project management as temporary, limited to the people that are actively engaged in the obstruction and not connected to their performance. Pessimists will view these signals of obstructions as a permanent problem for the whole development trajectory, exemplary for the mood of all the personal in the organization and caused by their own failures.

The differences in explanatory style can be predictive for the behavior of the person involved. The optimist will not be discouraged and will most likely continue their sustainability plan. The pessimist will be discouraged and will lose self confidence and is more likely to stop the plan.

An alternative approach towards optimism is proposed by Scheier and Carver (1992) with their concept of dispositional optimism. They define dispositional optimism as 'the global expectation that good things will be plentiful in the future and bad things scarce. Central in their theory is the pursue of goals, when people believe that the can reach a goal even when they face difficulties, there are seen as optimists, if not they are pessimists.

With this definition they focus on the expectations of the person involved. Where Seligman is using the explanations and perceived causalities of the past, Scheier and Carver look at the future expectations. In practice the two different approaches of optimism often correlate (Peterson, 2000).

The leading researcher on the topic of Hope is Snyder (2000). According to Snyder hope consists of two concepts: agency and pathways, these concepts foster hope that a goal can be achieved. Agency refers to the belief that you can influence or control what is happening with you, a concept related to the approach of Seligman. Pathways refers to the ability to see and follow different approaches to reach a goal, this concept is related with the concept of Scheier and Carver. In the theory of Snyder goals are central for hope. You can't have hope without a specific goal in mind. Snyder's theory can be seen as the combination of or the linking pin between the theories of Seligman and Scheier and Carver (Peterson 2000). In this chapter we will use the approach of Snyder as the central approach to hope and optimism.

Effects of Hope and Optimism

Various authors have researched the link between optimism and organizational performance, successful leadership and change (Henry, 2005; Amit, Popper, Gal, Mishkal-Sinai & Lisak, 2004). They show that optimistic managers are more effective compared to pessimistic managers.

Arakawa and Greenberg (2007) used the Life Orientation test revised (LOT_R) from Scheier, Carver and Bridges (1994) to research optimism amongst project managers and it's effect on (amongst others) project performance. There study suggests that the project manager's optimism is positively correlated with project performance. This effect is significant when the project members work for one project only. When project members work for various project managers at the same time the correlation of optimism and project performance is no longer significant.

Amit et al. (2004) researched the influence of (amongst others) optimism of Israeli soldiers on their perceived leadership competence. They found a positive correlation between optimism and perceived leadership competences. This finding was supported by other research on this topic (Chemers et al., 2000; George, 2000; Wunderley, Reddy and Dember, 1998; as cited by Amit et al., 2004). The relationship between optimism and leadership was no longer significant when a regression analysis was performed.

Avey, Wernsing, and Luthans (2008) studied the influence of psychological capital on positive emotions and attitudes behaviour during organisational change. Psychological capital consists of of the four components of hope, efficacy, resilience and optimism. Avey et al. (2004) found that psychological capital is related with both employee attitudes (engagement and cynicism) and employee behavior (organizational citizenship and deviance), these are attitudes and behavior that is important for dealing with organizational change. Psychological capital is positively related to engagement and organizational citizenship and negative to cynicism and deviance. The effect is mediated by positive emotions (except for cynicism). This research is showing the importance of optimism and hope both for the stimulation of positive emotions as for the stimulation of positive attitudes and behavior during organizational change.

Seligman has studied the relationship between optimistic leadership and success. Zullow and Seligman (1990) studied the influence of optimistic and pessimistic communication on the election success of president candidates in the USA. They found that between 1948-1984 candidates with the more pessimistic nomination acceptance speech lost 9 out of 10 elections.

Seligman (1991) studied basketball and baseball teams and found that the explanatory style of a team in a specific season predicts how much above or below their 'objective performance level' they will play in the next season. This study shows the direct relation between optimism and performance and at the same time show that teams can have an explanatory style at their own, meaning optimism or pessimism is not exclusively the domain of individuals.

Based on the research as described here the conclusion can be drawn that optimism is positively related to leadership in general and leadership during change processes in particular. Optimism and hope are also positively related to the way the subjects of change respond to it. Optimistic and hopeful people are responding in a more positive and supportive way to change compared to people who are more pessimistic and less hopeful.

But how do you stimulate optimism and hope in order to improve sustainable project management? What is the relevance of these concepts without a clear idea about the application in practice? Below various strategies will be described to stimulate hope and optimism of the individual sustainable project manager, of the sustainable project team and of the people involved in the sustainable change.

Hope and Optimism for the Sustainable Project Manager

The best researched intervention program for the stimulation of optimism and hope is based on the explanatory approach from Seligman (Seligman 1991). Since a high score on explanatory score has a strong correlation with the hope approach from Scheier and Carver (Peterson 2000), influencing the explanatory style of a project manager will most likely influence the scores on hope as well.

Improving optimism amongst individuals can be done by disputing the internal dialogue. This technique is based on the RET as originally developed by Albert Ellis. A cognitive approach to individual change that has shown his effectiveness in many studies (David, Szentagotia, & Macavei, 2005). This technique was originally used for therapeutic practices only but has evolved in an approach that is being used in many different areas as well.

Disputing is done by following a number of steps known as the ABCDE approach. What is the Adversity, what is the underlying (pessimistic) Belief? What is the Consequence of this belief? How can this belief be disputed? And finally what is an Energizing or Effective new Optimistic belief?

Disputing can be done by asking questions concerning the validity of the underlying belief (is it true?) or the usefulness of this belief (is it helping you to be optimistic)? Another approach is to look at the chance of something happening and the realistic consequences of an event happening. Seligman (1991) gives an extensive explanation of the practical application of the disputing technique.

Hope and Optimism for the Sustainable Project Team

A proven method to stimulate hope and optimism among project teams is to work with the solution focused method when problems have to be solved (Berg & Szabo, 2005). The mainstream method for problem solving is to analyze the source of the problem, develop several solutions based on this analysis and then choose the best one. The problem focused approach works very well for technical problems but is less suitable for problems with large uncertainties and problems regard humans and human interaction. These kinds of problems are some complex that trying to find the exact source of the problem is often very difficult and time and energy consuming. A focus on the sources of the problem doesn't foster hope and optimism.

The solution focus method has a different approach. One basic assumption of solution focused working is that analyzing problems will lead to a lot of knowledge about the problem but it doesn't lead to solutions. To find solutions you have to look for solutions instead of problems. When you start to look for solutions you start to find them. Solution focused work is a different approach that has proven to be effective (Franklin et al., 2012; Macdonald, 2011).

This means that project teams should start to look for sustainable solutions that can be integrated effectively in their project. Looking for solutions will stimulate optimism and hope. Sustainable project teams should not spend their time in analyzing all the problems and obstacles for sustainable project management. Studying the problems will lead to pessimism and will not focus the attention of the project team towards practical solutions.

To find sustainable solutions there are various solution focused methods that can be applied. An example is to look for exceptions. Even in very unsustainable environments there are moments that sustainable actions do take place (or at least less unsustainable actions took place). By deliberately searching for these exceptions sustainable approaches can be found that worked in het past in this particularly project environment or this particular company. By analyzing what made it work in the past, the application of the same approach in the present will probably lead to the same result.

A second example is to look at the future, by using optimism as a tool to look for practical approaches. A sustainable project team can work out a scenario in which they are very sustainable. By drawing this optimistic picture as concrete as possible it can stimulate hope and optimism and is fueling the development of small first steps towards this desired future (Bannik, 2012).

HOPE AND OPTIMISM FOR SUSTAINABLE CHANGE

For sustainable change, leadership is crucial, optimistic leadership. As previously described optimistic leaders influence the people around them in a positive way. People tend to follow optimistic leaders (Zullow & Seligman 1990). And optimistic followers tend to be more effective and are better equipped to deal with change

(Avey et al., 2008). This means that leaders of sustainable change have to be very well aware of the message they communicate. Messages that focus on the problems ahead will not stimulate hope and optimism and will be less likely to stimulate sustainability in projects. On the other hand, message that show optimism and have an explanatory style with a focus on self control and influence will most likely lead to support.

As mentioned before, the best example of this approach was probably Martin Luther King. His most famous words are from his speech at at Lincoln Memorial in Washington DC in 1963. These words are not about the racial problems, they were not about discrimination, he was actually focusing on a good future, stimulating and expressing hope and optimism. His "I have a dream' speech is a classical example of a speech that emphasizes hope and optimism even though at that time the racial problems were huge. Sustainable project managers have to spread the same kind of message in order to stimulate change.

At the same time sustainable project managers have to deal with criticism and sometimes cynicism about their sustainable plans. To tackle these pessimistic comments they can use the disputation technique as described by Seligman (1990). By externalizing and disputing pessimistic thoughts they can neutralize their effect. In this way they can use the individual approach in groups and reframe pessimistic ideas into optimistic ideas.

FUTURE RESEARCH DIRECTIONS

There is an enormous potential for research on the crossroad of positive psychology and sustainable project management .Two topics are of specific interest.

First of all research needs to be done on the empirical link between positive emotions, hope, optimism and project management in general. Most of the research on the effects of positive emotions is done in laboratory settings. The number of field studies is much smaller. Field research on positive psychology in the area of project management is very scarce. Testing whether the laboratory results are valid in 'real' project situation is crucial in order to be able to apply the knowledge of positive psychology in a proper way in the field of project management.

The second important research question regards the empirical research regarding the link between positive emotions and sustainable and environmental behavior. Especially the link between positive emotions and environmental behavior needs to be addressed. At this moment this link is indirect and it is unclear what the causal relationship between these two concepts is. Longitudinal empirical field research needs to be done to research this relationship.

CONCLUSION

A Disclaimer on Hope and Optimism

This chapter is a call for realistic optimism. But one should not be naive, too much optimism can kill. Every year people die on the Mount Everest due to too much optimism which makes them to pursue their climb even when all the objective signals are warning for a disaster. Optimism is a powerful way to stimulate sustainable project management. But it can backfire when it is used in an inappropriate way.

Optimism can hurt a project when it is applied in a situation in which the costs of failure are high. In this case too much optimism can lead to actions that can harm the project and or the people involved. Another risk is that optimism can lead to a lack of self-reflection. Looking at external causes for things that go wrong should not lead to a situation in which people are no longer accountable for their own behavior and decisions.

Finally hope and optimism shouldn't be reduced to simple 'positive thinking' as is often done in self-help books and popular articles on this subject. Events are not always positive, negative events are part of human live. And so are negative feelings like sadness and anger. Neglecting these kind of feelings isn't the message of this chapter. Using optimism and hope is a scientifically proved way to stimulate sustainable change and can be effective when it is being implemented in the appropriate way.

The Circular Effect of Positive Psychology and Sustainable Project Management

Positive psychology, and especially hope and optimism stimulate the development of positive emotions in individual project members and in project teams. These positive emotions stimulate the development of sustainable projects in three ways. First of all because stimulating positive emotions is part of sustainable people management in projects. Secondly because positive emotions stimulate environmental behavior. Thirdly because positive emotions stimulate effective and efficient project management.

Sustainable behavior in his turn stimulates positive emotions through various routes. Doing good deeds and helping other people leads to the stimulation of positive emotions (Cameron 2008). Working in green sustainable environments stimulates positive emotions (Berg, van den., Harting & Staats, 2007; Zelenski & Nisbet, 2012) and working with people with positive emotions leads to contagion effects in which the positive emotions of the project members contaminate other project members and the people around them (Fowler and Christakis 2008). These positive emotions in their turn stimulate sustainable behavior etc., creating a circular effect in which positive emotions and sustainable behavior might stimulate each other to prosper.

REFERENCES

Aitken, A., & Crawford. (2007). Coping with stress: Dispositional coping strategies of project managers. *International Journal of Project Management*, 666–673. doi:10.1016/j.ijproman.2007.02.003.

Aknin, L. B., Dunn, E. W., & Norton, M. I. (2011). Happiness runs in a circular motion: Evidence for a positive feedback loop between prosocial spending and happiness. *Journal of Happiness,* (13), 347-355.

Amit, K., Popper, M., Gal, R., Miskal-Sinai, M., & Lissak, A. (2006). The potential to lead: The difference between 'leaders' and 'non-leaders'. *Military Psychology, 16*(4), 245–263.

Arakawa, D., & Greenberg. (2007). Optimistic managers and their influence on productivity and employee engagement in a technology organisation: Implications for coaching psychologists. *International Coaching Psychology Review*, (2): 78–89.

Ashkanasy, N. M., & Ashton-James, C. E. (2007). Positive emotions in organizations: A multi-level framework. In Nelson & Cooper (Ed.), Positive Organizational Behavior. London: Sage.

Asquin, A., Garel, G., & Picq, T. (2010). When project-based management causes distress at work. *International Journal of Project Management*, 166–172. doi:10.1016/j.ijproman.2009.08.006.

Avey, J. B., Wernsing, T. A., & Luthans, F. (2008). Can positive employees help positive organizational change? Impact of psychological capital and emotions on relevant attitudes and behaviors. *The Journal of Applied Behavioral Science*, (44): 48–70. doi:10.1177/0021886307311470.

Bannik, F. (2012). *Practicing positive CBT, from reducing stress to building success.* West Sussex, UK: Wiley-Blackwell. doi:10.1002/9781118328941.

Bates, W. (2009). Gross national happiness. *Asian-Pacific Economic Literature*, *23*, 1–16. doi:10.1111/j.1467-8411.2009.01235.x.

Berg, A. E., Harting, T., & Staats, H. (2007). Preference for nature in urbanized societies: Stress, restoration, and the pursuit of sustainability. *The Journal of Social Issues*, *63*(1), 79–96. doi:10.1111/j.1540-4560.2007.00497.x.

Berg, I. K., & Szabo, P. (2005). *Brief coaching for lasting solutions*. New York, MY: WW Norton and Co..

Bono, J. E., & Ilies, R. (2006). Charisma, positive emotions and mood contagion. *The Leadership Quarterly*, (17): 317–334. doi:10.1016/j.leaqua.2006.04.008.

Brown, K., & Kasser, T. (2005). Are psychological and ecological wellbeing compatible? The role of values, mindfulness and lifestyle. *Social Indicators Research*, *74*, 349–368. doi:10.1007/s11205-004-8207-8.

Cameron, K. (2008). *Positive leadership, strategies for extraordinary performance*. San Francisco, CA: Berrett-Koehler Publishers.

Cameron, K. J., Dutton, J. E., & Quin, R. E. (Eds.). (2003). *Positive organizational scholarship: Foundations of a new discipline*. San Francisco, CA: Berrett-Koehler Publishers.

Cameron, K. S., & Spreitzer. (Ed.). (2012). *Oxford handbook of positive organizational scholarship*. Oxford, UK: Oxford University Press.

Corral-Verdugo, V., Mireles-Acosta, J., Tapia-Fonllem, C., & Fraijo-Sing, B. (2011). Happiness as correlate of sustainable behavior: A study of pro-ecological, frugal, equitable and altruistic actions that promote subjective wellbeing. *Human Ecology Review*, (18): 95–104.

Csikszentmihaiyi, M. (1990). *Flow: The psychology of optimal experience*. New York, NY: Quality Paperback.

Danner, D. D., Snowdon, D. A., & Friesen, W. V. (2001). Positive emotions in early live and longevity: Findings from the nun study. *Journal of Personality and Social Psychology*, (80): 804–813. doi:10.1037/0022-3514.80.5.804 PMID:11374751.

David, D., Szentagotia, A., & Macavei, B. (2005). A synopsis of rational-emotive behavior therapy (REBT), fundamental and applied research. *Journal of Rational-Emotive & Cognitive-Behavior Therapy*, *23*(3), 175–221. doi:10.1007/s10942-005-0011-0.

Dovers, S. R. (1995). A framework for scaling and framing policy problems in sustainability. *Ecological Economics*, *12*(2), 93–106. doi:10.1016/0921-8009(94)00042-T.

Dovido, J. F., Gaertner, S. L., Isen, A. M., & Lowrance, R. (1995). Group representations and intergroup bias: Positive effect, similarity, and group size. *Personality and Social Psychology Bulletin*, (21): 856–865. doi:10.1177/0146167295218009.

El-Sabaa, S. (2001). The skills and career path of an effective project manager. *International Journal of Project Management*, *19*(1), 1–7. doi:10.1016/S0263-7863(99)00034-4.

Elkington, J. (1997). *Canibals with forks: The triple botom line of the 21st century business*. Capstyone Publishing Ltc.

Fowler, J. H., & Christakis, N. A. (2008). Dynamic spread of happiness in a large social network: Longitudinal analysis over 20 years in the framingham Heart Study. *British Medical Journal*, 23–27. PMID:18174597.

Franklin, C., Trepper, T. S., Gingerich, W. J., & McCollum, E. E. (2012). *Solution-focused brief therapy: A handbook of evidence based practice.* New York: Oxford University Press.

Harker, L., & Keltner, D. (2001). Expressions of positive emotion in women's college yearbook pictures and their relationship to personality and life outcomes across adulthood. *Journal of Personality and Social Psychology,* 112–124. doi:10.1037/0022-3514.80.1.112 PMID:11195884.

Henry, P. C. (2005). Life stresses, explanatory style, hopelessness, and occupational class. *International Journal of Stress Management, 12*(3), 241–256. doi:10.1037/1072-5245.12.3.241.

IPMA. (2006). *ICB - IPMA competence baseline version 3.0.* The Netherlands: Nijkerk.

Isen, A. M., & Daubman, K. A. (1984). The influence of affect on categorization. *Journal of Personality and Social Psychology,* (47): 1206–1217. doi:10.1037/0022-3514.47.6.1206.

Johnson, K. J., & Frederickson, B. L. (2005). We all look te same to me: Positive emotions eliminate the own race bais in face recognition. *Psychological Science,* 875–881. doi:10.1111/j.1467-9280.2005.01631.x PMID:16262774.

Johnson, S. K. (2009). Do you feel what I feel? Mood contagion and leadership outcomes. *The Leadership Quarterly, 20,* 814–827. doi:10.1016/j.leaqua.2009.06.012.

Kahkonen, K., Kazi, A. S., & Rekola, M. (Eds.). (2009). The human side of projects in modern business. Helsinki, Finland: Project Management Association Finland (PMAF).

Kotter, J. P. (1996). *Leading change.* Boston, MA: Harvard Business School Press.

Linley, P. A. Harrington, & Garcea. (Eds.). (2010). Oxford handbook of positive psychology and work. Oxford, UK: Oxford University Press.

Lopez, S. J. (Ed.). (2013). *The encyclopedia of positive psychology.* West Sussex, UK: Wiley-Blackwell.

Lopez, S. J., Ciarlelli, R., Cofman, L., Stone, M., & Wyatt, L. (2000). Diagnosing for strengths, on measuring hope building blocks. In Snyder (Ed.), Handbook of hope: Theory, measures and applications. San Diego, CA: Academic Press.

Losada, M., & Heaphy, E. (2004). The role of positivity and connectivity in the performance of business teams: A nonlinear dynamics model. *The American Behavioral Scientist, 47*(6), 740–765. doi:10.1177/0002764203260208.

Loyd-Walker, B., & Walker, D. (2011). Authentic leadership for 21st century project delivery. *International Journal of Project Management,* (29): 282–295.

Lyubomirsky, S. (2001). Why are some people happier than others? The role of cognitive and motivational processes in well being. *The American Psychologist, 56,* 239–249. doi:10.1037/0003-066X.56.3.239 PMID:11315250.

Lyubomirsky, S. (2007). *The how of happiness: A practical guide to getting the life you want.* London: Piatkus.

Lyumbomirsky, S., King, L., & Diener, E. (2005). The benefits of positive affect: does happiness leads to success? *Psychological Bulletin,* (131): 803–855. doi:10.1037/0033-2909.131.6.803 PMID:16351326.

Macdonnald, A. J. (2011). *Solution-focused therapy: Theory, research& practice.* London: Sage.

Nelson, D. L., & Cooper, C. L. (Eds.). (2007). *Positive organizational behaviour.* Thousand Oaks, CA: Sage.

Pant, I., & Baroudi, B. (2008). Project management education: The human skills imperative. *International Journal of Project Management,* (26): 124–128. doi:10.1016/j.ijproman.2007.05.010.

Pasian, B. L. (2011). *Project management maturity: A critical analysis of existing and emergent factors.* (Unpublished doctoral dissertation). University of Technology, Sydney, Australia.

Peterson, C. (2000). The future of optimism. *The American Psychologist*, (55): 44–55. doi:10.1037/0003-066X.55.1.44 PMID:11392864.

Peterson, C., & Seligman, M. E. P. (2004). *Character strengths and virtues: A handbook and classification.* Washington, DC: APA Press and Oxford University Press.

Peterson, S. J., & Luthans, F. (2003). The positive impact and development of hopeful leaders. *Leadership and Organization Development Journal*, *24*(1), 26–31. doi:10.1108/01437730310457302.

Piderit, S. K. (2000). Rethinking resistance and recognizing ambivalence: A multidimensional view of attitudes toward an organizational change. *Academy of Management Review*, (25): 783–794.

Planko, J., & Silvius, G. (2012). Sustainability in business. In Silvius, Schipper, Planko, van den Brink, & Köhler (Ed.), Sustainability in Project Management. Farnham, UK: Gower Publishing.

Prat, M. G., & Ashforth, B. E. (2003). Fostering meaningfulness in working and at work. In Cameron, Dutton, & Quin (Ed.), Positive organizational scholarship: Foundations of a new discipline. San Francisco, CA: Berrett-Koehler Publishers.

Proudfoot, J.G., Corr, Guest, & Dunn. (2009). Cognitive-behavioural training to change attributional style improves employee well-being, job satisfaction, productivity, and turnover. *Personality and Individual Differences*, (46): 147–153. doi:10.1016/j.paid.2008.09.018.

Pryce-Jones, J. (2010). *Happiness at work, maximizing your psychological capital for success.* Chichester, UK: Wiley-Blackwell. doi:10.1002/9780470666845.

Raz, T., & Michael, E. (2001). Use and benefits of tools for project risk management. *International Journal of Project Management*, *19*(1), 9–17. doi:10.1016/S0263-7863(99)00036-8.

Rhee, S.Y., & Yoon. (2012). Group emotions, shared positive affect in workgroups. In Cameron & Spreitzer (Eds.), *Oxford Handbook of Positive Organizational Scholarship.* Oxford, UK: Oxford University Press.

Rothbard, N. P., & Patil, S. V. (2012). Being there: Work engagement and positive organizational scholarship. In Cameron & Spreitzer (Ed.), Oxford Handbook of Positive Organizational Scholarship. Oxford, UK: Oxford University Press.

Scheier, M. F., & Carver, C. S. (1992). Effects of optimism on psychological and physical well-being: Theoretical overview and empirical update. *Cognitive Therapy and Research*, *16*, 201–228. doi:10.1007/BF01173489.

Scheier, M. F., Carver, C. S., & Bridges, M. W. (1994). Distinguishing optimism from neuroticism (and trait anxiety, self-mastery, and self-esteem): A re-evaluation of the life orientation test. *Journal of Personality and Social Psychology*, *67*, 1063–1078. doi:10.1037/0022-3514.67.6.1063 PMID:7815302.

Schimmack, U., Oishi, S., Furr, R. M., & Funder, D. C. (2004). Personality and life satisfaction: A facet-level analysis. *Personality and Social Psychology Bulletin*, (30): 1062–1075. doi:10.1177/0146167204264292 PMID:15257789.

Seligman, M. E. P. (1991). *Learned optimism: How to change your mind and your life.* New York: Knopf.

Seligman, M. E. P. (1998). Building human strength: Psychology's forgotten mission. *APA Monitor*, *29*(1).

Silvius, G., & Schipper, R. (2012). Sustainability and projects. In Silvius, Schipper, Planko, van den Brink, & Köhler (Ed.), Sustainability in Project Management. Franham, UK: Gower Publishing.

Silvius, G., Schipper, R., & van den Brink, J. (2012). Incorporating sustainability in project management. In Silvius, Schipper, Planko, van den Brink, & Köhler (Ed.), Sustainability in Project Management. Franham, UK: Gower Publishing.

Snyder, C. R. (Ed.). (2000). *Handbook of hope: Theory, measures and applications.* San Diego, CA: Academic Press.

Spreitzer, G. M., & Sutcliffe, K. M. (2007). Thriving in organizations. In Nelson & Cooper (Ed.), Positive Organizational Behavior. London: Sage.

Staw, B. M., & Barsade, S. G. (1993). Affect and managerial performance: A test of the sadder-but-wiser vs. happier-and-smarter hypothesis. *Administrative Science Quarterly,* (38): 304–331. doi:10.2307/2393415.

Stroessner, S., Mackie, & Michalsen. (2005). Positive mood and the perception of variability within and between groups. *Group Processes & Intergroup Relations,* (8): 5–25. doi:10.1177/1368430205048619.

Suhonen, M., & Paasivaara, L. (2011). Shared human capital in project management: A systematic review of the literature. *Project Management Journal,* (42), 4-16.

Turner, J. R. (Ed.). (1993). *The handbook of project based management.* London: McGraw-Hill.

Van den Brink. (2013). *Project management? It's all about emotions: The positive psychology of project management.*

Westbrook, D., & Kennerly, H., & Kirk. (2007). *An introduction to cognitive behavioral therapy, skills and applications.* London. *Sage (Atlanta, Ga.).*

Wooten, L. P., & Cameron, K. S. (2010). Enablers of a positive strategy: Positively deviant leadership. In Liney, Harrington, & Garcea (Eds.), Oxford Handbook of Positive Psychology and Work. New York: Oxford University Press.

Wresniewski, A. (2003). Finding positive meaning in work. In Cameron, Dutton, & Quin (Eds.), Positive organizational scholarship: Foundations of a new discipline. San Francisco, CA: Berrett-Koehler Publishers.

Zelenski, J. M., & Nisbet, E. K. (2012). Happiness and feeling connected: The distinct role of nature relatedness. *Environment and Behavior,* 1–21.

Zelensky, J. M., Murphy, S. A., & Jenkins, D. A. (2008). The happy-productive worker thesis revisited. *Journal Happiness Studies,* (9), 521-537.

Zullow, H. M., & Seligman, M. E. P. (1990). Pessimistic rumination predicts defeat of Presidential candidates: 1900-1984. *Psychological Inquiry, 1,* 52–61. doi:10.1207/s15327965pli0101_13.

ADDITIONAL READING

Bannik, F. (2012). *Practicing positive CBT, from reducing stress to building success.* West Sussex, UK: Wiley-Blackwell. doi:10.1002/9781118328941.

Berg, I. K., & Szabo, P. (2005). *Brief coaching for lasting solutions.* New York, NY: WW Norton and Co..

Cameron, K. J., Dutton, J. E., & Quin, R. E. (Eds.). (2003). *Positive organizational scholarship: Foundations of a new discipline*. San Francisco, CA: Berrett-Koehler Publishers.

Cameron, K. S., & Spreitzer. (Eds.). (2012). *Oxford handbook of positive organizational scholarship*. Oxford, UK: Oxford University Press.

Linley, P. A. Harrington, & Garcea. (Eds.). (2010). *Oxford handbook of positive psychology and work*. Oxford, UK: Oxford University Press.

Losada, M., & Heaphy, E. (2004). The role of positivity and connectivity in the performance of business teams: A nonlinear dynamics model. *The American Behavioral Scientist*, *47*(6), 740–765. doi:10.1177/0002764203260208.

Lyumbomirsky, S., King, L., & Diener, E. (2005). The benefits of positive affect: Does happiness leads to success? *Psychological Bulletin*, (131): 803–855. doi:10.1037/0033-2909.131.6.803 PMID:16351326.

Nelson, D. L., & Cooper, C. L. (Eds.). (2007). *Positive organizational behaviour*. Thousand Oaks, CA: Sage.

Seligman, M. E. P. (1991). *Learned optimism: How to change your mind and your life*. New York: Knopf.

Silvius, G., Schipper, R., Planko, J., van den Brink, J., & Köhler, A. (Eds.). (2012). *Sustainability in project management*. Franham, UK: Gower Publishing.

Snyder, C. R. (Ed.). (2000). *Handbook of hope: Theory, measures and applications*. San Diego, CA: Academic Press.

KEY TERMS AND DEFINITIONS[2]

Explanatory Style: The way in which people interpret and explains the events that happen to him, based on three criteria: permanence, pervasiveness and personalization. Often a difference is made between an optimistic and a pessimistic explanatory style.

Hope: The expectancy to reach certain goals.

Optimism: A state of mind in which a person expect good things to happen to them.

Positive Emotions: Brief experiences that feel good in the present.

Positive Psychology: A movement in the (scientific) field of psychology with the aim to help people to lead a more productive and fulfilling life and to identify and nurture talent.

Positive Psychological Capital (PsyCap): A set of personality traits that have shown to be of relevance in the workplace consisting of: hope, optimism, efficacy, and resiliency.

ENDNOTES

[1] The 19 studied competences are: leadership, engagement and motivation, self control, assertiveness, relaxation, openness, creativity, results orientation, efficiency, consultation, negotiation, conflict and crisis, reliability, value appreciation, ethics, communication, teamwork, problem resolution, risk, and opportunity.

[2] The description of these key term is partly based on the definitions as described in *The encyclopedia of positive psychology*, Lopez (ed.), 2013.

Chapter 16
Project Manager as a Pivot Point for Implementing Sustainability in an Enterprise

Richard Maltzman
EarthPM, LLC, USA

David Shirley
EarthPM, LLC, USA

ABSTRACT

In this chapter, the authors provide a rationale for asserting a special importance of the project manager with respect to implementing sustainability at their enterprise, due to their being at a key "pivot point." This does not come without challenges, and here the authors convey those specific challenges for project managers. They show that one of these challenges is adopting a sustainability thinking mindset, a mindset that has its roots in the "larger scheme of things, and the long-haul," even though project managers are often (necessarily) focused on their immediate scope, and short-term deliverables for demanding stakeholders. Finally, the authors advise project managers with some specific techniques to overcome the prior challenges.

INTRODUCTION

Project managers may not see themselves this way, but they are at a significant advantage when it comes to bringing about sustainability integration for their enterprises. Project Managers, after all, are change agents. Projects themselves are all about change – we would never initiate a project to keep things exactly the same; and each project, by definition, is unique. So for starters, Project Managers are indeed agents of change. In this chapter, we will address the ways in which the project manager can invoke this role as change agent on their projects and within their enterprise.

DOI: 10.4018/978-1-4666-4177-8.ch016

BACKGROUND

Stanford University and IPS have created the Stanford Execution Framework which shows how projects, programs and portfolios 'connect' with the remainder of the enterprise. Recent case studies (Herazo et al., 2012) affirm that project managers can help align strategic and tactical management. Further, major project attributes such as risk management are heavily influenced by the interaction of the project manager and the project owner (Krane et al., 2012). Advice for how project managers can take on this role more effectively can be found in *Green Project Management* (Maltzman and Shirley, 2011). Despite the level of academic and theoretical support, however, project managers do not always recognize that they have the role, or, recognizing it, sometimes fail to *fully embrace* this role for a number of reasons which we'll discuss.

PROJECT MANAGER AS A PIVOT POINT FOR IMPLEMENTING SUSTAINABILITY IN AN ENTERPRISE

Your Project's Context

Why put this kind of pressure on a project manager? Don't project managers already have too much to do to bring their projects in on or under budget, meeting or exceeding customer expectations and on time or even earlier than promised? Isn't it bad enough that there is a beginning and an end to the temporary endeavor called *a project*? Why expand their role and give them the extra responsibilities to implement sustainability in an organization and even beyond their normal *project zone*? The simple answer is *because project managers are the best suited for the job*.

That begs the question as to why project managers are the best suited for the job and that requires a more complex answer. Project manag-ers have been and always will be *change agents*. It is just what they do. A project by definition is something "unique" and in addition is chartered to *change* something, whether it is process, procedure or product. This is what distinguishes project managers from operations managers, after all. Therefore it can be inferred that project managers are *change agents*. They plan, execute and then control the execution of a change. In addition, project managers are not only able to provide the mechanics for successful execution of a change, but can – or at least should - also see the "big picture." "Project Managers are traditionally recognized for providing the expertise to guide a company's endeavor to completion; on-time and on-budget; this is "PM 101". However for many organizations the PM is a *solution enabler; a process re-engineer; a project team facilitator*. To be an effective change agent, a well-seasoned PM should be part of the project team as a leader. Solving business problems often requires the cooperation and collaboration of multiple silos. The PM is in a unique position to span all the silos and lead the project to conclusion" (http://www.think-ebiz.com/2005/03/project_manager.html, emphasis provided by the authors).

That ability, to "span all silos," can also be related to one of the other important attributes of a project manager, the ability to see the "big picture." Because of that global view project managers are better able connect to the foundational aspects of sustainability, the Triple Bottom Line, people, planet and profits. Add to that projects and you have the quadruple bottom line or 4Ps of sustainability (people, planet, profits and projects). Projects are conducted in a larger, enterprise role; to make money, to gain an advantage over a competitor or for the greater good as examples. Project managers have an appreciation for that large role because they are stakeholders in their individual projects as well as the enterprise. It the project does well, it follows that the enterprise will do well and the employees share in that success. They can also see how the project fits into the overall business strategy. Few in the organization have that same impact or same appreciation. That appreciation also includes what everyone else in the organization should have; to further the business and keep the enterprise in business or as Auden Schendler (2009) says "sustainability is being in business forever."

The difficulty is that project management has been not been considered a business function. BA, or business analysis, is considered the function that identifies business needs and determines what is needed (projects) to satisfy those business needs. What is even more striking is that most project managers don't consider themselves business advocates. Let us look at where that intersection between the business and project management overlap.

The Overlap of Business and Projects

We are all aware that a project begins (or should begin) with a Project Charter. The best case is that the project charter is developed by the project manager with input from the project team. It can also be developed by a major stakeholder, like the funder, executive management or even a customer. But the most effective method to develop a project charter is with the project manager and the project team. So for our purposes let us assume that it is collaboration by the project manager and project team. Of course there will be input from key areas such as contracts, statements of work and the business case. More importantly, it will contain information critical to the understanding and success of the project; goal, objectives, high-level budget and schedule, assumptions and constraints (and other risk factors), project manager authority and project success criteria. As you can see by the data required for the project charter, there is an intersection or overlap with the business function. Let us look specifically at project sustainability (greenality) as it pertains to the project charter and synergy and potential conflict with business needs.

Why are projects initiated in the first place? Projects are initiated for a variety of reasons, two being customer demand and market demand. "Customer" here refers to those that are internal, upgrading an existing data center and external (upgrading an existing data center) and external (introducing a new product). Upgrading an existing data center can have two distinct objectives; giving the internal customers more efficient and modern computing facilities or providing a more efficient and effective use of the limited resources of energy. These two objectives can either be complementary or conflicting. If the point is to be more sustainable, then these two objectives can be complementary.

The Massachusetts Green High Performance Computing Center (MGHPCC) is being created with two objectives in mind; provide better, faster data crunching ability for specific data intense applications and provide a more efficient, less expensive, more sustainable computing environment. MGHPCC is collaboration between industry, the government of the Commonwealth of Massachusetts and five universities, University of Massachusetts, Boston University, Massachusetts Institute of Technology, and Northeastern University. All of those universities have their own sustainability missions. They also have a need for expanded research computing power; mining huge amounts of data and massive calculations. The facility will be located in Holyoke, Massachusetts, close to the Holyoke Gas and Electric hydro-electric dam for relatively inexpensive power. From the state's point of view, it is being located in a previously depressed area that could use rehabilitation and high tech jobs generated by the facility and its construction will benefit the local environment. From the business sponsors' points of view, the research facility allows for collaboration between industry and significant university resources.

Because it is new construction, better construction techniques, including building to Leadership in Energy and Environmental Design (LEED) Gold specifications, will be used. Because of the energy efficiency of new IT equipment and cost savings as a result of those efficiencies, most of the old computing equipment will be left at the various university campuses to be repurposed or recycled. More efficient cooling will also be designed and implemented in the new facility, saving even more of the energy costs. Energy savings not only translates to cost savings, but also to reduced green house gas emissions, a win for the universities and for the environment. This is a perfect example of where business sustainability, environmental needs intersect and overlap. In this instance, stakeholders; the university leadership, the computer users, industry leadership and the environmentally aware, all receive value.

But it may not have been this way. For example, because it is a shared environment, there will be a certain amount of shared resources. The project will need the integration of some monitoring and maintenance functions. It has been past procedure that the departments within the various universities had direct control over their own resources. Therefore, they had to give up some of that control for the shared environment. Their business needs would have been in conflict with business sustainability.

By being able to grasp the "big picture," the consortium is able to take advantage of all of the cost saving while protecting fragile resources. It could not have been easy getting buy-in from all of the different players in this scenario. However, it starts from the top down. In addition, the planning effort included windows of one to ten years and ten to twenty years looking at the long term. Unless that buy-in for both the project itself and the timing windows had been obtained, this project would not have the traction it does. The project continues to be on time and on budget.

While this is a large IT project, the concept can be applied across the entire "green spectrum" According to Maltzman and Shirley in their book *Green Project Management*, there is a "rainbow of green." "All projects have some element of 'green'." The spectrum is from a project that is green by intent, a project that is clearly "ecologically friendly", like constructing a wind turbine farm to a new software release, a project that one would not consider having an element of green, but in fact, does. In between there is the project that is green by the impact the project has on the environment, and green by product impact or the impact he product has in the longer term. The role of the project manager, as a sustainability advocate, increases as the project moves along the green spectrum. The sustainability of a project that is "green by intent" is well known by the stakeholders involved. The product of the project, constructing a wind farm, or bio-fuel processing facility is clearly green. At the other end of the scale is "green in general", and the sustainability of that type of project is not as clearly understood. Because as much as 90% of a project manager's job is communicating, it is only logical that the project manager help to articulate the sustainability of a project that, on the surface, has no sustainability element. The project manager, while having the communications skills to articulate the sustainability of a "green in general" project, also has the ability to see the "big picture" of a project. That ability allows the project manager to consider the larger issue of sustainability in that project that may appear not to have a sustainability element. As example, a software release would need to consider the method of delivery. Will it have to be packaged like a DVD or can it be delivered electronically, a much more sustainable method?

To further the argument that the project manager is the enterprise's sustainability advocate one only has to look to the Stanford University's Strategic Execution Framework (SEF). The SEF (See Figure 1) begins with the ideation phase and defines the enterprise's purpose, identity and the long term intentions. It progresses to the organizations culture and structure (nature), goals and metrics (vision) to strategy and portfolio (engagement). Finally it culminates in the "synthesis" of program and project to "transition" to operations.

Figure 1. Stanford's strategic execution framework

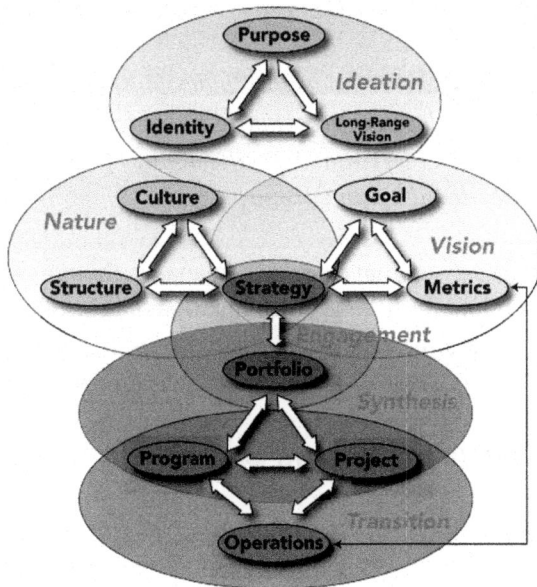

The key, however, is that all of the process flow to program and project and the interface to operations.

Project managers are key players at that intersection. It is the intersection with operations that allows the project manager to connect sustainability and the long term.

Your Project's Beginning and End

Dutch author Harry Mulisch organized one of his more famous books, "The Discovery of Heaven", into 4 big chunks. He entitled them:

- The Beginning of the Beginning
- The End of the Beginning
- The Beginning of the End
- The End of the End

It's an interesting way for us to think about the projects on which we work, but more importantly it's a good way to look at the *products* of the projects on which we work.

Our projects usually involve the first two chunks. We take an idea from its inception to the point to which it can be deployed *en masse* – put into operation, or the *steady state*. Whether it's a bridge, a sales training program, a new piece of software, or a wind farm, we, the project manager, get that *idea* to the *steady state* (to *operations* as discussed previously in "Your Project's Context"). So ironically, we tend to focus *not* on that steady state, but rather with the beginning of the beginning and the end of the beginning – the *getting to* the steady state. Here, in the first two chunks, there are indeed considerations for sustainability, but they are focused on the project and the resources the project team *itself* uses. They are not focused on longer-term issues like what happens to the product as it is 'manufactured', 'used', and 'disposed of'. We put these terms in quotes because they won't apply exactly that way for the product of every project, for example software releases.

But although we do that out of necessity (focus on getting to the steady state), the project does *not* stop when we hand it over. The wind farm, or bridge, or even the software release, has a life, and an end of life. It has a useful period of operation (during which there are side effects such as consumables and waste), and then finally, disposal of the product itself has to be considered as well. If you doubt the ability of software to contribute to reductions in carbon footprint, see the following press release from non-profit IT consortium GreenTouch:

AMSTERDAM: The GreenTouch Consortium, a global research initiative dedicated to dramatically improving network energy efficiency, introduced a major breakthrough for optical access -- Bit-Interleaved Passive Optical Network (Bi-PON) technology. GreenTouch estimates Bi-PON ultimately could deliver power reduction of 30 times over current technologies while improving performance and reducing cost.

In a Webcast, researchers from Alcatel-Lucent's Bell Labs, France's INRIA research lab and France Telecom Orange, described how the bit interleav-

ing passive optical network (BIPON) leverages a new protocol that cuts energy consumption in time division multiplexing (TDM) PON optical network units (ONUs) by a factor of 10 compared to today's protocols. The key observation is that 99% of data is unnecessarily processed in ONUs today. By modifying the protocol, an order of magnitude improvement in ONU performance can be attained.

The bit interleaving protocol reduces energy consumption in the ONU by reducing clock speed requirements, data processing requirements, voltage requirements, and memory requirements. The bits are spaced in time to match the clock rate. The bit interleaving protocol frame structure includes a header and a payload section. The header contains a synchronization code word and a unique identifier for each ONU on the PON. The header also contains information that allows the ONU to know where its payload bits are — at what offset and bit rate they are being sent in the payload section.

The consortium members said Bi-PON represents the next major leap in passive optical network (PON) technologies. It is expected to be a necessity as electronic processing will increase with future 40GPON systems.

With this demonstration, GreenTouch again shows why it is one of the most ambitious collaborative environments in sustainable network technologies," said Gee Rittenhouse, GreenTouch chairman. "We are committed to reducing energy consumption across all ICT networks and Bi-PON is a huge and critical step in helping us achieve that goal. The impact is clear and wide-ranging including wireless backhaul and fiber to the home. Implementing Bi-PON over current technologies will have the energy savings equivalent to the carbon impact of permanently taking all the cars in a city like San Francisco off the road. We are making great progress toward our goal and are planning

to make advances like this across all of our 25 research projects that are currently underway.

http://www.greentouch.org/index.php?mact=News,cntnt01,detail,0&cntnt01articleid=23&cntnt01origid=15&cntnt01detailtemplate=press_release_detail&cntnt01returnid=105

We assert that the project manager, though not traditionally tasked with doing so, should be thinking about the last two of Harry Mulisch' chunks: The *beginning of the end* and the *end of the end*.

Lifecycle Thinking Basics

The chart (EPA, 1993) in Figure 2, provides some orientation. In fact, to project managers this chart should look strikingly familiar – it is reflected the PMBOK® Guide diagram for any of its 42 processes – Inputs, Tools and Techniques, and Outputs. In this case, inputs are raw materials and energy, tools and techniques are the acquisition of those items, manufacturing processes, use/reuse and maintenance, and recycle and waste management. Outputs (other than the product itself, of course) are atmospheric emissions, waterborne and solid wastes, co-products, and other releases.

Figure 2 shows the basic "input-output" for a manufacturing process. Perhaps the most important part of this drawing is at the bottom: the system boundary. This will be discussed later when we get into the details of a Life Cycle Analysis or Life Cycle Assessment (LCA).

The basic tool which can be used for lifecycle thinking is an LCA or Life Cycle Analysis. LCA became popular in the early 1990s, at first mainly to help support environmental claims that could be directly used by companies in the marketing of their products or services, and indeed this is one use of an LCA. By the same token, a 1999 survey by Rubik and Frankl showed that LCA is most often used for internal purposes such as product improvement, support for strategic choices, and benchmarking. In fact, the best de-

Figure 2. The input- output system of a manufacturing process

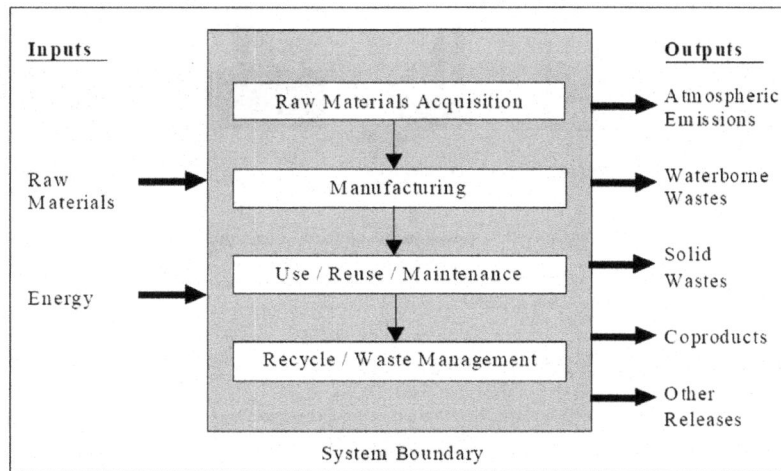

scription of an LCA (from the Carnegie-Mellon University site which provides a free LCA tool) is:

Life cycle assessment (LCA) is a way to investigate, estimate, and evaluate the environmental burdens caused by a material, product, process, or service throughout its life span. Environmental burdens include the materials and energy resources required to create the product, as well as the wastes and emissions generated during the process. By examining the entire life cycle, one gets a more complete picture of the environmental impact created and the trade-offs in impact from one period of the life cycle to another. Results of LCAs can be useful for identifying areas with high environmental impact, and for evaluating and improving product designs.

The Lifecycle of the Product of your Project

The product of your project will have different impacts on the environment during different stages of its life. Consider Figure 3.

The products of some projects will use materials that will have adverse environmental effects when extracted or processed, but when the product is deployed, it may be have relatively little effect in its use and may be very easy to recycle or reuse. Aluminum products are an example of this scenario. However, a printer or product powered by disposable batteries will create the bulk of its environmental impact while it is being used by the customer because of its "consumables" (cartridges or batteries).

Let's take the example of a washing machine[1]. It will be obvious to our readers that a washing machine uses energy and water. There is also, however, solid waste (packaging and end-of-life disposal). Most of the environmental impact is during its use (See Figure 4). Most of the solid waste impact comes from the two stages of delivery - first, when the packaging is removed and disposed of and secondly, the eventual end-of-life disposal of the machine. The solid waste levels are indeed significantly higher than other contributors at these stages, but notice that they total less than 15% of the solid waste produced by the washing machine. If this surprises you, a detailed LCA would reveal the many packets of washing powder and other consumables that are discarded as the

Figure 3. The lifecycle of a manufacturing process

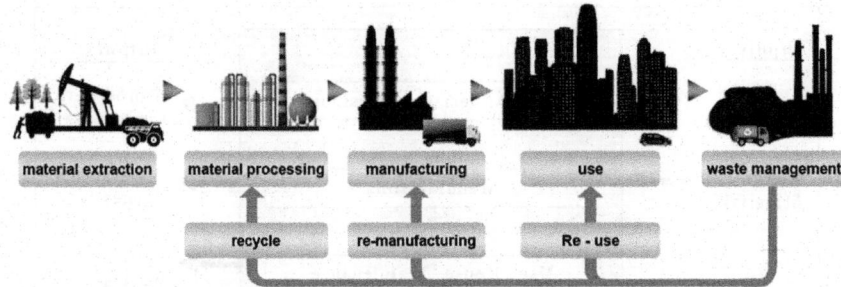

Figure 4. Impact of a washing machine over its lifecycle

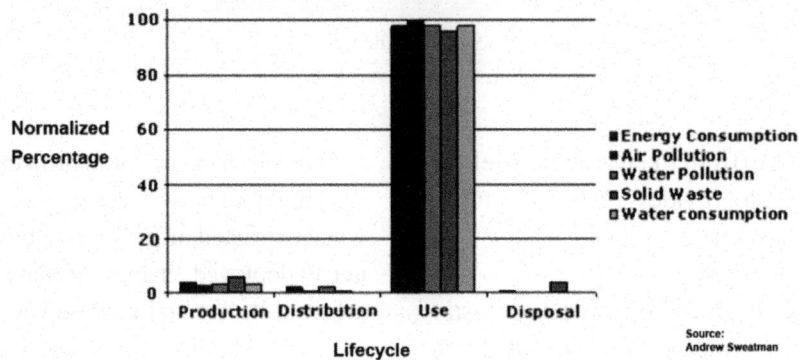

machine is used. This illustrates how careful we must be to consider every aspect of use, and to draw the 'system boundary' broadly enough to cover this aspect of the washing machine's use.

ENHANCING YOUR PROJECT WITH SUSTAINABILITY THINKING

In order to apply sustainability thinking to projects, this section discusses three concepts that refer to sustainability, and their potential application in projects. The concepts are Lean Thinking and Muda (wastes), the 5 Ss (Sort, Straighten, Shine, Standardize, Sustain), and the 4 Ls (Lean, Learn, Linked, Lasting).

LEAN THINKING AND YOUR PROJECT

Project managers should not consider themselves newcomers in lean thinking. Not by any stretch (excuse the pun). As project managers, we are constantly looking for ways to get more done with less. Uncertainty in projects often manifests itself in the following forms of threats:

- Suddenly unavailable resources.
- Reduced budget or overspends, yielding a reduced remaining budget.
- Unexpected increased scope or new requirements.
- A management or customer-imposed earlier project closing date.

Any or all of these things force us to be creative with schedule compression and resource leveling, each of which in turn are often about being more efficient, wasting less in other words, being lean.

Lean Thinking can and should be applied to the project itself as well as being folded into the planning for the product of the project. The PM can be a change agent not only for the project but for the long-term effects of the project (the operation of the project's product). In other words, they can make a lasting difference for the organization, and even beyond, to the population outside your organization and even beyond this generation.

One of the concepts threaded through Lean Thinking is the Theory of Constraints, which should not be a foreign concept to project managers because it has found its way into project management in the form of Critical Chain project management and is at the heart of Agile methodologies, such as those used in software development (Scrum, XP, DSDM).

As PMs we know that to use the critical chain, we revise the Critical Path project plan with resource constraints to get the Critical Chain project plan. Where the critical path is based on task dependencies, the critical chain is based on the additional (and important) information we get when we look at resource dependencies. The critical chain method (as illustrated by Herbie the slow hiker in Eliyahu Goldratt's *The Goal*) allows us to identify the bottleneck or constrained resource.

For those of you not familiar with The Goal, here is a summary of that portion of the book:

The protagonist of the book, Alex Rogo, takes his son and Boy Scout troop on a hike. The slowest hiker, Herbie, keeps falling behind the rest of the hikers, and the queue in front of him keeps stretching out, because the leaders (by definition) are walking much more quickly. The quickest hikers generally have no space between them and the Scout in front of them. Rogo realizes that even if the quickest hikers slow down or stop (to take a breath, have a snack, or to tie their shoes), they catch up because their average pace is faster

than that of the kid in front of them. However, if a Scout who is slower than the hiker in front of him pauses, he never regains his original spacing and the line of hikers continues to expand. Herbie is slowing down the whole group because Rogo (as the responsible adult) has to keep all of the kids in viewing distance and has to call ahead for them to wait. Rogo gets the inspired idea to place Herbie at the front of the line, which solves the problem of keeping the group together, since everyone has to walk as slowly as Herbie does. But he doesn't stop there. To increase the group's rate of speed, he redistributes what Herbie is carrying in his pack (cans of soda, a collapsible steel shovel, and a jar of pickles) into the quickest hikers' backpacks (as well as his own). The lighter load allows Herbie to walk more quickly. Rogo realizes that really, this is a system of hikers, hiking the trail together, and that any individual hiker's speed is dependent on the hiker's speed in front of him. He further realizes that the changes in pace are statistical fluctuations, and Herbie is the system constraint. He has slowed down his speediest hikers, and this intuitively seems quite wrong. However, the system is moving at its fastest collective rate because it is moving at the constraint's fastest speed. So, even though hikers are not individually efficient, the system's constraint is efficient and therefore the system is running at its highest possible efficiency. (Goldratt, 1992)

In critical chain project management we do not have individual safety buffers at each individual task; we instead move the buffering to the overall project date, to protect that team goal. Progress is measured by the use (or lack thereof) of buffers.

Let's translate this into action. Here are the "5 focusing steps" of the Theory of Constraints:

1. Identify the system's constraints. What's slowing things down? Where is the bottleneck?

2. Decide how to exploit the system's constraints.
3. Subordinate everything else to the constraint conclusions from Step 2.
4. Elevate the system's constraints.
5. If the constraint is broken, return to Step 1.

When you solve your worst problem, your next-worst problem gets a promotion, of sorts, and becomes the next big thing you'll work on. This is a continuous process.

What is Lean?

There are a variety of lean methods which can be adapted by organizations to become lean. Lean Thinking is about a *Continuous flow of value*, *Value defined by customer*, *Customer pulls value from provider* and this *All done in search of perfection* (Womack and Jones, 1996).

How can this be applied to projects? An illustration of lean thinking beyond a project:

A company wanted to increase its production capabilities as quickly as possible. As you know, the setup of a new or improved manufacturing line is a project. The ongoing running of the manufacturing line is an operation. As the pieces of major manufacturing equipment started to arrive, it was installed at the most convenient location available at that time. The location of the machines themselves was not considered part of the original project, and handover to operations occurred. At the time, the team was considering applying Lean Thinking to revise their manufacturing process. Lean thinking design called for the equipment to be relocated for reduced waste, improved efficiency and throughput. Had the project delivery considered this up front, the savings could have been instituted a year earlier at minimum.

This case helps illustrate the importance of connecting the project team's thinking with the long-term operation of the deliverable of the product – in this case, a manufacturing line.

Wastes

What are these wastes? The idea of the importance of eliminating waste was popularized as part of The Toyota Production System (TPS), and the identification of "The Seven Wastes". *Muda* is Japanese for waste – you will sometimes find this information referred to as the Seven Mudas. Here, in general, are the Seven Wastes:

1. **Overproduction:** Simply put, overproduction means producing an item for a process before it is actually required. Overproduction is highly costly to a process because it prohibits the smooth flow of materials or services and will tend to degrade quality and productivity. This is why you will also hear references to The Toyota Production System is also referred to as "Just in Time" (JIT) because every item is made just as it is needed. Overproduction is sometimes referred to as "Just in Case." Working on a "Just in Case" basis creates unnecessarily long lead times, results in unneeded storage costs, and makes it more difficult for the process to detect defects. One way to find out where overproduction is "hiding" is to turn off the supply to the system and see where the inventory is built up.

2. **Waiting:** If goods are not moving or being processed by the system, the waste of waiting occurs. Amazingly, the vast majority of a product's life in traditional batch-and-queue manufacture will be spent waiting to be processed in some way. Waiting can be caused by bad material flow, or production runs that are too long, or long distances between operations. A cure to this is to link the processes together (a la Goldratt) so that one process feeds directly into another.

3. **Transporting:** Moving product *between* processes incurs co*st and* adds no value to the operation. Excessive movement and handling may cause damage or decay in quality. This can be difficult to reduce, but mapping product or operations flows can make this easier to visualize.

4. **Inappropriate Processing:** In some cases, systems use expensive or unnecessarily high precision equipment where simpler equipment or operations would be sufficient. In some cases, investing in smaller, more flexible equipment or operations, or creating manufacturing cells; and combining steps can reduce the waste of inappropriate processing.

5. **Unnecessary Inventory:** Excess inventory – which makes us feel safe - tends to hide problems with a system. These problems should be identified and resolved in order to improve operating performance. Work in Progress (WIP), as stated before, is a direct result of overproduction and waiting. This WIP takes up floor space and can interfere with good communications by "numbing" the real problems of the system.

6. **Unnecessary or Excess Motion:** The classic Industrial Engineers will be familiar with this form of muda. This waste is related to the human-machine interface and is seen in bending, lifting, stretching, reaching, and walking. Activities with excessive motion should be analyzed and redesigned for improvement – and this should be done with the system personnel for ideal effectiveness and buy-in.

7. **Defects:** Having a direct impact to the bottom line, defects have a high cost to organizations. We know this as project managers when we study the Cost of Quality. These costs come from rework or scrap, from lost customers, and even lawsuits. There is, of course opportunity to reduce defects at many facilities

through involvement of employees, and continuous process improvement (kaizen).

A New Waste?

One further muda has been added in some treatments of this subject. For example, in the latest edition of Lean Thinking, *Underutilization of Employees* has been added as an eighth waste. This waste refers to not capitalizing on employees' creativity – and proposes that organizations can eliminate the other seven wastes more effectively if they better utilize their employees.

These wastes apply mainly to manufacturing. How might they apply to, say, software development? Mary Poppendieck (2002) translates this for us next.

-   The Basic Principles of Lean Development
    -   Add Nothing But Value (Eliminate Waste)
    -   Center On The People Who Add Value
    -   Flow Value From Demand (Delay Commitment)
    -   Optimize Across Organizations
-   The Seven Wastes of Software Development
    -   Overproduction = Extra Features
    -   Inventory = Requirements
    -   Extra Processing Steps = Extra Steps
    -   Motion = Finding Information
    -   Defects = Defects Not Caught by Tests
    -   Waiting = Waiting, Including Customers
    -   Transportation = Handoffs

What do we do about these wastes in software development? Agile methods, such as Extreme Programming, address these wastes as shown in Table 1.

What about the Service Sector? The EPA has looked at the seven wastes and produced this list-

Table 1. Wastes in software development

Waste In Software Development	How Extreme Programming Addresses Wastes
Extra Features	Develop only for today's stories
Requirements	Story cards are detailed only for the current iteration
Extra Steps	Code directly from stories: get verbal clarification directly from customers
Finding Information	Have everyone in the same room: customers included
Defects not caught by tests	Test first: both developer tests and customer tests
Waiting, Including Customers	Deliver in smaller increments
Handoffs	Developers work directly with customers

Table 2. Manufacturing and service wastes

Waste Type	Manufacturing Section Wastes	Service Sector Wastes
Defects	Scrap, rework, replacement production, reinspection	Order entry, design, engineering errors
Waiting	Stock-outs, lot processing delays, equipment downtime, capacity bottlenecks	System downtime, responses time, approvals
Overproduction	Manufacturing items for which there are no orders	Printing paperwork, purchasing items before they are needed, processing paperwork before the next person is ready for it
Transportation	Transporting Work-in-progress (WIP) long distances, tracking to and from an off-site storage facility	Multiple sites outside of walking distance, off-site training
Inventory	Excess raw material, WIP, or unfinished goods	Office supplies, sales literature, and reports
Complexity	More parts, process steps, or time than necessary to meet customer needs	Re-entry of data, extra copies, excessive reporting, etc.
Unused creativity	Lost time, ideas, skills, improvements, and suggestions from employees	Limited tools or authority available to employees to carry-out basic tasks

ing that shows them for both the manufacturing and service sectors (See Table 2).

Table 3 is a table from the US EPA which summarizes many of these methods and tools. Remember, these are typically applied to operations – the steady-state application of your project's product. However you should still consider applying them in your project for the direct environmental impact and benefit, and you'll want to understand these to have better connection points to your handoff to operations when that occurs.

A Case Study in Waste

(An illustration of wast involved in the production of cola cans in the UK)

First of all, note that a beverage can is more expensive than the beverage. Here's what happens on its journey to deliver your beverage to you.

1. Bauxite is minded in Autralia
2. Bauxite is truicked to chemical reduction mill, each ton of bauxite becomes ½ ton of aluminum oxide.
3. Aluminum Oxide is loaded on ore carrier and shipped to Scandinavia (where there is cheap hydroelectric power).
4. A smelter in Scandinavia turns each ton of aluminum oxide ¼ ton of aluminum ingots.
5. Ingots are shipped to Germany, heated to 900 degrees F and rolled to 1/8 inch.
6. Sheets of aluminum are shipped to another factory (in Germany or another country) and cold rolled to become 1/10 original thickness.
7. This aluminum is sent to England where sheets are punched and rolled into cans
8. Cans are washed, dried, and painted with a base coat.
9. Cans are painted with specific production branding and labeling.

Table 3. Lean methods as applied to environmental benefits (US EPA)

Lean Method	Potential Environmental Benefits
Kaizen Rapid Improvement Events	• continual improvement culture focused on eliminating waste • uncovering and eliminating hidden wastes and waste-generating activities • quick, sustained results without significant capital investment
5S (or 6S)	• decreased lighting, energy needs when windows are cleaned and equipment is painted light colors • spills and leaks noticed quickly • decreased potential for accidents and spills with clearly-marked and obstacle-free thoroughfares • reduced contamination of products results in fewer product defects (which reduces energy and resource needs; avoids waste) • reduced floor space needed for operations and storage; potential decrease in energy needs • less unneeded consumption of materials and chemicals when equipment, parts, and materials are organized, easy to find; less need for disposal of expired chemicals • visual cues can raise awareness of waste handling/management procedures, workplace hazards, and emergency response procedures
Cellular Manufacturing	• eliminates overproduction, thereby reducing waste and the use of energy and raw materials • fewer defects from processing and product changeovers- reduces energy and resource needs; avoids waste • defects are noticed earlier, preventing waste • less use of materials and energy (per unit of production) with right-sized equipment • less floor space needed; potential decrease in energy use and less need to construct new facilities • easier to focus on equipment maintenance, pollution prevention
Just-in-Time/ *Kanban*	• eliminates overproduction, thereby reducing waste and the use of energy and raw materials • less in-process and post-process inventory needed; avoids potential waste from damaged, spoiled, or deteriorated products • frequent inventory turns can eliminate the need for degreasing metal parts • less floor space needed; potential decrease in energy use and less need to construct new facilities • can facilitate worker-led process improvements • less excess inventory reduces energy use associated with transport and reorganization of unsold inventory
Total Productive Maintenance (TPM)	• fewer defects-reduces energy and resource needs; avoids waste • increased longevity of equipment decreases need for replacement equipment and associated environmental impacts (energy, raw materials, etc.) • decreased number and severity of spills, leaks, and upset conditions – less solid and hazardous waste
Six Sigma	• fewer defects – reduces energy and resource needs; avoids waste • can focus attention on reducing the conditions that result in accidents, spills, and malfunctions, thereby reducing solid and hazardous wastes • improving product durability and reliability can increase product lifespan, reducing environmental impact of meeting customer needs
Pre-Production Planning (3P)	• eliminates waste at product and process design stage, similar to "Design for Environment" methods • nature (inherently waste free) is used as a design model • right-sized equipment lowers material and energy requirements for production • reducing the complexity of the production process ("design for manufacturability") can eliminate or streamline process steps; environmentally sensitive processes can be targeted for elimination, since they are often time-, resource-, and capital-intensive • less complex product designs can use fewer parts and fewer types of materials, increasing the ease of disassembly and recycling
Lean Enterprise Supplier Networks	• magnification of environmental benefits of lean production (reduced waste through fewer defects, less scrap, less energy usage, etc.) across the network • environmental benefits are more broadly realized by introducing lean to existing suppliers rather than finding new, already lean suppliers

10. Cans are lacquered, flanged, sprayed inside with protective coating and inspected.
11. Cans are palletized, fork lifted, and warehoused until needed.
12. When needed, they are shipped to a bottler, washed and cleaned, and finally filled with beverage (this involved the mixed syrup, water, carbon dioxide, phosphorous and caffeine).
13. Filled cans are sealed with a pop-top and inserted into cardboard cartons, with matching color and proper promotional labeling.

14. Cartons are palletized again and shipped to regional warehouses and then to supermarkets.
15. A typical can is purchased with 3 days, consumed within minutes, and discarded in about one second.

The cartons come from forest pulp that may have originated anywhere from Sweden or Siberia to the old-growth, virgin forests of British Columbia that are the home of grizzly, wolverines, otters, and eagles. Beet fields in France provide the sugar, which undergoes significant trucking, milling, refining, and shipping. The phosphorus comes from the US state of Idaho, where it is excavated from deep open-pit mines—a process that also unearths cadmium and radioactive thorium. Round-the-clock, the mining company in Idaho uses the same amount of electricity as a city of 100,000 people in order produce food-grade phosphorous. The caffeine is shipped from a chemical manufacturer to the syrup manufacturer in England. In England, consumers discard 84 percent of all cans, which means that the overall rate of aluminum waste, after counting production losses, is 88 percent. The United States still gets three-fifths of its aluminum from virgin ore, at twenty times the energy intensity of recycled aluminum, and throws away enough aluminum to replace its entire commercial aircraft fleet every three months.

We realize that the example of the cola cans is a manufacturing process – an *operation*, and not a project – but we think it illustrates where a PM may be able to have a say in the reduction of waste, if the PM can become a change agent in the creation of the manufacturing process or if the PM can set an example in their projects that can be emulated by operations planning people in the organization.

The 5 Ss²

Let's look at one of these lean methods, "5S". This method actually focuses on a well lit, well-labeled, well cleaned workplace. We all sense that we'd work more efficiently (and have less waste) if our activities were more effective because, for example, we can see what we're doing, know where all of the components for the work are located, and don't have to look for documents or other items which are buried under other documents or items. The 5S method, which is Japanese in origin, uses these 5 "S" words (starting with S in Japanese and in loosely-translated English):

- Seiri → Sort
- Seiton → Straighten
- Seiso → Shine
- Seiketsu → Standardize
- Shitsuke → Sustain

Let's look at these in some detail (Figure 5)

- **Sort:** Clearly distinguish between components that are needed in a work area and components that are not, thereby eliminating sources of clutter and unwanted items.
- **Straighten:** Placing items in the work area in a logical arrangement, and establishing intuitive use guidelines; making the location visible and self-explanatory, so everyone knows what goes where.
- **Shine:** This refers literally to the cleanliness of floors, tools, machines, and equipment in the work place, and incorporates cleanliness into regular work duties.
- **Standardize:** Defines the standard activities, procedures, schedules, and the persons responsible for keeping the workplace clean and organized. As project managers, we're familiar with our tools for this, such as a WBS, a schedule and a RAM.
- **Sustain:** Make 5S an ingrained habit, spread the program to other functional and physical areas, and make it a company-wide routine.

Again, 5S is one of the many lean methods favored by organizations, refer to Table 3 for a

Figure 5. The 5S method

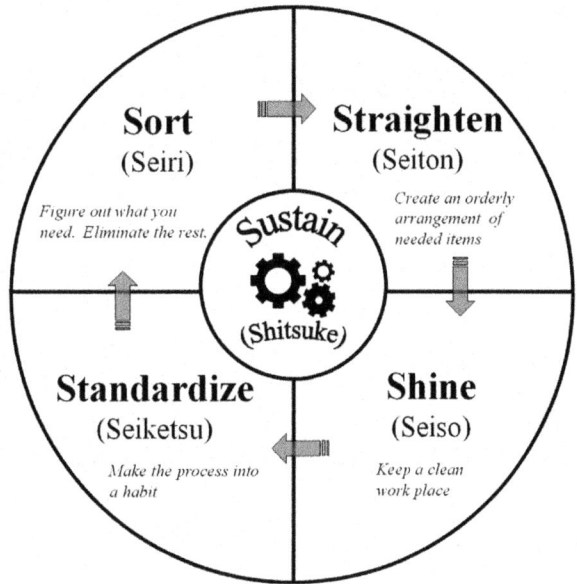

Source: *Green Project Management*, Richard Maltzman and David Shirley, CRC Press @2010, pg. 187.

Figure 6. EarthPM's 4L approach

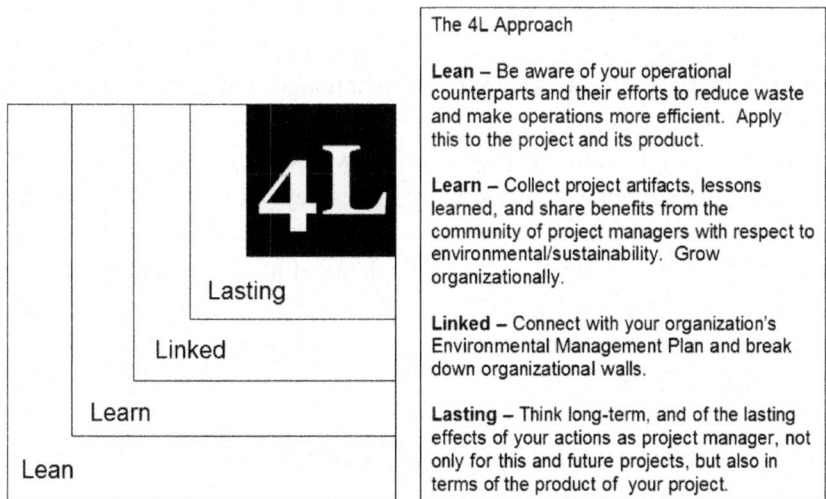

The 4L Approach

Lean – Be aware of your operational counterparts and their efforts to reduce waste and make operations more efficient. Apply this to the project and its product.

Learn – Collect project artifacts, lessons learned, and share benefits from the community of project managers with respect to environmental/sustainability. Grow organizationally.

Linked – Connect with your organization's Environmental Management Plan and break down organizational walls.

Lasting – Think long-term, and of the lasting effects of your actions as project manager, not only for this and future projects, but also in terms of the product of your project.

Source: *Green Project Management*, Richard Maltzman and David Shirley, CRC Press @2010, pg. 188

survey of the many others, and we urge you to understand how your organization uses these in the larger sense for operations.

Summary: The 4L Approach

To wrap up this section as well as to integrate other portions of our book we provide the 4L approach (Figure 6). The 4 Ls (Lean, Learn, Linked, and Lasting) describe how these aspects generally associated with operations can indeed be linked to the project and to the project managers and their team.

SOLUTIONS AND RECOMMENDATIONS

The authors, along with several other collaborators have formally suggested improvements to the Project Management Institute's PMBOK® Guide as well as PMI's Code of Ethics and Professional Responsibility.

We recommend that all of the organizational institutions that support the discipline of project management jointly issue a statement along the lines of that recently issued by The American Society of Civil Engineers (ASCE), the Canadian Society for Civil Engineering (CSCE) and the Institution of Civil Engineers (ICE):

ENVIRONMENTAL, SOCIAL AND ECONOMIC IMPACTS AND COSTS – THE TRIPLE BOTTOM LINE.

The three organizations are committed to improving methods for identifying and considering all of a project's environmental, social and economic costs and impacts throughout its life cycle. Practical approaches should be developed that would alter conventional accounting practices to factor in the direct and indirect environmental costs of a facility through its life-cycle of operations.

We think that the case ASCE, CSCE, and ICE have made for Civil Engineering is even truer and even more applicable for the project management discipline. As we have asserted in this chapter, we as PMs are at the pivot point between project ideation and operations. So, we further believe that the area of sustainability in project management needs more standardization so that, for example, meaningful credentials can be issued by a nonprofit organization truly dedicated to this focus.

To that end, the authors and other collaborators have established ISIS-PM (The International Society for the Integration of Sustainability and Project Management). More information about ISIS-PM can be found at http://www.isispm.org.

FUTURE RESEARCH DIRECTIONS

In order to be able to standardize, it is important that more research be done to help quantify the advantages of adopting (for example) long-term thinking in project management. In order to gain more support for the role that project managers play, it would be helpful to have more significant quantifiable data to prove that the effort spent in this area pays dividends not only for the environment, but for the enterprises themselves.

CONCLUSION

In this chapter, we highlighted the special significance of the project manager with respect to implementing sustainability, while identifying the challenges in taking on that role, and suggestions for overcoming those challenges. We have shown how adopting a sustainability thinking *mindset* goes beyond the natural focus of the PM on our immediate *scope*, and short-term *deliverables* for demanding *stakeholders*, and why that thinking is actually a strong advantage not only for the environment, but the enterprise.

REFERENCES

Goldratt, E. (1992). *The goal: A process of ongoing improvement*. Boston: North River Press.

Herazo, B., Lizarralde, G., & Paquin, R. (2012). Sustainable development in the building sector: A Canadian case study on the alignment of strategic and tactical management. *Project Management Journal, 43*(2).

Krane, H.P., Olsson, N.O.E., & Rolstadås, A. (2012). How project manager–Project owner interaction can work within and influence project risk management. *Project Management Journal, 43*(2).

Maltzman, R., & Shirley, D. (2010). *Green project management*. Boca Raton, FL: CRC Press. doi:10.1201/EBK1439830017.

Maltzman, R., & Shirley, D. (2011). *When unplugged is a bad thing*. Retrieved March 13, 2011 from http://www.earthpm.com

Poppendieck, M. (2002). *Principles of lean thinking*. Retrieved from http://www.poppendieck.com/papers/LeanThinking.pdf

Russo, M. V. (2010). *Companies on a mission*. Stanford, CA: Stanford University Press.

Schendler, A. (2009). *Getting green done*. New York, NY: Public Affairs Publishing.

Womack, J. P., & Jones, D. T. (1996). *Lean thinking: Banish waste and create wealth in your corporation*. New York: Simon and Schuster.

ADDITIONAL READING

Anderson, R. (2008). *Confessions of a radical industrialist*. New York, NY: St. Martins's Press.

Esty, D. C., & Simmons, P. J. (2011). *Green to gold business playbook*. Hoboken, NJ: John Wiley & Sons, Inc..

Esty, D. C., & Winston, A. S. (2009). *Green to gold*. Hoboken, NJ: Yale University Press.

Friedman, T. L. (2009). *Hot, flat and crowded*. New York, NY: Picador Press.

Friend, G. (2009). *The truth about green business*. Upper Saddle River, NJ: FT Press.

Hawken, P., Lovins, A., & Lovins, H. (1999). *Natural capitalism: Creating the next industrial revolution*. New York, NY: Little, Brown, and Company.

Phillips, P., & Phillips, J. (2011). *The green scorecard*. Boston, MA: Nicholas Brealey Publishing.

Smolen, D. (2010). *Tailoring the green suit*. Bloomington, IN: Author House.

Werbach, A. (2009). *Strategy for sustainability – Business manifesto*. Boston, MA: Harvard Business Press.

Wilhelm, K. (2009). *Return on sustainability*. Indianapolis, IN: Dog Ear Publishing.

KEY TERMS AND DEFINITIONS

Greenality: The degree to which an organization has considered environmental (green) factors that affects its projects during the entire life cycle and beyond.

Green IT: Considering sustainability (green) in information technology. It includes, but is not limited to, virtualization, cloud computing, energy efficient equipment, repurposing older equipment, etc.

Lean Thinking: A principle which takes into account (for any process) the continuous flow of value with value being defined by the customer). In this form of thinking, the customer "pulls" value from the provider and the process seeks to incrementally make improvements, seeking a perfect, waste-free process.

Life Cycle Assessment: A method, often accommodated with assistance from software, to determine how to minimize the environmental impact of a product or service taking into account the full effect of materials extracted, energy used, toxins produced, and so on, from the aspects of design, manufacturing, transportation, use, disposal, and reuse (a tool to assist in Long-Term Thinking).

Long-Term Thinking: Consideration of the product, service, or outcome from inception to disposal and possible re-use. See Life Cycle Assessment.

Muda: The Japanese word for waste. See text for discussion of The Seven Wastes.

Spectrum of Green: This is a scale for projects that goes from "*green by definition*" on one side of the spectrum to "*green in general*" on the other side.

Strategic Execution Framework: Stanford University's Strategic Execution Framework is used as a graphical illustration of the business process flow from the ideation phase to operations.

The 4 Ls: A mnemonic to remember a way increase the chances that sustainability in projects is ongoing, and made up of these four components – Lean (minimized wastes), Learn (using lessons learned to reduce project waste), Linked (connecting the project's goals to the enterprise's mission and operations), and Lasting (assuring that the project thinks in the long-term).

The 5S Philosophy: A way to organize a work area to minimize waste. The English translation of the 5 steps are: Sort, Straighten, Shine, Standardize, and Sustain.

ENDNOTES

[1] Based on: http://www.unep.org/resourceefficiency/Portals/24147/scp/presme/pdfs/UNEP_PRE_SME_ITH_Chapter_2.pdf

[2] Based on The U.S. Environmental Protection Agency, *Lean Manufacturing and the Environment*, 5S, 2009.

Chapter 17
Sustainability in Project Management:
Perceptions of Responsibility

Debby Goedknegt
HU University of Applied Sciences Utrecht, The Netherlands

ABSTRACT

When the project sponsor is responsible for the definition of the content of the project and the project manager for delivering this content, who then is responsible for incorporating sustainability in the process? Which project governance role has which responsibility to incorporate sustainability aspects in the project management process? This chapter shows how a project manager can influence the way sustainability is implemented in the project and the project management process. This perception is based on the notion that the project manager is intrinsically motivated to work on a sustainable project, and to achieve sustainable results.

INTRODUCTION

"In essence, sustainable development is a process of change in which the exploitation of resources, the direction of investments, the orientation of technological development; and institutional change are all in harmony and enhance both current and future potential to meet human needs and aspirations" (UN, 1987). This implies, as Nelmara Arbex has said, "We need to change the way we view things in order to change the way we do things." One of the key concepts of sustainability is that sustainability is about balancing or harmonizing social, environmental and economic interests, and it takes notice of both the short and the long term aspects. This is also known as the "Triple Bottom Line" (Elkington 1999); People (social), Planet (environmental), and Profit (economical).

DOI: 10.4018/978-1-4666-4177-8.ch017

Change towards sustainability asks for change on all three pillars of this triple bottom line. However, the question remains if it is necessary in all cases to give each of the three pillars an equal amount of attention or would that lead to non-realisable situations.

Project managers also have to ask themselves what the scope of sustainability is within their projects. Is the scope limited to the deliverables of the project, or does it concern more and does it also relate to the organization within which the project takes place? And are project managers able to integrate sustainability within the project's objectives and deliverables and in the project process? Silvius et al. (2010) say that the impact of sustainability is not really recognized yet. The way projects are managed, measured and reported does not reflect the different aspects of sustainability that can be derived from the concepts of sustainable development.

But then, what is sustainability? Sustainability is not a simple issue to grasp. Essentially it is not a methodology but a thinking dimension (Jaafari 2007). Alzami (2010) describes sustainability as each of us doing our part to build the kind of world – economically, environmentally and socially – that we want to live in, and one that we want our children and grandchildren to inherit. It means becoming aware of all interconnections – visible and invisible – in which our day-to-day choices affect the intricate balance of social, economic and ecological systems.

Thus, sustainability has to do with the use of resources that will not be exhausted over a reasonable period and that a system or process must not generate pollution. Furthermore, a definition of a project, OGC (2002) gives two definitions of a project:

1.   A management environment that is created for the purpose of delivering one or more business products according to a specific Business Case.

2.   A temporary organization that is needed to produce a unique and predefined outcome or result at a pre-specified time using pre-determined resources.

It is therefore assumed that a project is a temporary organization created for the purpose of delivering a unique and predefined outcome at a pre-specified time and within in pre-determined resources.

Within projects, the project sponsor is ultimately responsible for the project. He provides the finances, provides direction on the content of the project and ensures that the attention is kept focussed on the business justification (Hermarij 2010). This means that the project sponsor is also responsible for incorporating sustainability in the content and the business justification. The project manager takes responsibility for all activities necessary to provide the project deliverables (Hermarij 2010). This would imply that the project manager can incorporate sustainability within his project management process. To what extend is able to do so? Are there parts of the project management process where his influence is the biggest and in which the smallest? The research question is defined as follows:

What influence does a project manager have on the way sustainability is implemented in the project and in the project management process?

Approach

This chapter is based on a literature study and a case study. For this research, a case study seems appropriate because the main purpose is to show whether or not a project manager does have influence on the implementation of sustainability within the project management process. Little literature on this topic is yet available. This paper tries to contribute to the discussion which project management roles have what influence on aspects of sustainability within the project management process.

At first a literature study was conducted. Most literature was found through the 'Science Direct' data base. The key words that were used to find the papers were: 'sustainab*', 'sustainab* + project management', 'corporate social responsibility'. Other papers have been found by going to the reference list of the papers that were found.

After the literature review, a case study was prepared and executed. Data was collected from this case. The data was processed, analysed and compared to the theory. Finally a conclusion was drawn from the data.

LITERATURE REVIEW

Project managers are instrumental in achieving strategic goals, as they hold the path to execution. The project manager is in a position to perceive and analyse socially relevant issues and situations that may not be obvious to senior management. It is his responsibility to ensure that issues are raised appropriately. The social issues, like discrepancies between the minimums that the law requires and what is appropriate for the community (e.g. sustainability issues) can be ranked the same way as all other project risks, by probability and impact (Russell 2008). Does Russell imply that dealing with sustainability, as a social issue, is synonymous to other project risks?

Gareis et al. (2009) have a different opinion. Although they argue that they suspect that the consideration of sustainable development in project management supports the achievement of sustainable project results. They say that content related definitions of sustainable development are not relevant when it comes to discuss a possible integration into project management, however the context related definition should be further explored. It is the context where the project manager can make a difference. Silvius et al (2010) say that the general insight is that sustainability

in project management is about integrating economic, environmental and social aspects in the management of projects, and that sustainability in projects should be regarded on the level of the project, its results and its effect. Silvius et al. (2009) derived a the following definition of sustainable project management from combining the triple-P element of sustainability and the life cycle views:

Sustainable project management is the management of project-orientated change in policies, assets or organizations, with consideration of the economic, social, and environmental impact of the project, its result, and its effect, for now and for future generations.

Taylor (2008) argues succinctly that sustainability needs to be incorporated into every stage throughout the project life cycle.

Grevelman and Kluiwstra (2009) state, in line with Gareis et al. (2009) that the alignment between sustainability and project management is still very rare. Their case study revealed no attention to sustainability within the project management process. It did however reveal that attention to sustainability was given to the project's deliverables, however attention to sustainability within the project process was absent. They claim that the reason for this is the lack of attention to sustainability in project management deliverables. Although that particular finding is not of great interest to this case study, it is an interesting finding. Grevelman and Kluiwstra (2009) also found that although there is a lot of awareness regarding sustainability, the link to defining a sustainable process and methodology for project management is still absent.

Labuschagne and Brent (2006) state that projects are the means by which sustainability on all three corporate levels (strategic, methodological, and operational) can be made, and that business has the responsibility towards society to actively engage in the sustainable arena. Furthermore, they argue that the current project management frameworks do not effectively address the three goals of sustainable development (social equity, economic efficiency and environmental performance). This is underpinned by Silvius et al. (2010) who have found that sustainability is the big missing factor in major project management guidelines of PMBoK and ICB3. They give three reasons why they believe that sustainability should be on the agenda of project managers: (1) investments in projects that are considered sustainable are less prone to the financial crises as non-sustainable projects; (2) companies that have a strong sustainability image, like certain banks, show less loss of value than other banks; (3) public organizations are integrating criteria on sustainability in their procurement policies, thereby stimulating companies to be more active in this area.

Turner (2010) takes a different perspective towards sustainable development and project management. He does not point towards business as a large, rather anonymous group, but addresses all project governance roles. He has looked into the responsibilities for key players on projects and programs for the implementation of sustainable initiatives. He argues that in project management, sustainability can be gained both in the product of the project and in the process of delivering the product. He mentions six concepts of project management that are relevant for incorporating aspects of, sustainability: (1) project objectives; (2) project scope and schedule; (3) project resources, cost, income, and risk; (4)project organization; (5) project context; (6) design of the project management process. He also argues that no research has been done as yet on responsibility for different participants on projects and programs for the implementation of sustainability. However, using the six principles of sustainability: (1) holistic approach; (2) long term view; (3) large scale; (4) risk and uncertainty reduction; (5) values and ethics; (6) participation (Gareis et al. 2009), coupled with a governance model for projects and programs, suggests what may be the responsibility for some of the key players. Table

1 shows the relation between the six objectives of consideration and the six guiding principles of sustainable development.

Table 2 shows the responsibilities that some of the role performers may have for the six principles of sustainability. Turner (2010) has changed the position of Values and Ethics because he believes that this is where it starts. What are the corporate values of both the client organization and the delivery organization, what is their attitude towards corporate social responsibility, and what is their ethical position on preserving the environment for our grandchildren? In the final remarks of his paper, Turner (2010) furthermore mentions that the model presented is not offered as a solution, but as a suggested model to generate discussion.

CASE STUDY

Structure

Turner's model is interesting because it is the first model that tries to generate a discussion on the responsibilities that different project governance roles can have regarding the implementation of sustainability principles. He has made suggestions what may be the responsibilities of these key players. This paper will make a first attempt to test Turner's suggestions. For this, a case study approach has been chosen. The selected case is a project called "Duurzame Uithof"[1]. This project is a part of the program "De Omslag", which means "the turnaround" or similar. It is a program in which the University of Applied Science Utrecht intents to make the turnaround towards a sustainable educational institute. In this case study the PID and the Business Case of the project are studied and four interviews are conducted. The interviews are conducted from the program manager, the main project manager, one of the three minor project managers, and the client.

Table 1. Sustainable development and project management (after Gareis, et al., 2009; Turner, 2010)

Sustainability principles	Project management					
	Project objectives	Scope & Schedule	Resources & Income	Organization	Context	Design of the Process
1. Holistic approach	Hi	Hi	Hi	Hi	Hi	Hi
2. Long term view	Lo	Lo	Hi	Hi	Hi	Lo
3. Large scale	Hi	Lo	Lo	Lo	Hi	Lo
4. Risk reduction	Lo	Lo	Hi	Lo	Hi	Hi
5. Values and Ethics	Hi	Lo	Lo	Hi	Hi	Hi
6. Participation	Hi	Lo	Lo	Hi	Hi	Hi

Table 2. Sustainable development and project governance roles (Turner, 2010)

Sustainability principles	Project governance roles					
	Client Owner	Program Manager	Sponsor	Project Manager	Senior User	Senior Supplier
1. Values and Ethics	Hi	Med	Med	Med	Med	Med
2. Holistic approach	Hi	Med	Med	Lo	Lo	Lo
3. Long term view	Hi	Hi	Med	Lo	Lo	Lo
4. Large scale	Hi	Hi	Med	Med	Lo	Lo
5. Risk reduction	Lo	Hi	Med	Hi	Hi	Hi
6. Participation	Lo	Med	Med	Hi	Hi	Hi

Yin (2003) has defined a case study as an empirical inquiry within its real-life context, particularly when the boundaries between phenomena and context are not clearly evident. A case study can best be conducted when (Yin, 2003) (1) "how" or "why" questions are being posed, (2) when the investigator has little control over events, and (3) when the focus is on a contemporary phenomenon within some real life context. This paper is based on case study research because two of the three preconditions are met. The case study method allows the investigator to remain the holistic and meaningful characteristics of real life events (Yin, 2003) and is therefore extremely suitable for this research on the big theme of sustainability. Here the holistic and meaningful characteristics

are particularly important in trying to grasp the true meaning and preconditions and influence of sustainability in projects and project management.

The goal of a case study is, in general, to expand and generalize theories, called analytic generalization. In this type of generalization, the basis is formed by a theory which is used as a template with which the empirical results of the case study are compared. In this multiple case studies are preferred over single case studies, since the latter is found vulnerable in proving or rejecting theories (Yin, 2003).

Turner's (2010) model, which is partly based on the findings of Gareis et al (2009) is the theory that is going to be tested in a single case. Turner has showed the responsibilities that some of the role performers may have for the six principles of sustainability. In this case study only two of the sustainability principles and three of the project governance roles are taken into account (Table 3).

This is the starting point of the case study. It is investigated whether the assumptions made by Turner are also true for the project "Duurzame Uithof" of the University of Applied Sciences Utrecht.

Case Description

At first there was some confusion about the name of the project "Duurzame Uithof". There appear to be two projects/programs with this name. The objective of the program "Duurzame Uithof" is to develop the entire Uithof area towards a sustainable Utrecht Science Park in 2040. Participants in this program are Utrecht Science Park, Universiteit Utrecht, Hogeschool Utrecht and Utrecht Medisch Centrum. This program is in line with the intention to aspire a sustainable and alluring Utrecht region. The Uithof wants to be the laboratory for innovative sustainable measures regarding energy, water, mobility and construction. Moreover, Utrecht Science Park wants to be the centre of the knowledge economy of the Utrecht province. The focus of the project is on four subjects: energy, water, mobility and sustainable building. The project objectives are:

- **Energy:** Reducing the amount of energy used by businesses, promote the transition from fossil fuels towards sustainable energy sources.

- **Water:** Optimising the water cycle and minimising waste, the ultimate goal is a closed water cycle.
- **Mobility:** Stimulating the use of the bicycle and public transport, making the remaining car use energy-neutral.
- **Sustainable Building:** Developing sustainable new buildings and making existing buildings more sustainable in the area of recycling demolition and waste streams.

The project will deliver new concepts and methods regarding the sustainable development of the whole area. By developing and applying multi-disciplined knowledge, (system)innovations can be realised. Cooperation between the several partners is therefore an important prerequisite for the transition towards a sustainable Uithof.

The project is an initiative of the Faculty of Engineering that fits perfectly within their program "De Omslag". "De Omslag" means as much as "the turnaround", and is a program in which the University of Applied Science Utrecht intents to make the turnaround towards a sustainable educational institute. Within the program, several (student) projects are executed within the themes mobility, civil engineering and architecture, energy and installation engineering. The objectives of these projects were not determined beforehand. This project aims to deliver an inspirational document that will form the basis of future programs and projects within "De Omslag".

The project objectives all have to do with sustainability. Are just the objectives and with that the deliverables meant to be sustainable, or is it also important that these deliverables are developed in

Table 3. Case study starting point (derived from Turner, 2010)

Sustainability Principles	Project governance roles		
	Client/Owner	Program Manager	Project Manager
2. Holistic approach	High	Medium	Low
3. Long-term view	High	High	Low

a sustainable way? And then, who is responsible for achieving this? Does the project manager have any influence on the developing process of the deliverables? In this project, the project manager has not been involved in the writing of the project plan, which could imply that he has no or limited influence on the way sustainability is implemented in the project. But, does this also say something about the way sustainability is/can be implemented in the project management process?

Turner (2010) states that the owner is ultimately responsible for the holistic approach. And that the program manager has a responsibility for instructing and guiding the project manager in the holistic approach. On the long-term view he states that again the client should set the policy for the long-term view, but it is the role of the program manager to ensure it is implemented.

The data collection strategy that is used is that first the questionnaire was set up and the project was selected in discussion the program manager. After that the Business Case and the PID were studied and finally four interviews were conducted. However, first the questionnaire was tested in an interview with the program director. The date collected from this interview has not been implemented in this research.

CASE STUDY RESULTS

In this case study the Project Initiation Document and the Business Case of the project are studied and four interviews are conducted. The interviews are conducted with the program manager, the main project manager, one of the three minor project managers, and the client. Of these four interviews, only three are valid for this interview. In the interview with the perceived client/owner it became clear that she is responsible for the program "Duurzame Uithof" that is being set up by Utrecht Science Park, Universiteit Utrecht, Hogeschool Utrecht and Utrecht Medisch Cetrum,

but not for the project "Duurzame Uithof" of the Faculty of Engineering. The latter is not a part of the program "Duurzame Uithof" of these four major partners.

It is perceived by the interviewees that both holistic approach and long-term view are important aspects of sustainability and are both present within the project. However, a sustainability impact assessment has not been conducted, a baseline has not been set. That makes it difficult to really measure the impact of the projects within "De Omslag". Within the several projects multi-criteria analysis are used in order to make the right decision within the projects. For instance in the architectural project, multi-criteria analysis is used to make sure that all choices are not only based on sustainability aspects, but also on usability aspects. Unfortunately in this phase no other actors are involved in decision-making. Decisions are merely based on the expertise of the project managers and the input of the students working on the projects. In these decisions, and in the consideration of issues and risks the needs of future generations are addressed. This is perceived as something that comes natural when dealing with sustainability aspects. This perception also goes for social learning aspects, innovation and design.

All interviewees have been asked to fill out Turner's table. In Table 4 the deviations between Turner's assumptions and the outcomes of this case study are made visible. In this research it is perceived that the program manager has a high responsibility for regarding the holistic approach and the long-term view and that the project manager has a medium responsibility regarding these two aspects. So, the program manager is perceived to have more responsibility in both holistic approach and long-term view. This is perceived to be so, because the program manager is expected to have the overview. She knows the ultimate goal and expected benefits of the whole program. Both project managers only focus on their own project, on the delivering of the expected project results.

Table 4. Case study starting point (derived from Turner, 2010) and results

| | Project governance roles | | | | | |
| | Client/Owner | | Program Manager | | Project Manager | |
Sustainability Principles	*Turner*	*Case*	*Turner*	*Case*	*Turner*	*Case*
2. Holistic approach	High	High	Medium	High	Low	Medium
3. Long-term view	High	High	High	High	Low	Medium

The responsibility seems hierarchically defined. The program manager has more responsibility than the project manager and the client/owner has the highest responsibility as she sets the limits for the whole program. As one of the project managers said: "The client/owner has the highest responsibility for implementing sustainability in the project, because she has to determine whether or not to continue the program and thus to take the right steps. ... program and project managers must receive the right information from above". One of the project managers said about the influence of the program manager: "The long term view of the program manager must be high, the program must have a long term vision. This project is not a stand-alone within the University of Applied Sciences Utrecht. My long-term view is medium, because I am the general foreman". The program manager herself said about her perception of het holistic approach responsibility: "My responsibility for the holistic approach is high, because I am constantly switching between the different scale-levels."

CONCLUSION AND FUTURE RESEARCH RECOMMENDATIONS

It is perceived by the interviewer that the interviewees attribute a lot of intrinsic motivation and responsibility for sustainability to themselves and the other project governance roles. It is also perceived that they believe that one is being asked to fulfil a role in a sustainability project because of one's affinity with the context. The program manager only works with motivated project managers, because they are asked to do the job based on their affinity and expertise with the content and context of the project. The project managers are merely content project managers who do not have to execute project management tasks that do not connect with their profession, like communication with several stakeholders, budgeting, quality management.

The answer to the main research question of this paper is therefore that it is believed that a project manager can influence the way sustainability is implemented in the project and the project management process. His influence is regarded 'medium' for both holistic approach and long-term view. However, this perception is based on the notion that the project manager is intrinsically motivated to work on a sustainable project and achieve sustainable results. This is an interesting outcome that must be further explored in other case studies, because it also generates new questions. Does it mean that the degree to which sustainability is implemented on a project is dependent on the project manager's preferences. Is a project manager only appointed to obtain a predetermined project result? Does it mean that a project manager can have content related knowledge and influence? Or is this conclusion just a reflection of the chosen case?

REFERENCES

Alzamil, R. K. (2010). How project managers increase the sustainability of their projects. In *Proceeding s of IPMA Expert Seminar February 2010*. Zurich, Switzerland: IPMA.

Elkington, J. (1999). *Cannibals with forks: The triple bottom line of the 21st century business.* Sussex, UK: Wiley &Sons Ltd..

Gareis, R., Heumann, M., & Martinuzzi, A. (2009). *Relating sustainable development and project management.* Berlin: IRNOP IX.

Grevelman, L., & Kluiwstra, M. (2009). *Sustainability in project management: A case study on Enexis.* (Thesis). International MSc Real Estate Management at the University of Greenwich, Greenwich, UK.

Hermarij, J. (2010). *The better practices of project management.* The Netherlands: Dhirita B.V., Oudekerk a/d Amstel.

Jaafari, A. (2007). Thinking of sustainability as a dimension of managerial competency. *PM World Today, 9*(9).

Labuschagne, C., & Brent, A. C. (2006). Sustainable project life cycle management: The need to integrate life cycles in the manufacturing sector. *International Journal of Life Cycle Assessment, 11*(1), 3–15.

Office of Government Commerce (OGC). (2002). *Prince2.* London: The Stationary Office.

Russell, J. (2008). Corporate social responsibility: What it means for the project manager. In *Proceedings of PMI Europe Congress.* Philadelphia, PA: Project Management Institute.

Silvius, A. J. G., Brink, J., & Köhler, A. (2009). Views on sustainable project management. In *Human Side of Projects in Modern Business.* Kalle Kähköhnen, Abdul.

Silvius, A. J. G., Brink, J., & Köhler, A. (2010a). *The impact of sustainability on project management.* Paper presented at the Asia Pacific Research Conference on Project Management (APRPM). Melbourne, Australia.

Silvius, A. J. G., Brink, J., & Köhler, A. (2010b). The concept of sustainability and its application to project management. In *Proceeding s of IPMA Expert Seminar.* Zurich, Switzerland: IPMA.

Silvius, A. J. G., Brink, J., & Köhler, A. (2010c). *Sustainability in project management, questions and responsibilities.* Paper presented at the International Conference on Sustainability in Business (ICBS). Putrajaya, Kuala Lumpur.

Silvius, A. J. G., & Schipper, R. (2010). *A maturity model for integrating sustainability in projects and project management.* Paper presented at the 24th IPMA World Congress. Istanbul, Turkey.

Taylor, T. (2008). *A sustainability checklist for managers of projects.* Retrieved from http://www.pmforum.org/library/papers/2008/PDFs/Taylor-1-08.pdf

Turner, R. (2010). Responsibilities for sustainable development in project and program management. In *Proceeding s of IPMA Expert Seminar.* Zurich, Switzerland: IPMA.

Yin, R. K. (2003). *Case study research. design and methods.* Thousand Oaks, CA: Sage Publications.

ENDNOTES

[1] Duurzame Uithof means Sustainable Uithof. The Uithof is the area where most of the educational buildings of the Utrecht University and the University of Applied Sciences Utrecht are located as well as the Utrecht Medical Centre (a large hospital) and the Utrecht Botanical Gardes are located as well as some minor shops, a hockey club, and some student housing.

Chapter 18
Sustainability Assessment for Project Managers

Gilman C. K. Tam
Independent Researcher, Hong Kong

ABSTRACT

In the two decades since the Earth Summit in 1992, an increasing number of projects have built sustainability considerations into project design and implementation. Project managers without knowledge and guidance on sustainability assessment would find it difficult to drive projects and programs contributing towards a sustainable society. The purpose of this chapter is to devise an assessment tool for project managers incorporating the concept of pillar-based and principles-based sustainability approaches as well as the EIA-driven and objectives-led assessment methodologies. The definitions of sustainability in project management and program management are discussed as basis for the establishment of sustainability evaluation framework. The views of project management community regarding the role of project manager in handling project related sustainability activities are discussed. This chapter contributes to devising a practical assessment tool for project managers in managing project sustainability.

INTRODUCTION

Apart from the threat of hostilities and terrorism, it seems certain that climate change and the exhaustion of natural fossil fuel resources will provide the biggest challenges in the future. We shall need effective project managers to deal with these challenges if humankind is to survive (Lock, 2007, p. 5).

Lock raises concern about sustainability of humankind (Lock, 2007). He is well aware that project managers need to face the kind of challenges like climate change and lack of fossil fuel in the days to come. Project managers are becoming part of the solution to human survival or sustainable development – a popular term after Gro Harlem Brundtland releasing the well-known "Brundtland Report" in 1987. She puts down the definition of

DOI: 10.4018/978-1-4666-4177-8.ch018

sustainable development as "the development that meets the needs of the present without compromising the ability of future generations to meet their own needs" (Brundtland, 1987). Her basic emphases are on long-term aspects of the concept of sustainability and equity between the present and future generations. The context in which Brundtland's definition is embedded indicates that '*needs*' include a sound environment, a just society and a healthy economy (Diesendorf, 2000). It links to what people perceive for a change in behavior, attitudes, and consumption patterns, etc. towards sustainability and equity, and how society perceives and values the environment. In the eyes of Diesendorf, 'Development' covers social and economic improvement in a broad sense and which may or may not involve economic growth. The emphasis is on 'qualitative improvement in human-being' or 'unfolding of human potential' as discussed by the ecological economist, Herman Daly (Diesendorf, 2000).

The Agenda 21, which is a comprehensive blueprint of action as adopted by more than 178 governments at the United Nations in the 1992 Earth Summit in Rio de Janeiro, Brazil, called for global partnership and drove governments, business and industry for sustainable development (UNCED, 1992). While most discussions on sustainability and sustainable development focus on political or policy level issues and global concerns, a research supported by the U.S. Agency for International Development (USAID), the United Nations Environment Programme (UNEP) and the University of Minnesota addressed the equally important focus at the project level – how to conduct project for better performing sustainable development. Gregersen, Lundgren and White (1994) in their policy brief suggested changing the project approach to assure more sustainable benefit flows through project activities for the sake of improving the contribution of projects to sustainable development and avoiding unsustainability (Gregersen, Lundgren, & White, 1994).

Munier (2005, p. 21) in his book "Introduction to Sustainability: Road to a Better Future" mentions that "Sustainability as a process often involves making an analysis to determine the best course of action when several projects, plans, programs, and options are considered" (Munier, 2005). Project exists in a relatively turbulent environment and change is the purpose of the project itself and uncertainty is inherent in the objectives of that project. A Guide to the Project Management Body of Knowledge, PMBoK (4th edition) published by the Project Management Institute (PMI) recognizes "… Projects can also have social, economic, and environmental impacts that far outlast the projects themselves" (PMI, 2008). Since project management is becoming a common way of managing business (Bredillet, 2000; Turner, 2009), the awareness of project manager and his/her team members to meeting the challenges of sustainability in project delivery would have made contributions to mankind.

As a prerequisite, project managers need to understand sustainability and its relationship to project management before they can make contributions towards a sustainable world. In the project management community, sustainability emerges as a subject in the recent academic research. For instance, Gareis, Huemann and Martinuzzi (Gareis, Huemann, & Martinuzzi, 2009) presented a paper titled "Relating sustainable development and project management" at The International Research Network on Organizing by Projects (IRNOP) in the IRNOP IX Research Conference (Berlin, Germany, 11-13, October 2009) and another paper of related topic was presented at the Project Management Institute (PMI) Research and Education Conference 2010 (Washington, D.C., USA, 11-14, July 2010) (Gareis, Huemann, & Martinuzzi, 2010); and Silvius, van den Brink and Köhler (2010) presented a paper titled "The concept of sustainability and its application to project management" at the International Project Management Association (IPMA) International

Expert Seminar 2010 (Zurich, Switzerland, 18-19, February 2010) (Silvius, van den Brink, & Köhler, 2010). These research activities confirm the suggestion of Lock (2007) that effective project managers are required to deal with the challenges of climate change or sustainability for the well-being of humankind.

To deliver projects in a sustainable way, sustainability assessment within the project management process is important to drive for success. Though people understand the necessity of assessing sustainability, there is no unified approach to such assessment. Furthermore, except some authors such as Silvius and Schipper (Silvius & Schipper, 2010) wrote on sustainability assessment, there is generally a lack of guiding principles for project managers to conduct sustainability assessment which hinders the promotion of positive and minimization of negative project impacts towards a sustainable society.

The purpose of this chapter is to introduce the role of project managers and provide an assessment tool for managing project sustainability impacts whether by ways of ex-ante assessment or ex-post evaluation. It discusses the definitions of sustainability in project management and program management, sustainability approach, sustainability evaluation framework and assessment methodologies proposed for managing project sustainability impacts in the project management process.

THE ROLE OF PROJECT MANAGER

Mui and Sankaran (2004) suggest that sustainability development (e.g. urban renewal project) requires project managers to adopt a holistic perspective and a cradle-to-grave approach in managing projects. They have identified that current project management body of knowledge ignores the professional knowledge of sustainability and

that no guidance on suitability of *generalizing specialists* (project management specialist with general sustainability knowledge) or *specializing generalists* (sustainability manager with general project management knowledge) taking the role of project leader (Mui & Sankaran, 2004).

Mui et al. (2004) comment that project participants should possess sustainability knowledge and the infrastructure project team leader should have experience as generalizing specialist rather than specializing generalist. Furthermore, they find that sustainability is a contemporary issue considered by many global nations as an essential task for maintaining the future prosperity of human beings. To accomplish such a task, these nations adopt a multi-disciplinary and integrated project team approach to implement the change. Hence, Mui et al. suggest that the project management body of knowledge should include this essential knowledge area and should emphasize the importance of a multi-disciplinary and integrated approach (Mui & Sankaran, 2004).

I have conducted a survey in 2012 with 101 convenience samples received from the project management community and engineering institution. One of the questions focused on job responsibility of project sustainability activities as shown:

Care of project sustainability (economic, environmental and social) activities is the job of sustainability manager (professional specialized in sustainability activities) and not the job of project manager.

Out of the samples, sixty (60) responses did not agree with the statement (Strongly Disagree: 15; Disagree: 45; Neutral: 20; Agree: 16; Strongly Agree: 5). In other words, most respondents (59.4%) think that project related sustainability activities should be the responsibility of project manager. When I asked about whether *"Sustainability as essential knowledge area shall be included in the published guidebook of project management body of knowledge"*, seventy five (75) respondents responded either agree or strongly agree in a five points Likert Scale (Strongly Disagree: 1; Disagree: 3; Neutral: 22; Agree: 49; Strongly Agree: 26) which represented 74.3%. This indicates an urgent need for the inclusion of sustainability knowledge area in the project management body of knowledge to help project managers in this respect.

Though project managers are recognized by most of the survey respondents as responsible person for project sustainability works, they are not supported by the project management body of knowledge. The lack of literature covering sustainability in the realm of project management needs to be remedied to gain competitive advantages in today's world. Raising awareness and developing sustainability mindsets within the project team are important. Establishing a culture of care to the environment, people (stakeholders); and the communities involved in would help the delivery of project. Understanding of what sustainability means at a big picture level as well as what it means at a tangible day-to-day level is part of the challenge (Griffiths, 2007).

Nurturing sustainability competence as a managerial competency in professional people alongside other core competences resulting in outcomes that are financially sound, environmentally sustainable and socially responsible is important (Jaafari, 2007). It is also a capability requirement for project manager to assess sustainability impacts. Jaafari (2007) recommends teaching sustainability through project-based learning to professionals rather than discipline-based learning, as it provides a paradigm for creativity and achievement of balanced solutions through engagement in realistic assignments. The following sections would help project managers in building relevant sustainability skills for their upcoming projects.

THE SUSTAINABILITY APPROACH

The Three-Pillar Approach

Following to the Brundtland Report and Earth Summit, many researchers are researching the concept and meaning of sustainability. It typically considers three main areas of concern, namely: environmental (planet), social (people), and economic (prosperity) (Gibb, 2004). John Elkington in his 1998 book *"Cannibals with Forks: the Triple Bottom Line of 21st Century Business"* refers these main areas of concern to as the Triple Bottom Line (TBL) (Elkington, 2004). This TBL or three-pillar approach is commonly used in analyzing problems, nevertheless, some would prefer other pillar approaches such as the two intersecting pillars (the ecological and the human) or five-pillar approach (ecological, economic, political, social and cultural) to assess sustainability (R. B. Gibson, 2006).

Considering sustainability through a three-pillar approach, it involves the promotion of:

Economic sustainability – increasing profitability through efficient use of resources (human, materials, financial), effective design and good management, planning and control; Environmental sustainability – preventing harmful and irreversible effects on the environment by efficient use of natural resources, encouraging renewable resources, protecting the soil, water, air from contaminations and others; and Social sustainability – responding to the needs of society including users, neighbours, community, workers and other project stakeholders" (Zainul Abidin & Pasquire, 2007).

The TBL separating the concept of sustainability into three pillars tends to build up the so called "silo effect." It means that individual pillar tends to competing resource and always involving trade-off in decision-making. It is difficult to promote inter-linkages and interdependencies of various pillars (Pope, Annandale, & Morrison-Saunders, 2004) even though they are conceptualized as three intersecting circles representing the environment, society and the economy (Gibson, 2001). This reductionist approach dividing the holistic concept of sustainability into three pillars runs the risk of having the sum of the parts being less than the whole (Pope, et al., 2004).

The Principles-Based Approach

Other than pillars approach, Gibson (2001) promotes the use of principles-based approach to sustainability assessment. Sustainability criteria are generated from those principles in place rather than derived from TBL goals. He argues that the principles-based approach could handle the inter-linkages and interdependencies of pillars without the necessity of competing for resource and trade-offs. Gibson (2006) takes this approach and utilizes a set of general sustainability requirements (core obligations) for sustainability-oriented decision makers. These core generic criteria include: (1) socio-ecological system integrity; 2) livelihood sufficiency and opportunity; (3) intra-generational equity; (4) inter-generational equity; (5) resource maintenance and efficiency; (6) socio-ecological civility and democratic governance; (7) precaution and adaptation; and (8) immediate and long term integration (Gibson, 2006). The specific of each item and the package as a whole for the core generic criteria must be defined in context (define what and how as part of project specification). See Appendix 1 for detail requirements of core generic criteria.

Selection of different sustainability approach for assessment would lead to different sustainability outcomes in the route to a sustainable world. For instance, considering a land redevelopment project, social sustainability impact assessment under the three-pillar approach would many a time consider more on current impacts to residents in terms of provision of better environment to the community and jobs creation etc. But for the principles-based approach, it has to consider inter-generational and intra-generational equity, for example, preserving part of the heritage of the community for future generations. As a consequence, a different decision would be made. Although pillar view is easy to be conceptualized, it is not necessarily reflecting a holistic view of sustainability due to inherent difficulty in promoting the between pillars sustainability contributions. Principles-based view, on the other hand, covers a wider scope in assessing sustainability contributions on strategies, policies, plans, programs and projects. However, use of such view in the real world is still subject to limitations, for instance, unavoidable trade-offs and context dependent.

SUSTAINABILITY IN PROJECT MANAGEMENT

Sustainability is not a simple concept to define and there are a large number of interpretations (Epstein, 2008; Pope, et al., 2004; Robert, Daly, Hawken, & Holmberg, 1997). Early development was largely influenced by Brundtland (1987) through her report "Our Common Future" and her definition of sustainable development. She has pointed out intra-generational development and inter-generational equity; and the needs of sound environment, just society and healthy economy. In the last two decades since the 1992 Earth Summit, an increasing number of projects have built in sustainability considerations into project design and implementation. For instance, Mohamed Eid (2002) in his paper at the PMI Research Conference 2002 brought in an example of construction industry in the U.K. that construction companies have to face challenges to integrate the vital environmental and social considerations into their daily management.

According to Eid (2002, p. 206), "The goal of sustainability is the process of systematically and effectively integrating vital environmental and social concerns into economic development, financial planning, and project management". In his opinion, the integration of project management, sustainability and industry competitiveness (for example, quality, markets, equitable market conditions, etc.) would deliver a clearer business case for sustainable construction (Eid, 2002). Labuschagne & Brent (2004) describe clear understanding of the various project life cycles and their interactions between life cycles and the external environment and society as prerequisite for managing project sustainability (Labuschagne & Brent, 2004).

Project management as an evolving academic discipline and professional practice was developing in response to the needs of society. For instance, early days of modern project management focused on efficiency of managing project; and then focus has been changed to effective implementation of corporate strategy and effecting organizational change in the 1990s (Baccarini, 1999). The Shenhar and Dvir paper describe central concept of project management since 2000 as adaptation (one size does not fit all); strategic alignment (connect project management to business); and globalization (off-shore projects) (Shenhar & Dvir, 2004). External environmental influences including economic, political, community, and ecological impacts started to become essential dimensions on assessing policies, programs, plans, and projects after the Earth Summit. Public opposition to construction of nuclear power station due to safety reason was one manifestation (Baccarini, 1999). Project management plays a role in sustainability.

Project management with increasing emphasis on handling external environmental factors has set the tone for it being an active driver for sustainability. Projects delivered with well-structured sustainability impacts meet with the changing needs of a sustainable society. Typically, three-pillar approach is widely adopted in the project community. Take projects seeking project finance as example, the Equator Principles Financial Institutions (EPFIs) require projects to conduct

social and environmental assessment (Equator Principles). The EPFIs commit not to provide loans to projects where the borrower is unable to comply with their respective social and environmental policies and procedures. Hence, many project managers are working towards these goals without aware of taking the three-pillar approach in their assessment. In practice, it would be easier for project managers to assess project sustainability impacts by this approach due to ease of conceptualization (three intersecting circles). Other principles-based approach can also be selected if project managers find it appropriate to assess the same from a different perspective.

Definitions

Tam (2010a) suggests a definition of "Sustainability in Project Management" with reference to the definition of project management under the APM Body of Knowledge (APM BoK, 5th edition). The underlined portion next is taken out from the APM BoK (APM, 2006):

The promoting of positive and minimizing of negative sustainability impacts (economic; environmental; and social) within "the process by which projects are defined, planned, monitored, controlled and delivered such that the agreed benefits are realized" and contributing to a sustainable society (Tam, 2010a).

Two key components are included in this definition reflecting the attributes of sustainability in project management: (1) promoting positive impacts and minimizing negative impacts on economic sustainability; environmental sustainability; and social sustainability within the project development process; and (2) the recognition of such project benefits realized is contributing to a sustainable society.

To define "Sustainability in Program Management," Tam (2010b) is again making reference to the definition of program management under the APM BoK. He suggests that the emphasis on sustainability impacts and contribution to a sustainable society is the same as in the definition of "Sustainability in Project Management". The underlined portion next is taken out from the APM BoK (APM, 2006):

The promoting of positive and minimizing of negative sustainability impacts (economic; environmental; and social) within the process of "coordinated management of related projects, which may include related business-as-usual activities that together achieve a beneficial change of a strategic nature for an organization" and contributing to a sustainable society (Tam, 2010b).

The sustainability requirements are subject to the context of policies, programs, plans and projects. In other words, to be able to assess sustainability requirements with the aim of promoting positive impacts and minimizing negative impacts, project managers shall be able to develop competence in understanding various sustainability issues, identifying impacts due to the project, develop mitigation plan within the project life cycle process to which project manager shall make a balance or even trade-off on chosen solutions with a target to maximize overall positive sustainability effects.

Since project sustainability is context dependent, project managers working on nuclear power station project, for instance, would have focused on certain sustainability competence requirements. While other project managers (e.g. new product development project) may have chosen to develop a different set of competence. However, the basic needs of a sound environment, a just society and a healthy economy (Brundtland, 1987; Diesendorf, 2000) in project development are the same. These basic needs would drive project managers in identifying sustainability requirements during project reviews and that project managers shall exercise their sustainability competence in promoting positive impacts and minimizing negative

impacts overall whether adopting three-pillar or principles-based approach for assessing sustainability.

SUSTAINABILITY EVALUATION FRAMEWORK

Program management unlike project management concerns more about effectiveness (do the right project) than efficiency (do the project right). With emergent input in a turbulent environment, program manager makes use of current information (sensemaking) to identify options (ideation) for comparison (elaboration) and decision (choice). Once decision is made, project manager will at a later time takeover the project(s) where sustainability in project management is being observed. In other words, for the part of sustainability in program management, program manager shall make sure sustainability considerations are being taken care of and that such sustainability impacts are built in the learning loop leading to a 'Choice'. Detail discussion on program sustainability evaluation framework is beyond the scope of this chapter.

To facilitate project manager assessing sustainability impacts and devising mitigation plans during various stages of project life cycle, I have proposed a project sustainability evaluation framework as shown in Figure 1 (Tam, 2010a).

The project sustainability evaluation framework is based on the APM Body of Knowledge (5th edition) defined project life cycle (APM, 2006) which adopts the three-pillar approach. It shows that project economic sustainability; environmental sustainability; and social sustainability are part of the project review process where it has to be reviewed during various stages of project life cycle. Project managers shall make reference to previous project experience including the nature of the project and its context to identify appropriate potential impacts for review. The list under various sustainability dimensions of the evaluation

Figure 1. Sustainability evaluation framework for project management: three-pillar approach (Tam, 2010a)

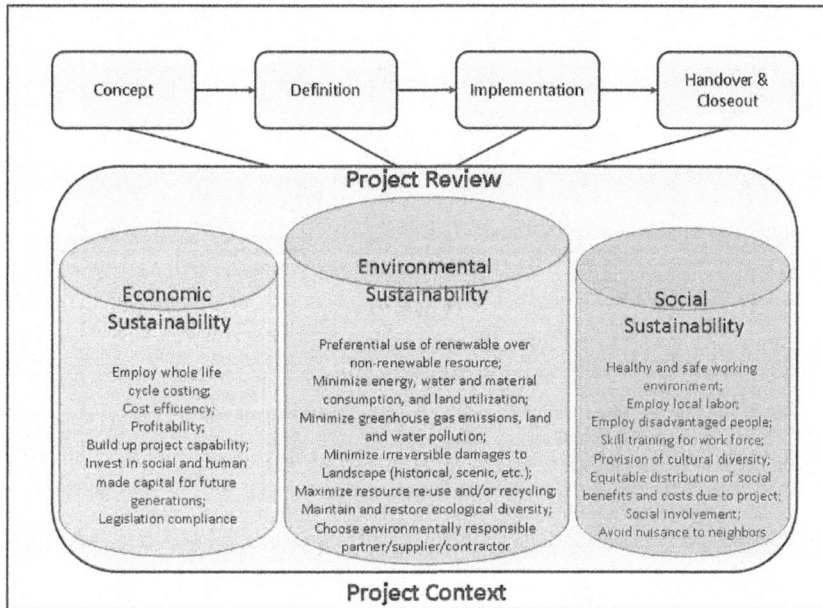

framework is non exhaustive, nevertheless, it can be taken as a starting point for sustainability competence development towards project manager as a generalizing specialist (defined in section before– "The Role of Project Manager").

Alternate to the framework based on the three-pillar approach, Figure 2 shows the same sustainability evaluation framework, however, making reference to the principles-based approach. The basic framework structure is the same but project manager needs to construct relevant sustainability assessment criteria for the project with the employed principles. Take socio-ecological system integrity (see Appendix 1 for requirement) for building a coal fired power station as example, project manager needs to make sure that a number of requirements has been put in place for project review, for example, monitoring extinction risk of endangered species, impact of acidic gas emissions to the nearby community, and proper design of zero discharge of waste water to river, etc. To cater for project complexity, project manager requires to develop assessment requirements with his/her

team members or subject specialists are invited to make contributions to such development.

THE ASSESSMENT METHODOLOGY

Approach

There are two forms of methodology applicable to assessing sustainability impacts of policies, plans, programs, and projects. They are "EIA-driven" (bottom-up from baseline) and "Objectives-led" (top-down with sustainability criteria for aspired state of society) (Pope, et al., 2004). As the name implies, EIA-driven is originating from environmental impact assessment which is typically a reactive, ex-post process with a view to evaluate the acceptability of sustainability impacts and to identify potential modifications to improve the outcomes. EIA-driven sustainability assessment needs benchmarking for comparison. To this end, industrial standards, best practices, and lessons learned from previous experience are taken as

295

Figure 2. Sustainability evaluation framework for project management: principles-based approach

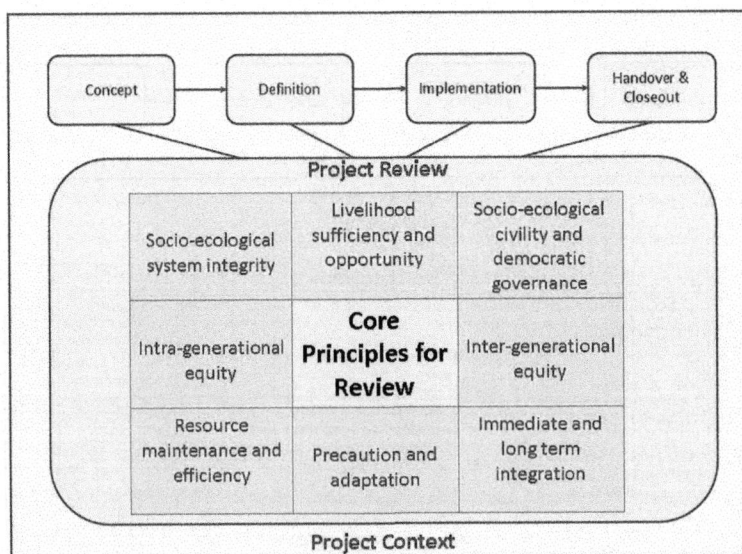

baselines for evaluation. It is argued that EIA-driven assessment tends to focus on reducing negative impacts against baseline conditions and minimizing mal-practices. It is not a tool to promote the concept of sustainability as a societal goal (Pope, et al., 2004). This sustainability assessment methodology aims to ensure that impacts are not unacceptably negative overall. It means that the project under assessment does not lead to a less sustainable outcome.

Unlike EIA-driven assessment, objectives-led assessment aims to be a proactive, ex-ante process being included as part of development process for policies, plans, programs and projects rather than evaluating them after the facts. It assesses the contributions of proposal to aspiration objectives, rather than against baseline conditions. Objectives-led assessment does not need baselines as in EIA-driven methodology. However, it is important to have the aspired criteria developed which lead the initiative towards the goal of a sustainable society. It requires clearly defined pillar objectives or outcomes derived from principles-based approach against which the assessment can be conducted. Thus it is found to be more compatible

to the concept of promoting sustainability (Pope, et al., 2004).

Depending on needs, both the EIA-driven and objectives-led methodologies can be applied to assess initiatives under either the pillar-based or principles-based approach. Hence, there are four different schemes available to assess project sustainability. They are: (1) pillar-based approach with EIA-driven assessment; (2) pillar-based approach with objectives-led assessment; (3) principles-based approach with objectives-led assessment; and 4) principles-based approach with EIA-driven assessment. Figure 3 shows the four schemes with applications.

Selection of sustainability assessment approach and methodology depends on need. There is no right or wrong in choosing assessment scheme. Whether be it required to evaluate completed projects or conduct assessment on initiatives, the tool described prior could be applied. However, commercial projects and government initiatives may have different requirements in choosing approach to fit for their purposes.

Generally speaking, commercial projects doing ex-post evaluation would seek to use pillar-based

Figure 3. Selection of sustainability impacts assessment methodology

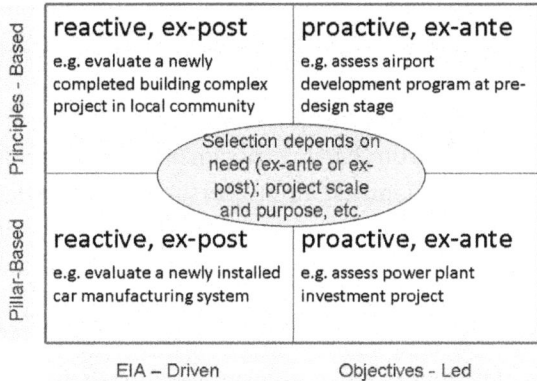

	reactive, ex-post	proactive, ex-ante
Principles - Based	e.g. evaluate a newly completed building complex project in local community	e.g. assess airport development program at pre-design stage
	Selection depends on need (ex-ante or ex-post); project scale and purpose, etc.	
Pillar-Based	reactive, ex-post	proactive, ex-ante
	e.g. evaluate a newly installed car manufacturing system	e.g. assess power plant investment project

EIA – Driven   Objectives - Led

EIA-driven assessment methodology. It can be understood that commercial project sponsors do not offer themselves to promote sustainability aspiration objectives. Hence, project managers are likely to compare their project performance to industry best practices. It naturally adopts industry benchmarks on economic, environmental and social sustainability performance as project TBL targets. For example, project manager would conduct sustainability performance evaluation upon completion of car manufacturing system project and that results are included in the Corporate Social Responsibility (CSR) report.

As before mentioned, project sponsors and project managers would tend to choose pillar-based approach for purely commercial project ex-post evaluation. In the same vein, commercial project initiative, e.g. power plant project to be invested by Independent Power Producer (IPP), they would also consider pillar-based ex-ante assessment. For major development in a community, local government may not be satisfied with taking minimum TBL baseline as targets. Some aspiration states of sustainability would likely be included as objectives for the initiative. Hence, for ex-ante assessment, pillar-based objectives-led methodology can be adopted.

Unlike commercial projects normally taking pillar-based assessment approach, other programs

or projects, e.g. government proposed airport development program, may choose principles-based approach for assessment. Since this assessment approach covers a wider scope than the pillar-based approach as aforementioned, it would be suitable for assessing large scale community projects where between pillars objectives can be covered. Furthermore, states of sustainability aspiration can be proposed and that principles-based objectives-led methodology can be utilized for such project assessment.

For those program or project taking ex-ante principles-based objectives-led assessment, results can be used as basis for ex-post evaluation upon project completion. For example, a building complex project within the airport development program has gone through ex-ante assessment utilizing principles-based objectives-led assessment. The results can be taken as basis for evaluation upon completion of project. Same principles-based approach should be observed in doing the ex-post principles-based EIA-driven assessment.

Selection Criteria

George (1999) suggests that the two principles of inter-generational equity and intra-generational equity are valid test for sustainable development across all people affected by the development. The inter-generational equity is a necessary condition for sustainability and the intra-generational equity is a necessary condition for development (George, 1999). These principles are embedded in Principle 3 of the Rio Declaration on Environment and Development of the Earth Summit for sustainable development "to equitably meet developmental and environmental needs of present and future generations" (United Nations, 1992).

When selecting an assessment scheme for assessing or evaluating a project or initiative, the following criteria have to be observed:

1. *Does the project or initiative likely to have issue of inter-generational equity? It is a key*

concern for managing project sustainability. If an initiative do have inter-generational issue (e.g. turning farmland into industrial park), pillar-based EIA-driven assessment methodology would not be a good choice due to between pillar issues could hardly be taken care of. Principles-based objectives-led assessment scheme with aspiration would provide a clear focus to address the inter-generational equity issue.

2. *Does it a project or initiative with obvious minor externality impact?* There are projects that have minor impacts on the external environment or community. For instance, a virtual project team building a computer model for analyzing job satisfaction of in house staff would prefer pillar-based EIA-driven assessment methodology. Other assessment schemes would not be suitable. Project managers may consider pillar-based EIA-driven scheme as basic assessment form for managing projects with minor externality impact.

3. *Does it an ex-ante assessment or ex-post evaluation?* Ex-ante assessment, which is in a sense of proactive in nature, would incorporate aspired objectives in the assessment. Hence, objectives-led assessment is adopted whether it is taken under the pillar-based or principles-based approach. On the other hand, ex-post evaluation is reactive in nature with pre-determined best practices or agreed criteria, EIA-driven assessment would match with the requirements.

4. *Does it a community project or project which is purely commercial?* Project objectives are different for those purely commercial projects and community (including government and NGO) projects. The impression that commercial organizations would preferably choose minimum requirements to satisfy laws and regulations and that pillar-based approach is chosen over the principles-based approach in managing project sustainability.

Though increasing amount of national and multi-national business organizations making exceptional sustainability contributions in recent decades, most organizations are driven by profitability as prime consideration over other sustainability goals. Further research on change in organizational behavior towards managing project sustainability after the Earth Summit would be necessary for project managers to learn more about the recent development in this respect.

The four criteria discussed previously reflect the guidance on selection of assessment approaches and methodologies. They are not absolute in nature and that variations can be accepted on conditions of "fit for purpose." For purpose of this chapter, "fit for purpose" covers not only the obvious purpose proposed by the project team but also any purpose determined at the time of assessment as a result of stakeholder consultation.

CONCLUSION

Managing project sustainability is important to building a sustainable world. The views of Mui et al. (2004) and the results of my recent research about the role of project managers in handling project sustainability activities and the inclusion of sustainability knowledge area in the project management body of knowledge have confirmed the necessity to develop sustainability assessment schemes for project managers. In this chapter, I have introduced definitions of sustainability in project management and program management, sustainability evaluation framework and assessment schemes. To effectively assess project sustainability impacts, pillar-based approach and principles-based approach are discussed and the philosophy of EIA-driven and objectives-led assessment is presented. Selection criteria are developed to help project managers in choosing appropriate sustainability impacts assessment methodology. Potential research opportunity related to this topic is recommended. Project managers need to develop relevant sustainability competence as part of their project management skills. This chapter contributes to devising a practical assessment tool for project managers in managing project sustainability.

REFERENCES

APM. (2006). *The APM body of knowledge* (5th ed.). The Association for Project Management.

Baccarini, D. (1999). *History of project management.* Curtin University of Technology.

Bredillet, C. N. (2000). *Proposition of a systemic and dynamic model to design life-long learning structure: The quest of the missing link between men, team, and organizational learning.* Paper presented at the PMI Research Conference 2000: Project Management Research at the Turn of the Millennium. Paris, France.

Brundtland, G. H. (1987). *Our common future.* Oxford, UK: Oxford University Press.

Diesendorf, M. (2000). Sustainability and sustainable development. In Dunphy, D., Benveniste, J., Griffiths, A., & Sutton, P. (Eds.), *Sustainability: The corporate challenge of the 21st century* (pp. 19–37). Sydney, Australia: Allen & Unwin.

Eid, M. (2002). *A sustainable approach to the project management odyssey.* Paper presented at the PMI Research Conference 2002: Frontiers of Project Management Research and Application. New York, NY.

Elkington, J. (2004). Enter the triple bottom line. In Henriques, A., & Richardson, J. (Eds.), *The triple bottom line, does it all add up? Assessing the sustainability of business and CSR* (pp. 1–16). London: Earthscan Publication Ltd..

Epstein, M. J. (2008). *Making sustainability work: Best practices in managing and measuring corporate social, environmental, and economic impacts.* San Francisco, CA: Berrett-Koehler Publishers, Inc..

Gareis, R., Huemann, M., & Martinuzzi, A. (2009). *Relating sustainable development and project management.* Paper presented at the IRNOP 2009. Berlin, Germany.

Gareis, R., Huemann, M., & Martinuzzi, A. (2010). *Relating sustainable development and project management: A conceptual model.* Paper presented at the PMI Research and Education Conference 2010. New York, NY.

George, C. (1999). Testing for sustainable development through environmental assessment. *Environmental Impact Assessment Review*, (19): 175–200. doi:10.1016/S0195-9255(98)00038-9.

Gibb, A. (2004). Safety, health, and environment. In Morris, P. W. G., & Pinto, J. K. (Eds.), *The Wiley guide to managing projects.* Hoboken, NJ: John Wiley & Sons, Inc..

Gibson, R. B. (2001). *Specification of sustainability-based environmental assessment decision criteria and implications for determining significance in environmental assessment.* Waterloo, Canada: University of Waterloo.

Gibson, R. B. (2006). Sustainability assessment: Basic components of a practical approach. *Impact Assessment and Project Appraisal*, 24(3), 170–182. doi:10.3152/147154606781765147.

Gregersen, H. M., Lundgren, A. L., & White, T. A. (1994). *Improving project management for sustainable development. Midwest Universities Consortium for International Activities, Inc.* MUCIA.

Griffiths, K. (2007). *Project sustainability management in infrastructure projects.* Paper presented at the 2nd International Conference on Sustainability Engineering and Science. Auckland, New Zealand.

Jaafari, A. (2007). Thinking of sustainability as a dimension of managerial competency. *PM World Today, 9*(9).

Labuschagne, C., & Brent, A. C. (2004). *Sustainable project life cycle management: Aligning project management methodologies with the principles of sustainable development.* Paper presented at the 2004 PMSA International Conference. Johannesburg, South Africa.

Lock, D. (2007). *Project management* (9th ed.). Gower Publishing Limited.

Mui, D. H. F., & Sankaran, S. (2004). An effective project management-based application model for sustainable urban renewal in Hong Kong. *Project Management Journal, 35*(4), 15–34.

Munier, N. (2005). *Introduction to sustainability: Road to a better future.* Berlin: Springer.

PMI. (2008). *A guide to the project management body of knowledge (PMBOK guide)* (4th ed.). Newtown Square, PA: Project Management Institute.

Pope, J., Annandale, D., & Morrison-Saunders, A. (2004). Conceptualising sustainability assessment. *Environmental Impact Assessment Review*, (24): 595–616. doi:10.1016/j.eiar.2004.03.001.

Robert, K.-H., Daly, H., Hawken, P., & Holmberg, J. (1997). A compass for sustainable development. *International Journal of Sustainable Development and World Ecology,* (4), 79-92.

Shenhar, A. J., & Dvir, D. (2004). Project management evolution: Past history and future research directions. In Slevin, D. P., Cleland, D. I., & Pinto, J. K. (Eds.), *Innovations: Project Management Research 2004* (pp. 57–64). Project Management Institute.

Silvius, A. J. G., & Schipper, R. (2010). *A maturity model for integrating sustainability in projects and project management.* Paper presented at the 24th IPMA World Congress. Istanbul, Turkey.

Silvius, A. J. G., van den Brink, J., & Köhler, A. (2010). *The concept of sustainability and its application to project management.* Paper presented at the IPMA International Expert Seminar 2010 - Survival and Sustainability as Challenges for Projects. Zurich, Switzerland.

Tam, G. C. K. (2010a). *Sustainability competence requirements for project manager.* Paper presented at the IPMA International Expert Seminar 2010 - Survival and Sustainability as Challenges for Projects. Zurich, Switzerland.

Tam, G. C. K. (2010b). The program management process with sustainability considerations. *Journal of Project. Program & Portfolio Management, 1*(1), 17–27.

Turner, J. R. (Ed.). (2009). *The handbook of project-based management: Leading strategic change in organizations* (3rd ed.). New York: McGraw-Hill.

UNCED. (1992). *Agenda 21: Preamble.* United Nations Conference on Environment & Development. New York: UNCED.

United Nations. (1992). *Rio declaration on environment and development.* Rio de Janeiro, Brazil: UN.

Zainul Abidin, N., & Pasquire, C. L. (2007). Revolutionize value management: A mode towards sustainability. *International Journal of Project Management*, (25): 275–282. doi:10.1016/j.ijproman.2006.10.005.

KEY TERMS AND DEFINITIONS

EIA-Driven Assessment: It is typically an assessment of bottom-up from baseline, reactive, ex-post process with a view to evaluate the acceptability of sustainability impacts and to identify potential modifications to improve the outcomes. EIA-driven sustainability assessment needs benchmarking for comparison. Thus industrial standards, best practices, and lessons learned from previous experience are taken as baselines for evaluation.

Generalizing Specialist: Project management specialist with general sustainability knowledge.

Objectives-Led Assessment: It is a top-down assessment with sustainability criteria for aspired state of society which aims to be a proactive, ex-ante process being included as part of development process for policies, plans, programs and projects rather than evaluating them after the facts. It assesses the contributions of proposal to aspiration objectives, rather than against baseline conditions.

Pillar-Based Approach: A reductionist approach dividing the holistic concept of sustainability into normally three pillars for project analysis and improvement. The three main areas of concern are, namely: environmental (planet), social (people), and economic (prosperity).

Principles-Based Approach: It utilizes a set of general principles to construct sustainability requirements for sustainability-oriented decision and assessment. Sustainability criteria are generated from those principles. It covers a wider scope than pillar-based approach, for instance it also addresses the between pillars issue, in assessing sustainability impacts on strategies, policies, plans, programs and projects.

Specializing Generalist: Sustainability manager with general project management knowledge.

Sustainability in Program Management: The promoting of positive and minimizing of negative sustainability impacts (economic; environmental; and social) within the process of coordinated management of related projects, which may include related business-as-usual activities that together achieve a beneficial change of a strategic nature for an organization and contributing to a sustainable society.

Sustainability in Project Management: The promoting of positive and minimizing of negative sustainability impacts (economic; environmental; and social) within the process by which projects are defined, planned, monitored, controlled and delivered such that the agreed benefits are realized and contributing to a sustainable society.

APPENDIX

Core Generic Criteria for Sustainability Assessment (Gibson, 2006)

Table 1. Core Generic Criteria for Sustainability Assessment (Gibson, 2006)

	Core Generic Criteria	Requirements
1	Socio-ecological system integrity	Build human-ecological relations to establish and maintain the long-term integrity of socio-biophysical systems and protect the irreplaceable life support functions upon which human and ecological well-being depends.
2	Livelihood sufficiency and opportunity	Ensure that everyone and every community has enough for a decent life and that everyone has opportunities to seek improvements in ways that do not compromise future generations' possibilities for sufficiency and opportunity.
3	Intra-generational equity	Ensure that sufficiency and effective choices for all are pursued in ways that reduce dangerous gaps in sufficiency and opportunity (and health, security, social recognition, political influence, and so on) between the rich and the poor.
4	Inter-generational equity	Favour present options and actions that are most likely to preserve or enhance the opportunities and capabilities of future generations to live sustainably.
5	Resource maintenance and efficiency	Provide a larger base for ensuring sustainable livelihoods for all, while reducing threats to the long-term integrity of socio-ecological systems by reducing extractive damage, avoiding waste and cutting overall material and energy use per unit of benefit.
6	Socio-ecological civility and democratic governance	Build the capacity, motivation and habitual inclination of individuals, communities and other collective decision-making bodies to apply sustainability requirements through more open and better informed deliberations, greater attention to fostering reciprocal awareness and collective responsibility, and more integrated use of administrative, market, customary and personal decision-making practices.
7	Precaution and adaptation	Respect uncertainty, avoid even poorly understood risks of serious or irreversible damage to the foundations for sustainability, plan to learn, design for surprise, and manage for adaption.
8	Immediate and long term integration	Apply all principles of sustainability at once, seeking mutually supportive benefits and multiple gains.

Section 4
Case Studies and Best Practices

Chapter 19
Changes of Projects by Considering the Principles of Sustainable Development Case Study:
Transforming the Project Hospital North

Roland Gareis
WU Vienna, Austria & Roland Gareis Consulting, Austria

ABSTRACT

Permanent organizations, such as companies, divisions, profit, and cost centres, as well as temporary organizations, i.e. projects and programmes, change. Reasons for changes might be new values of organizations such as transparency, empowerment, stakeholder participation, risk-orientation, etc., which are values on which sustainable development is based. Different change types, namely organizational learning, further developing, transforming, and radical re-positioning can be identified and can be described by specific chains of processes. For performing change processes of permanent organizations projects and programmes can be applied. The processes for managing the different changes of projects, in which the principles of SD might be considered, are described. The focus is on the management of transforming a project. The case study: Transforming the Project Hospital North is based on a comprehensive analysis of this project transformation in the book Project Management & Sustainable Development Principles by Roland Gareis, Martina Huemann, and André Martinuzzi (all WU Vienna) published by PMI (Gareis et al. 2013).

INTRODUCTION

The relationships between change management and projects were analyzed in a special issue of the International Journal of Project Management edited by the author and Martina Huemann (Gareis/ Huemann 2010). There the focus was on changes of permanent organizations, such as companies, divisions or profit centers, by projects or programs. The potential of projects and programs to deliver changes was demonstrated. Here the focus is on changes of projects. Not only permanent

DOI: 10.4018/978-1-4666-4177-8.ch019

organizations but also temporary organizations, i.e. projects and programs, are subject to change. Change management approaches can also be applied to projects and programs[1].

Projects are perceived as change objects and dimensions of projects to be changed are identified. SD principles might be a reason for changing a project. Different types of project changes, namely learning of a project, further developing a project, transforming a project, and radically new-positioning a project are introduced. These different change types require different approaches for their management. SD principles might be considered in managing changes of projects.

The case study: Transforming the *Project Hospital North* is based on a comprehensive analysis of this project transformation in the book "Project Management & Sustainable Development Principles" by Roland Gareis, Martina Huemann and André Martinuzzi (all WU Vienna) published by PMI (Gareis et al. 2013).

MANAGEMENT OF CHANGES OF PERMANENT ORGANIZATIONS

The term "change" relates to an important and basic development. Changes are of different intensity and speed, and can occur at the individual, the group, the organizational, or the societal level (Kasper/Mayrhofer 2002). Change has a strategic dimension, as it is "the movement of a company away from its present state toward some desired future state to increase its competitive advantage"(Hill/Jones 2001: 486). Different change types, namely learning, further developing, transforming, and radical new-positioning, which are requiring a different change management approaches, can be differentiated.

Change management is the management of a change. Change management tasks are to

- Define the change type, the change object and the change dimensions.

- Define the required change process.
- Design the change organization (change roles, communication structures, etc.) and culture.
- Plan and control the change processes and the change methods to be applied.
- Manage the transitions between the processes in a chain of change processes.
- Perform the change communication with internal and external stakeholders.

Change Objects and Reasons for a Change

Permanent organizations, such as companies, divisions, profit and cost centres, are objects of change. The internal structures and the contexts of these social systems define their identities. Dimensions of the internal structures of an organization are its objectives and strategies, its services, products, and technologies, its organizational structures and culture, its personnel and infrastructure as well as its budget and financing. Context dimensions are its stakeholders, its contribution to the higher social system it belongs to, as well as the history of the organization and its expectations regarding the future.

These identity dimensions are possible objects of change of an organization. The perception of an organization as a social system promotes this holistic consideration of it as a change object. The success of a 2nd order change depends on an integrated consideration of the previeously mentioned change dimensions (Whitington et al. 1999). For managing a change successfully, the change objects have to be clearly defined. This creates a basis for designing the change and planning the required change management interventions.

From a systemic point of view reasons for a change can either be interventions from stakeholders of an organization (e.g. its shareholders, clients, suppliers) or its internal dynamics, based on the self-organizational capabilities of a social system. Self-organizational processes of a company are e.g. strategic planning and controlling, monitoring the environment, new values, etc. Sustainable development was defined as a values-based concept[2]. If SD as a new set of values is developing in an organization, this might cause major changes in the services, technologies, the organizational structures, the personnel, etc. of the organization.

Change Types

Levy and Merry offer a development model for organizations which differentiates between 1st order and 2nd order change. The difference between these change types stems around the magnitude and the pace of change. 1st order changes are defined as "minor improvements and adjustments that do not change the system`s core and occur as the system naturally grows and develops" (Levy/Merry 1986: 5). 1st order changes are implemented in the context of an organization`s existing paradigm or meta-rules, which unnoticeably shape perceptions, procedures, and behaviors (Levy/Merry 1986). The 2nd order change is a multi-dimensional, multi-level, qualitative, discontinuous, radical change involving a paradigmatic shift. It leads to a new identity of the considered organization.

In a two-dimensional matrix, in which the vertical axes shows the demand for change and the horizontal axes shows the number of change dimensions to be considered the change types organizational learning, further developing, transforming and radical new-positioning can be differentiated (See Figure 1). This allows to categorize these changes in 1st and 2nd order changes.

Change Management Approaches

Defining phases of change processes has a long tradition. Lewin developed in 1947 a three phase model for transformations. A transformation should follow a three stages process of unfreezing, moving und re-freezing the organization. Another prominent change model is Kotter`s model (1996),

which includes the phases: Establish a sense of urgency, create a guiding coalition, develop a vision and a strategy, communicate the change vision, empower others to act on the vision, plan for and create short wins, consolidate improvements, produce more change, and anchor new approaches. Successful change for Kotter (1996) is influenced by appropriate motivation to overcome resistance to change and by high quality leadership.

Different change types require different management approaches. These are distinguished in the literature (Biedenbach/Söderholm 2008; By 2005; Gareis 2008; Heitger/Doujak 2008; Levy/Merry 1986).

Approaches for the management of the previously defined change types of permanent organizations are briefly summarized[3].

The objectives of the change "organizational learning" are the assurance of a continuous quality improvement in the daily business and the promotion of small innovations in an organization. In this change type a single or a few identity dimensions of an organization are considered (e.g. a process, a role, a relationship to a supplier). Incentives (e.g. for innovative ideas) as well as formal structures (processes, communication structures, databases, networks, training, etc.) are to be provided to assure organizational learning. Rituals for de-learning and introducing new knowledge have to be established. The challenge of organizational learning is to assure continuous reflections and the drive for improvement in the organization.

The process of organizational learning includes the tasks of identifying relevant new knowledge, securing this knowledge, providing the new knowledge to the employees, unlearning old, not relevant knowledge, and stabilizing the new knowledge.

The objectives of the change "further developing" are to maintain and/or to improve the business results by implementing major improvements and large innovations in products, or markets, or the organization, or the infrastructure, or in the management of relations with stakeholders. In managing this change the focus is on a few identity

Figure 1. Change types of permanent organizations (Gareis 2010)

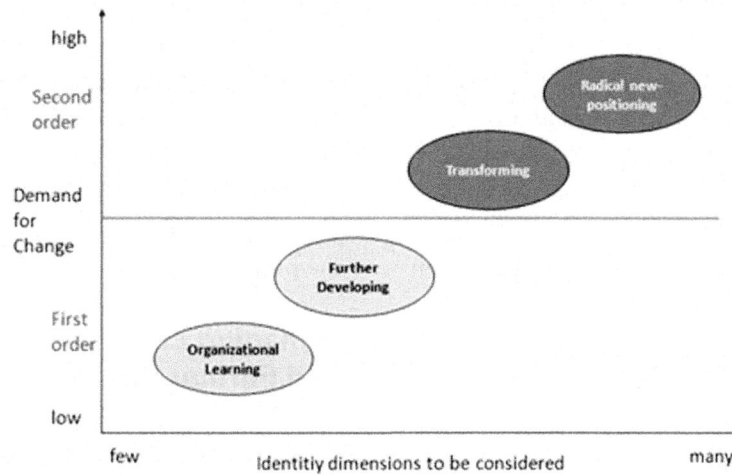

dimensions. If e.g. a new product is developed the consequences for the organizational processes and roles, the personnel and the infrastructure have to be considered too.

The performance of a further development often is managed by a chain of projects. The challenges of further developing are to assure appropriate resources, to assure (top) management commitment (e.g. for the performance of project sponsor role), and to align further developments with the overall strategies of the organization.

"Transforming" is a fundamental change as most or all identity dimensions of an organization have to be considered. As reasons for transformations often problems are coupled with new opportunities. The objectives of transforming an organization are on the one hand a rationalization and on the other hand growth and innovation. This is to be accomplished by a strategic and cultural new-orientation. In managing a transformation the focus is on redesigning the organization and on strengthening (new) core competences. A top down start for the strategic new-orientation is mandatory, comprehensive analyses and benchmarking are required, pilots, to assure broad involvement are to be organized, quick wins and management by projects (and programs) are musts. Similar to the change type „radical new-positioning" one has to

deal with a high social complexity, the uniqueness of the situation, the time pressure, and the high dynamics because of the ongoing daily business.

A reason for the change "radical new-positioning" is an existential threat to an organization, a crisis. The objectives of radically new-positioning an organization in a crisis situation are to assure its survival by improving the liquidity and achieving positive financial ratios. Potentials for future developments shall be regained. In managing this change all change dimensions have to be considered. Reductions of services and products, focusing on a few markets, re-engineering the organization, keeping good employees, improving the cash and liquidity management, focusing on the management of the relationships with the most important social environments are required. Stabilizing the daily business has the highest priority. Strict, results-oriented top down management shall assure quick wins. Management by projects (and programs) is possible, but only for the later phases of the change process. The challenges in the radical new-positioning are taking time for an appropriate crisis analysis, not losing competent employees, integrating new employees, and managing the crucial relations to stakeholders.

MANAGEMENT OF PROJECT CHANGES

Not only permanent organizations, but also temporary organizations, i.e. projects and programs, change. Due to the social complexities and dynamics of projects (and programs) their changes are structurally determined. Also for projects SD as a new set of values might cause major changes in the project structures and in the relations to project contexts. Different types of project changes can be defined, which require different approaches for their management.

Types of Project Changes

In analogy to the categorization of changes of permanent organizations (See Figure 1) the following types of project changes can be defined: learning of a project, further developing a project, transforming a project, and radical new-positioning a project. This change types are also differentiated by the demand for the project change and the number of project dimensions to be considered (See Figure 2).

Project dimensions to be considered in a project change are on the one hand the dimensions of the project structures, such as the project objectives, the project strategies, the project scope, the schedule, the resources, the costs, the income, the risks, the organizational structures, the culture, and the personnel as well as the project infrastructure. On the other hand, the dimensions of the project contexts, such as the pre-project and post-project phase, the project stakeholders, other projects and the company strategies as well as the costs and benefits of the investment, initiated by the project, can be subject to change.

Managing Learning of a Project and Further Developing a Project

Reasons for the change "learning of a project" are demands from project stakeholders for continuous improvements in the daily project performance. Objectives of this change are improving the quality of the project processes and of the project results by promoting little innovations.

The focus in the management of the change "learning of a project" is on integrating continuous improvements and small innovations into the project by concentrating on a single or a few project dimensions. By project controlling and lessons learned activities, the learning of a project can be organized. The challenges in managing this change are to provide incentives for learning of a project and to apply rituals for de-learning old knowledge.

Figure 2. Types of project changes (Gareis 2010)

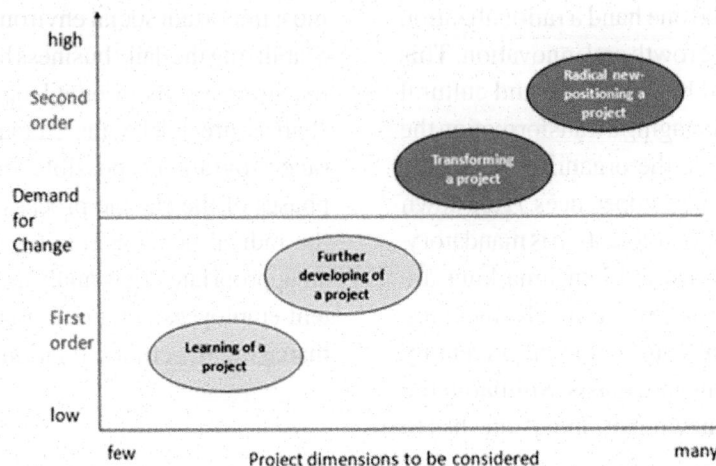

Learning of a project includes the processes acquiring new knowledge (identifying and documenting new knowledge), securing new project knowledge (providing new knowledge in meetings and trainings, unlearning old knowledge), and stabilizing the project by reflecting the application of the new knowledge and by adapting it. These processes are shown in Figure 3.

Reasons for the change "further developing a project" are the demands from project stakeholders to improve the project processes and/or the project results significantly. These demands might e.g. be expressed by change requests. Objectives of further developing a project are implementing major improvements and innovations. The focus in the management of this change is on changing the project scope, the schedule, and the costs. These changes might have consequences on the project objectives, the project organization, and the project context relations. Several project dimensions are affected. Challenges in managing the further developing of a project are to assure the appropriate project sponsor commitment and to provide the required resources for the further developing of the project.

The change of further developing a project includes the processes planning the further development, performing it, and stabilizing the project (See Figure 4). The planning of the further development includes information gathering and analyzing, impact analyzing, and planning of implementation actions. Implementing the further development of a project includes implementing the planned actions and controlling this implementation. To stabilize the project stakeholders have to be informed about the change, the change has to be evaluated, and possibly further optimizing is required.

Managing Transforming a Project and Radical New-Positioning a Project

Reasons for the change "transforming a project" are on the one hand signals about future threats for the project and on the other hand the identification of new project opportunities. The objectives of transforming a project are to rationalize by reducing the project scope and/or by cutting project costs, to implement major project innovations, and to assure a strategic and cultural new-orientation of the project.

The focus in managing a project transformation is on developing and implementing new project objectives, re-planning the project scope, the project schedule, and the project budget, re-designing the project organization and the relations to project contexts. By this the project structures and the project contexts relations shall be strengthened. Many or all project dimensions have to be considered. A top down strategic new-orientation of the project, assuring broad stakeholder involvement and quick wins, is required. The challenge is to manage the contradiction of hard cuts and new growth in the project.

The change "transforming a project" includes the processes planning the project transformation, implementing it, and stabilizing the project. Planning the project transformation includes interrupting the routine, analyzing the project situation,

Figure 3. Processes of the change "learning of a project"

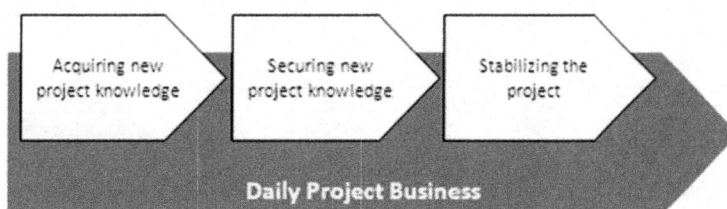

Figure 4. Processes of the change "further developing a project"

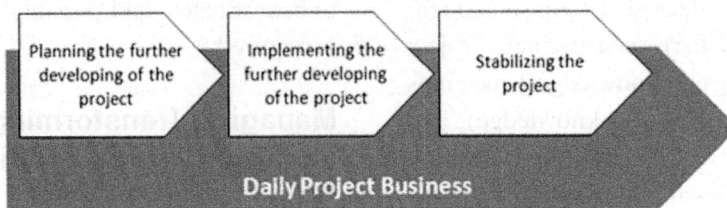

defining new project objectives, creating a sense of urgency for the change, developing transformation competences, and implementation planning. Implementing the project transformation includes changing the project strategies, objectives, scope, schedule, organization, etc., assuring quick wins, communicating the change and training, and planning the stabilization of the project. To stabilize the project adapting the changed project strategies, objectives, scope, schedule, organization, etc., further integrating the new values into the project, further communicating the change, and further training might be required (See Figure 5).

The reason for the change "radical new-positioning a project" is a project crisis situation based on an expected financial loss in an external project or a major increase in project costs, destructive relations with project stakeholders, an unfavorable cost-benefit ratio of the investment, initiated by the project, etc. Objectives of this change are to improve the project results, to achieve positive financial ratios, and to regain potentials for an efficient project performance.

The focus in the management of the change "radical new-positioning a project" is on reducing the project scope, on re-engineering the project,

and on liquidity and resource management. A project crisis is to be defined formally, all project dimensions are to be considered in the definition of crisis resolution measures, a strict, results-oriented top down management, involving additional external resources is required. Challenges in radically new positioning a project are to take time for an appropriate situation analysis and to assure that qualified project team members are not lost and new members of the project organization are integrated well.

The change "radical new-positioning a project" includes the processes planning the project crisis resolution, performing it, and stabilizing the project (See Figure 6). Planning the project crisis resolution includes the tasks interrupting the routine, defining the project crisis, rough project crisis analysis, implementing ad hoc measures, detailed planning of the project crisis resolution, defining the project communication strategy. Performing the project crisis resolution includes communicating the project crisis, developing organizational and individual competences for managing the crisis and performing the project, implementing selected crisis resolution strategies and measures, and controlling the measures.

Figure 5. Processes of the change "transforming a project"

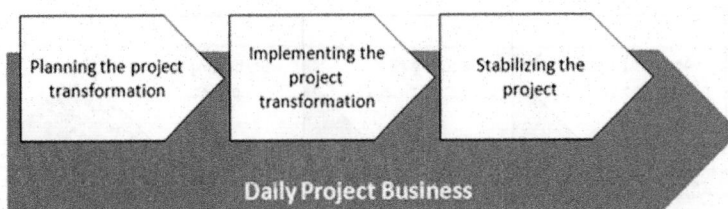

Figure 6. Processes of the change "radical new-positioning of a project"

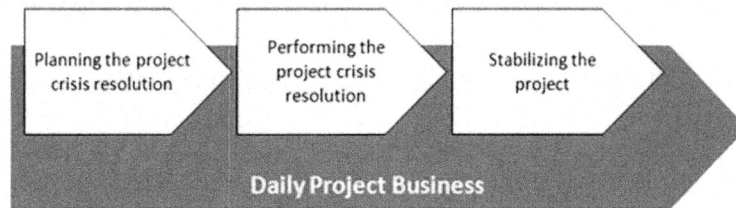

Stabilizing the project means to develop a project stabilization plan, to adapt the changed scope, schedule, etc., further integrating new values into the daily project business, and communicating the new project structures and contexts. In addition, a formal project crisis closedown is required.

CASE STUDY: TRANSFORMING THE PROJECT HOSPITAL NORTH CONSIDERING SD PRINCIPLES

Establishing the Hospital North of the Vienna Hospital Association in Vienna, Austria is performed by a chain of projects and a program. The *Project: Hospital North Planning*, which is described here, is preceded by the *Project: Hospital North Conception* and followed by the *Program: Hospital North Establishment*.

The transformation of the original *Project: Hospital North* into the chain of two projects and a program based on SD principles is demonstrated. This case study was developed in cooperation with members of the organization of the *Project: Hospital North*, who contributed to the *Research Project: SustPM* performed by the PROJEKT-MANAGEMENT GROUP of the WU Vienna.

Hospital North: Investment Object and Facts

The Vienna Hospital Association is one of the biggest hospital operators in Europe and is responsible for twelve hospitals, eleven geriatric centers and nursing homes, as well as training facilities for general healthcare and nursing care in Vienna. These competence centers offer 8.900 acute beds and 4.000 geriatric beds. The Vienna Hospital Association spends € 3.2 billion per year for business operations and invests some € 200 million each year in buildings, ICT, and medical technical equipment. The association employs nearly 32.000 people, who provide service for about 400.000 inpatients and 3.5 million outpatients (Vienna Hospital Association 2010: 6).

The Vienna Hospital Association has implemented SD principles in the fields of environmental management and ecological building. The "Otto Wagner Hospital", one of the hospitals of the association, successfully performed the project: The Sustainable Hospital in early 2010. Standards for the application of SD principles such as the "Catalogue of Criteria for Sustainable Building" and the "Green Guide for Health Care – GGHC" exist.

The Vienna Hospital Association establishes the new Hospital North with a capacity of some 800 beds. Some medical departments from other Viennese hospitals will be relocated into this new hospital. New organization concepts, such as surgery management, hospital bed management, and establishment of an emergency department will be implemented. Latest medical technical instruments will be installed, and the new ICT will be integrated in the existing systems according to the standards of the Association. Hospital personnel will be recruited and qualified, and facility management will be outsourced. The new hospital will cover approximately 160.000 m² with a park of about 45.000 m². In Figure 7 an overview of the buildings of the Hospital North is provided.

The new buildings shall be commissioned in two steps in 2015. The planning and building costs of the Hospital North are estimated to be € 825 million (Vienna Hospital Association 2010: 6).

In 2007 a team of the Vienna Hospital Association conceptualized the new central hospital. In a vision workshop the importance of integrating SD principles in the planning and construction processes of the new hospital was realized. In order to formalize the consideration of SD principles, the North Hospital's Charter on Sustainability was developed. This Charter represents 31 quality criteria for planning and constructing the hospital. Figure 8 shows the Vienna North Hospital's Charter on Sustainability.

The Hospital North is planned considering accessibility, gender mainstreaming, use of potable water and rainwater, and innovative medicine concepts. The Charter contains quality criteria for site, interior, energy, and construction. For each criterion specific goals measures are defined. SD principles are applied for planning and construction processes but not for the project initiation and the project management process. To demonstrate, how SD principles can be applied for these 2 processes, was the objective of the case study.

Definition of Project Boundaries and Contexts Considering SD Principles

Originally, the preliminary design, the design, and the construction of the hospital buildings were planned as one project. The project duration was estimated to be nine years, from 2007 to 2015. Figure 9 visualizes this original perception of the Project: Hospital North.

In this original definition of the project boundaries, the focus was on the hospital buildings. Just focusing on the buildings and not considering the medical-technical equipment, the ICT, the organization, and the personnel of the hospital resulted in a narrow definition of the project scope. This narrow perception of the project scope would have made a parallel management of additional objects of consideration necessary, which might have resulted in sub-optimal solutions. A holistic definition of the project boundaries integrating all closely coupled objects of consideration was required.

Further one project lasting for 9 years with major toll gates between phases, in which major scope decisions were to be made, did not allow the definition of operational project objectives. Therefore, a chain of two projects and a program for conceptualizing, planning, and establishing Hospital North as shown in Figure 10 was defined.

Figure 7. Hospital north: an overview of the buildings (Vienna Hospital Association, 2012)

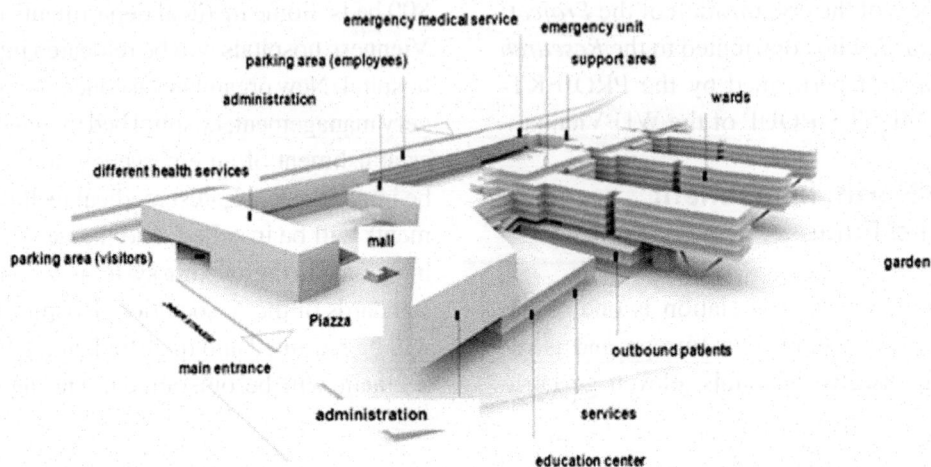

Figure 8. Vienna north hospital's charter on sustainability (Vienna Hospital Association, 2010, p. 1)

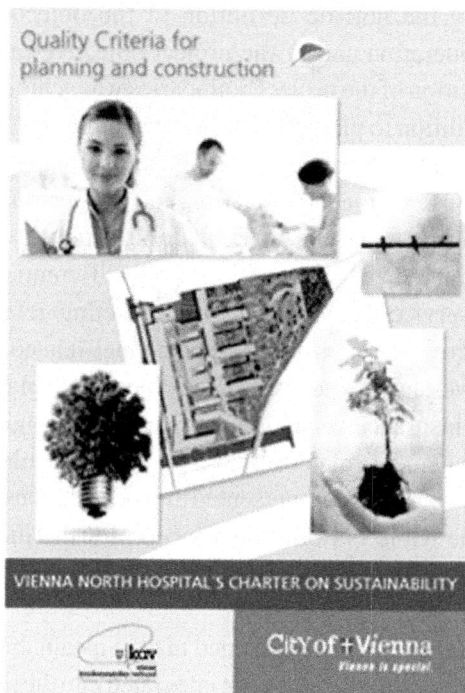

In each project, the contexts and structures of the following project or program were planned, which allowed transparent decisions and the operationalization of the objectives of each project or program. It was defined as one objective of a preceding project to initiate the following project or program.

This strategic project management decision to differentiate in two consecutive projects and a program considers SD principles in so far as:

- A holistic perception of the two projects and the program was assured (constructing of hospital buildings plus developing the organization, recruiting and qualifying the personnel of the hospital, etc.).
- A basis was provided for assuring transparency by differentiating between the investment in the hospital, the projects, and the program to initiate this investment.
- A basis was provided for giving orientation and empowerment to the members of the project organizations and the program organization by agreeing on operational objectives differentiated on the one hand by the investment, the single projects, and the program and on the other hand by economic, ecologic and social criteria.
- A basis for short-term, mid-term and long-term planning was provided by differentiating in short-term project schedules, budgets, etc. and mid-term program plans, as well as a long-term investment analysis.
- A basis for risk reduction was provided by reducing the complexity; instead of managing one huge "project" managing different projects, each of which to be understood, overseen, and documented.

Figure 9. Hospital north: original understanding of the project (see Gareis, et al., 2013)

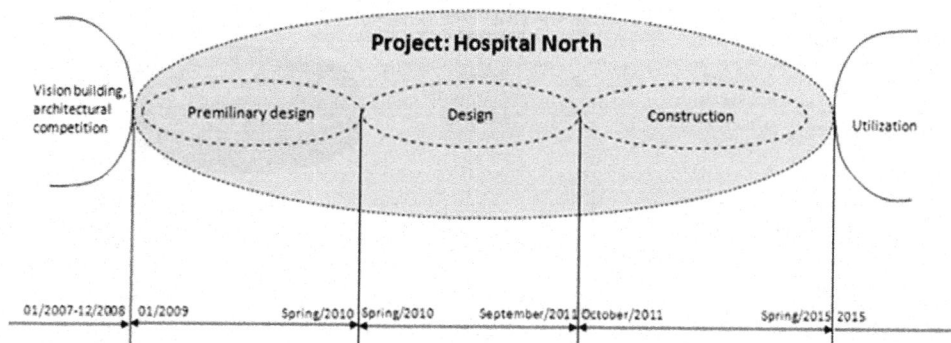

Structures of the Project: Hospital North Planning Considering SD Principles

The *Project: Hospital North Planning* started in summer 2010 and ended in September 2011. The main objective of this project was an integrated development of the architectural plans, medical-technical plans, and ICT plans. Also, rough plans regarding the hospital organization, the facility management, and the personnel recruiting and qualifying were developed. First construction contracts were prepared, and first agreements with cooperation partners were made. For initiating the Program: Hospital North Establishment also the program plans were developed in this project.

Based on the rough project management plan already developed in initiating the planning project, which happened by the *Project: Hospital North Conception*, the following project management documents were developed and regularly updated: project objectives plan, objects of consideration plan, work break-down structure, bar chart and milestone plan, project budget, project organization chart, project stakeholder analysis, and project risk analysis. Stakeholder participation was organized for. In addition to involving the Provisional Hospital Board and representatives of the City of Vienna and of cooperating hospitals the participation of future users, such as patients,

relatives, social organizations, religious groups, and future employees (doctors, nurses and non-medical hospital staff), were agreed on.

By the holistic definition of the objects of consideration and of the project objectives a re-definition of the project boundaries was achieved. In addition to planning the hospital buildings, the planning of the medical-technical equipment, of the ICT, of the organization and its personnel, its budget, and its stakeholder relations were considered. The objectives were differentiated into services, cooperations and marketing-related objectives, organization and personnel-related objectives, infrastructure-related objectives, finance and insurance-related objectives, and program management-related objectives. The stakeholder-related objectives represented the social dimension of the triple bottom-line concept. Furthermore, the objectives were differentiated into economic and ecologic objectives.

As the objectives defined in the Sustainability Charter were originally not integrated into the project objectives plan, by differentiating in economic, ecologic, and social objectives, this integration was achieved. Table 1 shows the structure of the objectives plan and as examples some objectives of the *Project: Hospital North Planning*.

The objectives plan defines the objectives of planning the Hospital North. By this transparency was assured and focusing on the objectives

Figure 10. Hospital north: chain of two projects and a program (see Gareis, et al., 2013)

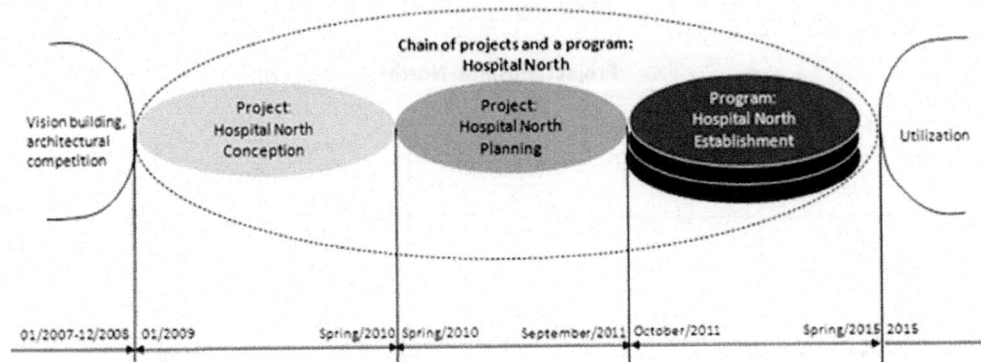

Table 1. Project hospital north planning: project objectives plan (see Gareis, et al., 2013)

Hospital North Planning: Project objectives plan		
Objective	Economic	Ecologic
Services, cooperations and marketing-related project objectives		
• Services of the hospital and its departments planned	x	
• Cooperations with other hospitals planned	x	
• Marketing strategies defined	x	
• Marketing plans developed	x	
• Environment friendly technologies for the services of the hospital considered		x
• …		
Organization, ICT and personnel –related project objectives		
• Facility management structures planned	x	
• Values of the hospital defined	x	
• ICT planned	x	
• Risk management strategies for the hospital defined	x	
• Mobility optimization planned		x
• …		
Infrastructure –related project objectives		
• Architectural plans developed	x	
• Medical-technical equipment plans developed	x	
• Alarm plan developed	x	
• Energy management in technical plans considered		x
• Rain water management in technical plans considered		x
• Park area concept developed		x
• …		
Finance and insurance-related project objectives		
• Procurement strategy defined	x	x
• Finance plan developed	x	
• Insurance plan developed	x	
• Operating cost plan developed	x	
• …		

continued on following column

Table 1. Continued

Hospital North Planning: Project objectives plan		
Objective	Economic	Ecologic
Program management- related project objectives		
• Program management plan for the program: Hospital North Establishment developed	x	
• Project management plans for the projects of the program developed	x	
• Basis for the assignment of the program: Hospital North Establishment created	x	
• …		
Stakeholder-related project objectives (social)		
• Vienna Hospital Association: Strategies of the association in the plans of the hospital implemented		
• Doctors, nurses, non-medical staff: Participated in the planning process		
• Patients and relatives: Participated in the planning process		
• Politicians: Integrated through periodic information		
• Local authorities: Early information, performed cooperation		
• Media: Periodically informed about project progress		
• Suppliers: Informed about cooperation possibilities		
• …		
Non-objectives		
• Stand-alone ICT solutions planned • Building permits and medical regulatory approvals obtained • ….		

of the planning project was possible. The members of the project organization were not lost in some comprehensive overall objectives to be achieved and measured at the end of the overall chain of the two projects and the program.

The basis for the development of the project objectives plan was the objects of consideration plan. This plan considers the project deliverables as well as additional objects, such as the hospital departments, contracts, documents, etc. In the objects of consideration also a differentiation between economic and ecologic objects was made (See Table 2).

Table 2. Project hospital north planning: objects of consideration (see Gareis, et al., 2013)

Object type	Object	Economic	Ecologic
Buildings	• Core hospital	x	
	• Venus building	x	
	• Mars building	x	
	• Park, courtyards	x	
	• Transportation areas	x	
Medical departments, institutions, centers and specialty areas	• Medical departments	x	
	• Medical centers	x	
	• Institutes	x	
	• Medical specialty areas	x	
Complementary departments	• Management departments, pharmacy, education center, simulation center, counseling, social worker, mall, employee representation	x	
	• Kindergarten, medical service for employees	x	
	• …		
Logistics	• Pharmacy	x	
	• Food logistic	x	
	• Laundry service	x	
	• Heating, cooling	x	x
	• Cleaning and maintenance service	x	x
	• Rain water management	x	x
	• Energy minimizing concept		x
	• …		
Other hospitals	• Hospital "Floridsdorf"	x	
	• Hospital "Semmelweis"	x	
	• Hospital "Gersthof"	x	
	• Hospital "Hietzing"	x	
	• Hospital "Otto-Wagner"	x	
Procurement strategy, contracts	• Procurement strategy	x	x
	• Contracts with contractors	x	
	• Contracts with suppliers	x	
	• …		
Finance and insurance documents	• Finance strategy and plan	x	
	• Insurance strategy and plan	x	
Services, cooperations	• Performance profiles for medical departments	x	
	• Performance profiles for institutions	x	
	• Performance profiles for medical centers	x	
	• Performance profiles for medical specialty areas	x	
	• Performance profiles for administrative departments	x	
	• Cooperation plans with other hospitals	x	
	• Cooperation strategy with the Medical University of Vienna	x	
	• Cooperation strategy health cluster	x	
	• Rental concept retail area	x	
	• …	x	

continued on following page

Table 2. Continued

Object type	Object	Economic	Ecologic
Organization	• Organization chart	x	
	• Role descriptions	x	
	• Communication structures plan	x	
	• Process descriptions	x	
	• Values description	x	
	• Risk management plan	x	
	• Facility management strategy	x	
	• …		
ICT	• IT hardware plan	x	
	• IT applications plan	x	
	• Phone, etc. plan	x	
Personnel	• Personnel groups: management, doctors, nurses, non-medical staff, technical staff	x	
	• Personnel plan	x	
	• Personnel recruitment plan	x	
	• Personnel development plan	x	
Technical plans (infrastructure)	• Architectural plans	x	
	• Room and functionality plans	x	
	• Medical-technical plans	x	
	• Room descriptions	x	
	• Alarm plans	x	
	• Logistic plans	x	
	• Ecologic construction standards/regulations		x
	• …		
Program management plan	• Program objectives plan	x	
	• Program breakdown structure	x	
	• …		
…	…		

This holistic definition of the objects of consideration and of the project objectives considering SD principles resulted in a comprehensive WBS, schedules and budgets.

The original project organization chart for the *Project: Hospital North* was hierarchically structured. It included persons of the line organization of the Vienna Hospital Association and of the City of Vienna. The project team representing the association was separated from the team of the technical planners. The technical planners were coordinated in technical project meetings. There were no integrative meetings. A project coordinator from the City of Vienna was responsible for the relationships to projects of the city municipality.

In order to meet the project demands and considering the SD principles of stakeholder participation and risk-orientation an integrated project organization was developed (See Figure 11). In this organization sub-teams, e.g. for architectural planning, ICT planning, services and organization planning, were defined. The communication between all sub-teams was organized in project team meetings. Specific project role descriptions for the

Figure 11. Project hospital north planning: project organization chart (see Gareis, et al., 2013)

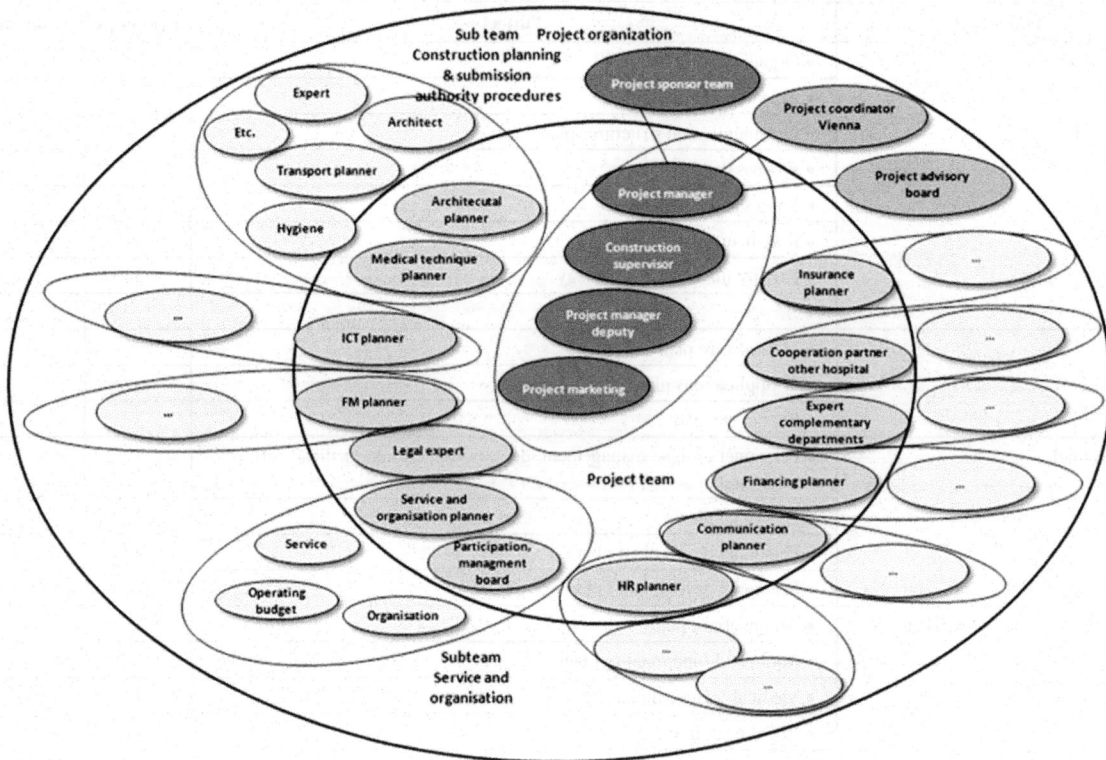

Project Dimensions Changed in the Transforming Process

Project: Hospital North Planning were developed. The responsibility of the project sponsor and of the project manager for achieving the objectives of SD, which were defined in the Sustainability Charter and in the project objectives plan, was included in these role descriptions.

In the *Project: Hospital North Planning* the program management plan for the following *Program: Hospital North Establishment*, including rough project management plans for the different projects to be started in October 2011, was developed. An overview of the *Program: Hospital North Establishment* is given in the program bar chart in Figure 12. It includes work packages such as program management, financing, insuring, etc. and it shows the different projects to be started at different points in time. There are several chains of preparation and following implementation projects for the different objects of consideration, such as organization, personnel, ICT, and facility management.

All project dimensions, i.e. scope, objectives, schedule, costs, risks, organization, personnel, etc., have been changed in the project transforming process. By not only considering the construction of hospital buildings but also the implementation of the ICT and the medical-technical equipment, the design of the hospital organization, the recruiting and qualifying of the personnel of the hospital, etc., the project scope was changed significantly. By not only considering overall "project" objectives but differentiating between the investment objectives, the objectives of the two consecutive projects, and the program objectives as well as by differentiating economic, ecologic and social criteria the original objectives plan was changed. The SD objectives defined in the Sustainability Charta were operationalized, were made measurable. The change in scope affected all short term

Figure 12. Program hospital north establishment: bar chart (see Gareis, et al., 2013)

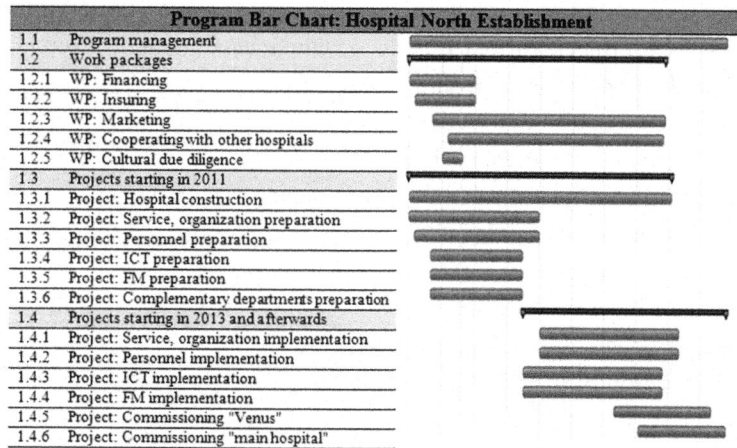

project plans, i.e. the WBS, the schedules, the budgets, the risk plans, etc. In addition to these project plans mid-term program plans and a long-term investment analysis were developed.

The project culture was changed by addressing explicitly values such as transparency, risk-orientation, empowerment, and stakeholder participation. A differentiation between the hospital values and the project/program values was made. The organization structures of the "project" were also changed significantly: Instead of one project organization a program organization plus several project organizations with different project sponsors, project managers, and project teams were established. Integrative responsibilities of the program sponsor and the program managers were defined, different communication structures for the different organizations were designed. Additional personnel for the program and for different projects was recruited and assigned.

The awareness was created that there are different stakeholders of the future hospital, of the program, and of single projects of the program. These different stakeholders require different engagements and different approaches for managing the relationships with them.

The main benefits of transforming the *Project: Hospital North* into a chain of projects and a program by considering SD principles were

- Assuring transparency and avoiding risks.
- Coping with the existing complexity and dynamics.
- Leading the program personnel and the personnel of the projects in a human and responsible way.

The transformation of the *Project: Hospital North* took about half a year. The author was involved as consultant and as researcher performing the role of a participating observer. The top management support from the CEO and CFO of the Vienna Hospital Association, who were the program sponsors, made this change possible.

CONCLUSION

Change management is not only of relevance for permanent organizations but also for projects. Given the characteristics of projects, being complex, dynamic, relatively unique and risky, changes of projects are structurally determined. SD relates to changes, as on the one hand the principles of SD shall be considered in changes of projects and on the other hand SD as a new set of values might cause major changes of projects. SD objectives might be a reason for change.

Differentiating the change types according to the change demand and the number of change dimensions in learning of a project, further developing a project, transforming a project, and radical new-positioning a project allows to apply adequate change management approaches. To perceive continuous and discontinuous developments of projects as changes promotes the application of professional change management methods, in order to deal with resistance appropriately, to focus on the change communication, and to assure the consideration of the important stabilization process.

REFERENCES

Biedenbach, T., & Söderholm, A. (2008). The challenge of organizing change in hypercompetitive industries: A literature review. *Journal of Change Management*, 8(2), 123–145. doi:10.1080/14697010801953967.

By, R. T. (2005). Organisational change management: A critical review. *Journal of Change Management*, 5(4), 369–380. doi:10.1080/14697010500359250.

Gareis, R. (2008). Change management und projekte. In Meyer, Wald, Gleich, & Wagner (Eds.), Advanced Project Management. Herausforderungen - Praxiserfahrungen - Perspektiven LIT-Verlag.

Gareis, R. (2010). Changes of organizations by projects. *International Journal of Project Management*. doi:10.1016/j.ijproman.2010.01.002.

Gareis, R., & Huemann, M. (2010). Changes & projects. *International Journal of Project Management*, 28(4), 311–412. doi:10.1016/j.ijproman.2010.02.005.

Gareis, R., Huemann, M., Martinuzzi, A., Weninger, C., & Sedlacko, M. (2013). *Project management & sustainable development principles*. Newtown Square, PA: Project Management Institute.

Heitger, B., & Doujak, A. (2008). *Management cuts and new growth - An innovative approach to change management*. Vienna, Austria: Goldegg.

Hill, C., & Jones, G. (2001). *Strategic management*. Boston: Houghton Mifflin.

Kasper, H., & Mayrhofer, W. (2002). *Personalmanagement, führung, organisation*. Vienna: Linde Verlag.

Kotter, J. (1996). Successful change and the force that drives it. *The Canadian Manager*, 21(3), 20–23.

Levy, A., & Merry, U. (1986). *Organizational transformation - Approaches, strategies, and theories*. New York: Greenwood Publishing Group.

Lewin, K. (1947). Frontiers in group dynamics. *Human Relations*, 1(1), 5–41. doi:10.1177/001872674700100103.

Vienna Hospital Association. (2010). *Vienna north hospital's charter on sustainability*. Vienna: Vienna Hospital Association.

Vienna Hospital Association. (2012). *Hospital north: Presentation of the Vienna hospital association*. Vienna: Author.

Whitington, R., Pettigrew, A., Peck, S., Fenton, E., & Conyon, M. (1999). Change and complementaries in the new competitive landscape. *Organization Science*, 10(5), 583–600.

ENDNOTES

[1] The approaches described refer to projects as well as to programs. To make the reading of the text easier, only projects will be addressed.

[2] See chapter "Re-thinking project initiation and project management by considering principles of sustainable development" by Roland Gareis.

[3] Please see Gareis (2010) for more details.

Chapter 20
Stakeholders' Perspectives on Sustainability in Project Management

Ramanda Achman
TU Delft, The Netherlands

ABSTRACT

More projects today are driven by sustainability goals than ever before. The need for sustainability as a critical factor for project success is clear. However, it is interesting to investigate the link between project management and sustainability more comprehensively. Especially by taking into account the importance of stakeholders' involvement in project management activities. Thus, this chapter examines whether stakeholders' perspectives on sustainability can provide a positive contribution to project management practices. Four different projects with goals related to sustainability in the Netherlands are studied and used as case studies to know the differences between the perspectives of stakeholders involved in the projects. One of the findings that was discovered is that the inclusion of "People" and "Planet" performance indicators in the management and delivery of projects is still rarely implemented, although the stakeholders categorize their projects as sustainable projects.

INTRODUCTION

Nowadays, there is an emerging concern and awareness on climate change. Consequently, the way in which governmental and business organizations operate is shifting significantly by putting more emphasis on societal and environmental issues. As an example of the environmental issues,

the report from Carbon Disclosure Project (CDP) for the year 2011 shows that 74% (294 companies) of *Global 500* respondents understand the need to have an active approach and also the benefits of accelerating Carbon Abatement Program (CAP) (PWC, 2011). This can be compared to 2010 where the value was at 65% (250 companies).

DOI: 10.4018/978-1-4666-4177-8.ch020

Furthermore, knowing that projects driven by sustainability involve various stakeholders, from government institutions, business organizations to environmental organizations, it means the quality requirement level of the project is also going to increase. Therefore, it is interesting to conduct a research on the perspectives of stakeholders involved in these projects. The reason is because the change of perspectives might affect the project execution and the project success factors. Moreover, it is expected by knowing, analyzing, and using these; problems or conflicts that arise in the project can be reduced by setting a better strategic plan at the earlier phase of a project.

BACKGROUND

The research used the definition of Sustainable Development (SD) from Brundtland's report, which leads to the formulation of three fundamental aspects of SD, known as the 3 Ps: People, Planet, and Profit. Sustainable solution can be achieved by balancing the 3P's. It means choices need to be made and priorities need to be set without any possibilities that one P will have more profit at the expense of another. Each P related to actors and interdependency among them is crucial. It shows that SD has multi-actor characteristics in nature. Therefore, sustainable solution is not a top down solution to balance among the Ps, but it is a consensus solution where stakeholders are involved in the decision making process (Bergmans, 2006). The involvement of different stakeholders needs to be taken into account more seriously, since they play a crucial role in the successful planning and implementation of project management activities. Stakeholders in this respect may consist of national or local government institutions, academia, Non-Governmental Organization (NGOs), business companies, locally affected residents or individuals.

Furthermore, the characteristics of SD projects or sustainable projects can be regarded as complex problems, in both technical and non-technical aspects, where various stakeholders with different interests, value structures, and expertise are affected by the problem. It is important to consider their interests and demands, especially in the decision making process, to ensure the success of a project (Cleland, 1986; Olander & Landin, 2005; Aaltonen, 2011). Because stakeholders can be considered as all parties or actors who either affect or who are affected by a corporation's actions, behavior, and policies (Mitroff, 1983). Different stakeholders do not share the same organization's definition of "problems" and thus they do not in general share the same solutions. Therefore their perspectives play an important role in this stage.

Understanding stakeholders' perspectives means understanding the whole of beliefs, values and presumptions that stakeholders use to cope with a particular problem (Cuppen, Breukers, Hisschemoller, & Bergsma, 2010). A perspective shapes a stakeholder's perceptions on a particular problem and its solution (Cuppen, Breukers, Hisschemoller, & Bergsma, 2010). The perceptions of the stakeholders are therefore particular to the individuals involved and are subjective (Bots, Twist, & Duin, 2000). Hence it implies that by understanding perspectives, stakeholders can have a better insight on what they should do to arrive at the same agreement.

Other than that, it is important to investigate stakeholders' perspectives on sustainability since these perspectives can be used as a supporting tool to stimulate the implementation of more sustainable projects. One such example is the formulation of new regulations by the government or the improvement of corporate strategic plan.

Therefore the main objective of this research is to investigate the perspectives of stakeholders on sustainability in projects and project management.

This research will answer the main question: *What are the stakeholders' perspectives on sustainability in projects and how could it be integrated into the project management practices?*

STAKEHOLDERS' PERSPECTIVES

Approach

The research question is an explorative research question. Thus, case studies are the suitable strategy. The research will be based from four case studies. However, considering the limitations to write this chapter, we will only analyze briefly each case study. The full extent of the research can be found from the research conducted by Ramanda (2011). A mixture of several data collection methods is implemented for a case study, namely: literature research or achieved data, observation, interviews, etc (Yin, 2003).

The research is conducted through a three-phase approach. First is to do literature research on the field of sustainable development, project management, and stakeholder analysis. It is mainly based on the review of existing literatures, Websites, and online news. A number of research have recognized the importance of implementing SD in projects and project management practices. Accordingly, literature on argumentative analysis as one of the method to analyze stakeholders' perspectives are also being studied. This could be a starting point for this research, especially to construct the theoretical framework.

In the second phase, four case studies on certain SDP from different knowledge expertise is selected to provide know how on different situations, problems, and stakeholders. Additionally, they can change the way stakeholders perceive on sustainability. The four projects that will be selected can come from usually known "Green Projects," "Social Projects," or "Economic Projects," since these projects are dominated by three fundamental aspects of SD: Ecology, Economics and Social Welfare (Capek & Westermayer, 2010).

Insight needs to be gained on the way stakeholders involved in the project think about sustainability. It is done through interviews with three stakeholders involved in the selected projects (e.g. project manager, sustainable manager, government, local community, etc). To support this, the Toulmin methodology as one of the methods for stakeholders' analysis is used. The model consists of six elements for argument analysis; ground (G), Claim (C), Warrant (W), Backing (B), Modality (M), and Rebuttal (R). It was introduced first time by Toulmin in his research about argumentative structures (1958) and continued with more detail elaboration in the study conducted by Toulmin, Rieke, and Janik in 1979.

The model was being adapted from the basic model of traditional formal logic, premises and conclusions, transformed into ground, warrant, and claims. It was then enhanced by three additional elements; a backing, modality and rebuttal, to be more coherent with the common practical use of arguments. Backing is used to verify assumptions from the warrant. Modality is used to qualify phrases that claim stated, while rebuttal is used to identified factors that might challenge the statement specified in claim.

Finally as the last approach, a comprehensive synthesis will be carried out from the interview results and Toulmin models that have been constructed. Through the cross case analysis, perspectives of each stakeholder from different cases will be grouped into three stakeholder groups: government group, project managers or project owners group, and third parties group. It will be used as a basis to determine the characteristics of a particular stakeholder group in projects especially project related to sustainability.

The Projects

For the purpose of this research and discussion about the topic, each project background will be discussed concisely. Following are the projects.

Project A: Energy Saving in Your Home Project (Steek Energie in je Woning)

This project was part of the Delft Climate Plan 2008-2012. The Delft Climate plan was translated into three scenarios (Municipality, 2008), as following:

- **Green Delft:** Focus on planer, both energy saving and sustainable energy promotion and realization on great scale.
- **United Delft:** Focus on People, cost reduction through energy saving in existing building stock, active energy saving campaigns.
- **Innovative Delft:** Focus on input for Dutch and international transition through intensive cooperation with local knowledge institutions.

The three scenarios were divided in more details into activities which can be seen in Table 1 by their share in percentages.

This project focus is reducing energy use in existing building stock combined with the improvement of indoor climate. In addition, the main goal is to stimulate individual homeowners to take actions in reducing their energy use, for instance; improved home insulation, installation of HR++glass, improved ventilation system, heat boiler, solar boiler, etc. The benefits for home owners are lower energy bills, more comfortable homes, and healthier indoor climate since it will reduce the dust quantity, contribution to make Delft become more sustainable, elevate the appreciation for the property, etc.

How does it actually work? At first houses in targeted area will be scanned to have an overview of recent conditions on the houses insulation and energy use. Next, an information evening will be held by Delft Municipality together with all involved parties so then the home owners can have better understanding about the project details. Later on, offers will be made by the building contractors to the home owners based on their

Table 1. Climate plan focus projects

Activities	Share (by %)
New residential building projects (Incl. Pilot project(s) climate neutral)	15
Existing housing stock	22
New utility and sustainable businesses	1
Existing utility	40
Municipal building and environmental care	2
District heat company Eneco Delft	10
Renewable energy sources	10

requirement. Execution will take place as soon as the time for the offers has ended. Finally, after the execution, architectural consultants will evaluate all the work done by building contractors in order to maintain the quality requirements. As a pilot project the area in Buitenhof was selected in 2010, followed by Tanthof in 2011 and continued with several other areas in Delft in the following year.

The project consists of four main stakeholders; (1) Delft Municipality as the project initiator and coordinator, (2) EREA (energy agency) as the party that provides support and information to the home owners, (3) BAM woningbouw as the building contractor, and (4) KOW Herstructurering as the architectural consultant that supervises the quality requirements. More detailed overview of the stakeholders in the project is depicted in Figure 1.

Three stakeholders interviewed for this project are as following: Project manager from government organizations (namely I1), Project Leader from consultancy firm in the renewable energy sector (namely I2), and General Manager from a construction firm in the housing sector (namely I3). Each stakeholder's argument or line of reasoning is translated into the Toulmin model to see the link between sustainability aspects and the project. Additionally, during the interview we also want to know what kind of environmental and social indicators define the project. This is established by requesting the respondents to identify these aspects from the list of possible indicators for an environmental and social criterion that was

Figure 1. Stakeholders in energy saving in your home project

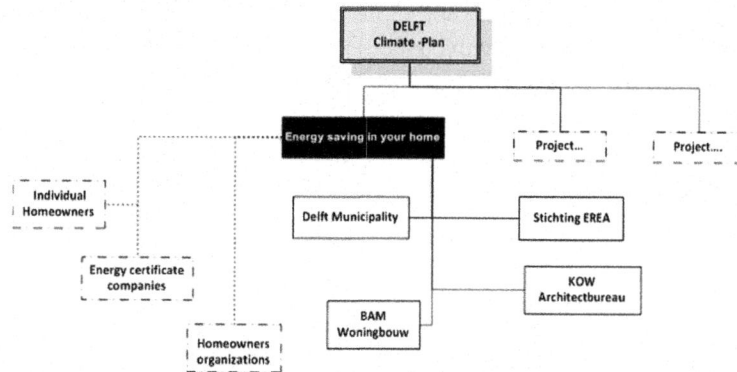

adapted from Labuschagne and Brent (2006, 2005). The indicators listed for this project can be found in Table 2.

Project B: Geothermal Heat The Hague (Geothermie Den Haag)

The scope of the project is to develop geothermal heat source and distribute it to 4000 houses in the area of The Hague Southwest (Den Haag Zuidwest). The project is executed as part of the fulfillment of The Hague municipality long term ambition to become a climate neutral city in 2040. It is projected that by generating geothermal heat, 5000 metrics tons of CO_2 emission will be reduced per year, which is approximately 70% less than regular heating methods, and save around 3 million m^3 of natural gas.

For this project, a partnership was formed consisting of six parties under an organization named Aardwarmte Den Haag v.o.f. These six parties are The Hague municipality (Gemeente Den Haag), 3

Table 2. Possible indicators for environmental and social criteria energy saving in your home project

Indicators for environmental and social criteria			Interviewee		
Main Criterion	**Sub Criteria**	**Possible Indicators**	**I1**	**I2**	**I3**
Air Resources	Global air quality	Global Warming Potential		+	
Mineral Resources	Energy reserves	Energy depletion	+	+	
Internal Human Resources	Employee Stability	Wages as percentage of project budget	+		+
	Employment practices	Average working hours	+		+
		Ratio of female and male workers	+		+
	Health and safety	(Post implementation review): number of health and safety incidents			+
Stakeholder Participation	Information provisioning	Number of planned stakeholder meetings			+
		Number of community forums			+
	Stakeholder influence	Number of channels for stakeholders to complaint through			+
Macro social performance	Socio-economic performance	Qualitative evaluation e.g., does supplier evaluation include environmental criteria?	+		
	Socio environmental performance	Increase in regional or national economic activity due to project	+		

housing corporations (Staedion, Vestia, and Haag Wonen), and 2 energy companies (Eneco, and E-ON). An overview of the stakeholders involved in this project can be seen from Figure 2.

The project started with the feasibility study in 2006 and is on target to finish building and connecting all the houses to the system in 2015 with an additional 1 to 2 years' time for maintenance period. However, because of the financial crisis in 2008 the finishing time might have a delay of approximately 5 years. Drilling of the well and constructing the boiler pump house started in 2010. At the end of 2011, the project aims to enable some houses in the neighborhood to use geothermal as the source of heat. Table 3 will show more detailed information of the project milestones.

The project costs are approximately € 45 million with around € 40 million for the system. The main question now is how the system actually works? The geothermal heat produces warm water from inside the earth with approximately 75 degree Celsius. Overall, the system consists of 4 parts. The first part is the geothermal heat source or also known as geothermal wells. It

Table 3. Geothermal heat The Hague project milestones (Haag, 2011)

Activities	Year
Parties first got together	2004
Feasibility study	2006
Creating the Business case	2007
Aardwarmte Den Haag v.o.f. established	2008
Laying of the piping alignment and delivery of the first houses	2009
Start the drilling and construction of the boiler pump house	2010
Grid construction, service level agreement with the energy companies for maintenance fault and production monitoring	2009-2014
All customers (houses) connected	2015

consists of two parts; production well-to pumps up the warm water- and the injection well to- inject back the cold water-. This is essential in order to keep the amount of the water inside the earth balanced. After that, the heat will be transferred to the second part, which is called geothermal Power Station or also known as boiler or geothermal heat plant. In this part the heat exchange units

Figure 2. Geothermal heat The Hague stakeholders

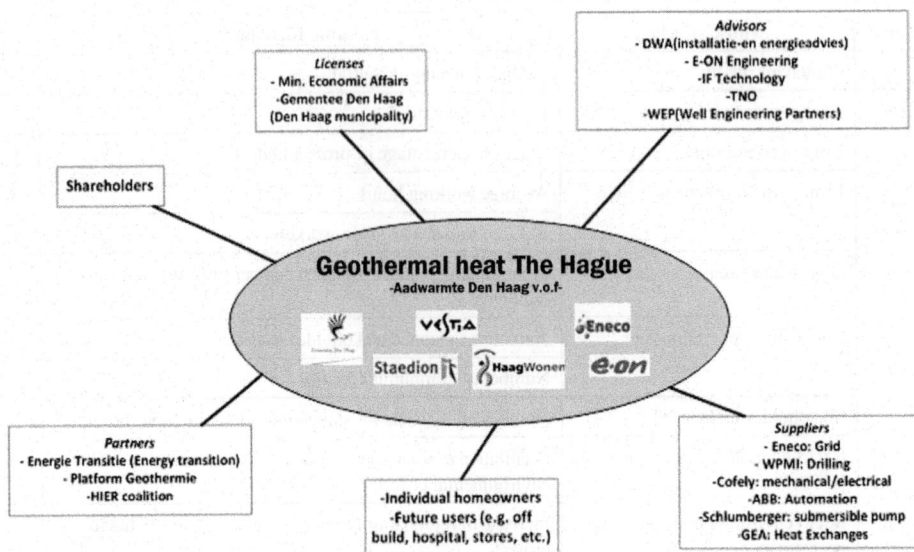

transfer the heat to the third part called distribution network or grid. The grid then distributes the heat to the houses via under floor heating systems and warm tap water. Figure 3 will give clearer overview on how it works.

Three stakeholders interviewed for this project are as following: Department heads from government organizations (namely I4), Director from service organizations in the housing and energy sector (namely I5), and a Chairman from a consultancy firm in the renewable energy sector (namely I6). Each stakeholder's argument or line of reasoning is translated into the Toulmin model to see the link between sustainability aspects and the project. Additionally, similar with the previous project the list of possible indicators for an environmental and social criterion that was adapted from Labuschagne & Brent (2006 & 2005) for this project can be found in Table 4. It is interesting to see that in this project more indicators were being measured not only by one stakeholder. Also it is still an interesting to analyze the various selections that were made.

Project C: Geothermal Heat TU Delft

The scope of the project is to develop geothermal heat source and use it to energize TU Delft Complex. Another important purpose of this project from TU Delft point of view is not only to have a facility that produces geothermal heat but also to use it as a research center. In which, advanced knowledge related to geothermal field can be developed.

The project arose after series of actions took place in Delft related to Geothermal heat by organization called DAP (Delft Aardwarmte Project). To realize this project, TU Delft together with DAP need to have an exploration license to drill geothermal well. In 2008, the license has been granted with an area of 61 square kilometers in the municipalities of Delft and Pijnacker-Nootdorp. Additionally, in 2010 two parties from the area of Pijnacker-Nootdorp; Ammerlaan and horticultural land (Tuinbouwbedrijf Ammerlaan Grond- en Hydrocultuur) and Tomato nursery Gebr. Duivesteijn (Tomaten-kwekerij Gebr. Duijvestijn), cooperated

Figure 3. Geothermal heat system work (adapted from Haag, 2011)

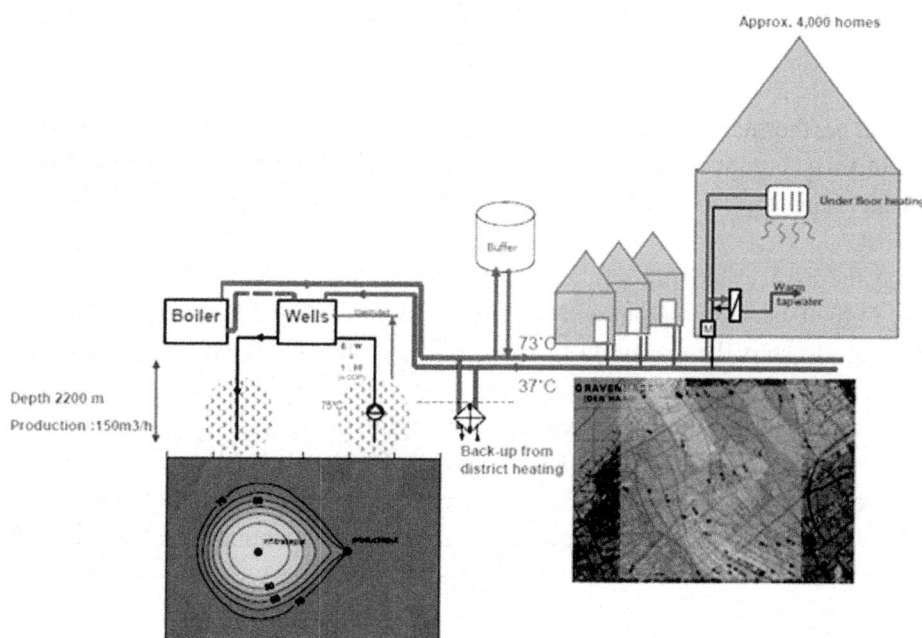

Table 4. Possible indicators for environmental and social criteria geothermal heat The Hague

Indicators for environmental and social criteria			Interviewee		
Main Criterion	**Sub Criteria**	**Possible Indicators**	**I4**	**I5**	**I6**
Air Resources	Global air quality	Global Warming Potential	+	+	+
Water resources	Water quantity	Water use: surface and ground water reserves	+		
Land Resources	Land quantity	Land use: occupation or transformation	+		+
Mineral Resources	Energy reserves	Energy depletion			+
Internal Human Resources	Employee Stability	Net numbers of permanent jobs created by project	+		
		Wages as percentage of project budget			+
	Employment practices	Average working hours	+		
	Health and safety	Percentage of project budget and project time spend on health and safety practices	+	+	+
		(Post implementation review): number of health and safety incidents		+	+
	Capacity development	Percentage of project budget allocated to training	+	+	
External Population	Human capital	Net impacts on house prices	+		
	Productive capital	Additional burden on water and electricity network	+	+	
	Community capital	Number of indirect job opportunities created	+	+	+
Stakeholder Participation	Information provisioning	Number of planned stakeholder meetings	+	+	+
		Number of community forums	+	+	+
	Stakeholder influence	Number of channels for stakeholders to complaint through	+	+	+
Macro social performance	Socio-economic performance	Qualitative evaluation e.g., does supplier evaluation include environmental criteria?	+	+	+
	Socio environmental performance	Increase in regional or national economic activity due to project	+		+
		Project's contribution to regional GDP	+		+

with DAP to drill geothermal wells and used it to energize their utilities. Figure 4 show the license area in 2008 including the location area of the TU Delft project.

At the time the case was being written the project is still in the business case phase. However, the plans are to start the execution phase within 2011 and have the full system running by the latest in the next two years. Three main parties that are involved in this phase are TU Delft, EBN, and Eneco. More detailed overview of the stakeholders involved in this project can be depicted from Figure 5.

The cost of this project is approximately € 10 million. The cost is calculated for the total project, from the start until it is finished, including all related infrastructure and cooling system, but excluding the renovation of existing building to be supplied by the geothermal heat. Additionally, the project has the possibility to capture the CO_2 and store it inside the well, as can be seen from Figure 6.

Three stakeholders interviewed for this project are as following: Department heads from government organizations (namely I7), Operational Manager from university (namely I8), and Project

Figure 4. Exploration license and TU Delft map location

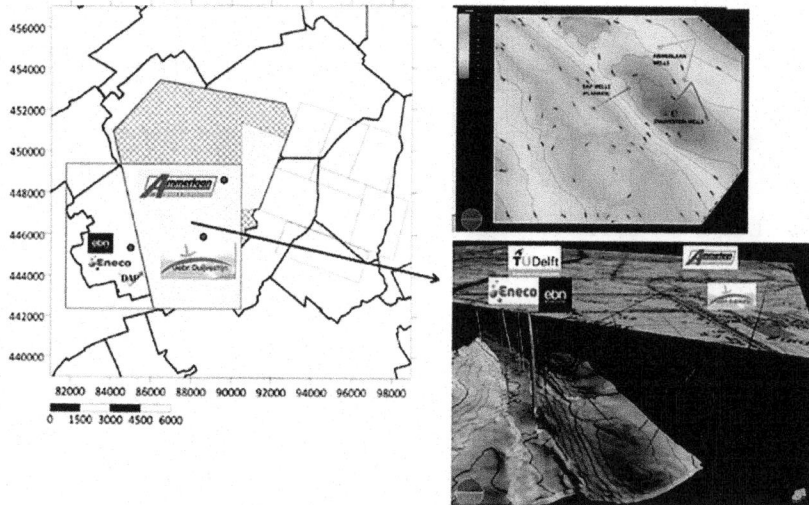

Figure 5. Geothermal heat TU Delft stakeholders

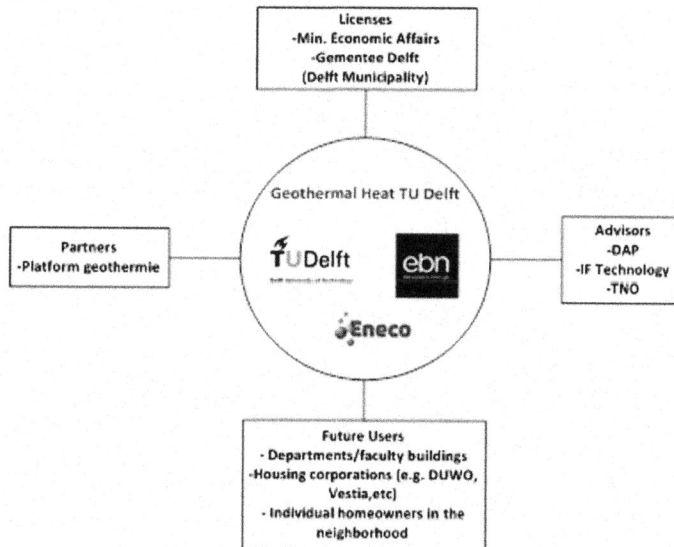

Developer from a services firm in the energy sector (namely I9). Each stakeholder's argument or line of reasoning is translated into the Toulmin model to see the link between sustainability aspects and the project. Additionally, in similar fashion with the previous two projects the list of possible indicators for an environmental and social criterion that was adapted from Labuschagne & Brent (2006 & 2005) for this project can be found in Table 5.

Project D: Modal Shift Project-Road to Barge

The project is to move Huntsman's (a chemical company located in Botlek, Rotterdam-the Netherlands), containers from road trucks, to barges. The goal is to reduce CO_2 emissions produced by the company by moving 2.600 containers/year to barges. This will reduce the CO_2 emissions from 145.080 kg to 64480 kg. This project is related to

Figure 6. Original and additional geothermal heat TU Delft project scopes

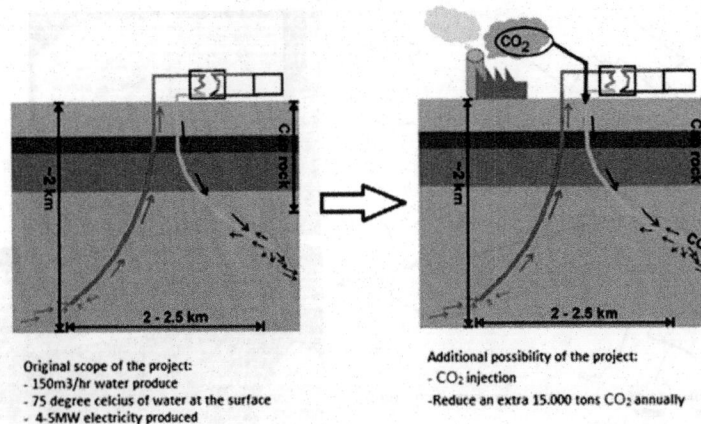

Table 5. Possible indicators for environmental and social criteria geothermal heat TU Delft

Indicators for environmental and social criteria			Interviewee		
Main Criterion	**Sub Criteria**	**Possible Indicators**	**I7**	**I8**	**I9**
Air Resources	Global air quality	Global Warming Potential	+		+
Mineral Resources	Energy reserves	Energy depletion	+	+	
Internal Human Resources	Employee Stability	Net numbers of permanent jobs created by project		+	+
		Wages as percentage of project budget		+	
	Employment practices	Average working hours		+	
	Health and safety	Percentage of project budget and project time spend on health and safety practices			+
		(Post implementation review): number of health and safety incidents			+
External population	Productive capital	Additional burden on water and electricity network		+	+
Stakeholder Participation	Information provisioning	Number of planned stakeholder meetings		+	+
		Number of community forums		+	+
	Stakeholder influence	Number of channels for stakeholders to complaint through		+	+
Macro social performance	Socio-economic performance	Qualitative evaluation e.g., does supplier evaluation include environmental criteria?	+		

Lean and Green program, which is a sustainable logistics program for the Netherlands organized by Connekt, an independent cooperation between companies and local government to improve sustainable mobility within the Netherlands.

There are 5 parties involved in the project. First is Huntsman as the producer/shipper (owner of the project), De Rijke (Warehouse), Agility, Waalhaven Botlek Terminal (WBT), and termi-

nal operators. More detailed information of the stakeholders involved in the project including the role of each stakeholder can be seen in Figure 7.

The project took a short time, lasting only a few months. It started in March 2011 and by June 2011, 70% of the shipments were managed to be delivered by barges except refrigerated containers, termed reefer containers. Table 6 shows the project time line.

Figure 7. Stakeholders' and their role in the road to barge project

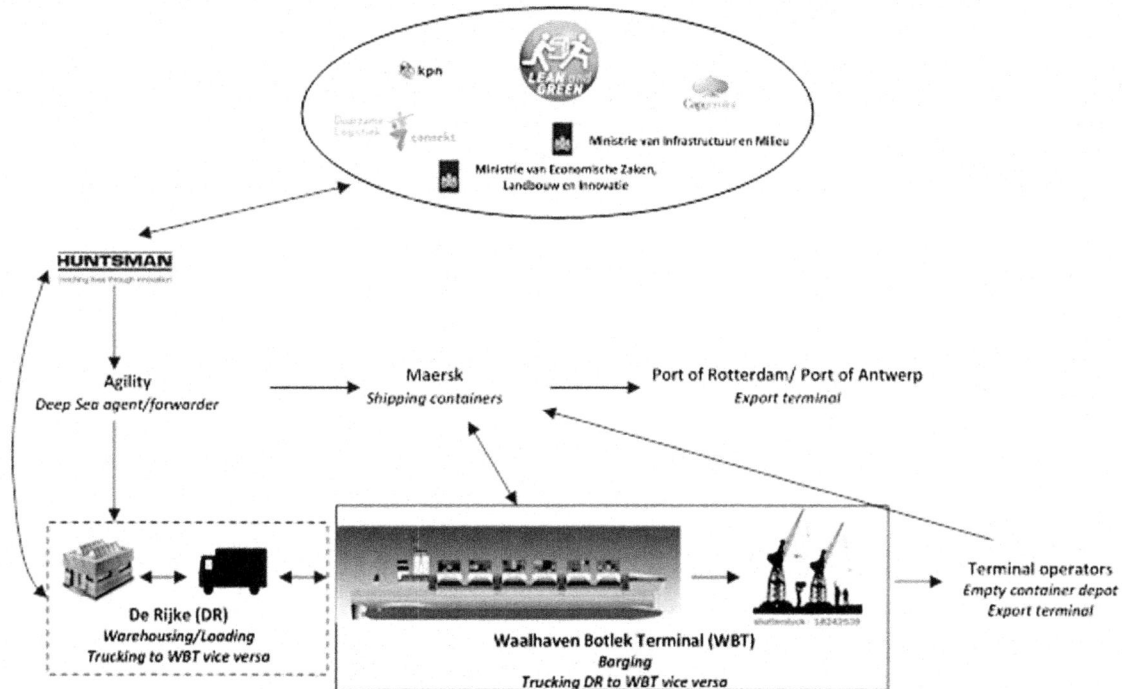

Table 6. Road to barge project time line

Activities	Date
First meetings were scheduled	March 2011
Meetings with all stakeholders. Financials and operational process was agreed	April 2011
First Trial shipments	May 2011
70% of the shipments to be handled by barge concept except reefer containers	June 2011

There were no specific costs spent for the project since it is mainly involved changing the containers shipment from warehouse to the terminal by a different mode of transport. However, through this shift Huntsman calculated to have saved 20% in costs for shipment. Additionally, with barges more containers can be delivered which leads to economies of scale. Assuming every year the company moves around 2.600 containers, it means around 217 containers per month and 10 containers per day. Whereas by using barges 20 containers can be moved while reducing the road traffic and CO_2 emission from the 10 trucks running every day from their plant to the port/terminal. Nevertheless, the shift required more advanced preparation as it took more time to move the containers.

Nevertheless, we cannot conduct interviews with the third party stakeholders for the case study D project because the organization could not be reached. Therefore the two stakeholders interviewed for this project are as following: Supply chain Manager from manufacturing firm in the chemical sector (namely I10) and Procurement Director from forwarder firm in the logistics sector (namely I11). Each stakeholder's argument or line of reasoning is translated into the Toulmin model to see the link between sustainability aspects and the project. Additionally, in similar fashion the list of possible indicators for an environmental and social criterion that was adapted from Labuschagne & Brent (2006 & 2005) for this project can be found in Table 7.

Table 7. Possible indicators for environmental and social criteria road to barge project

Indicators for environmental and social criteria			Interviewee	
Main Criterion	**Sub Criteria**	**Possible Indicators**	**I10**	**I11**
Air Resources	Global air quality	Global Warming Potential	+	
Land resources	Land quantity	Land use: occupation or transformation	+	
Internal human resources	Health and safety	(Post implementation review): number of health and safety incidents	+	
Stakeholder Participation	Information provisioning	Number of planned stakeholder meetings		+
Macro social performance	Socio-economic performance	Qualitative evaluation e.g., does supplier evaluation include environmental criteria?		+
	Socio environmental performance	Increase in regional or national economic activity due to project	+	

Summary

The stakeholder's perspectives can be summarized into three main perspectives as written in Table 8.

Furthermore, based on the sustainability factors we can conclude that most of the projects related to sustainability aspects executed in Netherlands, tend to have focus more in the environmental part particularly in reduction of CO_2 emissions. Even though the focus is more in the environmental part, sustainable projects in Netherlands still bring good contributions to many other aspects, for instance economic activity, education, policy, human resources, etc. For example, geothermal energy projects impact economic activities. Currently only few geothermal projects have been executed in the Netherlands, nevertheless I6 said "since geothermal projects

is now emerging in the Netherlands, in the coming next year the government will give an incentive scheme to support the development".

SOLUTIONS AND RECOMMENDATIONS

In this section the solutions and recommendations discussion from the problems presented in the preceding section will be presented. The results are generated from the involvement of all stakeholders. We found that in general, when it comes to the categorization of a project, most stakeholders justify their project as a sustainable project by judging the potential contribution of the project results or goals to the 3P's (People, Planet, and Profit) at the end and not solely from the project processes or from the environmental or social criteria indicators measured in the projects.

Moreover we also found that most of the stakeholders tend to categorize their projects as sustainable projects even for a normal or ordinary project. Another important finding in this research shows that even some stakeholders that are involved in the same project still have differences in selecting measured indicators.

Additionally we managed to group the stakeholders' perspectives into three groups; government, project owners or project managers, and third

Table 8. Three main stakeholders' perspectives

Stakeholders Code	Main Perspectives
I1, I2, I3, I6, I10, I11	It is a sustainable project because the end results contribute to the 3P's
I5, I9	It is sustainable looking at the end results of the project but the process probably are not entirely sustainable
I4, I7, I8	It is a sustainable project because the project used energy source that is sustainable and the project aim to reduce CO2 emissions

parties. First of all, perspectives of the government group show that their reason for participating in sustainable projects is to help realize their organization's long term vision. Generally speaking, their projects are part of a larger program that focuses on sustainability, such as the Delft municipality program named *Delft climate plan 2008-2012* and the Rotterdam municipality program named *Rotterdam climate initiative.*

Secondly, the perspectives of project owners or project managers group shows that in overall the reason for executing the project is because it fits with the organization's strategic goal. However, the project from case study D (*modal shift project-road to barge*) managed to show that external factors, for instance reconstruction works on a particular highway, can also force the execution of sustainable projects in order to keep their business in operation.

Thirdly, the perspectives of third party groups in general show the same positive support with the perspectives of the previous two groups in justifying their project as sustainable projects. However, when it relates to the reason they participate in the particular project, several factors arise (other than the appropriateness with the organizations strategic goal), for instance, to maintain long term relationship with the project owners, or because of lock-in situations due to agreements with other parties (for instance government institutions).

Moreover, related to one of the arguments from the research by Silvius et al. (2010) about sustainability in projects and project management, the total life-cycle of the project should be taken into account (initiation-development-execution-testing-launch) together with the asset and product life-cycle. In this research, the total life-cycle of the project is being narrowed into three phases; project pre-phase, execution, and operation of asset. However, because the selected projects in all case studies are not completed yet –most of it are still in the execution phase-, this research is not able to contribute to the analysis on the operation of asset phase. For the other two phases (project pre-phase and execution phase), the research was also able to indicate project communication management as the most important component to manage in reducing conflicts of interests between stakeholders. In general, compromising and confrontation-problem solving have been chosen by the stakeholders as the most favorable methods to be used from the five methods of conflict resolution proposed by Blake and Mouton (1964). Furthermore, stakeholders' perspectives managed to indicate the characteristics of project selection models used in projects related to sustainability.

Project selection decisions are often primarily based on the degree to which the financial goals of the organization are met (Meredith & Mantel, 2010). The book from Meredith and Mantel identified two basic types of project selection models; numeric and non-numeric. In practice, the combination of both models is often used. When it comes to the inclusion of sustainability aspects in projects, the level of uncertainty will increase. Therefore, we often see that in order to stimulate participation in such projects, government support, for instance; policies, funds, incentives, etc., plays an important role until this moment.

Our research indicated that financial aspects are still the most important factor for a project. This indication can be seen from the statements of the respondents towards the risks of the project. However, as the book of Meredith and Mantel said "It is not uncommon for the "minor side-effects" of a new product or process to have major impacts on the parent organization". It needs to be taken into account that for this type of project,, the ROI will be earned back after a longer period. In addition we suggest that if an organization wants to participate in such a type of project, the selection model should emphasize more in the non-numerical models, for instance; *the competitive necessity, the sacred crow, the operating necessity*, etc. (Meredith & Mantel, 2010), without neglecting the control of project costs and budgets.

FUTURE RESEARCH DIRECTIONS

In this section we will elaborate further in which issues the subsequent research should focus on. First of all, the research could focus on selecting completed projects for the case study. This will enrich the findings because not only all the stakeholders involved will have more experience from doing the project for a longer period of time but also because the research can learn from the process to get to the results regardless whether the research outcome meets its goals or not.

Secondly, the research could focus on doing interviews with more stakeholders from other types of organizations, for instance; non-governmental organizations (NGO), research organizations, financial institutions, local people or residents influenced by the project, different organizations inside the government, etc. The idea is to get either new perspectives from new types of stakeholders group or different perspectives from the existing stakeholders group due to involvement of other types of organizations under the same category.

Furthermore, the research could focus on doing the research with an ordinary project or normal project which goals are not related to sustainability. It will enrich the research findings because it is highly probable that the results will show that although these normal projects have nothing to do with sustainability, it turns out that unintentionally, they strictly measured several sustainable indicators during the project.

Finally, the research could focus on the extensive validation of the framework we developed. A combination of methodologies can be adopted to conduct the research. The combination of option analysis together with the Toulmin model would help to create a more comprehensive result of the stakeholders' perspectives then what it is shown from the research done by Leon Hermans (2005). Moreover, conducting a workshop session after doing the analysis of options will help to narrow down the focus of the stakeholders' perspectives when constructing the Toulmin model.

CONCLUSION

From our analysis of the stakeholders' perspectives on sustainability in projects, we argue that stakeholders' perspective is an important factor to the project management practices. The reason is because this research has found that stakeholders have many different perspectives, but that it would be better to have better aligned perspective. So the inclusion of 'People' and 'Planet' performance indicators in the management and delivery of projects would be aligned and similar for all stakeholders throughout the whole process. This can be done by laying more emphasis on the project communication management part, for instance by using compromising and confrontation-problem solving methods, to reduce conflicts of interests between stakeholders. Additionally, the way stakeholders' *frame* the project as a sustainable project will bring benefits not only to the involved organizations' brand image, but also benefits the project by the inclusion of sustainability indicators where it has not been done before.

REFERENCES

Aaltonen, K. (2011). Project stakeholder analysis as an environmental interpretation process. *International Journal of Project Management*, 165–183. doi:10.1016/j.ijproman.2010.02.001.

Achman, R. (2011). *Stakeholders' Perspectives on Sustainability in Project Management. Case studies of 4 different projects in the Netherlands.* Delft: Delft University of Technology.

Bergmans, F. (2006). Integrating People, Planet and Profit. In Jonker, J. (Ed.), *M. C. de Witte, Management models for corporate social responsibility.* Berlin, Heidelberg: Springer. doi:10.1007/3-540-33247-2_14.

Blake, R., Shepard, H., & Mouton, J. (1964). *Managing intergroup conflict in Industry.* Houston: Gulf Publishing Company.

Bots, P., Twist, M. v., & Duin, J. v. (2000). Automatic Pattern Detection in Stakeholder Networks. *The 33rd Hawaii International Conference on System Sciences* (pp. 1-10). Hawaii: IEEE.

Bruijn, H., & Heuvelhof, E. (2008). *Management in Networks on multi-actor decision making.* New York: Routledge.

Brundtland, G. (1987). *Our common future: The World Comission on Environment and Development.* Oxford: Oxford University Press.

Capek, B., & Westermayer, K. (2010). Sustainable Development Projects, Development of categorization. *PM World Today*, 1-15.

Cleland, D. (1986). Project stakeholder management. *Project Management Journal*, 36-44.

Cuppen, E., Breukers, S., Hisschemoller, M., & Bergsma, E. (2010). Q methodology to select participants for a stakeholder dialogue on energy options from biomass in the Netherlands. *Ecological Economics*, *69*(3), 579–591. doi:10.1016/j.ecolecon.2009.09.005.

DAP. D. (2011, July). *Home.* Retrieved July 26, 2011, from Delft Aardwamte Project: http://www.delftaardwarmteproject.nl/home/

Haag, G. D. (2011, June). *Geothermal heat for 4000 houses in The Hague, Dutch project example.* Retrieved July 2011, from www.aplu.org: http://www.aplu.org/document.doc?id=2938

Hermans, L. M. (2005). *Actor Analysis for water resources management.* Delft, the Netherlands: Eburon.

IEA. I. (2011). Technology Roadmap, Geothermal Heat and Power. Paris: IEA.

Labuschagne, C., & Brent, A. (2005). Environmental and Social Impact Considerations for Sustainable Project Life Cycle Management in the Process Industry. *Corporate Social Responsibility and Environmental Management*, *12*, 38–54. doi:10.1002/csr.76.

Labuschagne, C., & Brent, A. (2006). Social Indicators for sustainable project and technology life cycle management in the process industry. *International Journal of Life Cycle Assessment*, *11*(1), 3–15. doi:10.1065/lca2006.01.233.

Labuschagne, C., & Brent, A. (2006). Social Indicators for Sustainable Project and Technology Life Cycle Management in the Process Industry. *Process Industry*, 1-17.

Meredith, J., & Mantel, S. (2010). *Project Management, A managerial approach.* Hoboken: John Wiley & Sons, Inc..

Mitroff, I. (1983). *Stakeholders of the Organizational Mind. San Fransisco, Washington.* London: Jossey-Bass Publishers.

Municipality, D. (2008). Delft Climate Plan 2008-2012. Delft.

Olander, S., & Landin, A. (2005). Evaluation of stakeholder influence in the implementation of construction projects. *International Journal of Project Management*, 321–328. doi:10.1016/j.ijproman.2005.02.002.

PWC, P. (2011). *CDP Global 500 Report 2011; Accelerating Low Carbon Growth.* United Kingdom: CDProject.

Silvius, A. G., Brink, J. v., & Köhler, A. (2010). The concept of sustainability and its application to project management. *IPMA Expert Seminar*, pp. 130-144.

Toulmin, S. (1958). *The Uses of Argument.* Cambridge: Cambridge University Press.

Toulmin, S., Rieke, R., & Janik, A. (1979). *An introduction of reasoning.* New York: Macmillan Publishing Co, Inc..

Yin, R. (2003). *Case Study Research: Design and Method.* United States: Sage Publications Inc..

KEY TERMS AND DEFINITIONS

DAP (Delft Aardwarmte Project): Consist of various stakeholders for instance TU Delft, TNO, Eneco, Consultant (PanTerra), etc. The foundation was being formed by students and alumni from the department of Geotechnology with a goal to provide TU Delft a sustainable heat source through the realization of a geothermal project on the campus.

Delft Climate Plan 2008-2012: Is an environment program made by Delft Municipality. The goals are that in 2012 there will be 15% reduction in CO_2 emission, 15% reduction in energy use, and an additional 5% use of sustainable energy as compared to the 1990 levels. Additionally, the bigger goals are to achieve 50% reduction in CO_2 emission, 50% reduction in energy use, and an additional 25% use of sustainable energy by 2030 as compared with the year of 1990.

Framing: Concerns the language in which a goal is expressed; where in a project the content of a problem determines the framing of the goal (Bruijn & Heuvelhof, 2008).

The Competitive Necessity: Is the decision to undertake the project was based on a desire to maintain the organization's competitive position in a particular market.

The Global 500: Are the largest companies by market capitalization included in the FTSE Global Equity Index Series.

The Operating Necessity: Is the decision to undertake the project is based on the condition where the project is required in order to keep the organization in operation.

The Sacred Cow: Is the decision to undertake the project comes from the suggestion made by a senior and powerful official in the organization.

Chapter 21
Application of Sustainability Considerations in Practice:
The Open Remote Case

Ron Schipper
Van Aetsveld Project Management and Change, The Netherlands

Snezana Nedeski
Maastricht University, The Netherlands

ABSTRACT

Many articles have called attention to the concept of sustainability in project management. However, it still remains a challenge to tie all these very important principles to practice. In this chapter, the main issues with the practical application of sustainability to an actual project are identified, and a method for analysis is presented. Through this method, the authors answer the main question of this chapter: "How can a project and its project management be analyzed for sustainability and how can adequate actions be selected?" The proposed method is then applied to an actual case. In the analysis, an explicit distinction is made between the internal project view of sustainability and external view of sustainability. From the analysis, various conclusions can be drawn.

INTRODUCTION

Many articles have been provided to call attention to the concept of sustainability in project management. Some of them discuss the basic concepts that are involved; concepts like the triple bottom line (Elkington, 1997) and the six guiding principles to sustainability (Silvius, Van den Brink, & Köhler, 2010). Even with these concepts and theories in place it remains a challenge to tie all these very important principles to practice.

For this purpose, we have selected a single case study that we will use to bring some practicality into the largely theoretical field of sustainabil-

DOI: 10.4018/978-1-4666-4177-8.ch021

ity in project management. This case study will serve as an example of a project to be analyzed on sustainability. It will offer insights into how numerous sustainability theories are applicable to a project. By doing this, some general major pitfalls when it comes to sustainability in project management will come to light. With this we will also try to identify sustainability opportunities that are specific to the case study.

The case study focused on a project by the Beijing division of Finalist IT Group and was previously featured in an article by Silvius and Nedeski (2011), where the focus was more descriptive and on the connection to Green IS. The data collection for the case study took place in 2010 through semi-structured interviews with the general manager and the project manager of the project in question. Besides this the project manager filled in a maturity assessment questionnaire developed by Silvius and Schipper (2010). This maturity assessment measured the presence (and the lack) of sustainability in the project's project management process and end product. It measured both the actual situation and the desired situation. Finalist IT Group, the organization in question, is a Dutch IT service provider with several branches, amongst which their Beijing branch as visited in 2010. The Beijing office employed around 30 people.

The project in question, named 'OpenRemote', was an open source software development project where Finalist Beijing, with a core development team of 10 people, designed and implemented a software application for iPhone, iPad and other Mac-products. The project was destined for the US with a budget of over 1 million dollars. The goal of the project was to design and program an open source software application for controlling the lighting, air conditioning, entertainment equipment, and other electrical devices in the average home that normally require many separate remotes (and batteries). So in this case the product (remote control and batteries) is redesigned into a service (the software application).

Although this already suggests an inherent level of sustainability in the project's end-product, it should be kept in mind that creating a seemingly sustainable product could often have been significantly more sustainable. This due to the perception of inherent sustainability which leads to the overlooking of certain aspects that could have (less obviously) improved sustainability. Because this project is about replacing a product with a service, it already seems sustainable. But there are a lot more matters to take into account when it comes to creating a truly sustainable product. The design phase of a project can, for example, be utilized to create a sustainable end product. This is an advantage that should be used even when the end product already seems inherently sustainable. Thinking about the market, the use of the product, and so on, can also contribute to a more sustainable product. Because something is 'green' doesn't mean that it is completely sustainable. This is a mistake easily made.

This particular project is, for a case study on sustainability in project management, very interesting. As briefly mentioned, although it can be argued that this project (or at least the product) is inherently sustainable, this statement is actually slightly short-sighted. Simply observing that the end product of a project has a sustainable aspect or a sustainable impact hardly makes it (or the development process or the project management process!) sustainable. At the very least it lacks a full analysis of sustainability during the project. This can be clarified by looking at, for example, the product's entire life cycle, together with the project management life cycle. It has increasingly been argued that for a project and the product of that project to be truly sustainable, the entire process (from brainstorm to disposal) has to be taken into account (Labuschagne and Brent, 2007; Silvius et al., 2012).

When developing the 'OpenRemote' project, no thought was given to any aspect other than getting the project done. Project management in general, and this project is no exception, is often very short term and result-driven. Although obtaining your favored end-result is not a bad thing, narrowing your vision to that alone can have a negative impact on the end-product as a whole. This tunnel vision means that there is no time or effort set aside to think about what will happen *after* the project is finished. In this particular case, the Finalist team paid such specific (and limited) attention to their role within the product's life cycle, that many decisions that could have enhanced sustainability in both the product and the process were foregone. Even more so, these decisions weren't even thought of or considered. Therefore the main research question is: How can a project and its project management be analyzed for sustainability and how can adequate actions be selected?

In an attempt to answer this question we will have to look at important sustainability and project management concepts and apply them to an actual project. This will move theory into practice and provide a sense of understanding about how to use these concepts. Eventually we will draw several overall conclusions that represent some of the most important factors when it comes to analyzing your project for sustainability (and eventually using it to improve the sustainability of your project before it ends). It will contribute to a more focused understanding of what is important and necessary in order to analyze a project and its project management.

By using several tools and concepts that have been explored in sustainability literature, the case study will serve as a way of showing how these actually apply in practice. With this, we hope to clarify the importance of these aspects, show the complexity and extent of a project's sustainability, and hopefully discover some practical implications for projects, project managers, and all those involved in project processes.

First, we will start off by recapitulating general sustainability literature that is relevant for our analysis. The six principles of sustainability will be discussed, together with the sustainability checklist. After this we will discuss scoping within

theories on sustainability in project management. This section will explain the theoretical background necessary to gain a deeper understanding of the analysis. After this theoretical review the approach to our analysis will be clarified and structured.

BACKGROUND

Sustainable development has been defined by various people. The most common accepted one is the Brundtlandt definition in their report "Our common future" (1987): "development that meets the needs of the present without compromising the ability of future generations to meet their own needs". The linkage between sustainable development and project management has been defined by Schipper and Silvius (2012). They define sustainable project management as the "development, delivery and management of project-organized change in policies, processes, resources, assets or organizations, with consideration of the six principles of sustainability, in the project, its results and its effects".

This definition is the basis for observing the sustainability aspects of a project. The definition speaks about 3 important concepts. First, it's about delivering change. Second, it's about further operationalizing sustainability into 6 principles. Thirdly it's about changing the ordinary scope of projects. Taking sustainability and sustainable development as a starting point for organizing and doing business will obviously lead to change in these concepts -- change which is most commonly going to be delivered by projects. The Brundtland definition suggests changing our short-term perspective into a long-term perspective. Although this type of view often contradicts the very short-termed nature of projects, it needs to be applied there as well: do not limit yourself to looking at the project and its results, but also look at the effects of the project and its result. Maybe one of the most important things needed to reach this is guidance on making sustainability more practical.

This is done by the decomposition of the concept of sustainability into six principles (Silvius et al., 2012). These principles are:

1. **Sustainability is about balancing or harmonizing social, environmental and economic interests:** In order to contribute to sustainable development a company should satisfy all 'three pillars' of sustainability: social, environmental and economic also more well-known as people, planet and profit. The dimensions are interrelated, i.e. they influence each other in various ways. One way of considering sustainability is to 'balance' social, economic and environmental aspects by trading off the negative effects of doing business for a somewhat lower profit. This can be done, for example, by compensating CO2 emission by planting new trees or compensating unhealthy work pressure by higher salaries. A more proactive approach to sustainability looks at how organizations create a 'harmony' of social, environmental and economic aspects in their activities. This approach is not about compensating bad effects, but about creating good effects (Silvius and Schipper, 2010).

2. **Sustainability is about both short term and long term orientation:** A sustainable company should consider the long-term consequences of their actions and not only focus on short-term gains. Especially firms listed on the stock market have overemphasized the importance of short-term gains, trying to increase performance from quarterly report to quarterly report, and thereby losing long term vision. An important notion in this aspect is that the economical perspective, because of discount rates, tends to value short term effects more than long term effects, whereas social impacts or environmental degradation may not occur before the long-term.

3. **Sustainability is about local and global orientation:** The increasing globalization of economies *affect the* geographical area that organizations influence. Whether intentionally or not, many organizations are influenced by international stakeholders whether these are competitors, suppliers or (potential) customers. The behavior and actions of organizations therefore have an effect on economic, social and environmental aspects, both locally and globally. "In order to efficiently address these nested and inter-linked processes sustainable development has to be a coordinated effort playing out across several levels, ranging from the global to the regional and the local" (Gareis et al., 2011).

4. **Sustainability is about consuming the income, not the capital. Sustainability implies that "the natural capital remains intact:** This means that the source and sink functions of the environment should not be degraded. Therefore, the extraction of renewable resources should not exceed the rate at which they are renewed, and the absorptive capacity of the environment to assimilate waste, should not be exceeded." (Gilbert et al., 1996). This principle is common knowledge in business from the economic perspective. Finance managers know that a company which uses its capital instead of its income to pay for its costs will soon be insolvent. From a social or environmental perspective the impact of this kind of behavior may not be visible in the short-term. It will, however, cause degradation of resources in the long run. In order to be sustainable companies have to manage not only their economic capital but also their social and environmental capital.

5. **Sustainability is about transparency and accountability:** The principle of transparency implies that *an organizatio*n is open about its policies, decisions and actions, including the environmental and social effects of those actions and policies. This implies that organizations provide timely, clear and relevant information to their stakeholders so

that these stakeholders can evaluate the organization's actions and can address potential issues with these actions. The principle of accountability is logically connected to this. Accountability implies that an organization is responsible for its policies, decisions and actions and the effect of these on environment and society. The principle also implies that an organization accepts this responsibility and is willing to be held accountable for these policies, decisions and actions.

6. **Sustainability is also about personal values and ethics:** A key element of sustainability is change. Change towards more sustainable (business) practices. As argued by Robinson (2004) and Martens (2006), sustainable development is inevitably a normative concept, reflecting values and ethical considerations of the society. Part of the change that is needed to increase sustainable development will therefore also be the implicit or explicit set of values that we as professionals, business leaders or consumers have and that influence or lead our behavior. GRI Deputy Director Nelmara Arbex puts it clear and simple: "in order to change the way we DO things, we need to change the way we VIEW things".

The six principles, as explained previously, provide a powerful guidance to sustainability. The principles have not, however, offered a lot of practical guidance to sustainability. By operationalizing them, we can achieve this. This is done by knowledgeable selection of GRI-indicators. An IPMA project management Expert group selected the most appropriate GRI-indicators most suitable for project management (Silvius, 2010). These indicators were grouped together to form a checklist. This so-called sustainability checklist, which is divided to portray the triple-p concept, can be seen next.

In this checklist, sustainability indicators are portrayed for each triple-p aspect, after which they are explained in slightly more detail (See Table 1).

Table 1. Checklist

Economic Sustainability	Return on Investment	- Direct financial benefits - Net Present Value
	Business Agility	- Flexibility/Optionality in the project - Increased business flexibility
Environmental Sustainability	Transport	- Local procurement - Digital communication - Traveling - Transport
	Energy	- Energy used - Emission/CO2 from energy used
	Waste	- Recycling - Disposal
	Materials and resources	- Reusability - Incorporated energy Waste
Social sustainability	Labor Practices and Decent Work	- Employment - Labor/Management relations - Health and Safety - Training and Education - Organisational learning - Diversity and Equal opportunity
	Human Rights	- Non-discrimination - Freedom of association - Child labour - Forced and compulsory labor
	Society and Customers	- Community support - Public policy/ Compliance - Customer health and safety - Products and services labeling - Market communication and Advertising - Customer privacy - Investment and procurement practices
	Ethical Behaviour	- Bribery and corruption - Anti-competition behavior

The different studies and publications on sustainability and project management show that the question of what sustainability means for them cannot be answered without discussing the scope or system boundaries of project management.

What should be considered in scope and what shouldn't? In this question projects are, as temporary organizations, related to a non-temporary 'permanent' organization, and realize changes that benefit the strategy or goals of this organization. The permanent organization utilizes resources and assets in its operational business processes to deliver benefits or value to its customers and ultimately deliver business performance (e.g. profit, market share, return in capital, etc.) to the organization and its stakeholders. Its activities are based on goals that are developed or set in a strategic management process. The strategic management of the organization, however, does not just include setting goals. It also includes evaluating the business performance of the organization against these goals. If the performance is satisfactory, the operations may continue. But if the performance is unsatisfactory, because of lack of performance or because of changing goals, there may be reason to change something in the organization. In that case a temporary organization, in the form of a project, is commonly used to create this change. The change may concern the resources, assets or business processes of the permanent organization, but also the products/services rendered or the internal policies and procedures. The selection of the 'right' changes for the organization is usually part of a process called portfolio management. Figure 1 illustrates this relationship between projects as temporary organizations and the permanent organization (Silvius, et al., 2012).

When discussing the scopes and boundaries within sustainability and project management, it is important to specify what scope we will take into account. We make a comprehensive distinction between the *internal scope*, which is focused on the project (delivery and management, See Figure 2, the blackened fields are considered 'in scope') and the *external* scope, which is focused on the end product (the result and effect of the project; See Figure 3, the blackened fields are considered 'in scope').

APPLICATION OF SUSTAINABILITY

Issues

With respect to sustainability in project management three main issues can be identified.

First of all, project managers give no thought to sustainability in their project. This most commonly has to do with their attitude and position towards their sponsor and the fact that it often isn't viewed as their responsibility. But project managers are also not unfamiliar with the right attitude, and aren't taught to have this attitude, because of the various 'body of knowledge' and certification programs that do not yet make sustainability a part of their integral approach to the profession.

The second issue is that if an analysis is done, project managers tend to look at the project assignment (the project result) alone. This narrow project orientation leads to misunderstanding what the real change is. Because of this orientation possibilities or unintended outcomes are often missed when not observing the project from an holistic viewpoint.

The third issue is that there is no structural and documented approach (the combination of an action plan and knowledge) that can lead to a full analysis. Besides this, there is no guidance on the selection of adequate actions that is derived from a possibility list.

A first step in solving these issues, is developing adequate knowledge of sustainability as an integral and holistic perspective in development and project management. This chapter will contribute to this knowledge by defining an approach for the full analysis of sustainability in a project and its project management. Where the proof is in the eating, this approach is applied to the Open remote casus.

Method of Analysis

The method of analysis should meet three criteria. First it should identify all possibilities. We would not like to miss any opportunity to integrate sus-

Figure 1. Projects (temporary organizations) vs. permanent organizations

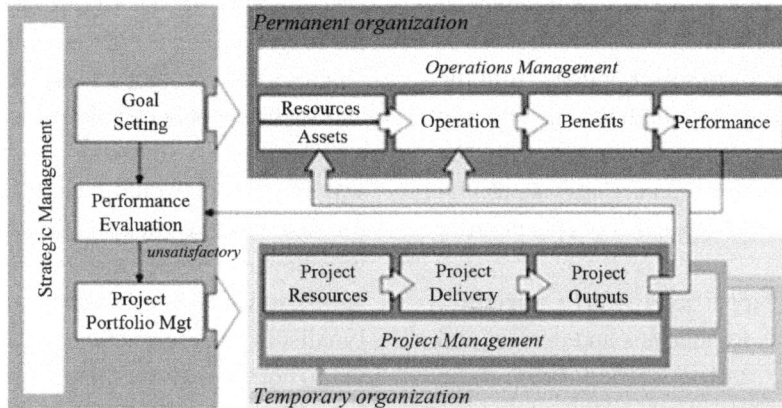

Figure 2. Internal scope

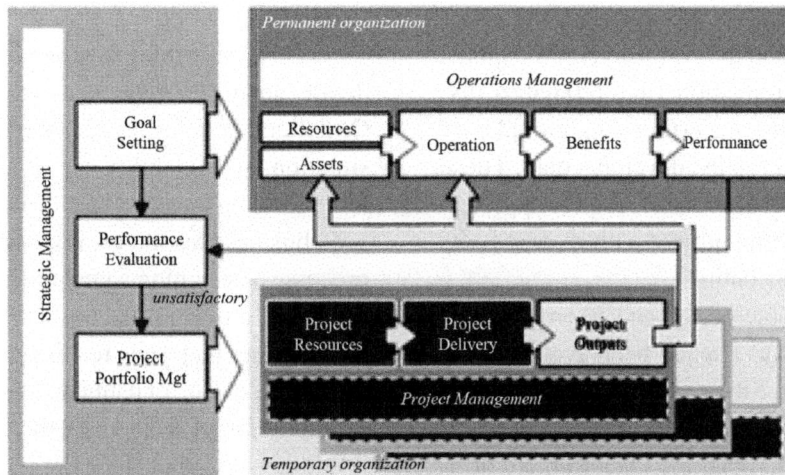

Figure 3. External scope

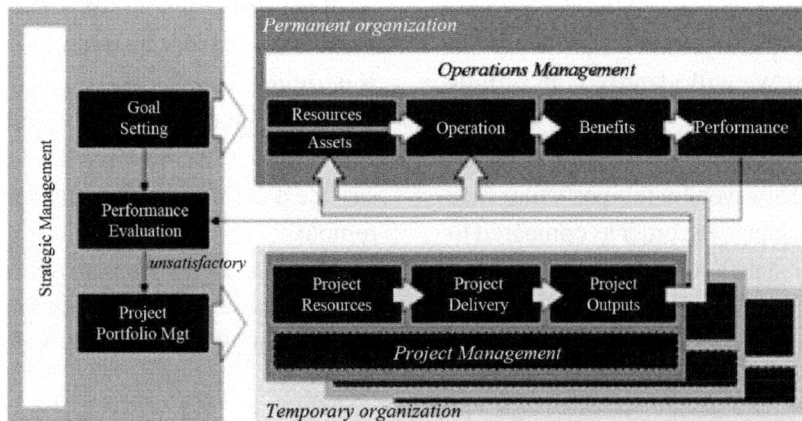

tainability in a (this) project. Second of all, an analysis method is in practice only useful when it leads towards actual action within real life, therefore the method needs to select options from the range of opportunities with high change of being applied by the project (and company). Thirdly, the method should combine the necessary steps and the appropriate knowledge and concepts in order to be successful.

Silvius and Schipper (2012) give a handful of meaningful tools for analysis and design, and includes a 'getting started' section. From these 'getting started' guidelines the chapter suggests (from the perspective of the project manager) that there are a number of actions to be taken to increase sustainability within project management. These are: take responsibility as a project manager; understand the company; set the goals; analyze the current situation; find and analyze discrepancies; assess the uncertainty and complexity of the project; and finally, develop a plan. These steps form a comprehensive and logical approach to analyze an existing project with respect to its sustainability contribution.

The 'OpenRemote' project and the project management process has already been analyzed and described detail in Silvius and Nedeski's (2011) paper, where the case was used as an example of a Green IS project. What the OpenRemote project team *has done*, thus, was already described. Although we use the same case, we will take a different approach. Instead of trying to analyze what they did (which has already been done) we will analyze the project in terms of what they could and/or should do. We will identify both pitfalls and opportunities.

In general these steps do meet our criteria for the analysis method. However, for this particular case we do somewhat change the order as compared to the original order stated, and leave some actions out as well that are irrelevant to the case. First, we leave out the first step, "Take responsibility

for sustainability". We analyze this case from a sustainability perspective so we are already taking responsibility for sustainability. Of course the OpenRemote project has already been finished and we have not been able to discuss our findings with Finalist IT. So it's not possible to see in what way Finalist IT would have taken responsibility for sustainability in real life with this case. We will however select the most probable options with knowledge we have about the ambition of Finalist IT with respect to sustainability. Second, we do not set goals for this case study. It's our goal to explore all possibilities so we would not limit our options. Our goal is to analyze and document. Next to changing the order, we also want to add actions that reflects the problems described in the "issues" paragraph.

Before describing our analysis approach in detail, an observation can be made about the OpenRemote solution compared to the original situation. Sustainability can be applied at various levels ranging from less bad to good: improving the used business resources, improving the business processes, designing a new business model up to designing a new product which is sustainable in itself. Using materials resulting in less pollution (reduction of $Co2$ or using less water) would be an example of improvements at the business resource level, this also counts for the prototypes of NEC who produced a prototype that uses no batteries, but generated energy from pressing the button, giving consumers a choice of delivery of a remote at all would be a choice of a new business model in this case and the Open Remote service solution is definitely an example of a product sustainable in itself. Some of these possibilities are shown in Figure 4. But this casus has the Open Remote service a starting point instead of the traditional remote.

With the Open Remote service as a starting viewpoint, we took the following concrete steps in analyzing this casus, which are listed next.

Figure 4. Overview of possibilities

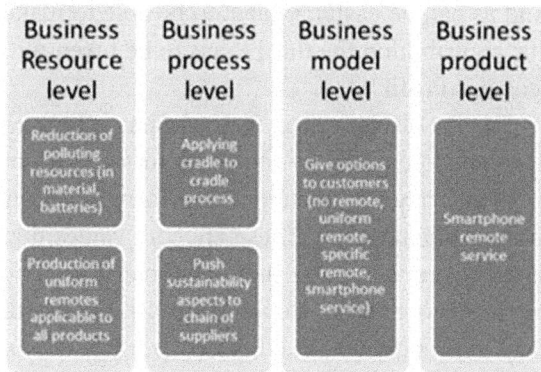

Business Resource level	Business process level	Business model level	Business product level
Reduction of polluting resources (in material, batteries)	Applying cradle to cradle process	Give options to customers (no remote, uniform remote, specific remote, smartphone service)	Smartphone remote service
Production of uniform remotes applicable to all products	Push sustainability aspects to chain of suppliers		

Step 1: Understanding Finalist IT with respect to sustainability.

Step 2: Understand the big picture:

    Step 2a: Be aware and document the real change.

    Step 2b: Life cycle analysis.

Step 3: Systematic confrontation of the sustainability project management knowledge to both the internal and external scope view of the casus.

Step 4: Analysis of the findings.

Step 5: Select realistic opportunities from the case situation.

With these steps all applicable actions from the company will be presented. The case is written from the perspective of within the company; therefore we will take the company as a starting point. After analyzing all possibilities, selecting the appropriate ones can only be done with a decision makers mind. This mind will, in the first step, be explored by analyzing the company culture to be able to make assumptions about the sustainability principles they would find important.

In order to explore all possibilities, the most important thing is to think about the big picture instead of just about the case context itself. Understanding the big picture consists of two sub-steps.

First of all, a common mistake is the identification of possibilities only from the project perspective. Certainly where a solution has already been defined, the analysis tends to have a result-orientation only. Although the focus is often on the result, in reality a project delivers change from a current situation towards a new situation, and this change can be delivered at 4 levels: resource improvement, process improvement, business model improvement and product or service improvement. So it is important to identify at what level the change is made and what extra possibilities or situations this will render. The second step consists of keeping (and documenting) the life cycle of both the current and new situation (the new situation being the result of this project) closely in mind. We take good care to look at both the life cycle chain from the economic, environmental, and social perspective. With this approach no information will be missed, or it will be excluded in awareness. The third step of the analysis is applying all sustainability knowledge to the internal and the external scope of the OpenRemote project with of course the broader context of the casus in mind. In this way, the project management process and the project result and its effects will be explored. This confrontation is about applying the six principles of sustainability and the project management checklist. It is expected that sometimes the outcomes seem to overlap. This is, for example, the case for the first principle of sustainability ("sustainability is about balancing the economic, environmental in social aspects") and the subcategories of the project management checklist (people, planet, profit). Because the checklist is an operationalization of the 6 principles and the 6 principles give powerful viewpoints and angles to the situation, we apply them rigorously. At the end we will summarize and analyze all possibilities and select realistic opportunities when the company situation has been taken into account.

CASE ANALYSIS

Step 1: Understanding Finalist IT with Respect to Sustainability

In exploring Finalist's view on sustainability, we can quite clearly look at aspects like their mission statement, their listed company values, and the activities they undertake that are related to sustainability. All information was found on their Website (http://www.finalist.nl) in March 2012.

Finalist's mission statement is a good starting point to uncover their stance towards sustainability: "We help our customers achieve long lasting competitive benefits by successfully implementing best of breed IT-solutions." There is a specific mention of a 'long lasting' view, which would imply that the company aims to look beyond simply the assignment of creating the product or service. This statement can be expected to be reflected in the use of extended life cycle models; so beyond the project life cycle. With this statement, you could expect a sense of long term planning and a long-term view in projects.

Finalist explicitly discusses their opinion on and action taken towards *Corporate Social Responsibility*. They help the foundation 'WorkMate' by donating 700 hours of software development to this charity. In their own opinion, in this way they can make a significant contribution to the growth and ambition that WorkMate has in mind. WorkMate arranges charity activities that, when viewed through the Triple-P eye, can be categorized as people and planet activities. These activities are aimed at improving both the environment and social conditions. Finalist mentions this activity on their Website in the "who are we" section. They view CSR as a part of who they are as a company, and obviously aim to make a significant contribution. According to their mission statement, they wish to make a contribution to their customers' long-term existence, and according to their CSR activity with WorkMate they wish to make a simi-lar contribution to society and nature in general. And as can be easily argued, to be able to make this contribution the third P has to be taken into account: Profit.

Finalist also states on their company Website that their core company values are very important to them. They, as a matter of fact, form the DNA of their organization. These are core values that they also recognize in their customers, as they say. Four core values are listed: Smart, Balanced, Dedicated and Reliable. *What do these values mean for Finalist's potential ambition of sustainability?*

From these simple pieces of information that are easily recovered, i.e. the mission statement, CSR activities and company values, we can make several observations about their (potential) sustainability ambition. In fact we try to relate the remarks to the 6 principles of sustainability.

First of all, the presence of sustainability within the company and the company strategy is already implied within their mission statement. This can matter-of-factly be derived from the fact that Finalist mentions achieving *long lasting* competitive benefits. Thinking about the long term instead of just the short term is, after all, one of the characteristics of sustainability. This connects to the principle `Sustainability is about the short term and the long term´. Sustainability is mentioned explicitly when it comes to their CSR activity. Nevertheless, this mentioning is from an 'idealistic' point of view, mainly by supplying software development hours to the WorkMate foundation. Although this CSR activity is explicitly placed as a section to describe 'who Finalist is' as a company, the term 'sustainability' does not seem to be a part of their business (process). It is, however, a hopeful thing that they would be spending time and resources on an activity that doesn't fall within their usual company activities. After all, it means that they are spending extra time and money to achieve sustainability. It is therefore not unlikely that they would be willing to do so to implement the concept within their company as well. This could be linked to the principle "sustainability is about personal values and ethics". Finalist (maybe unknowingly) includes the balancing of People and Profit in their company values. Their second company value is to be 'balanced'. They explain that the time pressure and hard work of the IT industry is balanced by allowing employees to have free time and relaxation. Also, in realizing a working relationship between management and employees there is room for the personal development of employees. This refers to the principle "sustainability is about balancing economic, environmental and social aspects". Another potentially interesting thing, which might be purely speculative, is the fact that Finalist mentions creativity as an opportunity to offer competitive benefits to their clients (they mention this in their company values). Both a focus on clients and creativity can be beneficial for sustainability. It, after all, often means that one has to come up with out of the box thinking to implement and understand the concept. If Finalist values creative thinking, and can empathize with their clients, they can think broader and look beyond the simple project borders. This is where the life and value chain would come into play; they imply looking beyond the simple project scope and looking to the product/service's entire life cycle.

With this information it can be suggested that Finalist tries to be transparent about their intentions as well as accountable for their actions and decision. This refers to the principle 'sustainability is about transparency and accountability".

So, by looking at a company's ambition towards sustainability you can create certain expectation. To recapitulate, we expect Finalist to be open for the following principles:

- A balance in People, Planet and Profits aspects.
- Both a short term and long term view.
- An emphasis on personal values and ethics.
- Transparency and accountability.

Step 2: Understand the Big Picture

Step 2a: Be Aware and Document the Real Change

An essential step in this analysis is describing and understanding the big picture. First one needs to understand the real change that is happening. Sustainability can be applied at various levels ranging from less bad to good: improving the used business resources, improving the business processes, designing a new business model up to designing a new product which is sustainable in itself. Using materials resulting in less pollution (reduction of CO_2 or using less water) would be an example of an improvement at the business resource level, this also counts for the prototypes of NEC who produced a prototype that uses no batteries, but generated energy from pressing the button, giving consumers a choice of delivery of a remote at all would be a choice of a new business model. In this case the Open Remote service solution is definitely an example of a product sustainable in itself. Some of these possibilities are shown in the earlier presented 'Overview of possibilities' (Figure 4). But instead of using the traditional remote as a starting point (which is what the project aims to change), the casus uses the Open Remote service a starting point.

Step 2b: Life Cycle Analysis

Sustainability is about the 'short term and the long term' and it's about 'local and global'. This view should be reflected in our analysis. Therefore, we cannot judge (dis)advantages and possibilities of one solution without comparing it with the current situation and their effects to the future and on a global scale. We describe the big picture by presenting the life cycle of both the current situation (in which ordinary remotes are used) and the life cycle of the service solution (in which remotes are replaced with a software application).

Assumptions made about the life cycle of this new service and the old product obviously play an important role in the concept of *sustainability*. It is useful to visualize the value change of both situations; the 'old' product of a remote control for all your entertainment products and the 'new' service 'OpenRemote' app. For the old product, it is doable to take the life cycle of one product; the television remote. Even though there are many more appliances that this would apply to (like air conditioning and a stereo set), it is possible to generalize these in the one life cycle visualization of the television remote. This can be done because in general, every appliance in an average home that requires a remote consists of the same parts. In general, appliances in your house that require a remote consist of the appliance itself, and then the remote. This is the case for the TV. It is useful to see what it takes to go from creation to destruction for both situations. Only then can we truly state that one is more sustainable than the other. Figure 5 shows the value chain, from creation to disposal, of the television remote.

As mentioned in the introduction the 'OpenRemote' project seems to be creating an inherently sustainable product. Namely, a service that replaces a product which, as the project's project manager argues, will reduce waste and thus lead to a more sustainable situation. From the perspective of the life cycle value chain, there are several early important observations that can be made.

- A remote and a TV more often than not come as one package. Every time a television is bought, a remote control is produced and standard packed with the TV.
- People often buy an extra remote, or a remote that is more to their taste than the one in the standard TV package, for their own convenience. This is not a product of necessity. In every household we will encounter several remotes (frequently unused).

- When a consumer installs the OpenRemote application, this does not automatically means the old physical remote is gone and therefore it doesn't instantly reduce the amount of waste (See Figure 6).

Now that we have identified Finalist's sustainability intentions and clarified the big picture, we can move on to the next step. In this step we will apply the six sustainability principles and the sustainability checklist, as explored in the beginning of this chapter, on both the internal and external scope (so on both the project's process and the end product). In doing this we will analyze what was possible within the case, what observations can be made and which opportunities can be identified. In doing this we will focus not so much on the details of what was going on in the OpenRemote project, but we will focus on the project in general terms and on identifying opportunities and pitfalls.

Step 3: Systematic Confrontation of the Sustainability Project (Management) Knowledge

In the next paragraphs, a systematic confrontation of sustainability knowledge will be done. First only with respect to the internal scope (3a), thereafter with respect to the external scope (3b).

Step 3a: Systematic Confrontation of the Sustainability Project (Management) Knowledge to the Internal Scope

By combining the sustainability knowledge explored in the beginning of this chapter, we can systematically confront this knowledge with each other in the broad context of the OpenRemote project. In this section, we apply it specifically to the internal scope. With the internal scope we focus on the project management approach,

Figure 5. Life cycle chain of TV remote ("old" situation)

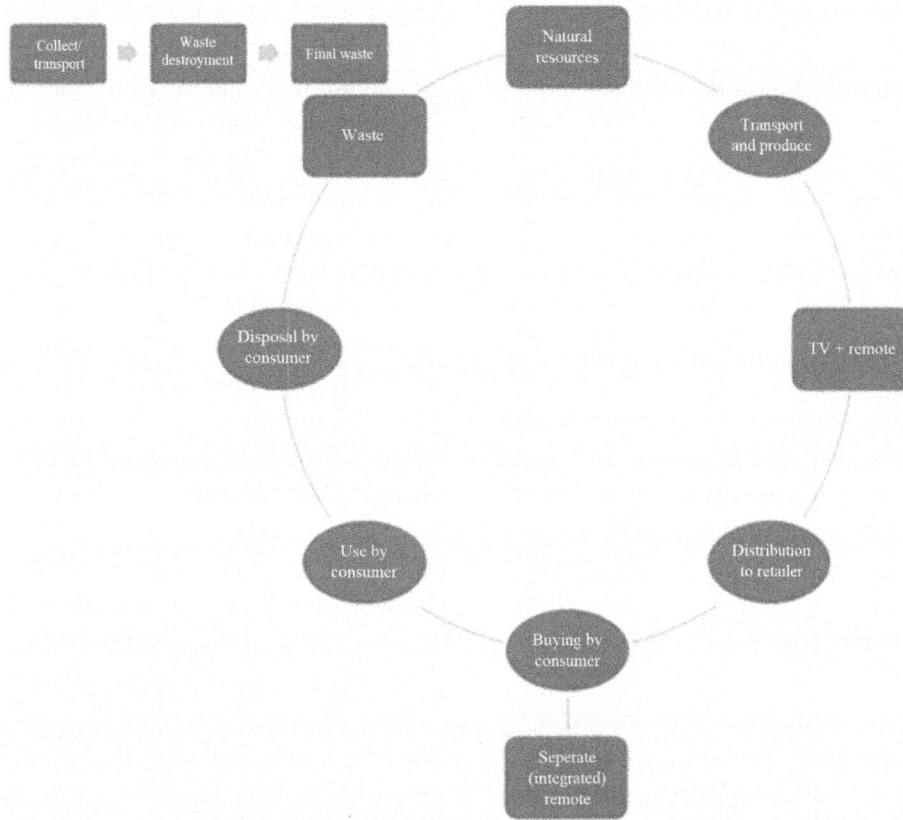

Figure 6. Life cycle chain of OpenRemote app ("new" situation)

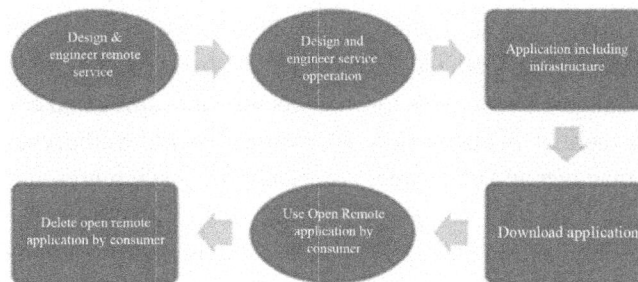

staffing, project delivery, materials used in the process etc. Aspects of the six principles of project management and the checklist that are relevant for this section will be portrayed. In this section, we will make critical observations that utilize the theories mentioned before, and go further by putting them into practice. This shows how the theories are applicable and shows a way of

thinking about these issues in an actual project. This should offer an example to project managers to thinking about sustainability possibilities and problems within their projects.

To categorize this confrontation and to keep a good overview, we will be categorizing by means of the sustainability principles. These principles envelop much of the relevant points that can be made. Since, when looking at a project through the lens of these principles, several observations, and categories seems to overlap and/or fit together, we ended up with four relevant categories:

- Triple bottom line.
- Short term and Long term/Local and Global.
- Consume income, not capital.
- Transparency, accountability, personal values and ethics.

In this section, then, we will analyze what the company *can do*, not what they have done (even though, inevitably, this is part of the analysis at times). This will provide valuable opportunities when it comes to thinking about sustainability.

Triple Bottom Line

There are a few interesting observations to be made when looking at the *social* aspect of the triple bottom line. Finalist Beijing, the creator of the OpenRemote project, is merely one of the locations of Finalist, which has its main office in the Netherland. The Dutch division, being the main office, can act as a leader through leading by example for the substantially smaller Beijing office. A good example when it comes to the social aspects of the projects. Think about standards for staff health, the encouragement of an open working relationship between manager and employee, the possibility for education for staff members and diversity in staff hire. By setting standards that might not be common in Asian companies, the Dutch company can provide their Beijing office with social advantages. In this way, they can influence the Asian community in its role as a leader of social conventions.

When it comes to the *environmental* aspect of the Triple-P, we can assume the presence of electronic communication, instead of environmentally harmful means of transportation like frequent flying. With the many boundaries that are crossed in this project (a foreign client, a main office in

the Netherlands, and a target group in the US), transportation and communication is definitely an issue to be considered. In this case, communication through e-mail, video and telephone conferencing is used instead to minimize transport (a way to reduce the harmful spreading of, e.g., CO2).

When trying to improve the company's *economic* sustainability, an agile approach as the project's business model (the way it delivers its value) is preferable. By allowing agility, the project (and its players) can react optimally to complexity and changing circumstances.

Short Term and Long term/ Local and Global

In recent decennia Asian countries have been known for their copying and low cost production labor. Of course this is still their main focus. Despite this the project is partly executed in Beijing. The requirement and design have probably been done in Europa and the actual development has been done in Beijing. In essence a regular form of outsourcing from Europe to Asian. This is made possible by the fast emerging educational possibilities in Asia and the low cost of labor and therefore attractive to cost-oriented European executives. This represents the short term orientation and local situations. But how about the future? With its big labor force and educational possibilities a situation can develop where knowledge orientated labor in Asia represents a necessary shift for European (Dutch) employees to be seen. This is perhaps premature, but the consequences need to be kept in mind.

Consuming Income, not the Capital

At first sight this principle is applied most logically towards physical resources or material used in the project. The most used example if of course the using of oil for fuel. We consume oil in a speed that nature is not able to refill the original resource, thereby weaken this natural resource. But the principle can and should also to be applied to human capital and even software. From a human capital viewpoint this principle therefore applies to good labor practices and the relationship between management and employees. In this situation, the Dutch company they can influence good labor practices by leading by example. They can show how business with European standards work and how this can also positively influence productivity. Practical application can be aimed at training and education. In knowledge oriented work, training and education of individual employees, the team and the company is crucial for everyone. The project manager can ask what employees want to learn (beyond the project) and how can the project help them. As a spin-off the project can ask the personnel how can they contribute to the community and to transferring knowledge and vision (e.g. through public educational services). Also within daily project work we can positively apply the aspect of human rights/and (non)forced labor. Forced labor is traditionally is identified with low-skilled work where employees are forced. But in knowledge oriented work where employees are given straight instructions what and how to (build software) this will not be productive. It's about giving freedom (and borders) to knowledge workers. But when a manager gives no opportunity for own interpretation of the assignment it's also forced. Here the Dutch can, yet again, set an example. These aspects will keep employees mentally fit, in a constant learning modus and thereby productive (now and in the future).

It is possible that another client or situation exists where a similar or extended version of the OpenRemote application is necessary. Not applying the principle of consuming income instead of capital would result in the situation where the company (or a new project) has to start from scratch therefore not using the results already available. This can be the situation where the software is built in a non-reusable way. Applying the principle would require the company to build in a software architecture with generic software components which could be (partly) reused.

Transparency, Accountability, Personal Values and Ethics

This principle is all about taking responsibility for sustainability and the choices one makes in the project delivery process (in this section we only view the internal aspects of the project). The principle is best shown in the project progress report where all information, decisions, and impacts should be shown. In this case specific we expect the project report will show the following indicators.

From an economical perspective the report is expected to contain how changes in e.g. market conditions may have an effect on the value and (economic) business case of the project's result. From social sustainability we expect indicators with respect to the project delivery process. These indicators can be about diversity, the number of learning goals that are met, lessons learned and improvements to the project. From an environmental perspective we expect indicators about travelling (or the use of electronic systems) to communicate.

Step 3b: Systematic Confrontation of the Sustainability Project (Management) Tools to the External Scope

This section looks specifically at the external scope. This means that we will be looking at the end product (the result and effect of the project).

Triple Bottom Line

Obviously, OpenRemote is a change at the level of the product. It is more sustainable than the 'old' situation. The project aims to be a profitable service on the one hand, and a service that produces less waste on the other. This profitability prospect is fed by the fact that consumers are very keen on smartphones and are willing to try out, use and even pay (a smart price) for smartphone applications. And at the end of the day, people watch TV with their smartphone next to them.

From and *environmental* viewpoint there is obviously a tremendous possibility to reduce waste. Remotes come with every apparatus in a household and usually people have unused remotes stored elsewhere. The Open Remote app can be downloaded numerous times for fraction of the energy used to produce a physical one. Two aspects however need to be considered. First: what are the effects of the extra use of a smartphone (they consume lot of energy). Secondly these waste reduction advantages will only be realized when TV producers stop producing physical remotes or give a choice to the customer to buy them separately. This will reduce production costs for the producers. So the OpenRemote service can also affect the business model and marketing possibilities (they can distinguish themselves) of the producers.

By introducing this service, there are still lot of physical remotes in use. This is where the problem of perceived inherent sustainability comes into play. By assuming that there is a certain level of sustainability inherent to the action of turning a product into service, a lot of opportunities are missed. Thinking from cradle to cradle concept would have made it possible to, e.g., make deals or promote with retail organizations about redelivering their old remotes. Taking a broader view than just the finishing the product in its simplest form can seriously enhance sustainability.

It is, in this light, important to explain that we're not stating that it's the responsibility of Finalist IT to actively change the business model of TV-producers (a business model in which remote controls are delivered as a standard service). Consumer choices and feedback would work most efficiently, but it would certainly count for responsibility when the company or the project takes an active initiative.

From an environmental viewpoint there are also less travelling costs to be expected because the physical goods do not need to be transported to shops and consumers do not need to transport themselves to purchase the service.

From a Green IS/Green IT abstraction we can learn that the delivery of the service (OpenRemote providing the software, data and regular updates to the consumer) could be designed in an eco-friendly way. For example: choose a location to host the application where temperature is low and natural cooling can be used to minimize energy use at the IT infrastructure level, the use of green energy etcetera. Although this is something that was not considered in the project, which can easily be accounted to short-term view and a lack of a broader scope and vision, it is an important point for the enhancement of Green IT in general.

From a *social responsibility* view the privacy aspect comes to mind. Smartphones are (very) easy to hack. In this way information about chosen channels can be obtain and published on for example the Internet. People can be put in compromising situation, possibly harming their reputation and image. So from social aspect the design should take this into account.

Short Term and Long Term/ Local and Global

But we see more and more 'addiction' towards smartphones. For example, in China there are now (April 2012) 1 billion smartphones. Most people have multiple smartphones of which the energy used to produce is high (the year production of all smartphones requires the same amount of energy as 2,8 million households use yearly) and they all use a lot of energy. Smartphones are more and more integrated in ordinary life. And people renew their smartphones very often, realizing waste and using a lot of rare resources (often obtained through non-social labor circumstances in Africa). There is a hardly any cradle-to-cradle concept for that. The question remains whether this realizes a better footprint at all. Solving all the world's problems is hardly possible for this company.. Nevertheless it's good to keep this impact in mind for future solutions.

Consume Income, not the Capital

Advantage can be gained through the fact that the OpenRemote project creates less waste by transferring remote controls (and batteries) into a service. As already touched upon, without further agreements there is double the waste! If this product is created *and* remote controls are still standardly included when buying home entertainment equipment, both will co-exist and thus the OpenRemote service won't replace anything at all. The software application's advantage of creating less waste will, then, not matter.

Transparency and Accountability and Personal Values and Ethics

This principle is all about taking responsibility for sustainability and the choices one makes in the project result, use and effect (remember: in this section we only view the external aspects of the project). The principle is best shown in the project progress report where all information, decision, and impact should be shown. In the report should show social and environmental sustainability indicators with respect to the use and disposal of the project deliverable or result.

Step 4: Analysis

So, loaded with a lot of ideas seen from various viewpoints, we can now analyze the possibilities. The starting point for the OpenRemote case is the OpenRemote service itself. Since in a few phases prior the six principles and the checklist lead to some similar observations about sustainability aspects, we've stripped away the ideas that occur in doubles.

In the diagrams next we've attempted to organize all the observations in a viewable way, for both the internal and external view. The diagrams are organized along two axes. First, there is the traditional division in economic, environmental and social aspects. We selected the appropriate components from the checklist, followed by the finding. Each finding is preceded by and "+" or a "-" indicating whether it makes a positive contribution towards sustainability or a negative (or less sustainable). The second axis represents the scope of the life cycle. Within the internal and extern scope one can view the sustainability aspects just within the context of the cases or also with an broader perspective. In the external scope, the case context will be about the OpenRemote service, the broader viewpoint will be about the manufactures part of cradle to cradle. In most situations, the potential initiatives of the broader view will be less realizable. Mostly these initiatives are out of the influence scope of the casus stakeholders (See Figure 7).

The Internal View

There are 8 initiatives identified which would contribute to a maximum sustainable contribution, One for the economic contribution, 2 environmentally oriented and 5 socially oriented. This being an information engineering project, it makes sense that most contributions are about social aspects. There is no environmental impactful material or resource flow, but the engineering business heavily depends on knowledge workers and their development tools. Therefore, most contributions can be done in creating safe and sound working environments and also about creating learning environments within and outside the project. These aspects contribute to employees performing optimally and contributes to productivity, which also contributes to economic aspects of sustainability. Of course knowledge workers who learn also contribute to their own development and their personal value of the labor market. The reusability of software components contributes to the economic aspects namely through the aspect of productivity. In new assignments Finalist IT can deliver the product quicker or against lower (human) costs.

Figure 7. Internal view summary

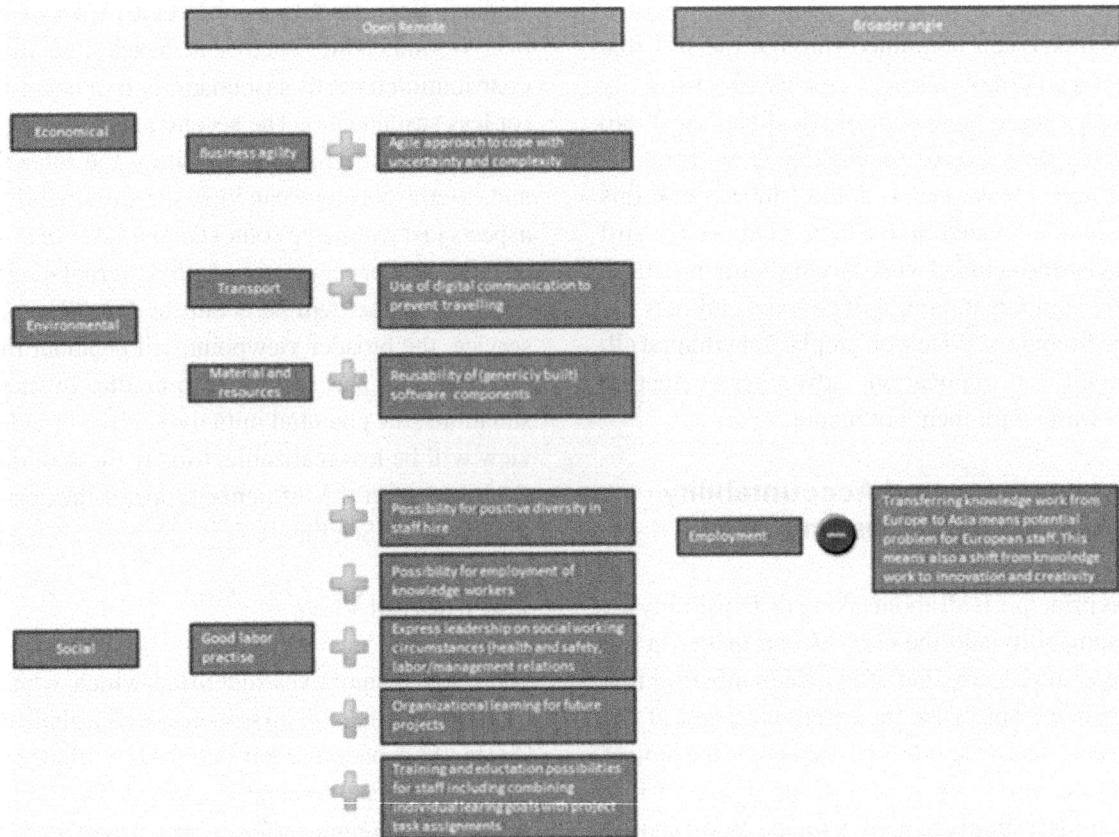

The External View

In analyzing the external view on this project, we can make some logical observations, but also some less obvious observations strike us as interesting. These observations are made merely due to the fact that we take a broader perspective on the situation. The overall finding are summarized in the Figure 8.

For the external view, there are eight positive contributions for sustainable (project management) development identified. Two for the economic orientation, and four for the environmental perspective. But there were also six aspects identified which need further attention in realizing the potential benefits of this service. They are marked with an "-" in the Figure. Except one, they all can be classified as aspects which are roughly out of

the direct influence of Finalist IT. They all can be classified as the consequence that the Open-Remote service doesn't mean that the old remotes are gone instantly, resulting in unused remotes. Although, it does give manufacturers the possibility to change their business model. The privacy aspect is the one aspect Finalist IT has direct influence. The privacy problem rests in the more or less open access to smartphones. It's not impossible to hostile connect to a smartphone, being able to obtain part of the data stored of transmitted or even influence the TV-channel being watched and to record this information. In this case, an outsider would be able to put this information on the Internet, thereby possibly sending compromising information to social media. The positive contribution directly originates from the fact that a physical product (the remote) is turned

Figure 8. External view summary

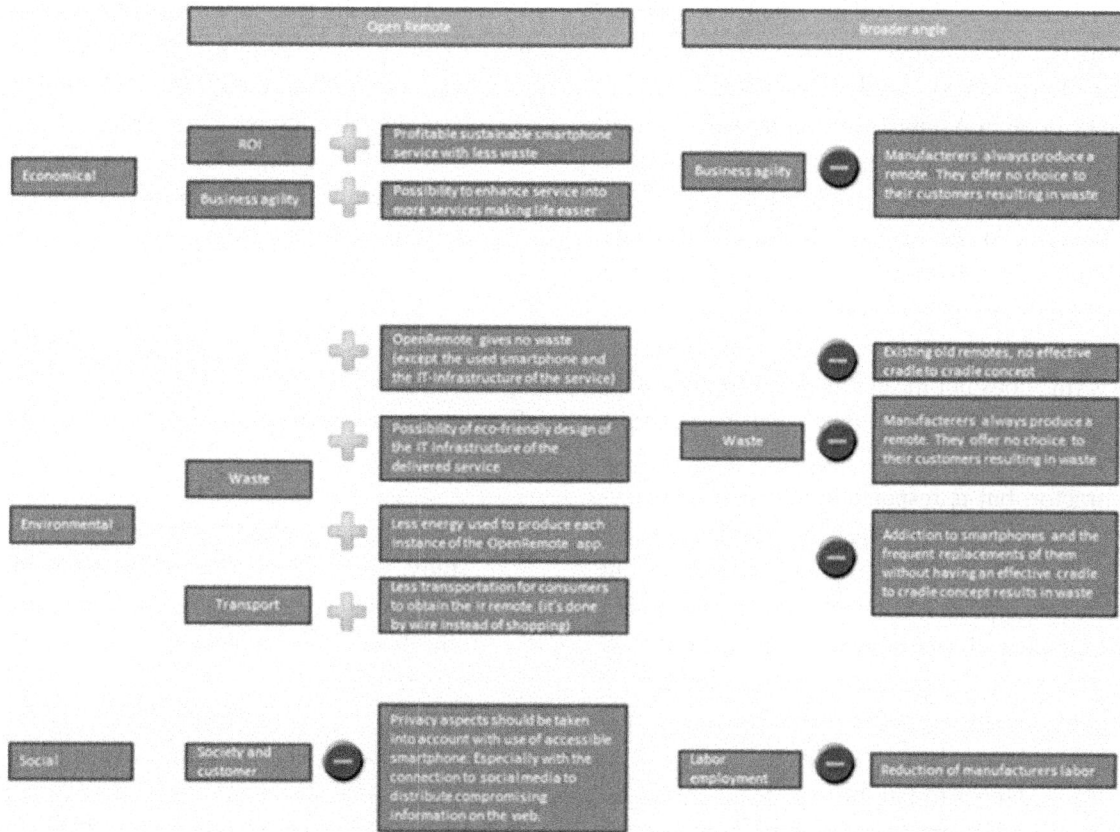

into a service. It means that less energy is used for manufacturing (of the service itself and the IT infrastructure) and transport (of the physical goods and even the transport of the consumer).

Step 5: Selecting Realistic Opportunities from the Ambition of Finalist IT

In the beginning of this analysis we looked at the ambition of Finalist IT with regards to sustainability. In that section we expected Finalist IT to actively apply and prefer the following sustainability principles:

- A balance in People, Planet and Profits aspects.
- Both a short term and long term view.

- An emphasis on personal values and ethics.
- Transparency and accountability.

With these principles in mind we do not think any possibility needs to be ruled out at first hand. Nevertheless we would like to say something about the identified sustainability aspects with respect to the business process and business model of manufacturers. Although the OpenRemote casus can result in less physical remotes, this will not be automatically the case. There is no efficient cradle-to-cradle process for old remotes resulting in reusability and less waste. The business model of manufactures, where consumers will be offered an option to buy a remote with their electronic device, will not be changed automatically. Secondly, the development of this OpenRemote service in China can be seen as an example of development of shifting labor. Where low cost production is mainly concentrated is Asiatic countries, the economic welfare and education possibilities lead to a situation where knowledge-orientated work can also be done in Asiatic countries as well (against lower costs). In the long run this will possibly lead to a new shift labor relations.

It is not in the realistic sphere of influence of Finalist IT (also being a contracting party) to expect them to take a leading role herewith and expect them to realize these goals (although naturally, this does not mean that there are measures within the project itself that Finalist can't take to improve sustainability!). Finalist IT is (just a) contractor, but is responsible for their delivery-process and has influencing power to other aspects. This doesn't mean they could win all battles, but making your points, can help. From a sustainable development viewpoint it would be great if they use their marketing power (including social media) to make this service noticeable to consumers and the general manufacturers market.

It is a danger to fall into an idealism trap. In order to implement sustainability, however, although the analysis of a project can be idealistic at some points, expectations should be realistic. This realistic view is significantly more useful to a company to be able to implement change. If we therefore apply our realistic expectations of Finalist IT to this case and the generated possibilities we would expect them to put (or continue to put) active effort into, we get the following list:

- Delivery of the OpenRemote service. It's clearly an example of a sustainable development.
- The realization of generic reusable software components for this service. Benefits of this will be the return on investment and less use of material and personal energy involved building the software.
- Design and realization of eco-friendly IT Infrastructure to service this application.

- Optimally protecting the privacy of consumers using this application.
- Express leadership in (and responsibility for) working conditions, learning and training and Chinese employees.
- Use digital equipment to communicate with employees and customers in order to prevent frequent flying.

FUTURE RESEARCH DIRECTIONS

There are many interesting directions for future research.

1. Since this chapter presents but a single case study, is recreating this analysis for other cases could provide interesting information and show if the conclusions drawn here are generalizable.
2. We saw the pitfall of only observing from the project result orientation. We must keep in mind that sustainability is about (organizational) change. So research could be done in applying the developed knowledge and skills to the organizational level (instead of the project level). By doing so, we move sustainability from the reputational level to the real business level and thereby contributing to a more sustainable society.
3. Make a sustainability checklist that is industry and/or county specific. The sustainability principles and checklist proved to be very powerful in analyzing the sustainability situation. These checklists can be made more powerful by targeting and adapting them to industry specific situations. In that case irrelevant items can be thrown out. Also, consistent and meaningful benchmarks can be set up. The checklists can also be targeted to countries where the checklist reflects positive and negative sustainability aspects.

4. Enhancement of life and value chain analysis techniques to reflect sustainability. The life cycle and value chain analysis techniques prove to be very successful in understanding current and changed situation. These techniques need to be adjusted to understand the full sustainability aspects.

5. Applying tools (like social media) as interventions to reach deeper influence. The case study showed that some outcomes can hardly be influenced by the project or the corresponding company. Influencing manufacturers to no longer automatically provide a remote control is an obvious example in this case. Nevertheless in the future customers might require projects (companies) to have a deeper influence. Social media might be an excellent and cost effective means to realize this. More research would be necessary to make this happen.

CONCLUSION

From the cases a number of conclusions can be made.

Conclusion 1: Sustainability in project management definitely stretches the scope of the project and project management.

The casus shows in practice that applying sustainability in project management will give a broader scope towards projects. There is far more to be observed and taken into account then the ordinary' product, the delivery process, the time/money/quality triangle and it's economic value view. Necessary for this is an open mind and the willingness to take a broader look that's further down the life cycle. It requires (project) managers to take responsibility transfers their role from "doing things right" towards "doing the right things". This corresponds with the observation that the role of the project manager will shift from behavioral competences towards contextual competences (PM2027). More options don't mean that every (sustainable) observation needs to be implemented. Therefore it makes decision-making and influencing more complex, while decision can't just be made from a Net Present Value (NPV) perspective alone anymore. Decision-making therefore needs transparency and accountability about the observed situation and the arguments why choices have been made.

Conclusion 2: Cyclic life cycle thinking is key to finding sustainability possibilities and implications.

More and more companies and consumers recognize the reduction of (physical) resources. Emerging welfare marks a growth in possibilities, but the resources necessary will reduce significantly if policy, way of thinking and innovation won't change. For the past decennia the way of thinking has been singular: from ground resource to waste resulting in the situation and forecast we are now in. No one really cared about the waste and disposal of natural resources. But we have become more aware and one of the real breakthroughs in sustainability thinking is thinking in circular resource flows from the cradle-to-cradle concept. The integrated life cycle analysis (from economic, environmental and social viewpoints) and putting the consumer use central (instead of the product/service) in the description of the current situation in the business processes, business model and products is an insightful technique of finding sustainability problems and possibilities.

Conclusion 3: Real (quantitative) valuation of possibilities or concern is difficult.

In the case analysis we encountered several situations where sustainability as solution can be questioned. The Open remote service declares being more sustainable because less natural resources are used in the production process. But, so we thought, the design en engineering costs electricity, probably using natural resources and there is also the servicing of the application and the smartphone. These example shows that real (and quantitative) valuating of various scenario's is difficult and in some way speculative.

Conclusion 4: Scope matters for your results.

Another important conclusion is that scope matters. Although many companies (and projects) have a tendency to limit their scope to the project itself, the scope should be broadened to be able to have a clear and complete overview of what is going on and what opportunities there are. This also holds for your starting point of analysis and corresponding opportunities for improvement. Starting from the old fashioned remote gives different opportunities when start from the service aspect.

We've specifically implemented theory on the scope in our analysis on several accounts. This is where the 'internal' and 'external' scope distinctions come into play. Although both scopes are important, they are often (if even used both) used to a certain limitation. When having an external scope, for example, there can be a tendency to look no further than the economic impact something would have on the project. Thinking about a product from creation to disposal, for example, isn't standard practice.

Conclusion 5: Sustainability requires leadership.

It was shown that after thinking about possibilities for sustainability improvements a selection was made, based on the companies ambition and values. We note that this was done based on Website information and without consulting the companies' responsible executives. Nevertheless we expect this reduces the list of directly applicable possibilities to the ones based on the direct influence a company has to take action. But to really make things more sustainable, leadership needs to be shown by taking action. In this case it's about contacting or influencing manufactures about offering choice to their consumers or even to

stop automatically producing traditional remotes. Networks and networking in general and probably social media especially could play in important role in this development and call for leadership.

REFERENCES

Brundtland, G. Harlem, et al. (1987). Our common future: World commission on environment and development. Oxford, UK: Oxford University Press.

Elkington, J. (1997). *Cannibals with forks: The triple bottom line of 21ˢᵗ century business*. Oxford, UK: Capstone Publishing Ltc.

Gareis, R., Huemann, M., & Martinuzzi, A. (2011). What can project management learn from considering sustainability principles? *Project Perspectives, 33*, 60–65.

Labuschagne, C., & Brent, A. C. (2007). Sustainable project life cycle management: The need to integrate life cycles in the manufacturing sector. In *Proceedings of OpenUp*. OpenUp.

Martens, P. (2006). Sustainability: Science or fiction? *Sustainability: Science, Practice, & Policy, 2*(1), 1–5. Retrieved from http://sspp. proquest.com/archives/vol2iss1/communityessay. martens.html

Robinson, J. (2004). Squaring the circle? Some thoughts on the idea of sustainable development. *Ecological Economics, 48*, 369–384. doi:10.1016/j.ecolecon.2003.10.017.

Silvius, A. J. G. (2010). Workshop report group 2. In H. Knoepfel (Ed.), *Survival and Sustainability as Challenges for Projects*, (pp. 155 – 160). International Project Management Association (IPMA).

Silvius, A. J. G., & Nedeski, S. (2011). Sustainability in IS projects: A case study. In *Proceedings of the 22nd Annual Conference of the International Information Management Association*. International Information Management Association.

Silvius, A. J. G., & Schipper, R. (2010). A maturity model for integrating sustainability in projects and project management. In *Proceedings of the 24th World Congress of the International Project Management Association (IPMA)*. Istanbul, Turkey: IPMA.

Silvius, A. J. G., & Schipper, R. (2012). Sustainability in the business case. In J.-P. Pantouvakis (Ed.), *26th World Congress of the International Project Management Association (IPMA)*, (pp. 1062-1069). Crete, Greece: IPMA.

Silvius, A. J. G., Schipper, R., Planko, J., Brink, J., & Köhler, A. (2012). *Sustainability in project management*. Farnham, UK: Gower Publishing.

Silvius, A. J. G., Van den Brink, J., & Köhler, A. (2012). The impact of sustainability on project management. In Linger, H., & Owen, J. (Eds.), *The Project as a Social System* (pp. 183–200). Victoria, Australia: Monash University Publishing.

ADDITIONAL READING

Association for Project Management. (2006). *APM support sustainability outlooks*. Retrieved from http://www.apm.org.uk/page.asp?categoryID=4

Buttrick, R. (2000). *The project workout: A toolkit for reaping the rewards from all your business projects*. London: Prentice Hall.

Crane, A., & Matten, D. (2004). *Business ethics: A European perspective: Managing corporate citizenship and sustainability in the age of globalization*. Oxford, UK: Oxford University Press.

Duncan, W. R. (1996). *A guide to the project management body of knowledge*. Retrieved from http://www.unipi.gr/akad_tmhm/biom_dioik_tech/files/pmbok.pdf

Dyllick, T., & Hockerts, K. (2002). Beyond the business case for corporate sustainability. *Business Strategy and the Environment, 11*, 130–141. doi:10.1002/bse.323.

Eid, M. (2009). *Sustainable development and project management*. Cologne, Germany: Lambert Academic Publishing.

Gareis, R., Heumann, M., & Martinuzzi, A. (2009). *Relating sustainable development and project management*. Berlin: IRNOP IX.

Gilbert, R., Stevenson, D., Girardet, H., & Stern, R. (Eds.). (1996). *Making cities work: The role of local authorities in the urban development*. Oxford, UK: Earthscan Publications Ltd..

Labuschagne, C., & Brent, A. C. (2006). Social indicators for sustainable project and technology life cycle management in the process industry. *International Journal of Life Cycle Assessment, 11*(1), 3–15. doi:10.1065/lca2006.01.233.

McKinley, M. (2008). *Where is project management running to…?* Paper presented at the International Project Management Association. Rome, Italy.

Russell, J. (2008). Corporate social responsibility: What it means for the project manager. In *Proceedings of the PMI Global Congress*. Denver, CO: PMI.

Silvius, A. J. G., Brink, J., & Köhler, A. (2010). Sustainability in project management, questions and responsibilities. In *Proceedings of the International Conference on Sustainability in Business (ICSB)*. Putrajaya, Malaysia: ICSB.

Taylor, T. (2008). A sustainability checklist for managers of projects. *PMWorldToday, 10*(1).

Wartick, S. L., & Wood, D. J. (1998). *International business and society*. Malden, MA: Blackwell.

World Commission on Environment and Development. (1987). *Our common future*. Oxford, UK: Oxford University Press.

Chapter 22

Drivers for Sustainable Project Management Behaviours in Facilities Management:
Fluorescent Tube Business Case Example

Stephanie Steele
USI Group, Australia

ABSTRACT

This chapter moves outside the traditional methodology of project management, looking more broadly at aspects that influence project sustainability initiatives, including regulation, legislation, brand reputation, government and non-government organisations, and client requirements. Using the example of mercury recycling from fluorescent tubes generated from the Facilities Management (FM) sector in Australia, the relationship between environmental management systems, specifically ISO 14001:2004, and project management aspects are highlighted. The importance of management support, both at a strategic and project level is discussed. The opportunity to create competitive advantage from the sales perspective is demonstrated, through a cost justification and review of client sensitivity to influencing factors, enabling reasoned decision making for a successful, environmentally sustainable initiative.

INTRODUCTION

The project initiation and planning phases are the key project focus areas of this chapter. They are crucial to establishing a framework for success in implementing sustainable environmental outcomes within projects, initiated within the bounds of a corporate structure.

This chapter explores the question 'can corporate sustainability be used to manage compliance and brand reputation within FM projects, while mitigating risk and leverage commercial opportunity?'

The interrelationship between social, environmental and economic sustainability are discussed and a proposal for a corporation is presented,

DOI: 10.4018/978-1-4666-4177-8.ch022

highlighting actions to be taken to achieve the desired outcome. These actions will influence individual project outcomes, taking into account environmental sustainability. The key contributors of Chief Executive Officer (CEO) support, legislation and regulation, Non-Government Organisations (NGOs), ISO 14001:2004 and changing behaviours are considered as the broad corporate drivers (or enablers/mechanisms) for a sustainable project.

The specific business case of fluorescent tube replacement is then presented, building on sustainable aspect identification, and highlighting recommendations for 'FMCo,' a representation of a typical large FM project and service supplier.

The business case covers recommendations which may potentially be outside of project management practitioners' sphere of influence, however suggestions to address this, for mature corporations, are included.

In conclusion, project environmental sustainability is highlighted as a vital but complex concept, involving both direct and indirect drivers, with sustainability, as a tool to manage risk and leverage opportunity. Environmental sustainability is highlighted as being reliant on corporate CEO and NGO support through environmental management systems, strong reputation and brand awareness, legislation, business planning, risk mitigation, effective project establishment and the ability to identify and execute micro projects addressing specific aspects of sustainability as the opportunity presents.

BACKGROUND TO SUSTAINABLE PROJECT MANAGEMENT IN THE FACILITIES MANAGEMENT SECTOR

Review of Sustainable Project Management

As summarised by Silvius and Schipper,(2012), project management has moved from the early acknowledgment of project management as discipline in the 1950s, to not only the consideration of sustainability as a core area of development, but further the stretching of the project boundaries as the full life cycle of the outcome of the project is considered, Labuschagne and Brent (2006). Although the full lifecycle model was developed for the manufacturing industry it is equally applicable to the FM industry and often FM contracts run from 5 to 20 years, with some project aspects requiring consideration over long time periods.

This chapter builds on the 'checklist for integrating sustainability in projects and project management' Silvius (2010) providing a business case (or project justification) as the next step where aspects for environmental sustainability are identified. While the business case is mentioned briefly by Silvius, Schipper and Van Den Brink (2012), indicating that the principles of sustainability need to be reflected in the project justification, the use of the business case to integrate sustainability across multiple 'sub' projects is not addressed. The business case example in this chapter demonstrates this link. Importantly as asserted by Maltzman and Shirley (2011) 'project management is a microcosm of business'(p23).

Two distinct but related areas are addressed:

1. The drivers for sustainability in the fluorescent tube example.
2. The business case required to achieve the sustainable outcome.

The drivers for sustainability establish the business conditions which contribute to the overall potential for success of a particular initiative. The drivers described in this chapter are derived from the specific example being examined, and as surmised by Maltzman and Shirley (2011) when considering project drivers, 'No matter what the impetus, organisations must respond to them with projects if they are to survive' (p. 73).

The description 'drivers' is used as a broader term than stakeholders, however it should be noted that for this example they are narrowly derived from the information available through audit, business interaction and informal site review by the author, rather than through a full stakeholder analysis as described in Achman (2011).

Facilities Management Background

FM is a niche market sector which arose in the 1980s outsourcing drive (Facilities Management Association of Australia, 2010), through the need for specialised skills in the management of all aspects of building operations, in both new and existing facilities. Government and private sector buildings such as hospitals, correction centres, railways and airport buildings are indicative of those who engage this service. According to the Facilities Management Association of Australia (2010) this sector is now considered one of the fastest growing business sectors with an annual turnover of more than AUD$20 billion to GDP.

The management of a facility encompasses two distinct projects concepts; the first is short term project covering six to eighteen months and is the initial fit-out or refit phase; the second may run from two years to thirty years, requiring much more in-depth planning, and often characterised by moving deliverables. It is a combination of project and maintenance work usually including the operation and maintenance of air conditioning, lifts, security systems, lighting, backup generators, waste management, gardens and pest control. The project aspects during this phase are either performance based, cover replacement or upgrade of key infrastructure. Any aspect of the 'built environment' may be included as part of FM. Each of these activities has a potential impact on the environment, with varying levels of Commonwealth and State regulation applying. Additionally recent FM contracts focus on energy, water and waste reduction often with a combination of penalties and bonuses to motivate desired supplier behaviour.

Sustainability as Challenge for Facilities Management Projects

The question 'can corporate sustainability be used to manage compliance and brand reputation within FM projects, while mitigating risk and leverage commercial opportunity?' has a number of different aspects; in this example five specific drivers for corporate environmental sustainability are identified. The term 'drivers' is used broadly to group aspects which influence sustainable outcomes; including stakeholders, enablers and mechanisms.

To answer this question the specific example of fluorescent tube use and disposal is considered. The specific drivers which contributed to identifying the need to change the existing practice for FMCo are presented, followed by the business case to achieve a more sustainable outcome.

Introduction to the Fluorescent Tube Business Case Example

To identify brand and reputation sensitivity, FMCo will be compared and contrasted with the case study examples of Patagonia and Starkist, highlighting what is in place and why it is or isn't effective, and what alternatives are available. FMCo achieved certification to the, ISO 14001:2004 standard, however the internal auditing process (Council of Standards Australia & Council of Standards New Zealand, 2004, p.8) has still identified locations where the regulatory and/or policy requirements are not being met. In particular, disposal of fluorescent tubes, while a seemingly simple problem, with a commercially available solution, continues to be identified as an issue at some sites. The corporate strategy in place and the effect on FM projects, along with possible changes, associated costs and drivers will be considered along with the risks and opportunities this situation provides.

The core influence for project performance in the FM industry is generally the clients or building owners/major lessees ('clients'). In addition, any corporation providing FM services is strongly influenced by the shareholders requirements and the board of directors through the CEO to the employees. Often the more convoluted the path is between the CEO and the actual facility project managers, the weaker the influence becomes, and the more likely other sub agendas are introduced. Suppliers, regulatory bodies, industry bodies, NGOs, real estate agents and competitors all influence the behaviours to varying degrees.

One of the key waste products produced by buildings is fluorescent tubes. The old T8 halophosphate tubes contain up to 15mg of mercury in a vapour form, and have a short life span of 12-24 months. This creates a waste product for landfill containing a heavy metal (mercury) deemed as dangerous to the environment and health (Skinner & Berger, 2003, p. 28). These tubes have been used historically as commercial building lighting since the late 1940s, and it is estimated by cmaecocycle (2010), Australia's only mercury recycling facility, that 50-60 million tubes are sent to landfill in Australia each year. The importation of these tubes has been banned since late 2009; however they still exist in legal stockpiles imported prior to the 2009 ban, which are still used in commercial buildings.

Adequate lighting for work environments is a health and safety, as well as comfort and aesthetic consideration for corporations. Commercial lighting is intrinsically intertwined with the search for lower energy usage. As carbon trading schemes permeate through all markets, the requirement to change behaviours to improve corporate bottom line performance will become more evident. A number of strategies have been put in place to address this issue including Government legislation, NGO motivation schemes and individual corporate strategies. These provide a framework within which FM projects need to operate, incorporating both constraints and opportunities.

In the fluorescent tube waste management and recycling market, proactive suppliers, those currently providing a service which is easy to undertake and has a self maintaining process, such as SITA, Transpacific and Veolia are more likely to not only to influence the industry behaviour, but additionally create and secure their market. These corporations have a choice of only two recycling plants in Australia, which are at this stage not capacity limited. Having established the market, smaller operators are now attempting to take market share through reduced price services. These services often only cover limited areas and market players, so are less attractive to large corporations who perceive (and often in real terms have) an add-on cost with maintaining multiple suppliers.

Regulatory bodies such as the Environmental Protection Agency (EPA) in most states of Australia, and the Department of Environmental Resource Management (DERM) in the state of Queensland are tasked with managing compliance to legislation. In the 2010-2011 annual report (Department of Environmental Resource Management, p. 17), DERM identified an increase of $29.4 million over the previous year's costs to assist with regulation of the coal seam gas industry, the 2009-2010 regulation of this industry redirected existing resources, effectively reducing the focus in other areas of environmental compliance, leading to these bodies being less influential in fluorescent tube recycling during this period.

The two key national NGO bodies for this activity are Facilities Management Australia (FMA), the FM industry association, and the Lighting Council of Australia. The Lighting Council of Australia administers the national "Fluorocycle" program, an initiative to provide motivation through reward and recognition for corporations participating in appropriate fluorescent tube recycling activities. This program is also supported by the FMA.

Large corporate Real Estate Agents, and their industry body exert some influence on property owners and builders, and many such as Jones,

Lang, LaSalle (2012) actively support sustainable behaviours in both new and retrofitted commercial buildings providing information and education through their online publication "Global Sustainability Perspective."

DRIVERS IN THE FM INDUSTRY

The methodology used to identify the drivers for sustainable behaviour for FMCo was a combination of review of business documentation presented by FMCo during systems audits (both internal and external), corrective action documentation and informal discussion with facilities project managers and business managers across multiple sites during audit and normal business interaction. Although predominately the identified drivers are stakeholders, it is important to note that in the FMCo context the drivers were not established through a stakeholder analysis. This is demonstrated by the inclusion of EMS as a driver, which is not a stakeholder, but a mechanism. For government contracts it could be argued that the EMS stakeholder is in fact the client, where they have specified ISO 14001 as a minimum requirement within the contract, or indeed the CEO where EMS is mandated as a corporate requirement. However, the environmental aspects identified within the EMS certainly provide 'impetus' for sustainability in this example, and as such is given independent status as a driver.

5 Key Drivers in the Fluorescent Tube Example

The five main drivers identified for the fluorescent tube case are:

- Client Requirements
- CEO Influence
- NGO Support
- Legislation and Regulation
- EMS

It is important to acknowledge that while some drivers may be repetitive they can also change with the changing circumstance of organisations, and as such will be described for each of these drivers. Some are actually groups of several drivers, mechanism and stakeholders. Each project could potentially have different drivers, both for different activities and different timeframes; hence, an example rather than a definitive solution is presented.

Client Requirements

In the FM Industry (and particularly for Public Private Partnerships) client requirements are well documented through contracts. While the high-level contracts are publicly available, for example, in the state of Victoria they are published to a website, the detailed performance measures are often not disclosed. Client requirements, particularly in the form of detailed performance measures with financial incentives, are key concerns for FM project performance having a direct effect on sustainable project performance.

Within the project teams these requirements are described as both client requirements and contract requirements, although in some instances the distinction is made that client requirements may include requirements outside the contract (or project scope) which are being negotiated for inclusion.

The type of driver for client requirements can be classified as 'stakeholder' and although the direct influence would be apparent through a stakeholder analysis, FMCo had not formally undertaken this exercise. However, the importance of the client as a driver was evident, both from the site priorities and more broadly from client satisfaction surveys.

CEO Influence

A key driver and/or influencer for corporate behaviour is the CEO, who is in turn influenced by shareholders and the board of directors for public corporations. The effect a change in CEO can have on an organisation is quite dramatic, with the focus and attention being moved from one part of the corporation's operation to another, as a new CEO brings different personal experience and is often tasked with changing or improving specific aspects of a corporation's performance. As resource (financial/ human capital/ physical) is moved, for example, from cost accounting to sales, a shift in organisational culture becomes evident, often resulting in an increased rate of personnel change. Health, Safety, and Environmental (HSE) issues are often not seen as core operational issues, but specialist areas, resulting in a lack of penetration of the core concepts and requirements of HSE into the operational areas. Organisational structure, and the status and depth of health, safety, and environmental roles within an organisation are an indicator of this lack of penetration. The CEO has the responsibility of placing the optimum focus on all areas to ensure the corporate operates not only profitably but ethically within the bounds of social and environmental acceptability. As identified by Reinhardt (1998) the more brand sensitive the organisation, the more likely they are to engage in socially and environmentally acceptable behaviours, promoting a sustainable organisation.

Corporations are organic entities, responding and growing to different stimuli. It is too simplistic to lay the entire responsibility for behaviour on the CEO. It is however important to note the significant influence they exert. Due to mergers, acquisitions and globalisation FMCo's structure has moved from a pyramid inside a country, where the country CEO was the clear leader in the organisation, to a structure which has in effect only those activities deemed as operational, for example direct sales, projects and service (including FM) as reporting within country. All other activities such as real estate, finance, travel, HSE, client management, information technology and supply chain are outside the core business operations. These report vertically through a global regional structure to the corporate head office. Potential for reduced sustainable functionality at the country level is evident by the horizontal interaction between these different aspects of the corporation, causing a diffusion of priorities. Individual projects are a further subset of this reporting structure creating a further diffusion of priorities from a corporate standpoint, but often with clear priorities from the client viewpoint, through the use of well defined contracts.

FMCo, like most large corporations, encapsulates the organisational priorities in the form of policies and codes of conduct. Environmental consideration, including beyond compliance behaviour is supported in FMCo's policy which identifies sustainability as a corporate imperative. To give the policy local credibility it is signed by the global CEO as well as the senior operational leaders (Australia), and is displayed prominently in all offices. This meets the ISO 14001:2004 requirements for Environmental Policy (Council of Standards Australia & Council of Standards New Zealand, 2004, p. 4). This policy is also included in tender documents and forms part of the project documentation.

The management style displayed at FMCo is 'Environmental Strategist' (Thornton, Kagen, & Gunningham, 2003, pp. 131-132). This is characterised by the concept of the environment being a business tactic in the political and market environment in which they operate, with a focus on the cost-benefit ratio, rather than being the 'True Believer' (Thornton, Kagen & Gunningham, 2003, pp. 131-132) where the focus is moved from the purely financial aspect of an undertaking in the first instance, to the environmental aspect being equally or preferentially considered.

The environmental sustainability deployment at the country project level is reinforced by structure and policy. A gap is apparent however, for the activities occurring out of the project based structure, driven vertically, through the corporate global real estate and finance groups. In effect FMCo's own facilities are not managed by the country project team, occasionally resulting in a disconnect between environmentally sustainable behaviours promoted through the country project team to clients and corporate behaviours exhibited through the vertically integrated groups. For example some of FMCo's leased office sites for their own employees have fluorescent tube disposal as the contractual responsibility of the building owner, therefore not subject to FMCo's policies. For newer sites FMCo adds these policy requirements to the lease contracts for their own facilities. This avoids brand damage which may occur where the building owner chooses the least cost option, resulting for example in fluorescent tubes being visible in a dump bin outside a building where FMCo's brand is displayed. Even though it is legal in most states, brand damage is more affected by the perception of what is acceptable, rather than the legality of actions.

In summary, as not only a stakeholder, but the representative of multiple stakeholders (shareholders and company board), the CEO influence even to an individual project level for FMCo is significant, but often convoluted, so while the influence is significant, for the FMCo project example, the effect is considered indirect.

NGO Support (Lighting Council, FM Industry Body)

As identified earlier, the FM sector industry body is the FMA. The gap in the recycling of fluorescent tubes was identified in the FM sector by the Environment Protection and Heritage Council (EPHC) who invited a number of NGO's to participate in the development of a solution. "FluoroCycle" was developed and funded federally with $500k over three years to focus entirely on addressing this issue within the commercial sector.

FMA supported the development of FluoroCycle although curiously there appears no evidence that the FluoroCycle scheme was presented to the members at any of the functions held by the FMA in 2008-2010. It is mentioned in the 2009-2010 annual report as an activity in which the FMA was invited to participate. The EPHC announcement confirmed 'The scheme will be delivered by the Lighting Council Australia and the Australian Government in collaboration with Property Council, the Facility Management Association of Australia, the council of Recyclers, the Australian Local Government and other key bodies.' (Environment Protection and Heritage Council, 2009, para.4). The purpose of the scheme is to provide independent recognition for corporations who can show evidence of fluorescent tube recycling. The recognition is provided through permission to use the FluoroCycle logo and advertising on the FluoroCycle Website.

It is important to note that both the property council, representing the clients and the FMA representing the FM corporations are participating in this initiative, giving a consistent recycling message. The level of support and effective behaviour change should become evident as the program matures. As identified by Gunningham (2002, p. 155), NGO initiatives are most likely to have a positive outcome where the offering is viewed as a win-win. Brand sensitive organisations are positively disposed to this initiative but are still likely to consider the cost of recycling in jurisdictions where it is not a regulatory requirement.

Fluorocycle, as an NGO, would normally be considered a potential stakeholder in a project, however for the FMCo example it is equally an enabler or mechanism for the sustainable outcome, the effect however is indirect with less significant recognition as a driver.

Legislation and Regulation (Political Acceptability)

Where legislation has been mandated, project managers are concerned with, at a minimum, meeting the basic requirements for compliance. This is reinforced in the "Legal and other requirements" section of ISO 14001:2004 process (Council of Standards Australia & Council of Standards New

Zealand, 2004, p. 5). As highlighted in the previous paragraph, brand and reputation sensitive corporations such as FMCo, often have a beyond-compliance policy as they are aware of the benefits and risk mitigation of sustainable behaviours. In Australia legislation and regulation for the disposal of tubes containing mercury is not consistent in identification, implementation or compliance. For example South Australia (SA) specifically identifies fluorescent tubes containing mercury as not being permitted to landfill through a legally binding policy (Law of South Australia, Environment Protection (Waste to Resources) Policy 2010, sch. 4, sec. 1, para. 15-16), whereas the other states allow it, but require it to be tracked. Queensland (Qld) has regulations in place for waste tracking (Law of Queensland, Environment Protection (Waste Management) 2000 Regulation, sec. 17, para. 1), but the extent to which the practical implementation and monitoring of this captures mercury from fluorescent tubes is not evident. These oversights undermine the effectiveness of the legislation, reducing the motivation for those corporations taking responsible action within their project scope, and supporting poor behaviours by corporations avoiding environmental responsibility. In contrast corporations embracing sustainable behaviours in the FM industry can use these differences as project sales differentiators, specifically creating opportunities where the client (including government organisations) is reputation sensitive, and therefore not necessarily as cost sensitive, for issues which affect reputation.

Legislation and regulation have a number of potential roles to play, while in the present Australian system, command and control is the predominant form and does not drive beyond-compliance behaviour. The fundamental underpinning or baseline performance, particularly where the regulation applies to an area of environmental sustainability which does not have a high profile, and is not a requirement of organisations which are not reputation or brand sensitive, is still however provided by legislation and regulation.

The regulatory and legislative requirements are important aspects of projects both as sales and scope drivers in the initial instance and as an important aspect of the monitoring and control phase, to ensure additional costs are not incurred, but more importantly to achieve sustainable outcomes which can be identified during the close phase and leveraged for later project sales. In the FMCo example these requirements are a mechanism for driving sustainability, however their perceived influence is variable across projects in most cases resulting in an indirect effect.

Role of Environmental Management Systems

Management systems provide frameworks for corporations to identify, prioritise and action issues. Specifically ISO 14001:2004 provides a framework for environmental management. For the FM sector this framework provides key 'product differentiation,' (Reinhardt, 2000, p.18), as clients are requesting elements of environmental management and few players in the sector have achieved certification. As ISO 14001:2004 requires a third party audit to maintain certification, tender documents and client appraisal processes often consider this as sufficient evidence of compliant sustainable environmental behaviour. FMCo's certification success was in part the reduction of the need for change management by leveraging existing and already ingrained processes and behaviours established through health and safety certification. In total only three new procedures and one new sub process were developed. Minimal change increases not only the likelihood of acceptance, but the long term sustainability and compliance to the processes, therefore makes good business sense and is a cost reduction driver.

A good framework such as ISO 14001:2004 assists corporations to identify risks, comply with legal requirements and consider their beyond-compliance activities at a high level, and ensures at a lower level that project methodologies are in place and are being utilised for all projects. It does not in its own right ensure sustainability, and in some cases such as the Benziger Family Winery' case study (Silverman & Lanphar, 2003), ISO 14001:2004 actually does not add value, as the cost of maintaining the certification (licence and external auditing) outweighs the value to the business. In the Benziger case study the corporation's target market is not demanding the certification, and in all likelihood a high percentage would not recognise ISO 14001:2004, therefore with no specific brand benefit to be gained, it is not financially sustainable.

The identification of the EMS by FMCo projects as a driver is likely due to the recency of implementation and also to the level of engagement of the project, program and other managers as internal auditors, in addition to the frequency and level of interaction with external auditors.

The process within the EMS for identifying environmental aspects of a project, and requiring actions to be formally instigated to address the impacts has given rise to the need for addressing the problem of fluorescent disposal and replacement. The Aspect identification aligns with and builds on the 'checklist for integrating sustainability in projects and project management' Silvius (2010), however the EMS drives the action by requiring the impacts to be instigated or eliminated, further reinforced by both the external and internal audit.

ISSUES, CONTROVERSIES, AND PROBLEMS

In summary Figure 1 shows the identified mix of both stakeholders and mechanisms as drivers affecting environmental sustainability with respect to fluorescent tube usage.

While stakeholders are well identified as driving project outcomes this example highlights the importance of understanding the effect of all potential drivers when looking for sustainable outcomes, particularly as the EMS implementation is within the direct control of FMCo.

Specifically for the fluorescent tube example, the environmental aspects of energy usage and waste management were identified through an aspect and impact analysis performed at the site project level. Similar to the checklist identified in Silvius (2010) this process comprises firstly a check list to determine what aspects are present, but secondarily once an aspect is identified, a risk analysis (refer ISO 31000:2009) to determine both the initial and residual risks is undertaken.

Under the EMS the result of this risk analysis is required to be translated into actions driving the provision of a solution to mitigate or eliminate the risk. In the fluorescent tube example the solution firstly required the development of a business case. In addition as part of the certification audit findings such as this, which are potentially applicable across multiple projects, are highlighted resulting in a better penetration of the outcome across multiple projects.

The real challenge then becomes to use corporate sustainability to both manage the risks associated with compliance and brand reputation, and turn this into an opportunity to leverage commercial gain across multiple projects.

In addition to the project risks highlighted, unwilling clients who do not see waste recycling as a core function or direction of their business may have an insurmountable resistance to an environmental concept which they perceive purely as a cost with no benefit. State governments without sufficient budget to rectify their own buildings (for example schools) may not support fluorescent tube recycling legislation due to the perceived cost and subsequent effect on their own budgets. This cost perception would be based on financial considerations only, rather than valuing sustainable environmental, health and safety and social considerations.

Emerging technology is a potential barrier to success as it can cause delayed decision making, or reduced priorities, while a potentially better solution may be available in the future. Low awareness of environmental responsibilities, imposed through changing legislation and regulation

Figure 1. Drivers, types, and effects for FMCo fluorescent tube example

Driver	Type	Effect
• Client Requirements	• Stakeholder	• Direct
• CEO Influence	• Stakeholder	• Indirect
• NGO Support	• Stakeholder/ Mechanism	• Indirect
• Legislation & Regulation	• Mechanism	• Indirect
• EMS	• Mechanism	• Indirect

potentially provides a barrier to success. Government and non government environmental groups have an important role in increasing community environmental awareness as well as targeting key groups.

SOLUTIONS AND RECOMMENDATIONS: EXAMPLE BUSINESS CASE FOR FLUORESCENT TUBE IMPACT

Scope

The business case for FMCo to address the potential opportunity created by the concept of correctly disposing of fluorescent light tubes from the commercial buildings which FMCo is contracted to manage for its clients, needs to address the resources, supply chain, sales strategy, social, economic and political factors and costing in addition to the potential risks. Only by considering all aspects can the plan be analysed to assess whether or not a sustainable model based on social, environmental, and economic attributes can be attained. Once the business case is established it can be redeployed into individual project plans, providing tailoring for State specific legislation, client requirements, market or site environmental

maturity and current tube disposal methods. It is at this stage that projects proposed for clients which do not adequately satisfy the business case criteria are formally discontinued; either permanently where there is no chance of recovery, or for review at a later date if the criteria is expected to be met. Most corporations have systems in place that manage this gated decision making and allow automated future review.

The business case is the logical progression from the impact findings within the EMS system and considers the following (See Figure 2):

Figure 2. Relationship between drivers, business case, and sustainable outcome

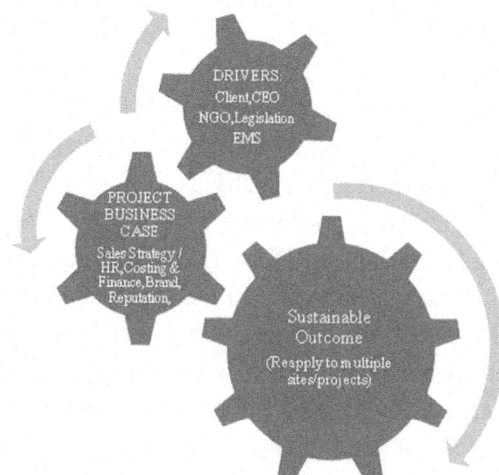

- Sales Strategy
- Human Resources
- Costing and Finance
- Brand, Reputation and Risk
- Other Considerations

Sales Strategy: Environmental Challenge to Competitive Advantage

Additional cost and effort of correctly disposing of fluorescent tubes does not present an obvious sales opportunity, in contrast it appears to be a direct cost. As a cost, the standard sales solution for FMCo (and many other corporations), is to build the cost of disposal into any contracts being negotiated. Unfortunately, for a relatively price sensitive industry, this may cause the price to become non competitive. In SA recycling of fluorescent tubes is already legislated (Law of South Australia, Environment Protection [Waste to Resources] Policy 2010), commencing 2012 in Adelaide metropolitan area and 2013 for the balance of the state. For this market an increase in contract price proportional to the cost of disposal is likely to be accepted, and can simply be effected through individually tailored project implementation plans per client site.

Sustainable policy's contain the direction to 'value add', not just 'on charge', to do this a number of alternatives are considered to cover different client sites, and provide alternatives to present to the clients, where the choice is guided as one of a number of sustainable alternatives, rather than the choice between sustainable or not. These include replacing existing old style fluorescent tubes with newer compact tubes, which have a longer life than the original tubes and therefore create less waste or using Light Emitting Diode (LED) tube lighting, which has a similar life to the newer compacts and contains no mercury, simply removing the issue by eliminating the mercury waste. In effect a combination of these will be used depending on the lifecycle stage of the contract, environmental maturity and receptiveness of the client to change.

As highlighted by Porter and Van der Linde (1995, p. 122), 'Customers bear additional costs when they use products that pollute or waste energy,' in this case the old fluorescent tubes do both.

For new clients, due to the long term nature of the contracts, it is easier to demonstrate the alternatives not only in terms of waste reduction and savings, but also energy savings, as both alternatives to traditional fluorescent lamps are more energy efficient. Environmentally responsible clients are likely to specify environmentally acceptable solutions in their tender documentation. For those less environmentally aware, bringing alternatives to their attention differentiates FMCo from any competitors who are simply providing a low cost short payback offering, which is not environmentally responsible and may in some jurisdictions have criminal penalties during the life of the contract.

Sales Strategy Recommendation

The contract between the FM service provider and their client is an important behaviour driver. Basic contracts drive compliance behaviour, leveraging legislation and regulation, however more innovative contracts set performance targets and use these as a method of driving performance beyond compliance. Innovative beyond-compliance contracts in the FM sector on work if sufficient reward (and/or penalty) is in place. As these are both established in the initiation phase of the project it is important to ensure sufficient time, consideration and expertise is allocated.

Human Resources

One of the key issues for FMCo is the human resources available. Many project, purchasing and sales personnel, despite the certification to ISO14001:2004, lack the expertise to identify or support environmental opportunities. While the processes have become ingrained, the depth of understanding still varies significantly by individual. The willingness to learn and embrace environmental progress is to some extent affected by an individual's external peer groups and interests.

The introduction of ISO 14001:2004 to FMCo in 2008, along with voluntary employee environmental participation programs has lifted awareness, and new initiatives through these programs are making progress. While the policy is clear and supported by senior management, the translation of the policy through the annual planning process to individual's goals is not widespread, with less than 1% of employees having environmentally sustainable improvements (or even compliance) as a goal.

Human Resources Recommendation

To introduce the change from traditional to environmentally sustainable goals the recommendation in the first instance is not to have a standalone environmental goal, but to include it as an aspect of the more traditional sales, marketing, project, and training based performance goals. Anecdotally smaller changes in these areas are often more readily accepted; therefore more likely to succeed, although the time to the desired outcome is potentially longer.

Costing and Finance

For any business proposal to be considered from the perspective of sustainability it must meet financial, environmental and social standards. In consideration of the problem presented, the main issue is evident in the cost of the tubes and end of life recycling. As identified in Zerk (2006, pp. 16-17), referring to the famous 1970s Friedman argument, it is the responsibility of corporations to deliver profit to their shareholders; unfortunately this is still prevalent, seen as the short term profit between annual reporting periods. For this sustainable fluorescent tube concept to enter its payback period an upfront expenditure (or sub finance) is

required to cover the initial cost resulting in gain in the long term.

Costing and Finance Recommendation

This can be overcome by either securing long term contracts or financing to cover the short term outlay, or a combination of both. For example Fantastic Lighting Pty. Ltd. (2012) offers a lease service on energy saving (LED) fluorescent tubes for $1.30 per month over 36 months, resulting in an additional cost of $13.80 per tube, however it avoids the initial outlay of $33.00 per tube and is often a preferred method to balance cash flow.

Further Costing Considerations

While the basic costing methodology and available technology is considered, each opportunity for mercury waste reduction needs to be individually and expertly designed to ensure there is no resultant loss in lighting amenity. Significant energy savings between 30-50% can be achieved contributing substantially to the cost benefit, however retrofitting existing operational lighting contributes to the mercury waste in potentially an earlier timeframe than necessary. As most T8 halophosphate tubes have a maximum 24 month life the period is not substantial in comparison to replacement of T8 triphosphor tubes which have a 5 year life. As halophosphate tubes are no longer allowed to be imported into Australia they are not a replacement option except where they have been stockpiled for that express purpose. The advantage of the T8 triphosphor tubes is they tend towards the lower mercury level of 5mg, offer significant savings due to the comparative energy efficiency and exhibit the more intangible savings of better employee amenity due to removal of 'flicker' associated with traditional lamps and fittings. The cost associated with recycling, rather than sending to landfill, of fluorescent tubes is however higher and therefore recycling is only more likely to be universally accepted in those states where it is mandated.

The supply chain function, in their project purchasing role, have a significant contribution to make not only in price negotiation but applying pressure to the tube manufactures to reduce or eliminate mercury vapour by using alternate technology. Many corporations, especially those with ISO 14001:2004 assess and review the environmental capability of their suppliers, identifying those with responsible and sustainable environmental practices as preferred suppliers. Suppliers are motivated to become 'preferred' as once a preferred supplier is identified by a corporation the process for purchasing from them becomes easier and the percentage of purchase orders they receive increases. Where legislation is in place defining a specific environmental requirement, a clear negotiating point is more easily established, often resulting in a reduction in the time for environmental improvements, through the combination of legislative need of the supplier to comply, and supply chain pressure to meet or exceed requirements.

Further Costing Considerations Recommendation

AusIndustry, a government body, has offered grants of $50,000 to $500,000 on a 50% of cost basis under the Green Building Fund program (AusIndustry, 2012), to commercial property owners who reduce their greenhouse gas emissions through a retrofit program. The program has been in place since 2008; in the Round 7 funding offers, for example, Stockland Green Hills Shopping Centre was granted $400,000 for the installation of solar panels, LED lighting, power sub-metering and a building tuning program to optimise operations. Of the 89 grants approved two specifically identified the replacement of fluorescent tubes and more than 45 indicated lighting efficiency upgrades; the 2012 details have not yet

been released. While this grant is not specifically aimed at fluorescent tubes, and the measurement criteria doesn't consider end of life recycling, it still provides an opportunity to reduce the cost of retrofit due to the energy saving characteristics of the triphosphor fluorescent or LED tubes. This cost saving can subsidise the cost for appropriate recycling of replaced tubes. The program itself has some associated costs in relation to auditing of energy consumption and may not be cost effective for all retrofit opportunities.

Brand, Reputation, and Risks

Brand and reputation are important factors in predicting how a corporation may react to a project proposal. Reinhardt's (1998, pp. 55-59) reported case study examples of StarKist and Patagonia both have similarities to FMCo. In the StarKist example the lack of differentiation in actual product offering between competitors is similar to FMCo's situation. However, FMCo's actual product offering does not suffer from the same additional negative environmental impacts as in the StarKist study. This means FMCo's offering is less open to the negative reputation effect suffered by StarKist. In fact additional positive benefits for both environmental and health concerns are evident through reduction in energy usage and the elimination of 'flicker' which is a known contributor to eye strain and other health issues. Although not to the same extent as in the Patagonia case highlighted by Reinhardt (1998, p. 56), FMCo has created brand loyal clients who are prepared to pay a premium. The difference is FMCo's clients consider a combination of brand and offering from a financial payback perspective, whereas Patagonia clients appear to pay simply for the brand name. The FMCo clients are willing to pay more, however require tangible evidence of, in proportion to, their perception of environmental value.

A risk for FMCo's project offerings is emerging technology. Changes in legislation which support new technology further cement this risk for existing technology owners. If, for example, the nanotechnology 'self lighting window' or a bioluminescent product are developed and are underpinned in the market by legislation during the payback period of the triphosphate fluorescent tube or LED tube, a potentially costly change would need to be undertaken to comply. To mitigate this risk, payback periods can be designed, not necessarily over the full life of the product, but over an estimated period of time for new technology to move from prototype to market, and then be legislated. Politically, a legislative change made too quickly, will disadvantage too many commercial operations, and is likely therefore to create a political disadvantage for the supporting party. A well-designed payback period estimate will effectively mitigate this issue of new technology in most cases.

A softer phased-in approach is usually more readily accepted and can be commercially addressed through a payback period, for example of 3 years, rather than 5 or more years. This project risk is additionally mitigated by a 'change in legislation' clause in contracts, whereby any additional cost arising from changes in legislation is the responsibility of the client.

Brand, Reputation, and Risks Recommendation

It is in far better interest of long-term client relationships, to plan well, using appropriate payback periods, and an understanding of the risks presented by emerging technologies, than to fall back on a contractual exclusion clause. Not only is client brand loyalty enhanced through adding value in this way, it allows FMCo and the client to respond well to the next environmental opportunity. In some cases, for example where large capital equipment is required, payback periods cannot necessarily be reduced, leaving a higher risk with a more difficult mitigation.

OTHER CONSIDERATIONS

Exchange Rates

Since the closure of the Electric Light Manufacturers Australia (ELMA) factory in Newcastle in 2002, there has been no manufacture of fluorescent or LED tubes in Australia. This leaves a potential risk due to currency fluctuations affecting imported tubes, resulting in increases in pricing.

Exchange Rate Recommendation

Again, for FMCo this can be mitigated through contractual exclusions or through supply chain agreements if the purchase volume or value is sufficient.

Criminal Penalties

While criminal penalties, for non compliance with legislation, need to be considered as a risk, they are also an opportunity to change behaviour. Senior executive's behaviour will be affected if they are aware and concerned about the likelihood and personal effect of penalties, in the event of an identified breach of legislation.

Criminal Penalty Recommendation

Project plans should clearly identify the relevant legislation, penalties and compliance action required. For ISO14001:2004 certified corporations this is a requirement under section 4.3.2 (Council of Standards Australia & Council of Standards New Zealand, 2004, p. 5).

Competitors

Competitors are seen as a real risk for FMCo, as with the exception of ISO 14001:2004 certification, the offerings being made are not unique and do not fully meet Reinhardt's (1999, p. 39) three conditions for success which are; clients willing to pay more, credible communication of a product's environmental benefits and the ability to avoid imitation. While brand and reputation sensitive clients may be willing to pay more, it is likely they will be looking for cost sharing with the supplier, rather than the full cost burden. ISO 14001:2004 provides credibility in the FM market, however is only likely to be a differentiator for a short period of time, as more tenders are demanding environmental criteria, the natural progression is for competitors to also identify ISO 14001:2004 as a solution, and become certified.

Competitor Recommendation 1

In addition to responsible waste management, reputation through successful energy management of FM client sites and the ability of FMCo to provide technical expertise are core differentiators. This supports the importance of brand and reputation as key drivers, as differentiators such as ISO14001 which can be copied and therefore has a short term effect.

Competitor Recommendation 2

An additional risk mitigation measure recommended for FMCo is partnering with FluoroCycle as it promotes FMCo's brand as environmentally responsible and prepared to undertake activities beyond- compliance, but which are already supported corporately through FMCo's own sustainability policy. The risk to the FMCo brand of an NGO identifying and publicizing evidence of illegal or not environmentally responsible disposal of waste tubes is high, particularly as some clients are in legislated states and would not necessarily be aware that the requirements in other states (or countries) are not as stringent.

New Technology Risk

LED tubes as an alternative to fluorescent tubes are relatively untried, information from manufacturers may be 'best case' and not necessarily reflected in the field. Some level of mitigation for this risk is through purchasing contracts for described performance; however any failure in the field has costs to reputation that cannot be justified through replacement policies.

New Technology Risk Recommendation

The recommendation for FMCo is to trial LED tubes in one of its own smaller facilities, where the potential issues can be assessed, and the tubes can be removed without potential brand or reputation damage if they do not perform to expectation.

Overall Comment on Implementing Recommendations

The recommendations presented are a combination of those which the project practitioner is likely to have control, for example identifying the legislation applicable to the project, and those which require additional influence, such as trialling LED tubes at an alternate site. As the initial driver for this business case was the EMS requirement to mitigate or eliminate the risk associated with fluorescent tubes, the business case itself, including all recommendations is subject to audit review.

While this is not a guarantee of acceptance of the recommendation, for FMCo it does require a response to each recommendation from the business area (or areas) which would have the responsibility for implementing the recommendation if accepted.

MANAGING CHANGE BEHAVIOURS

Management support at all levels from CEOs to project team leaders is crucial to the success of any environmentally sustainable initiative, firstly to provide the necessary resources but more importantly to provide the appropriate level of focus and motivation. The business strategy development for mature corporations is usually a defined and often open framework and process; however the detailed output forms a significant part of the corporation's intellectual property. This framework not only takes into account the 'client - business – supplier' relationship but extraneous factors such a market conditions, political and legislative constraints, internal and external community views. The implementation success of the strategy, particularly in large corporations is dependent on the methods used, and speed at which the requirements can be disseminated. These include details of actions required, goals, recognition and reward for achieving or over achieving requirements and the ongoing recognition for small advances throughout the project period.

While issued policies and verbal reinforcement from CEO's and members of the management team are key macro activities in achieving plan, the goals, reward and recognition provide the micro detail allowing the organisation to work towards an outcome. This tends to work well in a classical pyramid structure, or even in the flatter structures favoured in the 1980s and 1990s, however complex global matrix structures where vertical integration has weakened the horizontal country level structures which often subsequently suffer from a diffused interpretation of the original goals, or differing emphasis which can weaken the effectiveness of the intended goal. In addition Project Goals are conversely weakened (or strengthened) by the framework in which they operate. Initial stages of a project are key to sustainability, as is the inclusion of sustainability as a measure of success at this point. In the fluorescent tube example while T8 is a short term cheap option, both legislatively and environmentally it is not sustainable long term, if used it only defers the cost until a later date. For short term thinking project managers this appears as a cost saving, longer term focused managers understand that this type of decision results in poor client relationships and affects the opportunity for ongoing business. This means the focus provided by the project's direct leadership team is even more crucial in achieving environmentally sustainable outcomes.

FMCo uses a planning model which involves participation at all management levels, culminating, after considerable planning and negotiating, in an agreed path forward. Integration of non-operational aspects is still not well addressed, and there is often confusion between the number of tasks an individual manager takes on, and the ability of their team to address the requirement by sharing the load (Gunningham, 2009).

A solution to this for FMCo would be ensuring project managers and facility leaders, particularly those newly promoted, undertake training to assist them to change their behaviours to effectively delegate where appropriate, and to support their knowledge in the non operational areas such as HSE. In addition non operational areas need to support training by disseminating information in a way which integrates with normal workplace processes and behaviours and established project methodologies. The Project Management Institute, based in the USA publishes 'A guide to Project Management Body of Knowledge,' in the third edition, page 14 (2004) reference is given to the need to take the 'physical' environment into consideration in project management, while the 4th edition (2008) makes no specific mention of the physical environment, only referring to the operational environment. As this is the popular professional qualification for FMCo project employees, the removal of this aspect of sustainable project management, highlights the need for corporations to ensure any training gaps are identified and addressed. This can be achieved through including new information in existing processes, as well as leveraging FMCo's already established internal communication network.

A key recurring theme throughout this chapter is the need for a consistent sustainability focus, policy and communicated message. This is particularly important where competing internal drivers diffuse the concept of sustainability as a measure of success. This is most effectively addressed by aligning expected outcomes and success measures at both at a Project and Corporate level.

By including the broader aspects of environmental and sustainable solutions, behaviours and measures in the project management processes, more successful, environmentally sustainable outcomes will be evident. This will be most effective where environmental sustainability is emphasised early in the initiation phase, and is further reinforced in the planning phase of the project for FMCo. As this doesn't appear to be emphasised in current project management documentation or training offerings, corporations wanting to leverage sales from sustainable projects will need to provide this in-house in the short term. Developing tailored processes and training, including automated reminders and sustainability gates have the advantage of better integration and therefore a higher of level of acceptance, over introducing a new process. ISO 14001:2004 provides some guidelines as to the elements which should be included, and is further supported by Standards Australia AS/NZS ISO 9004: 2011 (2011, Managing for the sustained success of an organisation – A quality management approach).

Another important action is to leverage government and NGO funding to create solutions for clients, as an overall template which can be tailored within a project to specific client needs, circumstances or compliance requirements. Adequate time must be allocated to the training and communications aspect of the template development, and further, project experiences need to be reviewed and shared to continuously improve and refine solutions.

Importantly, factors that affect the success of sustainability initiatives such as emerging technologies, trends and regulations must be analysed, reviewed and have resulting actions taken. As described, these can be influenced through changing supplier behaviours and offerings, participating in industry bodies contributing to regulation development and analysing the outcomes of completed projects on an ongoing basis.

CONCLUSION

Corporate and project sustainability, encompassing financial, social and environmental aspects of decision making, provides a valuable method to manage risk and exploit opportunity; however it needs to be supported by all management levels, and be applied through rigorous business planning processes designed to take these aspects of an opportunity into consideration, to be successful.

As identified in the FMCo plan, while a good environmental goal, such as waste recycling, may be established, if the financial case, compliance and NGO support are not evident then failure is likely. In contrast as demonstrated, while the goal may be achievable for some clients it is not necessarily achievable, nor appropriate, in all circumstances.

In major retrofit, for example, removing a triphosphor fluorescent tube and replacing it with a LED tube in the early lifecycle of the fluorescent tube, while potentially financially attractive, could actually be counterproductive. This occurs when there is a lack of legislation and regulatory control, permitting the removed tubes to be directly dumped to landfill rather than recycled.

Environmental Management Systems such as ISO14001 provide a good framework for establishing environmental credentials, identifying risks and driving actions through the mandatory aspect and impact process. The cost of maintaining certification is justified when client demand is present.

Corporate sustainability is a key driver in the FM sector if it is linked to compliance, is a brand asset, or a marketing tool. Opportunity exists with 'brand aware' clients, who value public knowledge of their environmental credentials. Compliance also creates project opportunities in the FM sector and can be a key differentiator in market offerings. Strong focus on sustainability during the phases of project initiation and planning is crucial to establishing the framework for, and achieving, a sustainable outcome. Identifying that the sustainable outcome presented is impractical through early detection and action to change or even abandon the plan, allows an opportunity for a positive client outcome at a later time. A subsequent change in legislation or market conditions provides the trigger to re-explore the sustainability initiative.

The integration of behaviours and processes for environmental sustainability into project methodology at a detail level requires further consideration. The synergy with which environmental sustainability is incorporated into traditional practices and then integrated into corporate processes with good automation levels will affect both short and long-term success for corporations providing facilities project management services and their clients.

The outcome of changing regulation, standards, and behaviour motivation through government funding should be further independently analysed to identify if success in a particular geographical or market sector can be effectively extended to other sectors. Identification of further refinements in regulation and standards would be a valuable asset to this analysis.

The FMCo example is not definitive; however, highlights not all projects will fit existing definitions and therefore project practitioners should be flexible when considering what influences sustainable outcomes in a given circumstance.

REFERENCES

Achman, R. (2011). *Stakeholders' perspectives on sustainability in project management: Case studies of 4 different projects in The Netherlands.* (Unpublished master's thesis). Delft University of Technology, Delft, The Netherlands.

AusIndustry, Green Building Fund. (2011). Retrieved April 26, 2012 from http://www.ausindustry.gov.au/programs/innovation-rd/gbf/Documents/GBF-FundingOffers-Round7.pdf

Cmaecocycle. (n.d.). *Mercury and the environment.* Retrieved April 26, 2012 from http://www.cmaecocycle.net/mercury.html

Environment Protection and Heritage Council. (n.d.). *18th meeting of EPHC communiqué – Breakthrough on waste.* Retrieved April 26, 2012 from http://www.ephc.gov.au/sites/default/files/EPHC_Cmq__Communique_2009_05_22.pdf

Facilities Management Association of Australia. (n.d.). *What is facilities management?* Retrieved April 26, 2012 from http://www.fma.com.au/cms/index.php?option=com_content&task=view&id=45&Itemid=59

Fantastic Lighting. (n.d.). *Fantastic lighting's tube replacement service.* Retrieved April 25, 2012 from http://www.fantasticlighting.com.au/Products/Pricing/tabid/66/Default.aspx

Fluorocycle. (2010). *Launch of national scheme to reduce mercury-containing waste.* Retrieved April 26, 2012 from http://www.fluorocycle.org.au/news-detail.php?news_id=25

Gunningham, N. (2002). Green alliances: Conflict or cooperation in environmental policy? *Australasian Journal of Environmental Management, 9*(3), 148–157. doi:10.1080/14486563.2002.10648555.

Gunningham, N. (2009). Shaping corporate environmental performance: A review. *Environmental Policy and Governance, 19*(4), 215–231. doi:10.1002/eet.510.

Jones, L. Lasalle Inc. (2012). *Global property sustainability perspective.* Retrieved April 26, 2012 from http://www.joneslanglasalle.com/GSP/en-gb/Pages/Global-Sustainability-Perspective.aspx

Labuschagne, C., & Brent, A. (2006). Social indicators for sustainable project and technology life cycle management in the process industry. *The International Journal of Life Cycle Assessment, 11*(1), 3–15. doi:10.1065/lca2006.01.233.

Law of Queensland in force 1 December. (2011). *Environment Protection (Waste Management) 2000 Regulation, sec.17, para 1. (Austl.).*

Law of South Australia version 24.11. (2011). *Environment Protection (Waste to Resources) Policy 2010, sch. 4, sec.1, para.15-16. (Austl.).*

Maltzman, R., & Shirley, D. (2011). *Green project managemen*. Boca Raton, FL: CRC Press.

Porter, M., & Van der Linde, C. (1995). Green and competitive – Ending the stalemate. *Harvard Business Review, 73*(5), 120–134.

Reinhardt, F. L. (1998). Environmental product differentiation: Implications for corporate strategy. *California Management Review, 40*(4), 43–73. doi:10.2307/41165964.

Reinhardt, F. L. (2000). *Down to earth: Applying business principles to environmental management.* Boston: Harvard Business School.

Silverman, M., & Lanphar, T. (2003). *Benziger family winery.* Retrieved from http://www.bren. ucsb.edu/academics/courses/210/cases/benziger. pdf

Silvius, G., & Schipper, R. (2010). *A maturity model for integrating sustainability in projects and project management.* Paper presented at the 24th World Congress of the International Project Management Association (IPMA). Istanbul, Turkey. Retrieved from http://publicationslist. org/gilbert.silvius

Silvius, G., Schipper, R., Planko, J., Van Den Brink, J., & Kohler, A. (2012). *Sustainability in project management.* Great Britain, UK: MPG Books Group.

Skinner, C. W., & Berger, A. R. (Eds.). (2003). *Geology and health: Closing the gap.* New York, NY: Oxford University Press.

Standards Australia & Standards New Zealand. (2004a). *AS/NZS ISO 14001: 2004, environmental management systems- Requirements with guidance for use.* Sydney, Australia: Standards Australia.

Standards Australia & Standards New Zealand. (2004b). *AS/NZS ISO 31000: 2009, risk management- Principles and guidelines.* Sydney, Australia: Standards Australia.

Standards Australia & Standards New Zealand. (2011). *AS/NZS ISO 9004: 2011, Managing for the sustained success of an organisation – A quality management approach.* Sydney, Australia: SAI Global.

Thornton, D., Kagen, R., & Gunningham, N. (2003). Sources of corporate environmental performance. *California Management Review, 46*(1). doi:10.2307/41166235.

Zerk, J. A. (2006). *Multinationals and corporate social responsibility.* Cambridge, UK: Cambridge University Press. doi:10.1017/CBO9780511494864.

ADDITIONAL READING

Dunphy, D., Griffiths, A., & Benn, S. (2007). *Organizational change for corporate sustainability-A guide for leaders and change agents of the future.* London, UK: Routledge.

Ellis, M. (2003). *Regulatory impact statement: Minimum energy performance standards and alternative strategies for linear fluorescent lamps.* Retrieved April 26, 2012 from http:// www.legislation.qld.gov.au/LEGISLTN/SLS/ RIS_EN/2004/04SL223R2.pdf

Godden, L., & Peel, J. (2010). *Environmental law: Scientific, policy and regulatory dimensions.* Melbourne, Australia: Oxford University Press.

Grabosky, P. N., & Gant, F. (2000). *Improving environmental performance, preventing environmental crime*. Canberra, Australia: Australian Institute of Criminology.

Griffiths, A. (2004). Corporate sustainability and innovation. *Innovation: Management. Policy & Practice*, 6(2), vi–xiv. doi:10.5172/impp.2004.6.2.vi.

Jenkins, B. (2002). Organisation for sustainability. *Australasian Journal of Environmental Management*, 9(4), 243–251. doi:10.1080/14486563.2002.10648564.

Meredith, J. R., & Mantel, S. J. (2009). *Project management: A managerial approach*. New York: John Wiley & Sons.

Partnerships Victoria. (2010). *Ararat prison project, contract 016-09, schedules 5 & 14*. Retrieved April 26, 2012 from http://www.partnerships.vic.gov.au/CA25708500035EB6/0/FB6C6863455E4253CA2574980000DF5C?OpenDocument

SAI Global. (2007). *Implementing and maintaining an environmental management system*. Sydney, Australia: Standards Australia.

Schaltegger, S., Burritt, R., & Peterson, H. (2003). *An introduction to corporate environmental management – Striving for sustainability*. Sheffield, UK: Greenleaf.

Schwable, K. (2009). *An introduction to project management*. Boston, MA: Course Technology Cengage Learning.

Silverman, M., Marshall, R. S., & Cordano, M. (2005). The greening of the California wine industry: Implications for regulators and industry associations. *Journal of Wine Research*, 16(2), 151–169. doi:10.1080/09571260500331574.

Starik, M. (2004). The nexus between sustainability and innovation. In A. Griffiths (Ed.), Corporate Sustainability: Governance, Innovation Strategy, Development and Methods. Maleny, Australia: eContent Management.

Zwikael, O., & Smyrk, J. (2011). *Project management for the creation of organisational value*. London, UK: Springer. doi:10.1007/978-1-84996-516-3.

KEY TERMS AND DEFINITIONS

Beyond-Compliance: Individuals or corporations who are not limited by meeting regulations or standards but strive to achieve a better outcome than required.

Facilities Management: A broad range of services provided to address all functional elements of a building and the land it occupies.

FMCo: A corporate model representative of the large corporations providing services in the facilities management sector in Australia.

ISO 14001: An internationally recognised standard for environmental management based on the Quality management standard ISO 9001 (see references).

Non-Government Organisation (NGO): Organisation which may receive funding from the government but will act independently and is not bound by public service rules.

Non-Operational: Provides services which are not directly related to client contracts (for example employee services, real estate).

Sustainability Gate: Mandatory decision making and inclusion point in a process for sustainability initiatives to be considered.

Chapter 23
Experimenting with Project Stakeholder Analysis:
A Case Study

Claudia Weninger
WU Vienna, Austria

Jairo Cardoso de Oliveira
Siemens Ltd, Brazil

Martina Huemann
WU Vienna, Austria

Luis Fernando Mendonça Barros Filho
Siemens Ltd, Brazil

Erwin Weitlaner
Siemens AG, Germany

ABSTRACT

The chapter reports on the case study project of the Engineering, Procurement, and Construction (EPC) of a wind park farm in Brazil from the supplier perspective of Siemens Ltd. In the case study, researchers, together with practitioners, further developed project stakeholder analysis by explicitly integrating Sustainable Development (SD) principles. The chapter offers an operative approach and describes the working form systemic board to better handle the increasing dynamics and complexity in contemporary projects and contexts. For project stakeholder management, the consideration of SD principles means in particular: applying a more comprehensive stakeholder management approach with underpinning values that support sustainable development; integrating economic, ecologic, and social interests of project stakeholders into the project objectives to create shared benefit for the project investor and other project stakeholders; broadening the time perspective to consider not only current stakeholders but also future stakeholders of the investment initialized by the project; broadening the spatial perspective to consider local, regional as well as global impacts of the project for stakeholders; using systemic working forms to allow for making the dynamics and complexities of the project and the project contexts better visible to the project manager, the project team, and the project owner; taking consequences in the project organization which lead to more integrative project organization structures to support cooperation on a project and with its stakeholders.

DOI: 10.4018/978-1-4666-4177-8.ch023

INTRODUCTION

This chapter provides insights from a case study project of Siemens Ltd, in which the authors experimented with project stakeholder analysis to explicitly consider Sustainable Development (SD) principles and integrate these into project management. The cases study project is an Engineering, Procurement, and Construction (EPC) of a Wind Park Farm in a rural area of Brazil. The case study was part of an explorative research study which aimed to rethink project initiation and project management by considering SD principles (Gareis et al. 2013). A more comprehensive description of the research findings can be found in the chapter "Re-thinking project initiation and project management by considering principles of sustainable development" by Roland Gareis.

In this chapter, we concentrate on the case study of the project: EPC of a wind park farm.

In the notion of engaged scholarship (Van De Ven 2007) we took the approach of knowledge co-creation of researchers and practitioners. The case study team consisted of two researchers, the representatives of the case study project, two PMO (Project Management Office) managers and other interested senior project managers of the company, See Figure 1. Some of the practitioners engaged in the case study joined as authors of this chapter.

As the project manager of the case study projects said, we contributed to the demystification of Sustainable Development for project management, as we show an operative approach to consider SD in the project stakeholder analysis

The chapter is organized as following. After briefly providing a theoretical background on SD and project stakeholder management, we provide an example how SD principles can be explicitly integrated in project stakeholder management. We introduce the working form systemic board to deal with the complexity of the analysis in the dynamic and complex contemporary project contexts. We then further show the consequences of the findings in the project stakeholder analysis, which may for example result in an integrated project organization. Finally we reflect the case study results, opportunities and limits.

SUSTAINABLE DEVELOPMENT ON AND BY PROJECTS

Sustainable Development

The authors share an understanding of SD based on the one hand on an explicit consideration of *developing* sustainability and on the other hand based on the guiding principles of SD which are

Figure 1. Case study team

values based. SD includes the word "development," which implies that sustainability is an ultimate goal, which cannot be reached but we may provide a contribution to the development towards sustainability. While SD approaches are often defined topic related, we aimed for a more generic understanding to be applicable in all project types. SD is a development process guided by values to support sustainability. Relevant values include for example transparency, fairness, tractability, participation. Based on guiding principles, we define SD principles such as (Gareis et al. 2013):

- Economic, ecologic and social-orientation
- Short, mid and long term-orientation
- Local, regional and global-orientation
- Values based

These principles are further explained in the following sections.

Balancing Economic, Ecologic, and Social Orientation

To consider economic-orientation means that a project is managed economically successfully and contributes to continuing prosperity of the project investor(s). This prosperity may be expressed by competiveness, innovation, and resilience. Thus economic-oriented does not mean only to focus on short term financial gain, but to strive for long term economic success (Baumgartner/Ebner 2010).

To consider ecologic-orientation means that a project is managed in an ecologically responsible way. Ecological sustainability relates to the stability, diversity, and resilience of the ecological environment, as well as to resource conservation and sustainable resource utilization on the project and in the investment initiated by the project. Species and ecosystems should be utilized at levels and in ways that allow them renewing themselves (Allen 1980: 18) to ensure an equal and-long term access a resource base (Pearce 1987).

To consider social-orientation means that a project is managed in a socially responsible way. Social sustainability from a development-oriented perspective has an outcome dimension (e.g. social equity or poverty) and a process dimension (e.g. public participation in decision making). The recently launched ISO 26000 names fairness, equal opportunities and non-discrimination, workforce motivation and incentives, human capital development, and occupational health and safety. All of these are issues on a project.

These three dimensions economic, ecologic, and social-orientation, do not stand alone, but a balancing of this so called 'triple bottom line' or the 'holistic' approach is part of the values. A holistic understanding requires an integration of economic, social, and ecological perspectives, which is difficult to reach as the balancing between these dimension is especially challenged by the trade-offs between the dimensions (Elkington 1999:75; Steurer et al. 2005).

Broadening the Time Perspective

The consideration of SD broadens the time perspective. Companies often overemphasize short term profits by concentrating more on quarterly results than on creating the foundation for long term success. Valuing short term gains higher, for instance by economic discount rate is contrary to the spirit of sustainable development, which asks the organizations to meet the needs of its stakeholders in the future as well as today (Dyllick/Hockerts 2002: 132).

SD stresses the long term perspective, but as a project is a temporary organization there is a contradiction right away. Scholars researching SD in the context of project management (Gareis et al. 2013; Silvius et al. 2012) have explicitly added short and midterm-orientation as relevant for managing projects. Nevertheless, we can relate the long term-orientation to a project when we consider the investment initiated by the project.

Broadening the Spatial Perspective

The consideration of SD broadens the spatial perspective and adds to local-orientation, regional and global-orientation. For the organization to develop sustainably, it becomes necessary to balance its operations across geographic and institutional scales as well as through its entire value chain (see e.g. Wolters 2003). A project is a relatively small organization, nevertheless the project may have considerable effects on a region or beyond, due the results generated by project.

SD on a Project and by a Project

A project is a temporary organization, thus SD can be considered on a project. But as any organization a project is embedded in a wider context. SD by a project is of relevance, which allows for relating management decisions on a short term project to long term perspective and spatial scope beyond the project.

Money for Me, Here and Now!

The values described previously are the basis for SD related attitudes and behaviours in and by a project. SD behaviour stands in contrast to a non-SD behaviour, which emphasizes only short term, economic, and local-benefits for the investor organization(s). This may be represented with the slogan "Money for me, here and now" while mid and long term economic-orientation, ecologic and social impacts are not considered. A non-SD strategy internalizes benefits for the investor organization, but externalizes costs to other projects stakeholders.

In contrast, a SD strategy however would pursue shared benefit creation (Porter/Kramer 2011) and strives to balance the SD principles. From the perspective of the investor this means to also consider costs and benefits of other project stakeholders, such as the project personnel, suppliers, partners, communities.

PROJECT STAKEHOLDER MANAGEMENT

Insights from Contemporary Stakeholder Theory

While stakeholder management has been considered as core for creating project success (Cleland 1985), project management standards still do not reflect the importance of project stakeholder management, but remain superficial. SD principles and insights from contemporary stakeholder theory are not considered in stakeholder management as outlined in project management standards (Eskerod/Huemann 2013). Contemporary general stakeholder theory offers two approaches, i.e. a *management of stakeholders* approach and a *management for stakeholders* approach (Freeman et al. 2007), which can considered as the both extreme positions on a continuum.

The management of stakeholders approach sees stakeholders as providers of resources. Stakeholders are instrumemtailized and seen as means to specific aims in the organization, and managers influence the stakeholders to procure resources for the benefits of the organization. The management of stakeholders approach has been critizes for being manipulative, and for being without any ethical approach to stakeholders that are not considered important for the organization.

In contrast, the management for stakeholders does not consider stakeholders as means to specific aims of the organization but stakeholders are considered as valuable in their own rights. The basis for this more inclusive understanding of stakeholder interests is provided in a comprehensive stakeholder analysis.

In project management standards, a management of project stakeholders approach is advocated. While especially in the context of SD striving for a management for stakeholders is suggested as more appropriate (Eskerod/Huemann 2013) to increase the potential for a shared benefit creation (Porter/Kramer 2011).

Relating SD to Project Stakeholder Management

Stakeholder management is considered as having a high potential to consider SD principles in the management of a project (Gareis et al. 2013). Two possibilities to consider SD principles in project management exist. While one way is to take a project management method and put it into the context of SD values, which should lead to a different behavior of the project manager, project team and the project owner. The other way is to explicitly integrate SD principles into a project management approach. This approach explicitly asks the project manager, the project team and the project owner to consider SD principles in the plans and in their behavior. The latter approach was taken in the case study we report here. We experimented with project stakeholder analysis by explicitly integrating SD principles in the process of conducting a project stakeholder analysis as well as into the structures applied for a project stakeholder analysis.

THE CASE STUDY PROJECT AND ITS CONTEXT

Siemens has a long tradition in thinking long term oriented. As Werner von Siemens, one of the founders said in 1879 "I won't sell the future for instant profit". Since a couple of years the company explicitly pursues SD. While the primary strategy focuses on "greening" the project portfolio and SD principles have been integrated in some process like procurement to ensure SD in the supply chain. Siemens Ltd. in Brazil has been promoting SD in different initiatives relevant for projects such as national supplier regulations, the zero harm policy, capacity building, and the code of conduct for suppliers. The PMO supported the integration of SD into project management.

Specifically, the SD fitting values, efficiency, transparency, stakeholder-orientation, and risk-awareness were considered as relevant for projects.

The case study project was a pilot project for Siemens Ltd., who was one of three main suppliers for a client (utility company) who established the Wind Park Farm in the rural region of Brazil and who will then operate the wind park farm. Siemens Ltd. was responsible for Engineering, Procurement and Construction (EPC) of the wind turbines. Other suppliers were responsible for the foundations and the electrical network on site. The case study project comprises a typical EPC scope of engineering, procuring, constructing the wind turbines at several sites, and the planning for the maintenance service, the training of the future service personnel of the client and organizing the hand over to the service team. After the project a five year service contract follows, which is not considered as part of the project: EPC Wind Park Farm. The project was chosen as case study as the project manager and the core team members were open-minded regarding SD and curious as to how to integrate SD into project management. Further, it was considered as an opportunity as the project represented a pilot project with many more similar projects to be conducted in future.

THE PROCESS OF STAKEHOLDER ANALYSIS

The consideration of SD principles in the management of a project ensures that the complexity of the project in its specific context is perceived. SD broadens the perceptions in several aspects as discussed in the previous section. Using the lens of SD therefore shows the dynamics and complexity of the project and its context more comprehensively. Thus as a consequence, there is the need for different working forms that allow for dealing with the complexity of broadening the consideration of different stakeholders´ interests, time and spatial scales. Systemic working forms are considered to have potential to better grasp the complexity of the situation and allow the project manager and project team to better deal with the complex relation of the mutual relations of the project with stakeholders and the relation between the stakeholders.

Systemic Board as Adequate Working Form

While it is common practice that project management plans are solely developed by the project manager and then communicated in the project team, a more comprehensive approach was suggested and a systemic board was proposed to experiment with the integration of SD principles in project stakeholder analysis.

A workshop was performed. The project manager and two core team members of the case study project participated, as well as representatives of the PMO and other senior project managers. This setting allowed for different perceptions. This comprehensive setting was adequate as the project was explicitly considered as a pilot in two aspects. The case study project was a pilot for EPC wind park farms in Brazil, as well as for integrating SD principles into project management (See Figure 2).

A systemic board was applied to better deal with the complexity of the situation. It allows for visualization, abstraction, and systemic thinking. A systemic board uses a board or a table and material such as wooden blocks in different shapes and colors.

In the case study project, the project manager defined relevant project stakeholders and placed them represented by wooden blocks on a table which served as the board. While doing this he explained who the particular block represented. The project manager was supported by two core team members. The project manager positioned the blocks and explained the positioning, while the two core team members asked questions about

Figure 2. Systemic board work setting

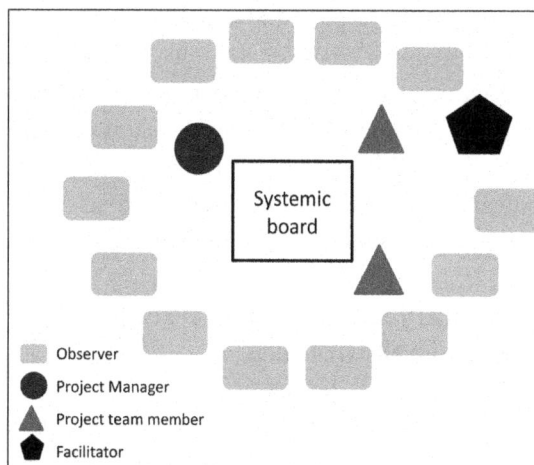

the position of the stakeholder and provided their points of view. One of the researchers acted as facilitator in this work setting and carefully steered the process. The other researcher was an observer and documented the process. The rest of the case study team acted as observers, and only in a final stage they were invited to ask questions and share their views. The work setting is visualized in Figure 3.

Figure 3 shows the final picture of the stakeholder analysis of the case study project. By using the wooden blocks of different colors and shapes

Figure 3. Systemic board with the project stakeholder analysis for the case study project

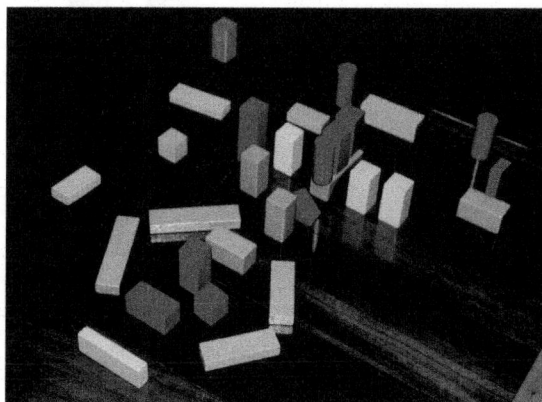

a holistic understanding of the project stakeholders relevant for the case study project was created. In the remainder of the chapter, we will abstract this picture even more to be better able to focus on selected specific issues. Figure 4 shows a more abstracted picture of the project stakeholder analysis. The stakeholders identified as most important for the case study project are shown.

Necessary Cooperation between Project Stakeholders

The constellation of the project stakeholders changed during the working process several times. These changes become visible when comparing Figure 5 and Figure 6. In Figure 5 all suppliers of the wind mill parts such as towers, hubs, blades, other parts (F1-F4) were positioned in one line. Interaction with the transportation supplier (G) and the police escorts (K) were not clear shown.

Figure 6 shows a different picture. This repositioning happened as the project team members responsible for procurement asked how they would organize the transportation of the wind mill parts.

What became clear was the necessary cooperation of the suppliers of the wind mill parts and the transportation suppliers. The suppliers of wind mill parts were repositioned (F1-F4) and grouped around the transportation supplier (G) and other organizations relevant to transportation such as police escorts (K). Finally, the picture created showed how representatives of these stakeholders can possibly work together as an integrated sub team led by the project team member procurement (L).

This is an example of how relationships between project stakeholders can be made visible on a systemic board. Further, it shows that possible solutions may be tried out by repositioning the wooden blocks representing the different

Figure 4. Selected stakeholders of case study project

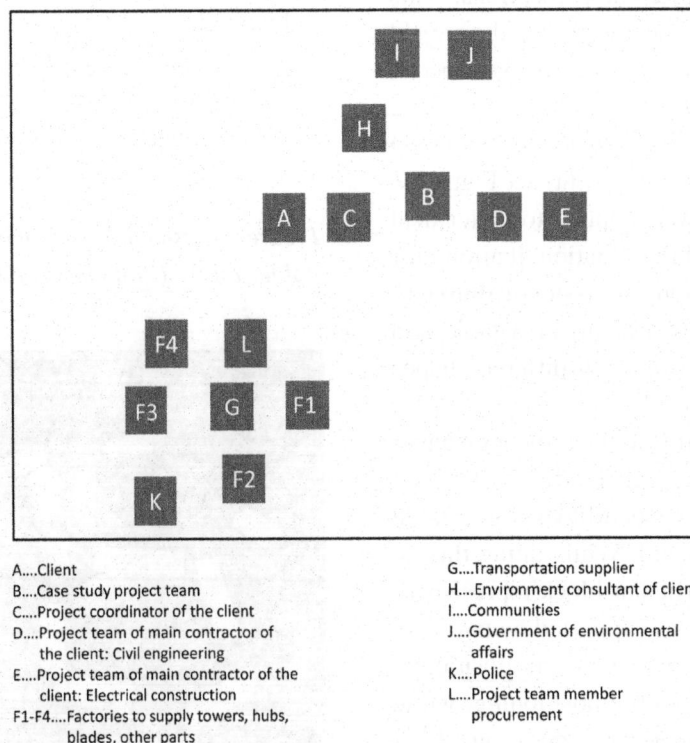

A....Client
B....Case study project team
C....Project coordinator of the client
D....Project team of main contractor of
   the client: Civil engineering
E....Project team of main contractor of the
   client: Electrical construction
F1-F4....Factories to supply towers, hubs,
   blades, other parts

G....Transportation supplier
H....Environment consultant of client
I....Communities
J....Government of environmental
   affairs
K....Police
L....Project team member
   procurement

Figure 5. Suppliers of wind mill parts

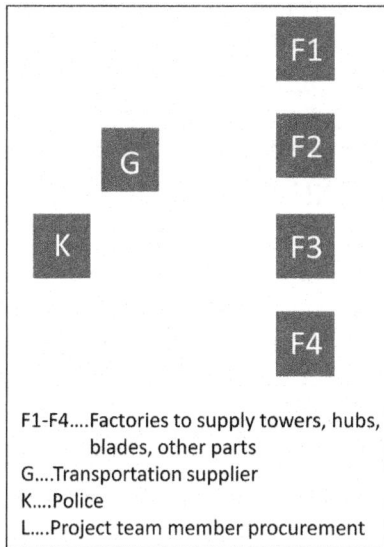

F1-F4....Factories to supply towers, hubs, blades, other parts
G....Transportation supplier
K....Police
L....Project team member procurement

Figure 6. Integrated transportation team

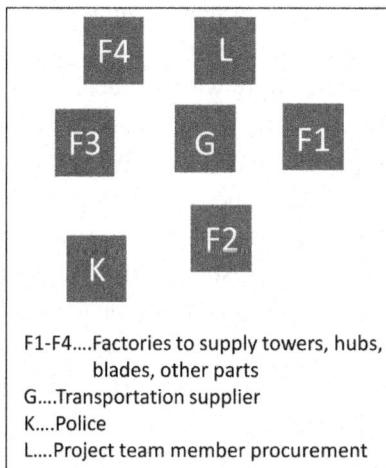

F1-F4....Factories to supply towers, hubs, blades, other parts
G....Transportation supplier
K....Police
L....Project team member procurement

stakeholders. The consideration of relationships between stakeholders may lead to a more appropriate project organization, which will be further discussed later in this chapter.

The Community and the Client

The stakeholder analysis was made from the perspective of the supplier project manager and two core team members. A closer look was taken on the communities, where the wind park farm was built. It was obvious that there is a mutual relation between the case study project and the communities where the wind park farm was being built. The acceptance of the project by the communities was vital to prepare for a good working environment on the construction site. It became clear that the case study project had limited influence on designing and managing the relationships with the communities. However, it strongly indicated the responsibility of the case study project raising the awareness with the client that it was his responsibility to organize for good relations with the communities.

Communication between Main Contractors and the Client

For the case study project the client is the utility company who will also run the wind park farm. To the investment of a wind park farm, several main contractors need to contribute. While Siemens Ltd. as one of the main contractors was responsible for Engineering, Procurement and Construction (EPC) of the wind turbines, other main contractors were responsible for the foundations and the electrical network on site. What became very clear in the analysis was that the cooperation between the utility company and the main contractors was essential for the project success (See Figure 7).

Figure 7. Client and main contractors

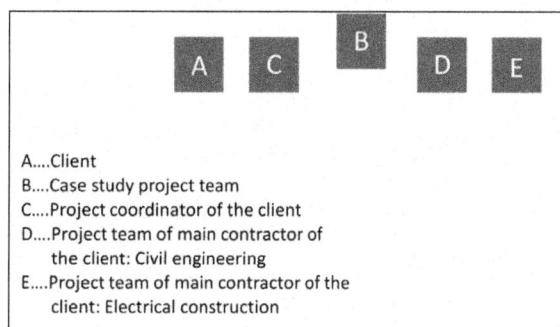

A....Client
B....Case study project team
C....Project coordinator of the client
D....Project team of main contractor of the client: Civil engineering
E....Project team of main contractor of the client: Electrical construction

While this necessary communication cannot be organized by the case study project, the analyzes strongly indicated the responsibility of the case study project to raise the awareness with the client that it was his responsibility to organize for a communication structure between the main suppliers and the investor to ensure cooperation.

Environmental License

An Environmental License was required, which included the consideration of environmental issues not only in the operations of the utility but also during the project. A communication structure including the project coordinator of the client (C), the project coordinator of the case study project (B1), the project coordinator of civil engineering (D1), the project coordinator of electrical construction (E1) and the environmental consultant (H) is a possible solution as visualized in Figure 8.

It became clear that the case study project had limited influence on designing and managing the interaction with the other main contractors and the environmental consultant of the client. However, it strongly indicated the responsibility of the case study project raising the awareness with the client that it was the responsibility of the project

Figure 8. Cooperation between client, main contractors, and environmental consultant

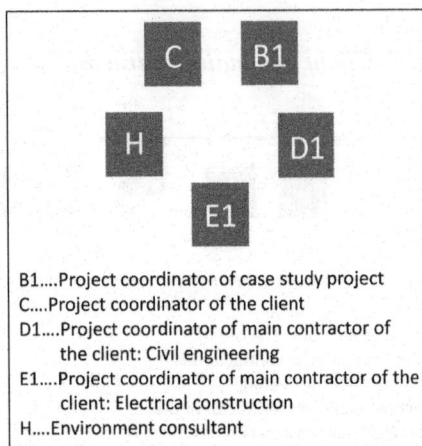

B1....Project coordinator of case study project
C....Project coordinator of the client
D1....Project coordinator of main contractor of the client: Civil engineering
E1....Project coordinator of main contractor of the client: Electrical construction
H....Environment consultant

coordinator to organize for the necessary interactions between client, main contractors, and environmental consultant.

THE EXPLICIT CONSIDERATION OF SD PRINCIPLES

In Table 1 an excerpt of the project stakeholder analysis is shown. A short term project perspective and a long term investment perspective for the analysis of the stakeholders were explicitly differentiated. The examples described in Table 1 relate to the project perspective. The form for the stakeholder analysis shows the explicit integration of the SD principles, social, economic and ecologic orientation.

In addition the structure provided introduces the possibility of classifying the expectations according to the spatial scale of an issue into local, regional, and global. Most of the issues in this particular case study were of local and regional relevance.

The expectations were analyzed from mutual perspectives. The expectations of the stakeholder towards the project and the expectations of the project towards the stakeholder were analyzed and documented. Based on this analysis measures were planned.

To consider the long term investment perspective, the project manager was asked to think beyond the project and to concentrate on the supplier investment as a long term relation between supplier and the client, who is also the future operator of the wind park farm. Also, from the perspective of the supplier, there exists a long term relationship, which goes beyond the project and relates to the investment into the relationship between supplier and client. This long term perspective allowed for the identification of further stakeholders. Despite they are future stakeholders they might have an impact on the project today.

One example for a future stakeholder was a government agency. The project manager con-

Table 1. Stakeholder analysis (project, short- and medium-term perspective, selected stakeholders, selected expectations) (Gareis, et al., 2013, p. 93)

Stakeholder	Project Expectations	Economic	Ecologic	Social	Local	Regional	Global	Stakeholder Expectations	Economic	Ecologic	Social	Local	Regional	Global
Client	Payment on time, fair working conditions	x		x	x			Technical excellence	x			x		
	Support with ecologic regulations on site		x		x			Compliance with environmental regulations			x	x		
	Client organizes communication between main suppliers	x		x	x			Trustworthiness	x			x		
	Client takes on responsibility for clean water on site	x	x		x			Find local staff for service and training			x	x		
Siemens Ltd	Support of project	x		x	x			Good pilot for establishment of new product line in Brazil					x	
								Compliance with environmental regulations					x	
								Compliance with HSE regulations, zero harm policy and other relevant Siemens policies		x	x		x	
Community A	Clean water		x	x		x		Water and waste solution during project	x	x		x		
	Adequate and healthy food		x			x		Job opportunities			x		x	
	Acceptance of project by community			x		x		Adequate behaviour of onsite staff in community			x		x	
Public finance agency	Clear standards	x				x		Use at least 50% national content in project			x	x		
	Payment on time	x			x									
Transportation supplier	On time delivery of parts to the sites	x			x			Payment on time	x			x		
	Optimized transport	x	x		x			Cooperation and clear communication with factories producing the parts	x		x		x	
	Clean roads		x		x			Availability of police escorts	x			x		

sidered at the very end of the utilization of the wind park farm and explained an uncertainty because of a newly issued regulation of a government agency. All suppliers will need to take their supply parts back when the utility is taken apart. The consideration of the abandonment of the wind park farm and the future relation to this particular government agency made the case study project consider of how the parts are installed today, so that they can be more easily dismantled in the future. As the supplier will need to take it back and is responsible for its recycling. Also the material was discussed.

IMPLICATIONS FOR THE PROJECT ORGANIZATION

In the systemic board, a definition of the social boarders of the case study project was performed. Thus it was defined who of the project stakeholders need to be represented in the project organization, and who will remain outside the project organization. By that, for instance, it became clear that within the procurement sub team the transportation teams need to work closely together with the police escorts. The organizational solution is made visible in Figure 9, which shows within the procurement sub team the integrated transportation team and the necessary close cooperation with the police escorts.

REFLECTIONS AND CONCLUSION

In the case study reported in this chapter, we experimented with the consideration of SD principles in a stakeholder analysis of the case study project: EPC Wind Park Farm. We provided an example how an explicit integration of SD principles in project stakeholder management can be organized and operationalized. We also showed some consequences the project stakeholder analysis may have on the project organization.

A systemic board was used as a working form for the project stakeholder analysis. This working form brought several potentials, which include

- **Building up and Reducing Complexity:** It allowed for better grasping the complexity of the project in the context of different stakeholders. As it helped the project manager to build up complexity and to reduce complexity by concentrating on selected relations and issues.

- **Positioning in Space Allows for Visibility of Relations:** It allowed for the consideration of relations between project stakeholders, and made relations better visible as space was added as a dimension. The working form made it able to consider directly and indirectly affected stakeholders and relationships between stakeholders. It provided a picture.

- **Communication Possibility to Create a Shared Reality:** As it provided a picture on a situation it helped the project manager and the project team members to communicate about. By the communication a shared understanding of the situation was created.

- **Simulation of Possible Solutions:** Using the possibility of repositioning, it helped to try out possible solutions. For example it helped to understand where integration of representatives of project stakeholders into a team was necessary. Thus it provided a basis for an adequate design of the project organization.

Table 1 provides a template for a project stakeholder analysis, which explicitly considers the project stakeholders' economic, ecologic, and social interests and their local, regional as well as global project stakeholders´ interests. For the broadening of the temporal scale to consider also a mid and long term perspective, and include the interests of future stakeholders for example of the utility, an additional analysis can be done. The same template can be used for the analyses of the stakeholders during the investment life cycle. By that the expectations and interests of future stakeholders can be analyzed, which might make a difference on decision taken today on the project.

Figure 9. Project organization chart

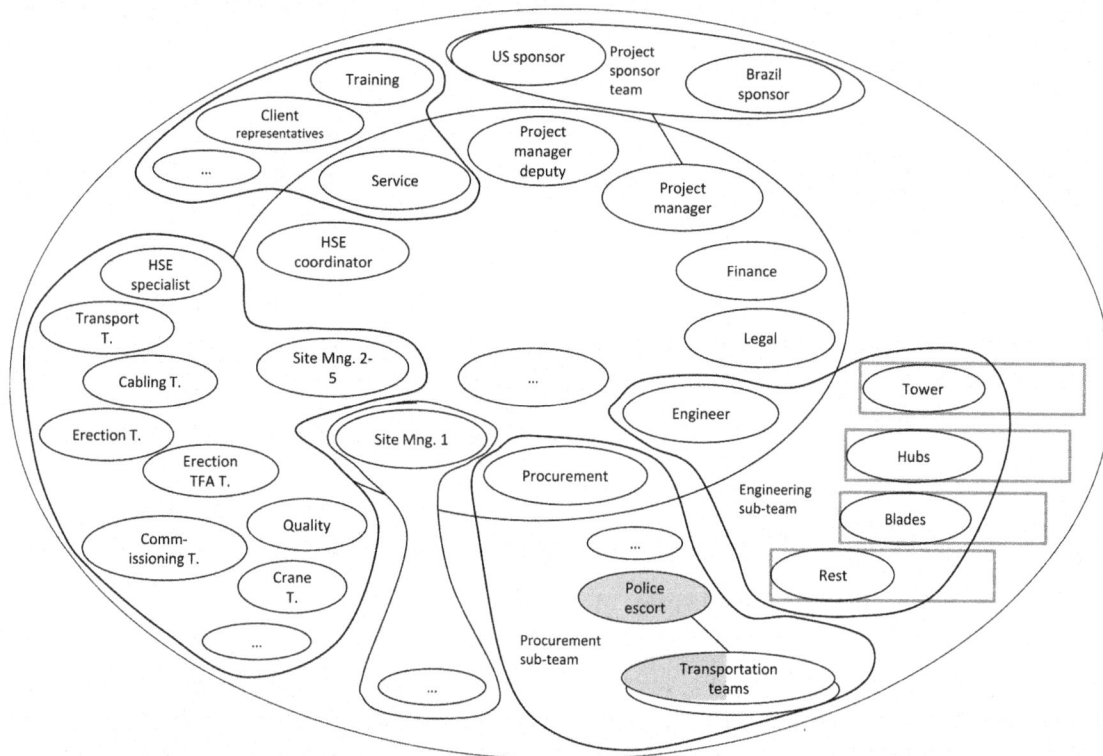

The main restriction nevertheless is the openness of the participants to allow for this working form and the need for experience in facilitating the systemic board. To allow for the integration of SD principles into project stakeholder analysis, SD fitting values like openness, strive for transparency, fairness, participation in the project are necessary. The case study project and more generally the context of Siemens Ltd. provided fitting values to support SD.

Limitations in integrating SD principles into project management are based on values and power position. The case study project reported here was a project of a main contractor contributing to the investment of a client. Thus, for example the establishment of adequate at least communication structures between client, main contractors and environmental consultant remains the responsibility of the client. There is therefore a limit of influence from the position of supplier. Nevertheless the case study clearly indicates that the consideration of SD principles advocates integrative organizational structures to be able to deal with the complexity of the project and its context.

From the practitioners point of view the main benefits gained from the cooperation included a demystification of SD for project management and particularly for the project stakeholder analysis. A development of an operational approach to consider SD principles in project stakeholder management was achieved. Other project teams have within Siemens Ltd have taken the systemic board to support to organize for a project stakeholder analysis that considers SD principles as outlined in this chapter.

Summarizing, for project stakeholder management the consideration of SD principles means in particular:

- Applying a more comprehensive stakeholder management approach with underpinning values that support sustainable development.
- Integrating economic, ecologic, and social interests of project stakeholders into the project objectives to create shared benefit for the project investor and other project stakeholders.
- Broadening the time perspective to consider not only current stakeholders but also future stakeholders of the investment initialized by the project.
- Broadening the spatial perspective to consider local, regional, as well as global impacts of the project for stakeholders.
- Using systemic working forms to allow for making the dynamics and complexities of the project and the project contexts better visible to the project manager, the project team and the project owner.
- Taking consequences in the project organization which lead to more integrative project organization structures to support cooperation on a project and with its stakeholders.

REFERENCES

Allen, R. (1980). *How to save the world: Strategy for world conservation*. London: Kogan Page.

Baumgartner, R. J., & Ebner, D. (2010). Corporate sustainability strategies: Sustainability profiles and maturity levels. *Sustainable Development, 18*(2), 76–89. doi:10.1002/sd.447.

Cleland, D. I. (1985). A strategy for ongoing project evaluation. *Project Management Journal, 16*(3), 11–17.

Dyllick, T., & Hockerts, K. (2002). Beyond the business case for corporate sustainability. *Business Strategy and the Environment, 11*(2), 130–141. doi:10.1002/bse.323.

Elkington, J. (1999). Triple bottom line revolution: Reporting for the third millennium. *Australian CPA, 95*, 75.

Eskerod, P., & Huemann, M. (2013). Sustainable development and project stakeholder management: What standards say. *International Journal of Managing Projects in Business, 6*(1) 36-50.

Freeman, R. E., Harrison, J. S., & Wicks, A. C. (2007). *Managing for stakeholders: Survival, reputation, and success*. New Haven, CT: Yale University Press.

Gareis, R., Huemann, M., Martinuzzi, A., Weninger, C., & Sedlacko, M. (2013). *Project management & sustainable development principles*. Newtown Square, PA: Project Management Institute.

Pearce, D. (1987). Foundations of an ecological economics. *Ecological Modelling, 38*(1-2), 9–18. doi:10.1016/0304-3800(87)90042-1.

Porter, M. E., & Kramer, M. R. (2011). Creating shared value. *Harvard Business Review, 89*(1/2), 62–77.

Silvius, G., Van Den Brink, J., Schipper, R., Köhler, A., & Planko, J. (2012). *Sustainability in project management*. Gower.

Steurer, R., Langer, M. E., Konrad, A., & Martinuzzi, A. (2005). Corporations, stakeholders and sustainable development I: A theoretical exploration of business–society relations. *Journal of Business Ethics, 61*(3), 263–281. doi:10.1007/s10551-005-7054-0.

Wolters, T. (2003). Transforming international product chains into channels of sustainable production: The imperative of sustainable chain management. *Greener Management International, 43*, 6–13.

KEY TERMS AND DEFINITIONS

Management for Stakeholders: The management-for-stakeholders does not consider stakeholders as means to specific aims of the organization but stakeholders are considered as valuable in their own rights.

Management of Stakeholders: The management-of-stakeholders approach sees stakeholders as providers of resources. Stakeholders are instrumemtalized and seen as means to specific aims in the organization, and managers influence the stakeholders to procure resources for the benefits of the organization.

Systemic Board: A systemic board is a working form consisting of a board and wooden blocks in different shapes (and sometimes in different colors). The wooden blocks are used to represent elements such as the project, project roles, organizations, stakeholders, but also interest, conflicts, values may be used as elements. A systemic board helps to visualize relations between these elements and helps to abstract a situations and simulate possible solutions.

Chapter 24

Instruments and Methods for the Integration of Sustainability in the Project Management:
Case Study from Slovenia

Aleksander Janeš
University of Primorska, Slovenia

Armand Faganel
University of Primorska, Slovenia

ABSTRACT

The purpose of this chapter is to propose a framework that is supporting achievement of the sustainable strategy of the organization. The research frames the methodology that integrates project management and Balanced Scorecard (BSC) in the management system of the organization. In this applicative project research, the authors identified and analyzed the Key Performance Indicators (KPIs) that significantly contribute to the benefits of the business processes exploitation. The involved company executes monitoring of its business performance in the four perspectives of the BSC. With this case study, the authors attempted to get deeper understanding, and to clarify and evaluate the causalities between strategic goals and their respective KPIs. For this purpose, they developed an Error Correction Model with which they performed application on the KPIs and estimated short and long term effects between them. The developed model also supports improvements of the performance management system and monitoring of projects.

INTRODUCTION

The theory and practices of Project Management (PM) have fundamentally changed over the past decades. The main concern regarding the changes in the PM is the need to ensure that it remains a useful management tool for academics and practitioners in today's fast-changing business environments. In order to stay relevant the academic and practical discipline of PM should be updated to reflect necessary changes in practice (Assiri, Zairi, & Eid, 2006; Bryde 2003). Janeš and Faganel (2008, p.

DOI: 10.4018/978-1-4666-4177-8.ch024

15) argued that already during the stages of the project planning, it would be wise to provide the development of integrative management system, which would connect quantitative and qualitative decision parameters in a dynamic environment, in order to rank and optimize basic processes. For this purpose, we explored the case study of the service company in which we considered the practical use of the Balanced Scorecard (BSC) as a managerial tool for selection and coordination of projects for achievement of the sustainable strategy.

The Port of Koper, PLC is recognized as a significant port and logistic system in the Adriatic maritime market. Port has an excellent location at the head of the Adriatic, the northernmost reach of the Mediterranean, which ensures Port of Koper with a leading position in servicing Central and South-eastern Europe, and in particular those EU markets with the highest growth potential. Port is strategically oriented towards vehicles, containers and other high value-added cargos. It has great potential to further increase handling and storage capacities, which should allow the company to further strengthen market share in Austria, Hungary, and Italy as well as the domestic market. Operating revenues in 2011 exceeded the 2010 performance for 13%, and operating profit (EBIT) increased for 58% regarding previous year (Port of Koper, 2012).

The company introduced their first Balanced Scorecard (BSC) system in 2006. Beside that the company entered the competition for the most prestigious European Business Excellence Award, and became an Excellence Award Finalist in 2006. System of performance measures or BSC, when used in practice, shows that it is difficult to determine transparent relations between perspectives. However, the implemented model does not allow the identification of all the information on relations (i.e. correlations, causalities) between process Key Performance Indicators (KPIs). In this manner, company does not have a transparent evaluation of resource inputs in efficiency of the implemented model in the management system

(Janeš & Dolinšek, 2010). Diagnostic activities, in this context, are usually "too expensive" to the company and it's usually overworked employees. Because of the latter's outlook, diagnostic is regarded as being time-consuming activity. With the development and application of the model for identification of the influential KPIs which give an important contribution to the business results, company can perform its own diagnostic activities and focus on improvements of the key processes and projects in a short and long-time period.

Many authors, such as Kaplan and Norton (1992), Bititci (1994), Bititci et al. (2006), Olve et al. (1999), and Robson (2004), argue that the establishment of a system of performance measurement must begin with the review of the strategy and not the actual outcome of business processes. Therefore, measures must be directly related to the strategies of the organization and should be selected on the basis of the strategic objectives of the organization. Knowledge about the relations and causality between the KPIs in the selection and composition of BSC is essential for efficient and effective management of the organizations. Namely, implementing and measuring effective sustainable strategies for future success represent continuous challenges for managers, researchers, and consultants.

The main goal of this study was to develop a quantitative approach that is useful in combination with a qualitative approach, as it is usual in determining the causal relations resulting in the strategic map of the BSC (Abernethy et al., 2005); causal knowledge can be gathered from employees that: "…through their experience and training have encoded relational or causal knowledge about complex systems; that is, they understand how things fit and work together, although they might not have articulated that knowledge."

Studies of many authors in the field of performance measurement systems show the actuality of this scientific field and the selected methodology provides support to organizations' decision-making process in real time. A link between BSC and

PM emanates from similar purposes i.e. business perspectives with the aim of meeting the requirements of customers and stakeholders, and on the other hand, satisfying customer and other project stakeholders' requirements. The development of the BSC strategy maps and integrated measures for project control based on KPIs is an essential step for successful project management (Assiri, Zairi, & Eid, 2006; Bryde 2003; Niebecker, Eager, & Kubitza 2008). Namely PM requires effective coordination and collaboration between multiple project teams which can be achieved by a real time information flow and effective communication between all participants.

Simulations of the presented model are possible on all levels of management, by combining the KPIs and consistently acquiring new knowledge about their relations. The developed model also supports improvements to the monitoring of implemented sustainable strategy and achievement of strategic objectives. In that context the contribution of an effective project management to the sustainability integration has been discussed (Assiri, Zairi, & Eid, 2006; Ittner et al., 2003; Janeš & Dolinšek, 2010; Kaplan & Norton, 2000; Kaplan & Norton, 2004; Modell, 2009; Poister, 1982; Vanita et al., 2010; Wang, 2005; Wisniewski & Dickson, 2001).

BACKGROUND

From the literature review, we can ascertain that the theory and practices of PM has fundamentally changed over the past decades. The main concern regarding the changes in the PM is the need to ensure that PM remains a useful management tool for practitioners in today's business environments. In order to stay relevant and useful the academic and practical discipline of PM must be updated to reflect necessary changes in practice. The authors of several case studies draw a common conclusion, that there is an emphasis on upstream activities, such as aligning a project with organi-

zation strategy and defining stakeholder requirements. There is also an emphasis on downstream activities, such as reviewing performance (e.g. implementing BSC) and learning from measurements analysis. A link between BSC and project management emanates from similar purposes i.e. business perspectives with the aim of meeting the requirements of customers and stakeholders, and on the other hand, satisfying customer and other project stakeholder requirements which is a primary aim of PM. The development of the BSC strategy maps and integrated measures for project control based on KPIs is an essential step for successful project management. In particular, the identification of relevant KPIs, which need to be exchanged and harmonized between the project teams and partners, needs attention before the start of the project (Assiri, Zairi, & Eid, 2006; Bryde 2003; Niebecker, Eager, & Kubitza 2008).

The origins of the BSC date back to the time when the management of organizations generally relied on a short-term perspective and only considered the historical data, which mainly represented the financial performance indicators (Johnson & Kaplan, 1987; Modell, 2009). Gradually, the need has arisen to take into account new perspectives, such as the customer satisfaction, the internal process perspective and the perspective of learning (innovation) and growth. In the 1990's, the role of various business-related perspectives and the associated financial and non-financial performance indicators has become an important topic for practitioners, experts and researchers.

The cause and effect relations among the different business perspectives are underlying for accomplishing the long term strategic goals of the organization. This can be achieved by a decomposition of the vision and strategic objectives of an organization into a set of causally related KPIs', which represent the financial perspective, the customers and internal processes, and the learning (innovation) and growth perspective. Such a set of indicators should be cascaded across all the levels of management so as to promote the understanding of the organization's objectives from the perspective of managers and employees (Assiri, Zairi, & Eid, 2006; Kaplan & Norton, 2000; Modell, 2009; Poister, 1982; Wisniewski & Dickson, 2001).

As a rule, the KPIs are determined based on the past experience and by regular reviewing. Where appropriate, an expanded range of KPIs' may be confirmed or some of them may also be phased out.

It is necessary to clarify why, what and how often we need to measure before we decide how to measure (Jones, 2009). Managers should be first asked the questions about what they really want to achieve, what their objectives are and how they can describe them. Therefore, we begin to set up the system of performance indicators by the consensus of managers regarding the description of their goals in the four perspectives. This will facilitate the determination of measurement, as well as defining and changing the KPIs themselves and the sources of data (Kaplan & Norton, 2004; Ittner et al., 2003; Poister, 1982). Historically, the processes in the organizations were investigated mainly as qualitative, verbal and linguistic. Previous research in the field of business processes and performance measurement systems was predominantly performed with the data within a short period of time.

Meanwhile, the longitudinal and dynamic researches for developing theories in this area are very rare. An example for updating the research methodology could be the theoretical physicists (e.g. Einstein or Hawkings), who think in the context of mathematical equations. Thus, the mathematical tools are appropriate to increase the exactness of the conceptual and empirical research. A completion of qualitative research of business processes with statistical tools holds great potential in this area. Namely, the inclusion of a process-based approach and the methodology of longitudinal treatment of business processes make a very important addition to the conceptual thinking of researchers (Brock & Durlauf, 2001; Fritz & Fritz, 1985; Monge, 1990).

Given the framework of the BSCs' strategy map, which consists of four perspectives, and within them a large number of related strategic objectives, it is considered that the added value to business processes is increased by direct and indirect mutual relations. The added value in business processes is manifested in the form of chains of cause and effect relations, ranging from nonfinancial and quantifiable KPIs in the learning (innovation) and growth perspective to the results in the customers' perspective (Ittner & Larcker, 1998) and in the financial perspective. Kaplan and Norton's Balanced Scorecard provides a comprehensive framework that translates the strategic goals of the organization into a coherent set of measures. The biggest advantage of the BSC, as compared to other approaches or models, is it's ability to integrate the capabilities of the various perspectives of the company - financial and nonfinancial, as well as internal and external (Kaplan & Norton, 2006).

Since we do not know the exact principles between the observed variables, which were taken into account in addition to the available literature, researches, documents and records, we especially applied the information contained in the time series of the observed variables (i.e. KPIs).

Already through the observation of linear regression between pairs of variables or KPIs, we can presume the causality which is then confirmed by the Granger causality test (Smith, 1993). It should be noted that from literature review to date, we have not found a similar case study. The knowledge about the correlations and causalities between the KPIs in the selection and composition of the BSC is essential for efficient and effective management of organizations (Janeš & Dolinšek, 2010). The BSC focuses attention of management on only a few KPIs and it links different functional areas, key processes, strategic initiatives and projects as it includes both financial and non-financial indicators. Studies of many authors in the field of performance management system show how topical this scientific field is and the selected methodology provides the support to organizations' decision-making process in real time. The BSC is an effective managerial tool for identification of a wide range of initiatives and projects related to strategy implementation (Bryde, 2003), new product/services development, processes improvements and adaptation of the business model towards achievement of the vision (Assiri, Zairi, & Eid, 2006). Since the BSC is a strategic tool for achieving sustainable development it can represent an excellent approach for harmonizing and coordinating projects in order to fulfill the selected sustainable strategy.

EMPIRICAL FINDINGS ON INTEGRATING SUSTAINABILITY IN PROJECT MANAGEMENT

System of performance measures or BSC, when used in practice, shows that it is difficult to determine transparent relations between perspectives. It is true that the implemented model usually doesn't enable the identification of all information on the relations (i.e. correlations, causalities) between process KPIs. And this is why the company can't provide a clear evaluation of resource inputs in efficiency of the implemented model in the management system (Janeš & Dolinšek, 2010). Very often it can be found that diagnostic activities, in this context, represent an excessive cost to the company and additional workload to its employees. Due to the latter's outlook, diagnostic is regarded as being time-consuming activity. With the development and application of a model for identification of the influential KPIs' which gives an important contribution to the business results, the company can perform its own diagnostic activities and focus on improvements of the key processes and strategic projects in a short and long-time period.

For the quantitative analysis we have chosen KPIs by which the company executes monitoring of its business performance in the four perspectives of the BSC. Among the indicators that were avail-

able, we were opting for those who are monitored in general cargo terminal (GT). All variables represent indicators which are monitored in the company's BSC system. We used six indicators which are: operating revenue OR1, revenue per unit of maritime throughput RU1, maritime throughput MT2, electricity consumption EC3, fossil fuel consumption FC3, and water consumption WACN3.

Purpose of the Research

The purpose of our research is to explore and clarify the cause and effect relations between KPIs. This will give us the basis for understanding these relations and understanding about the relations between business strategy and operations at all levels. This quantitative oriented research deals with the influence of the measured process KPI's on the company's strategy fulfillment. As a research method we have chosen the case study (Yin, 1994) of the Port of Koper, PLC, based on the following criteria:

- First BSC system has been introduced in 2006.
- Port of Koper, PLC entered the competition for the most prestigious European Business Excellence Award, and has become an Excellence Award Finalist in 2006.
- The project of identification of the KPI in collaboration with the UP Faculty of Management Koper has formally started in 2009.

Historically, the processes in the organizations were investigated mainly as qualitative, verbal and linguistic. Previous research in the field of business processes and performance measurement systems was predominantly performed with the data within a short period of time.

Meanwhile, the longitudinal and dynamic studies for developing theories in this area are very rare. A completion of qualitative research of business processes with statistical tools holds great potential in this area. Namely, the inclusion of a process-based approach and the methodology of longitudinal treatment of business processes make a very important addition to the conceptual thinking of researchers (Brock & Durlauf, 2001; Fritz & Fritz, 1985; Monge, 1990).

Main Goal and Methodology

Thus, our main goal is to develop a quantitative approach that is useful in the combination with a qualitative approach, which is a common practice in determining the causal relations resulting in the strategic map of the BSC (Abernethy et al., 2005).

For this purpose and goal we developed a single equation microeconomic Error Correction Model (ECM) with the Engle–Granger (1987) two step method. With the ECM approach we performed application on the KPIs and estimated short and long term effects between them. Final ECM indicates that that there is a lot of nonlinearity at the microeconomic level between KPIs and that a two step method should be used for the time series (i.e. KPIs) analyses at the microeconomic level. From the literature review it is evident that this kind of approach is not used very often with exception for the macroeconomic level.

Data for the model testing, application and analyses were gathered in the period between September and November 2010. From the collected data we constructed time series of KPIs' for one of the terminals for maritime throughput (i.e. GT) in the period from January 2003 to September 2010. In previous years of the project we already ascertained correlations between KPIs (Janeš & Dolinšek, 2010). But the research question about causality relations still remains: Which KPIs should be monitored and what are their causal relations which are enabling fulfillment of the strategy?

SOLUTIONS AND DISCUSSION

In order to set up the ECM model we have chosen KPIs by which the company executes monitoring of its business performance in the four perspectives of the BSC. Among the indicators that were available, we were opting for those who are monitored in GT terminal. We must emphasize that the KPIs have to be monitored on regularly basis (e.g. monthly) and that the period of measurements which is available should be long as much possible. As mentioned before we used six KPIs which are already monitored in the company's BSC system.

From the previous analyses in 2010 and 2011 we ascertained that selected KPIs are stationary, cointegrated between pairs and causally related. Stationarity means that the time series have an average value and constant variance during the observation period. Time series which are not stationary (e.g. random walk) have to be differentiated with the appropriate software (e.g. Eviews 7). Beside the ascertainment of stationarity we furthermore ascertained cointegration between the pairs of KPIs for the reason of excluding the possibility of false regression. Cointegration means that time series or KPIs have a common trend. If a pair of KPIs' is cointegrated then it is likely that, they have a common factor and that one of the KPI causes the other KPI. Namely, in order to set up an error correction model, without a spurious regression, KPIs have to be stationary and cointegrated. To this end, we used the Eviews 7 software (see Gujarati 1995; Janeš & Dolinšek, 2010; Janeš & Dolinšek, 2011).

Error Correction Model

In the first step, we estimated cointegration in accordance with the Engle-Granger procedure. To this end, we set the initial model of performance indicators, calculated regression by the least squares (LS) method and saved the residual value of the potential cointegration vector. Residual values were tested for stationarity which was ascertained by the Phillips-Peron test.

In the second step, we built an ECM model by using the seasonal differences of the indicators, and different time lags of KPIs' and residuals. When the KPIs are cointegrated, then according to the Engle-Granger procedure (1987), there must be an ECM model, which reconciles short-term changes of cointegrated KPIs' with their long-term behavior (Gujarati 1995, p. 730). In the following ECM model (See Table 1 and Equation 1) the value of u_{t-11} represents the error correction term u_{t-i}. The latter represents the residuals from the cointegration regression equation, which measures the speed of adjustment to long-term equilibrium.

In order to restore equilibrium, the sign of the coefficient of the u_{t-i} is expected to be negative (Engle and Granger 1987, Gujarati 1995, p. 730; Alkhathlan, 2011). Since we had monthly data

available we included 12 time lags for the initial model (Gujarati 1995, pp. 728-729). We evaluated the structure of the lags with the criteria for determining the order of lags and correlograms. In our case, 11th order of lags proved to be suitable. This was approved on the basis of five criteria, at the 5% level of statistical significance (i.e. Sequential modified LR test statistic, FPE - Final Prediction Error, AIC - Akaike information criteria, SC - Schwarz information Criterion and HQ - Hannan-Quinn information criterion).

$$\Delta OR1_t = \alpha_0 + \Sigma_{i=1}^{n} \alpha_1 \Delta OR1_{t-i} \\ + \Sigma_{i=1}^{n} \alpha_2 \Delta MT2_t + \Sigma_{i=1}^{n} \alpha_3 \Delta EC3_t \\ + \Sigma_{i=1}^{n} \alpha_4 \Delta FC3_t + \Sigma_{i=1}^{n} \alpha_5 \Delta WACN3_t \\ + \Sigma_{i=1}^{n} \alpha_6 \Delta RU1_t + \alpha_7 u_{t-i} + \varepsilon_t \qquad (1)$$

In activity of excluding lags we performed the visual analysis of time series and residuals with correlograms (Gujarati 1995, pp. 739-742).

Table 1. Final ECM

KPIs	Coefficient	Std. Error	t-Statistic	Prob.
D11MT2	16.91501	0.529441	31.94880	0.0000
D11EC3	-11.54019	1.222652	-9.438652	0.0000
D11FC3	6.149600	1.430026	4.300341	0.0001
D11WACN3	14.08760	2.065849	6.819277	0.0000
D11RU1	897.9722	101.5168	8.845557	0.0000
	-0.925361	0.030894	-29.95276	0.0000
OR1	0.836054	0.029701	28.14920	0.0000
MT2	-13.10256	1.049950	-12.47923	0.0000
EC3(-1)	9.172357	1.517075	6.046082	0.0000
FC3(-1)	-5.883652	1.374530	-4.280482	0.0001
RU1	-732.4894	142.9989	-5.122343	0.0000
C	-500897.6	55176.52	-9.078093	0.0000
R^2	0.990579	Schwarz criter.	26.34720	
Adj. R^2	0.989098	Hannan-Quinn criter.	26.13640	
Akaike info criter.	25.99499	Durbin-Watson stat	2.074189	

Note: Dependent variable is operating revenue denoted as D11OR1. Method: Least Squares. Used KPIs are: operating revenue OR1, revenue per unit of maritime throughput RU1, maritime throughput MT2, electricity consumption EC3, fossil fuel consumption FC3, and water consumption WACN3.

The number of lags was then gradually reduced on the basis of Wald test for exclusion of lags (excluding lags 2, 4, 7, 8, 10 and 12). By testing different KPIs time lags on the right side of the equation and decreasing of autocorrelation and serial correlation we have come to the final ECM model (Table 1).

The results of the final ECM model show that the operating revenue OR1 is dependent on several indicators. First and foremost, the causal indicators of the OR1 are maritime throughput MT2 and revenue per unit of maritime throughput RU1. The statistically significant causal relationship is contributed also by electricity consumption EC3, fossil fuel consumption FC3 and water consumption WACN3, which are exploited for the handling of all types of maritime throughput.

The final model has a high adjusted determination coefficient which is Adj. $R^2 = 0.9890$. For the cointegration regression it is generally recommended to choose the solutions that have the highest coefficient of determination R^2, because the latter reduces bias in the estimated cointegration parameters (Banerjee, Dolado, Hendry & Smith 1986; Hall 1986 as cited in Jiha & Orphee 1995, pp. 106-107).

In addition, the Durbin-Watson's statistic, which is 2.0741, indicates that we significantly reduced the impact of autocorrelation and serial correlation. All regression coefficients and constants of the KPIs' are statistically significant, the error correction term is negative and also statistically significant $u_{t-11} = -0.9253$. Error correction term shows how fast the model returns to the stability at any disturbance or shock. The result in Table 1 can be interpreted as follows: total turnover is increased, by increased maritime throughput. Increasing the maritime throughput means a reduction in electricity consumption per tonne reloaded and increasing consumption of fossil fuels and water.

Revenue per unit of maritime throughput RU1 has a negative regression coefficient, which may lead to an increase in income or increased amount of maritime throughput and simultaneously reducing the cost per tonne reloaded. Results are reflecting the impact of sharp declining in maritime throughput with greatest added value in the years 2007 and 2008. All these results and observations suggest that an error correction mechanism exists and that we set up a stable model, which describes the dynamics of the short-term determinants of the long-term service performance.

The final model with an ECM reflect Granger's causality caused by maritime throughput and energy consumption on the total sales revenue. Results of the analysis are also consistent with the developed procedure and the results of several authors on which we can tie our findings about cointegration between KPIs (Engle and Granger 1987, Granger 1983 Mon Miller 1991, 146; Jiha Orphee and 1995, p. 99; EViews, 2010).

From the methodological point of view it would be interesting to analyse the existence of cointegration and ECM with time series data sample divided into two parts. However, because of the relatively small number of measurements over the entire sample, which is n = 93, statistical analysis of the halved measurements indicates no cointegration between time series. Such a procedure is problematic due to the low number of available measurements and the error correction term that could be misleading. This was identified by the authors of several studies (Engle and Granger 1987; Stock & Watson 1988 as cited in Jiha & Orphee 1995, p. 101; Macunovich & Easterlin, 1988; Miller 1991, p. 146).

Diagnostics of the Error Correction Model

MT2 indicator of maritime throughput, which in this model appears on the right side of the equation, is substantively and statistically (Wald's test of independence) recognized as an independent indicator. Maritime throughput cannot be dependent on other indicators such as consumption of energy and consequently the revenue of maritime throughput. This happens because of the maritime throughput, which is shipped into port of Port of Koper, PLC. A share of throughput is also achieved due to the land transshipment of goods, which was not addressed in this study. The maritime throughput MT2 also includes seasonal component and random errors.

Correlogram of residuals showed that residuals did not induce serial correlation, as the Q statistic is not significant (from 0 to 36 lags). Breusch-Godfrey LM serial correlation test showed that between the residuals of the KPIs' there is no serial correlation, since we could not reject the null hypothesis that there is no serial correlation (up to 12th lag).

With the Breusch-Pagan-Godfrey, Glejser and White test we rejected the hypothesis of residuals heteroskedasticity. Examination of the stability of the model in breaking year 2006, with the Chow's test showed that we cannot reject the null hypothesis of no breaks at specified breakpoint. In the case of rejection of the null hypothesis, the Chow's test would indicate structural changes. This means that the coefficients of the model equation are stable. Using different tests we confirmed the relative stability of the final ECM. Performed test can be tied to procedures for testing models in studies of various authors (Engle and Granger 1987, Stock & Watson 1988; Jiha & Orphee 1995; Macunovich & Easterlin 1988, Miller 1991).

Described simulation and coefficients stability tests of the developed ECM model are possible on all levels of management, by combining the KPIs and consecutively acquire new knowledge about their relations. ECM modeling is primarily intended for forecasting the future values of the KPIs'. Because of these properties this kind of modeling can be used for evaluating causal relationships among the KPIs which are adding value for the customers and making a forecast of the future KPIs' values. Developed quantitative approach supports improving the monitoring of operational efficiency of an organization, improving quality, project efficiency, and achievement of the sustainable strategy and its objectives.

FUTURE RESEARCH DIRECTIONS

From the results of the final ECM model in Table 1, we can also assume the existence of certain nonlinearities which are reflecting their influence at the observed microeconomic level. Granger (1997) believed that there is a lot of nonlinearity in economics at the micro level. But there is not much left of that at the macro level, after temporal and cross-sectional aggregation. Granger was also of the opinion that more attention should be given to the nonlinearities (Phillips & Granger, 1997, p. 278). The ECM modeling approach should be used more often at the microeconomic level on various business areas (e.g. BSC, project management, process management, marketing, etc.).

Of course, it is appropriate to test and evaluate the final ECM model with the latest actual data and recalculate the ECM model and error correction term, which will further improve our model. It is also of our further research interest that the ECM approach should be deployed, first of all, on the BSC on the strategic level of the company. In the next step the BSC of the strategic level should be harmonized with the BSCs of all other terminals for the maritime throughput including their strategic initiatives and projects.

The results of the analyses are also consistent with the developed procedure and the research results of several authors to which we can tie our findings about the cointegration between KPIs with the error correction mechanism (Engle & Granger, 1987, Granger, 1983 as cited in Miller, 1991, p. 146; Jiha & Orphee, 1995, p. 99; EViews, 2010).

CONCLUSION

The discussed organization can be a model in terms of demonstrating the achieved level of business performance excellence. Using the model to identify KPIs is suitable for classification and assessment of the integration and causality between the performance indicators under the four perspectives of the BSC. The BSC is an effective managerial tool for identification of a wide range of initiatives and projects related to strategy implementation (Bryde, 2003), new product/services development, processes improvements and adaptation of the business model towards achievement of the vision. Namely, a link between BSC and project management emanates from similar purposes i.e. business perspectives with the aim of meeting the requirements of customers and stakeholders, and on the other hand, satisfying customer and other project stakeholder requirements, which is a primary aim of project management (Bryde 2003). Since the BSC is a strategic tool for achieving sustainable development it should be an excellent approach for harmonizing and coordinating projects in order to fulfill the selected strategy. Thus, a represented quantitative approach is useful in combination with a qualitative approach, which is common practice in determining the causal relations resulting in the strategic map of the BSC.

Simulations of the developed model are possible on all levels of management, by combining the KPIs and consecutively acquire new knowledge about their relations. Developed quantitative approach supports improving the monitoring of operational efficiency of an organization, improving quality, project efficiency and achievement of the sustainable strategy and its objectives. Some of the influences of specific factors that affect the unexplained part of the variables analyzed in the study are certainly random, but some may arise from current circumstances in the company and are not included in the model or we did not have available data. A case study of the port and logistic system Port of Koper, PLC has also some limitations. The first relates to sample size and quality of the data which were available. A second limitation is a quantitative analysis in the four perspectives of the BSC. Since this is the case study which investigates the impact of the KPIs' on the business results and causalities between them, we also encountered the data, which are treated as a business secret. We must also consider the impact of external factors, such as changing government regulations, access to public infrastructure such the second rail track to Divača and investment in the railway business, logistic centers, development of maritime passenger terminal and alcohol terminal and competing ports in the Mediterranean (in particular, Rijeka, Venezia and Trieste). The company has faced sharp decline in maritime throughput in 2007 as a result of the global financial crisis which is reflected through the KPI in the years 2008, 2009 and 2010.

Further research into the impact of introducing the four perspectives of the BSC to monitor the implementation of strategic projects for sustainable strategy fulfillment is definitely recommended. With research of case studies, as well as benchmarking between them, we contribute to clarify the position of Slovenian organizations among other organizations in the EU and beyond.

REFERENCES

Abernethy, M. A., Horne, M., Lillis, A. M., Malina, M. A., & Selto, F. H. (2005). A multi-method approach to building causal performance maps from expert knowledge. *Management Accounting Research*, *16*(2), 135–155. doi:10.1016/j.mar.2005.03.003.

Alkhathlan, K. A. (2011). Foreign direct investment and export growth in Saudi Arabia: A cointegration analysis. *China-USA Business Review*, *10*(2), 137–149.

Assiri, A., Zairi, M., & Eid, R. (2006). How to profit from the balanced scorecard: An implementation roadmap. *Industrial Management & Data Systems, 106*(7), 937–952. doi:10.1108/02635570610688869.

Banerjee, A., Dolado, J. J., Hendry, D. F., & Smith, G. W. (1986, August). Exploring equilibrium relationships in econometrics through static models: Some Monte Carlo evidence. *Oxford Bulletin of Economics and Statistics*, 253–277.

Bititci, U. S. (1994). Measuring your way to profit. *Management Decision, 32*(6), 16–24. doi:10.1108/00251749410065088.

Bititci, U. S., Mendibil, K., Nudurupati, S., Garengo, P., & Turner, T. (2006). Dynamics of performance measurement and organisational culture. *International Journal of Operations & Production Management, 26*(12), 1325–1350. doi:10.1108/01443570610710579.

Brock, W. A., & Durlauf, S. N. (2001). Growth empirics and reality. *The World Bank Economic Review, 15*(2), 229–272. doi:10.1093/wber/15.2.229.

Bryde, D. J. (2003). Project management concepts, methods, and application. *International Journal of Operations & Production Management, 23*(7), 775–793. doi:10.1108/01443570310481559.

Engle, R. F., & Granger, C. W. J. (1987). Cointegration and error correction: Representation, estimation, and testing. *Econometrica, 55*(2), 251–276. doi:10.2307/1913236.

EViews. (2010). *EViews 7*. Irvine, CA: Quantitative Micro Software, LLC.

Fritz, R. G., & Fritz, J. M. (1985). Linguistic structure and economic method. *Journal of Economic Issues, 19*(1), 75–101.

Granger, C. W. J. (1983). *Co-integrated variables and error-correcting models*. San Diego, CA: University of California.

Granger, C. W. J. (1997). On modelling the long run in applied economics. *The Economic Journal, 107*(440), 169–177. doi:10.1111/1468-0297.00150.

Gujarati, D. N. (1995). *Basic econometrics*. New York: McGraw-Hill.

Hall, S. G. (1986, August). An application of the granger and engle two-step estimation procedure to United Kingdom aggregate wage data. *Oxford Bulletin of Economics and Statistics*, 229–239.

Ittner, C. D., & Larcker, D. F. (1998). Indicators of financial performance? An analysis of customer satisfaction. *Journal of Accounting Research, 36*, 1–35. doi:10.2307/2491304.

Ittner, C. D., Larcker, D. F., & Meyer, M. W. (2003). Subjectivity and the weighting of performance measures: Evidence from a balanced scorecard. *Accounting Review, 78*(3), 725–758. doi:10.2308/accr.2003.78.3.725.

Janeš, A., & Dolinšek, S. (2010). Do we need a new compass for the journey through the global crisis? *Journal of Industrial Engineering and Management, 3*(2), 255–293. doi:10.3926/jiem.2010.v3n2.p255-293.

Janeš, A., & Dolinšek, S. (2011). *Can we use the statistical causality with the sufficient reliability?* Paper presented at the Knowledge and Learning International Conference 2011. Celje, Slovenia.

Janeš, A., & Faganel, A. (2008). Zadovoljstvo udeležencev projekta poslovne odličnosti v PS mercator, d.d. [Business excellence project in PS Mercator, P.l.c. participants' satisfaction]. *Projektna mreža Slovenije, 11*(1), 9-17.

Jiha, J., & Orphee, G. (1995). A note on inflation in Haiti: Evidence from cointegration analysis. *Social and Economic Studies, 44*(1), 95–115.

Johnson, H. T., & Kaplan, R. S. (1987). *Relevance lost: The rise and fall of management accounting*. Boston, MA: Harvard Business School Press.

Jones, P. (2009). *Avoiding problems and predicting recovery during the economic crisis*. Retrieved March 10, 2010, from http://www.excitant.co.uk

Kaplan, R., & Norton, D. (1992). The balanced scorecard - Measures that drive performance. *Harvard Business Review, 70*(1), 71–79. PMID:10119714.

Kaplan, R., & Norton, D. (2000). Having trouble with your strategy? Then map it. *Harvard Business Review, 78*(5), 167–176. PMID:11143152.

Kaplan, R. S., & Norton, D. P. (2004). *Strategy maps: Converting intangible assets into tangible outcomes*. Boston: Harvard Business School Publishing.

Kaplan, R. S., & Norton, D. P. (2006). *Alignment: Using the balanced scorecard to create corporate synergies*. Boston: Harvard Business School Publishing.

Macunovich, D. J., & Easterlin, R. A. (1988). Application of granger-sims causality tests to monthly fertility data, 1958-1984. *Journal of Population Economics, 1*(1), 71–88. doi:10.1007/BF00171511.

Miller, S. M. (1991). Monetary dynamics: An application of cointegration and error-correction modeling. *Journal of Money, Credit and Banking, 23*(2), 139–154. doi:10.2307/1992773.

Modell, S. (2009). Bundling management control innovations. *Accounting, Auditing & Accountability Journal, 22*(1), 59–90. doi:10.1108/09513570910923015.

Monge, P. R. (1990). Theoretical and analytical issues in studying organizational processes. *Organization Science, 1*(4), 406–430. doi:10.1287/orsc.1.4.406.

Olve, N., Roy, J., & Wetter, M. (1999). *Performance drivers: A practical guide to using the balanced scorecard*. Chichester, UK: John Wiley & Sons.

Phillips, P. C. B., & Granger, C. (1997). The ET interview: Professor Clive Granger. *Econometric Theory, 13*(2), 253–303. doi:10.1017/S0266466600005740.

Poister, T. H. (1982). Developing performance indicators for the Pennsylvania department of transportation. *Public Productivity Review, 6*(1/2), 51–77. doi:10.2307/3380402.

Port of Koper. (2012). *Annual report 2011*. Koper: Port of Koper.

Robson, I. (2004). From process measurement to performance improvement. *Business Process Management Journal, 10*(5), 510–521. doi:10.1108/14637150410559199.

Smith, P. K. (1993). Welfare as a cause of poverty: A time series analysis. *Public Choice, 75*(2), 157–170. doi:10.1007/BF01048360.

Stock, J. H., & Watson, M. W. (1988). Variable trends in economic time series. *The Journal of Economic Perspectives, 2*(3), 147–174. doi:10.1257/jep.2.3.147.

Vanita, A., Yang, J., Skitmore, M., & Shankar, R. (2010). An empirical test of causal relationships of factors affecting ICT adoption for building project management: An Indian SME case study. *Construction Innovation: Information, Process. Management, 10*(2), 164–180.

Wang, W. (2005). An evaluation of the balanced scorecard in equity valuation: The case of exchange ratio in the M&As of Taiwan's financial industry. *Journal of Intellectual Capital, 6*(2), 206–221. doi:10.1108/14691930510592807.

Wisniewski, M., & Dickson, A. (2001). Measuring performance in dumfries and galloway constabulary with the balanced scorecard. *The Journal of the Operational Research Society, 52*(10), 1057–1066. doi:10.1057/palgrave.jors.2601191.

Yin, R. K. (1994). *Case study research: Design and methods*. Thousand Oaks, CA: Sage.

ADDITIONAL READING

Aaltonen, P., & Ikavalko, H. (2002). Implementing strategies successfully. *Integrated Manufacturing Systems*, *13*(6), 415–418. doi:10.1108/09576060210436669.

Abernathy, W. (1997). Balanced scorecards make teamwork a reality. *Journal for Quality and Participation*, *20*(5), 58–59.

Agostino, D., & Arnaboldi, M. (2011). How the BSC implementation process shapes its outcome. *International Journal of Productivity and Performance Management*, *60*(2), 99–114. doi:10.1108/17410401111101458.

Alexander, L. D. (1985). Successfully implementing strategic decisions. *Long Range Planning*, *18*(3), 91–97. doi:10.1016/0024-6301(85)90161-X.

Atkinson, H. (2006). Strategy implementation: A role for the balanced scorecard? *Management Decision*, *44*(10), 1441–1460. doi:10.1108/00251740610715740.

Basu, R., Little, C., & Millard, C. (2009). Case study: A fresh approach of the balanced scorecard in the Heathrow terminal 5 project. *Measuring Business Excellence*, *13*(4), 22–33. doi:10.1108/13683040911006765.

Camacho, M., & Perez-Quiros, G. (2002). This is what the leading indicators lead. *Journal of Applied Econometrics*, *17*(1), 61–80. doi:10.1002/jae.641.

Caporale, G. M., Katsimi, M., & Pittis, N. (2002). Causality links between consumer and producer prices: Some empirical evidence. *Southern Economic Journal*, *68*(3), 703–711. doi:10.2307/1061728.

Denbaly, M., & Vroomen, H. (1993). Dynamic fertilizer nutrient demands for corn: A cointegrated and error-correcting system. *American Journal of Agricultural Economics*, *75*(1), 203–209. doi:10.2307/1242968.

Geweke, J., Meese, R., & Dent, W. (1983). Comparing alternative tests of causality in temporal systems. *Journal of Econometrics*, *21*, 161–194. doi:10.1016/0304-4076(83)90012-X.

Goold, M. (1991). Strategic control in the decentralised firm. *Sloan Management Review*, *32*(2), 69–81.

Granger, C. (1986). Statistics and causal inference: Comment source. *Journal of the American Statistical Association*, *81*(396), 967–968. doi:10.2307/2289068.

Granger, C. W. J. (2004). Time series analysis, cointegration, and applications. *The American Economic Review*, *94*(3), 421–425. doi:10.1257/0002828041464669.

Guilkey, D. K., & Salemi, M. K. (1982). Small sample properties of three tests for Granger-causal ordering in a bivariate stochastic system. *The Review of Economics and Statistics*, *64*, 668–680. doi:10.2307/1923951.

Holland, P. W. (1986). Statistics and causal inference. *Journal of the American Statistical Association*, *81*(396), 945–960. doi:10.1080/01621459.1986.10478354.

Hume, D. (1739). *A treatise of human nature*. Oxford, UK: Clarendon Press.

Hylleberg, S., Engle, R. F., Granger, C. W. J., & Yoo, B. S. (1990). Seasonal integration and cointegration. *Journal of Econometrics*, *44*, 215–238. doi:10.1016/0304-4076(90)90080-D.

Hylleberg, S., & Mizon, G. E. (1989). Cointegration and error correction mechanisms. *The Economic Journal*, *99*(395), 113–125. doi:10.2307/2234074.

Mooney Marini, M., & Singer, B. (1988). Causality in the social sciences. *Sociological Methodology*, *18*, 347–409. doi:10.2307/271053.

Murray, M. P. (1994). A drunk and her dog: An illustration of cointegration and error correction. *The American Statistician*, *48*(1), 37–39.

Neely, A. (2008). *Does the balanced scorecard work: An empirical investigation RP 1/08*. Retrieved May 6, 2008, from http:// www.som. cranfield.ac.uk/som/research/researchpapers.asp

Neely, A., Bourne, M., Mills, J., Platts, K., & Richards, H. (2002). *Strategy and performance: Getting the measure of your business*. Cambridge, UK: Cambridge University. doi:10.1017/ CBO9780511753695.

Neely, A., Mills, J., Platts, K., Richards, H., Gregory, M., Bourne, M., & Kennerley, M. (2000). Performance measurement system design: Developing and testing a process-based approach. *International Journal of Operations & Production Management*, *20*(10), 1119–1145. doi:10.1108/01443570010343708.

Niebecker, K., Eager, D., & Kubitza, K. (2008). Improving cross-company project management performance with a collaborative project scorecard. *International Journal of Managing Projects in Business*, *1*(3), 368–386. doi:10.1108/17538370810883828.

Singpurwalla, N. D. (2002). On causality and causal mechanisms: Comment on Dennis Lindley's seeing and doing: The concept of causation. *International Statistical Review*, *70*(2), 198–206.

Young, J. Z. (1978). *Programs of the brain*. Oxford, UK: Oxford University Press.

KEY TERMS AND DEFINITIONS

BSC: Balanced scorecard that includes perspectives, such as the customer satisfaction, the internal process perspective and the perspective of learning (innovation) and growth. BSC is a managerial tool which focuses attention of management on only a few most important KPIs and is a substantial component of the performance measurement system.

Cointegration: Cointegration means that series have a common trend. If a pair of variables is cointegrated then it is likely that, they have a common factor and that one of the variables causes the other variable.

Error Correction Model: If two or more time series (i.e. KPIs) are cointegrirated then there is an error correction mechanism or Error Correction Model. When the KPIs are cointegrated, there must be an ECM that describes the short run dynamics of the cointegrated variables towards their long run equilibrium values. In the ECM, usually, exists a lagged error correction term that measures the speed of adjustment to long run equilibrium between the KPIs.

KPIs: The most important key performance indicators of performance management system by which can be followed progress towards achievement of strategic goals.

Error Correction Term: Error correction term measures the speed of adjustment to long run equilibrium between the KPIs.

Microeconomic Level: Level that refers to research of a single case business.

Project Management: Management of the one time process which will become a regular business process when it will fulfill its purpose and goals. Multiple projects can be identified, monitored and managed through performance management system that supports the strategy fulfillment.

Overview of Literature on Sustainability in Projects and Project Management

BOOKS

Barnard, L. T., Ackles, B., & Haner, J. L. (2011). *Making sense of sustainability project management*. New York: Explorus Group Inc..

Brulin, G., & Svensson, L. (2012). *Managing sustainable development programmes: A learning approach to change*. London: Gower Publishing.

Eid, M. (2009). *Sustainable development & project management*. Cologne, Germany: Lambert Academic Publishing.

Gareis, R., Huemann, M., Martinuzzi, R.-A., Weninger, C., & Sedlacko, M. (2013). *Project management & sustainable development principles*. Newton Square, PA: Project Management Institute.

Haugan, G. (2012). *The new triple constraints for sustainable projects, programs, and portfolios*. Boca Raton, FL: CRC Press.

Ma, U. (2011). *No waste: Managing sustainability in construction*. London: Gower Publishing.

Maltzman, R., & Shirley, D. (2010). *Green project management*. Boca Raton, FL: CRC Press.

Morfaw, J.N. (2011). *Project sustainability: A comprehensive guide to sustaining projects, systems and organizations in a competitive marketplace*. New York: iUniverse Publishing.

Morfaw, J. N. (2012). *Fundamentals of project sustainability: Strategies, processes and plans*. New York: CreateSpace Independent Publishing Platform.

Müller-Pelzer, F. (2009). *Sustainability management in CDM project activities: How to demonstrate and assess the contribution to sustainable development of clean development mechanism (CDM) project activities*. Berlin: SVH-Verlag.

Oehlmann, I. (2011). *The sustainable footprint methodology*. Cologne, Germany: Lambert Academic Publishing.

Pelt, M. J. F. (1993). *Ecological sustainability and project appraisal: Case studies in developing countries*. Aldershot, UK: Avebury.

Silvius, A. J. G., Schipper, R., Planko, J., van den Brink, J., & Köhler, A. (2012). *Sustainability in project management*. London: Gower Publishing.

Taylor, T. (2010). *Sustainability interventions - For managers of projects and programmes*. New York: The Higher Education Academy – Centre for Education in the Built Environment.

BOOK CHAPTERS

Gareis, R., & Frank, A. (2010). ABS international: Sustainable project management. In Turner, Huemann, Anbari, & Bredillet (Eds.), Perspectives on Projects. London: Routledge.

Silvius, A. J. G. (2012). Change the game: Sustainability in projects and project management. In Brocke, Seidel, & Recker (Eds.), Green BPM - Towards the Environmentally Sustainable Enterprise. Berlin: Springer.

Silvius, A. J. G., van den Brink, J., & Köhler, A. (2009). Views on sustainable project management. In Kähköhnen, Samad Kazi, & Rekola (Eds.), Human Side of Projects in Modern Business. Helsinki, Finland: IPMA.

Silvius, A. J. G., van den Brink, J., & Köhler, A. (2012). The impact of sustainability on project management. In Linger & Owen (Eds.), The Project as a Social System, (pp. 183 – 200). Victoria, Australia: Monash University Publishing.

JOURNAL ARTICLES

Al-Saleh, Y. M., & Taleb, H. N. (2010). The integration of sustainability within value management practices: A study of experienced value managers in the GCC countries. *Project Management Journal*, *41*(2), 50–59.

Badiru, A. B. (2010). The many languages of sustainability. *Industrial Engineer*, *42*(11), 30–34.

Brent, A. C. (2005). The application of life cycle management in decision-making for sustainable development at government and corporate level: The integration of project, asset and product life cycles. *Progress in Industrial Ecology –. International Journal (Toronto, Ont.)*, *2*(2), 223–235.

Brent, A. C., van Erck, R. P. G., & Labuschagne, C. (2006). Sustainability cost accounting: Part 1 – A monetary procedure to evaluate the sustainability of technologies in the South African process industry. *South African Journal of Industrial Engineering*, *17*(2), 35–51.

Brent, A. C., van Erck, R. P. G., & Labuschagne, C. (2007). Sustainability cost accounting: Part 2 – A case study in the South African process industry. *South African Journal of Industrial Engineering*, *18*(1), 1–17.

Brent, A. C., Heuberger, R., & Manzini, D. (2005). Evaluating projects that are potentially eligible for clean development mechanism (CDM) funding in the South African context: A case study to establish weighting values for sustainable development criteria. *Environment and Development Economics*, *10*(5), 631–649.

Brent, A. C., & Labuschagne, C. (2007). An appraisal of social aspects in project and technology life cycle management in the process industry. *Management of Environmental Quality: An International Journal*, *18*(4), 413–426.

Brent, A. C., & Petrick, W. (2007). Environmental impact assessment (EIA) during project execution phases: Towards a stage-gate project management model for the raw materials processing industry of the energy sector. *Impact Assessment and Project Appraisal, 25*(2), 111–122.

Edum-Fotwe, F. T., & Price, A. D. F. (2009). A social ontology for appraising sustainability of construction projects and developments. *International Journal of Project Management, 27,* 313–322.

Fernández-Sánchez, G., & Rodríguez-López, F. (2010). A methodology to identify sustainability indicators in construction project management—Application to infrastructure projects in Spain. *Ecological Indicators, 10,* 1193–1201.

Gareis, R., Huemann, M., & Martinuzzi, R-A. (2011). What can project management learn from considering sustainability principles?. *Pabeles de Economia Espanola, 33.*

Goedknegt, D. (2012). Sustainability in project management: A case study at University of Applied Sciences Utrecht. *PM World Journal, 1*(4).

Jaafari, A. (2007). Thinking of sustainability as a dimension of managerial competency. *PMWorldToday, 9*(9).

Heuberger, R., Brent, A. C., Santos, L., Sutter, C., & Imboden, D. (2007). CDM projects under the Kyoto protocol: A methodology for sustainability assessment – Experiences from South Africa and Uruguay. *Environment, Development and Sustainability, 9,* 33–48.

Keeys, L.A. (2012). Emerging sustainable development strategy in projects: A theoretical framework. *PM World Journal, 1*(2).

Labuschagne, C., & Brent, A. C. (2005). Sustainable project life cycle management: The need to integrate life cycles in the manufacturing sector. *International Journal of Project Management, 23*(2), 159–168.

Labuschagne, C., & Brent, A. C. (2006). Social indicators for sustainable project and technology life cycle management in the process industry. *International Journal of Life Cycle Assessment, 11*(1), 3–15.

Labuschagne, C., & Brent, A. C. (2007). Sustainability assessment criteria for projects and technologies: Judgements of industry managers. *South African Journal of Industrial Engineering, 18*(1), 19–33.

Labuschagne, C., & Brent, A. C. (2008). An industry perspective of the completeness and relevance of a social assessment framework for project and technology management in the manufacturing sector. *Journal of Cleaner Production, 16,* 253–262.

Labuschagne, C., Brent, A. C., & Claasen, S. J. (2005). Environmental and social impact considerations for sustainable project life cycle management in the process industry. *Corporate Social Responsibility and Environmental Management, 12*(1), 38–54.

Lotz, M., Brent, A. C., & Steyn, H. (2009). Addressing the need for a clean development mechanism (CDM) specific project management strategy. *South African Journal of Economic and Management Sciences, 12*(2), 228–241.

Mulder, J., & Brent, A. C. (2006). Selection of sustainable agriculture projects in South Africa: Case studies in the LandCare programme. *Journal of Sustainable Agriculture, 28*(2), 55–84.

Pade-Knene, C.I., Mallinson, B., & Sewry, D. (2011). Sustainable rural ICT project management practice for developing countries: Investigating the Dwesa and RUMEP projects. *Information Technology for Development - Information Technology Success Factors and Models in Developing and Emerging Economies, 17*(3), 187-212.

Prieto, B. (2011). Sustainability on large, complex engineering & construction programs utilizing a program management approach. *PMWorldToday, 13*(7).

Raven, R. P. J. M., Mourik, R. M., Feenstra, C. F. J., & Heiskanen, E. (2009). Modulating societal acceptance in new energy projects: Towards a toolkit methodology for project managers. *Energy, 34*, 564–574.

Robichaud, L. R., & Anantatmula, V. S. (2011). Greening project management practices for sustainable construction. *Journal of Management Engineering, 27*(48), 48–57.

Scanlon, J., & Davis, A. (2011). The role of sustainability advisers in developing sustainability outcomes for an infrastructure project: Lessons from the Australian urban rail sector. *Impact Assessment and Project Appraisal, 29*(2), 121–133.

Schieg, M. (2009). The model of corporate social responsibility in project management. *Business: Theory & Practice, 10*(4), 315–321.

Shen, L.-Y., Hao, J. L., Wing-Yan Tam, V., & Yao, H. (2007). A checklist for assessing sustainability performance of construction projects. *Journal of Civil Engineering and Management, 13*(4), 273–281.

Silvius, A.J.G., & Nedeski, S. (2011). Sustainability in IS projects: A case study. *Communications of the IIMA, 11*(4).

Syal, M., Li, Q., Abdulrahman, K., & Mago, S. (2011). LEED® requirements and construction project management. *International Journal of Construction Project Management, 3*(3).

Tam, G. (2010). The program management process with sustainability considerations. *Journal of Project, Program & Portfolio Management, 1*(1).

Talbot, J., & Venkataraman, R. (2011). Integration of sustainability principles into project baselines using a comprehensive indicator set. *International Business & Economics Research Journal, 10*(9), 29–40.

Zainul-Abidin, N., & Pasquire, C. L. (2007). Revolutionize value management: A mode towards sustainability. *International Journal of Project Management, 25*(2), 275–282.

Zainul-Abidin, N. (2008). Achieving sustainability through value management: A passing opportunity?. *International Journal of Construction Management*, 79-91.

PROCEEDINGS AND CONFERENCE PAPERS

Alzamil, R. K. (2010). How project managers increase the sustainability of their projects. In Knoepfel (Ed.), Survival and Sustainability as Challenges for Projects. International Project Management Association.

Brent, A. C., & Labuschagne, C. (2004). Sustainable life cycle management: Indicators to assess the sustainability of engineering projects and technologies. In *Proceedings of the Engineering Management Conference*, (Vol. 1, pp. 99-103). EMC.

Carboni, J., & Reeson, M. (2012). The advent of the sustainability management plan: Practical activities that are long overdue. In *Proceedings of the 26th IPMA World Congress*, (pp. 1113 – 1117). IPMA.

Deland, D. (2009). *Sustainability through project management and net impact*. Paper presented at the PMI Global Congress North America. Philadelphia, PA.

Eid, M. (2002). *A sustainable approach to the project management odyssey*. Paper presented at the PMI Research Conference: Frontiers of Project Management Research and Application. Seattle, WA.

Gareis, R., Huemann, M., & Martinuzzi, R.-A. (2009). Relating sustainable development and project management. In *Proceedings of IRNOP IX*. Berlin: IRNOP.

Gareis, R., Huemann, M., & Weninger, C. (2010). *The consideration of sustainability principles in the project assignment process: An analysis of project management approaches*. Paper presented at the 24th IPMA World Congress. Istanbul, Turkey.

Gareis, R., Huemann, M., Martinuzzi, R.-A., Sedlacko, M., & Weninger, C. (2011). *The SustPM matrix: Relating sustainability principles to project assignment and project management*. Paper presented at EURAM11. Talinn, Estonia.

Gareis, R., Huemann, M., Martinuzzi, R.-A., Sedlacko, M., & Weninger, C. (2011). *The SustPM matrix: Relating sustainability principles to managing projects: First reflections on a case study project*. Paper presented at IRNOP XI. Montreal, Canada.

Goedknegt, D., & Silvius, A. J. G. (2012). The implementation of sustainability principles in project management. In *Proceedings of the 26th IPMA World Congress*, (pp. 875 – 882). IPMA.

Griffiths, K. (2007). *Project sustainability management in infrastructure projects*. Paper presented at the 2nd International Conference on Sustainability Engineering and Science. Auckland, New Zealand.

Gunter, G., & Hingst, R. (2009). *Project sustainability management and technology*. Paper presented at the PMoz Conference Incorporating the PMI Australia National Conference. Canberra, Australia.

Hulspas, L., & Maliepaard, F. (2011). *Sustainability in project management: Analyzing two projects within medisch spectrum twente*. Paper presented at the Happy Projects 2011 Conference. Vienna, Austria.

Karayaz, G., & Aydin, M. N. (2012). *Project management offices: Sustainable practices in project management*. Paper presented at the PM Summit 2012. Istanbul, Turkey.

Kirchhof, S., & Brandtweiner, R. (2011). Sustainability in projects: An analysis of relevant sustainability aspects in the project management process based on the three pillars model. In Brebbia & Beriatos (Eds.), *Sustainable Development And Planning V: Proceedings of the 5th Conference on Sustainable Regional Development*. Southampton, UK: WIT Press.

Kluiwstra, M., & Grevelman, L. (2010). *Sustainability in project management: A case study on Enexis*. Paper presented at the Happy Projects Conference 20'10. Vienna, Austria.

Knoepfel, H. (Ed.). (2010a). *Survival and sustainability as challenges for projects*. Paper presented at the International Project Management Association Conference. Zurich, Switzerland.

Knoepfel, H. (2010b). Sustainability and competence elements. In Knoepfel (Ed.), Survival and Sustainability as Challenges for Projects. Zurich, Switzerland: International Project Management Association.

Langdon, M., & Tsallas, S. (2010). *From single to triple bottom line and vice versa*. Paper presented at the 24th IPMA World Congress. Istanbul, Turkey.

Munksgaard, K. F., & Tinning, A. V. (2010). *Sustainability in virtual project management: A case study in social platforms*. Paper presented at Happy Projects Conference 20'10. Vienna, Austria.

Mishra, P., Dangayach, G. S., & Mittal, M. L. (2011). *An ethical approach towards sustainable project success*. Paper presented at the International Conference on Asia Pacific Business Innovation & Technology Management. New York, NY.

Ning, C., Zhang, S., & Li, L. (2009). *Sustainable project management: A balance analysis model of effect*. Paper presented at the International Conference on Management and Service Science. Wuhan, China.

Pade, C. I., Mallinson, B., & Sewry, D. (2006). An exploration of the categories associated with ICT project sustainability in rural areas of developing countries: A case study of the Dwesa project. In *Proceedings of the 2006 Annual Research Conference of the South African Institute of Computer Scientists and Information Technologists on IT Research in Developing Countries (SAICSIT)*, (pp. 100 – 106). SAICSIT.

Pade, C. I., Mallinson, B., & Sewry, D. (2008). Project management practice for rural ICT project sustainability in developing countries. In *Proceedings of the 2nd European Conference on Information Management and Evaluation (ECIME)*, (pp. 351-362). ECIME.

Pantouvakis, J.-P., & Panas, A. (2010). The contribution of health & safety management to sustainable development: A case study from the construction industry. In Knoepfel (Ed.), Survival and Sustainability as Challenges for Projects. Zurich, Switzerland: International Project Management Association.

Reeson, M. (2012). Measuring the convergence of sustainability and project management - Where the 'triple bottom line' falls short. In *Proceedings of the 26th IPMA World Congress*, (pp. 1107 – 1112). IPMA.

Russell Tharp, J. (2008). *Corporate social responsibility: What it means for the project manager*. Paper presented at the PMI EMEA Global Congress. Malta.

Sedlacko, M. (2010). *Sustainable development & corporate sustainability - A new paradigm or just another management fashion?* Paper presented at the PMI Research & Education Conference. Washington, DC.

Segers, D., & Van Hoeke, A. (2011). *The influence of a public private partnership on the maturity of sustainability during a building project*. Paper presented at the Happy Projects 2011 Conference. Vienna, Austria.

Sepehri, M. (2010). *The role of the project owner in project sustainability*. Paper presented at the 24th IPMA World Congress. Istanbul, Turkey.

Silvius, A. J. G. (2012). *Sustainability in project management: Vision, mission, ambition*. Paper presented at the PM Summit 2012. Istanbul, Turkey.

Silvius, A. J. G., van den Brink, J., & Köhler, A. (2010). The concept of sustainability and its application to project management. In Knoepfel (Ed.), Survival and Sustainability as Challenges for Projects. Zurich, Switzerland: International Project Management Association.

Silvius, A. J. G., & van den Brink, J. (2011). Taking responsibility: The integration of sustainability and project management. In Kettunen, Hyrkkänen, & Lehto (Eds.), *Applied Research and Professional Education: Proceedings from the First CARPE Networking Conference*. Utrecht, The Netherlands: CARPE.

Silvius, A. J. G., & Nedeski, S. (2011). *Sustainability in IS projects: A case study*. Paper presented at the 22nd Conference of the International Information Management Association. New Orleans, LA.

Silvius, A. J. G., & Schipper, R. (2010). A maturity model for integrating sustainability in projects and project management. Paper presented at the 24th IPMA World Congress. Istanbul, Turkey.

Silvius, A. J. G., & Schipper, R. (2012). Sustainability in the business case. In *Proceedings of the 26th IPMA World Congress*, (pp. 1062 – 1069). IPMA.

Silvius, A. J. G., Schipper, R., & Nedeski, S. (2012). Sustainability in project management: Reality bites. In *Proceedings of the 26th IPMA World Congress*, (pp. 1053 – 1061). IPMA.

Tanrikulu, Z., & Özturan, M. (2012). *Critical factors for sustainability in ICT projects*. Paper presented at the PM Summit 2012. Istanbul, Turkey.

Turner, J. R. (2010). Responsibilities for sustainable development in project and program management. In Knoepfel (Ed.), Survival and Sustainability as Challenges for Projects. Zurich, Switzerland: International Project Management Association.

Wang, W., Ding, R., Radosavljevic, M., & Sun, H. (2011). Practicing sustainability in PFI project management. In *Proceedings of the IEEE International Technology Management Conference (ITMC)*, (pp. 717 – 722). San Jose, CA: IEEE Press.

Xu, D., & Hua, X. (2011). The applications of sustainability in project management. In *Proceedings of the 2nd IEEE International Conference on Emergency Management and Management Sciences (ICEMMS)*, (pp. 693 – 697). Beijing, China.

OTHER ARTICLES

Balestrero, G. (2009, October). The shifting sands of the project management landscape. *Project Manager Today*.

Fister-Gale, S. (2007). The right shade of green. *PM Network, 21*(9), 30–39.

Fister-Gale, S. (2009). The real deal. *PM Network, 23*(12), 30–35.

Fister-Gale, S. (2012). From green to black. *PM Network, 26*(7), 28–35.

Fox, S. (2013). Sustainable beauty – Achieving sustainability goals by fulfilling materialistic aspirations. *Project Perspectives, 35*.

Gareis, R., Huemann, M., & Martinuzzi, R-A. (2011). What can project management learn from considering sustainability principles?. *Project Perspectives, 33.*

Howard, M. (2008, November). Climate change & the project manager. *Project Manager Today,* 6.

Taylor, T. (2008, November). Sustainable projects. *Project Manager Today,* 4.

Anonymous. (2008, November). Sustainability, carbon footprints and business. *Project Manager Today,* 10.

WHITE PAPERS AND ESSAYS

Association for Project Management. (2006). *APM supports sustainability outlooks.* New York: APM.

Project Management Institute. (2011). *The bottom line on sustainability.* Philadelphia, PA: Project Management Institute.

Taylor, T. (2008). *A sustainability checklist for managers of projects.* Retrieved from www.pmforum.org

Compilation of References

Aaltonen, K. (2011). Project stakeholder analysis as an environmental interpretation process. *International Journal of Project Management*, 165–183. doi:10.1016/j.ijproman.2010.02.001.

Abernethy, M. A., Horne, M., Lillis, A. M., Malina, M. A., & Selto, F. H. (2005). A multi-method approach to building causal performance maps from expert knowledge. *Management Accounting Research*, 16(2), 135–155. doi:10.1016/j.mar.2005.03.003.

Achman, R. (2011). *Stakeholders' perspectives on sustainability in project management: Case studies of 4 different projects in The Netherlands*. (Unpublished master's thesis). Delft University of Technology, Delft, The Netherlands.

Adams, D. (2005). *The hitchhiker's guide to the galaxy*. Toronto: Ballantine Books.

Adams, S., & Simnett, R. (2011). Integrated reporting: An opportunity for Australia's not-for-profit sector. *Australian Accounting Review*, 21(3), 292–301. doi:10.1111/j.1835-2561.2011.00143.x.

Adams, W. M. (2006). *The future of sustainability: Rethinking environment and development in the twenty-first century. The World Conservation Union*. IUCN.

Adebanjo, D. (2001). TQM and business excellence: Is there really a conflict? *Measuring Business Excellence*, 5(3), 37–40. doi:10.1108/13683040110403961.

Adebanjo, D., & Mann, R. (2008). Business excellence, part 1. *Progressing Business*, 1(3), 16–20.

AICPA/UNC Kenan-Flagler. (2008). *AICPA business and industry economic outlook survey 3Q 2008*. Retrieved from http://fmcenter.aicpa.org/NR/rdonlyres/2CAEEC67-79F4-4472-93B4-5AEB0502A1E1/0/3QEconomicOutlookSurveyChartsFinal.pdf

Aitken, A., & Crawford. (2007). Coping with stress: Dispositional coping strategies of project managers. *International Journal of Project Management*, 666–673. doi:10.1016/j.ijproman.2007.02.003.

Aknin, L. B., Dunn, E. W., & Norton, M. I. (2011). Happiness runs in a circular motion: Evidence for a positive feedback loop between prosocial spending and happiness. *Journal of Happiness*, (13), 347-355.

Alkhathlan, K. A. (2011). Foreign direct investment and export growth in Saudi Arabia: A cointegration analysis. *China-USA Business Review*, 10(2), 137–149.

Allen, R. (1980). *How to save the world: Strategy for world conservation*. London: Kogan Page.

Alzamil, R. K. (2010). How project managers increase the sustainability of their projects. In *Proceeding s of IPMA Expert Seminar February 2010*. Zurich, Switzerland: IPMA.

American Institute of Certified Public Accountants. (AICPA). (2007). *FAQs on sustainability reporting*. Retrieved from http://www.aicpa.org/innovation/baas/environ/faq.htm

Amit, K., Popper, M., Gal, R., Miskal-Sinai, M., & Lissak, A. (2006). The potential to lead: The difference between 'leaders' and 'non-leaders'. *Military Psychology*, 16(4), 245–263.

Andersen, E. (2008). *Rethinking project management–An organisational perspective*. FT Press.

APM. (2006). *The APM body of knowledge* (5th ed.). The Association for Project Management.

Arakawa, D., & Greenberg. (2007). Optimistic managers and their influence on productivity and employee engagement in a technology organisation: Implications for coaching psychologists. *International Coaching Psychology Review*, (2): 78–89.

Aras, G., & Crowther, D. (2009). Corporate sustainability reporting: A study in disingenuity? *Journal of Business Ethics*, *84*(1), 279–288. doi:10.1007/s10551-008-9806-0.

Archer, N., & Ghasemzadeh, E. (2004). Project portfolio selection and management. In Morris, P., & Pinto, J. (Eds.), *The Wiley guide to managing projects*. New York, NY: John Wiley & Sons, Inc..

Argyris, C., & Schon, D. (1978). *Organizational learning: A theory of action perspective*. Reading, MA: Addison-Wesley Publication.

Artto, K., Dietrich, P., & Martinsuo, M. (2008). What is project strategy? *International Journal of Project Management*, *26*, 4–12. doi:10.1016/j.ijproman.2007.07.006.

Ashkanasy, N. M., & Ashton-James, C. E. (2007). Positive emotions in organizations: A multi-level framework. In Nelson & Cooper (Ed.), Positive Organizational Behavior. London: Sage.

Asquin, A., Garel, G., & Picq, T. (2010). When project-based management causes distress at work. *International Journal of Project Management*, 166–172. doi:10.1016/j.ijproman.2009.08.006.

Assiri, A., Zairi, M., & Eid, R. (2006). How to profit from the balanced scorecard: An implementation roadmap. *Industrial Management & Data Systems*, *106*(7), 937–952. doi:10.1108/02635570610688869.

Association for Project Management. (2006). *APM supports sustainability outlooks*.

Association for Project Management. (2012). *Sustainability in project management*. Association for Project Management.

Association of Professional Engineering and Geoscience. B.C. (2004). Part 3e: Practice specific module - Consulting engineering and geosciences. In Sustainability in Professional Engineering and Geoscience: A Primer. Academic Press.

AusIndustry, Green Building Fund. (2011). Retrieved April 26, 2012 from http://www.ausindustry.gov.au/programs/innovation-rd/gbf/Documents/GBF-FundingOffers-Round7.pdf

Australia, C. P. A. (2005). *Sustainability reporting: Practices, performance and potential*. Melbourne, Australia: CPA Australia.

Avey, J. B., Wernsing, T. A., & Luthans, F. (2008). Can positive employees help positive organizational change? Impact of psychological capital and emotions on relevant attitudes and behaviors. *The Journal of Applied Behavioral Science*, (44): 48–70. doi:10.1177/0021886307311470.

Avram, D., & Kuhne, S. (2008). Implementing responsible business behaviour from a strategic management perspective: developing a framework for Austrian SMEs. *Journal of Business Ethics*, *82*, 463–475. doi:10.1007/s10551-008-9897-7.

Azcárate, F., Carrasco, F., & Fernández, M. (2011). The role of integrated indicators in exhibiting business contribution to sustainable development: A survey of sustainability reporting initiatives. *Spanish Accounting Review*, *14*, 213–240.

Baccarini, D. (1999). *History of project management*. Curtin University of Technology.

Badiru, A. B. (2010). The many languages of sustainability. *Industrial Engineer*, *42*(11), 30–34.

Bagheri, A., & Hjorth, P. (2007). Planning for sustainable development: a paradigm shift towards a process-based approach. *Sustainable Development*, *15*, 83–96. doi:10.1002/sd.310.

Bakshi, B. R., & Fiksel, J. (2003). The quest for sustainability: Challenges for process systems engineering. *AIChE Journal. American Institute of Chemical Engineers*, *49*(6), 1350–1358. doi:10.1002/aic.690490602.

Baldrige Performance Excellence Program. (n.d.a). *2000 criteria for performance excellence*. Gaithersburg, MD: National Institute of Standards and Technology, United States Department of Commerce.

Baldrige Performance Excellence Program. (n.d.b). *2011-2012 criteria for performance excellence*. Gaithersburg, MD: National Institute of Standards and Technology, United States Department of Commerce.

Balestrero, G., & Gedansky, L. (2008). *Contributing to a sustainable world: White Paper for setting PMI strategy on global sustainability and determining organizational social responsibility.* Draft document, unpublished.

Banerjee, A., Dolado, J. J., Hendry, D. F., & Smith, G. W. (1986, August). Exploring equilibrium relationships in econometrics through static models: Some Monte Carlo evidence. *Oxford Bulletin of Economics and Statistics,* 253–277.

Banerjee, S. B., & Bonnefous, A.-M. (2011). Stakeholder management and sustainability strategies in the French nuclear industry. *Business Strategy and the Environment, 2,* 124–140. doi:10.1002/bse.681.

Bannik, F. (2012). *Practicing positive CBT, from reducing stress to building success.* West Sussex, UK: Wiley-Blackwell. doi:10.1002/9781118328941.

Baratta, A. (2006). *The triple constraint, a triple illusion.* Paper presented at the PMI North America Global Congress. Seattle, WA.

Barker, J. A. (1989). *Discovering the future: The business of paradigms* (3rd ed.). St. Paul, MN: ILI Press.

Barnard, L. T., Ackles, B., & Haner, J. L. (2011). *Making sense of sustainability project management.* Explorus Group Inc..

Barthwal, R. R. (2002). *Environmental impact assessment.* New Delhi: New Age International.

Barton, D. (2011). Capitalism for the long term. *Harvard Business Review.* Retrieved on July 4, 2011 from http://hbr.org/2011/03/capitalism-for-the-long-term/ar/1

Bates, W. (2009). Gross national happiness. *Asian-Pacific Economic Literature, 23,* 1–16. doi:10.1111/j.1467-8411.2009.01235.x.

Baumgartner, R. J., & Ebner, D. (2010). Corporate sustainability strategies: Sustainability profiles and maturity levels. *Sustainable Development, 18*(2), 76–89. doi:10.1002/sd.447.

Bell, J., Masaoka, J., & Zimmerman, S. (2010). *Nonprofit sustainability: Making strategic decisions for financial viability.* San Francisco: Jossey-Bass.

Bell, S., & Morse, S. (2008). *Sustainability indicators: Measuring the immeasurable?* (2nd ed.). London: Earthscan.

Benoît, C., & Niederman, G. V. (2010). *Social sustainability assessment literature review.* Measurement Science.

Berg, A. E., Harting, T., & Staats, H. (2007). Preference for nature in urbanized societies: Stress, restoration, and the pursuit of sustainability. *The Journal of Social Issues, 63*(1), 79–96. doi:10.1111/j.1540-4560.2007.00497.x.

Berger, P., & Luckman, T. (1967). *The social construction of reality.* Hoboken, NJ: Anchor Publications.

Berg, I. K., & Szabo, P. (2005). *Brief coaching for lasting solutions.* New York, MY: WW Norton and Co..

Bergmans, F. (2006). Integrating People, Planet and Profit. In Jonker, J. (Ed.), *M. C. de Witte, Management models for corporate social responsibility.* Berlin, Heidelberg: Springer. doi:10.1007/3-540-33247-2_14.

Bernhart, M. S., & Maher, F. J. (2011). *ISO 26000 in practice: A user guide.* Milwaukee, WI: ASQ Quality Press.

Berns, M., Bussey, K., Murray, S., & Vismans, D. (2011, Winter). Sustainability: The 'embracers' seize advantage. *MIT Sloan Management Review.*

Berns, M., Townend, A., Khayat, Z., Balagopal, B., Reeves, M, Hopkins, M.S., & Kruschwitz, N. (2009, Fall). The business of sustainability: What it means to managers now. *MIT Sloan Management Review.*

Biedenbach, T., & Söderholm, A. (2008). The challenge of organizing change in hypercompetitive industries: A literature review. *Journal of Change Management, 8*(2), 123–145. doi:10.1080/14697010801953967.

Birkin, F., Polesi, T., & Lewis, L. (2009). A new business model for sustainable development: an exploratory study using the theory of constraints in Nordic organizations. *Business Strategy and the Environment, 18,* 277–290. doi:10.1002/bse.581.

Bititci, U. S. (1994). Measuring your way to profit. *Management Decision, 32*(6), 16–24. doi:10.1108/00251749410065088.

Bititci, U. S., Mendibil, K., Nudurupati, S., Garengo, P., & Turner, T. (2006). Dynamics of performance measurement and organisational culture. *International Journal of Operations & Production Management*, *26*(12), 1325–1350. doi:10.1108/01443570610710579.

Blake, R., Shepard, H., & Mouton, J. (1964). *Managing intergroup conflict in Industry*. Houston: Gulf Publishing Company.

Blignaut, J. N. (1995). *Environmental accounting in South Africa*. (Doctoral thesis) University of Pretoria, Pretoria, South Africa.

Bonini, S., Mendonca, L., & Oppenheim, J. (2006). When social issues become strategic. *McKinsey Quarterly*. Retrieved on July 4, 2011 from https://www.mckinseyquarterly.com/When_social_issues_become_strategic_1763

Bono, J. E., & Ilies, R. (2006). Charisma, positive emotions and mood contagion. *The Leadership Quarterly*, (17): 317–334. doi:10.1016/j.leaqua.2006.04.008.

Bots, P., Twist, M. v., & Duin, J. v. (2000). Automatic Pattern Detection in Stakeholder Networks. *The 33rd Hawaii International Conference on System Sciences* (pp. 1-10). Hawaii: IEEE.

Bourne, L. (2007). *Avoiding the successful failure*. Paper presented at the PMI Asia-Pacific Global Congress. Hong Kong.

Boutilier, R. G., & Svendsen, A. C. (2000). *From conflict to collaboration: Stakeholder bridging and bonding in clayoquot sound*. Burnaby, Canada: Simon Fraser University at Harbour Centre.

BRE Global Limited. (2012). *The world's leading design and assessment method for sustainable buildings*. Building Research Establishment Ltd (trading as BRE).

Bredillet, C. N. (2000). *Proposition of a systemic and dynamic model to design life-long learning structure: The quest of the missing link between men, team, and organizational learning*. Paper presented at the PMI Research Conference 2000: Project Management Research at the Turn of the Millennium. Paris, France.

Bredin, K. (2008). People capability of project-based organisations: A conceptual framework. *International Journal of Project Management*, *26*(5), 566–576. doi:10.1016/j.ijproman.2008.05.002.

Brent, A. C., & Pretorius, M. W. (2008). Sustainable development and technology management. In M.H. Sherif, & Khalil (Eds.), Management of technology innovation and value creation, (vol. 2, pp. 185-204). Hoboken, NJ: World Scientific.

Brent, A. C., & Labuschagne, C. (2007). An appraisal of social aspects in project and technology life cycle management in the process industry. *Management of Environmental Quality: An International Journal*, *18*(4), 413–426. doi:10.1108/14777830710753811.

Brent, A. C., van Erck, R. P. G., & Labuschagne, C. (2006). Sustainability cost accounting: Part 1 – A monetary procedure to evaluate the sustainability of technologies in the South African process industry. *South African Journal of Industrial Engineering*, *17*(2), 35–51.

Brent, A. C., van Erck, R. P. G., & Labuschagne, C. (2007). Sustainability cost accounting: Part 2 – A case study in the South African process industry. *South African Journal of Industrial Engineering*, *18*(1), 1–17.

Brent, A., & Labuschagne, C. (2006). Social indicators for sustainable project and technology life cycle management in the process industry. *The International Journal of Life Cycle Assessment*, *11*(1), 3–15. doi:10.1065/lca2006.01.233.

Brent, R. (2006). *Applied cost-benefit analysis*. Cheltenham, UK: Edward Elgar Publishing Limited.

Brock, W. A., & Durlauf, S. N. (2001). Growth empirics and reality. *The World Bank Economic Review*, *15*(2), 229–272. doi:10.1093/wber/15.2.229.

Brown Gooding, S. (n.d.). One company's shift to integrated reporting. *Communication World*. Retrieved from www.iabc.com/cw

Brown, K., & Kasser, T. (2005). Are psychological and ecological wellbeing compatible? The role of values, mindfulness and lifestyle. *Social Indicators Research*, *74*, 349–368. doi:10.1007/s11205-004-8207-8.

Bruijn, H., & Heuvelhof, E. (2008). *Management in Networks on multi-actor decision making*. New York: Routledge.

Brundtland, G. Harlem, et al. (1987). Our common future: World commission on environment and development. Oxford, UK: Oxford University Press.

Brundtland, G. (1987). *Our common future: The World Comission on Environment and Development.* Oxford: Oxford University Press.

Bryde, D. J. (2003). Modelling project management performance. *International Journal of Quality & Reliability Management, 20*(2), 228–253. doi:10.1108/02656710310456635.

Bryde, D. J. (2003). Project management concepts, methods, and application. *International Journal of Operations & Production Management, 23*(7), 775–793. doi:10.1108/01443570310481559.

Business Wire. (2008). *Four out of five college students and recent grads prefer jobs at green companies.* Retrieved from http://findarticles.com/p/articles/mi_m0EIN/is_2008_August_4/ai_n27968336

By, R. T. (2005). Organisational change management: A critical review. *Journal of Change Management, 5*(4), 369–380. doi:10.1080/14697010500359250.

Cameron, K.S., & Spreitzer. (Ed.). (2012). *Oxford handbook of positive organizational scholarship.* Oxford, UK: Oxford University Press.

Cameron, K. (2008). *Positive leadership, strategies for extraordinary performance.* San Francisco, CA: Berrett-Koehler Publishers.

Cameron, K. J., Dutton, J. E., & Quin, R. E. (Eds.). (2003). *Positive organizational scholarship: Foundations of a new discipline.* San Francisco, CA: Berrett-Koehler Publishers.

Canadian Green Building Council - LEED. (2009). Retrieved from http://www.cagbc.org/AM/Template.cfm?Section=LEED

Cano, J. L., & Lidon, I. (2011). Guided reflection on project definition. *International Journal of Project Management, 29*(5), 525–536. doi:10.1016/j.ijproman.2010.04.008.

Capek, B., & Westermayer, K. (2010). Sustainable Development Projects, Development of categorization. *PM World Today,* 1-15.

Carbon Disclosure Project (CDP). (2013). *CDP 2012 performance scores.* Retrieved from https://www.cdproject.net/en-US/Results/Pages/CDP-2012-performance-scores.aspx

Carnegie Mellon Software Engineering Institute. (2002). *Capability maturity models.* Retrieved from http://www.sei.cmu.edu/cmmi/

Caron, F., Marchet, G., & Perego, A. (1998). Project logistics: Integrating the procurement and construction processes. *International Journal of Project Management, 16*(5), 311–319. doi:10.1016/S0263-7863(97)00029-X.

Carson, R. (1962). *Silent spring.* Boston: Houghton Mifflin.

Castka, P., Bamber, C. F., Bamber, D. F., & Sharp, J. M. (2004). Integrating corporate social responsibility (CSR) into ISO management systems – In search of a feasible CSR management system framework. *The TQM Magazine, 16*(3), 216–224. doi:10.1108/09544780410532954.

Chambers, R. (1997). *Who's reality counts?* London: Intermediate Technology Publications.

Checkland, P., & Winter, M. (2005). Process and content: Two ways of using SSM. *The Journal of the Operational Research Society,* 1–7.

CIB. (1999). *Agenda 21 on sustainable construction.* CIB Report Publication 237.

Clark, C., Rosenzweig, W., Long, D., & Olsen, S. (2004). *Double bottom line project report: Addressing social impact in double bottom line methods.* New York: Rockerfeller Foundation.

Clayton, A. M. H., & Radcliffe, N. J. (1996). *Sustainability: A systems approach.* London: Earthscan Publications Limited.

Cleland, D. (1986). Project stakeholder management. *Project Management Journal,* 36-44.

Cleland, D. I. (1985). A strategy for ongoing project evaluation. *Project Management Journal, 16*(3), 11–17.

Cleland, D. I. (1998). Stakeholder management. In *Project Management Handbook.* San Francisco, CA: Jossey Bass.

Clifton, D., & Amran, A. (2011). The stakeholder approach: a sustainability perspective. *Journal of Business Ethics, 98,* 121–136. doi:10.1007/s10551-010-0538-6.

Cmaecocycle. (n.d.). *Mercury and the environment.* Retrieved April 26, 2012 from http://www.cmaecocycle.net/mercury.html

Cooke-Davies, T. (2002). The real success factors in projects. *International Journal of Project Management, 20*(3), 185–190. doi:10.1016/S0263-7863(01)00067-9.

Corral-Verdugo, V., Mireles-Acosta, J., Tapia-Fonllem, C., & Fraijo-Sing, B. (2011). Happiness as correlate of sustainable behavior: A study of pro-ecological, frugal, equitable and altruistic actions that promote subjective wellbeing. *Human Ecology Review*, (18): 95–104.

Crawford, L. (2007). Global body of project management knowledge and standards. In Morris & Pinto (Eds.), The Wiley Guide to Managing Projects. New York: Wiley.

Crawford, L. H., & Helm, J. (2009). Government and governance: The value of project management in the public sector. *Project Management Journal, 40*(1), 73–87. doi:10.1002/pmj.20107.

Csikszentmihaiyi, M. (1990). *Flow: The psychology of optimal experience*. New York, NY: Quality Paperback.

Cummings, T. (1980). *Systems theory of organizational development*. New York: Wiley Publications Ltd..

Cuppen, E., Breukers, S., Hisschemoller, M., & Bergsma, E. (2010). Q methodology to select participants for a stakeholder dialogue on energy options from biomass in the Netherlands. *Ecological Economics, 69*(3), 579–591. doi:10.1016/j.ecolecon.2009.09.005.

D'Amato, A., Henderson, S., & Florence, S. (2009). *Corporate social responsibility and sustainable business- A guide to leadership tasks and functions*. Greensboro, NC: CCL Press.

Dam, L. (2008). *Corporate social responsibility and financial markets*. (Unpublished doctoral dissertation). University of Rijks. Groningen, The Netherlands.

Danner, D. D., Snowdon, D. A., & Friesen, W. V. (2001). Positive emotions in early live and longevity: Findings from the nun study. *Journal of Personality and Social Psychology*, (80): 804–813. doi:10.1037/0022-3514.80.5.804 PMID:11374751.

DAP. D. (2011, July). *Home*. Retrieved July 26, 2011, from Delft Aardwamte Project: http://www.delftaardwarmteproject.nl/home/

Davenport, T. (1993). *Process innovation: Reengineering work through information technology*. Boston, MA: Harvard Publications.

David, D. K. (1949). Business responsibilities in an uncertain world. *Harvard Business Review, 27*(1), 1–8.

David, D., Szentagotia, A., & Macavei, B. (2005). A synopsis of rational-emotive behavior therapy (REBT), fundamental and applied research. *Journal of Rational-Emotive & Cognitive-Behavior Therapy, 23*(3), 175–221. doi:10.1007/s10942-005-0011-0.

Davidson, J. (2000). Sustainable development: Business as usual or a new way of living? *Environmental Ethics, 22*(1), 45–71.

Davis, K. (1973). The case for and against business assumption of social responsibility. *Academy of Management Journal, 16*, 312–322. doi:10.2307/255331.

De Piante Henriksen, A. (1997). A technology assessment primer for management of technology. *International Journal of Technology Management, 13*, 615–638. doi:10.1504/IJTM.1997.001681.

de Zoete, L. (2010, April). PMBOK of prince 2. *Automatisering Gids*.

Deland, D. (2009). *Sustainability through project management and net impact*. Paper presented at the PMI 2009 North America Global Congress. Orlando, FL.

Deloitte. (2011). *Integrated reporting: A better view?*. Deloitte.

Delone, W. H., & McLean, E. R. (2003). Model of information systems success: A ten-year update. *Journal of Management Information Systems, 19*(4), 9–30.

Dempsey, N., Bramley, G., Powe, S., & Brown, C. (2011). The social dimension of sustainable development: Defining urban social sustainability. *Sustainable Development, 19*(5), 289–300. doi:10.1002/sd.417.

Denis, J.-L., Langley, A., & Rouleau, L. (2007). Strategizing in pluralistic contexts: Rethinking theoretical frames. *Human Relations, 60*(1), 179–215. doi:10.1177/0018726707075288.

Diesendorf, M. (2000). Sustainability and sustainable development. In Dunphy, D., Benveniste, J., Griffiths, A., & Sutton, P. (Eds.), *Sustainability: The corporate challenge of the 21st century* (pp. 19–37). Sydney, Australia: Allen & Unwin.

Dietrich, P., & Lehtonen, P. (2005). Successful management of strategic intentions through multiple projects - Reflections from empirical study. *International Journal of Project Management, 23*(5), 386–391. doi:10.1016/j.ijproman.2005.03.002.

Dinsmore, P. C. (1998). How grown-up is your organization? *PM Network, 12*(6), 24–26.

Dovers, S. R. (1995). A framework for scaling and framing policy problems in sustainability. *Ecological Economics, 12*(2), 93–106. doi:10.1016/0921-8009(94)00042-T.

Dovido, J. F., Gaertner, S. L., Isen, A. M., & Lowrance, R. (1995). Group representations and intergroup bias: Positive effect, similarity, and group size. *Personality and Social Psychology Bulletin,* (21): 856–865. doi:10.1177/0146167295218009.

Drews, G., & Hillebrand, N. (2007). *Lexikon der projektmanagement-methoden.* Haufe Verlag.

Dunphy, D., Griffiths, A., & Benn, S. (2007). *Organizational change for corporate sustainability.* Abingdon, UK: Routledge.

Dyllick, T., & Hockerts, K. (2002). Beyond the business case for corporate sustainability. *Business Strategy and the Environment, 11*(2), 130–141. doi:10.1002/bse.323.

Ebner, D., & Baumgartner, R. J. (2006). *The relationship between sustainable development and corporate social responsibility.* Paper presented at the Corporate Responsibility Research Conference 2006. Dublin, Ireland. Retrieved from http://www.crrconference.org.

Ebner, D., & Baumgartner, R. (2010). Corporate sustainability strategies: Sustainability profiles and maturity levels. *Sustainable Development, 18,* 76–89. doi:10.1002/sd.447.

Eccles, R.G., Krzus, M.P., & Tapscott, D. (2010). *One report: Integrated reporting for sustainable strategy.*

Edum-Fotwoe, E., & Price, A. (2008). A social ontology for appraising sustainability of construction projects and developments. *International Journal of Project Management, 27*(4), 313–322. doi:10.1016/j.ijproman.2008.04.003.

Edwards, A. R. (2005). *The sustainability revolution: Portrait of a paradigm shift.* Gabriola Island, Canada: New Society Publishers.

EFQM. (2009). *EFQM excellence model: EFQM model 2010.* Brussels: EFQM.

Eid, M. (2000). A review of project management & sustainable development for construction projects. *EAR Journal, 27.*

Eid, M. (2002). *A sustainable approach to the project management odyssey.* Paper presented at the PMI Research Conference 2002: Frontiers of Project Management Research and Application. New York, NY.

Eid, M. (2009). *Sustainable development & project management.* Cologne, Germany: Lambert Academic Publishing.

Elkington, J. (2006). The triple bottom line. In M.J. Epstein & K.O. Hanson (Eds.), The Accountable Organization: Vol. 3: Corporate Social Responsibility (pp. 97-109). Westport, CT: Praeger Publishers.

Elkington, J., & Fennell, S. (1998). Partners for sustainability. *Greener Management International,* (24), 48-60.

Elkington, J. (1994). Towards the sustainable corporation: Win-win-win business strategies for sustainable development. *California Management Review, 36*(2), 90–100. Retrieved from http://search.ebscohost.com/login.aspx?direct=true&db=buh&AN=9410213932&site=ehost-live doi:10.2307/41165746.

Elkington, J. (1997). *Cannibals with forks: The triple bottom line of 21st century business.* Oxford, UK: Capstone Publishing.

Elkington, J. (1999). Triple bottom line revolution: Reporting for the third millennium. *Australian CPA, 95,* 75.

Elkington, J. (2004). Enter the triple bottom line. In Henriques, A., & Richardson, J. (Eds.), *The triple bottom line, does it all add up? Assessing the sustainability of business and CSR* (pp. 1–16). London: Earthscan Publication Ltd..

El-Sabaa, S. (2001). The skills and career path of an effective project manager. *International Journal of Project Management, 19*(1), 1–7. doi:10.1016/S0263-7863(99)00034-4.

Engle, R. F., & Granger, C. W. J. (1987). Co-integration and error correction: Representation, estimation, and testing. *Econometrica, 55*(2), 251–276. doi:10.2307/1913236.

Englund, R., & Graham, R. (1999). From experience: Linking projects to strategy. *Journal of Product Innovation Management, 16*, 52–64. doi:10.1016/S0737-6782(98)00046-0.

Engwall, M. (2003). No project is an island. *Research Policy, 32*, 789–808. doi:10.1016/S0048-7333(02)00088-4.

Environment Protection and Heritage Council. (n.d.). *18th meeting of EPHC communiqué – Breakthrough on waste.* Retrieved April 26, 2012 from http://www.ephc.gov.au/sites/default/files/EPHC_Cmq__Communique_2009_05_22.pdf

Environmental Leader. (2010). *Executives link sustainability with business strategy.* Retrieved from http://www.environmentalleader.com/2010/07/30/executives-link-sustainability-with-business-strategy/

Epstein, M. (2008). *Making sustainability work.* Sheffield, UK: Greenleaf Publishing.

Epstein, M. J. (2008). *Making sustainability work: Best practices in managing and measuring corporate social, environmental, and economic impacts.* San Francisco, CA: Berrett-Koehler Publishers, Inc..

Ernst & Young. (2011). *Climate change and sustainability: Shareholders press boards on social and environmental risks: Is your company prepared?* Ernst & Young LLP.

Eskerod, P., & Huemann, M. (2011). *Project management stakeholder practices—In the light of modern stakeholder theory and sustainability principles.* Paper presented at Nordic Academy of Management Meeting. Stockholm, Sweden.

Eskerod, P., & Huemann, M. (2013). Sustainable development and project stakeholder management: What standards say. *International Journal of Managing Projects in Business.*

Esty, D. C., & Winston, A. S. (2006). *Green to gold.* New Haven, CT: Yale University Press.

European Construction Industry Federation (FIEC). (n.d.). Retrieved June 2002, from http://www.fiec.org/main.html

European Council. (2006). *Review of the EU sustainable development strategy (EU SDS – renewed strategy).* European Council.

Evans, J. R., & Dean, J. W. Jr. (2000). *Total quality: Management, organization, and strategy* (2nd ed.). Cincinnati, OH: South-Western College Publishing.

Evans, R., Brereton, D., & Joy, J. (2007). Risk assessment as a tool to explore sustainable development issues: Lessons from the Australian coal industry. *International Journal of Risk Assessment and Management, 7*(5), 607–619. doi:10.1504/IJRAM.2007.014089.

EViews. (2010). *EViews 7.* Irvine, CA: Quantitative Micro Software, LLC.

Eweje, G. (2011). A shift in corporate practice? Facilitating sustainability strategy in companies. *Corporate Social Responsibility and Environmental Management, 18*, 125–136. doi:10.1002/csr.268.

Facilities Management Association of Australia. (n.d.). *What is facilities management?* Retrieved April 26, 2012 from http://www.fma.com.au/cms/index.php?option=com_content&task=view&id=45&Itemid=59

Facilities Reporting Project. (2004). Retrieved from https://www.ceres.org/resources/reports/facility-reporting-project-sustainability-reporting-guidance/view

Fanon, F. (1963). *The wretched of the earth.* Middlesex, UK: Penguin.

Fanon, F. (1970). *Toward the African revolution.* London: Penguin Books.

Fibuch, E., & Van Way, C. W. III. (2012). Sustainability: A fiduciary responsibility of senior leaders? *Physician Executive, 38*(2), 36–42.

Fluorocycle. (2010). *Launch of national scheme to reduce mercury-containing waste.* Retrieved April 26, 2012 from http://www.fluorocycle.org.au/news-detail.php?news_id=25

Fombrun, C. J., Gardberg, N. A., & Barnett, M. L. (2000). Opportunity platforms and safety nets: Corporate citizenship and reputational risk. *Business and Society Review, 105*(1), 85–106. doi:10.1111/0045-3609.00066.

Fonseca, A., Macdonald, A., Dandy, E., & Valenti, P. (2011). The state of sustainability reporting at Canadian universities. *International Journal of Sustainability in Higher Education, 12*(1). doi:10.1108/14676371111098285.

Fowler, J. H., & Christakis, N. A. (2008). Dynamic spread of happiness in a large social network: Longitudinal analysis over 20 years in the framingham Heart Study. *British Medical Journal*, 23–27. PMID:18174597.

Franklin, C., Trepper, T. S., Gingerich, W. J., & McCollum, E. E. (2012). *Solution-focused brief therapy: A handbook of evidence based practice*. New York: Oxford University Press.

Freeman, R. E., & McVea, J. (2001). *A stakeholder approach to strategic management*. Retrieved May 25, 2012, from http://papers.ssrn.com/paper.taf?abstract_id=263511

Freeman, R. E., Harrison, J. S., & Wicks, A. C. (2007). *Managing for stakeholders: Survival, reputation, and success*. New Haven, CT: Yale University Press.

Freeman, R. E., Harrison, J. S., Wicks, A. C., Parmar, B. L., & De Colle, S. (2010). *Stakeholder theory: The state of the art*. Cambridge, UK: Cambridge University Press. doi:10.1017/CBO9780511815768.

Fritz, R. G., & Fritz, J. M. (1985). Linguistic structure and economic method. *Journal of Economic Issues*, *19*(1), 75–101.

Garcia, S. (2005). How standards enable adoption of project management practice. *IEEE Software*, *22*(5), 22–29. doi:10.1109/MS.2005.122.

Gardner, B., & Demello, S. (1993). Systems thinking in action. *The Healthcare Forum Journal*, *36*(4). PMID:10127050.

Gareis, R. (2008). Change management und projekte. In Meyer, Wald, Gleich, & Wagner (Eds.), Advanced Project Management. Herausforderungen - Praxiserfahrungen - Perspektiven LIT-Verlag.

Gareis, R., Heumann, & Martinuzzi, A. (2010). *Relating sustainable development and project management: A conceptual model*.

Gareis, R., Huemann, M., & Martinuzzi, A. (2009). *Relating sustainable development and project management*. Paper presented at the IRNOP 2009. Berlin, Germany.

Gareis, R., Huemann, M., & Martinuzzi, A. (2011). What can project management learn from considering sustainability principles? *Project Perspectives*. ISSN 1445-4178

Gareis, R., Huemann, M., & Weninger, C. (2010). The consideration of sustainability principles in the project assignment process: An analysis of project management approaches. Paper presented at IPMA World Congress. Istanbul, Turkey.

Gareis, R., Huemann, M., Martinuzzi, R.-A., Sedlacko, M., & Weninger, C. (2011). *The SustPM matrix: Relating sustainability principles to project assignment and project management*. Paper presented at EURAM11. Talinn.

Gareis, R. (2005). *Happy projects!* Vienna: Manz Velog.

Gareis, R. (2010). Changes of organizations by projects. *International Journal of Project Management*. doi:10.1016/j.ijproman.2010.01.002.

Gareis, R., Heumann, M., & Martinuzzi, A. (2009). *Relating sustainable development and project management*. Berlin: IRNOP IX.

Gareis, R., & Huemann, M. (2010). Changes & projects. *International Journal of Project Management*, *28*(4), 311–412. doi:10.1016/j.ijproman.2010.02.005.

Gareis, R., Huemann, M., & Martinuzzi, A. (2011). What can project management learn from considering sustainability principles? *Project Perspectives*, *33*, 60–65.

Gareis, R., Huemann, M., Martinuzzi, A., Weninger, C., & Sedlacko, M. (2013). *Project management & sustainable development principles*. Newtown Square, PA: Project Management Institute.

Gareis, R., Huemann, M., Martinuzzi, A., Weninger, C., & Sedlacko, M. (2013). *Rethinking project management*. Newtown Square, PA: Project Management Institute.

Gareis, R., Huemann, M., & Martinuzzi, R.-A. (2009). *Relating sustainable development and project management*. Berlin: IRNOP IX.

Gareis, R., & Stummer, M. (2008). *Processes & projects*. Wien: Manz.

Garnaut, R. (2008). *Garnaut climate change review update: Bulletin 3*. Retrieved from http://www.garnautreview.org.au/CA25734E0016A131/WebObj/FINALAuguste-bulletin_29Aug08/$File/FINAL%20August%20e-bulletin_29%20Aug%2008.pdf

Garvare, R., & Isaksson, R. (2001). Sustainable development: Extending the scope of business excellence models. *Measuring Business Excellence, 5*(3), 11–15. doi:10.1108/13683040110403899.

Gary, C.M., Fagerström, A., & Hassel, L.G. (n.d.). Accounting for sustainability: What's next? A research agenda. *The Annals of the University of Oradea: Economic Sciences, 1*, 97-111.

George, C. (1999). Testing for sustainable development through environmental assessment. *Environmental Impact Assessment Review,* (19): 175–200. doi:10.1016/S0195-9255(98)00038-9.

Georgia State University. (2005). *Risk management.* Retrieved from http://www2.gsu.edu/~wwwpmo/risk_management.html

Geyer, A., Hanke, M., Littich, E., & Nettekoven, M. (2003). *Grundlagen der finanzierung.* Linde.

Ghobadian, A., Gallear, D., & Hopkins, M. (2007). TQM and the CSR nexus. *International Journal of Quality & Reliability Management, 24*(7), 704–721. doi:10.1108/02656710710774683.

Gibb, A. (2004). Safety, health, and environment. In Morris, P. W. G., & Pinto, J. K. (Eds.), *The Wiley guide to managing projects.* Hoboken, NJ: John Wiley & Sons, Inc..

Gibson, R. B. (2001). *Specification of sustainability-based environmental assessment decision criteria and implications for determining significance in environmental assessment.* Waterloo, Canada: University of Waterloo.

Gibson, R. B. (2006). Sustainability assessment: Basic components of a practical approach. *Impact Assessment and Project Appraisal, 24*(3), 170–182. doi:10.3152/147154606781765147.

Gido, J., & Clements, J. P. (2008). *Successful project management.* South-Western Pub..

Gilbert, R., Stevenson, D., Girardet, H., & Stern, R. (Eds.). (1996). *Making cities work: The role of local authorities in the urban environment.* Earthscan Publications Ltd..

Gilding, P. (2005). The profit motive is pure enough. *The Australian.* Retrieved June 6, 2012, from http://www.onlineopinion.com.au/author.asp?id=3806

Gladwin, T. N., Kennelly, J. J., & Krause, T.-S. (1995). Shifting paradigms for sustainable development: Implications for management theory and research. *Academy of Management Review, 20*(4), 874–907.

Glenn, J. C., & Gordon, T. J. (1998). *State of the future: Issues and opportunities.* Washington, DC: American Council for the United Nations University.

Global Compact-Accenture, U. N. (2010). *A new era of sustainability: UN global compact-accenture CEO Study.* New York: Accenture and UN Global Compact.

Global Compact, U. N.UNEP Finance Initiative. (2006). *Principles for Responsible investment.* Paris: UNEP.

Global Reporting Initiative (GRI). (2011). *Sustainability reporting guidelines.* Global Reporting Initiative.

Global Reporting Initiative (GRI). (2012). *A new phase: The growth of sustainability reporting: GRI's year in review 2010/11.* Global Reporting Initiative.

Godschalk, S. K. B. (2011). *An assessment of the relationship between environmental and financial reporting by South African listed companies in the mining sector.* (Unpublished doctoral dissertation). University of Pretoria. Pretoria, South Africa.

Goldratt, E. (1992). *The goal: A process of ongoing improvement.* Boston: North River Press.

Goleman, D. (2009). Why investors should consider sustainability risk management. *Harvard Business Review.* Retrieved on July 4, 2011 from http://blogs.hbr.org/cs/2009/10/investors_consider_sustainabil.html

Gonzales-Benito, J., & Gonzales-Benito, O. (2008). Operation management practices linked to the adoption of ISO 14001: An empirical analysis of Spanish manufacturers. *International Journal of Production Economics, 113*, 60–73. doi:10.1016/j.ijpe.2007.02.051.

Gormley, W. T. (1996, November). Counter-bureaucracies in theory and practice. *Administration & Society,* 275–298. doi:10.1177/009539979602800301.

Granger, C. W. J. (1983). *Co-integrated variables and error-correcting models.* San Diego, CA: University of California.

Granger, C. W. J. (1997). On modelling the long run in applied economics. *The Economic Journal, 107*(440), 169–177. doi:10.1111/1468-0297.00150.

Grant, R. (1996). Toward a knowledge based theory of the firm. *Strategic Management Journal, 17.*

Green Building Council of Australia (GBCA). (2013). *Green star overview.* Green Building Council of Australia.

Green, T. (2012). *The dictionary of global sustainability: With case studies on the environmental, economic technological, and social aspects of sustainability.* New York: McGraw-Hill.

Gregersen, H. M., Lundgren, A. L., & White, T. A. (1994). *Improving project management for sustainable development. Midwest Universities Consortium for International Activities, Inc.* MUCIA.

Grevelman, L., & Kluiwstra, M. (2009). *Sustainability in project management: A case study on Enexis.* (Thesis). International MSc Real Estate Management at the University of Greenwich, Greenwich, UK.

Griffiths, K. (2007). *Project sustainability management in infrastructure projects.* Paper presented at the 2nd International Conference on Sustainability Engineering and Science. Auckland, New Zealand.

Grigg, N., & Mann, R. (2008). Promoting excellence: An international study into creating awareness of business excellence models. *The TQM Journal, 20*(3), 233–248. doi:10.1108/17542730810867254.

Gujarati, D. N. (1995). *Basic econometrics.* New York: McGraw-Hill.

Gunningham, N. (2002). Green alliances: Conflict or cooperation in environmental policy? *Australasian Journal of Environmental Management, 9*(3), 148–157. doi:10.1080/14486563.2002.10648555.

Gunningham, N. (2009). Shaping corporate environmental performance: A review. *Environmental Policy and Governance, 19*(4), 215–231. doi:10.1002/eet.510.

Haag, G. D. (2011, June). *Geothermal heat for 4000 houses in The Hague, Dutch project example.* Retrieved July 2011, from www.aplu.org: http://www.aplu.org/document.doc?id=2938

Haanaes, K., Reeves, M., von Strengvelken, I., Audretsch, M., Kiron, D., & Kruschwitz, N. (2012, Winter). Sustainability nears a tipping point. *MIT Sloan Management Review.*

Hall, S. G. (1986, August). An application of the granger and engle two-step estimation procedure to United Kingdom aggregate wage data. *Oxford Bulletin of Economics and Statistics,* 229–239.

Hammer, M., & Champy, J. (1993). *Reengineering the corporation: A manifesto for business revolution.* New York: Harper Business School Press. doi:10.1016/S0007-6813(05)80064-3.

Hansmann, R. (2010). Sustainability learning: An introduction to the concept and its motivational aspects. *Sustainability, 2*(9), 2873–2897. doi:10.3390/su2092873.

Harker, L., & Keltner, D. (2001). Expressions of positive emotion in women's college yearbook pictures and their relationship to personality and life outcomes across adulthood. *Journal of Personality and Social Psychology,* 112–124. doi:10.1037/0022-3514.80.1.112 PMID:11195884.

Harrison, G. (2001). Administering market friendly growth? Liberal populism and the world bank's involvement in administrative reform in sub-Saharan Africa. *Review of International Political Economy, 8*(3), 528–547. doi:10.1080/09692290110055867.

Hartman, F. (1998). *The nature and role of projects in the next 20 years: Research issues and problems.* Calgary, Canada: Project Management Specialization, University of Calgary.

Hart, S. L. (1995). A natural-resource-based view of the firm. *Academy of Management Review, 20*(4), 986–1014.

Harvard Business School. (2010, October). *A workshop on integrated reporting- Framework and action plan.* Boston: Harvard.

Hawken, P. (1993). *The ecology of commerce: A declaration of sustainability.* New York: HarperBusiness.

Hazlett, S., McAdam, R., & Murray, L. (2007). From quality management to socially responsible organisations: The case for CSR. *International Journal of Quality & Reliability Management, 24*(7), 669–682. doi:10.1108/02656710710774665.

Hedberg, C., & von Malmborg. (2003). The global reporting initiative and corporate sustainability reporting in Swedish companies. *Corporate Social Responsibility and Environmental Management, 10*(3), 153–164. doi:10.1002/csr.38.

Heitger, B., & Doujak, A. (2008). *Management cuts and new growth - An innovative approach to change management*. Vienna, Austria: Goldegg.

Heltberg, R., Hossain, N., Reva, A., & Turk, C. (2012). *Anatomy of coping: Evidence from people living through the crises of 2008-11*. Washington, DC: World Bank.

Hendricks, K. B., & Singhal, V. R. (2001). Firm characteristics, total quality management, and financial performance. *Journal of Operations Management, 19*(3), 269–285. doi:10.1016/S0272-6963(00)00049-8.

Henry, P. C. (2005). Life stresses, explanatory style, hopelessness, and occupational class. *International Journal of Stress Management, 12*(3), 241–256. doi:10.1037/1072-5245.12.3.241.

Herazo, B., Lizarralde, G., & Paquin, R. (2012). Sustainable development in the building sector: A Canadian case study on the alignment of strategic and tactical management. *Project Management Journal, 43*(2).

Hermans, L. M. (2005). *Actor Analysis for water resources management*. Delft, the Netherlands: Eburon.

Hermarij, J. (2010). *The better practices of project management*. The Netherlands: Dhirita B.V., Oudekerk a/d Amstel.

Hill, C., & Jones, G. (2001). *Strategic management*. Boston: Houghton Mifflin.

Hirth, H. (2008). *Grundzüge der finanzierung und investition*. München, Germany: Oldenbourg Wissenschaftsverlag GmbH..

Hitchcock, D., & Willard, M. (2009). *The business guide to sustainability: Practical strategies and tools for organization* (2nd ed.). London: Earthscan.

Hodgson, D., & Muzio, D. (2011). Prospects for professionalism in project management. In Morris, Pinto, & Söderlund (Eds.), The Oxford Handbook of Project Management. New York: Oxford University Press.

Hoefer, R. (2000). Accountability in action? Program evaluation in nonprofit human service agencies. *Nonprofit Management & Leadership, 11*(2). doi:10.1002/nml.11203.

Holliday, C. (2001, September). Sustainable growth, the DuPont way. *Harvard Business Review*, 129–134. PMID:11550629.

Hopkins, M. (2011). From trust me to show me: Moving sustainability at shell oil from priority to core value. *MIT Sloan Management Review*. Retrieved on July 4, 2011 from http://sloanreview.mit.edu/the-magazine/2011-spring/52317/moving-sustainability-at-shell-oil-from-priority-to-core-value/?utm_source=Publicaster&utm_medium=email&utm_campaign=Sust%20Enews%20March%2017%202011&utm_term=Read+more+

Hopkins, W. E. (2011). Managing business from a values-based perspective. In S.G. McNall, J.C. Hershauer, & G. Basile (Eds.), The Business of Sustainability, Trends, Policies, Practices, and Stories of Success: Vol. 1: Global Challenges and Opportunities (pp. 143-158). Santa Barbara, CA: Praeger.

Hopkins, M. J. D. (2002). Sustainability in the internal operations of companies. *Corporate Environmental Strategy, 9*(4), 398–408. doi:10.1016/S1066-7938(02)00121-5.

Hossain, M., Islam, K., & Andrew, J. (2006). Corporate social and environmental disclosure in developing countries: Evidence from Bangladesh. In *Proceedings of the Asian Pacific Conference on International Accounting Issues*. Hawaii, HI: IEEE.

Htaybat, K. (2011). Corporate online reporting in 2010: A case study in Jordan. *Journal of Financial Reporting and Accounting, 9*(1).

Huemann, M., Eskerod, P., Weninger, C., & Aagaard, A. (2014). *Rethinking project stakeholder management*. Newtown Square, PA: Project Management Institute.

Hughes, A., & Halsall, D. N. (2002). Comparison of the 14 deadly diseases and the business excellence model. *Total Quality Management, 13*(2), 255–263. doi:10.1080/09544120120102487.

Hunsberger, K. (2008). The sustainability mandate. *PMI Voices on Project Management*. Retrieved on July 4, 2011 from http://blogs.pmi.org/blog/voices_on_project_management/2008/10/the-sustainability-mandate.html

IEA. I. (2011). Technology Roadmap, Geothermal Heat and Power. Paris: IEA.

Interbrand. (2012). *Methodology*. Retrieved from http://www.interbrand.com/en/best-global-brands/Best-Global-Green-Brands/2012-Report/bggb-2012-methodology.aspx

International Federation of Consulting Engineers. (2004). Retrieved from http://www1.fidic.org/bookshop/account/reading_pdf.asp?sesskey=0&productcode=FI-EN-T-AA-10&range=0&f=IENTAA&p=2&n=Project+Sustainability+Management+Guidelines%2C+2004

International Finance Corporation. (2006). Retrieved from http://www1.ifc.org/wps/wcm/connect/51591900 48855a4f85b4d76a6515bb18/SustainabilityPolicy.pdf? MOD=AJPERES&CACHEID=5159190048855a4f85b 4d76a6515bb18

International Institute for Sustainable Development & Deloitte and Touche. (1992). *Business strategy for sustainable development: Leadership and accountability for the 90s.* Winnipeg, Canada: International Institute for Sustainable Development.

International Organization for Standardization. (2010). *ISO 9001 certifications top one million mark, food safety and information security continue meteoric increase.* Retrieved from http://www.iso.org/iso/news.htm?refid=Ref1363

International Organization for Standardization. (2012). [Geneva: ISO.]. *ISO, 21500,* 2012.

International Organization for Standardization. (2012). *ISO 14001:2004.* Retrieved from http://www.iso.org/iso/iso_catalogue/catalogue_ics/catalogue_detail_ics.htm?csnumber=31807

International Organization for Standardization. (2012). *Management systems standards.* Retrieved from http://www.iso.org/iso/home/standards/management-standards.htm

International Project Management Association. (2006). *International Competency Baseline ver. 3.0.* Zürich: IPMA.

InvestorWords. (2011). *Definition investment.* Retrieved from http://www.investorwords.com/2599/investment.html

IPMA. (2006). *ICB - IPMA competence baseline version 3.0.* The Netherlands: Nijkerk.

Isen, A. M., & Daubman, K. A. (1984). The influence of affect on categorization. *Journal of Personality and Social Psychology,* (47): 1206–1217. doi:10.1037/0022-3514.47.6.1206.

ISO 26000. (2010). *Guidance on social responsibility.* Geneva: International Organization for Standardization.

Ittner, C. D., & Larcker, D. F. (1998). Indicators of financial performance? An analysis of customer satisfaction. *Journal of Accounting Research, 36,* 1–35. doi:10.2307/2491304.

Ittner, C. D., Larcker, D. F., & Meyer, M. W. (2003). Subjectivity and the weighting of performance measures: Evidence from a balanced scorecard. *Accounting Review, 78*(3), 725–758. doi:10.2308/accr.2003.78.3.725.

Jaafari, A. (2007). Thinking of sustainability as a dimension of managerial competency. *PM World Today, 9*(9).

James, P. (2000). *Business, eco-efficiency and sustainable development.* Lisbon: The European Commission.

Janeš, A., & Dolinšek, S. (2011). *Can we use the statistical causality with the sufficient reliability?* Paper presented at the Knowledge and Learning International Conference 2011. Celje, Slovenia.

Janeš, A., & Faganel, A. (2008). Zadovoljstvo udeležencev projekta poslovne odličnosti v PS mercator, d.d. [Business excellence project in PS Mercator, P.l.c. participants' satisfaction]. *Projektna mreža Slovenije, 11*(1), 9-17.

Janeš, A., & Dolinšek, S. (2010). Do we need a new compass for the journey through the global crisis? *Journal of Industrial Engineering and Management, 3*(2), 255–293. doi:10.3926/jiem.2010.v3n2.p255-293.

Jiha, J., & Orphee, G. (1995). A note on inflation in Haiti: Evidence from cointegration analysis. *Social and Economic Studies, 44*(1), 95–115.

Johnson, H. T., & Kaplan, R. S. (1987). *Relevance lost: The rise and fall of management accounting.* Boston, MA: Harvard Business School Press.

Johnson, K. J., & Frederickson, B. L. (2005). We all look te same to me: Positive emotions eliminate the own race bais in face recognition. *Psychological Science,* 875–881. doi:10.1111/j.1467-9280.2005.01631.x PMID:16262774.

Johnson, S. K. (2009). Do you feel what I feel? Mood contagion and leadership outcomes. *The Leadership Quarterly, 20,* 814–827. doi:10.1016/j.leaqua.2009.06.012.

Jones, L. Lasalle Inc. (2012). *Global property sustainability perspective*. Retrieved April 26, 2012 from http://www.joneslanglasalle.com/GSP/en-gb/Pages/Global-Sustainability-Perspective.aspx

Jones, P. (2009). *Avoiding problems and predicting recovery during the economic crisis*. Retrieved March 10, 2010, from http://www.excitant.co.uk

Jugdev, K., & Müller, R. (2005). A retrospective look at our evolving understanding of project success. *Project Management Journal, 36*(4), 19–31.

Juran, J. M., & De Feo, J. A. (2010). *Juran's quality handbook: The complete guide to performance excellence* (6th ed.). New York: McGraw-Hill.

Kahkonen, K., Kazi, A. S., & Rekola, M. (Eds.). (2009). The human side of projects in modern business. Helsinki, Finland: Project Management Association Finland (PMAF).

Kähkönen, K. (1999). Multi-character model of the construction project definition process. *Automation in Construction, 8*(6), 625–632. doi:10.1016/S0926-5805(98)00111-3.

Kamal, M. A.-S. A.-H. (2001). Application of the AHP in project management. *International Journal of Project Management, 19*, 19–27. doi:10.1016/S0263-7863(99)00038-1.

Kanter, R. M. (2010). How to do well and do good. *MIT Sloan Management Review*. Retrieved on July 4, 2011 from http://sloanreview.mit.edu/the-magazine/2010-fall/52118/how-to-do-well-and-do-good/

Kaplan, R. S., & Norton, D. P. (2004). *Strategy maps: Converting intangible assets into tangible outcomes*. Boston: Harvard Business School Publishing.

Kaplan, R. S., & Norton, D. P. (2006). *Alignment: Using the balanced scorecard to create corporate synergies*. Boston: Harvard Business School Publishing.

Kaplan, R., & Norton, D. (1992). The balanced scorecard - Measures that drive performance. *Harvard Business Review, 70*(1), 71–79. PMID:10119714.

Kaplan, R., & Norton, D. (2000). Having trouble with your strategy? Then map it. *Harvard Business Review, 78*(5), 167–176. PMID:11143152.

Kasper, H., & Mayrhofer, W. (2002). *Personalmanagement, führung, organisation*. Vienna: Linde Verlag.

Keating, M. (1993). *The earth summit's agenda for change*. Geneva: Centre for our Common Future.

Kennedy, A. (2000). *The end of shareholder value: Corporations at the crossroads*. New York: Basic Books.

Kim, D. Y., Kumar, V., & Murphy, S. A. (2010). European foundation for quality management business excellence model: An integrative review and research agenda. *International Journal of Quality & Reliability, 27*(6), 684–701. doi:10.1108/02656711011054551.

Klein, J. T. (2004). Prospects for transdisciplinarity. *Futures, 36*, 515–526. doi:10.1016/j.futures.2003.10.007.

Knoepfel, H. (Ed.). (2010). Survival and sustainability as challenges for projects. Zurich: International Project Management Association (IPMA).

Kolk, A. (2003). Trends in sustainability reporting by the fortune global 250. *Business Strategy and the Environment, 12*(5), 279–291. doi:10.1002/bse.370.

Kotter, J. (1996). Successful change and the force that drives it. *The Canadian Manager, 21*(3), 20–23.

Kotter, J. P. (1996). *Leading change*. Boston, MA: Harvard Business School Press.

KPMG. (2011). *Corporate sustainability: A progress report*. Retrieved May 20, 2012, from http://www.kpmg.com/sustainability

KPMG. (2012). *Expect the unexpected: Building business value in a changing world*. Retrieved May 20, 2012, from http://www.kpmg.com/sustainability

Krane, H.P., Olsson, N.O.E., & Rolstadås, A. (2012). How project manager–Project owner interaction can work within and influence project risk management. *Project Management Journal, 43*(2).

Kranjac, M., Henny, C., & Sikimić, U. (2011). European funds as fact of sustainable development in central eastern European countries. *Economics and Organization, 8*(3), 301–312.

Kuhlman, T., & Farrington, J. (2010). What is sustainability? *Sustainability, 2*(11), 3436–3448. doi:10.3390/su2113436.

Kujala, J., & Artto, K. (2000). *Developing corporate project management practices through quality award framework*. Paper presented at the Project Management Institute Annual Seminars & Symposium. Houston, TX.

Labuschagne, C., & Brent, A. (2004). *Sustainable project life cycle management: Aligning project management methodologies with the principles of sustainable development*. Paper presented at PMSA International Conference. Johannesburg, South Africa.

Labuschagne, C., & Brent, A. (2006). Social Indicators for Sustainable Project and Technology Life Cycle Management in the Process Industry. *Process Industry*, 1-17.

Labuschagne, C., Brent, A.C., & van Erck Ron, P.G. (2007). *Assessing performance of industries*. Pretoria, South Africa: University of Petroria openUP.

Labuschagne, C., & Brent, A. (2005). Environmental and Social Impact Considerations for Sustainable Project Life Cycle Management in the Process Industry. *Corporate Social Responsibility and Environmental Management*, *12*, 38–54. doi:10.1002/csr.76.

Labuschagne, C., & Brent, A. (2006). Social indicators for sustainable project and technology life cycle management in the process industry. *The International Journal of Life Cycle Assessment*, *11*(1), 3–15. doi:10.1065/lca2006.01.233.

Labuschagne, C., & Brent, A. C. (2005). Sustainable project life cycle management: The need to integrate life cycles in the manufacturing sector. *International Journal of Project Management*, *23*, 159–168. doi:10.1016/j.ijproman.2004.06.003.

Labuschagne, C., & Brent, A. C. (2008). An industry perspective of the completeness and relevance of a social assessment framework for project and technology management in the manufacturing sector. *Journal of Cleaner Production*, *16*, 253–262. doi:10.1016/j.jclepro.2006.07.028.

Labuschagne, C., Brent, A. C., & van Erck, R. P. G. (2005). Assessing the sustainability performance of industries. *Journal of Cleaner Production*, *13*(4), 373–385. doi:10.1016/j.jclepro.2003.10.007.

Labuschagne, C., Brent, A., & Claasen, S. J. (2005). Environmental and social impact considerations for sustainable project life cycle management in the process industry. *Corporate Social Responsibility and Environmental Management*, *12*, 38–54. doi:10.1002/csr.76.

Lacy, P., Cooper, T., Hayward, R., & Neuberger, L. (2010). A new era of sustainability: CEO reflections on progress to date, challenges ahead and the impact of the journey toward a sustainable economy. In UN Global Compact-Accenture CEO Study. New York: UN.

Law of Queensland in force 1 December. (2011). *Environment Protection (Waste Management) 2000 Regulation, sec.17, para 1. (Austl.)*.

Law of South Australia version 24.11. (2011). *Environment Protection (Waste to Resources) Policy 2010, sch. 4, sec.1, para.15-16. (Austl.)*.

Leonard, D., & McAdam, R. (2003). Corporate social responsibility. *Quality Progress*, *36*(10), 27–32.

Levy, A., & Merry, U. (1986). *Organizational transformation - Approaches, strategies, and theories*. New York: Greenwood Publishing Group.

Lewin, K. (1947). Frontiers in group dynamics. *Human Relations*, *1*(1), 5–41. doi:10.1177/001872674700100103.

Leys, C. (1996). *The rise and fall of development theory*. Bloomington, IN: Indiana University Press.

Lighting, F. (n.d.). *Fantastic lighting's tube replacement service*. Retrieved April 25, 2012 from http://www.fantasticlighting.com.au/Products/Pricing/tabid/66/Default.aspx

Lindgren, M., & Packendorff, J. (2006). What's new in new forms of organizing? On the construction of gender in project-based work. *Journal of Management Studies*, *43*(4), 841–866. doi:10.1111/j.1467-6486.2006.00613.x.

Linley, P. A. Harrington, & Garcea. (Eds.). (2010). *Oxford handbook of positive psychology and work*. Oxford, UK: Oxford University Press.

Linneluecke, M., Russell, S., & Griffiths, A. (2009). Subcultures and sustainability practices: The impact on understanding corporate sustainability. *Business Strategy and the Environment*, *18*, 432–452. doi:10.1002/bse.609.

Liverman, D. M., Hanson, M. E., Brown, B. J., & Meredith, R. W. Jr. (1988). Global sustainability: Toward measurement. *Environmental Management*, *20*(2), 133–143. doi:10.1007/BF01873382.

Lock, D. (2007). *Project management* (9th ed.). Gower Publishing Limited.

Loo, R. (2003). A multi-level casual model for best practices in project management. *Benchmarking: An International Journal, 10*, 29–36. doi:10.1108/14635770310457520.

Lopez, S. J., Ciarlelli, R., Cofman, L., Stone, M., & Wyatt, L. (2000). Diagnosing for strengths, on measuring hope building blocks. In Snyder (Ed.), Handbook of hope: Theory, measures and applications. San Diego, CA: Academic Press.

Lopez, S. J. (Ed.). (2013). *The encyclopedia of positive psychology*. West Sussex, UK: Wiley-Blackwell.

Lorbach, D., van Bakel, J., Whiteman, G., & Rotmans, J. (2010). Business strategies for transitions towards sustainable systems. *Business Strategy and the Environment, 133*, 133–146.

Losada, M., & Heaphy, E. (2004). The role of positivity and connectivity in the performance of business teams: A nonlinear dynamics model. *The American Behavioral Scientist, 47*(6), 740–765. doi:10.1177/0002764203260208.

Louche, C., & Lydenberg, S. D. (2011). *Dilemmas in responsible investment*. Greenleaf Publishing Limited.

Lovins, Lovins, & Hawken. (1999). *Natural capitalism: Creating the next industrial revolution*. New York: Little Brown and Company, UK.

Loyd-Walker, B., & Walker, D. (2011). Authentic leadership for 21st century project delivery. *International Journal of Project Management*, (29): 282–295.

Lubin, D. A., & Esty, D. C. (2010). Lessons for leaders from previous game-changing megatrends. *Harvard Business Review, 88*(5), 42–50.

Lundin, R. A., & Söderholm, A. (1995). A theory of the temporary organization. *Scandinavian Journal of Management, 11*, 437–455. doi:10.1016/0956-5221(95)00036-U.

Lyubomirsky, S. (2001). Why are some people happier than others? The role of cognitive and motivational processes in well being. *The American Psychologist, 56*, 239–249. doi:10.1037/0003-066X.56.3.239 PMID:11315250.

Lyubomirsky, S. (2007). *The how of happiness: A practical guide to getting the life you want*. London: Piatkus.

Lyumbomirsky, S., King, L., & Diener, E. (2005). The benefits of positive affect: does happiness leads to success? *Psychological Bulletin*, (131): 803–855. doi:10.1037/0033-2909.131.6.803 PMID:16351326.

Macalister, T. (2005). Browne lauds the noble purpose of making money. *The Guardian*. Retrieved June 6, 2012, from http://www.guardian.co.uk/business/2005/feb/oilandpetrol.news

Macdonnald, A. J. (2011). *Solution-focused therapy: Theory, research& practice*. London: Sage.

Macunovich, D. J., & Easterlin, R. A. (1988). Application of granger-sims causality tests to monthly fertility data, 1958-1984. *Journal of Population Economics, 1*(1), 71–88. doi:10.1007/BF00171511.

Malhotra, K. (2000). NGOs without aid: Beyond the global soup kitchen. *Third World Quarterly, 21*(4), 665–668. doi:10.1080/713701062.

Maltzman, R., & Shirley, D. (2011). *When unplugged is a bad thing*. Retrieved March 13, 2011 from http://www.earthpm.com

Maltzman, R., & Shirley, D. (2011). *Green project managemen*. Boca Raton, FL: CRC Press.

Martens, P. (2006). Sustainability: Science or fiction? *Sustainability: Science, Practice, &. Policy, 2*(1), 1–5.

Martinuzzi, A., & Krumay, B. (2012). The good, the bad and the successful - How CSR leads to competitive advantage and organizational transformation. *Journal of Organizational Change Management*.

Marx, B., & Dyk, V. (2011). Sustainability reporting and assurance: An analysis of assurance practices in South Africa. *Meditari Accountancy Research, 19*(1).

Material Handling Industry of America. (2007). *The green supply chain*. Retrieved from http://mhia.org/news/industry/7056/the-green-supply-chain

McKinlay, M. (2008). *Where is project management running to…?* Paper presented at the 22nd World Congress of the International Project Management Association. Rome, Italy.

McWilliams, A., & Siegel, D. (2001). Corporate social responsibility: A theory of the firm perspective. *Academy of Management Review, 26*(1), 117–127.

Meadowcroft, J. (2007). Who is in charge here? Governance for sustainable development in a complex world. *Journal of Environmental Policy and Planning, 9*(3), 299–314. doi:10.1080/15239080701631544.

Meadows, D. (1999). *Leverage points, places to intervene in a system*. New York: The Sustainability Institute.

Meadows, D. H., Meadows, D. L., Randers, J., & Behrens, W. W. (1972). *The limits to growth*. Universe Books.

Mell, E., & Mathiasen, C. (2011). *U.S. proxy season review 2011: Environmental & social issues*. Retrieved from http://www.issgovernance.com/files/private/2011ProxySeasonReviewES.pdf

Meredith, J., & Mantel, S. (2010). *Project Management, A managerial approach*. Hoboken: John Wiley & Sons, Inc..

Michael, J. (2009). *Best practice CR&S reporting in the real estate industry*. (Unpublished master's thesis). Ryerson University, Toronto, Canada.

Michelon, G. (2007). *Sustainability disclosure and reputation: A comparative study*. Paper presented at the IV Workshop on Disclosure to Financial Markets. Padova, Italy.

Michelson, G., Wailes, N., Van Der Laan, S., & Frost, G. (2004). Ethical investment processes and outcomes. *Journal of Business Ethics, 52*(1), 1–10. doi:10.1023/B:BUSI.0000033103.12560.be.

Miller, S. M. (1991). Monetary dynamics: An application of cointegration and error-correction modeling. *Journal of Money, Credit and Banking, 23*(2), 139–154. doi:10.2307/1992773.

Mills, K. (2008). *Demographic change has led to a shortage of skills and given employees the upper hand*. Retrieved from http://cio.co.nz/cio.nsf/focus/59F02885E3360D57CC25737E0082526F

Mills, R., & Turner, R. (1995). Projects for shareholder value. In Turner (Ed.), The commercial project manager. London: McGraw-Hill Book Company.

Minerals Council of Australia (MCA). (2004). *Enduring value: Guidance for implementation*. Canberra, Australia: MCA.

Mintzberg, H., Ahstrand, B., & Lampel, J. (1998). *Strategy safari*. Edinburgh, UK: Pearson Education Limited.

Mintzberg, H., & Walters, J. (1985). Of strategies, deliberate and emergent. *Strategic Management Journal, 6*, 257–272. doi:10.1002/smj.4250060306.

Mitchell, R., Agle, B., & Wood, D. (1997). Toward a theory of stakeholder identification and salience: Defining the principle of who and what really counts. *Academy of Management Review, 22*(4).

Mitroff, I. (1983). *Stakeholders of the Organizational Mind. San Fransisco, Washington*. London: Jossey-Bass Publishers.

Mochal, T., Krasnoff, A., Maltzman, R., & Shirley, D. (2010). Open letter to authors of PMI PMBOK guide V5 regarding green PM. *ICPM Blogs*. Retrieved July 11, 2011 from http://www.theicpm.com/component/content/article/152-blogs/3600-open-letter-to-authors-of-pmi-pmbok-guide-v5-regarding-green-pm

Modell, S. (2009). Bundling management control innovations. *Accounting, Auditing & Accountability Journal, 22*(1), 59–90. doi:10.1108/09513570910923015.

Moldan, & Billharz, S. (Eds.). (1997). Indicators and their use: Information for decision making sustainability indicators: Report on the project on indicators for sustainable development. Chichester, UK: Academic Press.

Molyneux, M. (2008). The 'neoliberal turn' and the new social policy in Latin America: How neoliberal, now new? *Development and Change, 39*(5), 775–797. doi:10.1111/j.1467-7660.2008.00505.x.

Monge, P. R. (1990). Theoretical and analytical issues in studying organizational processes. *Organization Science, 1*(4), 406–430. doi:10.1287/orsc.1.4.406.

Morgese, P. (n.d.). Integrating global sustainability into project management: The human resource knowledge area. *PMI Global Sustainability Community of Practice*. Retrieved July 11, 2011 from http://sustainability.vc.pmi.org/Community/Blogs/tabid/376/entryid/648/Integrating-global-sustainability-into-project-management-the-human-resource-knowledge-area.aspx

Morris, P. (2008). *Implementing strategy through project management: Managing the front-end*. Unpublished manuscript.

Morris, P. W. G., & Jamieson, A. (2005). Moving from corporate strategy to project strategy. *Project Management Journal, 36*(4), 5-18. Retrieved from http://search.ebscohost.com/login.aspx?direct=true&db=buh&AN=19561978&site=ehost-live

Morris, P., & Therivel, R. (1995). *Methods of environmental impact assessment.* Vancouver, Canada: University of British Columbia Press.

Mui, D. H. F., & Sankaran, S. (2004). An effective project management-based application model for sustainable urban renewal in Hong Kong. *Project Management Journal, 35*(4), 15–34.

Mulder, J. (2003). *Project selection criteria for LandCare projects.* (Masters dissertation). University of Pretoria, Pretoria, South Africa.

Mulder, J., & Brent, A. C. (2006). Selection of sustainable agriculture projects in South Africa: Case studies in the LandCare programme. *Journal of Sustainable Agriculture, 28*(2), 55–84. doi:10.1300/J064v28n02_06.

Municipality, D. (2008). Delft Climate Plan 2008-2012. Delft.

Munier, N. (2005). *Introduction to sustainability: Road to a better future.* Berlin: Springer.

Musango, J. K., & Brent, A. C. (2011). Assessing the sustainability of energy technological systems in Southern Africa: A review and way forward. *Technology in Society, 33,* 145–155. doi:10.1016/j.techsoc.2011.03.011.

Musango, J. K., Brent, A. C., Amigun, B., Pretorius, L., & Müller, H. (2011). Technology sustainability assessment of biodiesel development in South Africa: A system dynamics approach. *Energy, 36,* 6922–6940. doi:10.1016/j.energy.2011.09.028.

Natsios, A. (2010). The clash of the counter-bureaucracy and development. *Center for Global Development.* Retrieved from www.cgdev.org/content/publications/detail/1424271

Nelson, D. L., & Cooper, C. L. (Eds.). (2007). *Positive organizational behaviour.* Thousand Oaks, CA: Sage.

Nelson, R. R. (2005). Project retrospectives: Evaluating project success, failure, and everything in between. *MIS Quarterly Executive, 4*(3), 361–372.

NetImpact. (2009). Making your impact at work: A practical guide to changing the world from inside any company. *NetImpact.* Retrieved July 11, 2011 from http://netimpact.org/associations/4342/files/MakingYourImpactatWork.pdf

NetImpact. (2011). Corporate careers that make a difference. *NetImpact.* Retrieved July 11, 2011 from http://netimpact.org/associations/4342/files/CorporateCareersThatMakeaDifference_v2.pdf

Nidumolu, R., Prahalad, C. K., & Rangaswami, M. R. (2009). Why sustainability is now the key driver of innovation. *Harvard Business Review.*

Nieto, M., Lopez, F., & Cruz, F. (1998). Performance analysis of technology using the S curve model: The case of digital signal processing (DSP) technologies. *Technovation, 18,* 439–457. doi:10.1016/S0166-4972(98)00021-2.

NORAD. N. A. f. D. C. (1999). The logical framework approach: Handbook for objectives-oriented planning (4th ed.). Oslo, Norway: Tykk and Kopisenteret AS.

Norman, W., & MacDonald, C. (2003). Getting to the bottom of triple bottom line. *Business Ethics Quarterly.* Retrieved July 10 from www.businessethics.ca/3bl/triple-bottom-line.pdf

Norton, B. G. (2005). *Sustainability: A philosophy of adaptive ecosystem management.* Chicago: The University of Chicago Press. doi:10.7208/chicago/9780226595221.001.0001.

Nozick, R. (1974). *Anarchy, state and utopia.* Oxford, UK: Basil Blackwell.

Nyoka, M. (2005). *Internalising environmental costs: A case study of the minerals extraction industry in South Africa.* (Masters thesis). University of Pretoria, Pretoria, South Africa.

Nyoka, M., & Brent, A. C. (2007). Application of an environmental valuation approach to incorporate externality costs in decision making of the metallurgical sector. *Journal of the South African Institute of Mining and Metallurgy, 107*(10), 663–669.

Oberholzer, A. (n.d.). Integrated reporting: Why should you care? *Communication World.* Retrieved from www.iabc.com/cw

OECD. (2004). *OECD principles of corporate governance* (Revised ed.). Paris, France: OECD.

Oehlmann, I. (2010). *The sustainable footprint methodology: Including sustainability in the project management of the bergermeer gas storage project.* Delft, The Netherlands: Delft University of Technology Faculty of Technology, Policy and Management.

Office of Government Commerce (OGC). (2002). *Prince2*. London: The Stationary Office.

Office of Government Commerce. (2007). *Managing successful programmes*. London: The Stationery Office.

Office of Government Commerce. (2009). *Managing successful projects with PRINCE2*. London: Stationery Office.

Office of Government Commerce. (2010). *Management of value*. London: The Stationery Office.

Olander, S., & Landin, A. (2005). Evaluation of stakeholder influence in the implementation of construction projects. *International Journal of Project Management*, 321–328. doi:10.1016/j.ijproman.2005.02.002.

Olsson, J. A., Hilding-Rydevik, T., Aalbu, H., & Bradley, K. (2004). *Indicators for sustainable development. Discussion paper*. European Regional Network on Sustainable Development.

Olve, N., Roy, J., & Wetter, M. (1999). *Performance drivers: A practical guide to using the balanced scorecard*. Chichester, UK: John Wiley & Sons.

Organisation for Economic Co-Operation and Development. (2001). Corporate social responsibility: Partners for progress. *OECD Publishing*. Retrieved on July 6, 2011 from http://www.oecd.org/document/37/0,3746, en_2649_34417_2429925_1_1_1_1_,00.html

O'Rourke, A. (2003). The message and methods of ethical investment. *Journal of Cleaner Production*, *11*(6), 683–693. doi:10.1016/S0959-6526(02)00105-1.

Pant, I., & Baroudi, B. (2008). Project management education: The human skills imperative. *International Journal of Project Management*, (26): 124–128. doi:10.1016/j.ijproman.2007.05.010.

Pasian, B. L. (2011). *Project management maturity: A critical analysis of existing and emergent factors*. (Unpublished doctoral dissertation). University of Technology, Sydney, Australia.

Pearce, D. (1987). Foundations of an ecological economics. *Ecological Modelling*, *38*(1-2), 9–18. doi:10.1016/0304-3800(87)90042-1.

Peck, P., & Sinding, K. (2003). Environmental and social disclosure and data richness in the mining industry. *Business Strategy and the Environment*, *12*, 131–146. doi:10.1002/bse.358.

Perira, L. C. B. (1995). Development economics and the world banks' identity crisis. *Review of International Political Economy*, *2*(2), 218–219.

Peterson, C. (2000). The future of optimism. *The American Psychologist*, (55): 44–55. doi:10.1037/0003-066X.55.1.44 PMID:11392864.

Peterson, C., & Seligman, M. E. P. (2004). *Character strengths and virtues: A handbook and classification*. Washington, DC: APA Press and Oxford University Press.

Peterson, S. J., & Luthans, F. (2003). The positive impact and development of hopeful leaders. *Leadership and Organization Development Journal*, *24*(1), 26–31. doi:10.1108/01437730310457302.

Phillips, P. C. B., & Granger, C. (1997). The ET interview: Professor Clive Granger. *Econometric Theory*, *13*(2), 253–303. doi:10.1017/S0266466600005740.

Piderit, S. K. (2000). Rethinking resistance and recognizing ambivalence: A multidimensional view of attitudes toward an organizational change. *Academy of Management Review*, (25): 783–794.

Planko, J., & Silvius, G. (2012). Sustainability in business. In Silvius, Schipper, Planko, van den Brink, & Köhler (Ed.), Sustainability in Project Management. Farnham, UK: Gower Publishing.

PMI. (2008). *A guide to the project management body of knowledge (PMBOK guide)* (4th ed.). Newtown Square, PA: Project Management Institute.

Poister, T. H. (1982). Developing performance indicators for the Pennsylvania department of transportation. *Public Productivity Review*, *6*(1/2), 51–77. doi:10.2307/3380402.

Pojasek, R. B. (2007). A framework for business sustainability. *Environmental Quality Management*, *17*(2), 81–88. doi:10.1002/tqem.20168.

Pope, J., Annandale, D., & Morrison-Saunders, A. (2004). Conceptualising sustainability assessment. *Environmental Impact Assessment Review*, (24): 595–616. doi:10.1016/j.eiar.2004.03.001.

Poppendieck, M. (2002). *Principles of lean thinking.* Retrieved from http://www.poppendieck.com/papers/LeanThinking.pdf

Port of Koper. (2012). *Annual report 2011.* Koper: Port of Koper.

Porter, M. E., & Kramer, M. R. (2006). Strategy and society: The link between competitive advantage and corporate social responsibility. *Harvard Business Review,* 78–92. PMID:17183795.

Porter, M. E., & Kramer, M. R. (2011). Creating shared value. *Harvard Business Review, 89*(1/2), 62–77.

Porter, M. E., & Kramer, M. R. (2011). The big idea: Creating shared value. *Harvard Business Review, 89*(1-2).

Porter, M., & Van der Linde, C. (1995). Green and competitive – Ending the stalemate. *Harvard Business Review, 73*(5), 120–134.

Prairie, P. (2011, December 28). Top corporate sustainability trends to watch in 2012. *Fast Company.*

Prat, M. G., & Ashforth, B. E. (2003). Fostering meaningfulness in working and at work. In Cameron, Dutton, & Quin (Ed.), Positive organizational scholarship: Foundations of a new discipline. San Francisco, CA: Berrett-Koehler Publishers.

Presley, A., Meade, L., & Sarkis, J. (2007). A strategic sustainability methodology for organizational decisions: A reverse logistics illustration. *International Journal of Production Research, 45*(18-19), 4595–4620. doi:10.1080/00207540701440220.

Project Management Institute, Inc. (2012). *PMI today.* Newtown Square, PA: Project Management Institute, Inc..

Project Management Institute. (2006). *Code of ethics and professional conduct.* Newtown Square, PA: Project Management Institute.

Project Management Institute. (2008). *A guide to the project management body of knowledge.* Newtown Square, PA: Project Management Institute.

Project Management Institute. (2008). *The standard for program management.* Newton Square, PA: Project Management Institute.

Project Management Institute. (2009). *Strategic plan.* Newtown Square, PA: PMI.

Project Management Institute. (n.d.). *PMI code of ethics and professional conduct.* Newtown Square, PA: PMI. Retrieved from http://www.pmi.org/About-Us/Ethics/~/media/PDF/Ethics/ap_pmicodeofethics.ashx

Proudfoot, J.G., Corr, Guest, & Dunn. (2009). Cognitive-behavioural training to change attributional style improves employee well-being, job satisfaction, productivity, and turnover. *Personality and Individual Differences,* (46): 147–153. doi:10.1016/j.paid.2008.09.018.

Prugh, T., Costanza, R., & Daly, H. (2000). *The local politics of global sustainability.* Washington, DC: Island Press.

Pryce-Jones, J. (2010). *Happiness at work, maximizing your psychological capital for success.* Chichester, UK: Wiley-Blackwell. doi:10.1002/9780470666845.

PWC, P. (2011). *CDP Global 500 Report 2011; Accelerating Low Carbon Growth.* United Kingdom: CDProject.

Queensland Government. (2010). *Kingaroy groundwater test results remain at safe low levels.* Retrieved from http://www.derm.qld.gov.au/media-room/2010/08/kingaroy-testing-02-08.html

Raftery, J. (2003). *Risk analysis in project management.* London: Chapman and Hall.

Rand, A. (1964). *The virtue of selfishness: A new concept of egoism.* New York: New American Library.

Raz, T., & Michael, E. (2001). Use and benefits of tools for project risk management. *International Journal of Project Management, 19*(1), 9–17. doi:10.1016/S0263-7863(99)00036-8.

Reilly, A., & Weirup, A. (2010). Sustainability initiatives, social media activity, and organizational culture: An exploratory study. *Journal of Sustainability and Green Business.* Retrieved May 29, 2012, from http://ww.w.aabri.com/manuscripts/10621.pdf

Reinhardt, F. (1999). Market failure and the environmental policies of firms: Economic rationales for 'beyond compliance' behaviour. *Journal of Industrial Ecology, 3,* 9–21. doi:10.1162/108819899569368.

Reinhardt, F. L. (1998). Environmental product differentiation: Implications for corporate strategy. *California Management Review, 40*(4), 43–73. doi:10.2307/41165964.

Reinhardt, F. L. (2000). *Down to earth: Applying business principles to environmental management.* Boston: Harvard Business School.

Rhee, S. Y., & Yoon. (2012). Group emotions, shared positive affect in workgroups. In Cameron & Spreitzer (Eds.), *Oxford Handbook of Positive Organizational Scholarship.* Oxford, UK: Oxford University Press.

Riemer, S., & Meyer, S. (2009, October 15). Integrating sustainability in project management- A practical approach. *Strategies to Sustainability.*

Robb, L. (2007). Project proposal and initiation. In Turner (Ed.), Gower Handbook of Project Management. Aderlshot, UK: Gower.

Robert, K.-H., Daly, H., Hawken, P., & Holmberg, J. (1997). A compass for sustainable development. *International Journal of Sustainable Development and World Ecology,* (4), 79-92.

Robert, K.-H., Schmidt-Bleek, B., de Larderel, A., Basile, G., Jansen, J. L., & Kuehr, R. et al. (2002). Strategic sustainable development—Selection, design and synergies of applied tools. *Journal of Cleaner Production, 10,* 197–214. doi:10.1016/S0959-6526(01)00061-0.

Robinson, J. (2004). Squaring the circle: On the very idea of sustainable development. *Ecological Economics, 48*(4), 369–384. doi:10.1016/j.ecolecon.2003.10.017.

Robson, I. (2004). From process measurement to performance improvement. *Business Process Management Journal, 10*(5), 510–521. doi:10.1108/14637150410559199.

Rodney, W. (1972). How Europe underdeveloped Africa. Dar es Salaam, Tanzalia: Tanzania Publishing House.

Roelofse, A. J., & Pretorius, M. W. (2003). A generalised innovation model for large organizations. In *Proceedings of PICMET.* Portland, OR: PICMET.

Rostow, W. (1964). *The stages of economic growth: A noncommunist manifesto.* Cambridge, UK: Cambridge University Press.

Rostow, W. (1971). *Politics and the Stages of growth.* Cambridge, UK: Cambridge University Press. doi:10.1017/CBO9780511562778.

Rothbard, N. P., & Patil, S. V. (2012). Being there: Work engagement and positive organizational scholarship. In Cameron & Spreitzer (Ed.), Oxford Handbook of Positive Organizational Scholarship. Oxford, UK: Oxford University Press.

Royal Commission on Environmental Pollution (RCEP). (2000). *Energy - The changing climate.* London: RCEP.

Russell, J. (2008). Corporate social responsibility: What it means for the project manager. In *Proceedings of PMI Europe Congress.* Malta: Project Management Institute.

Russo, M. V. (2010). *Companies on a mission.* Stanford, CA: Stanford University Press.

Saaty, T. T. (1990). *The analytic hierarchy process.* New York: McGraw-Hill.

Sahlin-Andersson, K., & Söderholm, A. (2002). *Beyond project management: New perspectives on the temporary-permanent dilemma.* Malmö: Liber.

Salt, B. (2007). *Beyond the baby boomers: The rise of generation Y - Opportunities and challenges for the funds management industry.* Melbourne, Australia: KPMG International. Retrieved from http://www.bernardsalt.com.au/pdf/Beyond_the_Baby_Boomers.pdf

Samset, K. (2008). How to overcome major weaknesses in mega-projects: The Norwegian approach. In Decision-making on mega-projects: Cost-benefit analysis, planning and innovation, (pp. 173-188).

Savitz, A. W., & Weber, K. (2006). *The triple bottom line: How today's best-run companies are achieving economic, social, and environmental success – And how you can too.* San Francisco: Jossey-Bass.

Scheier, M. F., & Carver, C. S. (1992). Effects of optimism on psychological and physical well-being: Theoretical overview and empirical update. *Cognitive Therapy and Research, 16,* 201–228. doi:10.1007/BF01173489.

Scheier, M. F., Carver, C. S., & Bridges, M. W. (1994). Distinguishing optimism from neuroticism (and trait anxiety, self-mastery, and self-esteem): A re-evaluation of the life orientation test. *Journal of Personality and Social Psychology, 67,* 1063–1078. doi:10.1037/0022-3514.67.6.1063 PMID:7815302.

Schendler, A. (2009). *Getting green done.* New York, NY: Public Affairs Publishing.

Schimmack, U., Oishi, S., Furr, R. M., & Funder, D. C. (2004). Personality and life satisfaction: A facet-level analysis. *Personality and Social Psychology Bulletin,* (30): 1062–1075. doi:10.1177/0146167204264292 PMID:15257789.

Schmitz, O. J. (2010). Perspectives on sustainability of ecosystem services and functions. In Graedel, T. E., & van der Voet, E. (Eds.), *Linkages of Sustainability* (pp. 33–46). Cambridge, MA: The MIT Press.

Seligman, M. E. P. (1991). *Learned optimism: How to change your mind and your life.* New York: Knopf.

Seligman, M. E. P. (1998). Building human strength: Psychology's forgotten mission. *APA Monitor, 29*(1).

Senge, P. (1999). *The fifth discipline field book, strategies and tools for building a learning organization.* London: Nicholas Braeley Publishing Limited.

Sharma, A. K., & Talwar, B. (2007). Evolution of universal business excellence model incorporating Vedic philosophy. *Measuring Business Excellence, 11*(3), 4–20. doi:10.1108/13683040710820719.

Shenhar, A., Dvir, D., Guth, W., Lechler, T., Milosevic, D., & Patanakul, P. Stefanovic, J. (2007). Project strategy: The missing link. In A. J. Shenhar, D. Milosev, D. Dvir, & H. Thamhain (Eds.), Linking Project Management to Business Strategy. Newtown Square, PA: Project Management Institute.

Shenhar, A. J., & Dvir, D. (2004). Project management evolution: Past history and future research directions. In Slevin, D. P., Cleland, D. I., & Pinto, J. K. (Eds.), *Innovations: Project Management Research 2004* (pp. 57–64). Project Management Institute.

Siegelaub, J. M. (2007). *Six (yes six!) constraints: An enhanced model for project control.* Paper presented at the PMI North America Global Congress. Atlanta, GA.

Sijtsma, F. (2006). *Project evaluation, sustainability and accountability.* REG- publication 27.

Silva, P., & Pagiola, S. (2003). A review of the valuation of environmental costs and benefits in World Bank projects. *Environmental Economic Series, 94.* Retrieved June 2, 2012, from http://econwpa.wustl.edu:80/eps/othr/papers/0502/0502007.pdf

Silverman, M., & Lanphar, T. (2003). *Benziger family winery.* Retrieved from http://www.bren.ucsb.edu/academics/courses/210/cases/benziger.pdf

Silvius, A. J. G. (2010). Workshop report group 2. In H. Knoepfel (Ed.), *Survival and Sustainability as Challenges for Projects,* (pp. 155 – 160). International Project Management Association (IPMA).

Silvius, A. J. G. (2012). *Update May 2012 overview of literature on sustainability in projects and project management.* Retrieved from http://www.slideshare.net/GilbertSilvius/update-may-2012-overview-of-literature-on-sustainability-in-projects-and-project-management

Silvius, A. J. G., & Nedeski, S. (2011). Sustainability in IS projects: A case study. In *Proceedings of the 22nd Annual Conference of the International Information Management Association.* International Information Management Association.

Silvius, A. J. G., & Schipper, R. (2012). Sustainability in the business case. In J.-P. Pantouvakis (Ed.), *26th World Congress of the International Project Management Association (IPMA),* (pp. 1062-1069). Crete, Greece: IPMA.

Silvius, A. J. G., & van den Brink, J. (2011). Taking responsibility: The integration of sustainability and project management. In J. Kettunen, U. Hyrkkänen, & A. Lehto (Eds.), *Proceedings from the First CARPE Networking Conference.* Utrecht, The Netherlands: CARPE.

Silvius, G., & Schipper, R. (2010). *A maturity model for integrating sustainability in projects and project management.* Paper presented at the 24th World Congress of the International Project Management Association (IPMA). Istanbul, Turkey. Retrieved from http://publicationslist.org/gilbert.silvius

Silvius, A. J. G., van der Brink, J., & Köhler, A. (2009). Views on sustainable project management. In Kähköhnen, K., Kazi, A. S., & Rekola, M. (Eds.), *Human Side of Projects in Modern Business.* Helsinki, Finland: IPMA Scientific Research Paper Series.

Silvius, G., Van Den Brink, J., Schipper, R., Köhler, A., & Planko, J. (2012). *Sustainability in project management.* Gower.

Simon, D. (1997). Reconsidered: New directions in development thinking. *Geografiska Annaler. Series B, Human Geography, 79*(4), 183–201. doi:10.1111/j.0435-3684.1997.00018.x.

Skinner, C. W., & Berger, A. R. (Eds.). (2003). *Geology and health: Closing the gap*. New York, NY: Oxford University Press.

Smith, P. K. (1993). Welfare as a cause of poverty: A time series analysis. *Public Choice, 75*(2), 157–170. doi:10.1007/BF01048360.

Smithson, C. W. (1998). *Managing financial risk: A guide to derivative products, financial engineering and value maximisation* (3rd ed.). New York: McGraw Hill Professional.

Sneider, K. F., & Nissen, M. E. (2003). Beyond the body of knowledge: Knowledge-flow approach to project management theory and practice. *Project Management Journal, 34*(2).

Snyder, C. R. (Ed.). (2000). *Handbook of hope: Theory, measures and applications*. San Diego, CA: Academic Press.

Spee, A. P., & Jarzabkowski, P. (2009). Using strategy tools as boundary objects. *Strategic Organization, 7*(2), 223–232. doi:10.1177/1476127009102674.

Spender, J. (1996). Making knowledge the basis of a dynamic theory of the firm. *Strategic Management Journal, 17*.

Spreitzer, G. M., & Sutcliffe, K. M. (2007). Thriving in organizations. In Nelson & Cooper (Ed.), Positive Organizational Behavior. London: Sage.

Standards Australia & Standards New Zealand. (2004). *AS/NZS ISO 14001: 2004, environmental management systems- Requirements with guidance for use*. Sydney, Australia: Standards Australia.

Standards Australia & Standards New Zealand. (2004). *AS/NZS ISO 31000: 2009, risk management- Principles and guidelines*. Sydney, Australia: Standards Australia.

Standards Australia & Standards New Zealand. (2011). *AS/NZS ISO 9004: 2011, Managing for the sustained success of an organisation – A quality management approach*. Sydney, Australia: SAI Global.

Staw, B. M., & Barsade, S. G. (1993). Affect and managerial performance: A test of the sadder-but-wiser vs. happier-and-smarter hypothesis. *Administrative Science Quarterly, (38)*: 304–331. doi:10.2307/2393415.

Sterman, J. D. (2000). *Business dynamics: Systems thinking and modelling for a complex world*. New York: McGraw-Hill/Irwin.

Steurer, R., Langer, M. E., Konrad, A., & Martinuzzi, A. (2005). Corporations, stakeholders and sustainable development I: A theoretical exploration of business–society relations. *Journal of Business Ethics, 61*(3), 263–281. doi:10.1007/s10551-005-7054-0.

Steyn, H. (2003). *Project management: A multi-disciplinary approach*. Pretoria, South Africa: FPM Publisher.

Stock, J. H., & Watson, M. W. (1988). Variable trends in economic time series. *The Journal of Economic Perspectives, 2*(3), 147–174. doi:10.1257/jep.2.3.147.

Stockmann, R. (1997). The sustainability of development projects: An impact assessment of German vocational-training projects in Latin America. *World Development, 25*(11), 1767–1784. doi:10.1016/S0305-750X(97)00067-3.

Stranger, C. (2002). *Sustainability accounting in the construction industry*. London: Ciria Publishing Services.

Stroessner, S., Mackie, & Michalsen. (2005). Positive mood and the perception of variability within and between groups. *Group Processes & Intergroup Relations, (8)*: 5–25. doi:10.1177/1368430205048619.

Suhonen, M., & Paasivaara, L. (2011). Shared human capital in project management: A systematic review of the literature. *Project Management Journal, (42)*, 4-16.

Sunter, W. V. A. C. (2002). *Beyond reasonable greed: Why sustainable business is a much better idea*. Cape Town, South Africa: Human & Rousseau Tafelberg.

Sustainability SA. (n.d.). Retrieved from http://www.sustainabilitysa.org/IntegratedReporting/ReferenceSourcesonIntegratedReporting.aspx

Sustainable Infrastructure. (2012). Retrieved from http://www.sustainableinfrastructure.org/rating/index.cfm

Swasdio, U., Islam, N., & Krairit, D. (2004). Commercialization of technologies developed in public research and development institutes: The case of Thailand. *IEEE Engineering Management Conference Proceedings, 2*, 617-621.

Talwar, B. (2011). Business excellence models and the path ahead.... *The TQM Journal, 23*(1), 21–35. doi:10.1108/17542731111097461.

Tam, G. C. K. (2010). *Sustainability competence requirements for project manager.* Paper presented at the IPMA International Expert Seminar 2010 - Survival and Sustainability as Challenges for Projects. Zurich, Switzerland.

Tam, G. C. K. (2010). The program management process with sustainability considerations. *Journal of Project. Program & Portfolio Management, 1*(1), 17–27.

Taylor, T. (2008). *A sustainability checklist for managers of projects.* Retrieved from http://www.pmforum.org/library/papers/2008/PDFs/Taylor-1-08.pdf

Tharp, J. (2007). *Align project management with organizational strategy.* Hong Kong: PMI Global Congress.

Tharp, J. (2008). Corporate social responsibility: What it means for the project manager. In *Proceedings of PMI Europe Congress.* Philadelphia, PA: Project Management Insitute.

Tharp, J. (2012). *Project management and global sustainability.* Paper presented at the PMI 2012 EMEA Global Congress. Marseille, France.

The Commission of the European Parliament. (2002). *The competitiveness of the construction industry.* Brussels: European Union.

The Construction Task Force. (1998). *Rethinking construction.* London: DETR.

The European Union Online. Europa. (n.d.). *The European commission.* Retrieved June 2002, from http://europa.eu.int/comm/enterprise/construction/it/connet/connet.htm

The World Bank. (1997). *The logframe handbook: A logical framework approach to project cycle management.* Washington, DC: OECD.

The, U. K. Government. (2003). Sustainable development fact sheets: The UK government's policy for SD for UK businesses. London: Her Majesty's Stationery Office (DETR).

Thornton, D., Kagen, R., & Gunningham, N. (2003). Sources of corporate environmental performance. *California Management Review, 46*(1). doi:10.2307/41166235.

Toulmin, S. (1958). *The Uses of Argument.* Cambridge: Cambridge University Press.

Toulmin, S., Rieke, R., & Janik, A. (1979). *An introduction of reasoning.* New York: Macmillan Publishing Co, Inc..

Tovey, H. (2009). Sustainability: A platform for debate. *Sustainability, 1*(1), 14–18. doi:10.3390/su1010014.

Tran, T. A. (2007). Review of methods and tools applied in technology assessment literature. In *Proceedings of PICMET.* Portland, OR: PICMET.

Turner, R. (2010). Responsibilities for sustainable development in project and program management. In *Proceedings of IPMA Expert Seminar.* Zurich, Switzerland: IPMA.

Turner, J. R. (Ed.). (2009). *The handbook of project-based management: Leading strategic change in organizations* (3rd ed.). New York: McGraw-Hill.

Turner, J. R., & Müller, R. (2003). On the nature of the project as a temporary organization. *International Journal of Project Management, 21*(3), 1–8. doi:10.1016/S0263-7863(02)00020-0.

Turner, R. J., Huemann, M., Anbari, F. T., & Bredillet, C. N. (2010). *Perspectives on projects.* New York: Routledge.

U.S.Green Building Council. (2013). *LEED rating systems. U.S.* Green Building Council.

UNCED. (1992). *Agenda 21: Preamble.* Paper presented at the United Nations Conference on Environment & Development. New York: UNCED.

United Nations. (1992). *Rio declaration on environment and development.* Rio de Janeiro, Brazil: UN.

United Nations. (2005). [World Summit Outcome. New York: UN.]. *Resolution, 60*(1), 2005.

United States of America Defense Acquisition. (2006). *Risk management guide for department of defense acquisition* (6th ed.). Washington, DC: United States of America Defense Acquisition University.

Uwuigbe, U., Uwuigbe, O., & Aiayi, A. O. (2011). Corporate social responsibility disclosures by environmentally visible corporations: A study of selected firms in Nigeria. *European Journal of Business and Management*, *3*(9), 9–17.

Van den Brink. (2013). *Project management? It's all about emotions: The positive psychology of project management.*

Van Der Merwe, S., & Bussin, M. (2006). An evaluation of a communication, facilitation and project management tool to enhance the effectiveness of project execution. *Journal of Human Resource Management*, *4*(3), 48–54.

Van Erck, R. P. G. (2003). *Monetary evaluation of business sustainability, case study: GTL fuel production in South Africa*. (Masters thesis). Technical University of Eindhoven, Eindhoven, The Netherlands.

Van Marrewijk, M. (2003). Concepts and definitions of CSR and corporate sustainability: Between agency and communion. *Journal of Business Ethics*, *44*(2), 95–105. doi:10.1023/A:1023331212247.

Van Pelt, M. J. F. (1993). Ecologically sustainable development and project appraisal in developing countries. *Ecological Economics*, *7*, 19–42. doi:10.1016/0921-8009(93)90018-2.

Vancaly, F. (2004). International principles for social impact assessment. *Impact Assessment and Project Appraisal*, *21*(1), 5–12. doi:10.3152/147154603781766491.

Vanita, A., Yang, J., Skitmore, M., & Shankar, R. (2010). An empirical test of causal relationships of factors affecting ICT adoption for building project management: An Indian SME case study. *Construction Innovation: Information, Process. Management*, *10*(2), 164–180.

Velis, E., & Linich, D. (2012). *The evolving supply chain: Lean and green*. Retrieved from http://www.interbrand.com/en/best-global-brands/Best-Global-Green-Brands/2012-Report/the-evolving-supply-chain.aspx

Vienna Hospital Association. (2010). *Vienna north hospital's charter on sustainability*. Vienna: Vienna Hospital Association.

Vienna Hospital Association. (2012). *Hospital north: Presentation of the Vienna hospital association*. Vienna: Author.

Visser, W. T. (2002). Sustainability reporting in South Africa. *Corporate Environmental Strategy*, *9*(1), 79–85. doi:10.1016/S1066-7938(01)00157-9.

Wang, W. (2005). An evaluation of the balanced scorecard in equity valuation: The case of exchange ratio in the M&As of Taiwan's financial industry. *Journal of Intellectual Capital*, *6*(2), 206–221. doi:10.1108/14691930510592807.

Ward, J. L. (2008). *Dictionary of project management terms* (3rd ed.). Arlington, VA: ESI International.

Warhurst, A. (2003). *Sustainability indicators and sustainability performance management*. Mining, Minerals and Sustainable Development.

Wartick, S. L. W. D. J. (Ed.). (1998). International business and society. Malden, MA: Blackwell.

WBCSD. (2000). Corporate social responsibility: Making good business sense. *World Business Council for Sustainable Development*. Retrieved on June 30, 2011 from http://www.wbcsd.org/templates/TemplateWBCSD5/layout.asp?type=p&MenuId=MTE0OQ

WebFinance. I. (2010). *InvestorWords - Investment*. Retrieved from http://www.investorwords.com/2599/investment.html

Weingaertner, C., & Moberg, A. (2011). Exploring social sustainability: Learning from perspectives on urban development and companies and products. *Sustainable Development*, 10.

Werbach, A. (2009). *Strategy for sustainability*. Boston: Harvard Business Press.

Westbrook, D., & Kennerly, H., & Kirk. (2007). *An introduction to cognitive behavioral therapy, skills and applications*. London. *Sage (Atlanta, Ga.)*.

Westerveld, E. (2003). The project excellence model®: Linking success criteria and critical success factors. *International Journal of Project Management*, *21*(6), 411–418. doi:10.1016/S0263-7863(02)00112-6.

Wheeler, R., Fabig, H., & Boele, R. (2000). Shell, Nigeria and the Ogoni: A study in unsustainable development: In analysis and implications of Royal Dutch/Shell group strategy. *Sustainable Development*, *9*(4), 177–196. doi:10.1002/sd.172.

Wheelwright, S. C., & Clark, K. B. (1992). *Revolutionizing product development*. New York: The Free Press.

White, D., & Fortune, J. (2002). Current practice in project management: An empirical study. *International Journal of Project Management, 20*(1), 1–11. doi:10.1016/S0263-7863(00)00029-6.

Whitington, R., Pettigrew, A., Peck, S., Fenton, E., & Conyon, M. (1999). Change and complementaries in the new competitive landscape. *Organization Science, 10*(5), 583–600.

Whittington, R. (2003). The work of strategizing and organizing: For a practice perspective. *Strategic Organization, 1*(1), 117–125.

Wideman, R. M. (1995). Criteria for a project management body of knowledge. *International Journal of Project Management, 13*(2), 72. doi:10.1016/0263-7863(94)00020-D.

Wijnen, G., & Kor, R. (2000). *Managing unique assignments: A team approach to projects and programmes*. Aldershot, UK: Gower.

Willard, B. (2002). *The sustainability advantage: Seven business case benefits of a triple bottom line*. Gabriola Island, Canada: New Society Publishers.

Williams, T., & Samset, K. (2010). Issues in front-end decision-making on projects. *Project Management Journal, 41*(2), 38–49. doi:10.1002/pmj.20160.

Wiltbank, R., Dew, N., Read, S., & Sarasvathy, S. (2006). What to do next? The case for non-prescriptive strategy. *Strategic Management Journal, 27*, 981–998. doi:10.1002/smj.555.

Winch, G. M. (2004). *Managing project stakeholders*. Hoboken, NJ: John Wiley & Sons.

Wingard, C. H. (2001). *Financial performance of environmentally responsible South African listed companies*. (Doctoral thesis). University of Pretoria, Pretoria, South Africa.

Winter, M., Smith, C., Morris, P., & Cicmil, S. (2006). Directions for future research in project management: The main findings of a UK government-funded research network. *International Journal of Project Management, 24*, 638–649. doi:10.1016/j.ijproman.2006.08.009.

Wirtenberg, J. (2011). Sustainable enterprise for the 21st century. In S.G. McNall, J.C. Hershauer, & G. Basile (Eds.). The Business of Sustainability, Trends, Policies, Practices, and Stories of Success: Vol. 1: Global Challenges and Opportunities (pp. 67-88). Santa Barbara, CA: Praeger.

Wirth, I., & Tryloff, D. (1995). Preliminary comparison of six efforts to document the project management body of knowledge. *International Journal of Project Management, 13*, 109–118. doi:10.1016/0263-7863(95)00003-9.

Wisniewski, M., & Dickson, A. (2001). Measuring performance in dumfries and galloway constabulary with the balanced scorecard. *The Journal of the Operational Research Society, 52*(10), 1057–1066. doi:10.1057/palgrave.jors.2601191.

Wolstenholme, E. F. (2003). The use of system dynamics as a tool for intermediate level technology evaluation: Three case studies. *Journal of Engineering and Technology Management, 20*, 193–204. doi:10.1016/S0923-4748(03)00018-3.

Wolters, T. (2003). Transforming international product chains into channels of sustainable production: The imperative of sustainable chain management. *Greener Management International, 43*, 6–13.

Womack, J. P., & Jones, D. T. (1996). *Lean thinking: Banish waste and create wealth in your corporation*. New York: Simon and Schuster.

Wooten, L. P., & Cameron, K. S. (2010). Enablers of a positive strategy: Positively deviant leadership. In Liney, Harrington, & Garcea (Eds.), Oxford Handbook of Positive Psychology and Work. New York: Oxford University Press.

World Business Council for Sustainable Development (WBCSD). (2002). *The business case for sustainable development, making a difference toward the Johannesburg summit 2002 and beyond*. Switzerland: WBCSD.

World Business Council for Sustainable Development (WBCSD). (2008). *Guidelines for identifying business risks and opportunities arising from ecosystem change*. Conches-Geneva: WBCSD.

World Business Council for Sustainable Development (WBCSD). (2010). *Vision 2050: The new agenda for business*. Retrieved May 20, 2012, from http://www.wbcsd.org/vision2050.aspx

World Commission on Environment and Development. (1987). *Our common future*. Oxford, UK: Oxford University Press.

Wresniewski, A. (2003). Finding positive meaning in work. In Cameron, Dutton, & Quin (Eds.), Positive organizational scholarship: Foundations of a new discipline. San Francisco, CA: Berrett-Koehler Publishers.

Yin, R. (2003). *Case Study Research: Design and Method*. United States: Sage Publications Inc..

Yin, R. K. (1994). *Case study research: Design and methods*. Thousand Oaks, CA: Sage.

Zainul Abidin, N., & Pasquire, C. L. (2007). Revolutionize value management: A mode towards sustainability. *International Journal of Project Management*, (25): 275–282. doi:10.1016/j.ijproman.2006.10.005.

Zelenski, J. M., & Nisbet, E. K. (2012). Happiness and feeling connected: The distinct role of nature relatedness. *Environment and Behavior*, 1–21.

Zelensky, J. M., Murphy, S. A., & Jenkins, D. A. (2008). The happy-productive worker thesis revisited. *Journal Happiness Studies,* (9), 521-537.

Zerk, J. A. (2006). *Multinationals and corporate social responsibility*. Cambridge, UK: Cambridge University Press. doi:10.1017/CBO9780511494864.

Zhao, F. (2004). Siemens' business excellence model and sustainable development. *Measuring Business Excellence*, 8(2), 55–64. doi:10.1108/13683040410539436.

Zullow, H. M., & Seligman, M. E. P. (1990). Pessimistic rumination predicts defeat of Presidential candidates: 1900-1984. *Psychological Inquiry*, *1*, 52–61. doi:10.1207/s15327965pli0101_13.

About the Contributors

Gilbert Silvius (1963) is professor at HU University of Applied Sciences Utrecht in The Netherlands. He is program director of the first Master of Project Management program in The Netherlands. This innovative program focuses on project management from an organizational change perspective. The Master of Project Management has a special focus on the integration of the concepts of sustainability in Projects and Project Management. In research, Gilbert focuses on sustainability in Projects and Project Management. He is the lead author of *Sustainability in Project Management*, published by Gower publishing, 2012. Besides being an established academic, Gilbert is an experienced project manager with over 20 years of experience in various business and IT projects. As a principal consultant at Van Aetsveld, project and change management; he advises numerous organizations on the development of their project managers and their project management capabilities. Gilbert is a member of IPMA, PMI, and the ISO TC236 that develops the ISO 21.500 guideline on project management. In the Dutch IPMA chapter, Gilbert is board representative for higher education.

Jennifer Tharp is President of Mastodon Consulting in San Francisco, CA, USA. She uses project management to drive good corporate governance practices in regulatory compliance, strategic execution, and sustainability. Ms. Tharp has over 20 years experience advising high-tech multinational corporations such as Genentech, Nikon, Vodafone, and Thomson on technology infrastructure, organizational development, and change management. Profiled by Ziff-Davis Media as a "Great Mind in Development," Jennifer speaks frequently on sustainability and strategy. A Past President of the San Francisco Chapter of Project Management Institute (PMI SFBAC), she teaches project management and sustainability at University of California, Berkeley.

* * *

Ramanda Achman is a globally minded, talented consultant in the fields of project management, energy, and sustainability. His business acumen is complemented by his vast knowledge of the technological and regulatory issues in the utilities and pharmaceutical industries. He is an excellent strategic planner with a proven track record in project management. Moreover, he feels comfortable working in a multidisciplinary and multicultural setting. Ramanda received his Masters from the prestigious Delft University of Technology, The Netherlands, specializing in the confluence of project management and sustainability on the energy sector, especially power sector. He now lives in Jakarta, Indonesia and works as a consultant, with his latest project providing analytics of Indonesia's Industrial Estates for the Ministry of State-Owned Corporations. Ramanda is your go-to guy if you are looking for a consultant having expertise in managing for-profit and not for-profit projects especially in the energy, infrastructure, and environmental sectors.

Luis F. M. Barros, PMP®, is a Mechanical Engineer with 15 years of experience in Power Generation and Renewable Energy business, specialized and certified in Project Management. Leading multicultural project teams in USA, Latin America, and Europe, his background includes greenfield development and project management of industrial biomass power plants and wind farms in Brazil and Latin America. He is currently Head of Project Management and Development at EDP Renewables, located in São Paulo, Brazil.

Alan Brent is a chemical engineer with Masters degrees in environmental engineering, technology management, and sustainable development, and a PhD in engineering management. Since 1995, he consulted to a variety of industry and public sectors in South Africa and other developing countries in the fields of environmental engineering and management. Currently, he is appointed as a professor in the Sustainable Development programme of the School of Public Leadership (SPL) of the Faculty of Economic and Management Sciences of Stellenbosch University, where he is also the associate director of the Centre for Renewable and Sustainable Energy Studies (CRSES) in the Faculty of Engineering. He is also appointed as a part-time professor of Sustainable Life Cycle Management in the Graduate School of Technology Management (GSTM), University of Pretoria.

William T. Craddock, Ed.D., PE, PMP, is an international trainer and management consultant with over 30 years of experience in progressive leadership assignments in functions such as process improvements and systems implementations. He led staff and operations groups for a Fortune 500 company before forming Craddock & Associates, Inc. Bill is a member of the Board of Examiners for both the Arkansas Governor's Quality Award and the Malcolm Baldrige National Quality Award. He is also affiliated with Project Auditors, LLC, an international training and consulting firm. Bill is an active Project Management Institute (PMI) Volunteer, serving as the former Chair of the Consulting Specific Interest Group and former VP Finance for the Central Arkansas Chapter. He has made numerous presentations at PMI Global Congresses and Leadership Meetings. Bill also teaches graduate classes at the University of Central Arkansas and the University of Arkansas at Little Rock.

Lynn Crawford, through Human Systems International Limited, works globally with corporations and government agencies concerned with improving their project management capability. As Professor in the Institute for Sustainable Development and Architecture at Bond University, she has focused on the embedding of sustainability in project management practice. Ongoing research includes project management competence, business change, contextual variation, public sector project governance, and management of disasters as projects. She is an Honorary Member of IPMA, Life Member of AIPM, Co-Vice-Chair of PMI's Global Accreditation Center Board, a director of the Global Alliance for Project Performance Standards (GAPPS) and was recipient of the 2011 IPMA Research Achievement Award.

Ioana Dragu is a PhD Candidate at Babes-Bolyai University, Faculty of Economics and Business Administration, Accounting and Audit Department. She graduated Finance and Banking English Line of Study within Faculty of Economics and Business Administration and then followed an MBA of two years in Managerial Accounting, Audit, and Control. She started her research in corporate reporting and disclosure when she was still a student. Currently, she is writing her thesis on Integrated Reporting as the mixture between financial and non-financial information brought together, including in her topic sustainability and corporate social responsibility disclosure practices. She published a series of papers on reporting practices and disclosure regarding financial and non-financial information. Her research interests incorporate CSR insights and their integration into standard reporting practices and information disclosure.

Mohamed Eid is the Former Faculty Coordinator for Learning & Teaching at the British University in Egypt (BUE). He was also the Joint Head of the Business Administration Department. He joined BUE in 2006 as an Assistant Professor in Management, Business Ethics & Corporate Social Responsibility, Sustainable Development & Sustainable Businesses, Organisation Development, and Public Policy & Administration. He led the faculty team working on the validation from Loughborough University successfully both in 2007 and the revalidation in 2010. Dr. Eid also worked as an independent consultant for the United Nations Human Settlements Programme (UN-Habitat) and as a member of the Egyptian team for Rapid Urban Profiling for Sustainability (RUSPS). His focus was on the issues of governance and sustainable development. Dr. Eid was awarded the PhD degree in 2004 from the University of Edinburgh, his research focused on sustainable development, project management (PMBOK) and systems thinking theories. He has publications on sustainable industries, project management practices, sustainable quality of life in developing countries, strategic level of sustainability in decision making, the ecological footprint and governance approach to public participation in decision making, as well as several published UN-Habitat reports for Egyptian Cities Profiles. He has published his first book on Sustainable Development & Project Management entitled *Sustainable Development: Rethinking Relationships in the Construction Industry; Integrating Sustainable Development (SD) into Project Management (PM)*.

Armand Faganel gained his Master's degree in the area of marketing from the Faculty of Economics and Business in Maribor. He is a PhD student at the Faculty of management, where he teaches as a senior lecturer in marketing. Before taking up teaching at the faculty he had gained working experience in the field of commerce, he was a marketing director, sales director, and a business unit manager in different international companies. He is the head of Marketing institute at the Faculty of management. His research areas include marketing, communication, intercultural competences, quality, and evaluation of tertiary education.

Roland Gareis conducted his studies at the University of Economics and Business Administration, Vienna, and did his habilitation at University of Technology, Vienna, Department of Construction Industry. He was Professor at the Georgia Institute of Technology in Atlanta and Visiting Professor at the ETH, Zurich, at the Georgia State University, Atlanta, and at the University of Quebec, Montreal. Professor Roland Gareis is Professor of Project Management at the University of Economics and Business, Vienna Austria. There he established the post graduate program "International Project Management" in 1983. Currently, he chairs the PROJEKTMANAGEMENT GROUP, which was founded at the Vienna University of Economics and Business in 1994 and is director of the professional MBA program "Project and Process Management." From 1986 to 2002, he was president of PROJEKT MANAGEMENT AUSTRIA, the Austrian project management association. In 1990, he organized the IPMA World Congress on "Management by Projects" in Vienna. He is former director of research of the IPMA-International Project Management Association.

Debby Goedknegt is lecturer and project manager at the Institute for the Built Environment of the HU University of Applied Sciences Utrecht. Sustainability is the main theme in her work (in both education and practice). She is, for instance, the manager of the bachelor minor period called "People-Planet-Profit" in which students participate and execute practice based research on for instance the improvement of the waste management system in municipalities in South Africa. Debby is the first graduate of the Master of Project Management program in The Netherlands, that is focused around the theme of sustainability. The chapter she contributed to this book, is based on her master's thesis.

Martina Huemann is Assistant Professor at the PORJEKTMANAGEMENT GROUP, WU Vienna, and Adjunct Professor of Project Management at SKEMA, Business School, France. Her research addresses Project Management & Sustainable Development as well as specifics of the project-oriented organization including Human Resource Management. She has project management experience in research, marketing, and organizational development projects. Since 2003, Martina is board member of Project Management Austria. Between 2005 and 2012, she was member of the IPMA Research Management Board. Since 2007, she is director of the IPMA Research Awards. Since 2009, she is a member of the PMI Academic Advisory Group. Martina trains project management personnel and consults projects, programs, and project-oriented organizations internationally.

Aleksander Janeš holds a Masters degree received from the University of Primorska, Faculty of Management Koper. He is a PhD student at the Faculty of Management Koper. From diversity of experiences in economy, with emphasis on project work, he continues upgrading his professional experiences and skills in a tertiary education with lecturing, as a researcher in projects with economy, and as a Licensed External Evaluator in HE and EFQM assessor. He received the Breakthrough certificate for Leadership Initiative for Excellence from Consortium Institute of Management and Business Analysis (CIMBA). His research fields are leadership, management of technology, management of quality, and business excellence.

Lynn A. Keeys is a Ph.D. candidate in strategy, programme and project management at the SKEMA Business School (Lille, France) and an independent international consultant in strategy and project management. She has extensive experience in international cooperation and sustainable development programs, specializing in programme and project strategy, design and planning, project & strategy facilitation, and organizational project management. She has headed project and programme offices for international development assistance programs and consulted on projects and programmes in various sectors with bilateral and international donors and organizations. Her special interest is relationship between organizational strategy and projects, especially emergent strategy in multi stakeholder environments. She has a master's degree in international development and completed advanced studies in organizational leadership. Her doctoral research focuses on the emergence of project sustainable development strategy in the context of corporate sustainability strategy. She is a member of the Project Management Institute and a certified Project Management Professional (PMP).

Andrea Krasnoff, PMP, is Director of Consulting Services of TenStep, Inc., a global methodology development, consulting, and training company. She is a member of the Atlanta, Georgia (USA) chapter of the Project Management Institute (PMI). Krasnoff has more than 20 years in project management, program management, PMOs, and portfolio management. She has managed and delivered projects of various sizes, including rescuing and successfully delivering troubled projects for several clients. Prior to TenStep, Krasnoff was responsible for application development groups comprised of project managers and developers, and consistently delivered business-related systems to meet strategic business needs. She has leveraged her experience into training and consulting in her areas of expertise. While at TenStep, Krasnoff has spoken on the subjects of project management, GreenPM, project management offices, and portfolio management.

Rich Maltzman, PMP, has been an engineer since 1978 and a Project Management supervisor since 1988, including a recent 2-year assignment in The Netherlands in which he built a team of PMs overseeing deployments of telecom networks in Europe and the Middle East. His project work has been diverse, including projects such as the successful deployment of the entire video and telecom infrastructure for the 1996 Summer Olympic Games in Atlanta, to the 2006 integration of the PMOs of two large merging corporations. As a second, but intertwined career, Rich has also focused on consulting and teaching. Rich has also professionally developed PMP-exam prep courseware, including exams and books. He even edited and was "the voice" for a set of 8 Audio CDs – a major part of a PMP prep course for an international company, for whom he has also facilitated PMP exam study groups. Rich was selected for the Modeling Team for the 4th Edition *PMBOK Guide* published by PMI in 2008, and contributed to the chapters on Quality and Risk. Currently, Rich is Senior Manager, Learning and Professional Advancement, at the Global Program Management Office of a major telecom concern. He is also co-authoring a book with Ranjit Biswas, PMP, entitled *The Fiddler on the Project*, a portion of which is being collaboratively written on the Web via a wiki, http://fiddlerontheproject.wikidot.com, and posts regularly on his blog, Scope Crêpe, http://scopccrcpc.blogspot.com.

Tom Mochal, PgMP, PMP is President of TenStep, Inc., a global methodology development, consulting, and training company. He is also the head of The TenStep Group, a network of TenStep offices supporting the TenStep process in numerous languages and countries around the world. Mochal is author of a book on managing people called *Lessons in People Management* and a companion book on project management called *Lesson in Project Management*. Mochal also authored all of the TenStep methodology products. Mochal won the Distinguished Contribution Award from the Project Management Institute for his work spreading knowledge of project management around the world. Mochal is a speaker, lecturer, instructor, and consultant to companies and organizations around the world. He is a member of the Atlanta, Georgia (USA) chapter of the Project Management Institute (PMI), the American Management Association (AMA), and the American Society for the Advancement of Project Management (asapm®).

Snezana Nedeski has a MSc in International Business from Maastricht University. During this time, she also taught the class Sustainability in Project Management at the School of Applied Sciences in Utrecht. Her interest in this topic led to additional research in this area, and several co-authored conference and journal papers. Her goal is to implement this theory in the future, starting with a tech startup in Amsterdam, where she will be part of the management team and will aim to create a platform for sustainability principles. While implementing the theory in practice in this setting, she hopes to continue theoretical research on an academic level as well.

Jairo Cardoso de Oliveira, professional with over 30 years of experience in the telecommunications and information technology industries, having worked in large companies in the areas of project management, engineering, service management, and operations management. Graduated in Electrical Technology at Universidade Presbiteriana Mackenzie and post graduated in Business Management with emphasis in information technology at Fundacao Getulio Vargas and University of California Irvine. Currently undertaking Master Degree in Project Management at Universidade Nove de Julho. Also dedicated in teaching classes in graduate courses for project management and telecommunications at Brazilian universities. Certified PMP© by the Project Management Institute (PMI©) in 2003. Since July 2011 is the head of Project Management Office (Corporate PMO) of Siemens in Brazil, with focus in portfolio management, project controlling and reporting, corporate governance actions, evaluation of maturity in project management, training and support.

Ron Schipper (1971) is project manager and principal consultant at Van Aetsveld, a leading consulting firm in project and change management in The Netherlands. He has more than 15 years of experience as a project manager in realising (organizational) change in various organizations. As well as executing projects, he is interested in developing the profession of project management and transferring this knowledge to other people in the Netherlands and developing countries. As sustainability emerges as a theme for the world, his attention has focused on the implications for projects and project management. Ron is also an external examiner in the Master of Informatics programme at HU University of Applied Sciences Utrecht in The Netherlands.

Dave Shirley, PMP, has been an instructor and consultant, with more than 30 years experience in management and project management, in the corporate, public, and small business arenas. He has presented at such prestigious organizations as The Conference Board and the PMI® Global Congress. Dave has also focused on consulting and teaching at the graduate level. As a Distinguished Member of Technical Staff with AT&T and Lucent Technologies Bell Laboratories, Dave was responsible for managing the first light-wave transmission products as well as several quality efforts. He was also AT&T's project manager for the first fiber-to-the-home effort in Connecticut and was the Lucent Technologies program management director managing several large telecommunications companies' equipment deployment. Dave has many years experience in developing, leading, and managing teams as well as experience in environmental regulation compliance.

Stephanie Steele (1964) works as a senior consultant for The USI Group, covering business system design, environmental and quality management, and systems implementation for clients in the manufacturing, service, and facilities management sectors. She has a Master of Environmental Law from the Australian National University, and has project managed facilities, business system integration, manufacturing control, and organisational change projects over the past twenty years for a number of corporations and SMEs.

Jude Talbot is a project manager and sustainability champion at AMEC, an international engineering and project management services company. His current research focuses on the intersection of sustainability and project management in an effort to normalize the incorporation of sustainability on projects. He completed his Masters studies at Penn State University where he earned a Masters Degree in Project Management. He is a professional engineer, a PMI certified Project Management Professional, and a LEED accredited professional. He lives in Vancouver, Canada, where he enjoys the west coast life style and the wide-open wild spaces at his doorstep.

Gilman Tam is an independent researcher and is currently taking asset management role for a multinational independent power producer. He has gained extensive practical experience in power plant project development, construction, commissioning, and maintenance both in Hong Kong and China. Gilman is a member of The Institution of Engineering and Technology (IET) in the UK; member of The American Society of Heating, Refrigerating, and Air-Conditioning Engineers (ASHRAE); and member of Project Management Institute (PMI) in the US. He is a Project Management Professional (PMP). Gilman holds MSc degree with distinction in Energy from the Heriot-Watt University in the UK and MBA degree from the Newport University in the US. Gilman is working on project management research at doctoral level with a focus on sustainability in project management. His major research interests include the development of practical sustainability tools for project managers.

Adriana Tiron-Tudor is a PhD, Full Professor, at Babes-Bolyai University, Faculty of Economics and Business Administration, Accounting, and Audit Department, where she coordinates doctoral students in accounting, and is actively involved in the development of the Romanian accounting profession. A graduate of Babes Bolyai University with a Ph.D. in accounting, Mrs. Tiron-Tudor received her expert accountant designation from CECCAR in 1995. She has lectured extensively at a national level on financial management, internal audit and control topics for public entities, and on public sector accounting standards. In 2006, she contributed to the implementation of the accrual accounting system in Romania by being involved in the training of practitioners, especially for local governmental administrations. Since 2008, she has also been a member of the Fédération des Experts Comptables Européens (Federation of European Accountants, or FEE) Public Sector Committee. She became a member of the International Public Sector Accounting Standards Board (IPSASB) in January 2012. She was nominated by the Body of Expert and Licensed Accountants of Romania (CECCAR). She has also written several publications relating to government accounting and standard setting in the public sector.

Carin Tredoux is an industrial engineer with a Masters degree in industrial and systems engineering, and a PhD in engineering management. Since 2006, she has worked on the sustainability aspects of a variety of industrial projects in Sasol – as part of the Environmental and Risk Engineering group in Sasol Technology, and from 2012, she is the engineering manager responsible for a large alternative energy project in Sasol. She is also involved in postgraduate programme of the Graduate School of Technology Management (GSTM) of the University of Pretoria.

J. Rodney Turner, MA, MSc, DPhil (Oxon), BE (Auck), CEng, FIMechE, FAPM, MInstD. Rodney Turner is managing consultant at EuroProjex Ltd and Academic Director to the PhD in Project and Programme Management at SKEMA Business School, in Lille France. He is Adjunct Professor at the University of Technology Sydney, and the Kemmy Business School, Limerick. Rodney is the author or editor of sixteen books, and over 30 peer reviewed journal articles. He is editor of *The International Journal of Project Management*. He lectures on project management worldwide. Rodney is Vice President, Honorary Fellow, and former chairman of the UK's Association for Project Management, and former President and Chairman of the International Project Management Association. His research interests are leadership and human resource management in project-oriented organizations, the management of projects in SMEs, the success of complex projects, and governance, ethics, and trust on projects.

Jasper van den Brink (1970) studied Social Sciences at the University of Utrecht and did a second master study at the Faculty of Law of the Catholic University of Leuven (Belgium). Jasper worked for many years as a project and program manager. In 2008, he started at the HU University of Applied Sciences Utrecht, where he is conducting research at the intersection of positive psychology and project management. He is a teacher and trainer on subjects related to the behavioral part of project management such as leadership, project management skills, and (team) coaching and he is coaching both students and project managers on their professional development. He is the owner of MWP Coaching, a Dutch coaching firm based in Utrecht, The Netherlands. He was one of the authors and editors of the book *Sustainability in Project Managers*.

Ray Venkataraman is a Professor of Supply Chain and Project Management at Penn State University, Erie, PA. He has a Ph. D. in Management Science from Illinois Institute of Technology and over thirty years of teaching experience. His teaching interests are in the areas of Supply Chain and Project Management. He won an award for excellence in business teaching and has several publications in top Operations Management journals and has published a book – *Cost and Value Management in Projects*. His current research is in Manufacturing Planning and Control Systems and Supply Chain issues in Project Management.

Erwin Weitlaner, Ing. (Electrical Engineering), certified Projects Director (IPMA Level A), Project Director, Siemens cert. works for Siemens AG since 1982 in various national and long-term international project business assignments in e.g. Libya, Iran, and Taiwan. From 1999 until 2006, Head of Subdivision Turn-Key in Transportation Systems, Railway Electrification, thereafter Head of Project Management Office for Transportation Systems. In 2010 and 2011, Head of Project Management Office Cluster Brazil, and since January 2012, Member of the PM@Siemens Core Team in Munich, Germany.

Claudia Weninger, since 2009, has been a junior researcher of the Project Management Group, Vienna University of Economics and Business (WU Vienna), and is currently writing her PhD thesis on project management. Born in 1985, Claudia holds a Magister Degree in Project Management and IT from the University of Applied Sciences bfi Vienna. Her research focuses on sustainable development in project management. She was a project team member of the research project "SustPM" and currently, she is the project manager of the PMI-sponsored research project, "Rethink!PSM (Rethink project stakeholder management). She is a certified IPMA, junior project manager, and active member of PMI. In the PMI Austria Chapter, Claudia is responsible for project management research and education at universities and universities of applied sciences throughout Austria.

Jessica-Louise Winnall has been managing complex projects, providing monitoring and evaluation support, undertaking evaluations and social risk analysis for projects in development and resources sectors for eight years. She has a further 6 years of voluntary Project Management experience in the community sector. Jessica-Louise is experienced in development of strategic initiatives, reporting and planning, with a proven track record of delivering effective solutions from complex problems. Her experience extends to the provision of training and capacity development solutions to a range of audiences. She also has extensive stakeholder engagement experience. Ms Winnall specialises in fragile communities, including experience in Timor-Leste, Papua New Guinea, Indonesia, Ethiopia, and Iraq.

Index

A

accountability 58, 60-61, 66, 74, 96, 100, 104, 114, 123, 126-127, 236, 240, 340-341, 347, 350-351, 353, 355, 357, 405
adaptive capacity 181
adaptive management 176, 181
American Psychological Association (APA) 246
Analytical Hierarchy Process (AHP) 163

B

Balanced Scorecard (BSC) 394-395
biodiversity conservation 199
Bioenergy Technology Sustainability Assessment (BIOTSA) 173
Business Excellence Model (BEM) 1-2, 5-13, 15-19
business model 35, 213, 215-216, 219, 221, 344-345, 347, 350, 352, 354-355, 357, 398, 403

C

Capability Maturity Model Integrated (CMMI) 46
Carbon Abatement Program (CAP) 321
Carbon Disclosure Project (CDP) 237, 240, 243, 321
carbon footprint 239, 241-242, 265
Catalogue of Criteria for Sustainable Building 311
change agents 261-262, 378
change management 35, 142, 245, 249, 304-306, 319-320, 367
Chief Executive Officer (CEO) 361
circular effect 255
Civil Right Act 250
cointegration 399-407
communication management 186, 190, 333-334
community involvement 186
company strategies 132, 308
Competitive Necessity 333, 336

construction industry 76-83, 92-94, 207, 292
consumer issues 186
corporate carbon footprint 241
corporate disclosure 106, 109, 116, 123-124, 127
Corporate Social Responsibility (CSR) 1, 5, 14, 19, 24, 161, 236-237, 297
Corporate Sustainable Development 37-38
Cost Benefit Analysis (CBA) 170
Criteria for Performance Excellence (CPE) 2, 7
cultural heritage 199
cyclic life cycle thinking 357

D

Delft Climate Plan 324, 333, 335-336
De Omslag 282, 284-285
Department of Environmental Resource Management (DERM) 363
Duurzame Uithof 282, 284-285, 287

E

eco-friendly 65-66, 101, 222, 352, 356
economical indicators 248
electric hydro-electric dam 263
emergent strategy 38
endorsement 62
Engineering, Procurement, and Construction (EPC) 380-381
Environmental License 388
environmentally friendly 39-42, 50, 52, 54-55, 241
Environmental Management System (EMS) 42, 49, 52-53
Environmental Protection Agency (EPA) 363
environmental viewpoint 352
Equator Principles Financial Institution (EPFI) 293
Error Correction Model 394, 399, 401, 407
European Foundation for Quality Management (EFQM) 2, 6-7

P

R

S

T

U

W

Lightning Source UK Ltd.
Milton Keynes UK
UKOW04n0456140217

294344UK00023B/308/P